Tolley's Company Secretary's Handbook

21st Edition

by

Jerry P L Lai FCIS

Members of the LexisNexis Group worldwide

United Kingdom	LexisNexis, a Division of Reed Elsevier (UK) Ltd, Halsbury House, 35 Chancery Lane, London, WC2A 1EL, and London House, 20–22 East London Street, Edinburgh EH7 4BQ
Australia	LexisNexis Butterworths, Chatswood, New South Wales
Austria	LexisNexis Verlag ARD Orac GmbH & Co KG, Vienna
Benelux	LexisNexis Benelux, Amsterdam
Canada	LexisNexis Canada, Markham, Ontario
China	LexisNexis China, Beijing and Shanghai
France	LexisNexis SA, Paris
Germany	LexisNexis Deutschland GmbH, Munster
Hong Kong	LexisNexis Hong Kong, Hong Kong
India	LexisNexis India, New Delhi
Italy	Giuffrè Editore, Milan
Japan	LexisNexis Japan, Tokyo
Malaysia	Malayan Law Journal Sdn Bhd, Kuala Lumpur
New Zealand	LexisNexis NZ Ltd, Wellington
Poland	Wydawnictwo Prawnicze LexisNexis Sp, Warsaw
Singapore	LexisNexis Singapore, Singapore
South Africa	LexisNexis Butterworths, Durban
USA	LexisNexis, Dayton, Ohio

First published in 1991

© Reed Elsevier (UK) Ltd 2011

Published by LexisNexis

A CIP Catalogue record for this book is available from the British Library.

ISBN: 9781405757560

Printed and bound by CPI Group (UK) Ltd, Croydon, CR0 4YY

Visit LexisNexis at www.lexisnexis.co.uk

Preface

The role and responsibilities of the company secretary continue to evolve as the legislation and other regulations affecting companies change to meet the demands of today's ever competitive business environment. The Cadbury Committee, the Hampel Committee, and the Higgs Review, recognise the important role of the secretary. The secretary is responsible for ensuring that corporate governance procedures are appropriate for the company, as well as interpreting and applying the Code of Best Practice drafted by the Committee. Inevitably, this places more demands upon the knowledge and expertise required of the secretary, who must therefore be suitably qualified and well informed to fulfil this role.

Although under the Companies Act 2006 the requirement to appoint a company secretary is no longer mandatory for private companies, the choice as to whether to have one is left very much to the private companies themselves. Bearing in mind that some private companies can be very substantial in size and the wide role that a company secretary can play in companies, it is unlikely that these companies will choose not to have a company secretary.

The purpose of this book is to provide the company secretary with a comprehensive handbook on the wide range of duties and responsibilities which typically fall to the secretary. It is intended that this book should be an initial source of advice on company secretarial matters and other business issues. Where further explanation is required, I would recommend that recourse is made to the relevant statutes or to the company's professional advisers. As before, we seek to improve on future editions of the book and would very much welcome readers' comments and suggestions.

For this edition, I have once again maintained overall editorial control whilst still updating some of the chapters. Steve Martin FCIS has once again continued to provide significant contribution in the update of this edition.

This 21st edition seeks to encompass *inter alia* the changes made by legislation during 2010/11 and reflect the changes brought about by the Companies Act 2006. As this Act is fully in force, I have updated this edition to show the changes accordingly. Information on the Bribery Act 2010, the UK Corporate Governance Code, and their impact is also included. The important role that the company secretary plays in corporate governance continues to be highlighted and I hope that this will be useful in assisting the secretary to keep up to date with the changes. This edition also includes changes in tax legislation, employment, health and safety and pensions regulations, and draws readers' attention to the various consultative documents issued by the relevant authorities. Again, based on the feedback that I have continued to receive, I have kept the chapters very much in the same order as the previous edition.

Finally, I would like to thank Mike Conroy of Tricor-ATC Europe LLP for his contribution to the Tax and Pensions Chapters, Andrew Scrimshaw from KPMG LLP on the Pensions Chapter, Diana Reid, Solicitor, Anglia Ruskin University (Legal Practice Course) on the Employment, Health and Safety

Chapter, and, for their valued support whilst updating this edition, all the members of the Company Secretarial team of Tricor-ATC Europe LLP.

Jerry P L Lai FCIS

Tricor-ATC Europe LLP

Contents

Contents

Contents

Abbreviations and References

Abbreviations

AAL	Additional Adoption Leave
ACAS	Advisory, Conciliation and Arbitration Service
ACOP	Approved Code of Practice
ACT	Advance Corporation Tax
AGM	Annual General Meeting
AIM	Alternative Investment Market
AML	Additional Maternity Leave
APL	Additional Paternity Leave
ASPP	Additional Statutory Paternity Pay
(FS)AVC	(Free Standing) Additional Voluntary Contribution
BIS	Department for Business, Innovation and Skills
CA 1948	Companies Act 1948
CA 1967	Companies Act 1967
CA 1980	Companies Act 1980
CA 1981	Companies Act 1981
CA 1985	Companies Act 1985
CA 1989	Companies Act 1989
CA 2006	Companies Act 2006
CFC	Controlled Foreign Company
CIC	Community Interest Company
CIHC	Close Investment Holding Company
CPI	Consumer Price Index
CTSA	Corporation Tax Self-Assessment
DDA 1995	Disability Discrimination Act 1995
DDA 2005	Disability Discrimination Act 2005

DPA 1998	Data Protection Act 1998
DSS	Department of Social Services
DTI	Department of Trade and Industry
DWP	Department for Work and Pensions
EA 2002	Employment Act 2002
ECJ	European Court of Justice
EEIG	European Economic Interest Grouping
EGM	Extraordinary General Meeting
EnA 2002	Enterprise Act 2002
EPA 1970	Equal Pay Act 1970
EP(C)A 1978	Employment Protection (Consolidation) Act 1978
ERA 1996	Employment Rights Act 1996
ERA 1999	Employment Relations Act 1989
ESLs	EC Sales Lists
ETA 1996	Employment Tribunals Act 1996
EU	European Union
EWC	Expected week of confinement
FAS	Financial Assistance Scheme
FSA	Financial Services Authority
FSA 1986	Financial Services Act 1986
FSMA 2000	Financial Services and Markets Act 2000
GAT	Gross Amount of Tax
GMP	Guaranteed Minimum Pension
HMRC	Her Majesty's Revenue and Customs
HRA 1998	Human Rights Act 1998
HSWA 1974	Health and Safety at Work etc. Act 1974
IA 1986	Insolvency Act 1986
ICTA 1988	Income and Corporation Taxes Act 1988
LEL	Lower Earnings Limit
LGHA 1989	Local Government and Housing Act 1989
LLPA 2000	Limited Liability Partnerships Act 2000
LPI	Limited price indexation

LTA 1954	Landlord and Tenant Act 1954
Ltd	Limited
MFR	Minimum Fund Requirement
NEST	National Employment Savings Trust
NI	National Insurance
NICs	National Insurance contributions
NMWA 1998	National Minimum Wage Act 1998
OAL	Ordinary Adoption Leave
OML	Ordinary Maternity Leave
OPAS	Occupational Pensions Advisory Service
OPB	Occupational Pensions Board
OPL	Ordinary Paternity Leave
OPRA	Occupational Pensions Regulatory Authority
PAYE	Pay As You Earn
PLC	Public Limited Company
PPF	Pension Protection Fund
PSO	Pension Schemes Office
PTS	Percentage Threshold Scheme
R&D	Research and Development
Reg	Regulation
RPI	Retail Price Index
RRA 1976	Race Relations Act 1976
S2P	State Second Pension
S(s)	Section(s)
SAP	Statutory Adoption Pay
SAS	Statement of Auditing Standard
Sch	Schedule
SDA 1975	Sex Discrimination Act 1975
SDRT	Stamp Duty Reserve Tax
SERPS	State Earnings Related Pension Scheme
SI	Statutory Instrument
SMA	State Maternity Allowance

SMEs	Small and Medium-Sized Enterprises
SMP	Statutory Maternity Pay
SPP	Statutory Paternity Pay
SSAS	Small Self-Administered Schemes
SSCBA 1992	Social Security Contributions and Benefits Act 1992
SSP	Statutory Sick Pay
Table A	Table A to the Companies (Tables A to F) Regulations 1985
TAT	True Amount of Tax
TUPE	Transfer of Undertakings (Protection of Employment)
TURERA 1993	Trade Union Reform and Employment Rights Act 1993
UEL	Upper Earnings Limit
VAT	Value Added Tax
WA 1986	Wages Act 1986

References

AC	Law Reports, Appeal Cases
AER	All England Law Reports
All ER	All England Law Reports
BCC	British Company Law Cases (CCH Editions Ltd)
BCLC	Butterworths Company Law Cases
Ch/ChD	Law Reports, Chancery Division
ECR	European Court Reports
EGLR	Estates Gazette Law Reports
EWCA Civ	Court of Appeal Civil Division
EWHC	High Court (followed by court abbreviation)
ICR	Industrial Cases Reports
IRLR	Industrial Relations Law Reports
KB	Law Reports, King's Bench Division
LR	Law Reports (followed by court abbreviation)

QB/QBD	Law Reports, Queen's Bench Division
UKHL	House of Lords
WLR	Weekly Law Reports

Chapter 1

The Company Secretary

Definition and authority

General

[1.1] The Companies Act 2006 (CA 2006) has brought about a change in the position of the company secretary in private companies. With effect from April 2008 there is no longer a requirement for a company secretary to be appointed, although this requirement remains unchanged for public companies. A private company may continue to appoint a company secretary if it so wishes and CA 2006, ss 270, 274–280 will apply to such a secretary. The appointee would be able to carry out the function of that office with the full authority that a company secretary has hitherto had under the Companies Act 1985 (CA 1985). Existing companies who have company secretaries can continue unaffected until such time as the company decides to take on the permissible change, whereby the secretary either resigns in the usual way or by decision by the directors.

It should be noted that the tasks performed by the company secretary will continue, ie the maintenance of the statutory registers and filing statutory returns, and it is important that companies that have decided not to appoint a company secretary have considered this.

Where a company has decided not to appoint a company secretary:

(a)   anything authorised or required to be given or sent to, or served on, the company by being sent to the company secretary:
    (i)   may be given or sent to, or served on, the company itself; and
    (ii)   if addressed to the company secretary shall be treated as addressed to the company; and
(b)   anything else required or authorised to be done by or to the company secretary of the company may be done by or to:
    (i)   a director; or
    (ii)   a person authorised generally or specifically in that behalf by the directors.

Many companies still consider the role of the company secretary as an important one, particularly with the attention being placed on corporate governance.

In 1877 the Master of the Rolls described the company secretary as:

> 'a mere servant; his position is that he is to do what he is told, and no person can assume that he has any authority to represent anything at all.'

This view of the ostensible authority of the company secretary in law remained for some considerable time. However, since the beginning of the century, the company secretary's profile has risen considerably.

The first recognition of this increasing importance by the courts came in the case of *Panorama Developments (Guildford) Ltd v Fidelis Furnishing Fabrics Ltd* [1971] 2 QB 711 where, in the Court of Appeal, Salmon LJ described the company secretary as:

> 'the chief administrative officer of the company.'

Lord Denning MR said:

> 'He regularly makes representations on behalf of the company and enters into contracts on its behalf which come within the day-to-day running of the company's business . . . He is certainly entitled to sign contracts connected with the administrative side of a company's affairs . . . All such matters now come within the ostensible authority of a company's secretary.'

Thus, the company secretary can be said to have an ostensible authority on behalf of a company to enter into contracts which are of an administrative nature. This authority could be said to extend to such matters as the employment of administrative staff (eg accounting staff), ordering of office/factory equipment and stationery and the arrangement of the company's insurance. The secretary's ostensible authority does not, however, extend to contracts of a managerial nature. To enter into such contracts the secretary must be given express authority by the directors.

The position of the modern company secretary's authority would therefore appear to be as follows:

(a)   If the secretary has express authority from the board, he may enter into contracts of both an administrative and managerial nature on behalf of the company, and the company will be bound by his acts.

(b)   When the secretary has no express authority, his ostensible authority will allow him to enter into contracts of an administrative nature on behalf of the company, and the company will be bound by such acts.

Should the secretary act beyond his ostensible authority, and without an express authority, the position appears to be that the company will be bound by his acts but he may be held personally liable by the company for any resultant loss.

Since the publication of the 'Cadbury Report', incorporating recommendations on corporate governance, even greater emphasis has been placed on the role of the company secretary. An example of this is that the code stipulates that all directors should have access to the company secretary, and that any question regarding his removal should be a matter for all the board.

It goes further to suggest that the company secretary has a key role to play in ensuring that board procedures are both followed regularly and reviewed and that the company secretary will be a source of advice to the chairman and to the board on the implementation of the Code of Best Practice (see **CHAPTER 6 THE DIRECTORS**).

The Higgs Review, published in January 2003, further strengthened the role of the company secretary with regard to corporate governance (see **6.13 THE DIRECTORS**).

Statutory recognition

[1.2] The recognition of the authority of the secretary also extends to legislation, with the company secretary being recognised by several Acts of Parliament.

Companies Act 2006 (with effect from April 2008)

[1.3] Section 270 of CA 2006 states that a private company is not required to have a secretary. For companies that continue to have a secretary the Act shall be construed accordingly. There is no requirement for the company secretary to be a natural person. Whilst not imposing any specific duties upon him, the secretary is authorised to sign various documents on behalf of a company (for example, the directors' report may be signed on behalf of the board by the secretary).

As an officer of the company the secretary can be held jointly liable for defaults which the company commits under the Act. Accordingly, a common assumption is that the secretary is the person responsible for maintaining a company's statutory books and records which are required to be maintained under the Act. Interestingly, the Act does not specify this as being a duty of the secretary but of the company. However, the directors will usually delegate this duty to the secretary and, as an officer of the company, the secretary would be liable for any default in carrying out those duties.

Insolvency Act 1986 and Company Directors Disqualification Act 1986

[1.4] Both of these Acts provide that where a body corporate is guilty of a certain offence and it is proved that the offence was committed with the consent or connivance of, or was attributable to any neglect on the part of, any director, manager, company secretary or other similar officer, that person will be guilty of an offence and may be proceeded against and punished accordingly.

Other legislation

[1.5] The company secretary is also recognised as a responsible officer of the company in other miscellaneous Acts of Parliament, examples being:

(a)   the Trade Descriptions Act 1968;
(b)   the Unsolicited Goods and Services Act 1971;
(c)   the Data Protection Act 1998; and
(d)   the Taxes Management Act 1970.

Other roles

[1.6] As well as the recognition that the company secretary now has in law, in modern practice it is increasingly common for the company secretary to have considerable managerial responsibilities within a company and also to be given certain express powers in areas such as investments and commercial contract arrangements. The additional roles will usually be defined in the secretary's contract, or terms and conditions of employment. Thus, today, the secretary can, in many ways, be described as forming the backbone of the organisation.

Appointment and qualifications

General

[1.7] Where a company has a company secretary, the following should be noted:

(a)   A sole director of a company may not also be the secretary (CA 2006, s 280).

(b)   No company may have as secretary, a corporation, the sole director of which is a sole director of the company.

(c)   Similarly, a company is prohibited from having as sole director, a corporation, the sole director of which is secretary to the company.

Regulation 99 of Table A 1985 provides model regulations surrounding the appointment of the company secretary:

> 'Subject to the provisions of the Act, the secretary shall be appointed by the directors for such term, at such remuneration and upon such conditions as they may think fit; and any secretary so appointed may be removed by them.'

Thus, under Table A 1985, the directors of a company have the power to appoint and remove the secretary. For a private company this causes no particular problem so long as the provisions above are not contravened.

The new Table A brought about by CA 2006 is silent on the procedure to appoint and remove the company secretary. As the company secretary is regarded as an officer of the company, it would be prudent to assume that his appointment or removal will continue unchanged.

In the case of a *public company*, CA 2006, s 273 imposes a further duty upon the directors to ensure that the secretary is a person who appears to them to have the requisite experience and knowledge to fulfil the role and who either:

(i)   for at least three out of the five years preceding his appointment as secretary, held the office of secretary of a company other than a private company;

(ii)   is a person who, by virtue of previous offices held, appears to the directors to be capable of discharging the functions required of the secretary;

(iii)   is a barrister, advocate or solicitor called or admitted in any part of the United Kingdom; or

(iv)   is a member of any of the following bodies:

    (A)   Institute of Chartered Secretaries and Administrators (ICSA);

    (B)   Institute of Chartered Accountants in England and Wales (ICAEW);

(C)   Institute of Chartered Accountants in Scotland (ICAS);

(D)   Institute of Chartered Accountants in Ireland (ICAI);

(E)   Chartered Institute of Management Accountants (CIMA);

(F)   Chartered Association of Certified Accountants (ACCA);

(G)   Chartered Institute of Public Finance and Accountancy (CIPFA).

These qualifications would also appear to apply in the circumstances where a private company re-registers as a public company (see **2.43 THE COMPANY CONSTITUTION**).

A company may, if it wishes, make further regulations in its articles of association for the appointment and removal of the secretary.

Procedure on appointment

[1.8] The first secretary of a company is appointed by the completion of the appropriate section on form IN01 submitted to Companies House in the application for registration (see **2.36 THE COMPANY CONSTITUTION**). His appointment is deemed to commence from the date the company is incorporated.

Subsequent appointments are made by the appropriate resolution of the board and in accordance with the articles of association, ie:

'It was resolved that [   ] be and is hereby appointed Secretary of the company in the place of [   ] who resigned as Secretary on [   ] 200[   ].'

Following appointment, the details of the new secretary must be entered in the register of secretaries (CA 2006, s 275) and a return in the prescribed form (form AP03, or AP04 for corporate secretary) must be made to Companies House within 14 days of the date of the change (CA 2006, s 276).

Similarly, any change in the details of the secretary must also be notified to Companies House on form CH03 within 14 days of their occurrence and the details entered in the register of secretaries.

The Criminal Justice and Police Act 2001 introduced new sections 723B–723F to CA 1985 to enable residential addresses of both directors and secretaries to be kept secure on a separate register maintained at Companies House. The said changes came into force on 2 April 2002. The individual had to apply for a Confidentiality Order using a form 723B and pay a statutory fee of £100. The application was sent to the Administrator at Companies House who would, if satisfied that the individual, or any person living with them, was at serious risk of violence or intimidation, grant an exemption from having to disclose a home address. A director had to provide an alternative service address for public disclosure, whilst his home address was kept on a separate confidential register, with restricted access (eg for the Police). Any historic records held at Companies House were not removed.

Sections 162–167 of CA 2006 came into effect in October 2009 to, by default, allow all directors and secretaries to provide a service address (which may be the registered office address) when registering their appointments with Companies House. Their usual residential address will still be required but will be kept on a separate confidential register.

Where the company is listed, it may be thought appropriate to notify the London Stock Exchange of the appointment as it could be regarded as an important change in the holding of an executive office, however this is not obligatory.

Removal and resignation

[1.9] Unless otherwise stated in a company's articles of association the secretary may be removed by a resolution of the board, ie:

> 'It was resolved that [   ] be and is hereby removed as Secretary of the company with immediate effect.'

The Companies Act 2006 makes no special procedure which must be followed, as in the removal of a director (see **6.11 THE DIRECTORS**).

A secretary may also resign office at any time.

The resignation or removal of a secretary must be notified to Companies House on form TM02 within 14 days of the date of resignation or removal.

Although removal from office is a remarkably simple procedure the secretary may have recourse against the company under any service contract or contract of employment for breach of contract.

It should be noted, however, that the 'Cadbury Report' recommends that in the case of the removal of a secretary this should be an item for the whole of the board to decide.

Joint secretary

[1.10] Where a company has joint secretaries then CA 2006, s 275 requires the details of each to be entered in the register of secretaries and accordingly notified to Companies House (on form AP03). It follows then that their authority is joint, and hence all acts should be done together, eg signing and giving of notices. However, if it is the company's intention for the joint secretaries to act jointly and severally, express authority to that effect should be given in the articles or recorded in the board minute appointing them.

Scope of duties and responsibilities

General

[1.11] The duties and responsibilities of a company secretary vary widely from company to company and will commonly be defined in the secretary's contract of employment or by the board of directors of the company. The secretary has become increasingly recognised by statute as being the officer of the company responsible for certain activities (see **1.1** above). However, in general, the extent and nature of a company secretary's duties are not defined in law and, accordingly, the secretary must look to his contract of employment and the company's articles of association to ascertain his precise responsibilities in any company. The secretary as an 'officer' of the company can be said to be jointly and severally liable with the other officers of a company for ensuring the performance of certain activities.

The Companies Act 2006 imposes a number of duties on the secretary (where one is appointed) or upon him as an alternative to another person including:

(a)   the completion and signing of the annual return of the company;
(b)   the signing of the directors' report in the company's annual accounts;
(c)   the completion and signing of various Companies House forms;
(d)   the making of applications on behalf of the company to Companies House; and
(e)   the making of various statutory declarations on behalf of the company.

These are the basic duties; the actual scope of the secretary's duties will differ from company to company but will normally include:

(i)   the maintenance of the statutory registers of the company;
(ii)   attendance at board meetings, the formulation of agendas, taking minutes of the meeting, preparation of articles and notices to shareholders, and ensuring that correct procedures are followed both at board and general meetings;
(iii)   the custody of the company seal; and
(iv)   the authentication and retention of documents.

Maintenance of the statutory registers

[1.12] The Companies Act 2006 requires that every company maintain the following registers:

(a)   register of members;
(b)   register of charges;
(c)   minute books of the proceedings of meetings of the members of the company;
(d)   accounting records;
(e)   register of directors;
(f)   register of directors' residential addresses;
(g)   register of secretaries;
(h)   if the company is a public company, a register of interests in voting shares.

The secretary should ensure that all the registers are correctly maintained and that they are kept at the location specified by the Act. The secretary must also ensure that the requirements of the Act relating to the inspection of the registers are complied with at all times and, where notifiable changes are made, that Companies House is informed within the time limits specified in the Act (see **CHAPTER 3 THE STATUTORY RECORDS** for details).

Meetings and minutes

[1.13] The secretary of a company is usually expected to make the arrangements for meetings of the directors and members of the company. He is also expected to attend the meetings and take minutes. At general meetings it is usual for the secretary to read the notice to the meeting. Where possible a secretary should attempt to prepare agendas prior to meetings, setting out the items of business that are to be considered in a logical, clear and concise order.

The secretary should keep a file of documents that require the attention of the directors so that no items of concern are overlooked at board meetings. Agendas for board meetings should be prepared and circulated in advance, together with any papers or reports relating to the proposed items of discussion. The chairman's and secretary's copies of the agenda should have spaces, so as to allow notes to be made.

At the end of the meeting the secretary should use the chairman's copy of the agenda and his own to prepare the minutes.

The minutes should be completely impartial and in most circumstances should not include details of the discussions leading to decisions.

Extreme care should be taken in preparing minutes so as to make them as clear and concise as possible. The chairman of the meeting should then sign the minutes presented at the next board meeting, and the secretary should place them in the minute book.

Minutes do not need to be read out at the next meeting or approved by anybody other than the chairman but should, as a matter of good practice, be circulated to the other persons present at the meeting to allow them to comment on their content.

No amendments should be made to the minutes except to correct obvious errors and these should be initialled by the chairman before he signs them. Once the minutes have been signed they cannot be altered and any subsequent changes must be approved by a resolution at a meeting.

The statutory requirements relating to minutes are contained in **3.43–3.47 THE STATUTORY RECORDS.**

The company seal

[1.14] Section 45 of CA 2006 no longer makes it compulsory for a company to have a common seal. It may, however, have one if it so wishes. If a company has a seal it must have the name of the company engraved in legible characters on it.

The seal will normally be kept by the secretary who should keep a record of all the documents to which the seal is affixed. This may be conveniently done in a register of sealings.

Where a company does not have a seal, documents which are expressed as being executed 'on behalf of the company' and signed by a director and the secretary (or by two directors) and which are accordingly treated as being under seal, should be entered in the record of sealings (see **CHAPTER 11 COMMERCIAL CONSIDERATIONS**).

The directors of a company should authorise the execution of such documents and those under seal.

If a company transacts business abroad, it may (if permitted by its articles of association) have one or more seals for use overseas and may authorise a person overseas to affix it to any document. Such a seal will be a facsimile of the common seal with the addition of the name of the place where it is to be used.

The secretary should, at all times, ensure the adequacy of the security of the seal to prevent it being fraudulently affixed to documents.

Authentication and retention of documents

[1.15] The secretary is authorised by CA 2006, s 44 to authenticate any document requiring authentication by the company. Such authentication need not be under the seal of the company. As such authentications are requested frequently by banks etc and many secretaries have stamps made which state that a document is 'certified to be a true original copy . . . . Secretary'.

One of the main administrative duties of a secretary may be to ensure that documents that need to be retained for a requisite period are so retained and then destroyed at the appropriate time.

Stationery

[1.16] Sections 82 and 84 of CA 2006 require every company to mention certain details in its business stationery. Failure to do so renders every officer of the company in default liable to a fine. Thus the main responsibility for ensuring that a company's stationery meets the requirements of the Act will usually fall to the secretary (see **2.19 THE COMPANY CONSTITUTION**).

Administrative responsibilities

[1.17] In addition to the statutory duties detailed above, the modern day company secretary will also find himself engaged in the following administrative responsibilities.

Compliance

(a)   Making certain that the company complies with the memorandum and articles of association and drafting amendments to ensure that they are kept up to date.

(b)   Where the company's securities are listed on the Stock Exchange, ensuring compliance with the 'Listing Rules', releasing information to the market and ensuring security in respect of unreleased price-sensitive information.

Shares/shareholders

(i)   Dealing with transfers, transmissions and forfeiture of shares, issuing share certificates, attending to shareholders' queries and requests, and where some of these functions are delegated to Registrars, the secretary will be responsible for liaison with them to settle matters of particular sensitivity.

(ii)   Communicating with the shareholders through the issue of circulars, payment of dividends, distribution of documentation regarding rights/capitalisation issues and general shareholder relations.

(iii)   Monitoring movements on the register of members to identify any possible 'stake-building' in the company's shares, making enquiries of shareholders as to beneficial ownership of holdings under CA 2006, s 793, maintaining a register of material interests, and making timely announcements to the Stock Exchange.

(iv)   Implementing changes in the company's share and loan structure, and administering directors' and employees' share option schemes.

(v)   Where the company is involved in an acquisition or disposal, the secretary will have a number of responsibilities, especially in ensuring the effectiveness of all documentation and due diligence disclosures.

Directors

(A)   Preparing the directors' report and co-ordinating the printing and distribution of the company's interim statements and annual report and accounts in consultation with the company's advisers.

(B)   Keeping directors up to date on new developments in corporate governance and advising directors of their duties, responsibilities and personal obligations.

(C)   Acting as a channel of communication for non-executive directors and providing them with relevant information.

Miscellaneous

(I)   Administering the registered office, including dealing with official correspondence received.

(II)   Maintaining a record of the group structure.

(III)   Involvement in payroll, credit control, corporate finance, commercial law, contract vetting/drafting/negotiating, litigation, property management, employment law, personnel administration, pensions, insurance and risk management, office administration and company car schemes.

Liabilities

[1.18] The secretary, as an officer of the company, may be liable with the directors to default fines for non-compliance with the Companies Act in several of the aforementioned situations (see **1.17** above). The penalties vary accordingly and are governed by CA 2006, s 1121. He will, without doubt, fall within the meaning of the expression 'any officer of the company who knowingly or wilfully authorised or permits the default, refusal or contravention mentioned in the enactment' (CA 2006, s 1121(3)).

The fiduciary duties owed by a director are not dissimilar to those which may be applied to the position held by the company secretary. Therefore, the company secretary must, as an officer of the company, act in good faith in the interests of the company and not act for any collateral person. He must avoid any conflicts of interest and must not make profits from dealings for and on behalf of the company.

It should be noted that a company can take out and maintain insurance for its officers against any liability arising from negligence, default and breach of duty, subject to the appropriate provision being contained within the company's articles.

As a cautionary note, the secretary when making contracts on behalf of the company should always ensure that he does so as the company's agent otherwise he could be held personally liable.

Chapter 2

The Company Constitution

The limited company

General

[2.1] The Companies Act 2006 (CA 2006) introduces changes in the method of incorporating companies. These changes came into effect on 1 October 2009 and although the requirements are largely the same in that individuals wishing to form a company must subscribe their names to the memorandum of association, CA 2006, s 7(1) states that a single person is able to form any sort of company, including a public limited company.

Incorporation is the process by which a company may be formed and become a separate legal entity in its own right; distinct from its owners. This principle of the company being a separate legal person was established in 1897 in the case of *Salomon v Salomon and Co Ltd* [1897] AC 22. The Companies Acts have since established the procedure by which a company can be created and this is specified in Part I of CA 1985, section 1(1) of which states:

> 'Any two or more persons associated for a lawful purpose may, by subscribing their names to a memorandum of association and otherwise complying with the requirements of this Act in respect of registration, form an incorporated company, with or without limited liability.'

Section 1(3A) of CA 1985 (inserted by the Schedule to the Companies (Single Member Private Limited Companies) Regulations 1992 (SI 1992/1699)) allowed one person to form a private company limited by shares or by guarantee by subscribing his name to the memorandum, so long as he complied with the registration requirements of the Act. These provisions were introduced on 15 July 1992. The single person may be a natural or a legal person.

The responsibility for recording minutes and decisions made in general meetings, together with the drawing up of any contract in writing outside of normal conditions between himself and the company, then lay with the sole member or his representative. Single member private limited companies are considered more fully later (see **CHAPTER 7 MEMBERSHIP**).

To effect the incorporation of a limited liability company, CA 2006, like its predecessors, requires the preparation and presentation of certain documents to Companies House. When the Registrar is satisfied that the documents fulfil the requirements of the Act, a certificate of incorporation will be issued. This can be regarded as a company's 'birth certificate' and is conclusive evidence that the requirements of the Act in respect of registration have been complied with and that the company is authorised to be registered (CA 2006, s 17). The basic aim of the incorporation process is to ensure that sufficient information appears on the public file, maintained by Companies House, to enable the public to make an assessment of the company and of the risks attendant in dealing with it (see **CHAPTER 5 DISCLOSURE AND REPORTING REQUIREMENTS**).

Reasons for incorporation

[2.2] In Great Britain, businesses may take many different legal forms. For most people considering which form of business to use, the choice usually faced is whether to go into business as:

(a)   a sole trader;
(b)   a partnership;
(c)   a limited liability company; or
(d)   a limited liability partnership.

Other types of business organisation do exist, for example, Industrial and Provident Societies and Building Societies. However, in comparison to (*a*) to (*d*) above, their use is limited for most purposes. There have recently been two new types of companies that can be incorporated, namely the European Public Liability Company – Societas Europea – and Community Interest Companies.

European Public Liability Company (SE) – these companies are suitable for businesses that operate in more than one Member State and can be set up by registration with Companies House using the appropriate forms SE FM01, 02, 03, 04 and 05. The minimum capital requirement for an SE is 120,000 euros.

Community Interest Companies (CIC) – these companies are a new type of company that can be set up for social enterprises that want to use their profits and assets for the public good. From 1 July 2005, the Companies (Audit Investigation and Community Enterprises) Act 2004, in its provisions, established the statutory framework for the creation, conduct and supervision of CICs. Together with the Community Interest Company Regulations 2005 (SI 2005/1788), it covers in detail the mechanics for applying to set up a new CIC or convert an existing company into a CIC.

Many factors exist in deciding what identity a business should take, for example, taxation considerations. In this decision process the advantages and disadvantages of the incorporation must be examined carefully, and professional advice should be sought where appropriate. The main advantages and disadvantages of incorporation are as follows.

Advantages

(i)   The limited liability of the members, where the company is limited.
(ii)   The ability to raise capital from outside the existing membership.
(iii) The ability to borrow money in the company's name.
(iv)   A company is taxed in its own right as distinct from its members.
(v)   The continuance of the existence of the business notwithstanding the death or bankruptcy of all or any of its existing members.

Disadvantages

(A)   Requirements of the Companies Acts to disclose information about the company.

(B)   A greater formality is involved in setting up, running and winding up a company.
(C)   Various tax considerations may prove a disincentive.
(D)   The requirement to undergo a formal audit of the accounts each year (subject to exemptions for certain categories of small company and dormant companies (see **4.14** and **4.22** ACCOUNTS AND AUDITORS).

Classification of companies

[2.3] Under the Act there exist three basic types of company which may be incorporated, being:

(a)   a company limited by shares;
(b)   an unlimited company; and
(c)   a company limited by guarantee and having no share capital.

Of the three types, the most commonly used for trading entities in Great Britain is the company limited by shares. However, there are two distinct classifications of company within this type, being the private limited company and the public limited company. Both unlimited companies and companies limited by guarantee are (by virtue of the definition given by CA 2006 to public companies) private companies.

The Act does, however, provide for the registration of certain other classifications of company. These companies fall into the following categories:

(i)   oversea companies having a place of business in Great Britain;
(ii)   an Isle of Man or Channel Islands company having a place of business in England and Wales and/or Scotland.

The registration of these types of company are discussed more fully in **2.48** below.

Additionally CA 2006, s 1040 allows for the registration of companies:

(A)   consisting of two or more members, which were in existence on 2 November 1862, including any company registered under the Joint Stock Companies Acts; and
(B)   any company formed after 2 November 1862, in pursuance of any Act of Parliament, or of letters patent, or being otherwise duly constituted according to law, and consisting of two or more members.

The Act also makes provision for the re-registration of companies as follows:

(I)   of a private company limited by shares as a public company limited by shares (CA 2006, ss 90–95);
(II)   of a public company limited by shares as a private company limited by shares (CA 2006, ss 97–100);
(III) of a limited company as an unlimited company (CA 2006, ss 102, 103); and
(IV)   of an unlimited company as a limited company (CA 2006, ss 105, 106).

The re-registration of companies is dealt with in **2.43–2.46** below.

The public limited company

[2.4] Section 4(2) of CA 2006 states that a public company is a company whose certificate of incorporation states that it is a public company.

The provisions of the Act as regards the registration of public companies are basically the same as for private companies. However, certain significant differences exist in relation to:

(a)   capital; and
(b)   commencement of trading.

These points are discussed more fully in **2.42** below.

The private limited company

[2.5] Section 4(1) of CA 2006 states that by definition a private company is a company 'that is not a public company'.

The differences in the classification of companies limited by shares were first introduced by the Companies Act 1980, the provisions of which were then incorporated in CA 1985, to give effect to the European Community 2nd Company Law Directive of 1976 which was aimed at public companies.

The reasons why the classifications were introduced are now mainly historic. However, the basic difference between the two is that under CA 2006, s 755 it is an offence for a private company to offer or to allot any of its shares or debentures to the public, whether for cash or otherwise. Section 81 was repealed for most purposes by sections 143(3) and 170(1) of the Financial Services Act 1986 but the basic principles introduced by CA 1985, s 81 remain the same.

Liability

[2.6] The concept of limited liability is one which relates to the liability of the membership of a company to contribute to the assets of the company should it be wound up. The amount of the members' liability is determined by the liability clause contained in the company's memorandum of association and differs in its nature according to whether the company is one which is limited by shares, limited by guarantee or unlimited.

(a)   **Limited by shares**
        A company limited by shares is formed on the basis that the liability of the members is limited to the amount (if any) unpaid on the shares held by them. A member's liability does not extend beyond any amounts unpaid on shares should the company be wound up.
(b)   **Limited by guarantee**
        The liability of the members is limited to an amount which the members each undertake to contribute to the assets of the company should it be wound up. In effect, each member makes a guarantee to pay a specified amount to the company.
(c)   **Unlimited**

No limit to the liability of the members exists, thus the meml
such a company may, in the event of the company being woun
themselves liable to pay or contribute towards the debts of the
and the winding-up costs.

The privilege of obtaining limited liability, however, is only available where a company is limited by shares or by guarantee.

It should be borne in mind that, given the current practice of the banks to seek personal guarantees from directors and/or shareholders, the attractions of limited liability may be somewhat short-lived.

Nature of companies

[2.7] The Register of Companies maintained by Companies House currently contains around one million companies which have been registered under the Companies Acts. Of this figure, around 99% are private companies (of which private companies limited by shares form the overwhelming majority). Public companies represent only 1% of companies registered. However, this is an increase from previous years. In 1985 public companies represented only 0.5% of companies registered.

The reason for this overwhelming use of the private company limited by shares comes out of the balance of the ability of the company to raise initial capital compared with the company limited by guarantee and the less onerous requirements of the Act compared with the public company (see CHAPTER 7 MEMBERSHIP).

(a) **Capital**
     By definition, the members of a company limited by guarantee do not contribute any funds to the capital of the company on the assumption of their membership. They instead make a guarantee to do so should the company be wound up. Thus, the introduction of new members to the company will not, in itself, assist the company to raise capital.
     For a company limited by shares, subject to certain requirements imposed by the Act (see **8.8 CAPITAL**), members are usually asked to pay a cash consideration to the company in return for the allotment of shares.
     Thus, the incorporation and use of a company limited by guarantee will only be appropriate where the company will be obtaining its funds by other means than the issue of shares. As such, the guarantee company is commonly used where funds are raised by fees or subscriptions and thus is suited to the incorporation of a club, society, association, institute or other 'not for profit' organisation. Guarantee companies are commonly used where charitable status will be required.
(b) **Companies Act requirements**
     The requirements of the Act vary in certain respects in relation to private and public limited companies in that the Act imposes additional requirements upon public companies in the disclosure of information and capital requirements.

Incorporation requirements

General

[2.8] The registration of a limited company is effected by the delivery to the Registrar of Companies of the documents specified by CA 2006, the company's compliance with the various procedures contained therein and the payment to the Registrar of Companies of the appropriate fee (£40 as at the time of this publication for paper incorporation, or £14 for electronic incorporation).

Prior to proceeding to registration, however, several matters must first be considered.

The company name

[2.9] In general, a company may register itself under any name it chooses. The Companies Act 2006, the Business Names Act 1985 and common law do, however, place certain restrictions on the use of company and business names.

Companies Act 2006

[2.10] Section 65 of CA 2006 defines several circumstances in which a company shall not be registered under CA 2006 by a name:

(a)   which includes, otherwise than at the end of the name, any of the following words or expressions – 'Limited', 'Unlimited' or 'Public Limited Company' (CA 2006, s 58 allows the abbreviations 'Ltd' and 'PLC' to be used as alternatives to the full forms);

(b)   which is the same as a name already appearing on the index of company names maintained by the Registrar of Companies; or

(c)   the use of which, in the opinion of the Secretary of State, would constitute a criminal offence or is considered offensive.

When considering whether to refuse to register a name which is the 'same as' an existing name, Companies House will apply a strict CA 2006, s 66 test. Therefore, when comparing names punctuation will be ignored, as will differences between 'and' and '&', abbreviations of company/limited, and the use of accents, capital letters and spaces.

Also, without the prior approval of the Secretary of State, a company may not be registered by a name:

(d)   which in the opinion of the Secretary of State would be likely to give the impression that the company is connected in any way with HM Government or with any local authority (CA 2006, s 56 now extends this to cover the Scottish administration and HM Government in Northern Ireland); or

(e)   which includes any word or expression which is specified for the time being by the Secretary of State (see **APPENDIX 2B**).

Prior to registration of a company, it is important that a check be undertaken on the index of names maintained by the Registrar of Companies under CA

2006, s 1099, to ensure that the name required is not already being used. However, the Registrar also maintains a 'proposed name' index for companies which have lodged the relevant documents for registration but which have not yet been processed. While a name may not appear on the statutory index, it still may not be available for use.

It should be noted that the Registrar does not consult the Trade Marks Index when considering an application for a company name, and the registration of a name does not mean that trade marks do not already exist. It is therefore advisable to make a search at the Trade Marks Registry if in doubt. (See **11.16** COMMERCIAL CONSIDERATIONS.)

Business Names Act 1985

[2.11] As well as the restrictions placed on the use of company names under CA 2006, the Business Names Act 1985 further introduces a system for regulating the use of names under which companies, partnerships and individuals may carry on business in Great Britain. As regards a company registered under the Companies Act these regulations apply to it in circumstances where the company carries on business in a name other than its corporate name.

The main provisions of this Act as it applies to companies are as follows:

(a)   Except with the prior written approval of the Secretary of State a company may not carry on business under a name which would be likely to give the impression that the business is connected with Her Majesty's Government or with any local authority or the name includes any word or expression specified in regulations made by Statutory Instrument. Failure to acquire consent by the Secretary of State for a name needing approval is a criminal offence.

(b)   Where a company is using a name other than its corporate name it must state in legible characters on all its business letters, written orders for the supply of goods and services, invoices, receipts and demands for payment of debts arising in the course of business, the corporate name of the company and an address within Great Britain at which the service of documents relating to the business will be effective (usually the registered office address). This is in addition to a company's stationery requirements as specified in the Companies Act (CA 2006, ss 82 and 84).

(c)   At any premises where the business is carried on to which the customers of the business or suppliers of any goods or services to the business have access, to display in a prominent position so that it may easily be read, a notice containing those names and addresses specified above. The company must also, on request, supply such names and addresses to any person who, in the course of business, may ask for them.

It should also be noted that it is an offence for any person who is not a public company to carry on any trade, profession or business with a name which contains the words 'Public Limited Company' (or its abbreviation).

Further, any person trading or carrying on a business is prevented to use the word 'Limited' (or its abbreviation) unless duly incorporated with limited liability.

Too like names

[2.12] Section 67 of CA 2006 gives the Secretary of State a power, in certain circumstances, to direct a company to change its name. This power is exercisable where a company has been registered with a name that is either 'the same as' or 'too like' a name already appearing on the Register of Companies at the time the name was first registered.

Names which are considered 'the same as' or 'too like' will usually be brought to the Registrar's attention by the company for whom the name is 'the same as' or 'too like' lodging an objection and requesting that the company name be changed. In submitting an objection, the objecting party should give support to his objection by detailing his reasons for the application and giving evidence of any confusion between the companies that has arisen.

It is important to note that the power of the Secretary of State to direct a company to change its name in these circumstances is only exercisable for a period of twelve months from the date of registration of the name which is 'the same as' or 'too like' an existing name. Thus, objections lodged after this twelve-month period will be disregarded. However, in circumstances where the Secretary of State considers that misleading information was provided to him for the purpose of securing the registration of a company with a particular name or that undertakings or assurances given in this connection were not fulfilled, then the power of the Secretary of State to direct that the name of a company be changed is extended to five years from the date of registration in that name.

Failure to comply with a direction from the Secretary of State to change a company name may render the directors of the company so directed liable to a fine. The criteria which the Registrar will apply in determining whether a company is 'too like' an existing name is that of a visual comparison, although phonetic similarities will also be considered. When issuing a section 67 direction to change a company name, Companies House will not take into account the intended or existing types of business carried on or geographical location.

Examples of circumstances, subject to the above criteria, in which names will be considered 'the same as' or 'too like' others are where:

(a) *The names are the same*
eg PL Lai Limited and PL Lai Company, Limited.

(b) *The names are phonetically identical*
eg Tricor UK Limited and Trycor UK Limited.

(c) *The names contain only a slight variation in spelling which does not make a significant difference*
eg Aquiss Limited and Aquis Limited.

(d) *The names contain a word (or words) which are regarded as a distinctive element and that element is not sufficiently qualified*
eg Aquis Limited and Aquis <u>Holdings</u> Limited.
In this circumstance the addition of the word 'Holdings' to the name would not sufficiently qualify the name, the word 'Aquis' being considered the distinctive element.
Should a more distinctive qualification be added, then the names may then be considered sufficiently distinctive

eg Aquis <u>Engineers</u> Limited and Aquis <u>Secretaries</u> Limited.

Company Names Adjudicator

[2.13] Section 70 of CA 2006 is a new provision that enables the Secretary of State to appoint persons to the office of Company Names Adjudicator. Appointees must have such legal or other experience as, in the Secretary of State's opinion, makes them suitable for appointment. One adjudicator must be appointed as Chief Adjudicator. The function of such adjudicators will be to hear objections brought about under CA 2006, s 69.

The Company Names Adjudicator Rules 2008 (SI 2008/1738) came into force on 1 October 2008. The purpose of these rules is to regulate the proceedings before a Company Names Adjudicator under CA 2006, s 69 and prescribe the procedure for objecting to a company's registered name, set out the general powers of the Adjudicator in relation to proceedings, and include provisions relating to extension of time limits, evidence and costs or expenses of the proceedings.

Overseas company names

[2.14] In the case of an overseas company (see **2.48** below), such registration will not be permitted in the overseas company's name if it differs from an existing registered company name only by the substitution of the overseas equivalent of 'Limited', 'Unlimited' or 'Public Limited Company' (or their permitted abbreviations).

eg Aquis <u>S.A.</u> and Aquis <u>PLC.</u>

Additionally, the provisions of CA 2006, s 65 (see **2.10** above) apply to the registration of overseas company names.

Misleading name

[2.15] Pursuant to the power given to him by CA 2006, s 76, the Secretary of State (acting through the Registrar of Companies) may *at any time* direct a company to change its name if, in his opinion, the continued use of the name gives a misleading indication of the nature of the activities a company undertakes and that this is likely to cause harm to the public.

Where such a direction is made it must normally be complied with within six weeks. The company receiving the direction does, however, in such circumstances, have a right of appeal to the court, within three weeks of receiving the direction, to have it set aside. This contrasts with any direction to change a company name given under CA 2006, s 77 where no right of appeal to the court exists.

Exemption from using the word 'Limited' in a company name

[2.16] Section 60 of CA 2006 specifies certain circumstances in which a company may be exempted from the use of the word 'Limited' in its name.

To qualify for such an exemption the company making the application must be a private company *limited by guarantee* and must satisfy the following conditions:

(a)   the objects of the company are the promotion of either commerce, art, science, education, religion, charity or of any profession;

(b)   the memorandum and articles of association state that:

    (i)   any profits or other income will be applied in promoting the company's objects;

    (ii)   the payment of dividends to the members is prohibited; and

    (iii)   on a winding-up, all the assets of the company will be transferred to another body having similar objects or of which the objects are the promotion of a charity.

Furthermore, a company which was a private company limited by shares on 25 February 1982, may also be exempt, but only if it did not include the word 'Limited' in its name due to a licence it had under section 19 of the Companies Act 1948 and it complies with the above conditions: (*a*) and (*b*).

In support of the application a company must submit to the Registrar of Companies a statutory declaration made by either a director or secretary of the company (or a solicitor engaged in the company's formation) on form NE01 which confirms that the above requirements have been met.

Should a company which has obtained an exemption from using the word 'Limited' in its name fail to continue to fulfil the conditions required to so exempt it, then the Registrar of Companies may direct the company to change its name to include the word 'Limited' at its end.

Passing off

[2.17] Although through the various means and protections afforded by CA 2006, a company can protect its name by objecting to the registration of a company with a similar name, such protections are not open to a company when faced with the position that an *unincorporated* business is using a similar name (for example, possibly the same name with the exception of the words 'Limited' or 'Public Limited Company').

In such circumstances, no right of objection exists through the Registrar of Companies. However, the common law principle of 'passing off' may apply. Action may be taken by the objecting company through the courts which seeks to restrain the use of a particular name by another party, on the basis that a person may not represent himself as carrying on the trade or business of another. Such actions will usually succeed where it can be shown that the use of a particular name has or will mislead the public (*Ewing v Buttercup Margarine Co Ltd* [1917] 2 Ch 1).

Insolvency Act 1986

[2.18] Under section 216 of the Insolvency Act 1986 a person who at any time in the preceding twelve months has been a director of a company which has gone into insolvent liquidation, is disallowed:

(a)   from being a director of any other company which is known by a prohibited name;

(b)   from taking part in the promotion, formation and management of any such company; or

(c)   from being involved in the carrying on of a business, which is not a company, under a prohibited name.

A prohibited name is the name by which the company was known in the twelve months prior to the liquidation or one which is so similar to suggest association with that company.

The restriction lasts for five years from the day the company went into liquidation and if a director contravenes any of the above regulations he is liable to imprisonment, or a fine, or both.

Publication of company name

[2.19] Under the provisions of CA 2006 a company must fulfil certain obligations imposed by the Act to publish its name, and other prescribed details, on its business stationery. Failure to do so renders every officer of the company in default, liable to a fine.

Section 82 of CA 2006 requires that a company's name must appear in legible characters upon:

(a)   all business letters;

(b)   all notices and other official publications;

(c)   all bills of exchange, promissory notes, endorsements, cheques and orders for money or goods purporting to be signed by or on behalf of the company; and

(d)   all bills of parcels, invoices, receipts and letters of credit.

There is a further requirement under the Companies (Trading Disclosures) Regulations 2008 (SI 2008/495) that the following details appear in legible characters on companies' business letters and order forms:

(i)   place of registration (ie England and Wales or Scotland);

(ii)   registered number;

(iii)   registered office address;

(iv)   where the company is exempt from the use of the word 'Limited' as part of its name, a statement that the company is limited (eg 'a company limited by guarantee');

(v)   if the company is an 'investment company' (within the definition of CA 2006, s 833), a statement that it is such a company.

There is no obligation on companies to state on their business stationery the names of any of the directors. However, should a company opt to do so (otherwise than as the signatory or in the text) then the names of *all* the directors must appear, including those of any shadow directors.

Similarly, a company having a share capital is under no obligation to state its share capital on its stationery. However, should it choose to do so, then any reference made must be to the *paid-up* share capital.

Companies using e-mail as a means of communication, should note that business letters and order forms sent by electronic messaging should still comply with the statutory requirements laid down by CA 2006. The Criminal Evidence Act 1985, which came into force on 31 January 1997, makes it clear that computer generated documents are admissible in proceedings and can be treated in the same way as paper documents.

Similarly it is considered best practice to include on faxes the information you would show on business letters and with an order form placed on a website the same details as required by CA 2006.

Section 111 of the Companies Act 1989 substituted sections 30, 30A, 30B and 30C for the original section 30 in the Charities Act 1960. The 1960 Act has since been consolidated into the Charities Act 1993 (see **11.9 COMMERCIAL CONSIDERATIONS**). Section 68 of the 1993 Act requires that a charity incorporated under the Companies Act (or to which the provisions of the Companies Act apply), where its name does not include the word 'charity' or the word 'charitable', must state the fact that it is a charity on all business stationery and in all conveyances purporting to be executed by the company. Section 84(1)–(3) of CA 2006 applies in relation to a contravention of this section.

Section 82 of CA 2006 further requires a company to paint or affix its name outside every office or place from which it carries on business. The name painted or affixed must be placed in a conspicuous position and be legible. Failure to comply with this section renders the company and every officer of that company who is in default liable to a fine.

It should be noted that these provisions are in addition to any provisions with which a company must comply pursuant to the Business Names Act 1985 (see **2.11** above).

Change of company name

[2.20] In accordance with CA 2006, s 77 a company may, by a special resolution of its members, change its name (see **PRECEDENT A, APPENDIX 2D**). When changing a company name, a similar process to that described above must be undertaken to ensure the name's availability and acceptability. When passed, a copy of the special resolution changing the company name must be filed at Companies House (CA 2006, s 30) within 15 days of its passing, together with a cheque for £10 (as at the time of this publication) in payment of the appropriate fee.

Section 79 of CA 2006 is a new provision which provides that a company may change its name by any means provided for in its articles.

Once the name has been approved, the Registrar of Companies will issue to the company a Certificate of Incorporation on Change of Name and alter the name of the company on the Register of Companies. The new company name becomes effective as from the date of issue of the Certificate of Incorporation on Change of Name (CA 2006, s 80).

During company reorganisations it is often preferable for companies simultaneously to swap their names. This can be achieved by writing an explanatory letter to the Registrar enclosing the respective special resolutions.

A company which is listed must inform the Listing Authority of the name change and date from which it takes effect without delay and send them a copy of the change of name certificate (Listing Rules, para 9.40).

The memorandum of association

[2.21] Section 7 of CA 2006, which came into effect from October 2009, states that a company is formed by one or more person subscribing their names to a memorandum of association. The memorandum looks very different to the previous format to reflect the simplification ethos of the new Act. It must be in the prescribed form and must be authenticated by each subscriber. In addition it will not be possible to amend or update the memorandum of a company formed under CA 2006. The previous clauses no longer appear but will instead be dealt with under CA 2006, ss 9–13.

For existing companies, CA 2006, s 28 deals with this as follows:

(a) Provisions that immediately before the commencement of this Part were contained in a company's memorandum but are not provisions of the kind mentioned in section 8 (provisions of new style memorandum) are to be treated after the commencement of this Part as provisions of the company's articles. This document constitutes a company's charter with the outside world, being more particularly the persons with whom a company will transact, either directly or indirectly, in the course of its business.

(b) This applies not only to substantive provisions but also to provision for entrenchment (as defined by CA 2006, s 22).

(c) The provisions of this Part about provision for entrenchment apply to such provision as they apply to provision made on the company's formation, except that the duty under section 23(1)(a) to give notice to the Registrar does not apply.

Previously, CA 1985, s 2 provided that the memorandum of association of a company must state:

(i) the name of the company;

(ii) in the case of public companies only, a statement that the company is a Public Limited Company (CA 1985, s 25);

(iii) whether the domicile of the company is to be in England and Wales, or in Scotland;

(iv) the objects of the company;

(v) that the liability of the members is limited;

(vi) in the case of a company limited by shares, the amount of authorised share capital with which the company is to be incorporated and how the shares are to be divided, or for a company limited by guarantee, the amount each member undertakes to contribute to the assets of the company in the event of it being wound up;

(vii) the names of the subscribers and, in the case of a company limited by shares, the number of shares to be taken by each (a minimum of one share must be taken by each subscriber).

Sub-paragraphs (v) to (vii) above do not apply in the case of an unlimited company.

Companies Act 2006 – objects clause

[2.22] With effect from October 2009, unless a company's articles of association specifically restrict its objects, a company's objects are unrestricted. Thus, unless a company chooses to restrict its objects in its articles, it will be able to do anything lawful. Some companies, eg charities and CICs, will continue to restrict their objects.

The Companies Act 2006 takes a different approach to corporate capacity by allowing companies the choice of restricting their objects if they so wish. If they choose the unrestricted route, then those transacting business with such a company will no longer need to be concerned as to whether the company has capacity to enter into a transaction.

Companies formed under CA 2006 will have unlimited objects unless its articles specifically restrict its objects. For existing companies, the objects clause in the memorandum of association will be treated as a provision of the articles. If it has not adopted the 'general commercial company' clause, the company's capacity will continue to be restricted.

The authorised share capital

[2.23] The Companies Act 2006 removed the requirement for a company to have an authorised share capital. For existing companies their current authorised share capital will be treated as a restriction in their articles of association which can be removed by ordinary resolution. Different currency denomination and different classes of shares denominated in different currencies will be permitted by the new Act. The only exception is that the initial minimum share capital requirement for a public company can only be met by shares denominated in either sterling or the equivalent in euros.

Public companies

[2.24] Section 763 of CA 2006 defines the authorised minimum as being £50,000 (or such other figure as the Secretary of State may from time to time determine). The new Act recognises the euro equivalent to the prescribed sterling amount.

Further requirements exist as to the paid-up capital of a public company before it may commence trading activities. These are discussed in **2.42** below.

The articles of association

[2.25] This document sets out a company's regulations for its internal management, and will commonly cover such matters as the rights of shareholders, procedure upon an issue or transfer of shares, rights attaching to shares, the appointment, removal and powers of the directors, and the conduct of board and general meetings. There have been radical changes that have been proposed by Government which are outlined in **2.27** below.

Table A

[2.26] This is contained in the Companies (Tables A to F) Regulations 1985 (SI 1985/805) and is a model set of articles for a company limited by shares. It applies to both public and private companies limited by shares and, with certain modifications as introduced by Tables C and E, to private companies limited by guarantee and unlimited companies respectively. This version of Table A was modified on 22 December 2000 by the Companies Act 1985 (Electronic Communications) Order 2000 (SI 2000/3373) to allow for the use of electronic communications for statutory purposes and therefore is appropriate to companies incorporated on or after 22 December 2000. For companies registered prior to the modifications to Table A, the Table A contained in the Companies Act under which the company was registered applies, unless the current form of Table A has been adopted by the company into its articles.

Pursuant to CA 1985, s 8 a company may adopt all or any of the regulations contained in Table A as its articles of association. Table A will therefore only apply to the extent that it is not modified or excluded by a company's articles of association.

Thus a company may either:

(a) register its own articles, in which case the provisions of Table A will only apply where matters detailed in Table A are not omitted from, or specifically included in, the articles; or

(b) adopt Table A in its entirety, or in a modified form.

If no articles are registered, then Table A will apply in its entirety and will automatically become the regulations of the company.

Thus, companies have a fairly free hand to draft such provisions as they may require into their articles of association. However, in constructing articles the following overriding principles should be borne in mind:

(i) no effect can be given to any regulations in the articles which conflict with any statutory requirements; and

(ii) should any regulations in the articles conflict with any provisions in its memorandum of association, then the provisions of the memorandum prevail.

Should a company on incorporation decide that it wishes to register its own articles, CA 1985, s 7(3) states that they must be printed, divided into paragraphs, numbered consecutively, signed by each subscriber to the memorandum of association in the presence of a witness and dated.

The Companies Act 1989 prospectively inserted a new section 8A into CA 1985. This section provides that regulations may be prescribed for a Table G containing model articles of association for partnership companies. A partnership company is defined as a company limited by shares whose shares are intended to be held to a substantial extent by or on behalf of its employees.

Radical changes to Table A

[2.27] Over the past hundred years or so Table A has been revised several times and whilst many new provisions have been added to it, redundant provisions have rarely been removed, resulting in a 'one size fits all' approach to the model articles. This has given rise to a number of problems. From a private company perspective, much of Table A is taken up with matters which are remote to them and creates unnecessary burden in its management.

The Companies Act 2006 has introduced the following:

(a) a simplified set of model articles for private companies limited by shares, which is more suited to the way smaller companies operate (see **APPENDIX 2C** for a model set of articles);

(b) a separate set of model articles for public companies limited by shares with a clearer layout and drafting; and

(c)   a set of model articles for private companies limited by guarantee.

Section 18 of CA 2006 carries forward the requirement that all registered companies must have articles and they must be contained in a single document divided into consecutively numbered paragraphs. The companies can elect to use model articles, of which there will be several versions for different types of companies as abovementioned. Under CA 2006, s 19 the Secretary of State may prescribe model articles for different types of companies and this will act as a default where a company has not registered articles or where its registered articles do not cover a particular matter.

Existing companies can continue without change to their articles or will be able to replace them with the new model articles if their members pass a special resolution to do so.

Entrenchment

[2.28] Section 22 of CA 2006 is a new provision which replaces the current practice enabling companies to entrench certain elements of their constitution by putting them in their memoranda and providing that they cannot be altered. This new section permits companies to have provisions in their articles that specified provisions may be amended or repealed only if conditions are met; these conditions may be more restrictive than would apply in the case of a special resolution.

Notice of entrenchment must be given to the Registrar and entrenchment is only possible on the formation of a company or with the consent of all members. When a company alters such an entrenching provision, notice must be given to the Registrar together with a statement of compliance certifying that the amendment has been made in accordance with the company's articles.

Private companies

[2.29] Many private companies limited by shares find it convenient to adopt articles of association in a shortened format to the 1985 Table A. The reason for this is to simplify, as far as possible, the administration surrounding the company. This applies both where the company is a subsidiary within a group of companies or is in a 'stand alone' situation. The new model Table A will provide a much shorter version of the old Table A and is intended to be more user-friendly.

Many companies, however, may deem it necessary to have strict procedures laid down for the administration of their affairs in such matters as:

(a)   share capital and class rights;
(b)   allotment and transfer of shares;
(c)   meetings of members and directors;
(d)   appointment and removal of directors;
(e)   powers of directors; and
(f)   general administration.

Due consideration must be given to such matters in giving instructions for the drafting of articles of association.

Public companies

[2.30] No additional requirements are imposed on public companies to have included in their articles of association any specific provisions. However, should a public company be intending to apply for a listing on the London Stock Exchange or Alternative Investment Market, then the articles must comply with the regulations contained in the Financial Services Authority's 'Listing Rules' or AIM rules. For example, no restrictions may exist on the transferability of fully paid shares.

Companies limited by guarantee

[2.31] The rules on articles of association apply equally to a company limited by guarantee as they do to a company limited by shares. However, as a basic difference exists in the nature of the companies' memberships in so far as a company limited by guarantee has no shares, it is necessary for Table A to be modified in this respect. Accordingly Table C in the Companies (Tables A to F) Regulations 1985 was drawn up to accommodate these necessary modifications.

Alteration of articles

[2.32] Under CA 1985, s 9 a company may at any time, but subject to its memorandum of association, by special resolution alter all or any of the conditions contained in its articles of association (see **PRECEDENTS B** and **C**, **APPENDIX 2D**). No reason for the alteration need be given and any alterations made are deemed as valid as if they had been originally contained in the articles and are also subject to further alteration by a special resolution (see **7.57 MEMBERSHIP**). A company may not deprive itself or fetter its ability to alter its articles by any arrangement contained in its articles, in favour of its members or a third party. Thus, any attempt to make part of the articles unalterable is void (*Allen v Gold Reefs of West Africa* [1900] 7 Ch 656). Any article requiring a greater majority than is necessary to pass a special resolution is also void. When altered, a copy of the amended articles of association, together with a print of the special resolution which effected the alteration, must be delivered to Companies House (CA 1985, ss 18 and 380).

Only if a listed company is proposing to make unusual alterations to the articles will prior approval be required from the Listing Authority. However, the final version of the amended articles, associated circular, notice and proxy terms which have been sent to the members must be delivered to the UK Listing Authority followed by copies of the resolution and articles once approved by the members.

Section 21 of CA 2006 has largely preserved the existing ability for a company to amend its articles although it is modified in the case of a company that is a charity in that the consent of the Commissioners will be required for charitable companies in England and Wales, in Northern Ireland and in Scotland.

Completion and filing of the incorporation documents

Companies Act 2006 – the changes to registration requirements

[2.33] With effect from October 2009 there are new registration requirements as set out in CA 2006, ss 9–13. These sections replaced CA 1985, ss 2
and 10. Section 9 of CA 2006 prescribes the types of information or
documents that must be delivered to the Registrar when an application for
registration is made.

The incorporation of companies under CA 2006 is largely similar to the
previous process and the following will have to be delivered to the Registrar:

(a)   the new simplified form of memorandum of association in the pre-
       scribed form authenticated by each subscriber (at the time of writing,
       the form has yet to be prescribed);
(b)   an application for registration stating:
       (i)   the proposed name of the company;
       (ii)   the domicile of the registered office (ie England and Wales,
               Wales, Scotland or Northern Ireland);
       (iii)   whether the liability of the members is to be limited and, if so,
               whether by shares or by guarantee;
       (iv)   whether the company is to be public or private;
       (v)   a statement of capital and initial share holdings or a statement of
               guarantee;
       (vi)   a statement of the proposed officers;
       (vii)   a statement of the intended address of the registered office;
       (viii) a copy of the articles of association (to the extent that these are
               not supplied by the default application of model articles).

In line with the Registrar of Companies' intention to encourage greater
participation in the use of electronic filings, in future it will be possible to form
a company online and the various types of information referred to above will
be capable of being delivered as a series of data entries as well as the
conventional paper or other form as the Registrar may permit or prescribe.

Particulars of the first directors, secretary and registered office

[2.34] In accordance with CA 2006, s 12 the following details are required to
be given to the Registrar of Companies on form IN01.

Directors

[2.35] The details which must be given are as follows:

(a)   full name and any former name;
(b)   service address (with effect from October 2009) or residential address;
(c)   business occupation;
(d)   nationality;
(e)   date of birth.

The Companies Act 1985 was amended and new regulations came into force
on 2 April 2002 to allow private addresses of directors and secretaries to be
kept on a secure register (see **1.8 THE COMPANY SECRETARY** and **6.4
DIRECTORS**). In addition the final report published by the Company Law

Review Steering Group recommended that all directors should be allowed the right to file a service address for the public records whilst still providing a home address to be kept on a restricted access register. Section 163 of CA 2006 has captured this and, in addition, states that particulars of any other directorships held are no longer required to be registered.

For a public company, CA 2006, s 154 imposes the requirement that the minimum number of directors needed is two. No such requirement exists for private companies where, subject to any provisions in the company's articles of association, the minimum number of directors needed is one.

Changes to the directors of a company (appointment, removal and resignation) subsequent to registration are dealt with in **6.3** and **6.11** THE DIRECTORS.

Company secretary

[2.36] The particulars required to be disclosed about the secretary of a company are his full name and service address (with effect from October 2009) or residential address. For further developments on the requirement to provide a residential address for the public record see **1.8** THE COMPANY SECRETARY and **6.4** the directors.

The position and qualifications of the company secretary are dealt with more fully in **CHAPTER 1**.

Registered office

[2.37] The full postal address of the first registered office of the company must be detailed.

If the company is to be domiciled and accordingly registered in England and Wales, the address of the registered office must be in either England or Wales. Similarly if the company is to be domiciled in Scotland the address of the registered office must be in Scotland. Accordingly, the address given must be consistent with the domicile stated in the company's memorandum of association.

Currently the address of the registered office (but not the country of domicile) may subsequently be changed by resolution of the directors of the company. Section 88 of CA 2006 will allow a Welsh company, by special resolution, to determine that it shall be registered in England and Wales. No such privilege is afforded to English companies which must always state that they are registered in England and Wales.

Where a change in the location of a company's registered office occurs, CA 2006, s 87 requires notice of the change to be given to the Registrar of Companies on the prescribed form AD01. The change does not become effective until the form of notification is filed at Companies House. However, until the end of a period of 14 days, beginning with the date on which notification of the change is filed at Companies House, a person may validly serve upon the company any document at its previous registered office address (CA 2006, s 87(2)).

Memorandum and articles of association

[2.38] Section 9 of CA 2006 requires the memorandum and articles of association to be in the form and executed as specified by the Act (see **2.21** above and also note the new format as introduced by CA 2006).

An important point to note about the memorandum and articles of association is that when they are registered at Companies House they bind the members of a company to the same extent as they would have been bound had they been signed and sealed by each member. Thus, anyone entering into membership of the company, subsequent to the company's registration, is as bound to observe the provisions contained in the company's memorandum and articles as the subscribers who signed the original documents.

Declaration of compliance

[2.39] Section 13 of CA 2006 has simplified this process by requiring only a statement of compliance (signed by all the subscribers) which is essentially a statement that the requirements of the Act as to registration have been complied with.

Electronic incorporations

[2.40] When the Companies Act 1985 (Electronic Communications) Order 2000 (SI 2000/3373) came into force it provided for companies to be incorporated electronically and made it possible for both the memorandum and articles of association to be delivered otherwise than in legible form and thus dispenses with the requirement for the said documents to be signed and witnessed. Section 13 of CA 2006 allows for a statement of compliance to be delivered instead of the statutory declaration.

Once the company has been incorporated the Registrar will transmit the certificate of incorporation to the presenter electronically under CA 2006, s 1115.

Certificate of incorporation

[2.41] Upon the submission of form IN01 and the memorandum and articles of association, together with payment of the appropriate fee to the Registrar of Companies (£40 as at the time of publication), the Registrar will issue to the company its certificate of incorporation. This certificate contains details of the company's name and allocates to it a registered number, which is unique to that company. Should the name of the company subsequently be changed, this registered number will remain the same. There is one change introduced by CA 2006, s 15 and that is, the certificate of incorporation will be required to state whether the company's registered office is situated in England and Wales (or in Wales), in Scotland or in Northern Ireland. If the company is a limited company, it should also state whether it is limited by shares or by guarantee.

The certificate of incorporation is conclusive evidence that the requirements of the Act have been complied with and that a company is duly registered (in the case of a public company the certificate is also conclusive proof that the company is a public company) (CA 2006, s 15(2)(d)). It is effectively the 'birth certificate' of a company and from the date of its issue a company becomes a body corporate in its own right with all the attendant rights attached. Thus a company will have obtained its own legal identity which is distinct from that of its members.

A *private company* may commence trading activities from the date of issue of this certificate. However, a *public company* may not commence trading activities or exercise any of its borrowing powers until the provisions of CA 2006, s 761, relating to a public company's minimum share capital requirements, have been fulfilled.

Minimum share capital requirements for a public company

[2.42] Pursuant to CA 2006, s 762, a *public company* may not commence business or exercise any of its borrowing powers unless the Registrar of Companies has issued to it a certificate under this section (commonly known as the 'trading certificate').

Previously, to apply for a trading certificate a public company had to submit to the Registrar of Companies a statutory declaration in the prescribed paper or electronic form, stating:

(a)   that the nominal value of the company's allotted share capital is not less than the authorised minimum (currently being £50,000 sterling or euro equivalent);
(b)   the amount of the share capital which is paid up;
(c)   the amount (or an estimate) of the preliminary expenses payable by the company and to whom they have been paid or are payable; and
(d)   the amount of or benefit paid, given or intended to be paid or given to any promoter of the company and the consideration for the payment of the benefit.

The statutory declaration must be made by a director or secretary of the company in the presence of a Notary Public, Commissioner of Oaths or Justice of the Peace.

Section 762 of CA 2006 replaces the statutory declaration with a statement of compliance which does not need to be witnessed. It can continue to be made in paper or electronic form and at the time of writing, it is still unclear as to what the Registrar's rules are on who may make this statement and the form of it.

An application for a trading certificate under the CA 2006 must:

(i)   state that the nominal value of the company's allotted share capital is not less than the authorised minimum;
(ii)   specify the amount, or estimated amount, of the company's preliminary expenses;
(iii)   specify any amount or the benefit paid or given, or intended to be paid or given, to any promoter of the company, and the consideration for the payment or benefit; and
(iv)   be accompanied by a statement of compliance.

The Registrar of Companies further requires that, before the issue of the trading certificate, at least one-quarter of the nominal value of each issued share pursuant to (i) above is paid up (ie at least £12,500 in aggregate). Furthermore, the Registrar will refuse to issue the trading certificate unless all of the minimum paid up capital requirements have been strictly complied with. Section 586 of CA 2006 further provides that a public company shall not allot a share except as paid up to one-quarter of its nominal value.

Upon the issue of the trading certificate a public company may commence its business activities.

Re-registration

Re-registration of a private limited company as a public limited company

[2.43] Under CA 2006, s 90 a private company having a share capital and which has not previously been re-registered as unlimited may, by special resolution of its members, re-register as a public company. The resolution must be delivered to the Registrar within 15 days of it being passed, and the company must make an application in the prescribed form RR01 to the Registrar of Companies.

The special resolution must alter the name and articles so as to bring them into line with that suitable for use by a public company (see **PRECEDENT D**, **APPENDIX 2D**). It should thus be altered so that:

(a)   the name states that the company is to be a public company (ie insertion of a 'public company' clause);

(b)   the allotted share capital is increased if, prior to the application for re-registration being made, it is below the statutory minimum (currently £50,000 or euro equivalent). The allotted share capital must be paid up to at least one-quarter of the nominal value of each share (see **2.42** above) as well as the whole of any premium on it (or an undertaking to pay the premium); and

(c)   appropriate alterations are made in the company's articles in the circumstances (eg minimum number of directors as two).

Once the articles have been amended as appropriate an application can then be made in the prescribed form RR01), signed by a director or secretary (if there is one) of the company and delivered to the Registrar of Companies together with:

(i)   a printed copy of the articles as altered;

(ii)   a copy of the company's balance sheet prepared to a date being not more than seven months before the company's application for re-registration, together with a copy of an unqualified report by the company's auditors in relation to that balance sheet;

(iii)   a copy of a written statement made by the company's auditors, certifying that the balance sheet ((ii) above) shows that the company's net assets were not less than the aggregate of its called-up share capital and its undistributable reserves;

(iv)   a copy of the valuation report relating to the value of the consideration if shares have recently been allotted in accordance with CA 2006, s 93;

(v)   if there is no company secretary appointed, a statement of the company's proposed secretary; and

(vi)   a remittance filing fee of £20 (as at the time of this publication).

It should also be noted that a new provision under CA 2006, s 95 covers the scenario where the company does not have a company secretary. In such instances, an application for re-registration from a private limited company to a public limited company should also include details of the person or persons who will act as company secretary or joint secretaries on re-registration.

Once satisfied that the requirements of CA 2006, s 90 have been complied with, the Registrar of Companies will issue a new certificate of incorporation stating that the company is a public limited company. Such a change in status being effective as from the date of issue of the certificate. The certificate is conclusive evidence that the company is a public company and any alterations in the articles of association take effect accordingly and the person(s) named as secretary (or joint secretaries) will be deemed to have been appointed as such. The company can commence business immediately without having to obtain a trading certificate.

Re-registration of a public limited company as a private limited company

[2.44] Under CA 2006, s 97, a public company may re-register as a private company by passing a special resolution to alter its name so that it no longer states that the company is a public company (see **PRECEDENT E, APPENDIX 2D**). The resolution must also make any other alteration to the articles which are requisite in the circumstances to bring it into line with a private company.

A copy of the special resolution should be sent to the Registrar of Companies within 15 days of it being passed together with an application on the prescribed form RR02, signed by a director or secretary of the company and accompanied by a registration fee of £20 (as at the time of this publication). A printed copy of the altered articles of association must also be attached together with a statement of compliance under CA 2006, s 97.

Where the above special resolution has been passed, an application can be made to the court for its cancellation within 28 days by:

(a)   the holders of no less than 5% in nominal value of the company's issued share capital or any class thereof;

(b)   5% of its members if it is not limited by shares; or

(c)   not less than 50 of the company's members.

If such an application has been made the company must notify the Registrar of Companies on the prescribed form RR04.

The courts, on hearing the application, have the power to either cancel or confirm the resolution or make such order as it considers appropriate. Additionally, the company must deliver to the Registrar an office copy of the court order cancelling or confirming the resolution (if appropriate).

Once the period of 28 days after the passing of the resolution has expired and there is no application or the courts have confirmed the resolution, and the Registrar is satisfied that the company can be re-registered, he will issue a certificate of incorporation stating that the company is a private company. Such change in status takes effect from the date of the issue of the certificate (CA 2006, s 101).

The certificate is conclusive evidence that the company is a private company and the alterations in the articles as set out in the resolution become effective.

Re-registration of an unlimited company as a private company

[2.45] Under CA 2006, s 105 an unlimited company may, by passing a special resolution, re-register as a private limited company (see PRECEDENT F, APPENDIX 2D). It is not possible for a company which has previously re-registered itself as unlimited under CA 1985, s 49 (see **2.46** below) to re-register as a private limited company again.

The special resolution must state whether the company is to be limited by shares or by guarantee. Alterations must be made to the name and articles of association to comply with the requirements of CA 2006 in respect of a company limited by shares or a company limited by guarantee.

A copy of the special resolution should be lodged with the Registrar of Companies within 15 days of its passing, together with the application on the prescribed form RR06 and a printed copy of the altered articles of association. Under CA 2006, a statement of compliance will be required.

The fee for re-registration is £20 (as at the time of this publication).

The Registrar will issue a certificate of incorporation appropriate to the circumstances, which is conclusive evidence that the company is limited.

Re-registration of a private limited company as an unlimited company

[2.46] Under CA 2006, s 102, a private limited company may make an application to the Registrar for the company to be re-registered as unlimited, so long as it has not been registered as limited by virtue of CA 2006, s 105 (see **2.45** above).

The difference with this type of re-registration is that all the members must approve the registration by signing the prescribed form of assent, form RR05. The name and articles of association must also be altered to bring them in line with those of an unlimited company with or without a share capital.

As with the other re-registrations as abovementioned, a statement of compliance will be required (CA 2006, s 103).

The fee for re-registration is £20 (as at the time of this publication).

Upon receipt of the various documents the Registrar will issue a certificate of incorporation appropriate to the changed status of the company, being conclusive evidence that the requirements of the Act have been complied with.

Same day registration

[2.47] Companies House offers a same day service where incorporations, change of name and re-registration of companies can be effected on the same day.

The appropriate completed statutory documents can be taken to Companies House offices at London, Cardiff or Edinburgh before 3pm (see **APPENDIX 5B DISCLOSURE AND REPORTING REQUIREMENTS** for addresses). The documents are inspected at the counter and providing the necessary requirements are met, a certificate is issued on the same day. The fee for this service is £50 (as at the time of this publication) or £100 in the case of a re-registration accompanied by a change of name. It should be noted that registration of a place of business or branch can only be effected on the same day if the documents are taken to Cardiff or Edinburgh.

Registration of an overseas company

General

[2.48] Registration of an overseas company conducting business in the UK is only required if there is some physical or visible appearance in connection with a particular premises, a degree of permanence or some identification as being a location of the company's business.

It should be noted that CA 2006 has introduced changes to overseas companies. Section 1044 of CA 2006 states that an 'overseas company' means a company incorporated outside the United Kingdom. Previously, under CA 1985, there were two forms of registration of an oversea company, ie either as a 'place of business' or 'branch'. With effect from October 2009, there is only one form of registration which is based on the branch regime (CA 2006, ss 1044–1059).

Particulars required for registration

[2.49] Within one month of opening a UK establishment, an overseas company must deliver to Companies House the following information:

(a)   a completed 'Registration of an overseas company opening a UK establishment' application form (form OS IN01);
(b)   the registration fee (£20).

If the company is registering its first UK establishment, it must also deliver the following with the application:

(i)   a certified copy of the company's constitutional documents (eg charter, statute, memorandum and articles of association) with a certified translation in English if the original is in a language other than English;
(ii)   a copy of the company's latest set of accounts (with a certified translation in English if the original is in a language other than English) if:

> - they are required to be filed under parent law; or
> - the company is incorporated in an EEA state and is required by its parent law to prepare and disclose accounts but its parent law does not require such accounts to be audited or delivered.

When an overseas company registers a further UK establishment, it is not required to again deliver these documents and may instead state in the return that they have been delivered in respect of another UK establishment, giving the registered number of that establishment.

The office of the Registrar of Companies to which the documents must be delivered will depend upon whether the company has established its presence in England and Wales (documents sent to Companies House in Cardiff) or Scotland (documents sent to Companies House in Edinburgh). Where a company has its presence in both parts of Great Britain the documents are required to be delivered to both Registrars. It is also possible for the registration to take place on the same day if the documents are taken to Cardiff or Edinburgh.

Name of the company

[2.50] An overseas company required to register itself as a place of business must effect the registration in the name of the corporate body which is registered overseas. Section 1048 of CA 2006 enables an overseas company to be registered under a name that is different to its corporate name and to subsequently change its registered name if it so wishes.

Section 66 of CA 2006 relating to the prohibition of registration of certain company names applies equally to the registration of a company name by an overseas company as it does to a UK company (see **2.9–2.19** above).

Should the company's name be unacceptable for use in the UK, notice may be served on the company to adopt a business name for use in the UK. The notice will be issued by the Secretary of State within twelve months of the date of registration or within twelve months of notifying the Registrar of any change of name. The notice will state the reasons given why the name is unacceptable, and will prevent the company from carrying on business in the UK using that name, after normally two months of the notice being served. A company may then send in form OS NM01 stating the name, other than its corporate name, under which it proposes to carry on business in the UK, and will be subject to the Business Names Act 1985 as any person of a UK incorporated company operating under a business name (see **2.11** above).

Alteration of registered particulars

[2.51] Should any changes occur in any of the particulars registered at Companies House then a return in the prescribed form must be made to the Registrar of Companies within 21 days.

The changes and the prescribed forms specified for notification are:

(a)   form OS CC01 – any alteration to the constitutional particulars;

(b)   form OS CH02 – any alteration of company particulars;

(c)   form OS CH03, 04 and 05 – any change of directors or secretary or of their particulars;

(d)   form OS CH01 – any change of address or branch particulars;

(e)   form OS CH07 or 09 – any change of person authorised to accept service or to represent the branch or any change in their particulars; and

(f)   form OS AD01 – any change in the branch where the constitutional documents have been registered.

Disclosure requirements

[2.52] The company must comply with the following:

(a)   at every place of business the company's registered name and its country of incorporation must be displayed;

(b)   the company's name and country of incorporation must be stated on all billheads, letter paper and all notices and other official publications;

(c)   if the liability of the company's members is limited, this must be stated at (*a*) above and on (*b*) above; and

(d)   the place of registration and registration number of the company must be stated on letter paper and order forms.

Also, every company incorporated outside the EU must state the following on its letter paper and order forms:

(i)   the legal form of the company;

(ii)   the location of its head office; and

(iii)   the fact that it is being wound up if applicable.

Additionally, if the company is not incorporated in the EU and which is required by the law of the country in which it is incorporated to be registered it shall also state on its letter paper and order forms:

(A)   the company's registration number; and

(B)   the identity of the registry in which it is registered in its home state.

Closing an overseas company

[2.53] A company must notify the Registrar of Companies if it closes its establishment in Great Britain. Notice should be given on form OS DS01 and signed by a director, secretary or permanent representative of the company. The obligations on the company for delivery of documents will cease only from the date that this fact is notified to the Registrar.

General requirements for overseas companies

Registration of charges by an overseas company

[2.54] Previously all overseas companies registered with Companies House had to register specified charges created by the company over property situated in the UK. The onus to register fell on either the overseas company or the party taking the charge and was done on form OS MG01 (Particulars of a mortgage or charge by an overseas company).

However the Government has confirmed its intention to revise the scheme for registration of company charges in its response to the March 2010 consultation which will exclude overseas companies from 1 October 2011. Therefore overseas companies will no longer be required to register their charges from that date.

Service of documents on an overseas company

[2.55] Any process or notice served on an overseas company is sufficiently served if:

(a) addressed to any person whose name has been delivered to the Registrar to accept service of process on the company's behalf; and

(b) left at or sent by post to the address for that person which has been so delivered.

If, at any time, the appropriate person's name and address has not been delivered to the Registrar; or this information has been delivered but the person has died or ceased to reside at the address given; or the named person has refused to accept service on the company's behalf; or for any reason service cannot be given, then the document may be served by either leaving it or sending it by post to any place of business established by the company in the UK.

Northern Ireland registration

[2.56] Previously Northern Ireland has had its own regimes with respect to place of business and branch registration. An overseas company having a branch in Northern Ireland and a place of business in Great Britain must register the branch in Northern Ireland but need not register as a place of business in Great Britain.

If a Northern Ireland company has a place of business in Great Britain, then it is required to register as a place of business (however large its operations) as the branch registration regime only applies to limited companies incorporated outside the UK.

The Companies Act 2006 extends to Northern Ireland by virtue of section 1284 and will repeal the principal pieces of Northern Ireland legislation. Section 1044 of CA 2006 removes Northern Ireland companies from the definition of overseas companies since the new Act creates a single company law regime for the whole of the United Kingdom.

Isle of Man and Channel Islands companies

[2.57] As already mentioned in **2.48** above, the definition of 'overseas company' under CA 2006, s 1044 will effectively treat Isle of Man and Channel Islands companies as 'overseas companies'.

Limited Liability Partnerships

[2.58] The Limited Liability Partnerships Act 2000 (LLPA 2000), which was passed in July 2000, created a new form of business entity, namely the Limited Liability Partnership (LLP). The new vehicle functions as a partnership but with limited liability for its members. Whilst it was originally intended to restrict the use of LLPs to regulated professions, the LLPA 2000 permits any two or more persons carrying on a lawful business to establish an LLP. The liability of each partner is limited, however a negligent members' personal assets may still be at risk in a claim for negligence.

Incorporation

[2.59] To form an LLP, there must be at least two people associated for carrying on a lawful business with a view to profit and who subscribe to the incorporation document (Form LLP2). The form needs to be submitted to the Registrar of Companies together with a statement of compliance signed by a solicitor or proposed member, and the registration fee of £20.

Information required to comply with the LLP2 form includes the LLP's name which must end with the words 'Limited Liability Partnership', 'LLP' or the Welsh equivalent (similar restrictions apply to use of a name as with companies – see **2.12** above), situation and address of the registered office, full names and addresses of the persons who are to be members on incorporation, and details of the designated members. The Registrar, once satisfied that the incorporation documents are correct, will issue a certificate of incorporation which is conclusive evidence that all the legal requirements have been complied with.

Members

[2.60] Subscribers to the incorporation documents automatically become members on incorporation. Any new members may be admitted by agreement of the existing members. Members may cease to act by following agreed procedures. Any changes in membership must be notified to Companies House on the prescribed form (see **APPENDIX 5D DISCLOSURE AND REPORTING REQUIREMENTS**).

Designated members

[2.61] LLPs are required to have at least two designated members at all times. They will carry out similar administrative duties to that of a director or company secretary. Under LLPA 2000 designated members are responsible for appointing auditors, signing and delivery of accounts, signing and delivery of the annual return and notifying the Registrar of changes to members, registered office and the LLP name. Again, any changes must be notified to the Registrar on the prescribed form (see **APPENDIX 5D DISCLOSURE AND REPORTING REQUIREMENTS**). Furthermore, the designated members will be liable under LLPA 2000 for failure to carry out these defined duties.

Partnership agreement

[2.62] Although there is no legal requirement for LLPs to have a partnership agreement, members would probably want to have an agreement in place. The agreement would set out the rights and duties of the LLP and its members with regards to management of internal affairs (similar to articles of association of a company). The formal agreement does not have to be filed with Companies House. Where there is no such agreement the Act provides for default provisions on matters such as members rights to a share of the profits.

Tax treatment

[2.63] The profits of an LLP will be taxed as if the business were carried on by partners in partnership rather than a body corporate.

The European Economic Interest Grouping

General

[2.64] Created on 25 July 1985 by the Council of Ministers of the European Community, the European Economic Interest Grouping (EEIG) facilitates cross-frontier co-operation between firms engaged in similar activities within the European Union (EU). The instrument became available on 1 July 1989, and is part of the construction of the single European market programme.

The idea behind the instrument is to enable firms within the EU, particularly small and medium-sized firms, to group together in order to develop their own common activities and to increase profits by combining resources and services. The instrument provides a pre-established legal framework and flexible operational procedures. The purpose of a grouping is consequently not to make profits for itself, but to allow member companies to organise and co-ordinate projects, and to monitor their execution. Moreover, companies wishing to participate in cross-border co-operation will be able to overcome the difficulties presented by the legal systems of individual EU States.

Regulations

[2.65] All legal bodies governed by public or private law can become members of EEIGs and a grouping may be created in any sector, be it agriculture, trade, industry or services. The official address of the EEIG must be within a EU Member State although it need not correspond to the place where the principal activity is carried out. Members of an EEIG should be active within the Union prior to the creation of the grouping. Companies and other legal entities should be incorporated according to the legislation of a Member State. In addition, at least two members of a grouping should be based in different Member States, and a manager(s) must be appointed to operate the EEIG on a day-to-day basis. EEIGs are governed by EU law, although only minimal obligations with regard to the organisation and management of the grouping are imposed.

Organisation

[2.66] The grouping must have at least two 'organs'.

(a) *College of members.* This is the ruling body and is analogous to a company acting in general meeting with each member having the right to vote. The conditions for the taking of decisions are largely left to the grouping contract, and the college may take any decision in order to achieve the objectives of the grouping.

(b) *Management.* The managers are responsible for the day-to-day running of the grouping and may represent the EEIG in dealing with third parties. The contract of the grouping will determine the conditions for the appointment and removal of management.

Finance

[2.67] An EEIG may be formed without capital, and is not even required to have any assets. Members have great flexibility regarding the method of financing the activities of the grouping, thus enabling funds to be used more effectively. As a result of this, members' liability is joint and several for the grouping's debts to third parties.

Taxation

[2.68] The relevant EU regulations state that EEIGs are to be 'fiscally transparent'; properties are to be taxable and losses allowable only in the hands of their members. This is given effect in the UK by provisions included in the Finance Act 1990.

Where an EEIG is trading, the trade is regarded as being carried on by the members in partnership, and its profits are taxed accordingly. Thus, for capital gains purposes the existing partnership rules apply, ie gains realised by the partnership are apportioned to the partners, but no gain or loss is treated as arising where a partner joins or leaves the partnership, or where there is a change in profit-sharing ratios, unless payment is made (except in certain cases where assets are revalued in the partnership accounts).

Normal rules (such as the requirement for expenditure to be incurred wholly and exclusively for the purpose of the member's trade) apply when considering the availability of relief for contributions by a member to the EEIG's running expenses, or entitlement to capital allowances on the member's share of the grouping's assets.

Legal capacity

[2.69] The instrument gives full legal capacity to the grouping from the date of its registration. To register, the grouping must request enrolment at the appropriate Registry of the Member State where it has its official address. For example, if the grouping is in the UK it will be registered with the Registrar of Companies at Companies House, Cardiff and, within one month, in the Official Journal of the EU. Certain information about the grouping will then be published in a journal carrying legal notices, for example, the *London Gazette*.

An EEIG may have rights and obligations, place contracts and carry out legal acts in accordance with the objects determined by the members, in all EU Member States. It may also operate outside the Union in the exploration, research and penetration of new markets.

Post incorporation considerations

[2.70] Shortly after a company has been duly registered and its certificate of incorporation issued, the directors of the company (as detailed on form IN01) should hold their first board meeting. The purpose of this meeting is to record the position of the company at incorporation and to make the decisions necessary to enable the company to commence its business.

Accordingly, items which will commonly appear on the agenda for the first board meeting for consideration are:

(a) the election of a chairman;
(b) the certificate of incorporation and memorandum and articles of association produced to the meeting and, if a public limited company, the obtaining of a trading certificate discussed;
(c) any further appointments of directors considered;
(d) the common seal of the company adopted;
(e) the registered office address confirmed or changed;
(f) the company's accounting reference date fixed and the appropriate notification prepared and filed with the Registrar of Companies (see **4.2–4.5 ACCOUNTS AND AUDITORS**);
(g) auditors appointed;
(h) bankers appointed to the company and an account opened;
(i) statutory registers obtained and written up (see **CHAPTER 3 THE STATUTORY RECORDS**);
(j) any arrangements for obtaining further capital discussed. If necessary, the relevant instructions should be given for the preparation of a prospectus and for application to be made to the Stock Exchange for a listing and if appropriate brokers, underwriters and share registrars appointed (public companies only, see **8.24–8.31 CAPITAL**);
(k) if the company was formed to acquire a business then the terms of the purchase agreement should be agreed;
(l) any pre-incorporation contracts made by the promoters of the company should be adopted and the need for directors' service contracts considered;

(m)   VAT registration application considered and also the company's arrangements for the payment of corporation tax, PAYE and National Insurance and the company's insurance arrangements discussed;

(n)   the necessity of applying for the registration of any trade or service marks discussed and, if required, trade mark agents instructed; and

(o)   business stationery complying with the Companies Act 2006 and the Business Names Act 1985 ordered (see **2.19** above).

It should be noted that upon incorporation the directors and secretary of the company named in form IN01 submitted to the Registrar of Companies are deemed appointed. Likewise, the subscribers to the memorandum of association are deemed the first members of the company. Any subsequent changes must then be made in accordance with the company's memorandum and articles of association and CA 2006.

Appendix 2A

Checklist for incorporation

General

The following guide is designed purely as a reference point in ensuring the completeness of the documents required to be filed with the Registrar of Companies in applying for the registration of a private or public limited company. Reference to the detailed notes in the main text of this chapter is recommended.

Type of company

Is the company to be a private or public company limited by shares, or a private company limited by guarantee? Determine the purpose and capital requirements of the company.

Company name

(a)   Is the proposed name available? Check index at Companies House for availability. (See **2.9** above.)
(b)   Does the proposed name require prior approval? (See **2.10** above.)
(c)   Would the use of the name constitute a criminal offence or is it forbidden? (See **2.10** above.)

Statement of first directors, secretary and registered office (form IN01)

(i)   Have all the details required for the directors and secretary been entered and the form signed by each? (See **2.34** above.)
(ii)   Is the registered office address within the country of domicile stated in the memorandum of association? (See **2.37** above.)
(iii)   Has the form been signed by the subscribers to the memorandum of association *or* by an agent acting on their behalf?

Memorandum of association

(A)   Has the name of the company been correctly stated?
(B)   Have the names and addresses of the subscriber or subscribers been clearly stated, their signatures obtained and the number of shares they have each agreed to take been entered against their names?
(C)   Has the name and address of the witness to the subscribers' signatures been entered and his signature obtained?
(D)   Has the date of signature by the subscribers been stated?

Articles of association

(I)   Are they in the correct format for the type of company
(II)   As (B), (C) and (D) in 'memorandum of association' above.

Fees

A cheque for £20 (this is the amount as at the date of publication) made payable to 'Companies House' must be submitted with the incorporation documents.

Appendix 2B

Restricted company names

Prescribed words that require the support of the body shown in the second column

Abortion	To use this word you must obtain the written support of: Sexual Health Policy Team Department of Health Wellington House 133-155 Waterloo Road London SE1 8UG
Accounts Commission for Scotland	To use this expression you must obtain the written support of: The Secretary Accounts Commission for Scotland 110 George Street Edinburgh EH2 4LH
Accredit Accreditation Accredited Accrediting	To use these words you must obtain the written support of: Department for Business Innovation & Skills Accreditation Policy 1 Victoria Street London SW1H 0ET
Adjudicator	This word implies the same or similar status of an official ombudsman and therefore an implied connection with a representative body or government department. To use this word you must obtain the written support of the appropriate representative body or government department.
Alba Na h-Alba	If you wish to use any of these words at the beginning of your company name, you would need to show that the company is pre-eminent in its field by providing independent support from a representative body, trade association or the Scottish Government. If the words are used elsewhere in the name, you would be expected to show that your company is substantial in relation to its activity or product and that it is eminent in its own field. If you want to use the words because it is a surname, you will usually be given approval if the company name includes forenames or initials.

Registered names only	Unless the word is a surname the company's registered office must be in Scotland.
Albannach	If you wish to use this word at the beginning of your company name, you would need to show that the company is pre-eminent in its field by providing independent support from a representative body, trade association or the Scottish Government.
	If the word is used elsewhere in the name, you would be expected to show that your company is substantial in relation to its activity or product and that it is eminent in its own field.
Registered names only	The company's registered office must be in Scotland.
Association	To use this word the company should normally be limited by guarantee with each member having one vote and include a non-profit distribution clause in the articles of association. These requirements do not apply if the company is a residents or tenants association.
Assurance Assurer	To use these words you must obtain the written support of: Financial Services Authority Perimeter Guidance 25 The North Colonnade Canary Wharf London E14 5HS Email: perimeterguidance@fsa.gov.uk
Audit Commission for Local Authorities and the National Health Service in England	To use this expression you must obtain the written support of:
Audit Commission	Chief Executive's Office Audit Commission for Local Authorities and the National Health Service in England 1st Floor, Millbank Tower Millbank London SW1P 4HQ
Audit Scotland	To use these expressions you must obtain the written support of:
Auditor General for Scotland	The Secretary Auditor General for Scotland 110 George Street Edinburgh EH2 4LH

Audit Office	To use these expressions you must obtain the written support of:
Auditor General	*England:* Comptroller & Auditor General Corporate Secretariat National Audit Office 157-159 Buckingham Palace Road London SW1W 9SP *Wales:* Wales Audit Office 24 Cathedral Road Cardiff CF11 9L *Scotland:* Audit Scotland 110 George Street Edinburgh EH2 4LH *Northern Ireland:* Northern Ireland Audit Office 106 University Street Belfast BT7 1EU
Auditor General for Wales	To use this expression you must obtain the written support of: Auditor General for Wales 24 Cathedral Road Cardiff CF11 9LJ *In Welsh:* Archwilydd Cyffredinol Cymru 24 Heol y Gadeirlan Caerdydd CF11 9LJ
Authority	To use this word the company must be either: (a) a governing, supervisory or representative body of an activity (for example, sport or religion), trade, business, profession; or (b) a body with recognised expertise.

Evidence must be produced to show that the company will be what it claims, and that it has the support of whoever it claims it will govern, supervise, or look to it for expertise. Any applicant should produce evidence of support from a representative body or government department.

Banc Bank Banking	To use these words you must obtain the written support of: Financial Services Authority Perimeter Guidance 25 The North Colonnade Canary Wharf London E14 5HS Email: perimeterguidance@fsa.gov.uk
The Governor and Company of the Bank of England	To use this expression you must obtain the written support of: Bank of England Threadneedle Street London EC2R 8AH
Banknote	To use this word you must obtain the written support of: The Governor and Company of the Bank of England Threadneedle Street London EC2R 8AH
Benevolent	The inclusion of this word in a company name will normally be refused if it wrongly implies that the company has charitable status. If the company is limited by guarantee and has a non-profit distribution clause in the articles of association the name will normally be approved.
Board	To use this word the company must be: 1. a governing, supervisory or representative body of an activity, trade, business, profession; or 2. an independent advisory body; or 3. a deliberative assembly. Evidence must be produced to show that the company will be what it claims, and that it has the support of whoever it claims it will govern, supervise, or look to it for expertise. In addition, the applicant should produce independent support from a representative body or government department

Breatannach Bhreatanach BhreatanaichBreatannaich	If you wish to use any of these words at the beginning of your company name you would need to show that the company is pre-eminent in its field by providing independent support from a representative body, trade association or the Scottish Government. If the word is used elsewhere in the name, you would be expected to show that your company is substantial in relation to its activity or product and that it is eminent in its own field. The company's registered office must be in Scotland.
Breatainn Bhreatainn	If you wish to use any of these words at the start of your company name you would need to show that the company is pre-eminent in its field by providing independent support from a representative body, trade association or the Scottish Government. If the word is used elsewhere in the name, you would be expected to show that your company is substantial in relation to its activity or product and that it is eminent in its own field. If you want to use the word because it is a surname, you will usually be given approval if the company name includes forenames or initials. Unless the word is a surname the company's registered office must be in Scotland.
Brenin Frenin Brenhines Frenhines	To use these words you must obtain the written support of: The Welsh Assembly Government Public Administration and Honours Unit Crown Buildings Cathays Park CARDIFF CF10 3NQ
Brenhinol Frenhinol Brenhiniaeth Frenhiniaeth	To use these words you must obtain the written support of: The Welsh Assembly Government Public Administration and Honours Unit Crown Buildings Cathays Park CARDIFF CF10 3NQ
Britain	If you wish to use this word at the start of your company name you would need to show that the company is pre-eminent in its field by providing independent support from a representative body, trade association or government department. If the word is used elsewhere in the name, you would be expected to show that your company is substantial in relation to its activity or product and that it is eminent in its own field. If you want to use the word because it is a surname, you will usually be given approval if the company name includes forenames or initials.

Unless the word is a surname the company's registered office must be in England and Wales.

British

If you wish to use the word at the beginning of your company name you would need to show that the company is pre-eminent in its field by providing independent support from a representative body, trade association or government department.

If the word is used elsewhere in the name, you would be expected to show that your company is substantial in relation to its activity or product and that it is eminent in its own field.

The company's registered office must be in England and Wales.

Cenedlaethol
Chenedlaethol
Genedlaethol
Gwladol Wladol

If you wish to use any of these words at the beginning of your company name you would need to show that the company is pre-eminent in its field by providing independent support from a representative body, trade association or the Welsh Assembly Government.

If the word is used elsewhere in the name, you would be expected to show that your company is substantial in relation to its activity or product and that it is pre-minent in its own field.

Chamber of

This expression implies representative status such as that associated with a Chamber of Commerce or Trade. To use this expression you would normally need to obtain written support from a Chamber of Commerce or other representative body.

Charitable
Charity

To use these words you must obtain the written support of:
England, Wales & Northern Ireland:
Head of Registration
Charity Commission Direct
PO Box 1227
Liverpool
L69 3UG

Scotland:
Office of the Scottish Charity Regulator
2nd Floor Quadrant House
9 Riverside Drive
Dundee
DD1 4NY

Charter
Chartered

Names that include these words will be refused if they unjustifiably give the impression that the company has a Royal Charter. If the words are used to qualify a profession, you should obtain the written support of the appropriate governing body.

Child
Maintenance
Child Support

To use any of these expressions you must obtain the written support of:
Child Maintenance and Enforcement Commission

Child Mainte- nance and Enforce- ment Commission	PO Box 239
	Holbeck Leeds S11 1EB

Coimisean Choimisean Chomisein Coimisein	These words imply that the company has a regulatory role such as a:

1. a governing, supervisory or representative body of an activity, trade, business, profession; or

2. an independent advisory body; or

3. a deliberative assembly

Evidence must be produced to show that the company will be what it claims, and that it has the support of whoever it claims it will govern, supervise, or look to it for expertise. In addition, the applicant should produce independent support from a representative body or the Scottish Government

Comhairle Chomhairle Comhairlean Chomhairlean	These words imply that the company has a regulatory role such as a:

1. a governing, supervisory or representative body of an activity, trade, business, profession; or

2. an independent advisory body; or

3. a deliberative assembly

Evidence must be produced to show that the company will be what it claims, and that it has the support of whoever it claims it will govern, supervise, or look to it for expertise. In addition, the applicant should produce independent support from a representative body or the Scottish Government.

Comisiwn Gomisiwn Chomisiwn	These words imply that the company has a regulatory role such as a:

1. a governing, supervisory or representative body of an activity, trade, business, profession; or

2. an independent advisory body; or

3. a deliberative assembly.

Evidence must be produced to show that the company will be what it claims, and that it has the support of whoever it claims it will govern, supervise, or look to it for expertise. In addition, the applicant should produce independent support from a representative body or the Welsh Assembly Government.

Commission	This word implies that the company has a regulatory role such as a:

1. a governing, supervisory or representative body of an activity, trade, business, profession; or

2. an independent advisory body; or

3. a deliberative assembly.

Evidence must be produced to show that the company will be what it claims, and that it has the support of whoever it claims it will govern, supervise, or look to it for expertise. In addition, the applicant should produce independent support from a representative body or government department.

Comptroller and Auditor General

To use this expression you must obtain the written support of:

Comptroller and Auditor General
Corporate Secretariat
National Audit Office
Elizabeth 2
151 Buckingham Palace Road
London
SW1W 9SS

Comptroller and Auditor General for Northern Ireland

To use this expression you must obtain the written support of:

Comptroller and Auditor General for Northern Ireland
Northern Ireland Audit Office
106 University Street
Belfast
BT7 1EU

Co-operative

To use this word the company should normally be limited by guarantee with each member having one vote and include a non-profit distribution clause in the articles of association.

Council

To use this word the company must be:

1. a governing, supervisory or representative body of an activity, trade, business, profession; or

2. an independent advisory body; or

3. a deliberative assembly.

Evidence must be produced to show that the company will be what it claims, and that it has the support of whoever it claims it will govern, supervise, or look to it for expertise. In addition, the applicant should produce independent support from a representative body, local authority or government department.

Cymru
Gymru
Chymru
Nghymru

If you wish to use any of these words at the beginning of your company name you would need to show that the company is pre-eminent in its field by providing independent support from a representative body, trade association or the Welsh Assembly Government.

If the word is used elsewhere in the name, you would be expected to show that your company is substantial in relation to its activity or product and that it is eminent in its own field.

	If you want to use the words because it is a surname, you will usually be given approval if the company name includes forenames or initials.
Registered names only	Unless the word is a surname the company's registered office must be in Wales.
Cymreig Cymraeg Chymraeg	If you wish to use any of these words at the beginning of your company name you would need to show that the company is pre-eminent in its field by providing independent support from a representative body, trade association or the Welsh Assembly Government.
Chymreig	If the word is used elsewhere in the name, you would be expected to show that your company is substantial in relation to its activity or product and that it is eminent in its own field.
Gymraeg Gymreig Chymreig	
Registered names only	The company's registered office must be in Wales.
Cyngor Chyngor	To use any of these words the company must be: 1. a governing, supervisory or representative body of an activity, trade, business, profession; or
Gyngor	2. an independent advisory body; or
	3. a deliberative assembly.
	Evidence must be produced to show that the company will be what it claims, and that it has the support of whoever it claims it will govern, supervise, or look to it for expertise. In addition, the applicant should produce independent support from a representative body, local authority or the Welsh Assembly Government
Data protection	To use this expression you must obtain the written support of: Information Commissioner's Office Wycliffe House Water Lane Wilmslow SK9 5AF
Dental Dentistry	To use any of these words you must obtain the written support of: General Dental Council Registration Development 37 Wimpole Street London W1G 8DG
Disciplinary	These words imply that the company has a regulatory role such as a governing, supervisory or representative body.

Discipline	Evidence must be produced to show that the company will be what it claims, and that it has the support of whoever it claims it will govern or supervise. In addition, the applicant should produce independent support from a representative body or government department.

Diùc	To use these words you must obtain the written support of:
Dhiùc	The Scottish Government
Diùcan	Protocol Team
Dhiùcan	Victoria Quay
Ban-diùc	Edinburgh
Bhan-dhiùc	EH6 6QQ
Bhan-dhiùcan	
Ban-diùcan	

Dug	To use these words you must obtain the written support of:
Ddug	The Welsh Assembly Government
Duges	Public Administration and Honours Unit
Dduges	Crown Buildings
	Cathays Park
	Cardiff
	CF10 3NQ

Duke	To use these words you must obtain the written support of:
Duchess	*England & Northern Ireland:*
	Ministry of Justice
	Constitutional Settlement Division
	Ministry of Justice
	Postal Point 5.25
	102 Petty France
	London
	SW1H 9AJ
	Wales:
	The Welsh Assembly Government
	Public Administration and Honours Unit
	Crown Buildings
	Cathays Park
	Cardiff
	CF10 3NQ
	Scotland:
	The Scottish Government
	Protocol Team
	Victoria Quay
	Edinburgh

EH6 6QQ

Ei Fawrhydi	To use these expressions you must obtain the written support of:
Ei Mawrhydi	The Welsh Assembly Government
	Public Administration and Honours Unit
	Crown Buildings
	Cathays Park
	Cardiff
	CF10 3NQ

England

If you wish to use this word at the beginning of your company name, you would need to show that the company is pre-eminent in its field by providing independent support from a representative body, trade association or government department.

If the word is used elsewhere in the name, you would be expected to show that your company is substantial in relation to its activity or product and that it is eminent in its own field.

If you want to use the word because it is a surname, you will usually be given approval if the company name includes forenames or initials.

Unless the word is a surname the company's registered office must be in England and Wales.

English

If you wish to use the word at the beginning of your company name, you would need to show that the company is pre-eminent in its field by providing independent support from a representative body, trade association or government department.

If the word is used elsewhere in the name, you would be expected to show that your company is substantial in relation to its activity or product and that it is eminent in its own field.

The company's registered office must be in England and Wales.

European

Names which include this word will not be approved if they unjustifiably imply a connection with official bodies of the European Union. If there is a genuine connection with an official body, the name may be allowed if the appropriate body supports the application.

Federation

To use this word the company should normally be limited by guarantee with each member having one vote, and include a non-profit distribution clause in the articles of association. If the company is limited by shares its articles would still need to include a clause stating each member has one vote and also a not for profit distribution clause.

Financial Reporting Council

To use this expression you must obtain the written support of:

General Counsel & Company Secretary
Financial Reporting Council

5th Floor, Aldwych House
71-91 Aldwych
London
WC2B 4HN

Financial Services Authority	To use this expression you must obtain the written support of: Financial Services Authority The General Counsel's Division Perimeter Guidance 25 The North Colonnade Canary Wharf London E14 5HS Email: perimeterguidance@fsa.gov.uk
Foundation	This word will normally be refused if it wongly implies that the company has charitable status. If the company is limited by guarantee and has a non-profit distribution clause in the articles of association then the name will normally be approved.
Friendly Society	To use this expression you must obtain the written support of: Financial Services Authority Perimeter Guidance 25 The North Colonnade Canary Wharf London E14 5HS Email: perimeterguidance@fsa.gov.uk
Fund	To use this word you must obtain the written support of: Financial Services Authority Perimeter Guidance 25 The North Colonnade Canary Wharf London E14 5HS Email: perimeterguidance@fsa.gov.uk
Giro	This word implies a connection with an official or private banking organisation or activity. Please provide support from an appropriate body or further information about why you want to use this word.
Government	This word implies a connection with Her Majesty's Government. To use this word you will need the consent of the appropriate government department

	The use of this word normally implies more than one company under the same corporate ownership. If the company cannot satisfy these conditions on registration, it must provide a written undertaking that it will do so within 3 months.
Group	If the name clearly shows that the company is to promote the interests of a group of individuals, then the name will normally be approved.

Gwasanaeth iechyd	To use any of these expressions you must obtain the written support of:
Wasanaeth iechyd	The Welsh Assembly Government
	Head of Communications
	Health & Social Services Directorate
	General Head of Corporate Management
	South Wing, 4th Floor
	Cathays Park
	Cardiff
	CF10 3NQ

Gwladol	If you wish to use any of these words at the beginning of your company name you would need to show that the company is pre-eminent in its field by providing independent support from an independent source such as a representative body, trade association or the Welsh Assembly Government.
Wladol	If the word is used elsewhere in the name, you would be expected to show that your company is substantial in relation to its activity or product and that it is eminent in its own field.
	The company's registered office must be in Wales.

Health and Safety Executive	To use this expression you must obtain the written support of:
	Health and Safety Executive
	Redgrave Court
	Merton Road
	Bootle
	Merseyside
	L20 7HS

Health centre Health service	To use any of these expressions you must obtain the written support of:
	England:
	Department of Health
	Head of Brand Management
	Skipton House
	80 London Road
	London
	SE1 6LH

Wales:
The Welsh Assembly Government
Head of Communications
Health & Social Services Directorate General
General Head of Corporate Management
South Wing,4th Floor
Cathays Park
Cardiff
CF10 3NQ

Scotland:
The Scottish Government
Health Directorate
Business Management and Support
Floor 2N.11
St Andrew's House
Regent Road
Edinburgh
EH1 3DG

Northern Ireland:
Department of Health, Social Services and Public Safety
Office of the Permanent Secretary
DHSSPS
Room C4.15, Castle Buildings
Stormont Estate
Belfast
BT4 3SQ

Health visitor	To use this expression you must obtain the written support of: Nursing & Midwifery Council The Registrar and Chief Executive 23 Portland Place London W1B 1PZ
His Majesty Her Majesty	To use these expressions you must obtain the written support of: *England and Northern Ireland:* Ministry of Justice Constitutional Settlement Division Ministry of Justice Postal Point 5.25 102 Petty France London

SW1H 9AJ

Wales:
The Welsh Assembly Government
Public Administration and Honours Unit
Crown Buildings
Cathays Park
Cardiff
CF10 3NQ

Scotland:
The Scottish Government
Protocol Team
Victoria Quay
Edinburgh
EH6 6QQ

Holding	A company wishing to use this word must be a holding company as defined under section 1159 of the Companies Act 2006. The Companies Act can be viewed on the publications page of our website at www.companieshouse.gov.uk
	If the company cannot satisfy these conditions on registration, when it returns the application, it must confirm that it will do so within 3 months.
House of Commons	To use this expression you must obtain the written support of:
	Corporate Officer of the House of Commons, House of Commons Legal Services Office, London SW1 0AA
House of Lords	To use this expression you must obtain the written support of: Corporate Officer of the House of Lords Houses of Parliament London SW1A 0AA
HPSS HSC	To use these expressions you must obtain the written support of: Office of the Permanent Secretary Department of Health, Social Services and Public Safety (DHSSPS) C.4.15, Castle Buildings Stormont Estate Belfast BT4 3SQ

Human rights	To use this expression the public would expect the company to be:
	1. working or campaigning for the better protection or
	2. promotion of human rights, at home or abroad; or
	3. providing a legal, advice or training service in relation to human rights.
	Prior approval will be given for a name that includes these words by any charitable or not-for-profit body provided that the full name does not unjustifiably suggest a special status in relation to the Council of Europe, the Human Rights Act, or one of the human rights commissions.
Inspectorate	This word implies the company has a quasi-judicial role similar to decisions made by a court of law, administrative tribunal or government officials.
	To use this word you will need to provide support from the appropriate representative body or government department.
Institute	Approval for use of these words is normally given only to those organisations which are carrying out research at the highest level or to professional bodies of the highest standing.
Institution	You will need to explain why there is a need for the proposed institute or institution and that it has appropriate regulations or examination standards. You will need evidence of support from other representative and independent bodies.
Insurance	To use any of these words you must obtain the written support of:
Insurer	Financial Services Authority
	Perimeter Guidance
	25 The North Colonnade
	Canary Wharf
	London
	E14 5HS
	Email: perimeterguidance@fsa.gov.uk
International	If you wish to use this word at the start of the name you will need to show at the time of registration that the major part of the company's activities is in trading overseas.
	If you wish to use the word at the end of the name, you will need to show that the company operates in two or more overseas countries. If the company cannot satisfy these conditions on registration, you must confirm that it will do so within 3 months when you return the application,
Judicial appointment	To use this expression you must obtain the written support of:
	Ministry of Justice
	Democracy, Constitution and Law Group
	102 Petty France

London
SW1H 9A

King   To use this word you must obtain the written support of:
England and Northern Ireland:
Ministry of Justice
Constitutional Settlement Division
Ministry of Justice
Postal Point 5.25
102 Petty France
London
SW1H 9AJ

Wales:
The Welsh Assembly Government
Public Administration and Honours Unit
Crown Buildings
Cathays Park
Cardiff
CF10 3NQ

Scotland:
The Scottish Government
Protocol Team
Victoria Quay
Edinburgh
EH6 6QQ

Law Commission   To use this expression you must obtain the written support of:
Ministry of Justice
Democracy, Constitution and Law Group
102 Petty France
London
SW1H 9AJ

Licensing   This word implies that the company has a regulatory role such as a governing, supervisory or representative body.

Evidence must be produced to show that the company will be what it claims, and that it has the support of whoever it claims it will govern or supervise. In addition, the applicant should produce independent evidence of support from a representative body or government department.

Llywodraeth   To use any of these words you must obtain the written support
Lywodraeth   of:
Welsh Assembly Government
Head of Communications

	Cathays Park Cardiff CF10 3NQ
Medical centre	To use this expression you must obtain the written support of: Office of the Permanent Secretary Department of Health, Social Services and Public Safety (DHSSPS) C.4.15, Castle Buildings Stormont Estate Belfast BT4 3SQ
Midwife Midwifery	To use any of these words you must obtain the written support of: The Registrar and Chief Executive Nursing & Midwifery Council 23 Portland Place London W1B 1PZ
Mòrachd' Mhòrachd'	To use any of these words you must obtain the written support of: The Scottish Government Protocol Team Victoria Quay Edinburgh EH6 6QQ
Mutual	To use this word you must obtain the written support of: Financial Services Authority Perimeter Guidance 25 The North Colonnade Canary Wharf London E14 5HS Email: perimeterguidance@fsa.gov.uk
National	If you wish to use this word at the beginning of your company name you would need to show that the company is pre-eminent in its field by providing independent support from a representative body, trade association or government department. If the word is used elsewhere in the name, you would be expected to show that your company is substantial in relation to its activity or product and that it is eminent in its own field.

National Assembly for Wales National Assembly for Wales Commission	To use any of these expressions you must obtain the written support of:
	The National Assembly for Wales Cardiff Bay Cardiff CF99 1NA
NHS	To use this expression you must obtain the written support of: Department of Health Head of Brand Management Skipton House 80 London Road London SE1 6LH
Northern Ireland Northern Irish	If you wish to use any of these expressions at the beginning of your company name you would need to show that the company is pre-eminent in its field by providing independent support from a representative body, trade association or the Northern Ireland Assembly If the expressions are used elsewhere in the name, you would be expected to show that your company is substantial in relation to its activity or product and that it is eminent in its own field. The company's registered office must be in Northern Ireland.
Northern Ireland Assembly Northern Ireland Assembly Commission	To use any of these expressions you must obtain the written support of: Northern Ireland Assembly Parliament Buildings Belfast BT4 3XX
Northern Ireland Audit Office	To use this expression you must obtain the written support of: Northern Ireland Audit Office 106 University Street Belfast BT7 1EU
Nurse Nursing	To use these words you must obtain the written support of: The Registrar and Chief Executive Nursing & Midwifery Council 23 Portland Place

London
W1B 1PZ

Oifis sgrùdaidh	To use this expression you must obtain the written support of: The Secretary Audit Scotland 110 George Street Edinburgh EH2 4LH
Oilthigh t-Oilthigh Oilthighean h-Oilthighean	To use these words you must obtain the written support of: The Scottish Government Protocol Team Victoria Quay Edinburgh EH6 6QQ
Ombudsman Ombwdsmon	These words imply an official organisation appointed by government to investigate complaints, generally on behalf of individuals such as consumers or taxpayers, against private or public institutions. These organisations also have access rights to sensitive personal information. To use this word you need to provide support from the appropriate government department.
Oversight	This word implies that the company has a regulatory role such as a governing, supervisory or representative body. Evidence must be produced to show that the company will be what it claims, and that it has the support of whoever it claims it will govern or supervise. In addition, the applicant should produce independent support from a representative body or government department.
Parlamaid Pharlamaid Parlamaidean Pharlamaidean	To use these words you must obtain the written support of: The Secretary Scottish Parliamentary Corporate Body The Scottish Parliament Edinburgh EH99 1SP
Parliament Parliamentarian Parliamentary	To use these words you must obtain the written support of: The Corporate Officer of the House of Lords and separately The Corporate Officer of the House of Commons Houses of Parliament London SW1A 0AA

Patent Patentee	To use these words, including Patent Agent(s) or Patent Attorney(s), you must obtain the written support of the Intellectual Property Office (IPO) by emailing ipenforcement@ipo.gov.uk or by writing to the following address; Legal Framework Team Copyright and Enforcement Directorate Intellectual Property Office Concept House Cardiff Road Newport NP10 8QQ
The Pensions Advisory Service	To use this expression you must obtain the written support of: Department for Work and Pensions Protection and Stewardship, 7 floor, Caxton House London SW1H 9NA
Police	To use this word you must obtain the written support of: *England & Wales:* Home Office Policing Strategy Team Police Reform Unit Crime and Policing Group 6th Floor, Fry Building 2 Marsham Street London SW1P 4DF *Scotland:* Scottish Government Police Division St Andrews House Regent Road Edinburgh EH1 3DG *Northern Ireland:* Private Secretary to the Secretary of State Northern Ireland Office Stormont House, Stormont Estate Belfast BT4 3SH
Polytechnic	To use this word you must obtain the written support of:

Department for Business, Innovation & Skills
Higher Education Governance
Level 3, Kingsgate House
66-74 Victoria Street
London
SW1E 6SW

Post Office

This expression will not be allowed in a company name without the approval of the Royal Mail Group.

Pregnancy termination

To use this expression you must obtain the written support of:

Sexual Health Policy Team
Department of Health
Wellington House
133 -155 Waterloo Road
London
SE1 8UG

Prifysgol
Brifysgol
Phrifysgol

To use these words you must obtain the written support of:
The Welsh Assembly Government
Public Administration and Honours Unit
Crown Buildings
Cathays Park
Cardiff
CF10 3NQ

Prince

To use any of these words you must obtain the written support of:

Princess

England and Northern Ireland:
Ministry of Justice
Constitutional Settlement Division
Ministry of Justice
Postal Point 5.25
102 Petty France
London
SW1H 9AJ

Wales:
The Welsh Assembly Government
Public Administration and Honours Unit
Crown Buildings
Cathays Park
Cardiff
CF10 3NQ

Scotland:
The Scottish Government
Protocol Team
Victoria Quay
Edinburgh
EH6 6QQ

Prionnsa	To use any of these words you must obtain the written support of:
Phrionnsa	The Scottish Government
Prionnsaichean	Protocol Team
Phrionnsaichean	Victoria Quay
Bana-phrionnsa	Edinburgh
Bhana-Phrionnsa	EH6 6QQ
Bana-Prionnsaichean	
Bhana-Phrionnsaichean	

Prydain	If you wish to use this word at the beginning of your company name, you would need to show that the company is pre-eminent in its field by providing independent support from a representative body, trade association or Welsh Assembly Government.
Phrydain	If the word is used elsewhere in the name, you would be expected to show that your company is substantial in relation to its activity or product and that it is eminent in its own field.
Brydain	If you want to use the word because it is a surname, you will usually be given approval if the company name includes forenames or initials.
	Unless the word is a surname the company's registered office must be in Wales.

Prydeinig	If you wish to use this word at the beginning of your company name, you would need to show that the company is pre-eminent in its field by providing independent support from a representative body, trade association or Welsh Assembly Government.
Phrydeinig	If the word is used elsewhere in the name, you would be expected to show that your company is substantial in relation to its activity or product and that it is eminent in its own field.
Brydeinig	The company's registered office must be in Wales.

Queen	To use this word you must obtain the written support of:
	England and Northern Ireland
	Ministry of Justice
	Constitutional Settlement Division
	Ministry of Justice
	Postal Point 5.25

102 Petty France
London
SW1H 9AJ

Wales:
The Welsh Assembly Government
Public Administration and Honours Unit
Crown Buildings
Cathays Park
Cardiff
CF10 3NQ

Scotland:
The Scottish Government
Protocol Team
Victoria Quay
Edinburgh
EH6 6QQ

To use any of these expressions you must obtain the written support of:

Regional Agency for	Office of the Permanent Secretary
Public Health and	Department of Health, Social Services and Public Safety
Social Well-being	Room C4.15, Castle Buildings
Regional Health and	Stormont Estate,
Social Care Board	Belfast
	BT4 3SQ

To use any of these words you must obtain the written support of:

Reassurance	Financial Services Authority
Reassurer	Perimeter Guidance
Reinsurance	25 The North Colonnade
Reinsurer	Canary Wharf
	London
	E14 5HS

Register	These words imply a connection with a regulatory body, government department or devolved administration. The proposed name will not be allowed unless the appropriate body supports the application,
Registered	
Registrar	
Registration	
Registry	

Regulator Regulation	These words imply an official organisation appointed by government to regulate public and private organisations or investigate complaints made by consumers or taxpayers, against private or public institutions. To use these words you need to provide support from the appropriate body or government department.
Riaghaltas Riaghaltais Riaghaltasan	To use these words you must obtain the written support of: The Secretary Scottish Parliamentary Corporate Body The Scottish Parliament Edinburgh EH99 1SP
Rìgh Banrigh Bhanrigh Bhanrighrean Banrighrean	To use these words you must obtain the written support of: The Scottish Government Protocol Team Victoria Quay Edinburgh EH6 6QQ
Rìoghachd Aonaichte	If you wish to use this expression at the beginning of your company name you would need to show that the company is pre-eminent in its field by providing evidence of support from a representative body, trade association or Scottish Government. If the expression is used elsewhere in the name, you would be expected to show that your company is substantial in relation to its activity or product and that it is eminent in its own field. Approval is not required for RA.
Rìoghail Rìoghalachd	To use these words you must obtain the written support of: The Scottish Government Protocol Team Victoria Quay Edinburgh EH6 6QQ
Royal Royalty	To use these words you must obtain the written support of: *England & Northern Ireland:* Ministry of Justice Constitutional Settlement Division Ministry of Justice Postal Point 5.25 102 Petty France London SW1H 9AJ *Wales:* The Welsh Assembly Government

Public Administration and Honours Unit
Crown Buildings
Cathays Park
Cardiff
CF10 3NQ

Scotland:
The Scottish Government
Protocol Team
Victoria Quay
Edinburgh
EH6 6QQ

Rule committee	To use this expression you must obtain the written support of: Ministry of Justice Democracy, Constitution and Law Group 102 Petty France London SW1H 9A
Scotland	If you wish to use this word at the beginning of your company name, you would need to show that the company is pre-eminent in its field by providing independent support from a representative body, trade association or the Scottish Government. If the word is used elsewhere in the name, you would be expected to show that your company is substantial in relation to its activity or product and that it is eminent in its own field. If you want to use the word because it is a surname, you will usually be given approval if the company name includes forenames or initials. Unless the word is a surname the company's registered office must be in Scotland.
Scottish	If you wish to use this word at the beginning of your company name, you would need to show that the company is pre-eminent in its field by providing independent support from a representative body, trade association or the Scottish Government. If the word is used elsewhere in the name, you would be expected to show that your company is substantial in relation to its activity or product and that it is eminent in its own field. The company's registered office must be in Scotland.
Scottish Law Commission	To use this expression you must obtain the written support of: Chief Executive Scottish Law Commission

140 Causewayside
Edinburgh
EH9 1PR

The Scottish Parliament	To use any of these expressions you must obtain the written support of:

The Scottish
Parliamentary
Corporate Body

To use any of these expressions you must obtain the written support of:
The Secretary
Scottish Parliamentary Corporate Body

The Scottish Parliament
Edinburgh
EH99 1SP

Senedd
To use this word you must obtain the written support of:
The National Assembly for Wales
Cardiff Bay
Cardiff
CF99 1NA

Sheffield
To use this word you must obtain the written support of:
The Company of Cutlers in Hallamshire
c/o Hulse & Co.
St. James House
Vicar Lane
Sheffield
South Yorkshire
S1 2EX.

Siambr
This word implies representative status such as that associated with a Chamber of Commerce or Trade. To use this word you would normally need to obtain written support from a Chamber of Commerce or other representative body.

Social Service
This expression implies a connection with a local authority Social Services department with access rights to sensitive personal information. To use this expression you should obtain support from the appropriate local authority.

Society
To use this word the company should normally be limited by guarantee with each member having one vote, and include a non-profit distribution clause in the articles of association. If the company is limited by shares its articles would still need to include a clause stating each member had one vote and also a not for profit distribution clause.

To use this expression you must obtain the written support of:
England:
Department for Children, Schools and Families

SEN and Disability Division
Sanctuary Buildings
20 Great Smith Street
London
SW1P 3BT

Special School *Wales:*
The Welsh Assembly Government
Cathays Park
Cardiff
CF10 3NQ

Scotland:
The Scottish Government
Edinburgh
EH99 1SP

Northern Ireland:
Department of Education
Special Education Policy Advisory Group
Rathgael House
43 Balloo Road
Bangor
County. Down
BT19 7PR

Standards This word implies that the company has a regulatory role such as a governing, supervisory or representative body.

Evidence must be produced to show that the company will be what it claims, and that it has the support of whoever it claims it will govern or supervise. In addition, the applicant should produce independent support from a representative body or government department.

Stock exchange This expression implies that the company is part of, or connected with the official "Stock Exchange".

Swyddfa archwilio To use this expression you must obtain the written support of:
Auditor General for Wales
Cathedral Road
Cardiff CF11 9LJ

in Welsh:
Archwilydd Cyffredinol Cymru
24 Heol y Gadeirlan
Caerdydd
CF11 9LJ

Teyrnas Unedig Teyrnas Gyfunol Deyrnas Unedig	If you wish to use this expression at the beginning of your company name you would need to show that the company is pre-eminent in its field by providing evidence of support from a representative body, trade association or government department.
Theyrnas Unedig	If the expression is used elsewhere in the name, you would be expected to show that your company is substantial in relation to its activity or product and that it is eminent in its own field.
Deyrnas Gyfunol Theyrnas Gyfunol	
Trade Union	This expression will normally be refused unless it conforms to legislation relating to trade unions.
Tribunal	This word implies the company has a quasi-judicial role similar to decisions made by an administrative tribunal or other institution with the authority to judge, adjudicate on, or determine claims or disputes. To use this word you will need to provide support from the appropriate representative body or government department.
Trust	Trust is prescribed and will normally require the approval or support of a representative body. The requirements for individual trusts are set out below:

Artistic Trust and Educational Trust:

The company should have a non-profit distribution clause in the articles of association and the name should reflect the nature of the trust. The promoters should be of high standing in the field.

Charitable Trust:

The company should have charitable objects and a non-profit distribution clause in the articles of association. You will be asked for confirmation that you have made, or will make, an application for registration as a charity with the Charity Commission (England, Wales and Northern Ireland) or the Office of the Scottish Charity Regulator (Scotland).

Enterprise Trust:

The company should have a non-profit distribution clause in the articles of association and you must provide evidence of support from, for example, local authorities, businesses or banks.

Family Trust:

The company should have a non-profit distribution clause in the articles of association and the objects should reflect the nature of the trust. Names of family trusts will usually be approved if the name as a whole identifies the company as such.

Financial Trust and Investment Trust:

If you wish to use one of these expressions you will need to provide a written assurance that substantial paid up share capital or other funds will be achieved within a reasonable period after incorporation.

Pensions Trust and Staff Trust:

The name of the company must include the name of the parent company and the objects of the company must include the operation of pension funds.

Unit Trust:

To use this expression you must obtain the written support of:
Financial Services Authority
Perimeter Guidance
25 The North Colonnade
Canary Wharf
London
E14 5HS.
Email: perimeterguidance@fsa.gov.uk

Tywysog Dywysog Thywysog Tywysoges Dywysoges Thywysoges	To use these words you must obtain the written support of: The Welsh Assembly Government Public Administration and Honours Unit Crown Buildings Cathays Park Cardiff CF10 3NQ
Underwrite Underwriting	To use these words you must obtain the written support of: Financial Services Authority 25 The North Colonnade Canary Wharf London E14 5HS Email: perimeterguidance@fsa.gov.uk
United Kingdom	If you wish to use this expression at the beginning of your company name you would need to show that the company is pre-eminent in its field by providing evidence of support from a representative body, trade association or government department. If the expression is used elsewhere in the name, you would be expected to show that your company is substantial in relation to its activity or product and that it is eminent in its own field. Approval is not required for UK.

University	To use this word you must obtain the written support of:

England:
Department for Business, Innovation & Skills
Higher Education Governance
1 Victoria Street
London
SW1H 0ET

Wales:
The Welsh Assembly Government
Cathays Park
Cardiff
CF10 3NQ

Scotland:
The Scottish Government
Higher Education Governance Team
Atlantic Quay
150 Broomielaw
Glasgow
G2 8LG

Northern Ireland:
Department for Employment and Learning
Head of Higher Education, Finance & Governance
39-49 Adelaide Street
BELFAST
BT2 FD8

Wales

If you wish to use this word at the beginning of your company name you would need to show that the company is pre-eminent in its field by providing independent support from a representative body, trade association or the Welsh Assembly Government.

If the word is used elsewhere in the name, you would be expected to show that your company is substantial in relation to its activity or product and that it is eminent in its own field.

If you want to use the word because it is a surname, you will usually be given approval if the company name includes fore-names or initials.

Unless the word is a surname the company's registered office must be in Wales.

Watchdog

This word implies that the company has a regulatory role such as a governing, supervisory or representative body.

Evidence must be produced to show that the company will be what it claims, and that it has the support of whoever it claims it will govern or supervise. In addition, the applicant should produce independent support from a representative body or government department.

Welsh

If you wish to use this word at the beginning of your company name you would need to show that the company is pre-eminent in its field by providing providing independent support from a representative body, trade association or the Welsh Assembly Government.

If the word is used elsewhere in the name, you would be expected to show that your company is substantial in relation to its activity or product and that it is eminent in its own field.

The company's registered office must be in Wales.

Welsh Assembly Government

This expression suggests the company is a part of the Welsh Assembly Government. To use this expression you must obtain the written support of:

The Welsh Assembly Government
Cathays Park
Cardiff
CF10 3NQ

Windsor

To use this word you must obtain the written support of:

England & Northern Ireland:
Ministry of Justice
Constitutional Settlement Division
Ministry of Justice
Postal Point 5.25
102 Petty France
London
SW1H 9AJ

Wales:
The Welsh Assembly Government
Public Administration and Honours Unit
Crown Buildings
Cathays Park
Cardiff
CF10 3NQ

Scotland:
The Scottish Government
Protocol Team
Victoria Quay
Edinburgh
EH6 6QQ

Sensitive words and expressions that require the approval of the Secretary of the State

Agency	This word will not be allowed if it implies a connection with a government department, devolved administration or other representative body.
Accountancy and Actuarial Discipline Board	To use any of these expressions you must obtain the written support of:
Accounting Standards Board	Comptroller and Auditor General
Auditing Practices Board	Corporate Secretariat
Board for Actuarial Standards	National Audit Office

Elizabeth 2
151 Buckingham Palace Road
London
SW1W 9SS

Archwilydd Cyffredinol Cymru	To use this expression you must obtain the written support of:

Auditor General for Wales
24 Cathedral Road
Cardiff
CF11 9LJ
or
Archwilydd Cyffredinol Cymru
24 Heol y Gadeirlan
Caerdydd
CF11 9LJ

Assembly	This word implies a connection with a government department, devolved administration or other representative body. To use this word you must obtain the written support of the appropriate body.
Border Agency	These expressions imply a connection with The UK Border Agency. To use any of these expressions you must obtain the written support of:
UKBA	UK Border Agency

Lunar House
40 Wellesley Road
Croydon
CR9 2BY

Cabinet Office	This expression implies a connection with the government's official Cabinet Office. Further information can be found on the Cabinet Office website at www.cabinetoffice.gov.uk
Cadw	To use this name you must obtain the written support of: Cadw Welsh Assembly Government Plas Carew Unit 5/7 Cefn Coed Parc Nantgarw Cardiff CF15 7QQ
Care and Social Services Inspectorate Wales CISSW	To use any of these expressions you must obtain the written support of: Care and Social Services Inspectorate Wales Cathays Park Cardiff CF10 3NQ
Chamber of Commerce	To use this expression you must obtain the written support of: The British Chambers of Commerce Oak Tree Court Binley Business Park Harry Weston Road Coventry CV3 2UN
Chartered Accountant ICAEW	To use these expressions you must obtain the written support of: The Institute of Chartered Accountants in England and Wales Chartered Accountants' Hall Moorgate Place London EC2P 2BJ
Chartered Secretary	To use this expression you must obtain the written support of: The Institute of Chartered Secretaries and Administrators 16 Park Crescent London W1B 1AH
Chartered Surveyor	To use this expression you must obtain the written support of: Royal Institution of Chartered Surveyors

RICS
Parliament Square
London
SW1P 3AD

Comisiwn Cynulliad Cenedlaethol Cymru	This expression implies a connection with the National Assembly for Wales or the National Assembly for Wales Commission. To use this expression you must obtain the written support of:

Clerk of the Assembly
National Assembly for Wales Commission
Cardiff Bay
Cardiff
CF99 1NA
or
Clerc y Cynulliad
Comisiwn Cynulliad Cenedlaethol Cymru
Bae Caerdydd
Caerdydd
CF99 1NA

Commissioner	These expressions imply a connection with an official body set up to investigate complaints made by consumers or taxpayers, against private or public institutions. To use this word you need to provide support from the appropriate body or government department.
Commonhold Association	This expression may only be used at the end of the company name to indicate that the company is a Commonhold Association in accordance with the Commonhold and Leasehold Reform Act 2002.
Copyright Design	These words and expressions will be allowed if they do not imply a connection with the Intellectual Property Office, a government department or representative body. If we believe the use of these expressions suggests a connection with her Majesty's Government then we may ask the Intellectual Property Office to comment.
Crime Squad	This expression implies a connection with The Serious Organised Crime Agency (SOCA). Please see entry for 'Serious Organised Crime'.
Criminal Intelligence Service	This expression implies a connection with the UK's official criminal intelligence services such as the Police, National Criminal Intelligence Service and the Serious Organised Crime Agency.
Cynulliad Cenedlaethol Cymru	This expression implies a connection with the National Assembly for Wales or the National Assembly for Wales Commission. To use this expression you must obtain the written support of:

Clerk of the Assembly
National Assembly for Wales Commission
Cardiff Bay
Cardiff
CF99 1NA
or
Clerc y Cynulliad
Comisiwn Cynulliad Cenedlaethol Cymru
Bae Caerdydd
Caerdydd
CF99 1NA

Department for Department of	The use of these expressions may imply a connection with a government department.
Employment Medical Advisory Service EMAS	These expressions imply a connection with the Health and Safety Executive. To use these expressions you must obtain the written support of: Health and Safety Executive Redgrave Court Merton Road Bootle L20 7HS
Financial Report- ing Review Panel	To use this expression you must obtain the written support of: Financial Reporting Review Panel 5th Floor Aldwych House 71-91 Aldwych London WC2B 4HN
Health and Safety HSE	These expressions imply a connection with the Health and Safety Executive. To use these expression you must obtain the written support of: Health and Safety Executive Redgrave Court Merton Road Bootle L20 7HS
Home Office	This expression implies a connection with the Home Office government department

HMRC — This expression implies a connection with a Her Majesty's Revenue and Customs.

HSE — This expression will be allowed provided it does not imply a connection with the Health and Safety Executive.

Industrial and Provident Society — To use this expression you must obtain the written support of:

Financial Services Authority
Perimeter Guidance
25 The North Colonnade
Canary Wharf
London
E14 5HS
Email: perimeterguidance.gov.uk

Intellectual Property — These words and expressions will be allowed if they do not imply a connection with the Intellectual Property Office, a government department or representative body.

IPO
UKIPO — If we believe the use of these expressions suggests a connection with Her Majesty's Government then we may ask the Intellectual Property Office to comment.

Licensing Authority Assets Recovery — This expression implies a connection with The Serious Organised Crime Agency (SOCA). Please see entry for Serious Organised Crime'.

Ministry
Ministry of — The use of this word or expression may imply a connection with a government department.

National Accounts — These expressions and the abbreviation imply a connection with the National Audit Office. To use these expressions you must obtain the written support of:

National Accounting
NAO — Comptroller & Auditor General

Corporate Secretariat
National Audit Office
157-159 Buckingham Palace Road
London
SW1W 9SP

NAW
NAWC
NAFW
NAFWC — These expressions will be allowed provided they do not imply a connection with the National Assembly for Wales.

Nuclear Installation — This expression implies a connection with the Health and Safety Executive. To use this expression you must obtain the written support of:

Health and Safety Executive
Redgrave Court
Merton Road
Bootle
L20 7HS

Professional
Oversight Board

To use this expression you must obtain the written support of:

General Counsel & Company Secretary
Financial Reporting Council
5th Floor, Aldwych House
71-91 Aldwych
London
WC2B 4HN

Public Health

This expression implies a connection with the Department of Health. To use this expression you must obtain the written support of:
Office of the Permanent Secretary
Department of Health, Social Services and Public Safety
Room C4.15, Castle Buildings
Stormont Estate
Belfast
BT4 3SQ

Select Committee

This expression implies a connection with the House of Commons. To use this expression you must obtain the written support of:
Corporate Officer of the House of Commons
Houses of Commons Legal Services Office
London
SW1A 0AA

Serious Organised
Crime

SOCA

These expressions imply a connection with The Serious Organised Crime Agency (SOCA).

To use any of these expressions you must obtain the written support of:
Serious Organised Crime Agency
PO Box 8000
London
SE11 5EN

Scottish Chamber
of Commerce

To use this expression you must obtain the written support of:

Scottish Chambers of Commerce
30 George Square
Glasgow

G2 1EQ

WAG | This expression will be allowed provided it does not imply a connection with the Welsh Assembly Government

Words and expressions governed by other legislation.

2012
(Olympic Games)
| "2012" is one of several words and expressions which are protected under the London Olympic Games and Paralympic Games Act 2006. These words and expressions can be found under "Olympic Games" later in this table.

Anzac | This word is controlled by section 1 of the Anzac Act 1916 and will not be allowed in a company name.

Architect | With the exception of 'naval architect', 'landscape architect' or 'golf-course architect', the use of this word is controlled by the Architects Registration Act 1997 (Section 20). To use this word you must obtain the written support of:

Architects Registration Board
8 Weymouth Street
London W1W 5BU

Art
psychotherapist.
Art therapist.
Biomedical
scientist.
Chiropodist.
Clinical scientist.
Clinical
psychologist.
Counselling
psychologist.
Drama therapist.
Dietician.
Dietitian
Educational
psychologist.
Diagnostic
radiographer.
Forensic
psychologist.
Health
psychologist.
Music therapist.
Podiatrist.
Occupational
psychologist.
| These expressions are protected titles and require the approval of the Health Professions Council who can be contacted at:

Registration Department

Health Professions Council
184 Kennington Park Road
London SE11 4BU

Email: registration@hpc-uk.org

Occupational therapist.

Operating department. Practitioner.

Orthoptist.

Orthotist.

Paramedic.

Physical therapist.

Physiotherapist.

Practitioner psychologist.

Prosthetist.

Radiographer.

Registered psychologist.

Speech and language therapist.

Speech therapist.

Sport and exercise psychologist.

Therapeutic radiographer.

Building Society	To use this expression you must obtain the written support of: Financial Services Authority Perimeter Guidance 25 North Colonnade Canary Wharf London E14 5HS Email: perimeterguidance@fsa.gov.uk
Chemist	These words are controlled by section 78 of the Medicines Act 1968
Druggist	To use any of these words you must obtain the written support of:
Pharmaceutical	*England and Wales:*
Pharmaceutist	The Director of Legal Services
Pharmacist	The Royal Pharmaceutical
Pharmacy	Society of Great Britain 1 Lambeth High Street London SE1 7JN *Scotland:* The Pharmaceutical Society 36 York Place Edinburgh

EH13HU

Northern Ireland:
The Pharmaceutical Society of Northern Ireland
73 University Street
Belfast
BT7 1HL

Chiropractor	This word is controlled by the Chiropractors Act 1994. To use this name you must obtain the written support of: The Chief Executive General Chiropractic Council 44 Wicklow Street London WC1X 9HL
Credit Union	This expression is controlled by the Credit Union Act 1979 To use this expression you must obtain the written support of: Financial Services Authority Perimeter Guidance 25 The North Colonnade Canary Wharf London E14 5HS Email: perimeterguidance@fsa.gov.uk
Dentist	These words and expressions are controlled by the Dental Act 1984. To use these words and expressions you must obtain the written support of:
Dental Surgeon	The Registrar
Dental Practitioner	General Dental Council
	37 Wimpole Street London W1G 8DG
Housing Corporation	To use this expression you must obtain the written support of Tenant Services Authority Maple House 149 Tottenham Court Road London W1T 7BN
Olympic words and expressions	These words and expressions (including similar words) are controlled by the London Olympic Games and Paralympic Games Act 2006:

Olympiad	To use any of these words and expressions you must obtain the written support of:
Olympiads	The London Organising Committee of the Olympic Games Limited (LOCOG)
Olympian	23rd Floor
Olympians	1 Churchill Place
Olympic	Canary Wharf
Olympics	London
Paralympic	E14 5LN
Paralympics	www.london2012.com/
Paralympiad	
Paralympiads	
Paralympian	
Paralympians	
2012	
Citius Altius Fortius ('Faster, Higher Stronger')	
Spirit in Motion	
Twenty twelve	
Two thousand and twelve	
Optician.	These words and expressions are controlled by the Opticians Act 1989
Ophthalmic Optician.	To use these words and expressions you must obtain the written support of:
Dispensing Optician.	The Registrar
Enrolled Optician.	General Optical Council
Registered Optician	41 Harley Street
Optometrist.	London
	W1N 2DJ
Patent Attorney	The words 'Patent', Patentee and 'Registered' are prescribed words (see Table A).
Patent Agent	The expressions 'Trade Mark' and 'Trade Mark Agent' will be allowed provided their use does not imply a connection with the Intellectual Property Office, a government department or representative body.
Registered trade mark agent	
Trade Mark	
Trade Mark Agent	
Physician.	If we believe the use of these expressions suggests a connection with Her Majesty's Government then we may ask the Intellectual Property Office to comment.

Doctor of medicine. Licentiate in medicine and surgery. Bachelor of medicine. Surgeon. General practitioner Red Cross,	The use of these words and expressions in a company name could be in breach of the Medical Act 1983. If you are qualified to use any of these words and expressions your application should include a letter or email from your representative body confirming it has no objection to the proposed name.
Geneva Cross Red Crescent Red Lion and Sun	These expressions are controlled by the Geneva Convention Act 1957 and will not be permitted for use in a company name.
Solicitor	*England and Wales:* This word is controlled by sections 20-21 of the Solicitors Act 1974. If you are an existing firm of solicitors (i.e. a sole proprietor or partnership) you will already be regulated by the Solicitors regulatory authority. Your application to form a company must include a copy of your firms letterhead which includes the statement 'regulated by the Solicitors Regulatory Authority' (or SRA). No additional information is required. If you are a new firm your application must include a letter of support from: The Solicitors Regulatory Authority Operations Ipsley Court Berrington Close Redditch B98 0TD *Scotland:* This word is controlled by section 31 of the Solicitors (Scotland) Act 1980. To use this word you must obtain the written support of: The Law Society of Scotland 26 Drumsheugh Gardens Edinburgh EH3 7YR. *Northern Ireland:* To use this word in a company name you must obtain the written support of: The Law Society of Northern Ireland

96 Victoria Street
Belfast
BT1 3GN

Veterinary Surgeon	These words and expressions are controlled by sections 19/20 of the Veterinary Surgeons Act 1966.
Vet	To use any of these words and expressions you must obtain the written support of:

The Registrar
Royal College of Veterinary Surgeons
62-64 Horseferry Rd
London
SW1P 2AF

Appendix 2C

Model Articles of Association

Model articles for private companies limited by shares

53.   Insurance

Part 1
Interpretation and limitation of liability

1. Defined terms

1 In the articles, unless the context requires otherwise—

"articles" means the company's articles of association;

"bankruptcy" includes individual insolvency proceedings in a jurisdiction other than England and Wales or Northern Ireland which have an effect similar to that of bankruptcy;

"chairman" has the meaning given in article 12;

"chairman of the meeting" has the meaning given in article 39;

"Companies Acts" means the Companies Acts (as defined in section 2 of the Companies Act 2006), in so far as they apply to the company;

"director" means a director of the company, and includes any person occupying the position of director, by whatever name called;

"distribution recipient" has the meaning given in article 31;

"document" includes, unless otherwise specified, any document sent or supplied in electronic form;

"electronic form" has the meaning given in section 1168 of the Companies Act 2006;

"fully paid" in relation to a share, means that the nominal value and any premium to be paid to the company in respect of that share have been paid to the company;

"hard copy form" has the meaning given in section 1168 of the Companies Act 2006;

"holder" in relation to shares means the person whose name is entered in the register of

members as the holder of the shares;

"instrument" means a document in hard copy form;

"ordinary resolution" has the meaning given in section 282 of the Companies Act 2006;

"paid" means paid or credited as paid;

"participate", in relation to a directors' meeting, has the meaning given in article 10;

"proxy notice" has the meaning given in article 45;

"shareholder" means a person who is the holder of a share;

"shares" means shares in the company;

"special resolution" has the meaning given in section 283 of the Companies Act 2006;

"subsidiary" has the meaning given in section 1159 of the Companies Act 2006;

"transmittee" means a person entitled to a share by reason of the death or bankruptcy of a

shareholder or otherwise by operation of law; and

"writing" means the representation or reproduction of words, symbols or other information in a visible form by any method or combination of methods, whether sent or supplied in electronic form or otherwise.

Unless the context otherwise requires, other words or expressions contained in these articles bear the same meaning as in the Companies Act 2006 as in force on the date when these articles become binding on the company.

2. Liability of members

The liability of the members is limited to the amount, if any, unpaid on the shares held by them.

Part 2
Directors

Directors' powers and responsibilities

3. Directors' general authority

Subject to the articles, the directors are responsible for the management of the company's business, for which purpose they may exercise all the powers of the company.

4. Shareholders' reserve power

(1)   The shareholders may, by special resolution, direct the directors to take, or refrain from taking, specified action.

(2)   No such special resolution invalidates anything which the directors have done before the passing of the resolution.

5. Directors may delegate

(1)   Subject to the articles, the directors may delegate any of the powers which are conferred on them under the articles—

        (a)   to such person or committee;

(b)   by such means (including by power of attorney);

(c)   to such an extent;

(d)   in relation to such matters or territories; and

(e)   on such terms and conditions;

as they think fit.

(2)   If the directors so specify, any such delegation may authorise further delegation of the directors' powers by any person to whom they are delegated.

(3)   The directors may revoke any delegation in whole or part, or alter its terms and conditions.

6. Committees

(1)   Committees to which the directors delegate any of their powers must follow procedures which are based as far as they are applicable on those provisions of the articles which govern the taking of decisions by directors.

(2)   The directors may make rules of procedure for all or any committees, which prevail over rules derived from the articles if they are not consistent with them.

Decision-making by Directors

7. Directors to take decisions collectively

(1)   The general rule about decision-making by directors is that any decision of the directors must be either a majority decision at a meeting or a decision taken in accordance with article 8.

(2)   If—

(a)   the company only has one director, and

(b)   no provision of the articles requires it to have more than one director,

the general rule does not apply, and the director may take decisions without regard to any of the provisions of the articles relating to directors' decision-making.

8. Unanimous decisions

(1)   A decision of the directors is taken in accordance with this article when all eligible directors indicate to each other by any means that they share a common view on a matter.

(2)   Such a decision may take the form of a resolution in writing, copies of which have been signed by each eligible director or to which each eligible director has otherwise indicated agreement in writing.

(3)   References in this article to eligible directors are to directors who would have been entitled to vote on the matter had it been proposed as a resolution at a directors' meeting.

(4)   A decision may not be taken in accordance with this article if the eligible directors would not have formed a quorum at such a meeting.

9. Calling a directors' meeting

(1)   Any director may call a directors' meeting by giving notice of the meeting to the directors or by authorising the company secretary (if any) to give such notice.

(2)   Notice of any directors' meeting must indicate—

(a)   its proposed date and time;

(b)   where it is to take place; and

(c)   if it is anticipated that directors participating in the meeting will not be in the same place, how it is proposed that they should communicate with each other during the meeting.

(3)   Notice of a directors' meeting must be given to each director, but need not be in writing.

(4)   Notice of a directors' meeting need not be given to directors who waive their entitlement to notice of that meeting, by giving notice to that effect to the company not more than 7 days after the date on which the meeting is held. Where such notice is given after the meeting has been held, that does not affect the validity of the meeting, or of any business conducted at it.

10. Participation in directors' meetings

(1)   Subject to the articles, directors participate in a directors' meeting, or part of a directors' meeting, when—

(a)   the meeting has been called and takes place in accordance with the articles, and

(b)   they can each communicate to the others any information or opinions they have on any particular item of the business of the meeting.

(2)   In determining whether directors are participating in a directors' meeting, it is irrelevant where any director is or how they communicate with each other.

(3)   If all the directors participating in a meeting are not in the same place, they may decide that the meeting is to be treated as taking place wherever any of them is.

11. Quorum for directors' meetings

(1)   At a directors' meeting, unless a quorum is participating, no proposal is to be voted on, except a proposal to call another meeting.

(2)   The quorum for directors' meetings may be fixed from time to time by a decision of the directors, but it must never be less than two, and unless otherwise fixed it is two.

(3)   If the total number of directors for the time being is less than the quorum required, the directors must not take any decision other than a decision—

(a)   to appoint further directors, or

(b)   to call a general meeting so as to enable the shareholders to appoint further directors.

12. Chairing of directors' meetings

(1)   The directors may appoint a director to chair their meetings.

(2)   The person so appointed for the time being is known as the chairman.

(3)   The directors may terminate the chairman's appointment at any time.

(4)   If the chairman is not participating in a directors' meeting within ten minutes of the time at which it was to start, the participating directors must appoint one of themselves to chair it.

13. Casting vote

(1)   If the numbers of votes for and against a proposal are equal, the chairman or other director chairing the meeting has a casting vote.

(2)   But this does not apply if, in accordance with the articles, the chairman or other director is not to be counted as participating in the decision-making process for quorum or voting purposes.

14. Conflicts of interest

(1)   If a proposed decision of the directors is concerned with an actual or proposed transaction or arrangement with the company in which a director is interested, that director is not to be counted as participating in the decision-making process for quorum or voting purposes.

(2)   But if paragraph (3) applies, a director who is interested in an actual or proposed transaction or arrangement with the company is to be counted as participating in the decision-making process for quorum and voting purposes.

(3)   This paragraph applies when—

(a)   the company by ordinary resolution disapplies the provision of the articles which would otherwise prevent a director from being counted as participating in the decision-making process;

(b)   the director's interest cannot reasonably be regarded as likely to give rise to a conflict of interest; or

(c)   the director's conflict of interest arises from a permitted cause.

(4)   For the purposes of this article, the following are permitted causes—

(a)   a guarantee given, or to be given, by or to a director in respect of an obligation incurred by or on behalf of the company or any of its subsidiaries;

(b)   subscription, or an agreement to subscribe, for shares or other securities of the company or any of its subsidiaries, or to underwrite, sub-underwrite, or guarantee subscription for any such shares or securities; and

(c)   arrangements pursuant to which benefits are made available to employees and directors or former employees and directors of the company or any of its subsidiaries which do not provide special benefits for directors or former directors.

(5)   For the purposes of this article, references to proposed decisions and decision-making processes include any directors' meeting or part of a directors' meeting.

(6)   Subject to paragraph (7), if a question arises at a meeting of directors or of a committee of directors as to the right of a director to participate in the meeting (or part of the meeting) for voting or quorum purposes, the question may, before the conclusion of the meeting, be referred to the chairman whose ruling in relation to any director other than the chairman is to be final and conclusive.

(7)   If any question as to the right to participate in the meeting (or part of the meeting) should arise in respect of the chairman, the question is to be decided by a decision of the directors at that meeting, for which purpose the chairman is not to be counted as participating in the meeting (or that part of the meeting) for voting or quorum purposes.

15. Records of decisions to be kept

The directors must ensure that the company keeps a record, in writing, for at least 10 years from the date of the decision recorded, of every unanimous or majority decision taken by the directors.

16. Directors' discretion to make further rules

Subject to the articles, the directors may make any rule which they think fit about how they take decisions, and about how such rules are to be recorded or communicated to directors.

Appointment of directors

17. Methods of appointing directors

(1)   Any person who is willing to act as a director, and is permitted by law to do so, may be appointed to be a director—

(a)   by ordinary resolution, or

(b)   by a decision of the directors.

(2)   In any case where, as a result of death, the company has no shareholders and no directors, the personal representatives of the last shareholder to have died have the right, by notice in writing, to appoint a person to be a director.

(3)   For the purposes of paragraph (2), where 2 or more shareholders die in circumstances rendering it uncertain who was the last to die, a younger shareholder is deemed to have survived an older shareholder.

18. Termination of director's appointment

A person ceases to be a director as soon as—

(a)   that person ceases to be a director by virtue of any provision of the Companies Act 2006 or is prohibited from being a director by law;

(b)   a bankruptcy order is made against that person;

(c)   a composition is made with that person's creditors generally in satisfaction of that person's debts;

(d)   a registered medical practitioner who is treating that person gives a written opinion to the company stating that that person has become physically or mentally incapable of acting as a director and may remain so for more than three months;

(e)   by reason of that person's mental health, a court makes an order which wholly or partly prevents that person from personally exercising any powers or rights which that person would otherwise have;

(f)   notification is received by the company from the director that the director is resigning from office, and such resignation has taken effect in accordance with its terms.

19. Directors' remuneration

(1)   Directors may undertake any services for the company that the directors decide.

(2)   Directors are entitled to such remuneration as the directors determine—

(a)   for their services to the company as directors, and

(b)   for any other service which they undertake for the company.

(3)   Subject to the articles, a director's remuneration may—

(a)   take any form, and

(b)   include any arrangements in connection with the payment of a pension, allowance or gratuity, or any death, sickness or disability benefits, to or in respect of that director.

(4)   Unless the directors decide otherwise, directors' remuneration accrues from day to day.

(5)   Unless the directors decide otherwise, directors are not accountable to the company for any remuneration which they receive as directors or other officers or employees of the company's subsidiaries or of any other body corporate in which the company is interested.

20. Directors' expenses

The company may pay any reasonable expenses which the directors properly incur in connection with their attendance at—

(a)   meetings of directors or committees of directors,

(b)   general meetings, or

(c)   separate meetings of the holders of any class of shares or of debentures of the company, or otherwise in connection with the exercise of their powers and the discharge of their responsibilities in relation to the company.

Part 3
Shares and distributions

Shares

21. All shares to be fully paid up

(1)   No share is to be issued for less than the aggregate of its nominal value and any premium to be paid to the company in consideration for its issue.

(2)   This does not apply to shares taken on the formation of the company by the subscribers to the company's memorandum.

22. Powers to issue different classes of share

(1)   Subject to the articles, but without prejudice to the rights attached to any existing share, the company may issue shares with such rights or restrictions as may be determined by ordinary resolution.

(2)   The company may issue shares which are to be redeemed, or are liable to be redeemed at the option of the company or the holder, and the directors may determine the terms, conditions and manner of redemption of any such shares.

23. Company not bound by less than absolute interests

Except as required by law, no person is to be recognised by the company as holding any share upon any trust, and except as otherwise required by law or the articles, the company is not in any way to be bound by or recognise any interest in a share other than the holder's absolute ownership of it and all the rights attaching to it.

24. Share certificates

(1)   The company must issue each shareholder, free of charge, with one or more certificates in respect of the shares which that shareholder holds.

(2)   Every certificate must specify—

    (a)   in respect of how many shares, of what class, it is issued;

    (b)   the nominal value of those shares;

    (c)   that the shares are fully paid; and

    (d)   any distinguishing numbers assigned to them.

(3)   No certificate may be issued in respect of shares of more than one class.

(4)   If more than one person holds a share, only one certificate may be issued in respect of it.

(5)   Certificates must—

    (a)   have affixed to them the company's common seal, or

    (b)   be otherwise executed in accordance with the Companies Acts.

25. Replacement share certificates

(1)   If a certificate issued in respect of a shareholder's shares is—

    (a)   damaged or defaced, or

    (b)   said to be lost, stolen or destroyed, that shareholder is entitled to be issued with a replacement certificate in respect of the same shares.

(2)   A shareholder exercising the right to be issued with such a replacement certificate—

    (a)   may at the same time exercise the right to be issued with a single certificate or separate certificates;

    (b)   must return the certificate which is to be replaced to the company if it is damaged or defaced; and

    (c)   must comply with such conditions as to evidence, indemnity and the payment of a reasonable fee as the directors decide.

26. Share transfers

(1)   Shares may be transferred by means of an instrument of transfer in any usual form or any other form approved by the directors, which is executed by or on behalf of the transferor.

(2)   No fee may be charged for registering any instrument of transfer or other document relating to or affecting the title to any share.

(3)   The company may retain any instrument of transfer which is registered.

(4)   The transferor remains the holder of a share until the transferee's name is entered in the register of members as holder of it.

(5)   The directors may refuse to register the transfer of a share, and if they do so, the instrument of transfer must be returned to the transferee with the notice of refusal unless they suspect that the proposed transfer may be fraudulent.

27. Transmission of shares

(1)   If title to a share passes to a transmittee, the company may only recognise the transmittee as having any title to that share.

(2)   A transmittee who produces such evidence of entitlement to shares as the directors may properly require—

(a)   may, subject to the articles, choose either to become the holder of those shares or to have them transferred to another person, and

(b)   subject to the articles, and pending any transfer of the shares to another person, has the same rights as the holder had.

(3)   But transmittees do not have the right to attend or vote at a general meeting, or agree to a proposed written resolution, in respect of shares to which they are entitled, by reason of the holder's death or bankruptcy or otherwise, unless they become the holders of those shares.

28. Exercise of transmittees' rights

(1)   Transmittees who wish to become the holders of shares to which they have become entitled must notify the company in writing of that wish.

(2)   If the transmittee wishes to have a share transferred to another person, the transmittee must execute an instrument of transfer in respect of it.

(3)   Any transfer made or executed under this article is to be treated as if it were made or executed by the person from whom the transmittee has derived rights in respect of the share, and as if the event which gave rise to the transmission had not occurred.

29. Transmittees bound by prior notices

If a notice is given to a shareholder in respect of shares and a transmittee is entitled to those shares, the transmittee is bound by the notice if it was given to the shareholder before the transmittee's name has been entered in the register of members.

Dividends and other distributions

30. Procedure for declaring dividends

(1)   The company may by ordinary resolution declare dividends, and the directors may decide to pay interim dividends.

(2)   A dividend must not be declared unless the directors have made a recommendation as to its amount. Such a dividend must not exceed the amount recommended by the directors.

(3)   No dividend may be declared or paid unless it is in accordance with shareholders' respective rights.

(4)   Unless the shareholders' resolution to declare or directors' decision to pay a dividend, or the terms on which shares are issued, specify otherwise, it must be

paid by reference to each shareholder's holding of shares on the date of the resolution or decision to declare or pay it.

(5) If the company's share capital is divided into different classes, no interim dividend may be paid on shares carrying deferred or non-preferred rights if, at the time of payment, any preferential dividend is in arrear.

(6) The directors may pay at intervals any dividend payable at a fixed rate if it appears to them that the profits available for distribution justify the payment.

(7) If the directors act in good faith, they do not incur any liability to the holders of shares conferring preferred rights for any loss they may suffer by the lawful payment of an interim dividend on shares with deferred or non-preferred rights.

31. Payment of dividends and other distributions

(1) Where a dividend or other sum which is a distribution is payable in respect of a share, it must be paid by one or more of the following means—

    (a) transfer to a bank or building society account specified by the distribution recipient either in writing or as the directors may otherwise decide;

    (b) sending a cheque made payable to the distribution recipient by post to the distribution recipient at the distribution recipient's registered address (if the distribution recipient is a holder of the share), or (in any other case) to an address specified by the distribution recipient either in writing or as the directors may otherwise decide;

    (c) sending a cheque made payable to such person by post to such person at such address as the distribution recipient has specified either in writing or as the directors may otherwise decide; or

    (d) any other means of payment as the directors agree with the distribution recipient either in writing or by such other means as the directors decide.

(2) In the articles, "the distribution recipient" means, in respect of a share in respect of which a dividend or other sum is payable—

    (a) the holder of the share; or

    (b) if the share has two or more joint holders, whichever of them is named first in the register of members; or

    (c) if the holder is no longer entitled to the share by reason of death or bankruptcy, or

    otherwise by operation of law, the transmittee.

32. No interest on distributions

The company may not pay interest on any dividend or other sum payable in respect of a share unless otherwise provided by—

(a) the terms on which the share was issued, or

(b) the provisions of another agreement between the holder of that share and the company.

33. Unclaimed distributions

(1) All dividends or other sums which are—

    (a) payable in respect of shares, and

(b) unclaimed after having been declared or become payable,

may be invested or otherwise made use of by the directors for the benefit of the company until claimed.

(2) The payment of any such dividend or other sum into a separate account does not make the company a trustee in respect of it.

(3) If—

. (a) twelve years have passed from the date on which a dividend or other sum became due for payment, and

(b) the distribution recipient has not claimed it,

the distribution recipient is no longer entitled to that dividend or other sum and it ceases to remain owing by the company.

34. Non-cash distributions

(1) Subject to the terms of issue of the share in question, the company may, by ordinary resolution on the recommendation of the directors, decide to pay all or part of a dividend or other distribution payable in respect of a share by transferring non-cash assets of equivalent value (including, without limitation, shares or other securities in any company).

(2) For the purposes of paying a non-cash distribution, the directors may make whatever arrangements they think fit, including, where any difficulty arises regarding the distribution—

(a) fixing the value of any assets;

(b) paying cash to any distribution recipient on the basis of that value in order to adjust the rights of recipients; and

(c) vesting any assets in trustees.

35. Waiver of distributions

Distribution recipients may waive their entitlement to a dividend or other distribution payable in respect of a share by giving the company notice in writing to that effect, but if—

(a) the share has more than one holder, or

(b) more than one person is entitled to the share, whether by reason of the death or

bankruptcy of one or more joint holders, or otherwise,

the notice is not effective unless it is expressed to be given, and signed, by all the holders or persons otherwise entitled to the share.

Capitalisation of profits

36. Authority to capitalise and appropriation of capitalised sums

(1) Subject to the articles, the directors may, if they are so authorised by an ordinary resolution—

(a) decide to capitalise any profits of the company (whether or not they are available for distribution) which are not required for paying a preferential dividend, or any sum standing to the credit of the company's share premium account or capital redemption reserve; and

  (b) appropriate any sum which they so decide to capitalise (a "capitalised sum") to the persons who would have been entitled to it if it were distributed by way of dividend (the "persons entitled") and in the same proportions.

(2) Capitalised sums must be applied—

  (a) on behalf of the persons entitled, and

  (b) in the same proportions as a dividend would have been distributed to them.

(3) Any capitalised sum may be applied in paying up new shares of a nominal amount equal to the capitalised sum which are then allotted credited as fully paid to the persons entitled or as they may direct.

(4) A capitalised sum which was appropriated from profits available for distribution may be applied in paying up new debentures of the company which are then allotted credited as fully paid to the persons entitled or as they may direct.

(5) Subject to the articles the directors may—

  (a) apply capitalised sums in accordance with paragraphs (3) and (4) partly in one way and partly in another;

  (b) make such arrangements as they think fit to deal with shares or debentures becoming distributable in fractions under this article (including the issuing of fractional certificates or the making of cash payments); and

  (c) authorise any person to enter into an agreement with the company on behalf of all the persons entitled which is binding on them in respect of the allotment of shares and debentures to them under this article.

Part 4
Decision-making by shareholders

Organisation of general meetings

37. Attendance and speaking at general meetings

(1) A person is able to exercise the right to speak at a general meeting when that person is in a position to communicate to all those attending the meeting, during the meeting, any information or opinions which that person has on the business of the meeting.

(2) A person is able to exercise the right to vote at a general meeting when—

  (a) that person is able to vote, during the meeting, on resolutions put to the vote at the meeting, and

  (b) that person's vote can be taken into account in determining whether or not such resolutions are passed at the same time as the votes of all the other persons attending the meeting.

(3)   The directors may make whatever arrangements they consider appropriate to enable those attending a general meeting to exercise their rights to speak or vote at it.

(4)   In determining attendance at a general meeting, it is immaterial whether any two or more members attending it are in the same place as each other.

(5)   Two or more persons who are not in the same place as each other attend a general meeting if their circumstances are such that if they have (or were to have) rights to speak and vote at that meeting, they are (or would be) able to exercise them.

38. Quorum for general meetings

No business other than the appointment of the chairman of the meeting is to be transacted at a general meeting if the persons attending it do not constitute a quorum.

39. Chairing general meetings

(1)   If the directors have appointed a chairman, the chairman shall chair general meetings if present and willing to do so.

(2)   If the directors have not appointed a chairman, or if the chairman is unwilling to chair the meeting or is not present within ten minutes of the time at which a meeting was due to start—

   (a)   the directors present, or

   (b)   (if no directors are present), the meeting,

           must appoint a director or shareholder to chair the meeting, and the appointment of the chairman of the meeting must be the first business of the meeting.

(3)   The person chairing a meeting in accordance with this article is referred to as "the chairman of the meeting".

40. Attendance and speaking by directors and non-shareholders

(1)   Directors may attend and speak at general meetings, whether or not they are shareholders.

(2)   The chairman of the meeting may permit other persons who are not—

   (a)   shareholders of the company, or

   (b)   otherwise entitled to exercise the rights of shareholders in relation to general meetings,

   to attend and speak at a general meeting.

41. Adjournment

(1)   If the persons attending a general meeting within half an hour of the time at which the meeting was due to start do not constitute a quorum, or if during a meeting a quorum ceases to be present, the chairman of the meeting must adjourn it.

(2)   The chairman of the meeting may adjourn a general meeting at which a quorum is present if—

   (a)   the meeting consents to an adjournment, or

(b)   it appears to the chairman of the meeting that an adjournment is necessary to protect the safety of any person attending the meeting or ensure that the business of the meeting is conducted in an orderly manner.

(3)   The chairman of the meeting must adjourn a general meeting if directed to do so by the meeting.

(4)   When adjourning a general meeting, the chairman of the meeting must—

(a)   either specify the time and place to which it is adjourned or state that it is to continue at a time and place to be fixed by the directors, and

(b)   have regard to any directions as to the time and place of any adjournment which have been given by the meeting.

(5)   If the continuation of an adjourned meeting is to take place more than 14 days after it was adjourned, the company must give at least 7 clear days' notice of it (that is, excluding the day of the adjourned meeting and the day on which the notice is given)—

(a)   to the same persons to whom notice of the company's general meetings is required to be given, and

(b)   containing the same information which such notice is required to contain.

(6)   No business may be transacted at an adjourned general meeting which could not properly have been transacted at the meeting if the adjournment had not taken place.

Voting at general meetings

42. Voting: general

A resolution put to the vote of a general meeting must be decided on a show of hands unless a poll is duly demanded in accordance with the articles.

43. Errors and disputes

(1)   No objection may be raised to the qualification of any person voting at a general meeting except at the meeting or adjourned meeting at which the vote objected to is tendered, and every vote not disallowed at the meeting is valid.

(2)   Any such objection must be referred to the chairman of the meeting, whose decision is final.

44. Poll votes

(1)   A poll on a resolution may be demanded—

(a)   in advance of the general meeting where it is to be put to the vote, or

(b)   at a general meeting, either before a show of hands on that resolution or immediately after the result of a show of hands on that resolution is declared.

(2)   A poll may be demanded by—

(a)   the chairman of the meeting;

(b)   the directors;

(c)   two or more persons having the right to vote on the resolution; or

(d)   a person or persons representing not less than one tenth of the total voting rights of all the shareholders having the right to vote on the resolution.

(3)   A demand for a poll may be withdrawn if—

(a)   the poll has not yet been taken, and

(b)   the chairman of the meeting consents to the withdrawal.

(4)   Polls must be taken immediately and in such manner as the chairman of the meeting directs.

45. Content of proxy notices

(1)   Proxies may only validly be appointed by a notice in writing (a "proxy notice") which—

(a)   states the name and address of the shareholder appointing the proxy;

(b)   identifies the person appointed to be that shareholder's proxy and the general meeting in relation to which that person is appointed;

(c)   is signed by or on behalf of the shareholder appointing the proxy, or is authenticated in such manner as the directors may determine; and

(d)   is delivered to the company in accordance with the articles and any instructions contained in the notice of the general meeting to which they relate.

(2)   The company may require proxy notices to be delivered in a particular form, and may specify different forms for different purposes.

(3)   Proxy notices may specify how the proxy appointed under them is to vote (or that the proxy is to abstain from voting) on one or more resolutions.

(4)   Unless a proxy notice indicates otherwise, it must be treated as—

(a)   allowing the person appointed under it as a proxy discretion as to how to vote on any ancillary or procedural resolutions put to the meeting, and

(b)   appointing that person as a proxy in relation to any adjournment of the general meeting to which it relates as well as the meeting itself.

46. Delivery of proxy notices

(1)   A person who is entitled to attend, speak or vote (either on a show of hands or on a poll) at a general meeting remains so entitled in respect of that meeting or any adjournment of it, even though a valid proxy notice has been delivered to the company by or on behalf of that person.

(2)   An appointment under a proxy notice may be revoked by delivering to the company a notice in writing given by or on behalf of the person by whom or on whose behalf the proxy notice was given.

(3)   A notice revoking a proxy appointment only takes effect if it is delivered before the start of the meeting or adjourned meeting to which it relates.

(4)   If a proxy notice is not executed by the person appointing the proxy, it must be accompanied by written evidence of the authority of the person who executed it to execute it on the appointor's behalf.

47. Amendments to resolutions

(1)   An ordinary resolution to be proposed at a general meeting may be amended by ordinary resolution if—

    (a)   notice of the proposed amendment is given to the company in writing by a person entitled to vote at the general meeting at which it is to be proposed not less than 48 hours before the meeting is to take place (or such later time as the chairman of the meeting may determine), and

    (b)   the proposed amendment does not, in the reasonable opinion of the chairman of the meeting, materially alter the scope of the resolution.

(2)   A special resolution to be proposed at a general meeting may be amended by ordinary resolution, if—

    (a)   the chairman of the meeting proposes the amendment at the general meeting at which the resolution is to be proposed, and

    (b)   the amendment does not go beyond what is necessary to correct a grammatical or other non-substantive error in the resolution.

(3)   If the chairman of the meeting, acting in good faith, wrongly decides that an amendment to a resolution is out of order, the chairman's error does not invalidate the vote on that resolution.

Part 5
Administrative arrangements

48. Means of communication to be used

(1)   Subject to the articles, anything sent or supplied by or to the company under the articles may be sent or supplied in any way in which the Companies Act 2006 provides for documents or information which are authorised or required by any provision of that Act to be sent or supplied by or to the company.

(2)   Subject to the articles, any notice or document to be sent or supplied to a director in connection with the taking of decisions by directors may also be sent or supplied by the means by which that director has asked to be sent or supplied with such notices or documents for the time being.

(3)   A director may agree with the company that notices or documents sent to that director in a particular way are to be deemed to have been received within a specified time of their being sent, and for the specified time to be less than 48 hours.

49. Company seals

(1)   Any common seal may only be used by the authority of the directors.

(2)   The directors may decide by what means and in what form any common seal is to be used.

(3)   Unless otherwise decided by the directors, if the company has a common seal and it is affixed to a document, the document must also be signed by at least one authorised person in the presence of a witness who attests the signature.

(4)   For the purposes of this article, an authorised person is—

    (a)   any director of the company;

    (b)   the company secretary (if any); or

    (c)   any person authorised by the directors for the purpose of signing documents to which the common seal is applied.

50. No right to inspect accounts and other records

Except as provided by law or authorised by the directors or an ordinary resolution of the company, no person is entitled to inspect any of the company's accounting or other records or documents merely by virtue of being a shareholder.

51. Provision for employees on cessation of business

The directors may decide to make provision for the benefit of persons employed or formerly employed by the company or any of its subsidiaries (other than a director or former director or shadow director) in connection with the cessation or transfer to any person of the whole or part of the undertaking of the company or that subsidiary.

Directors' indemnity and insurance

52. Indemnity

(1)   Subject to paragraph (2), a relevant director of the company or an associated company may be indemnified out of the company's assets against—

    (a)   any liability incurred by that director in connection with any negligence, default, breach of duty or breach of trust in relation to the company or an associated company,

    (b)   any liability incurred by that director in connection with the activities of the company or an associated company in its capacity as a trustee of an occupational pension scheme (as defined in section 235(6) of the Companies Act 2006),

    (c)   any other liability incurred by that director as an officer of the company or an associated company.

(2)   This article does not authorise any indemnity which would be prohibited or rendered void by any provision of the Companies Acts or by any other provision of law.

(3)   In this article—

    (a)   companies are associated if one is a subsidiary of the other or both are subsidiaries of the same body corporate, and

    (b)   a "relevant director" means any director or former director of the company or an associated company.

53. Insurance

(1)   The directors may decide to purchase and maintain insurance, at the expense of the company, for the benefit of any relevant director in respect of any relevant loss.

(2)   In this article—

    (a)   a "relevant director" means any director or former director of the company or an associated company,

(b)   a "relevant loss" means any loss or liability which has been or may be incurred by a relevant director in connection with that director's duties or powers in relation to the company, any associated company or any pension fund or employees' share scheme of the company or associated company, and

(c)   companies are associated if one is a subsidiary of the other or both are subsidiaries of the same body corporate.

Appendix 2D

Precedents

Form of Resolution for Submission to Companies House

Number of Company [   ]
THE COMPANIES ACT 2006
COMPANY LIMITED BY SHARES
ORDINARY/SPECIAL RESOLUTION[1]
OF
[   ] LIMITED/PUBLIC LIMITED COMPANY[1]

Passed
[   ]
200[].

At a GENERAL MEETING of the above named Company, duly convened and held at [ADDRESS] on [DATE] at [TIME] the following resolution was duly passed as an ORDINARY/SPECIAL[1][*] RESOLUTION.

viz:

RESOLUTION

[TEXT OF RESOLUTION][*]

. . . .

Chairman

---

[1]   Delete as appropriate.
[*]   See overleaf for the special resolutions relevant to this chapter.

A.   **Special Resolution for Change of Company Name**

'That with the sanction of the Department for Business, Innovation and Skills the name of the company be and is hereby changed to [   ].'

B.   **Special Resolution for the Alteration of part of the Articles of Association**

'That regulations [to   ] in the existing Articles of Association be and are hereby deleted and that the following regulations be and are hereby inserted in their stead:

New Regulations [to   ]

(Detail)'

C.   **Special Resolution for the Adoption of new Articles of Association**

'That the existing Articles of Association be and are hereby deleted in their entirety and that the new Articles of Association as initialled by the Chairman and presented to the meeting be and are hereby adopted in place thereof.'

D.   **Special Resolution for the Re-registration of a Private Company as a Public Company**

'That pursuant to the provisions of Section 90 of the Companies Act 2006 the Company be and is hereby re-registered as a public company and that the following alterations be made:

(a)   The name of the company is [   ] PUBLIC LIMITED COMPANY.

(b)   the existing articles of association be and are hereby deleted in their entirety and that the new articles of association as initialled by the chairman and presented to the meeting be and are hereby adopted in place thereof.

E.   **Special Resolution for the Re-registration of a Public Company as a Private Company**

'That the Company make an application to the Registrar of Companies pursuant to the provisions of Section 97 of the Companies Act 2006 to be re-registered as a private company and that the following alterations be made:

(a)   The name of the Company is [   ] LIMITED.

(b)   the existing articles of association be and are hereby deleted in their entirety and that the new articles of association as initialled by the chairman and presented to the meeting be and are hereby adopted in place thereof.

F.   **Special resolution of the Re-registration of an unlimited company as a Private Limited Company**

'That pursuant to the provisions of Section 105 of the Companies Act 2006 the company be and is hereby re-registered as a private company limited by shares with share capital of £100 and that the following alterations be made:

(a)   The name of the Company is [   ] LIMITED.

(b)   the existing articles of association be and are hereby deleted in their entirety and that the new articles of association as initialled by the chairman and presented to the meeting be and are hereby adopted in place thereof.

Chapter 3

The Statutory Records

Form and inspection of registers

[3.1] The concept underlying the regulations set down in the Companies Act 2006 (CA 2006) is that information should be readily available to shareholders and other interested persons, and thus CA 2006 requires every company to keep certain information in the form of registers. The registers must be in a form which allows them to be examined easily and it is important that care is taken to maintain the registers properly as this will be the best safeguard against accusations of impropriety.

Section 1135 of CA 2006 provides that any register required to be kept under the Act may be kept either by recording entries in bound books/hard copies or recording the matters in question in any other manner including in electronic form. CA 2006, s 1135 further provides that if entries are recorded otherwise than in bound books/hard copies, then appropriate precautions must be taken to guard against falsification and facilitating their discovery.

Section 1135(2) of CA 2006 requires that if any register kept pursuant to the Act is otherwise than in legible form (ie stored on a computer), then it must be capable of being produced in a legible form, eg a print-out. The Companies (Registers and Other Records) Regulations 1985 (SI 1985/724) introduced provisions about the location of registers kept otherwise than in legible form and notification that the registers are in a non-legible form must be given to the Registrar of Companies together with notification of the place for inspection.

Inspection rights were introduced by section 723A of the Companies Act 1985 (CA 1985) and the Companies (Inspection and Copying of Registers, Indices and Documents) Regulations 1991 (SI 1991/1998), from 1 November 1991. This has been continued in CA 2006, s 1137 (which replaces CA 1985, s 723A) and a number of regulations have been made (the Companies (Fees for Inspection of Company Records) Regulations 2007 (SI 2007/2612); the Companies (Fees for Inspection of Company Records) (No 2) Regulations (SI 2007/3535); the Companies (Company Records) Regulations 2008 (SI 2008/3006); and the Companies (Fees for Inspection of Company Records) Regulations 2008 (SI 2008/3007)).

The regulations set out certain obligations of companies in relation to the inspection and copying of their records by members and non-members. They set out the circumstances in which companies are obliged to provide copies of entries on the various registers and prescribe the fees that they may charge for the provision of copies of entries on registers and for copies of other documents. Section 1137(5) of CA 2006 provides that companies can provide more extensive facilities than they are obliged to provide under these regulations or charge fees that are less than those prescribed under these regulations.

The regulations apply an obligation to make a register, index or document available for inspection when required by the following sections of CA 2006:

(a) CA 2006, s 702 – contract for purchase by company of its own shares;
(b) CA 2006, s 720 – statutory declaration and auditors' report relating to payment out of capital;
(c) CA 2006, s 743 – register of debenture holders;
(d) CA 2006, s 809 – register of interests in shares and reports;
(e) CA 2006, ss 162 and 275 – register of directors and register of secretaries;
(f) CA 2006, s 228 – directors' service contracts;
(g) CA 2006, s 115 – register and index of members; and
(h) CA 2006, s 358 – minute books.

The company must permit a person inspecting the register, index or document to copy any information made available for inspection by means of taking notes or by transcribing the information, but the company is not obliged to provide any additional facilities for this purpose, other than those provided for the purposes of facilitating inspection.

Register of members

General

[3.2] Section 113 of CA 2006 requires every company to keep a register of its members. For a company limited by shares, the section further provides that the following particulars be kept in respect of each member:

(a) name and address (the section does not detail the exact particulars required but the intent of the Act is that members should be sufficiently identified to avoid doubt);
(b) date upon which each person was first registered as a member;
(c) number of shares held by each member and the class of share held (if distinguished);
(d) amount paid, or agreed to be considered as paid, on each share held;
(e) date upon which each person ceased to be a member; and
(f) amount and class of stock held by each member (this applies where a company has converted some of its shares into stock).

In the case of joint holders, all their names must be entered although the joint holders are regarded as a single member and only one address need to be shown.

Section 127 of CA 2006 states that entry of these particulars in the register is *prima facie* evidence of them but is not conclusive, and thus anyone dealing with the company will be taken to know that:

(i) shares may be transferred in accordance with the articles;
(ii) a member may, in certain circumstances, repudiate his shares and have his name removed from the register;

(iii)   there may be persons registered without their consent who may have their names removed;

(iv)   a person who has been incorrectly entered may be removed; and

(v)   where the entry is conditional, membership is not complete.

Single member companies

[3.3] If the number of members of a private company limited by shares or by guarantee falls to one, there shall upon the occurrence of that event be entered in the company's register of members with the name and address of the sole member:

(a)   a statement that the company has only one member; and

(b)   the date on which the company became a company having only one member.

If the membership increases from one to two or more members, there shall upon the occurrence of that event be entered in the company's register of members, with the name and address of the same member, a statement that the company has ceased to have only one member together with the date on which that event occurred.

Index of members

[3.4] Section 115 of CA 2006 requires that every company having more than 50 members (usually only public companies) must keep an index of the names of its members, unless the register is in such a form as to constitute an index on its own (eg alphabetical order).

The index must be updated in accordance with any changes in the register of members within 14 days of the updating of the register and must, at all times, be kept at the same place as the register.

Designated accounts

[3.5] Members sometimes request that accounts in the register of members of companies be split into separately designated accounts in the same name with each account bearing a different reference. A company is not bound to grant such requests unless the articles expressly provide for this. No formal instrument is required to move shares from one account to another as there is no change of ownership.

Care must be taken when splitting an account into designated accounts as no entry must appear to give expressed, implied or constructive notice of a trust as this is contrary to the provisions of CA 2006, s 126.

Location and inspection

[3.6] The register of members is required to be kept at the company's registered office. However, if the work of making up the register is done at another office of the company, it may be kept there. Furthermore, if the company arranges with some other person (eg share registrars) to maintain the register for the company, then it may be kept at that person's office. Section 114 of CA 2006 states that the register of members must be kept available for inspection at its registered office address or at a place specified in regulations under CA 2006, s 1136, whereby the Secretary of State can make provisions by regulations specifying places other than the registered office address where the records can be kept available for inspection. Those seeking to inspect the register must make a request to the company and provide their names and addresses and the purpose for which the information will be used, and if access is sought on behalf of others, similar information for them.

Section 114(2) of CA 2006 provides that if the register is kept otherwise than at the registered office, then the Registrar of Companies must be notified of the location at which it is kept, except where the register has always been held at the registered office or if the register was in existence on 1 July 1948 in the case of a company registered in Great Britain or 1 April 1961 in the case of a company registered in Northern Ireland. In such cases no notice need be sent until there is a change (CA 2006, s 114(3)).

If the company defaults in respect of this obligation, the company and every officer are liable to a default fine (CA 2006, s 114(5)).

Section 116 of CA 2006 requires that the register must be open for inspection:

(a)   by any member of the company without charge; and
(b)   by any other person on payment of such charge as the company may prescribe.

Neither the index of members' names nor the register of members is required to be laid out to show whether a member has given an address in a particular geographical location, has a holding of a certain size, is of a particular nationality, is a natural person or not, or is of a particular gender.

The company is not obliged, when providing copies of the whole or any part of the register of members, to extract entries by reference to any of the matters listed above.

When copies are requested they do not have to be provided by the company immediately, but within five working days following the day upon which the request was received by the company (CA 2006, s 117).

Where a register is kept in a non-legible form as permitted by CA 2006, s 1135, the right of inspection is construed as a right to inspect a reproduction of the register in a legible form.

Penalties are imposed in case of default of the above provisions and, in addition, a judge may order an immediate inspection of the register or may direct that the copies requested be sent to the persons requiring them.

Rectification of the register

[3.7] The underlying purpose of the public disclosure of the members of a company is to allow creditors to be aware of whom and what they are dealing with. It is, therefore, vital that the register of members is maintained correctly at all times.

An error cannot be corrected by the company without applying to the court. Section 125 of CA 2006 grants the court power to order the correction of a company's register of members if:

(a)   the name of any person is, without sufficient cause, entered in or omitted from the register; or

(b)   default is made or an unnecessary delay occurs in entering the fact that a person has ceased to be a member.

The court may order such a rectification before and after the winding-up of a company. Any person may apply to the court, as may the company itself, and in fact this facility is frequently invoked.

When making an order for rectification the court can appoint any person to rectify the register. There must, of course, be a register to be rectified and thus, if the register has been destroyed, a new register will have to be prepared.

Removal of names

[3.8] An entry relating to a former member may be removed from the register of members after the end of 20 years from the date on which he ceased to be a member (CA 1985, s 352(6)). Section 121 of CA 2006 has reduced this to 10 years.

Entries of share warrants

[3.9] A company may issue share warrants to members in respect of any fully-paid shares if so authorised by its articles. The share warrant entitles the bearer to the shares specified within it.

When a warrant is to be issued, the name of the member should be struck out of the register of members (CA 2006, s 122).

The following information should then be entered in the register:

(a)   the issue of the warrant;
(b)   the shares included in the warrant; and
(c)   the date of issue of the warrant.

Subject to the company's articles a bearer can become a member of the company by surrendering his warrant and will be entered on the register.

Changes in registered particulars

[3.10] In order to prevent the register of members gradually becoming inaccurate due to changes in the registered particulars of members, it is necessary that all such changes are notified to the company. The most common types of changes requiring registration are as follows:

(a)   a change in a member's address; and
(b)   a change in a member's name.

Any notice of change of address should be signed by the appropriate member so as to reduce the risk of fraud and, in practice, it is advisable for a company to send out a form for the member to complete and return.

A change of the name of a member will require more formal documentary proof before the register of members is amended, such as the production of a marriage certificate, together with a written request by the member for the amendment to be made. Where a corporate member has changed its name, the usual procedure will be the production of the change of name certificate.

All alterations in the register of members should only be made after the directors of the company have approved them, as the secretary (or such other nominated person) has no power to alter the register without the authority of the board of directors.

Registration of trusts

[3.11] Section 126 of CA 2006 prohibits the entry of any notice of any trust on the register of members of the company. The section has the following effects:

(a)   the company is relieved of the duty of enquiring whether a transfer of shares by a trustee is within his powers;

(b)   the beneficiary who is not registered as the holder of shares has no connection with, or rights in, a company in which shares are held on trust for him; and

(c)   the registered holder is liable to the company for calls on the shares.

The section should be read in conjunction with the articles of the company which usually go beyond the provisions of the section by stating that the company is not required to recognise any right in a share except an absolute right in the registered holder. This will, however, not prohibit a company from recognising such rights should it so wish.

Overseas branch registers

[3.12] A company which has a share capital and which transacts business in any of the countries in any part of Her Majesty's dominions outside the United Kingdom, the Channel Islands and the Isle of Man, and the countries or territories specified section 129(2)(b) of CA 2006, may maintain a branch register of members who are resident there (CA 2006, s 129).

Prior to CA 1985 such registers were called 'Dominion Registers'. It is at the discretion of the company whether it maintains such registers; it is not obliged to do so.

Any company which establishes an overseas branch register is required, within 14 days of such establishment, to give notice to the Registrar of Companies of the situation of the office where it is kept. Any changes or the discontinuance of the register must also be notified in the same manner.

The overseas branch register is deemed to be part of the register of the company and can be rectified by any competent court. Overseas branch registers must be maintained in the same manner as the register, with the exception that notice of the closing of the overseas branch register should be inserted in a newspaper circulating in the district where the overseas branch register is kept.

No transaction in respect of shares registered in an existing overseas branch register may be registered in another register and the shares must be distinguished from those appearing in the principal register.

A copy of every entry in an overseas branch register must be sent to the company's registered office as soon as practicable and a duplicate of this register kept at the office where the company's principal register is kept.

Duplicate registers

[3.13] A company may keep its complete register in two places; one at the registered office and another at an office abroad. The 'duplicate' register has no statutory basis and should not be confused with the copy of an overseas branch register.

In law only one register exists, ie the original register at the registered office of the company.

Register of directors and register of secretaries

General

[3.14] Every company has to keep a register of directors and register of secretaries (in the case of a private company who has appointed a secretary), in which the following details for every person who is a director or secretary of the company must be shown (CA 2006, ss 162 and 275).

(a)   If the director is an individual:
  (i)   his present Christian name (this includes a forename) (CA 2006, s 163(2)) and surname (surname in the case of a peer or person usually known by a title means that title) (CA 2006, s 163(2)(a));
  (ii)   any former Christian name or surname (this does not include, in the case of a peer or person having a British title, the name by which he was known before taking or succeeding to the title). The requirement also does not apply where a person's name was changed before he reached 18 or was changed or disused not less than 20 years ago. A married woman does not have to show her maiden name;
  (iii)   his usual residential address (a Confidentiality Order may be applied where appropriate, see **6.4 THE DIRECTORS**) (CA 2006 requires a service address, which may be the registered office address);
  (iv)   his nationality;
  (v)   his business occupation;
  (vi)   date of birth.

Should the director be a corporation, then the details required are its corporate name and the address of its registered or principal office.

It should also be noted that CA 2006, s 162 also extends to shadow directors who are treated as officers of the company and their particulars should be registered as above.

The Companies Act 2006 has introduced section 165 which requires companies, who have individual directors, to keep a register of directors' usual residential addresses. This register is not open to public inspection.

(b)   For each secretary:
  (i)   present Christian name and surname (and any former names); and
  (ii)   residential address (see (iii) above). A service address, which may be the registered office, is required under CA 2006, s 277(5).

Should a corporation be a secretary then the same details are required as those for a corporate director.

The register should also note the dates of appointment and resignation/removal of each director and secretary.

Location and inspection

[3.15] The register must be kept at the company's registered office or at a place specified in regulations under CA 2006, s 1136 (CA 2006, s 162(3)).

The register must be open to the inspection of the members of the company without charge and by other persons on the payment of such sum as the company may determine.

Changes

[3.16] The Registrar of Companies must be notified (and the register of directors and register of secretaries accordingly updated) if there is:

(a)   a change in the directors or the secretary of the company; or
(b)   a change in any of the information contained in the register.

The notification must show the date of change (CA 2006, s 167) and where a new director or secretary is being appointed it must include a consent to act in the appropriate capacity. If a corporation is being appointed, the consent should be signed on its behalf by an officer of that corporation.

CA 2006 also requires that such notifications are forwarded in the prescribed form (forms AP01 or AP02 (appointment), TM01 or TM02 (termination) and CH01 to CH04 (change of particulars)) to Companies House within 14 days of the date of the change.

Register of directors' interests

General

[3.17] Up until 6 April 2007, every company was obliged to maintain a register of directors' interests in the shares or debentures of the company or a related company (CA 1985, s 325) and for this purpose, under CA 1985, s 324, a director had to notify the company in writing of his interests in the shares or debentures of the company and its associated companies and state that the notice was given in fulfilment of the obligation. Directors also had to notify companies of the interests of their wives and children (CA 1985, s 328), and shadow directors were also included.

The Companies Act 2006 repealed CA 1985, s 324 and most of sections 325 and 326–329 with effect from 6 April 2007. This is to avoid duplication with FSA rules. However, directors of companies traded on the regulated market, and their connected persons will continue to have to disclose dealings and shareholdings above 3% under the FSA's Disclosure and Transparency Rules.

Directors of companies which have a listing on either the full securities market or Alternative Investment Market should, in dealing with shares of that company or any of its subsidiaries, further comply with the provisions of the 'Model Code for Securities Transactions by Directors of Listed Companies' as set out in the appendix of Chapter 16 of the Listing Rules or the AIM rules as appropriate.

The purpose of the register of directors' interests is to allow members and the general public to be aware of the extent that the directors of the company are interested in the shares and debentures and have rights to subscribe for further shares and debentures of the company.

With CA 1985, s 324 being repealed, companies may find themselves in a position of deciding what course of action to take as regards the register of interests. Companies may well decide that although there is no longer the requirement to keep the register, common sense might suggest that it may be prudent to keep it in case of any historical problems that may arise as to its compliance prior to abolition.

Register of charges

General

[3.18] This was an area which was supposed to undergo alteration and sections changed and renumbered by the Companies Act 1989 (CA 1989), although it never really materialised. The Companies Act 2006 has basically restated the existing provisions in CA 1985 and will also extend to companies registered in Northern Ireland.

Section 876 of CA 2006 imposes an obligation upon all limited companies to keep a register of all fixed and floating charges.

Section 875 of CA 2006 further requires companies to keep copies of every instrument creating a charge which requires registration with the Registrar of Companies.

However, the Government has confirmed its intention to revise the scheme for the registration of company charges in its response to the March 2010 consultation. The new regime will apply to all companies incorporated under CA 2006 or its predecessors and to unregistered companies and limited liability partnerships, but will not apply to overseas companies.

The Government intends to bring the new regime into force in 2012 or 2013 and its response can be found at www.bis.gov.uk/Consultations/registrat ion-of-charges.

Location

[3.19] Sections 406(1) and 407(1) of CA 1985 respectively required that a company keep copies of all charges which must be registered pursuant to the Act and the register of charges at its registered office. Section 877 of CA 2006 has relaxed this by providing that it may be kept at its registered office or at a place specified in regulations under CA 2006, s 1136.

Contents of register

[3.20] Section 876 of CA 2006 requires that the following details be entered in the register of charges for each charge affecting the property or undertaking of a company:

(a)   short description of the property charged;
(b)   amount of the charge; and
(c)   name(s) of the person(s) entitled to the charge (except in the case of bearer securities).

Charges for the purposes of CA 2006, s 876 (1)(a), (b) are charges specifically affecting the property of the company and floating charges on the company's undertaking or property. However, this does not only mean charges required to be registered at Companies House but extends to all charges which fit the definition.

Inspection

[3.21] Section 877 of CA 2006 requires that a company have available for inspection at its registered office or a place specified in regulations under CA 2006, s 1136, the register of charges and copies of any charge documents.

Creditors and members of the company have the right to inspect the register and any copy charge documents required to be kept by the company without payment. However, any other person wishing to inspect them may be charged a prescribed fee under CA 2006, s 1167. The right to obtain copies of the charges register and any charge documents of which the company has to maintain copies will be extended to all persons. Previously this right was restricted to members and creditors.

Register of interests in shares

General

[3.22] Section 808 of CA 2006 requires a *public company* only to maintain a register for the purpose of recording notifications of interests in shares. Sections 198–211 of CA 1985 were replaced by Financial Services and Markets Act 2000 regulations in implementing the Transparency Obligations Directive.

Under CA 2006, s 793 a public company may give notice to any person whom the company knows or has reasonable cause to believe to be interested in the company's shares. The company must keep a register of information received in pursuant of the notice.

The underlying purpose of the register is to prevent takeovers by stealth.

Contents of register of interests

[3.23] When a company receives a notification from a person in satisfaction of the above obligation the company must within three days record the following information:

(a)   the fact that the requirement was imposed and the date on which it was imposed;
(b)   the information received; and
(c)   the name of the present holder.

The entries must be in chronological order (CA 2006, s 808).

Location and inspection

[3.24] The register is required to be kept at the company's registered office or at a place specified in regulations under CA 2006, s 1136.

The register of interests in shares is required to be made available to any person without charge (CA 2006, s 811). Any person is entitled on request and on payment of such fee as may be prescribed, to be provided with a copy of any entry in the register. A person wishing to inspect the register must make a request to the company to that effect and provide the information as set out in CA 2006, s 811(4).

However, an exemption exists in CA 2006, s 826 which allows a company not to make the register available for inspection in certain circumstances. The relevant exemption is the exemption of a company from the requirement to disclose in its accounts particulars of shareholdings in subsidiaries or other bodies corporate incorporated or carrying on business outside the United Kingdom, in circumstances where disclosure would be harmful to the business of the company.

Removal of entries from the register

[3.25] Under CA 2006, s 815, entries in the register of interests must not be deleted except in accordance with CA 2006, ss 816 and 817 which permit deletions in the following circumstances:

(a)   a company may remove an entry where more than six years have elapsed since the date of inscription;

(b)   where a notification gives the name and address of another person and states that the person is interested in its shares, the other person may then apply to the company to have his name removed from the register on the grounds that the entry was incorrect; and

(c)   where a person who is identified in the register as party to a concert party agreement ceases to be such a party, he may apply to have the information recorded that he is no longer party to the agreement.

If the company fails to make the alterations requested an application may be made to the court who may order the appropriate amendment to be made.

Any entry wrongly removed must be restored to the register as soon as is reasonably practicable. Unauthorised deletions and failure to restore are punishable by default fines (CA 2006, s 815(3), (4)).

Penalties for non-compliance

[3.26] If default is made in complying with the requirements to maintain a register of interests in shares, the company and every officer who is in default is liable on summary conviction to a fine not exceeding level 3 on the standard scale or, for continued contravention, a daily default fine not exceeding one-tenth of level 3 on the standard scale.

Investigations by a company of interests in its own shares

[3.27] Under CA 2006, s 793 a public company may issue a notice in writing to any person whom it knows, or has reasonable cause to believe, to be interested in the shares of the company (or has been so interested in the three years prior to the notice). It does not, however, have to show real ground for its belief as long as it is not frivolously or vexatiously sought.

Such notice may require the recipient to:

(a)   indicate whether he is or was so interested;

(b)   give particulars of his own past or present interest in shares in the company held by him at any time during the previous three years;

(c)   give particulars of any other interests subsisting in the shares; and

(d)   in relation to past interests, to provide particulars and the identity of any person who held the interest immediately upon the addressee ceasing to hold it.

Members holding not less than one-tenth of the voting rights of the company may require the company to exercise its powers under section 793 of CA 2006 (CA 2006, s 803).

The members making the requisition must not only specify the manner in which they wish the powers to be exercised but also give reasonable grounds for requiring the company to exercise the powers (CA 2006, s 803(3)). On the conclusion of the investigation the company must then prepare a report of the information received. Such a report must then be made available at the registered office of the company or at a place specified in regulations under CA 2006, s 1136 within a reasonable time after the end of the investigation (CA 2006, s 805).

There are further provisions relating to the time scale for investigations and reports contained in CA 2006, ss 803, 805 and there is a default fine for non-compliance (CA 2006, s 806).

Penalties for failure to provide information under CA 2006, s 793

[3.28] There are two types of penalty for failure to provide the information required under CA 2006, s 793.

First, failure to supply the information permits the company to apply to the court for an order directing that the shares in question shall be subject to the restrictions imposed by CA 2006, s 794. Such restrictions are as follows:

(a)   the shares may not be transferred;
(b)   no voting rights shall be exercisable in respect of the shares;
(c)   no bonus shares may be issued in respect of the shares; and
(d)   no payments whatsoever in respect of the shares shall be made except in liquidation.

Second, there are criminal penalties in respect of failure to comply with a CA 2006, s 793 request and the making of statements known to be false in a material matter or recklessly made.

There is a statutory defence if the defendant can prove that the requirement to give the information was vexatious or frivolous (CA 2006, s 795(2)). There is also a provision for exemption from the obligation to give information, with the exemption being made by the Secretary of State (CA 2006, s 796).

Register of debenture holders

General

[3.29] The Companies Acts do not impose a requirement to keep a register of debenture holders. However, when a debenture is created, the terms of the document constituting the debenture invariably include an obligation to maintain such a register.

Once such an obligation has arisen CA 2006, s 743 applies. This contains provisions relating to where the register may be kept, rights of inspection and the duty to notify the Registrar of the register's location.

Contents of register of debenture holders

[3.30] The Companies Act 2006 does not specify the information that must be included in a register of debenture holders, as such requirements are normally included in the debenture document.

Location and inspection

[3.31] The register of debenture holders must be kept at either of the following two locations:

(a)   at the company's registered office; or
(b)   at a place specified in regulations under CA 2006, s 1136.

If the register is not kept at the registered office, notice of its location must be given to the Registrar, as should notice of any change in its location.

Previously, under CA 1985, s 190(1) and (2), a company registered in England and Wales was not able to keep such a register in Scotland, nor was a company registered in Scotland able to keep a register of debenture holders in England or Wales.

The register of debenture holders must be open to the inspection of a registered debenture holder or shareholder without payment of a fee and to any other person on payment of such fee as may be prescribed. Those seeking to inspect the register must make a request to the company and provide their names and addresses, the purpose and if access is sought on behalf of others, similar information for them.

The register must be available for inspection subject to such reasonable restrictions as the company in general meeting may impose, provided that a minimum of two hours in each day shall be allowed for inspection. The register can, however, be closed (and thus not available for inspection) in accordance with the articles of the company or the document(s) securing the debenture(s) during such period or periods not exceeding 30 days in total in any year.

The company is not obliged to present its register of debenture holders for inspection in a manner which groups together entries by reference to whether a debenture holder has given an address in a particular geographical location, is of a particular nationality or gender, has a holding of a certain size, or is a natural person or not).

The company must provide any registered debenture holder or any shareholder with a copy of the register or part of it on payment of exactly the same fee as with the register of members (see **3.6** above). The company is not obliged, when providing such copies, to extract entries by reference to any of the matters listed above.

In addition, every debenture holder is entitled to have forwarded to him a copy of any trust deed securing any issue of debentures on payment of such fee as may be prescribed (see **3.6** above for inspection and copying requirements).

Accounting records

General

[3.32] Every company is required to maintain accounting records which must be sufficient to show and explain the company's transactions and must be such as to:

(a) disclose with reasonable accuracy at any time, the financial position of the company at that time; and

(b) enable the directors to ensure that any balance sheet and profit and loss account prepared under CA 2006 and, where applicable, Article 4 of the IAS regulation, comply with the requirements.

(CA 2006, s 386.)

The accounting records must contain entries from day to day of all sums of money received and expended by the company and the matters in respect of which the receipt and expenditure takes place, and a record of all the assets and liabilities of the company.

If a company deals in goods the records must also contain:

(i) statements of stock held by the company at the end of each financial year of the company;

(ii) all statements of stocktakings from which any such statement of stock has been or is to be prepared; and

(iii) except in the case of goods sold by way of ordinary retail trade, statements of all goods sold and purchased, showing the goods and the buyers and sellers in sufficient detail to enable all these to be identified.

(CA 2006, s 386(4).)

Form of accounting records

[3.33] Although CA 2006 does not prescribe any precise form that accounting records should take, it does however provide that accounting records may be kept either by making entries in bound books or by recording the matters in any other manner (CA 2006, s 1135). Where the accounting records do not take the form of entries in a bound book adequate precautions must be taken to guard against falsification and to facilitate their discovery (CA 2006, s 1138).

Section 1135(2) of CA 2006 permits data to be recorded otherwise than in a legible form provided it is capable of being reproduced in legible form, thereby allowing such information to be stored electronically.

In practice, the method chosen will depend on many factors such as the size of the company and the degree of sophistication required for management purposes.

Duty in relation to subsidiary undertakings

[3.34] A parent company which has a subsidiary undertaking to which the consolidation requirements of CA 2006 do not apply, must take reasonable steps to secure that the undertaking keeps such accounting records as to enable the directors of the parent company to ensure that any balance sheet and profit and loss account prepared in accordance with CA 2006.

Retention of accounting records

[3.35] Accounting records must be retained for three years by a private company and for six years by a public company; the period running from the date on which the records were made. There is an exception to this, ie where a direction as to the disposal of records is made under the winding-up rules under section 411 of the Insolvency Act 1986. In addition, a company must ensure that it complies with any other statutory requirements relating to the retention of accounting records, for example, the Taxes Management Act 1970, the Value Added Tax Act 1983 and PAYE Regulations etc (see **11.14** and **APPENDIX 11A COMMERCIAL CONSIDERATIONS**).

Location and inspection of accounting records

[3.36] A company's accounting records must be kept at the company's registered office or such place as the directors consider fit. They must at all times be open to inspection by the company's officers (CA 2006, s 388(1)) which include all directors and managers, as well as the secretary of the company. It has been held that an auditor who is appointed under the Act is an officer of the company but he also has a specific right of access at all times enshrined in CA 2006, s 499 (*R v Shacter* [1960] 2 QB 252).

A member of a company does not have such a right of inspection and Article 109 of the 1985 Table A (as set out in SI 1985/805) states that 'No member shall (as such) have any right of inspecting any accounting records or other book or document of the company except as conferred by statute or authorised by the directors or by ordinary resolution of the company'. It is, however, open to a company's articles of association to give members a right to inspect the company's accounting records although this right ceases on the voluntary winding-up of a company. (See also **4.21 ACCOUNTS AND AUDITORS** and **7.7 MEMBERSHIP** for members' rights in respect of the accounts.)

If the accounting records of a company are kept outside the United Kingdom, accounts and returns with respect to the business dealt with in those accounting records must be sent to, and kept at, a place in the United Kingdom, and must at all times be open to inspection by the company's officers (CA 2006, s 388(2)).

These accounts and returns must:

(a)   disclose with reasonable accuracy the financial position of the business at intervals of not more than six months; and

(b)   enable the directors to ensure that the company's balance sheet and profit and loss account comply with the requirements of CA 2006.

(CA 2006, s 388(3).)

Failure to keep proper accounting records

[**3.37**] Every officer of a company who is in default in respect of accounting records is guilty of an offence unless he acted honestly and his default is excusable. The officer will also be guilty of an offence if he has intentionally caused default by the company in relation to the provisions for maintenance of accounting records, or if he has failed to take all reasonable steps to secure compliance with them (CA 2006, s 389).

Anyone summarily convicted of an offence under this section is liable to imprisonment for up to twelve months (in the England and Wales, six months in Scotland and Northern Ireland), or a fine or both; and on conviction on indictment liable to imprisonment for up to two years, or a fine or both (CA 2006, s 387(3)).

Apart from the liability arising from the failure to carry out the statutory obligation outlined above, penalties may also arise for offences antecedent to or in the course of the winding-up of the company.

Directors' service contracts

General

[**3.38**] Every company must make available for inspection of its members the terms of service contracts with its directors, including shadow directors (CA 2006, s 228). Previously this requirement did not include contracts which have less than twelve months to run or which can be terminated by the company within the following twelve months without payment of compensation. The Companies Act 2006 has not carried this forward.

The following must be available:

(a)   if the service contract is in writing, a copy of the contract; and
(b)   if the service contract is not in writing, a written memorandum of its terms.

(CA 2006, s 228(1)(a), (b).)

Any amendments to the contract must also be shown (CA 2006, s 228(7)). It is important that this obligation is fulfilled with fairness so as to give the members an accurate understanding of the obligations of the company to the director and thus, if all the terms of the contract are not contained in the contract, then a memorandum detailing the additional terms should be provided.

The obligation extends to service contracts with subsidiaries of the company (CA 2006, s 228(1)(a)). Previously if the contract required the director to work mainly or completely outside the United Kingdom the company needed only to make available a memorandum stating the name of the director, the provisions of the contract concerning its duration and, if appropriate, the name of and place of incorporation of the subsidiary (CA 1985, s 318(5)). The Companies Act 2006 has not carried this forward.

Location and inspection of service contracts

[3.39] Copies of all service contracts and memoranda must be kept together (CA 2006, s 228(2)) by companies at one of the following places:

(a)   the registered office;
(b)   any other place specified in regulations under CA 2006, s 1136.

If the documents are not kept at the registered office, then the Registrar of Companies must be notified of the address at which they are held (CA 2006, s 228(4)).

All members of the company are entitled to inspect the documents without payment of a fee (CA 2006, s 229(1)). The court can compel an immediate inspection in the case of refusal to allow such inspection (CA 2006, s 229(5)).

Penalties

[3.40] Failure to comply with the obligations relating to inspection of the above documents has penal consequences for the company and every officer in default (CA 2006, s 229(4))).

Contracts for the purchase of the company's own shares

[3.41] Should a company have entered into any contracts for the purchase of its own shares, they must be held at the registered office of a company for a period of ten years after the contract is completed (CA 2006, s 702). In a public company any person may inspect them, but if the company is private, the right of inspection is confined to members.

Redemption or purchase of shares

[3.42] Where a company has passed a resolution to redeem or purchase its shares out of capital under CA 2006, s 716, a copy of the statutory declaration and auditors' report must be retained at the company's registered office from the date of publication of notice in the *Gazette* until five weeks after the date of the resolution for payment out of capital. These documents must be available for inspection by any member or creditor of the company without charge (CA 2006, s 720(2), (4)).

Minutes

General

[3.43] Section 355 of CA 2006 requires every company to keep minutes of the proceedings of its general meetings and, under CA 2006, s 248, of the meetings of its directors and managers. These must be kept for at least ten years from the date of the meetings. If it fails to do so, the company and every officer in default may be liable to a fine.

Form and security of minutes

[3.44] The minutes (like other company registers and records covered by CA 2006, s 1135) can be kept either in a bound book or in some other manner, for example, in a loose-leaf folder into which typed sheets can be inserted as a record of each successive meeting.

If the minutes are not kept in the form of a bound book, CA 2006, s 1138 states that adequate precautions must be taken for safeguarding against falsification and facilitating its discovery.

Minutes as evidence

[3.45] Sections 249 and 356 of CA 2006 state that the minutes of a meeting, which have been signed by the chairman of the meeting (or signed at the next meeting by the chairman), are evidence of its proceedings.

As sections uses the simple word 'evidence', the implication is that in the case of a dispute as to the content of a minute further proof may be needed. Other evidence may, therefore, be produced to rebut or correct the minutes, even though they may have been signed by the chairman. For example, a member who was present at a meeting might testify that a resolution was not put to the vote, although it is recorded in the minutes as having been done.

To prevent subsequent argument over a matter which cannot be proved or disproved afterwards, the articles of association of the company may introduce a regulation to provide that the minutes are 'conclusive evidence' of the business transacted at a meeting in certain circumstances.

The matter most likely to give rise to argument is whether the chairman's declaration of a result of a vote on a show of hands was correct (ie that a resolution was carried or not carried, or that a required majority was or was not obtained).

A member may, however, still challenge the minutes of a meeting, even if they have been declared to be conclusive evidence, if he can show that they are a false record or have been fraudulently prepared or that the chairman's declaration is incorrect by its own terms (ie in conflict with the result which it purports to verify).

Written resolutions

[3.46] In place of a board meeting, the directors of a company may substitute 'resolutions in writing'. The power to do so must, however, be contained in a company's articles of association. Regulation 93 of Table A 1985 provides a model for this authority:

> 'A resolution in writing signed by all the directors entitled to receive notice of a meeting of directors or of a committee of directors shall be as valid and effectual as if it had been passed at a meeting of directors or (as the case may be) a committee of directors duly convened and held and may consist of several documents in the like form each signed by one or more directors . . . '

A similar procedure can be adopted for general meetings. However, for private companies, they are regulated in this respect by the provisions of CA 2006, s 288, and public companies by the power in their articles of association.

Resolutions in writing of the directors and the members must be recorded in a company's minute books in the same way as minutes.

Location and inspection of minutes

[3.47] Pursuant to CA 2006, s 358 a company is required to keep the minutes of its general meetings at its registered office or at a place specified in regulations under CA 2006, s 1136 and to make them available for inspection by members without charge.

The section grants members a right to inspect the minutes of general meetings of a company of which they are members and to be supplied with a copy of any minutes of a general meeting within 14 days of making the request. In providing such copies a company may levy a prescribed fee.

It should be noted that the rights of members to inspect minutes are confined solely to minutes of general meetings. Members have no right to inspect the minutes of board meetings; this is a right that only extends to the directors.

Chapter 4

Accounts and Auditors

Annual accounts

General

[4.1] Section 394 of the Companies Act 2006 (CA 2006) requires the directors of a company to prepare a profit and loss account in respect of each financial year and a balance sheet as at the end of the financial year; these are referred to as the company's individual accounts. The Companies Act 2006 draws a distinction between 'Companies Act individual accounts' and 'IAS individual accounts' where the accounts are prepared in accordance with CA 2006, s 396 on the one hand and international accounting standards on the other.

A company's first financial year begins on its date of incorporation and ends on the last day of its first accounting reference period (the 'accounting reference date' see **4.2** below) or, if the directors so wish, on a day which is not more than seven days before or after the end of that period. Each successive financial year begins on the day after the date to which the preceding balance sheet was made up and ends.

Accounting reference date

[4.2] A company's accounting reference periods are determined according to its accounting reference date.

Section 391 of CA 2006 states that the accounting reference date of a company is the last day of the month in which the anniversary of its incorporation falls. A company's accounting reference period must not exceed 18 months and while CA 2006, s 391(5) states that a company's first such period must be more than six months, this is subject to the provisions of CA 2006, s 392 (see **4.3** below). Subsequent accounting reference periods are successive periods of twelve months beginning immediately after the end of the previous accounting reference period and ending with the company's accounting reference date.

Companies House will not accept accounts which for the relevant accounting period are made up to a date other than the accounting reference date shown on the public file. A company may, however, treat its accounting reference period as ending at any time within seven days either side of its given accounting reference date by virtue of CA 2006, s 390(2) and (3) (see **4.1** above).

Alteration of the accounting reference date

[4.3] Section 392 of CA 2006 governs any subsequent changes to lengthen or shorten the accounting period of a company. The rules for the alteration of an accounting reference date whether during or after the end of an accounting reference period are now broadly similar and the form (form AA01) prescribed to notify the change to Companies House is the same in each case.

Form AA01 must state whether the current or previous accounting reference period is to be shortened, so as to come to an end on the first occasion on which the new accounting reference date falls or fell after the beginning of the period, or is to be extended, so as to come to an end on the second occasion on which that date falls or fell after the beginning of the period.

A notice stating that the current or previous accounting reference period is to be extended is ineffective if given less than five years after the end of an earlier accounting reference period of the company which was extended under CA 2006, s 392, unless:

(a) form AA01 was given by a company which is a subsidiary undertaking or parent undertaking of another EEA undertaking and the new accounting reference date coincides with that of the other EEA undertaking or, where that undertaking is not a company, with the last day of its financial year;

(b) an administration order is in force under Part II of the Insolvency Act 1986; or

(c) the Secretary of State directs that it should not apply, which he may do with respect to a notice which has been given or which may be given.

An 'EEA undertaking' is defined as an undertaking established under the law of any part of the United Kingdom (UK) or the law of any other EEA State. An 'EEA State' is a State which is a Contracting Party to the Agreement on the European Economic Area signed at Oporto on 2 May 1992, as adjusted by the Protocol signed at Brussels on 17 March 1993 and by Council Decision Number 1/95 of 10 March 1995. The Companies (EEA State) Regulations 2007 (SI 2007/732), which came into force on 9 March 2007, amended the definition of 'EEA State' in companies' legislation to include Bulgaria and Romania following their entry as Community Member States on 1 January 2007. These amendments apply to CA 2006, s 1170.

Alteration during an accounting reference period

[4.4] A company may by notice in the prescribed form (form AA01) given to the Registrar, specify a new accounting reference date having effect in relation to the company's current accounting reference period and subsequent periods.

Alteration after the end of an accounting reference period

[4.5] A company may by notice in the prescribed form (form AA01) given to the Registrar, specify a new accounting reference date having effect in relation to the company's previous accounting reference period and subsequent periods. A company's 'previous accounting reference period' means that immediately preceding its current accounting reference period.

A notice may not be given for a previous accounting reference period if the period allowed for laying and delivering accounts and reports in relation to that period has already expired.

Form and content of accounts

[4.6] For financial years beginning on or after 6 April 2008, the relevant provisions for the purpose of section 396(3) of CA 2006 appear in the Small Companies and Groups (Accounts and Directors' Report) Regulations 2008 (SI 2008/409) and the Large and Medium-sized Companies and Groups (Accounts and Reports) Regulations 2008 (SI 2008/410).

'A true and fair view'

[4.7] Section 393 of CA 2006 requires that the balance sheet gives a true and fair view of the company's state of affairs as at the end of the financial year and the profit and loss account gives a true and fair view of the company's profit or loss for the financial year.

Accounts must be prepared with regard to the accounting standards issued by the Accounting Standards Board (ASB). When the ASB replaced the Accounting Standards Committee on 1 August 1990, it adopted the Statements of Standard Accounting Practice (SSAPs) existing on that date. The ASB has developed and issued Financial Reporting Standards with a view to superseding the SSAPs. The ASB issued its first standard, FRS 1 – Cashflow statements, on 26 September 1991, to replace SSAP10 (Statement of source and application of funds). Further standards have since been issued, the most recent of which is FRS 30 – Heritage Assets issued in June 2009.

Listed companies are required to adopt International Financial Reporting Standards (IFRS) for accounting periods beginning on or after 1 January 2005. In addition, CA 2006 contains provisions which allow, or in some cases require, companies to prepare their accounts in accordance with International Accounting Standards (CA 2006, s 395).

The Companies Act 2006 draws a distinction between companies which are small (and therefore subject to the small companies' regime) and those which are not, as well as companies which are quoted and those which are not (CA 2006, s 380). In essence, CA 2006 sets out a separate comprehensive code for each of the different sizes of company, starting with small, private companies (addressed in the Small Companies and Groups (Accounts and Directors' Report) Regulations 2008 (SI 2008/409)) which can be read independently of the provisions applying to larger companies (covered by the Large and Medium-sized Companies and Groups (Accounts and Reports) Regulations 2008 (SI 2008/410)).

Group accounts

[4.8] In addition to the requirement to prepare individual accounts, the directors of a company must, if at the end of the financial year the company is a UK registered parent company, prepare group accounts pursuant to CA 2006, s 399(2). Group accounts must be consolidated accounts comprising:

(a)   a consolidated balance sheet dealing with the state of affairs of the parent company and its subsidiary undertakings; and

(b)   a consolidated profit and loss account dealing with the profit or loss of the parent company and its subsidiary undertakings.

(CA 2006, 404(1)(a), (b).)

An exemption does, however, exist for companies within the small companies' regime (CA 2006, s 398).

Under the definitions in CA 2006, s 1162, an undertaking is a parent undertaking in relation to another undertaking, a subsidiary undertaking, if it:

(i)   holds a majority of the voting rights in the undertaking;

(ii)   is a member of the undertaking and has the right to appoint or remove a majority of its board of directors;

(iii)   has the right to exercise a dominant influence over the undertaking:

     (A)   by virtue of provisions contained in the undertaking's articles; or

     (B)   by virtue of a control contract;

(iv)   is a member of the undertaking and controls alone, pursuant to an agreement with other shareholders or members, a majority of the voting rights in the undertaking; or

(v)   has a participating interest (being around 20% of the issued share capital) in the undertaking, and:

     (I)   it actually exercises a dominant influence over it; or

     (II)   it and the subsidiary undertaking are managed on a unified basis.

These definitions apply only for the purposes of determining whether group accounts should be prepared. For general purposes the definitions of subsidiary, holding company and wholly-owned subsidiary given in CA 2006, s 1159 apply.

The group accounts prepared must represent a true and fair view of the group's affairs.

Exemption for subsidiaries of EEA undertakings

[4.9] Section 400 of CA 2006 provides that a parent company is exempt from the requirement to prepare group accounts if it is itself a subsidiary undertaking and its immediate parent undertaking is established under the law of an EEA State, where:

(a)   the company is a wholly-owned subsidiary of that parent undertaking;

(b)   the parent undertaking holds more than 50% of the allotted shares in the company and notice requesting the preparation of group accounts has not been served on the company by shareholders holding in aggregate:

     (i)   more than half of the remaining allotted shares in the company; or

     (ii)   5% of the total shares in the company.

     Such notice must be served no later than six months after the end of the financial year to which it relates.

The exemption does not apply to a company any of whose securities are listed on a stock exchange in any EEA State and is also conditional upon compliance with all of the following conditions.

(A) The company is included in consolidated accounts for a larger group drawn up to the same date, or to an earlier date in the same financial year, by a parent undertaking established under the law of an EEA State.

(B) Those accounts are drawn up and audited, and that parent undertaking's annual report is drawn up, according to that law, in accordance with the provisions of the Seventh Directive, or in accordance with international accounting standards.

(C) The company discloses in its individual accounts that it is exempt from the obligation to prepare and deliver group accounts, and the name of the parent undertaking is disclosed as well as:
(i)   its country of incorporation, if outside the United Kingdom, or
(ii) the address of its principal place of business, if unincorporated.

(D) The company delivers to the Registrar of Companies, within the period allowed for delivering its individual accounts, copies of those group accounts and of the parent undertaking's annual report, together with the auditors' report on them. A certified translation of these documents is required if they are in a language other than English.

Exemption for subsidiaries of non-EEA undertakings

[4.10] The exemption available to subsidiaries of EEA undertakings is also available to subsidiaries of non-EEA undertakings. Under CA 2006, s 401, a parent company is exempt if it is itself a subsidiary undertaking and its immediate parent undertaking is established under the law of a non EEA State and meets the same requirements as specified in 4.9 (a) and (b) above. The exemption does not apply to a company any of whose securities are listed on a stock exchange in any EEA State, and conditions (A) and (C) are relevant. However, the conditions differ slightly in that conditions (B) and (D) are expressed as follows:

(a) Those accounts are drawn up and audited, and that parent undertaking's annual report is drawn up, according to that law, in accordance with the provisions of the Seventh Directive, *or in a manner equivalent to consolidated accounts and consolidated annual reports so drawn up.*

(b) The company delivers to the Registrar of Companies, within the period allowed for delivering its individual accounts, copies of those group accounts and, where appropriate, *the consolidated annual report,* together with the auditors' report on them. A certified translation of these documents is required if they are in a language other than English.

Small and medium-sized companies

[4.11] Section 380 of CA 2006 draws a distinction between companies which are subject to the small companies' regime and those that are not, as well as between quoted companies and companies that are not quoted. In addition, the form and content of the accounts required for small and medium-sized companies are now dealt with separately in the following regulations:

(a)   Small Companies and Groups (Accounts and Directors' Report) Regulations 2008 (SI 2008/409) for companies that subject to the small companies' regime; and

(b)   Large and Medium-sized Companies and Groups (Accounts and Reports) Regulations 2008 (SI 2008/410) for companies that are outside of the small companies' regime.

A company subject to the small companies' regime or a medium-sized company is entitled to deliver abbreviated accounts to Companies House and prepare and issue full accounts to its members.

To qualify as a small or medium-sized company the company may not be:

(i)   a public company; or

(ii)   a company which is a member of an ineligible group.

(CA 2006, ss 384(1) and 467(1).)

An ineligible group is defined by CA 2006, ss 384(2) and 467(2) as a group which contains:

(I)   a public company;

(II)   a body corporate (other than a company) whose shares are admitted to trading on a regulated market (restricted to regulated markets in an EEA State for small companies);

(III)   a person (other than a small company) who has permission under Part 4 of the Financial Services and Markets Act 2000 to carry on a regulated activity;

(IV)   a small company that is an authorised insurance company, a banking company, an e-money issuer, a MiFiD investment firm or a UCITS management company; or

(V)   a person who carries on an insurance market activity.

Small company

[4.12] In order to qualify as small in relation to a particular year, a company must have been:

(a)   small since incorporation;

(b)   small in that year, and in the year before;

(c)   small in the two years before that year; or

(d)   small in that year, and small in any two years out of the three years before that year.

'Small' means that at least two of the following three conditions are fulfilled:

(i)   turnover does not exceed £6.5 million;

(ii)   balance sheet total does not exceed £3.26 million;

(iii)   average number of employees during the relevant period does not exceed 50.

(CA 2006, s 382(3).)

The term 'balance sheet total' for the purpose of the small company qualification means the aggregate of the amounts shown as assets in the company's balance sheet as set out in the Small Companies and Groups (Accounts and Directors' Report) Regulations 2008 (SI 2008/409).

The above regulations set out the form and content of the individual accounts of a company which is subject to the small companies' regime and which is preparing Companies Act individual accounts, as well as the form and content of group accounts which a parent company subject to the small companies' regime may opt to prepare. The regulations also make provision for the accounts which a company may deliver to the Registrar of Companies and identify the information to be included in the directors' report.

Form of accounts

[4.13] A company subject to the small companies' regime must deliver to Companies House a balance sheet for the year in question and may deliver a profit and loss account and directors' report for that year. An auditor's report is required on those accounts and any directors' report delivered with those accounts, unless the company is exempt from audit and the directors have taken advantage of those exemptions.

(a)   Where a company prepares Companies Act accounts, the directors may deliver a balance sheet drawn up in accordance with SI 2008/409 and may omit from the profit and loss account such items as are specified in these regulations. These accounts are referred to as 'abbreviated accounts'. In this case, a special auditor's report is required by section 449 of CA 2006.

(b)   Where a company delivers to Companies House IAS accounts or Companies Act accounts that are not abbreviated accounts which do not include the profit and loss account or the directors' report, a statement is required in the balance sheet to the effect that the annual accounts and reports have been delivered in accordance with the provisions applicable to companies subject to the small companies' regime.

The form and content of accounts prepared for companies subject to the small companies' regime is set out in the Small Companies and Groups (Accounts and Directors' Report) Regulations 2008 (SI 2008/409).

Audit exemption

[4.14] A small company is entitled to a total exemption from an audit of its accounts under CA 2006, s 477. For a company to take advantage of this exemption, it must satisfy the following conditions:

(a)   it must qualify as a small company in relation to that year for the purposes of section 246 (see **4.12** above);

(b)   its turnover in that year must be not more than £6.5 million;

(c)   its balance sheet total for that year must be not more than £3.26 million; and

(d)   the company must not have been at any time within that year:

(i)   a public company;

(ii)   an authorised insurance company, a banking company, an e-money issuer, a MiFID investment firm or a UCITS management company, or have carried on insurance market activity; or

(iii)   a special register body as defined in section 117(1) of the Trade Union and Labour Relations (Consolidation) Act 1992.

A company which is a parent company or subsidiary undertaking for any period within a financial year may take advantage of the audit exemption if it was a member of a group satisfying the following conditions:

(i)   the group qualifies as a small group, in relation to that financial year, and was not at any time within that year an ineligible group;

(ii)   the group's aggregate turnover in that year is not more than £6.5 million net or £7.8 million gross; and

(iii)   the group's aggregate balance sheet total for that year is not more than £3.26 million net or £3.9 million gross.

The Companies Act 2006 (Amendment) (Accounts and Reports) Regulations 2008 (SI 2008/393) apply the financial thresholds for turnover and the balance sheet total (of £6.5 million net and £3.26 million net respectively) for financial years beginning on or after 6 April 2008.

Additionally, a company which is a subsidiary undertaking and was dormant within the meaning of CA 2006, s 480 throughout the financial period in question (see **4.22** below) is entitled to the audit exemption under CA 2006, s 480.

Directors' statement in accounts

[4.15] The directors of a company entitled to the exemptions in CA 2006, s 475 must state in the company's balance sheet that for the year in question the company was entitled to the audit exemption and that no notice has been deposited by the members in relation to the accounts for that financial year (see **4.16** below). They must also acknowledge their responsibilities for complying with the requirements of the Act in relation to accounting records (CA 2006, s 386) and the preparation of accounts. A statement to this effect must appear in the balance sheet immediately above the signature of the director signing the accounts on behalf of the board of directors.

Notice by members requiring audit

[4.16] Section 476(2) of CA 2006 provides that any member or members holding not less than 10% in the aggregate in nominal value of the company's issued share capital or any class of it or, if the company does not have a share capital, of not less than 10% in number of the members of the company, may by notice in writing deposited at the company's registered office require the company to obtain an audit of its accounts for that year. The notice must be given during the financial year but no later than one month before the end of that year and where such a notice has been deposited, the company is not entitled to the audit exemptions.

Medium-sized company

[4.17] In order to qualify as medium-sized in relation to a particular year, a company must have been:

(a)   medium-sized since incorporation;

(b)   medium-sized in that year, and in the year before;
(c)   medium-sized in the two years before that year; or
(d)   medium-sized in that year, and medium-sized in any two years out of the three years before that year.

Medium-sized qualification requires at least two of the following three conditions to be satisfied:

(i)   turnover does not exceed £25.9 million;
(ii)   balance sheet total does not exceed £12.9 million;
(iii)   number of employees during the relevant period does not exceed 250.

(CA 2006, s 465(3).)

The term 'balance sheet total' for the purpose of the medium-sized company qualification means the aggregate of the amounts shown as assets in the company's balance sheet as set out in the Large and Medium-sized Companies and Groups (Accounts and Reports) Regulations 2008 (SI 2008/410).

The abbreviated accounts of a medium-sized company require:

(I)   a balance sheet (as for a small company) (see **4.12** above);
(II)   a profit and loss account, which may be abbreviated but must disclose turnover;
(III)   a special auditors' report; and
(IV)   a directors' report.

(CA 2006, s 445.)

The Large and Medium-sized Companies and Groups (Accounts and Reports) Regulations 2008 (SI 2008/410) specify the form and content of the individual accounts of a company (IAS individual accounts in the case of banking and insurance companies and Companies Act individual accounts for other companies) which fall outside the small companies' regime.

Small and medium-sized groups

[4.18] A parent company subject to the small companies' regime may prepare, or deliver, group accounts for the financial year, although CA 2006, s 398 provides that this is at the option of the directors. The Companies Act 2006 does not include the option for a medium-sized company to prepare group accounts.

In order to qualify as small in relation to a particular year, the group must have been:

(i)   small or medium-sized since incorporation;
(ii)   small or medium-sized in that year, and in the year before;
(iii)   small or medium-sized in the two years before that year; or
(iv)   small or medium-sized in that year, and small or medium-sized in any two years out of the three years before that year.

(CA 2006, s 383 (for small companies).)

Small group

[4.19] In order to qualify as a small group, a group must meet at least two of the following three conditions:

(a)   aggregate turnover does not exceed £6.5 million net or £7.8 million gross);

(b)   aggregate balance sheet total does not exceed £3.26 million net or £3.9 million gross;

(c)   aggregate average number of employees does not exceed 50.

(CA 2006, s 383(4).)

Medium-sized group

[4.20] In order to qualify as a medium-sized group, a group must meet at least two of the following three conditions:

(a)   aggregate turnover does not exceed £25.9 million net or £31.1 million gross;

(b)   aggregate balance sheet total does not exceed £12.9 million net or £15.5 million gross;

(c)   aggregate average number of employees does not exceed 250.

(CA 2006, s 466(4).)

Disclosure requirements

[4.21] If a parent company is exempt from the requirement to prepare group accounts, it is entitled to issue full individual accounts to its members and to lodge abbreviated individual accounts with Companies House (see **4.13** and **4.17** above). Where the auditors are of the opinion that the directors were not entitled to the exemption conferred by CA 2006, s 398, the auditors must state that fact in their report (CA 2006, s 498(5)).

Dormant companies

[4.22] Under CA 2006, s 480, a company other than a company that at any time during the financial year in question:

(a)   was an authorised insurance company, a banking company, an e-money issuer, a MiFiD investment firm or a UCITS management company; or

(b)   carried on insurance market activity,

may, in the circumstances defined by this section, exempt itself from the obligation to appoint auditors.

A company which is exempt from this obligation is entitled to prepare accounts which are not subject to audit and do not contain an audit report, and to deliver such accounts to the Registrar of Companies. In addition, a company which is not entitled to prepare abbreviated accounts for a small company, by virtue of the restrictions on a company which is a member of an ineligible group (see **4.11** above), may nonetheless take advantage of the exemption from the obligation to appoint auditors afforded to the company by its dormant status.

The circumstances defined by CA 2006, s 480 in which a company can take advantage of this exemption are that:

(a)   the company has been dormant since its incorporation; or
(b)   the company has been dormant since the end of the previous financial year, qualifies as a 'small' company and is not required to produce group accounts.

'Dormant' is defined by CA 2006, s 1169 as meaning that no significant accounting transactions which would be required by CA 2006, s 386 to be entered in the accounting records of the company have occurred during the relevant period (ie either since incorporation ((a) above) or the end of the previous financial year ((b) above)). For this purpose, any amounts paid for the subscriber shares issued on the incorporation of a company will be disregarded as well as any payment for a fee to the registrar of companies for a change of name, on the re-registration of a company and for the registration of the company's annual return. In addition, the payment of a civil penalty arising from the failure to file the company's accounts by the due date will not affect the company's dormant status (CA 2006, s 1169).

A company which satisfies the conditions for dormant status will automatically qualify for exemption from audit provided that 10% of the members have not required the company to obtain an audit of its accounts for the year in question (under the rights available to members in CA 2006, s 476).

Dormant companies which act as agents (eg for the purpose of acting as a nominee secretary) must disclose the fact that the company has acted as an agent for the financial year in question in the notes to their accounts.

If the company ceases to be dormant and exceeds the thresholds for entitlement to audit exemption as a small company, or becomes a company not entitled to take advantage of dormancy, the directors must appoint an auditor to serve until the next occasion when the appointment of an auditor falls due for a private company or, in the case of a public company, the general meeting at which accounts are laid. Failing this, the members of the company may appoint an auditor.

Overseas companies

[4.23] The Overseas Companies Regulations 2009 (SI 2009/1801) sets out the accounting requirements for an overseas company that has an establishment in the United Kingdom (a UK establishment). The regulations differentiate between the accounting requirements for:

(a)   a company that it required by its parent law to prepare, have audited and disclose accounts, or is incorporated in an EEA State and is required by it parent law to prepare and disclose accounts but is not required by its parent law to have its accounts audited or delivered to a registry; or
(b)   a credit or financial institution, or a company whose constitution does not limit the liability of its members.

Disclosure required under parent law

[4.24] The directors of the company must deliver to the Registrar of Companies a copy of all the accounting documents prepared for a financial period that are disclosed in accordance with its parent law. Where the company's parent law allows the company to fulfil this disclosure requirement by delivering such documents in modified form then the directors are permitted to deliver such modified accounts to the Registrar. Where the company is incorporated in an EEA State the directors are not required to deliver accounting documents to the Registrar if the company is not required to do deliver such documents under its own parent law, or may deliver these documents to the Registrar without an audit report if the company's parent law does not require it to have its accounts audited.

The accounting documents delivered to the Registrar must be accompanied by a statement giving the following information:

(i)   the legislation under which the accounts have been prepared and, if applicable, audited;
(ii)   whether those accounts have been prepared in accordance with a set of generally accepted accounting principles and, if so, the name of the organisation or other body which issued those principles;
(iii)   whether the accounts have been audited, and if they have:
   (a) whether they have been audited in accordance with a set of generally accepted standards; and
   (b) in which case, the name of the organisation or other body which issued those standards; and
(iv)   if they have not been audited, whether the company is not required to have its accounts audited.

The period allowed for delivery to Companies House is three months from the date on which the accounting documents are required to be disclosed under the parent company's law.

Disclosure not required under parent law

[4.25] Sections 390–397, 399 and 402–406 of CA 2006 (which deal with how the company's financial year and corresponding accounting reference date are determined, and the duty to prepare accounts) are modified by SI 2009/1801 in relation to the application of these provisions to overseas companies which are not required to prepare and disclose accounts under their parent law. In particular, an overseas company's individual accounts may be prepared in accordance with its parent law, international accounting standards or CA 2006, s 396 (as modified). Such accounts must comprise:

(a)   a balance sheet as at the last day of the financial year; and
(b)   a profit and loss account,

which comply with Schedule 4 of SI 2009/1801 as to the content of these accounting documents, the additional information to be provided by way of notes to the accounts.

The directors must state in the notes to the accounts for a company that prepares:

(A)   IAS individual accounts:
   (i) that the accounts have been prepared in accordance with international accounting standards;

(ii)   whether the accounts have been audited, and if they have:
- (a)   whether they have been audited in accordance with a set of generally accepted standards; and
- (b)   in which case, the name of the organisation or other body which issued those standards; and

(iii)   if they have not been audited, whether the company is not required to have its accounts audited.

(B)   parent law individual accounts:

In addition to (A)(ii) and (iii) above:

(i)   that the accounts have been prepared in accordance with the company's parent law;

(ii)   the legislation under which the accounts have been prepared; and

(iii)   whether those accounts have been prepared in accordance with a set of generally accepted accounting principles and, if so, the name of the organisation or other body which issued those principles.

(C)   overseas company individual accounts:

In addition to (A)(ii) and (iii), and (B)(iii) above:

(i)   that the accounts have been prepared in accordance with section 396 of CA 2006.

The period allowed for delivery to Companies House is 13 months from the end of the accounting reference period to which the accounts relate. However, if the overseas company's first accounting reference period is for more than 12 months, the period allowed in respect of that first period is 13 months from the anniversary of the company having an establishment in the United Kingdom.

Credit or financial institutions

[4.26] The requirements for a credit or financial institution that has an establishment in the United Kingdom will depend on whether the institution is required to prepare accounts under its parent law or not. For a company that:

(a)   is required by its parent law to prepare, have audited and disclose accounts, or is incorporated in an EEA State and is required by its parent law to prepare and disclose accounts but is not required by its parent law to have its accounts audited or delivered to a registry, the period allowed for delivery of such accounting documents is three months from the date on which the document is required to be disclosed in accordance with the institution's parent law; and

(b)   is not required by its parent law to have its accounts audited or delivered to a registry, sections 390–397, 399 and 402–406 of CA 2006 are modified by SI 2009/1801 in relation to the application of these provisions in a similar manner to overseas companies which fall within the circumstances specified in **4.25** above. The period allowed for delivery to Companies House is 13 months from the end of the accounting reference period to which the accounts relate. However, if the overseas company's first accounting reference period is for more than 12 months, the period allowed in respect of that first period is 13 months from the anniversary of the company having an establishment in the United Kingdom.

Approval of accounts

[4.27] Under CA 2006, s 414(1), a company's annual accounts must be approved by the board of directors and signed on behalf of the board by a director of the company. For this purpose, the company's annual accounts comprise its individual balance sheet and profit and loss account, together with any group accounts. The signature must be on the company's individual balance sheet (CA 2006, s 414(2)) and although the consolidated balance sheet is often signed there is not a requirement to do so.

Every copy of a company's balance sheet which is laid before a company's general meeting or is otherwise published, circulated or issued, must state the name of the person who signed the balance sheet on behalf of the board.

The accounts must also bear a statement as to the date they were signed. This is commonly stated above the director's signature on the balance sheet, or is sometimes given in a note to the accounts.

The directors' report

[4.28] Pursuant to CA 2006, s 415(1), all companies must prepare a directors' report in respect of each financial year. The contents of the report are set out in CA 2006, s 416 and 417 and the relevant regulations (SI 2008/409 or SI 2008/410 as appropriate) setting out the form and content of the company's accounts. In summary the contents required are:

(a)   a fair review of the development of the business of the company during the financial year and of its position at the end of it;
(b)   the principal activities of the company during the year;
(c)   the names of the persons who were directors at any time during the year and their interests (if any) in any shares and debentures (or options) of the company;
(d)   the amount (if any) which the directors propose should be paid as a dividend;
(e)   a statement of the market value of fixed assets where this is substantially different from the balance sheet amount;
(f)   details of any political or charitable contributions made, exceeding in aggregate £2,000 during the year; and
(g)   details of any acquisitions of its own shares which a company has made during the year.

For companies which employ an average of more than 250 employees in each week of the financial year, the directors' report must also give details as to the employment of disabled persons and of employee involvement in the company's management. Further, public companies or large subsidiaries of public companies must disclose the company's payment policy and practice.

Section 417 of CA 2006 requires that a company, other than one subject to the small companies' regime, includes a business review in the directors' report.

The business review enables the members of the company to assess the extent to which the directors promoted the success of the company, and must therefore contain a fair review of the company's business, together with a description of the principal risks and uncertainties facing the company. The review should provide a balanced and comprehensive analysis of:

(i) the development and performance of the company's business during the financial year;

(ii) the position of the company's business at the end of that year, consistent with the size and complexity of the business;

(iii) for a quoted company, sufficient information to allow an understanding of the development, performance or position of the company's business, comprising:

    (a) the main trends and factors likely to affect the future development, performance and position of the company's business;

    (b) information about environmental matters (including the impact of the company's business on the environment), the company's employees, and social and community issues, along with information about the company's policies in these areas and their effectiveness; and

    (c) information about persons with whom the company has contractual or other arrangements which are essential to the business of the company; and

(iv) financial (and, where appropriate, non-financial) key performance indicators (although non-financial information is not required in relation to medium-sized companies).

The directors are not required to disclose any information of a commercial nature (such as impending developments or ongoing negotiations), the disclosure of which, in the directors' opinion, would seriously prejudice the company's interests.

Pursuant to CA 2006, s 419, the directors' report must be approved by the board of directors and signed on their behalf by either a director or the secretary of the company. Every copy of the report which is laid before the company in general meeting or which is published, circulated or issued, must bear the name of the person who signed it on behalf of the board (CA 2006, s 433). It is usual for the directors' report to be approved and signed on the same date as the balance sheet.

A corporate governance statement may form part of the directors' report or be produced as a separate statement. Where it is not included in the directors' report, the Companies Act 2006 (Accounts, Report and Audit) Regulations 2009 (SI 2009/1581) require it to be filed with the Registrar of Companies and for the auditor to give an opinion as to whether the information required to be shown in the statement as to internal control and risk management systems in relation to the financial reporting process and certain disclosures required by the Takeovers Directive (Directive 2004/25/EEC), is consistent with the annual accounts for the year in question. Under CA 2006, s 419A, the corporate governance statement must be approved by the board of directors and signed on their behalf by either a director or the company secretary.

The auditors' report

[4.29] Under CA 2006, ss 485 and 489, every company except companies exempt from audit (ie small companies) and dormant companies are required to appoint an auditor (see **4.40** below). The auditor, pursuant to CA 2006, s 495, is required to make a report to the company's members on all annual accounts of the company, of which copies are to be laid before the company in general meeting, or sent to the members during their tenure of office (see **4.49** below).

The report is required to state whether in the auditors' opinion the annual accounts have been properly prepared in accordance with the relevant financial reporting framework and the requirements of the CA 2006, and where applicable Article 4 of the IAS Regulation, and whether a true and fair representation of the state of affairs of the company is given. The auditors' report must state the name(s) of the auditors and be signed by them pursuant to CA 2006, s 503(1). Every copy of the report which is delivered to the members or is published, issued or circulated, must bear the name of the auditors who signed it (CA 2006, s 503(1)), and must be signed on a date on or after the date the balance sheet and directors' report are approved by the board of directors.

Where the auditor is a firm, the report must be signed by the senior statutory auditor in his own name, for and on behalf of the auditor (CA 2006, s 503(3)). This is the individual identified by the firm as senior statutory auditor in relation to a company's audit in accordance with standards issued by the European Commission, or in the absence of any applicable standard, any relevant guidance issued by the Secretary of State, or a body appointed by order of the Secretary of State. The person concerned must be eligible for appointment as auditor of the company in question. He is not subject to any civil liability to which he would not otherwise have been subject by virtue of being named or identified as senior statutory auditor or by virtue of signing the auditor's report.

However, the auditor's name and, where the auditor is a firm, the name of the senior statutory auditor, may be omitted from published copies of the report, and the copy of the report delivered to the Registrar of Companies in circumstances where the auditor or senior statutory auditor may reasonably be subject to violence or intimidation (CA 2006, s 506). To take advantage of this, the company must pass a resolution such that the name of the auditor or senior statutory auditor should not be stated in the report, and give notice to the Secretary of State to this effect, identifying the name and registered number of the company, the financial year to which the report relates, and the name of the auditor or senior statutory auditor concerned.

It should be noted that the Auditing Practices Board (APB) in the first of its Statements of Auditing Standards (SASs), 'Auditors' Report on Financial Statements', dispensed with the common practice of auditors to sign the audit report as made at an effective date. The SAS has additionally adopted the recommendations of the Cadbury Report in relation to directors' and auditors' responsibilities (see **4.30** below) and has given auditors greater flexibility over the wording to be used in expressing an opinion on a set of accounts.

Corporate governance

Cadbury

[4.30] The report of the Cadbury Committee (see **6.15 THE DIRECTORS**) made several recommendations relating to statements to be made in a company's report and accounts by the directors and the auditors in their respective reports. All listed companies registered in the UK were advised to comply with the Code of Best Practice developed by the Committee and were required to indicate in their report and accounts their compliance with the Code and identify with supporting reasons any areas of non-compliance.

The Combined Code, as published on 25 June 1998, applied to companies listed on the London Stock Exchange and continues to apply to such companies following subsequent revisions to the Code. As a consequence, Rule 12.43A was introduced into the Listing Rules which required companies to produce the following:

(1)   A narrative statement which describes how the principles in section 1 of the Code have been applied by the company and provides an explanation so that shareholders can evaluate how the principles have been applied.

(2)   A statement of compliance which indicates the extent to which the company has complied with section 1 of the Code during the accounting period. In particular, a company will be required to disclose its compliance with the Code provisions while identifying those provisions with which it has not complied. The statement should also indicate the period during which the company did not comply with the Code provisions.

(3)   A report on the directors' remuneration which provides certain specified information about the remuneration packages paid to directors. This requirement of the Listing Rules is disapplied in the case of investment companies (including investment trusts) with boards of non-executive directors.

The statement of compliance, and its review by the company's auditors, is a continuing listing obligation of the Listing Rules (now in Chapter LR9). In addition, the directors' report should contain a statement of their responsibilities for the accounts, the effectiveness of the company's system of internal control, and indicate whether the business is a going concern, together with any assumptions or qualifications to support this statement.

Likewise, the auditors are required to provide a statement of their reporting responsibilities and to give an opinion on the directors' statement, as well as reviewing the compliance statement as far as it is possible for them to objectively verify compliance with the Code.

Turnbull

[4.31] The ICAEW published guidance (in September 1999) to assist companies in implementing the internal controls requirements of the Combined Code ('Internal Control: Guidance for Directors on the Combined Code'). The Code has extended the internal control so that in addition to financial controls, companies are required to report on their operational controls, compliance controls and risk management. The guidance prepared by the Turnbull Committee applies in respect of accounting periods ending on or after 23 December 2000.

The Turnbull Review Group subsequently proposed certain limited changes to those parts of the Turnbull guidance dealing with maintaining and reviewing the internal control system, and the disclosures companies are required to include in the annual report. The Review Group considered that the disclosure requirements of section 404 of the Sarbanes Oxley Act 2002 (US Act) – which requires the company's management to make a statement on the effectiveness of internal controls over financial reporting, and the external auditor to issue an attestation report on that statement – did not constitute an appropriate model for disclosures made in the UK under the Combined Code and Turnbull guidance.

In October 2005, the FRC published its revised guidance based on the Review Group's key recommendations for updating the Turnbull guidance set out in their consultation paper, 'Review of the Turnbull Guidance on Internal Control: Proposals for Updating the Guidance' (available at www.frc.org.uk/corp orate/internalcontrol.cfm). Their recommendations which were incorporated into 'Internal Control: Revised Guidance for Directors on the Combined Code' are summarised below.

Guidance

(a)   Significant changes to the Turnbull guidance are not required.

(b)   The guidance should continue to cover all internal controls.

(c)   No changes should be made to the guidance that would have the effect of restricting a company's ability to apply the guidance in a manner suitable to its own particular circumstances.

(d)   A new preface should be added to the guidance to encourage boards regularly to reassess their application of the guidance and use the internal control statement to communicate to their shareholders how they manage risk effectively.

Board

(a)   Amendments should be made to require the board to exercise reasonable care, skill and diligence when forming a view on the effectiveness of the internal control system (as opposed to forming a view 'after due and careful enquiry'), to reflect the proposed statement of directors' duties in the draft Company Law Reform Bill;

(b)   Boards should be required to:

(i)   confirm that, in their opinion, necessary action has been or is being taken to remedy any significant failings or weaknesses identified from the reviews of the effectiveness of the internal control system; and

(ii)   include in the annual report and accounts such information as is considered necessary to assist shareholders' understanding of the main features of the company's risk management processes and system of internal control.

Audit

(a) The section relating to internal audit, dealt with in provision C.3.5 of the Combined Code, should be removed and incorporated into the Smith guidance on audit committees.

(b) It would not be appropriate to require boards to make a statement in the annual report and accounts on the effectiveness of the company's internal control system.

(c) There should be no need for companies that are already applying the Turnbull guidance to develop additional processes in order to comply with the requirement to identify principal risks in the Operating and Financial Review (OFR). Nevertheless, companies are encouraged to ensure that the OFR and the internal control statement are complementary.

(d) There should be no expansion of the external auditors' responsibilities in relation to the company's internal control statement.

Smith and Higgs

[4.32] The report produced by the committee chaired by Sir Robert Smith, 'Audit Committees: Combined Code Guidance' ('the Smith Report'), provides further guidance to audit committees in applying corporate governance principles. The recommendations of the Smith Report (together with those of the Higgs Review on the role of non-executive directors) were incorporated into a new Combined Code produced by the FRC in July 2003. The Code applied to listed companies for reporting years beginning on or after 1 November 2003. The Code was updated in June 2006 (applicable for reporting years beginning on or after 1 November 2006) and again in June 2008 (applicable for reporting years beginning on or after 29 June 2008).

Recent developments

[4.33] The UK Corporate Governance Code (formerly the Combined Code) was published by the FRC in May 2010. The Code retains the key elements of the earlier versions of the Code but builds in further refinements to board effectiveness, accountability and transparency. The Code is applicable for reporting years beginning on or after 29 June 2010 and is reproduced in full at **APPENDIX 6G**. Aligned to this, the FRC published the Stewardship Code in July 2010 with the aim of enhancing 'the quality of engagement between institutional investors and companies to help improve long-term returns to shareholders and the efficient exercise of governance responsibilities'.

In addition, the ICAEW, at the invitation of the FRC, formed a working group to develop a code of good governance practice for audit firms involved in the audit of listed companies. The outcome of this, the Audit Firm Governance Code, was published in January 2010. While the Code primarily provides a formal benchmark of good governance practice against which such firms can be measured, the FRC anticipates that it will benefit other stakeholders, including:

(a) directors, particularly audit committee members, with responsibilities for the appointment of auditors;

(b) regulators with responsibilities for confidence in audit quality; and

(c)   partners and employees of audit firms.

The Code addresses six key areas of governance: leadership, values, independent non-executives, operations, reporting and dialogue, and comprises 20 provisions and 31 principles. It is intended that the Code should apply for financial years beginning on or after 1 June 2010.

In December 2010 the FRC published its 'Guidance on Audit Committees' which serves to support the audit committees of listed companies in applying the principles in this area of the UK Corporate Governance Code. This is available on the FRC website at www.frc.org.uk/corporate/auditcommittees. cfm.

Duty to lay accounts

[4.34] In respect of each financial year, CA 2006, s 437 requires the directors of a company to lay copies of the company's annual accounts and the directors' and auditors' reports for that year before the company in general meeting. It is common practice for a company's accounts to be laid before the annual general meeting, although this is not a specific requirement. The Companies Act 2006 imposes the requirement to lay accounts on public companies only with effect from 1 October 2007, since private companies will not generally be required to hold annual general meetings under the new Act.

Duty to file accounts

[4.35] Section 441 of CA 2006 requires the directors, in respect of each financial year, to deliver to the Registrar of Companies a copy of the company's annual accounts together with directors' and auditors' reports. The individual balance sheet and directors' report must bear the live signatures of the persons who signed them on behalf of the board. The auditors' report must also bear the live signatures of the auditors who signed it. The Companies Act 2006 imposes different filing requirements upon the company, depending on whether the company is subject to the small companies' regime, is medium-sized, or is a quoted or unquoted public company.

Section 1104 of CA 2006 permits any company which is shown on the register of companies as having its registered office is to be situated in Wales (defined as a Welsh company by CA 2006, s 88) to deliver to Companies House its accounts and reports in Welsh only. The Registrar of Companies is required under the Act to obtain a translation of these documents into English, although such companies may provide a certified translation on a voluntary basis. Under CA 2006, s 469, a company is permitted to deliver and publish an additional copy of its accounts in which the amounts have been translated into euros, together with the accounts required to be lodged with Companies House under CA 2006, s 441.

Time limits for laying and filing accounts

[4.36] Section 442 of CA 2006 fixes the periods allowed from the end of a company's financial year on its accounting reference date, to lay and file its accounts and report. These are:

(a)   for a *private* company, nine months after the end of the relevant accounting reference period; and

(b)   for a *public* company, six months after the end of the relevant accounting reference period.

Where a company's first accounting reference period exceeds twelve months, the period allowed for laying and delivering the accounts and reports is nine months for a private company and six months for a public company from the first anniversary of the company's incorporation, or, for both types of company, three months from the end of the accounting reference period, whichever expires last. The impact of this rule is that for private companies the maximum period between the date of the company's incorporation and the date it must file its first accounts at Companies House is 21 months. For public companies, the maximum period between these two dates is 18 months.

These time limits are strictly interpreted by reference to calendar months with the deadline for delivery being calculated to the exact day, although where the accounting reference date for a private company is 30 April, the company is required to file its annual accounts by midnight on 31 January of the following year, not 30 January. On the other hand, where the accounts of a private company are for a financial year ending on 30 May, the accounts must be lodged with Companies House by 28 February in the following year. These rules must be interpreted correctly in view of the civil penalties which apply in relation to accounts which are filed late.

Companies may seek an extension of three months beyond the normal period allowed for filing accounts by application to the Secretary of State under CA 2006, s 442(5). The application must be made before the end of the period for filing the accounts and detail the circumstances which prevent the company from filings its accounts on time. An extension under these provisions is difficult to obtain since it is usually granted in extenuating circumstances, which by definition are wholly outside the company's control, such as the death of all of the company's officers.

Failure to file the accounts within the above periods can result in the Registrar of Companies using one of the sanctions available under the Act (see **5.2 DISCLOSURE AND REPORTING REQUIREMENTS**).

Revision of defective accounts

[4.37] The directors of a company may prepare revised accounts and reports where it appears to them that these documents do not comply with the requirements of the Companies Act (CA 2006, s 454). If these have been laid before the members in general meeting or delivered to the Registrar of Companies, the revisions to be made are restricted to:

(a)   the correction of any part of the accounts or report which does not comply with the requirements of the Act (or Article 4 of the IAS Regulation where applicable); and

(b)   the making of any necessary consequential amendments.

The Companies (Revision of Defective Accounts and Report) Regulations 2008 (SI 2008/373) specify the requirements which apply to the preparation, laying and delivery of revised accounts or a revised report. The requirements will depend in part on whether revision is by *replacement* of the original accounts and report or revision by a *supplementary note* indicating the corrections made to the original accounting documents.

Sections 414 and 419 of CA 2006, which relate to the approval and signing of the accounts and directors' report, shall apply to the revised accounts and report respectively, except that where revision is by supplementary note, the signature shall apply in respect of the supplementary note. Where the accounts and report have been laid before the members in general meeting or delivered to the Registrar of Companies, the following statements are required in the revised accounting documents:

(i)   in the case of revision by replacement:
- (A)   that the revised accounts or report replace the original accounting documents for the financial year in question;
- (B)   that, in respect of revised accounts, they are now the statutory accounts of the company for that financial year;
- (C)   that the revised accounts or report have been prepared as at the date of the original accounting documents and not at the date of revision;
- (D)   the defects in the original accounts or report which caused them not to comply with the requirements of CA 2006; and
- (E)   any significant amendments made consequential upon the remedying of those defects;

(ii)   in the case of revision by supplementary note:
- (A)   that the note revises certain aspects of the original accounts or report of the company and is to be treated as forming part of the document in question; and
- (B)   that the accounts or report have been revised as at the date of the original accounting documents and not as at the date of revision.

A company's current auditors are required to make a report, or (as the case may be) a further report under CA 2006, s 495 to the members of the company under these regulations, on any revised accounts or reports prepared under CA 2006, s 454. If the auditors' report on the original annual accounts was not made by the company's current auditors, the directors of the company may resolve that the auditors' report on the revised accounts and report is made by the company's previous auditors, provided that they agree to do so and continue to be qualified for appointment as auditor of the company.

Following approval of the revised accounting documents, the directors shall:

(1)   where the original accounts and report were sent to all persons entitled to receive such documents under CA 2006, s 423:
- (a)   send to any person who was entitled to receive the original documents under CA 2006, s 423, a copy of the revised accounts or report in the case of revision by replacement, or a copy of the supplementary note where revision is by supplementary note, together with a copy of the auditors' report on those documents, not more than 28 days after the date of the revision; and

(b) send to any person who at the date of revision is entitled to receive copies of accounts and reports under CA 2006, s 423/, the documents referred to in (1)(*a*) above not more than 28 days after the revision;

(2) where the original accounts and report have been laid before the members in general meeting in compliance with CA 2006, s 437, for public companies, lay the documents referred to in (1)(*a*) above before the next general meeting held after the date of revision at which any annual accounts for a financial year are laid, unless the revised documents have been laid before an earlier general meeting;

(3) where the original accounts and report have been delivered to the Registrar of Companies as required by CA 2006, s 441, deliver to the Registrar within 28 days of the revision, copies of the documents referred to in (1)(*a*) above.

The statutory instrument also contains similar regulations affecting the abbreviated accounts of small and medium-sized companies, summary financial statements and the unaudited accounts of dormant companies.

The Secretary of State may give notice to the directors of a company under CA 2006, s 455 where a question arises as to the compliance of the company's accounts and report with the requirements of the Act. Following notice under this section, the Secretary of State or a person authorised under CA 2006, s 456 may make application to the court for a declaration that the accounts do not comply with the Act and an order requiring the directors to prepare revised accounts.

The Financial Reporting Review Panel is an authorised person for the purpose of CA 2006, s 456, by virtue of the Companies (Defective Accounts and Directors' Reports) (Authorised Person) and Supervision of Accounts and Reports (Prescribed Body) Order 2008 (SI 2008/623). The effect of this statutory instrument was that the Financial Reporting Review Panel established under the articles of association of The Financial Reporting Review Panel Limited is deemed a person authorised to receive and investigate complaints about the annual accounts of companies (CA 2006, s 457). Any accounts referred to the Panel may result in the auditors being reported to their professional body, who as recognised supervisory bodies may exercise their ultimate sanction to deregister auditors.

The Companies (Revision of Defective Accounts and Reports) Regulations 2008 (SI 2008/373) apply in respect of financial years beginning on or after 6 April 2008 and set out how the provisions of CA 2006 are to apply to revised annual accounts, directors' reports, directors' remuneration reports and summary financial statements. They recognise the differences between public and private companies in relation to the laying and delivering of revised accounts, as well the provisions for those companies which are exempt from audit. The regulations also extend the application of these provisions to persons nominated to enjoy information rights under CA 2006, s 146.

Partnerships and unlimited companies

[4.38] The Partnerships and Unlimited Companies (Accounts) Regulations 1993 (SI 1993/1820) came into force on 21 July 1993 and applied, until their revocation and replacement by later regulations (see below), to limited and unlimited companies which fall within the following definitions of a 'qualifying partnership' and a 'qualifying company'.

(a)   A qualifying partnership is a partnership governed by the laws of any part of Great Britain in which each of its members is either:

    (i)   a limited company; or

    (ii)   an unlimited company, or a Scottish firm, each of whose members is a limited company.

(b)   A qualifying company is an unlimited company incorporated in Great Britain in which each of its members is:

    (i)   a limited company; or

    (ii)   another unlimited company, or a Scottish firm, each of whose members is a limited company.

The regulations require members of a qualifying partnership to prepare, deliver and publish audited accounts for financial years commencing on or after 23 December 1994, and an unlimited company which is a qualifying company by virtue of these regulations is required to deliver accounts and reports to the Registrar of Companies. The regulations are drafted so that any member of a qualifying partnership or a qualifying company which is a comparable undertaking incorporated in or formed under the law of any country or territory outside Great Britain is subject to the requirements of these regulations.

The members of a qualifying partnership at the end of any financial year of the partnership are required for that year to prepare in respect of the partnership the same annual accounts and reports as are required to be prepared by companies formed and registered under the Companies Act within ten months after the end of the financial year. Each limited company which is a member of a qualifying partnership at the end of any financial year of the partnership must append to the copy of its annual accounts, which is next delivered to the Registrar of Companies in compliance with CA 2006, s 441, a copy of the accounts of the partnership prepared for that year.

The members of a qualifying partnership are exempt from the requirements to prepare, deliver and publish the partnership's accounts if the partnership is dealt with on a consolidated basis in group accounts prepared by a member of the partnership which is established under the law of an EU Member State, or a parent undertaking of such a member which is so established (see **4.9** above). Where a qualifying partnership's head office is in Great Britain and each of its members is an undertaking comparable to a limited company which is incorporated in a country or territory outside the UK but not within the EU, or an undertaking comparable to an unlimited company or partnership, which is incorporated in or formed under the law of such a country or territory, and each of whose members is such an undertaking, the latest accounts of the partnership must be available for inspection by any person at the head office of the partnership.

The Partnerships and Unlimited Companies (Accounts) (Amendment) Regulations 2005 (SI 2005/1987) came into force on 1 October 2005 and made minor amendments to the principal regulations (SI 1993/1820). These ensured that the 1993 Regulations refer to the correct statutory references following changes made by other accounting regulations, and also extended the application of the exemption available under the regulations to group accounts prepared in accordance with international accounting standards.

The Partnerships (Accounts) Regulations 2008 (SI 2008/569) revoke the Partnerships and Unlimited Companies (Accounts) Regulations 1993 (SI 1993/1820) as amended by Partnerships and Unlimited Companies (Accounts) (Amendment) Regulations 2005 (SI 2005/1987) and consequently separate out the requirements for partnerships and unlimited companies. SI 2008/569 relate to partnerships with a financial year beginning on or after 6 April 2008 and apply the principles established in the earlier regulations which are still relevant, while section 448 of CA 2006 applies in respect of unlimited companies and requires the delivery to the Registrar of Companies of annual reports and accounts where:

(i)   the company is a banking or insurance company or the parent company of a banking or insurance group; or

(ii)   each of its members is:

(a)   a limited company; or

(b)   another unlimited company, or a Scottish partnership, each of whose members is a limited company.

Summary financial statements

[4.39] Under CA 2006, s 426, a company is authorised to issue summary financial statements in place of full accounts. The Companies (Summary Financial Statement) Regulations 2008 (SI 2008/374) enable any company that has its full accounts audited to distribute a summary financial statement to shareholders (provided that consent has been given to receive them). Consequently, any company which has had audited its full accounts and reports for the year in question may issue summary financial statements to any entitled person, being those persons specified in CA 2006, s 423(1), namely:

(a)   every member of the company;

(b)   every holder of the company's debentures; and

(c)   every person who is entitled to receive notice of general meetings.

The procedure under which summary financial statements may be prepared and issued is set out in SI 2008/374, while Schedules 1 to 3 of the regulations detail the form and content required of these statements. The requirements which a company wishing to issue summary financial statements must fulfil are as follows:

(i)   The company must have ascertained that the entitled person does not wish to continue to receive copies of the full accounts.

(ii)   The time limits specified by CA 2006, s 442 must not have expired (see **4.36** above).

(iii) The summary statements must be approved by the board. The original must be signed by a director and all copies must state the name of the director who signed.

(iv)   The summary statements must contain a prominent statement that the entitled persons have a right to the full report and accounts if they so wish, and that they should consult them for a full understanding of the affairs of the company which the summary does not provide.

(v)   The statements must contain a clear and conspicuous statement of how members and debenture holders can obtain a copy of the company's last full accounts and reports, and of how they can elect to receive such accounts in place of summary financial statements for future years.

The regulations prescribe the manner in which the wishes of entitled persons can be ascertained as to whether or not they wish to receive summary financial statements, ie:

(A)   Any relevant notification in writing by the entitled person to the company that he wishes to receive summary financial statements only (or full accounts in place of them). Such notice must be received by the company before the first date on which copies of the full accounts are sent out in compliance with CA 2006, s 423.

(B)   Consultation by notice accompanied by a printed reply card or form, specifying a date by which the company must receive a response to the consultation. The date must be at least 21 days after the service of the notice and not less than 28 days before the first date on which copies of the full accounts for the next financial year are sent out in compliance with CA 2006, s 423.

(C)   A relevant consultation comprising a copy of the full accounts and reports, a specimen of the summary financial statements on those accounts and a printed card or form to notify the company that he wishes to receive full accounts for the next and future years. If no response is received to this consultation, he will receive summary financial statements.

Shareholders may also receive the full accounts or the summary financial statements by electronic communications at an address notified to the company by the shareholder. In these circumstances, the statements are treated as being sent to the shareholder where:

(I)   the company and that person have agreed to his having access to summary financial statements on a website (instead of them being sent to him);

(II)   the statement is a statement to which that agreement applies; and

(III)   that person is notified, in a manner for the time being agreed for the purpose between him and the company, of:

    (a)   the publication of the statement on a website;

    (b)   the address of that website; and

    (c)   the place on that website where the statement may be accessed, and how it may be accessed.

The company may ascertain from its shareholders whether or not they wish to receive the full accounts or the summary financial statements in electronic format in a similar manner as they would be required to do so in relation to the receipt of summary financial statements.

The Companies (Summary Financial Statement) Regulations 2008 (SI 2008/374) apply for financial years beginning on or after 6 April 2008. In summary, the regulations set out the conditions for sending out summary financial statements and the manner in which it is to be ascertained whether a person entitled to receive copies of the full accounts and reports wishes to receive summary financial statements in their place. The regulations define the form and content of the summary financial statements regardless of whether the full accounts are prepared as Companies Act accounts or as IAS accounts. The regulations extend the persons to whom summary financial statements may be sent beyond members, debenture holders and persons entitled to receive notice of general meetings, to cover persons nominated to enjoy information rights under CA 2006, s 146.

The auditor

General

[4.40] Sections 485 and 489 of CA 2006 require that every company must appoint an auditor. However, exemptions do exist for small companies and dormant companies. Section 25(1) of the Companies Act 1989 introduced the qualification that a person to be eligible for appointment as a company auditor must be a member of a recognised supervisory body, as defined by CA 1989, s 30 (see **4.42** below). However, no person may be appointed as auditor of a company if he is an officer or employee of the company, or a partner or employee of an officer or employee of that company. A partnership of which such a person is a partner or a body corporate may also not be appointed as an auditor (see **4.44** below).

Appointment

[4.41] Under CA 2006, s 489(3) for public companies, the first auditors of a company may be appointed by the directors at any time, to hold office until the *first* general meeting of the company at which accounts are presented (see **PRECEDENT A, APPENDIX 4A**). The directors may also appoint an auditor to fill a casual vacancy in the office of auditor which has been caused by the death or resignation of the previous auditor (CA 2006, s 489(3)).

Section 489(2) of CA 2006 requires a company in general meeting to appoint (or re-appoint) auditors at each general meeting at which accounts are laid, to hold office until the next such general meeting (see **PRECEDENT B, APPENDIX 4A**). A *private company* is not required to hold an annual general meeting under CA 2006; the provisions for the appointment of auditors by a private company therefore allow 'deemed' or 'automatic' re-appointment of auditors. Under CA 2006, s 485, the appointment must be made before the end of the period of 28 days beginning with the end of the time allowed for sending out copies of the company's annual accounts and reports for the previous financial year (CA 2006, s 424), or, if earlier, the day on which copies of such accounts and reports are sent out to those entitled to receive them (CA 2006, s 423). This is defined as the 'period for appointing auditors'.

Section 485 of CA 2006 enables the directors to appoint auditors at any time before the company's first period for appointing auditors, at any time before the company's next period for appointing auditors where the company was previously exempt from audit, or to fill a casual vacancy in the office of auditor. The members are similarly empowered and may appoint auditors by ordinary resolution during a period for appointing auditors or to remedy the failure of the directors to appoint auditors during this period. For a private company, the term of office of an auditor takes effect immediately after any previous auditor ceases to hold office and continues until the end of the next period for appointing auditors unless re-appointed (CA 2006, s 487). If no auditor has been appointed at this point, any auditor in office immediately before that time is deemed to be re-appointed at that time. Such deemed appointment will not occur where the auditor was appointed by the directors or the directors or members have resolved that he should not be re-appointed, or the company's articles of association contain provisions requiring actual appointment. Additionally, members representing at least 5% (or a lower percentage if allowed by the company's articles) of the total voting rights of all members who would be entitled to vote on a resolution that the auditor should not be re-appointed, may prevent the deemed re-appointment by serving notice on the company (CA 2006, s 488). Such notice may be in hard copy or electronic form, must be authenticated by those giving it, and must be received by the company before the end of the accounting reference period immediately preceding the time when the deemed reappointment would have effect.

The Act places primary responsibility for appointing the auditors on the directors but also allows the members to appoint auditors during the 'period for appointing auditors' (where there is no irregularity) and in two instances where there has been a failure to appoint auditors. Such a failure is likely to arise where the directors have failed to appoint auditors or the members have not appointed auditors in circumstances where a deemed reappointment cannot occur (eg following an earlier appointment by the directors). In these circumstances, the members of a private company may remedy the failure using the special written resolution procedure in CA 2006, s 514 or in general meeting under CA 2006, s 515 if the matter is to be addressed in this way. Section 515 of CA 2006 requires the special notice procedure to be followed where the resolution is considered in general meeting, while section 514 indicates that use of the special notice is not applicable to this procedure.

Should the members fail to appoint or re-appoint auditors, the company must, within seven days, give notice of the fact to the Secretary of State who may exercise his power under CA 2006, ss 486 and 490 to appoint an auditor.

The provisions apply to the appointment as company auditor of a partnership constituted under the law of England and Wales or Northern Ireland, or under the law of any other country or territory in which a partnership is not a legal person (CA 2006, s 1216(1)). In Scotland, a partnership is a legal person and, thus, any change in the partners does not affect the appointment of the partnership.

The appointment is (unless a contrary intention appears) an appointment of the partnership as such and not of the partners (CA 2006, s 1216(2)). Where the partnership ceases, the appointment is to be treated as extending to:

(a)   any partnership which succeeds to the practice of that partnership and which is eligible for the appointment; and

(b)   any person who succeeds to that practice having previously carried it on in partnership and who is eligible for the appointment.

For this purpose, a partnership is to be regarded as succeeding to the practice of another partnership only if the members of the successor partnership are substantially the same as those of the former partnership; and a partnership or other person is to be regarded as succeeding to the practice of a partnership only if it or he succeeds to the whole or substantially the whole of the business of the former partnership (CA 2006, s 1216(4)).

Thus, in order for a partnership automatically to succeed to another partnership which has ceased, it is necessary for the partners of the successor partnership to consist 'substantially' of the same persons as the former partnership and for the whole or substantially the whole of the business of the former partnership to be taken by the new partnership. A partnership in England and Wales ceases where there is any change in the composition of the partnership, or on its dissolution.

Where the partnership ceases and no person succeeds to the appointment, the appointment may with the consent of a client company be treated as extending to a partnership or other person (that is, an individual or body corporate) eligible for the appointment, who succeeds to the business of the former partnership or to such part of it as it is agreed by the company shall be treated as comprising the appointment (CA 2006, s 1216(5)).

Eligibility for appointment

[**4.42**] Under CA 2006, s 1212, a person is eligible for appointment as a company auditor only if he:

(a)   is a member of a recognised supervisory body (that is, recognised by the Secretary of State); and

(b)   is eligible for the appointment under the rules of that body.

By virtue of Schedule 10, Part 2 of CA 2006, a recognised supervisory body must have rules to the effect that a person is not eligible for appointment as a company auditor unless:

(i)   in the case of an individual (other than an EEA auditor), he holds an appropriate qualification, or in the case of an individual who is an EEA auditor:

    (A)   he holds an appropriate qualification;

    (B)   he has been authorised on or before 5 April 2008 to practise the profession of company auditor pursuant to the European Communities (Recognition of Professional Qualifications) (First General System) Regulations 2005 (SI 2005/18) and has fulfilled any requirements imposed pursuant to regulation 6 of those Regulations; or

    (C)   he has passed an aptitude test which tests the person's knowledge of subjects:

      (i)   that are covered by a recognised professional qualification;

      (ii)   that are not covered by the professional qualification already held by that person; and

      (iii)   the knowledge of which is essential for the pursuit of the profession of statutory auditor; and

may test the person's knowledge of rules of professional conduct but must not test their knowledge of any other matters.

(ii)   in the case of a firm:

      (A)   the individuals responsible for statutory audit work on behalf of the firm are eligible for appointment as a statutory auditor hold an 'appropriate qualification'; and

      (B)   the firm is controlled by 'qualified persons'.

A 'qualified person' is deemed under Schedule 10 to be a person who:

(I)   in the case of an individual, holds an appropriate qualification or a corresponding qualification under the law of an EEA State (or part of an EEA State), other than the UK; and

(II)   in the case of a firm, is eligible for appointment as a statutory auditor or is eligible for a corresponding appointment under the law of an EEA State (or part of an EEA State), other than the UK. and:

      (a)   a majority of the members of the firm are qualified persons; and

      (b)   the firm's affairs are managed by a board of directors, committee or other management body, a majority of which are qualified persons, or where the body consists of only two individuals at least one of them is a qualified person.

The bodies of accountants which are designated as recognised supervisory bodies are:

(1)   Institute of Chartered Accountants in England and Wales (ICAEW);

(2)   Institute of Chartered Accountants of Scotland (ICAS);

(3)   Association of Chartered Certified Accountants (ACCA);

(4)   Institute of Chartered Accountants in Ireland (ICAI); and

(5)   Association of Authorised Public Accountants (AAPA).

A 'recognised supervisory body' is a body corporate or unincorporated association which is recognised by the Secretary of State, is established in the UK, and which maintains and enforces rules as to:

–   the eligibility of persons to seek appointment as company auditors; and

–   the conduct of statutory audit work;

which are binding on persons seeking appointment or acting as company auditors, either because they are members of that body or because they are otherwise subject to its control (CA 2006, s 1217).

Register of auditors

[4.43] Section 1239 of CA 2006 requires recognised supervisory bodies to keep and maintain a register of individuals and firms eligible for appointment as company auditor, and of individuals holding an appropriate qualification, who are responsible for statutory audit work on behalf of such firms (see **4.18** above).

Such registers must be maintained at the principal UK office of the relevant body and must be available for inspection by any person for at least two hours between 9 am and 5 pm on any business day. The recognised supervisory body must ensure that the entries in the register are arranged, for inspection purposes, alphabetically and by reference to recognised supervisory bodies. An obligation is imposed by statutory instrument upon all such bodies to co-operate with each other to ensure that each recognised supervisory body enters the required information on the register maintained by that body.

Such bodies are also required to provide to the public the names and addresses of the directors and members of the firm, where the firm is a body corporate, and of the partners, in the case of a partnership. This information must be available for inspection alphabetically and by reference to the firm.

In maintaining the register of auditors, each recognised supervisory body must exercise reasonable care to ensure the accuracy of the register and to ensure that all persons or firms named in the register are eligible for appointment as company auditor. Any amendments to entries in the register must be effected within ten business days of the body becoming aware of the relevant change.

Independence of auditors

[4.44] A person is ineligible for appointment as company auditor of a company if he is:

(a)   an officer or employee of the company; or

(b)   a partner or employee of such a person, or a partnership of which such a person is a partner;

or if he is ineligible, by virtue of the above, for appointment as company auditor of any associated undertaking of the company (CA 2006, s 1214(1)).

An 'officer' of a company includes a director, manager or company secretary (CA 2006, s 1173). Because an auditor is for some purposes regarded as an officer of the company, for the purpose of the foregoing, an auditor of a company is not to be regarded as an officer or employee of the company (CA 2006, s 1214(5)). It follows that an auditor cannot also be secretary of the same company.

A person is also ineligible for appointment as auditor of a company if there exists between:

(i)   him or any associate of his; and

(ii)   the company or any associated undertaking,

a connection of any such description as may be specified by regulations, in the form of a statutory instrument, made by the Secretary of State. The regulations may make different provisions for different cases (CA 2006, s 1214(4)).

Pursuant to CA 2006, s 1214(6), 'associated undertaking', in relation to a company, means:

(A)   a parent undertaking or subsidiary undertaking of the company (see **4.8** above); or

(B)   a subsidiary undertaking of any parent undertaking of the company.

'Associate' is defined as follows:

(I)   In relation to an individual 'associate' means:
      (1)   that individual's spouse, civil partner or minor child or stepchild;
      (2)   any body corporate of which that individual is a director; and
      (3)   any employee or partner of that individual.

(II)   In relation to a body corporate 'associate' means:
      (1)   any body corporate of which that body is a director;
      (2)   any body corporate in the same group as that body; and
      (3)   any employee or partner of that body or of any body corporate in the same group.

(III)   In relation to a Scottish partnership, or a partnership constituted under the law of any other country or territory in which a partnership is a legal person, 'associate' means:
      (1)   any body corporate of which the partnership is a director;
      (2)   any employee of or partner in the partnership; and
      (3)   any person who is an associate of a partner in the partnership.

(IV)   In relation to a partnership constituted under the law of England and Wales or Northern Ireland, or the law of any other country or territory in which a partnership is not a legal person, 'associate' means any person who is an associate of any of the partners.

(CA 2006, s 1260.)

Acting when disqualified

[4.45] A person may not act as statutory auditor if he is ineligible for appointment to that office (CA 2006, s 1213). If during his term of office a company auditor becomes ineligible for appointment to the office, he must thereupon vacate office and must forthwith give notice in writing to the company concerned that he has vacated it by reason of ineligibility (CA 2006, s 1213(2)). An auditor is also required to resign by reason of lack of independence (CA 2006, s 1215).

Contravention of these provisions carries a penalty (CA 2006, s 1215(3) and (6)), but it is a defence for a person to show that he did not know and had no reason to believe that he was, or had become, ineligible for appointment (CA 2006, s 1215(7)). The onus of proof is thus on the defendant.

Vacation of office through ineligibility requires a statement of any circumstances which the outgoing auditor considers should be brought to the attention of members or creditors of the company (see **4.47** below).

Power of Secretary of State to require second audit

[4.46] Where a person appointed auditor of a company was, for any part of the period during which the audit was conducted, ineligible for appointment as auditor of the company, the Secretary of State may require the company to engage the services of someone who is eligible for that appointment. The company has 21 days in which to comply with the direction (CA 2006, 1248).

Pursuant to CA 2006, s 1248(1) the person engaged must either:

(a)   audit the relevant accounts again; or
(b)   review the first audit and report (giving his reasons) whether a second audit is needed.

Removal and resignation

[4.47] Section 510 of CA 2006 allows for the removal from office of an auditor before the expiry of his term of appointment by the passing of an ordinary resolution by the company in general meeting (see PRECEDENT C, APPENDIX 4A). However, special notice (see **7.40** MEMBERSHIP) must be given to the company (see PRECEDENT D, APPENDIX 4A), and the company must notify its members whenever a resolution is to be proposed at a general meeting, for the appointment of an auditor who was not the previously appointed auditor of the company or for the removal of an auditor before the expiry of his term of office.

Special notice is required to be given of the proposal of such a resolution (CA 2006, s 511) and notification must be given to Companies House in the prescribed form within 14 days of the passing of the resolution (CA 2006, s 512). In practice, this procedure is rarely used as the directors of a company seeking to change its auditors will often request the auditors to resign voluntarily. The directors will then exercise their power to appoint new auditors to fill the resulting casual vacancy.

Under CA 2006, s 516, whenever an auditor ceases to hold office, *for whatever reason*, he is required to deposit at the registered office of the company a statement that there are no circumstances connected with his ceasing to hold office which he considers should be brought to the notice of members or creditors of the company, or otherwise disclose any such circumstances. Where the auditor discloses any circumstances a copy of the statement must be filed with the Registrar of Companies within 28 days. The auditor of a quoted company is required to deposit a statement of circumstances connected with his ceasing to hold office in all cases.

Where an auditor resigns his office, the company must within 14 days of receipt of the auditor's notice of resignation file a copy with Companies House (CA 2006, s 517(1)). Should the auditor's notice contain a statement of circumstances connected with his resignation, the company must also (unless the court holds it to be defamatory) send a copy to every person entitled to receive a copy of the accounts.

Section 518 of CA 2006 allows an auditor, who has included in the notice of his resignation a statement of the circumstances connected with it, the following discretionary rights:

(a)   to circulate to members a statement, of reasonable length, of the reasons for his resignation (unless, upon application to the court, it is held to be defamatory);

(b)   to requisition a general meeting, at which he may explain the reasons for his resignation; and

(c)   to attend and speak at the general meeting at which his resignation or the appointment of his successor is to be considered.

Under CA 2006, s 522, an auditor ceasing to hold office is required to notify the appropriate audit authority (eg ICAEW) when, in the case of a major audit, he ceases to hold office for any reason, or where it is a not a major audit, the auditor ceases to hold office before the end of his term of office. The notice must be accompanied by a copy of the statement of circumstances deposited by the auditor at the company's registered office.

Meetings and resolutions

[4.48] A company's auditors are entitled to receive all notices of, and other communications relating to, any general meeting which a member of the company is entitled to receive, to attend any general meeting of the company and to be heard at any general meeting which they attend on any part of the business of the meeting which concerns them as auditors (CA 2006, s 502). The auditors of a private company are entitled to receive a copy of the resolution and all such communications relating to that resolution as are supplied to a member for signature (CA 2006, s 502(1)).

Auditors' report

[4.49] The auditors are required to report to the company's members on all accounts of the company, copies of which are to be laid before the company in general meeting, or sent to the members of a private company, during their tenure of office (CA 2006, s 495(1)) (see **4.29** above).

The auditors' report is required to state:

(a)   whether, in the opinion of the auditors, the annual accounts have been properly prepared in accordance with the Companies Act 2006; and, in particular,

(b)   whether a 'true and fair view' is given (see **4.7** above):

    (i)   in the case of an individual balance sheet, of the state of affairs of the company as at the end of the financial year;

    (ii)   in the case of an individual profit and loss account (see below), of the profit or loss of the company for the financial year; and

    (iii) in the case of group accounts, of the state of affairs as at the end of the financial year, and the profit or loss for the financial year, of the undertakings included in the consolidation as a whole, so far as concerns members of the company.

The Statement of Auditing Standards, 'Auditors' Report on Financial Statements', requires auditors to report on their audit responsibilities as well as those of the directors and to provide a full description of their audit opinion (see **4.29** above).

The annual accounts are defined as the company's individual accounts and, where applicable, its group accounts (CA 2006, s 474(1)). The auditor is not required to report on a company's individual profit and loss account where the company is required to prepare, and does prepare, group accounts (CA 2006, s 408(3)).

Under CA 2006, s 505(1), the auditors' report must state the names of the auditors and be signed by them.

Every copy of the auditors' report which is laid before the company in general meeting, or which is otherwise circulated, published or issued, must state the names of the auditors (CA 2006, s 505(1)). The 'names of the auditors' refer to the name under which a partnership or body corporate practises, as well as the name of the person who signed it as the senior statutory auditor, and, in the case where an individual is the auditor, the individual's name must be referred to (CA 2006, s 505(1)).

The copy of the auditors' report which is delivered to the Registrar of Companies must state the names of the auditors and be signed by them (CA 2006, s 444(7)). The company and its officers (which could include the auditor) are exposed to penalties for non-compliance with the foregoing.

Consistency of directors' report with accounts

[4.50] Pursuant to CA 2006, s 498(1), in preparing their report, the auditors must carry out such investigations as will enable them to form an opinion as to:

(a)   whether proper accounting records have been kept by the company and proper returns adequate for their audit have been received from branches not visited by them;

(b)   whether the company's individual accounts are in agreement with the accounting records returns; and

(c)   in the case of a quoted company, whether the auditable part of the company's directors' remuneration report is in agreement with the accounting records returns.

If the auditors form a negative opinion in relation to any of these matters, they must state that fact in their report (CA 2006, s 498(2)).

Information and explanations not received

[4.51] If the auditors fail to obtain all the information and explanations which, to the best of their knowledge and belief, are necessary for the purposes of their audit, they must state that fact in their report (CA 2006, s 498(3)).

SAS 120 – Consideration of law and regulations, requires the auditors to obtain written confirmation from the directors on non-compliance with relevant law and regulations; this may be by way of board resolution passed at the same time as the accounts are approved by the directors. The auditors should ensure that the directors giving the representation have taken appropriate steps to inform themselves by making the necessary enquiries.

Remuneration of directors and transactions with directors and officers

[4.52] If the requirements of the Companies Act 2006 relating to the disclosure of directors' remuneration and the disclosure of particulars of transactions with directors and officers are not complied with in the accounts, the auditors are required to include in their report, so far as they are reasonably able to do so, a statement giving the required particulars (CA 2006, s 498(4)).

Auditors' rights to information

[4.53] The auditors of a company have right of access at all times to the company's books, accounts and vouchers, and are entitled to require from the company's officers such information and explanations as they think necessary for the performance of their duties as auditors (CA 2006, s 499(1)).

It is an offence, punishable by imprisonment or a fine (or both), if an officer of a company knowingly or recklessly makes to the company's auditors a statement (whether orally or in writing) which conveys or purports to convey any information or explanations which the auditors require, or are entitled to require, as auditors of the company, and which is misleading, false or deceptive in a material particular (CA 2006, s 501).

Remuneration of auditors

[4.54] The remuneration (including expenses) of auditors appointed by the company in general meeting must be fixed by the company in general meeting, or in such manner as the company in general meeting may determine (CA 2006, s 492). In practice, the shareholders in general meeting give authority to the directors to fix the remuneration of the auditors.

Where the auditor is appointed by the directors (for example, as first auditor or to fill a casual vacancy) or by the Secretary of State, the remuneration (including expenses) of the auditors may be fixed by the directors or by the Secretary of State, as the case may be. The amount of the remuneration (including expenses) of the company's auditors in their capacity as such must be stated in a note to the company's annual accounts (CA 2006, s 494).

The amount for remuneration is to include the estimated money value of benefits in kind. The nature of any such benefit must also be disclosed.

The Companies (Disclosure of Auditor Remuneration and Liability Limitation Agreements) Regulations 2008 (SI 2008/489) apply for financial years beginning on or after 6 April 2008 and require companies to disclose the fees receivable by their auditors and their auditors' associates by a note in the company's annual accounts. Small and medium-sized companies must disclose the fee paid to their auditors for the audit itself, while the Secretary of State (or any body to whom the Secretary of State's functions are delegated) may require the auditors of a medium-sized company to give him limited information about other fees paid to them unless the company voluntarily discloses that information. Every other company must disclose both the audit fee and all other fees paid to the auditors for services (as set out in the regulations) provided by them and their associates to the company, its subsidiaries (except where its control over a subsidiary is subject to severe long-term restrictions) and associated pension schemes. Auditors are required to provide this information to the company's directors to enable them to make the necessary disclosures in the accounts.

Remuneration for non-audit work

[4.55] Under CA 2006, s 494, the Secretary of State for Business, Innovation and Skills has the power to require the disclosure of the amount of any remuneration received by a company's auditors or their associates in respect of services other than those as auditor of the company. Regulations requiring such disclosure are set out in the Companies (Disclosure of Auditor Remuneration and Liability Limitation Agreements) Regulations 2008 (SI 2008/489) for financial years beginning on or after 6 April 2008.

The regulations require disclosure of the total remuneration paid to the company's auditors or their associates during the financial year in question in respect of non-audit services provided to the company, its subsidiaries and associated pension schemes. Such disclosure is to be made in the notes to the annual accounts of a company. The regulations define sums paid in respect of expenses as forming part of the auditors' remuneration and apply in relation to benefits in kind as to payments in money, (and for any such benefit requires disclosure of its nature and its estimated money value) as well as the types of services provided to the company.

The definition of an 'associate' is widely drafted and an associate of a company's auditors in the relevant financial year, at any time in the financial year, will depend upon the form in which the auditors exist, and is:

(a) where the company's auditor is an individual:
  (i) any person controlled by the company's auditors or by any associate of the company's auditors (whether alone or through two or more persons acting together to secure or exercise control), but only if that control does not arise solely by virtue of the company's auditors or any associate of the company's auditors acting:
    • as an insolvency practitioner in relation to any person;
    • in the capacity of a receiver, or a receiver or manager, of the property of a company or other body corporate; or
    • as a judicial factor on the estate of any person;
  (ii) any person who, or group of persons acting together which, has control of the company's auditors;
  (iii) any person using a trading name which is the same as or similar to a trading name used by the company's auditors, but only if the company's auditors use that trading name with the intention of creating the impression of a connection between them and that other person; and

(iv) any person who is party to an arrangement with the company's auditors, with or without any other person, under which costs, profits, quality control, business strategy or significant professional resources are shared.

(b) where the company's auditors are a partnership:

(i) any other partnership which had a partner in common with the company's auditors;

(ii) any partner in the company's auditors;

(iii) any body corporate which is in the same group as a body corporate which is a partner in the company's auditors or in a partnership which has a partner in common with the company's auditors; and whether

(iv) any body corporate of which a partner in the company's auditors is a director.

(c) where the company's auditors are a body corporate:

(i) any other body corporate which has a director in common with the company's auditors;

(ii) any director of the company's auditors;

(iii) any body corporate which is in the same group as a body corporate which is a director of, or has a director in common with, the company's auditors;

(iv) any partnership in which the auditors were a partner;

(v) any partnership in which a director of the company's auditors is a partner;

(vi) any body corporate which is in the same group as the company's auditors;

(vii) any partnership in which any such body corporate which is in the same group as the company's auditors is a partner.

The auditors of a company are under an obligation to provide the directors of the company with any information necessary to identify the auditors' associates for the purposes of disclosure in the accounts of the company.

The FRC's 'Guidance on Audit Committees' and the UK Corporate Governance Code require the audit committees of listed companies to approve the purchase of non-audit services from the company's auditors and to justify this to shareholders. Changes to the rules governing non-audit services that apply from 30 April 2011 require enhanced disclosure in the annual report of a listed company to more fully explain the application by the audit committee of the company's policy on non-audit services.

Liability of auditors

[4.56] Section 532 of CA 2006 makes void any provision exempting an auditor from liability or indemnity, except where the auditor is successful in defending the proceedings brought against him. Under section 532, a limitation agreement must not apply in respect of acts or omissions occurring in the course of the audit of accounts for more than one financial year and must specify the financial year to which it relates. The Companies (Disclosure of Auditor Remuneration and Liability Limitation Agreements) Regulations 2008 (SI 2008/489) requires companies to disclose any liability limitation agreements they make with their auditors by a note in the company's annual accounts. The company must disclose the principal terms of such an agreement and the date the resolution approving the agreement was passed (or for a private company the date of the resolution waiving the need for approval).

Appendix 4A

Precedents

A. Resolution for Appointment of First Auditors

'That [name of individual auditors or partnership] be and are hereby appointed auditors of the company to hold office until the conclusion of the first general meeting at which accounts are laid before the company.'

B. Resolution for Re-appointment of Auditors

'That [name of individual auditors or partnership] be and are hereby re-appointed auditors of the company to hold office until the conclusion of the next general meeting at which accounts are laid before the company and that the Directors be and are hereby authorised to fix their remuneration.'

C. Resolution for Removal of Auditors

'That [existing auditors' name] be and are hereby removed as auditors of the company with immediate effect and that [new auditors' name] be and are hereby appointed as auditors of the company in their stead to hold office until the conclusion of the next general meeting at which accounts are laid before the company and that the Directors be and are hereby authorised to fix their remuneration.'

D. Special Notice for the Removal of Auditors

'The Directors
[
                        ]
Limited

Dear Sirs

I hereby give notice pursuant to Section 312 and Section 511 of the Companies Act 2006 of my intention to propose the following ordinary resolution at the next Annual General Meeting of the Company.

RESOLUTION

That [existing auditors' name] be and are hereby removed from office as auditors of the company [and that [new auditors' name] be appointed as auditors of the company in their place to hold office until the conclusion of the next General Meeting at which Accounts are laid before the company at a remuneration to be fixed by the Directors].

Dated this day of [   ]

. . . . ,

Chapter 5

Disclosure and Reporting Requirements

Disclosure and Companies House

General

[5.1] An essential element of the incorporation process and the subsequent operation of a limited liability company is that of the disclosure of information about it. The principle behind this is that, in dealing with a company which has been granted limited liability status, the public must be able to make an assessment of the company and of any risks attendant in dealing with it.

The legislation which sets down the majority of disclosure requirements for limited liability companies is now the Companies Act 2006 (CA 2006) which amends and consolidates previous companies legislation. The CA 2006 has replaced much of the earlier legislation, with the provisions of the new Act relating to the functions of the Registrar of Companies and the disclosures to be made by companies fully implemented with the remaining provisions having come into force with effect from 1 October 2009.

The disclosure requirements of the Act are basically twofold. Firstly, a company is required to place certain information about itself (broadly relating to its management, capital structure and activities), on a public file maintained at Companies House and secondly, it is also required to make certain disclosures in statutory registers which it must maintain itself (see CHAPTER 3 THE STATUTORY RECORDS).

Companies House is an Executive Agency of the Department for Business, Innovation and Skills, commonly referred to as 'BIS', for whom it performs two basic roles:

(a) the incorporation, re-registration and striking off of companies and the registration of documents required to be filed under companies, insolvency and related legislation; and

(b) the provision to the public of information about these companies, for which Companies House enforces compliance with statutory requirements.

Companies House also provides assistance and information to those involved in the administration of companies and has produced a series of publications in this connection (see APPENDIX 5A).

The main office of Companies House is located in Cardiff where the Registrar of Companies for England and Wales is based, while a separate Registrar of Companies is based in offices in Edinburgh to administer companies incorporated in Scotland. The remaining office outside of Wales and Scotland is the Companies House Information Centre based in London. The addresses of these offices and the services provided at each of them can be found in **APPENDIX 5B**.

Information about companies on the public register is available either electronically or in paper form. Document images and information are extensively available through Companies House Direct (or commercial providers that draw down information from Companies House), as all documents registered since 1995 have been placed onto an on-line system. The Companies House website offers a large degree of information (both free and paid for) on companies on the public register.

Membership of the European Business Register (EBR) as an information provider enables Companies House to provide basic company information via the EBR database. The benefit of this is that company information is more accessible across Europe and the format of the information allows easy comparison of companies incorporated in countries which have signed up to EBR.

Companies Act compliance and enforcement

[5.2] The Companies Act requires each company registered under the Companies Acts to disclose certain specified information about itself. These requirements can be split into two broad categories being:

(a) annual filing requirements (see **5.6** below); and
(b) transactional or event-driven filing requirements (see **5.10** and **APPENDIX 5C** below).

Companies House continues to devote considerable efforts to ensuring that companies fulfil their annual filing and this has resulted in an increase of companies being compliant. Companies House has generally achieved a high rate of compliance with in excess of 90% of companies in England and Wales submitting their accounts and annual returns. Companies House continues to maintain a high level of compliance with both accounts and annual returns.

To ensure companies comply with their disclosure requirements, Companies House has considerable powers under the Act, reinforced by the statutory authority given in Part 35 of the Companies Act 2006 for the Registrar of Companies to establish rules and powers in relation to:

(a) the form, manner of delivery and authentication of documents;
(b) entering into agreements with companies for filing of certain documents by electronic means only (the PROOF scheme);
(c) amending or annotating the register in specified circumstances; and
(d) setting fees for the performance of any of the Registrar's functions.

The main sanctions available to Companies House are as follows.

(i) *Default order*
     Under the provisions of CA 2006, ss 1113 and 452, the Registrar of Companies may, after service of notice on the company where the default continues for more than 14 days from the date of the notice, apply to the court for an order requiring the officers of a company to deliver a specified document within a given time.

(ii) *Penalties*

(A) *Criminal penalties*

The Registrar of Companies may proceed through the courts to prosecute any company officers who have failed to file at Companies House any documents which they are obliged to file under the Act. Successful prosecutions result in the officers concerned receiving a criminal record and render them liable to a fine as specified under the relevant section of CA 2006.

The statutory maximum prescribed under section 32 of the Magistrates' Courts Act 1980 is currently £5,000 by virtue of the Criminal Justice Act 1991 (Commencement No 3) Order 1992 (SI 1992/333) which brought into force section 17 of the Criminal Justice Act 1991. In addition, various offences in CA 2006 refer to the standard scale which under the Criminal Justice Act 1991, s 17 is as follows:

Level on the Scale	Amount of Fine
1	£200
2	£500
3	£1,000
4	£2,500
5	£5,000

A maximum fine of £5,000 per offence exists for failing to deliver, in the specified time, an annual return or the annual financial statements. After conviction, continued default in the delivery of the above overdue documents can result in additional fines of up to £500 per day from the date of default being imposed.

(B) *Civil penalties*

The Registrar of Companies is empowered under CA 2006, s 453 to impose upon a company a civil penalty without recourse to the court for its failure to file the annual financial statements within the required period. The penalties set out in the Companies (Late Filing Penalties and Limited Liability Partnerships (Filing Periods and Late Filing Penalties) Regulations 2008 (SI 2008/497) apply with effect from 1 February 2009 in relation to accounts filed under the previous Act (Companies Act 1985), while the penalty imposed on a company will be doubled in relation to any accounts filed under the Companies Act 2006 where the company filed its accounts late in the previous year. The level of penalties applicable to public and private companies are as indicated below.

Length of Period	Public Company	Private Company
Not more than 1 month	£750	£150
1 to 3 months	£1,500	£375
3 to 6 months	£3,000	£750

Length of Period	Public Company	Private Company
More than 6 months	£7,500	£1,500

Such penalties can be enforced from the first day of default and are calculated by reference to the length of default. These penalties are strictly enforced and no mitigating circumstances, such as the size of the company or the nature of its business, will be taken into account.

Upon receipt of the accounts by Companies House, a notice will be issued to the company at its registered office, followed by a final notice two weeks later. Any penalties still outstanding after 30 days from the date of notification of the amount due will be referred to the Lewis Group, the debt collection agency appointed by Companies House, who will pursue such debts in the courts if necessary.

The collection agents have applied a range of measures to ensure the effectiveness of their collection procedures. These include garnishee orders, oral examinations and for persistent late filing the prosecution of individual directors. Under a garnishee order, the court will be asked to grant an order requiring the company's bank to pay the penalty and any associated legal costs from the company's bank account. An oral examination will involve a director of the company attending court to undergo a strict examination of the assets, liabilities and means of the company.

(iii) *Disqualification*

Under the provisions of section 3 of the Company Directors Disqualification Act 1986, a director who has been prosecuted and convicted three or more times in a five-year period for a failure to deliver documents to Companies House may be disqualified by the court from being a director or taking part in the management of a company for up to five years.

Similarly, the court may also make a disqualification order against any director who has received three or more default orders under the provisions of CA 2006, ss 452 and 1113, in the last five years.

(iv) *Dissolution*

Where the Registrar of Companies believes that a company is no longer in business or in operation, the Registrar is empowered under CA 2006, 1000 to remove a company from the Register of Companies. This has the effect of deregistering the company and thus depriving it of its legal status. Reinstatement of a company in such circumstances can be both costly and time-consuming. However, without reinstatement any property or rights held by the company prior to its dissolution become bona vacantia and pass to the Crown. Application for reinstatement may be made by either the company, a director or member at any time up to six years from the date of dissolution. (See **9.15–9.32 BORROWING AND SECURITY**.)

A company's failure to file annual returns, accounts, or to respond to any communication from Companies House, will commonly result in the company being struck off.

Thus, it can be seen that Companies House has considerable powers to enforce the disclosure requirements of CA 2006.

Registrar's rules and powers

[5.3] Some issues previously covered by secondary legislation will in future be set out in 'rules' made by the Registrar of Companies, with the aim of providing more flexibility and a less administratively complex procedure for making future changes. The extent of the Registrar's powers specified in its rules and in CA 2006 are set out below.

(1) **Delivery of information**

Companies must deliver to the Registrar, either electronically or in paper format, documents which meet the Registrar's requirements as to the format of the document, and the way in which it is delivered and signed, as well as any other requirements set out in CA 2006. Companies House will now accept documents at any of its offices, regardless of where the company is registered. For the purpose of proper delivery, such documents must comply with the requirements of CA 2006, s 1072 and, in particular:

(a) meet all requirements of CA 2006 and/or the Registrar's rules in respect of:

(i) the content of the document;

(ii) its form, authentication (ie it has been signed or electronically authenticated) and manner of delivery, while also ensuring that it is capable of being scanned or copied;

(iii) inclusion of the company name and number; and

(iv) delivery of the document, such as being sent electronically where the company has agreed with the Registrar to use this as the only method of delivery for specified documents;

(b) comply with legislative and/or the Registrar's requirements in relation to:

(i) presentation of such documents either in English or along with a certified translation of that document if it is not in English;

(ii) the use of permitted characters, letters and symbols in names and addresses; and

(iii) certification or verification of the document as an accurate or correct copy or translation; and

(c) be accompanied by the correct fee (where required).

On receipt of the correct form, the Registrar may remove the original document from the register of companies, unless he is of the view that it serves the public interest better to retain the document on the register. The Registrar will reject any document which has not been properly delivered but may accept and register a document where it is not apparent from the document that something is missing or incorrect. In these circumstances, the obligation to file the document continues and any liabilities that arise from not doing so will still apply. Where the company is required to remedy the filing, the Registrar will issue a notice to this effect, and the company will be required to file the correct document along with a form RP01 within 14 days of the notice.

(2) **Amendment of the public register**

(a) *Unnecessary material (CA 2006, s 1074)*

Where a company delivers material that is neither necessary to fulfil a statutory obligation nor specifically authorised to be delivered (for example, a detailed profit and loss account attached to the statutory accounts), the Registrar may remove such unnecessary material prior to registration of the document. However, this assumes that the Registrar has identified that such material forms part of the document submitted for registration and that it is easily removable from the document in question. Alternatively, the Registrar will normally reject the document if he cannot easily remove such unnecessary material.

(b) *Informal correction of documents (CA 2006, s 1075)*

The Registrar is authorised to informally correct a document before accepting it for registration, where it is:

(i) incomplete, for instance, the particulars of a mortgage or charge on a form MG01 do not reflect the details in the deed itself; or

(ii) internally inconsistent, in that information contained within the document is not consistent.

The Registrar may ask the person who is authorised to correct it to provide appropriate instructions to correct the document, following which the Registrar may correct the document and treat it as properly delivered. However, he will only exercise this power in relation to the registration of charges, in view of the significant consequences for a company, particularly in the event of a subsequent liquidation, and the statutory time constraints for the delivery of charges for registration.

(c) *Annotation of the register (CA 2006, s 1081)*

The Registrar is empowered to annotate the register of companies to enable anyone searching the register to more easily understand the information on the register about a particular company. When exercising his powers under this section, the Registrar must annotate the register to record:

(i) the date an original document was delivered;

(ii) the nature and date of a correction if he has informally corrected a document under CA 2006, s 1075;

(iii) the date of the replacement of a document and the fact that it has been replaced; and

(iv) the date and under what power he removed any material, and a description of the material.

The Registrar may also annotate the register if he considers that information on it is misleading or confusing, or remove an annotation if it no longer serves a useful purpose.

(d) *Inconsistency on the register (CA 2006, s 1093)*

The Registrar must accept for registration any document he considers contains information that appears to be inconsistent with other information on the register of companies, such as the inclusion of a director on an annual return whose appointment has not been previously notified.

However, the Registrar can subsequently take steps to resolve the inconsistency by requiring the company to file replacement or additional documents to correct it, failing which the Registrar is empowered to issue a formal notice of inconsistency that:

(i)   states how the information contained in the document appears to be inconsistent with other information on the register; and

(ii)   requires the company to deliver the required replacement or additional documents within 14 days of the issue of a notice.

Failure to comply with the notice of inconsistency will render the company and every officer of it who is in default guilty of an offence and liable, on summary conviction, to a fine.

(e)   *Second filing*

Companies House now allows companies and LLPs to resubmit previously registered forms to more easily correct inaccuracies such as an incorrect date of birth. The new procedure (known as 'Second Filing') is currently restricted to the most commonly used company and LLP forms, with a view to broadening its application at an unspecified time in the future. At present, this procedure will apply to the following form types submitted under CA 2006:

(i)   forms for the appointment or termination of a director or secretary (or a member in the case of an LLP), or any change in their details (eg forms AP01, TM01 and CH01);

(ii)   return of allotment of shares (form SH01) in the case of a company; and

(iii)   annual returns for a company or an LLP (ie forms AR01 and LL AR01).

There is no fee payable for a second filing. A second filing will be rejected by Companies House if the original form had not been properly delivered and registered.

(3)   **Removal of material from the register**

(a)   *Administrative removal (CA 2006, s 1094)*

The Registrar is empowered to administratively remove from the register of companies any material that is:

(i)   unnecessary (ie any material sent in error to the Registrar that is not required to fulfil a statutory obligation and is not specifically authorised to be delivered to him); and

(ii)   derived from a document that has been replaced because it was not properly delivered or was replaced following the issue of an inconsistency notice.

However, the Registrar cannot remove from the register anything he was required to accept, nor material the registration of which has had legal consequences in relation to matters, such as:

(i)   a company's formation, change of name or re-registration;

(ii)   a reduction of capital;

(iii)   a change of registered office;

(iv)   registration of a charge; and

(v)   dissolution of the company.

The Registrar is also not permitted to administratively remove from the register a person's registered service address (CA 2006, s 1140).

Unless the removal has been requested by the company in question, the Registrar must notify the person who delivered the material or the company to which it relates of what material is to be, or has been, removed and on what grounds.

(b)   *Rectification by the Registrar (CA 2006, s 1095)*

The Registrar is permitted to remove specified material from the register of companies, as set out in the Registrar of Companies and Applications for Striking Off Regulations 2009 (SI 2009/1803), that:

(i)   derives from anything invalid or ineffective, or was done without the authority of the company; or

(ii)   is factually inaccurate or is derived from something that is factually inaccurate or forged.

The Registrar is therefore allowed to remove material relating to company hijacks or false filings where the matter is straightforward and uncontested, and consequently this now avoids the need to obtain a court order to achieve this. These powers also allow the Registrar to remove certain documents or information derived from them which contain factual inaccuracies such as an incorrect date of birth for a director.

The company may apply for rectification of the register using form RP02a for rectification of notices dealing with a proposed director or secretary on incorporation, or the subsequent appointment, change of details or termination of a director or secretary, and a form RP02b where rectification relates to a change of the company's registered office.

On receipt of an application, the Registrar will give notice in writing to all directors and secretaries of the company known to the Registrar at the time of the application, the company's registered office, the presenter of the document (if known), and any other person to whom the material relates, of his intention to remove the material set out in form RP02a or RP02b unless he receives an objection within 28 days of the date of the issue of the notice.

A valid objection will prevent the Registrar from rectifying the register in this manner, in which case he will inform the company and all other persons he had previously notified that the rectification has stopped. The company may consider reapplying to the Registrar or seeking rectification through the courts under CA 2006, s 1096. If no objections are received, the Registrar will remove the material and annotate the register accordingly.

(c)   *Rectification under court order (CA 2006, ss 1096 and 1097)*

The Registrar must remove from the register of companies any material:

(i) that derives from anything that the court has declared to be invalid or ineffective, or to have been done without the authority of the company; or

(ii) that a court declares to be factually inaccurate, or to be derived from something factually inaccurate, or forged; and

(iii) that the court directs to be removed from the register.

However the court cannot use this power to rectify where the court has other specific powers to deal with the matter, such as in relation to the revision of defective accounts (CA 2006, Part 15) or the rectification of the register of charges (CA 2006, ss 873 and 888).

The court order must specify what the Registrar must remove from the register and indicate where on the register it is. The court must not order the removal of material the registration of which had legal consequences for the company, unless it is satisfied that:

(A) the presence of the material has caused, or may cause, damage to the company; and

(B) the company's interest in removing the material outweighs the interest of any other person in the material continuing to appear on the register.

If the court is so satisfied, it may also direct that the Registrar:

(I) must remove any note on the register which relates to the material which is the subject of the order;

(II) shall not make available for public inspection the order itself;

(III) shall make no note on the register as a result of the order, or restrict any such note to the matters specified by the court.

The court can also direct the removal of a person's registered service address (CA 2006, s 1140).

(4) **Other powers of the Registrar**

(a) *Delivery by electronic means (section 1070)*

A company can enter into an agreement with the Registrar to file certain specified documents by electronic means only using PROOF ('PROtected On line Filing'). In these circumstances, the Registrar will not accept any documents delivered in paper form other than as agreed between the company and the Registrar. This provides a measure of protection for companies seeking to minimise the risk of being hijacked or other false filings.

(b) *Retention of documents (section 1083)*

The Registrar must normally retain original paper documents for companies for three years, after which he can destroy them provided that he has recorded the information contained in them. This requirement is fulfilled by the Registrar keeping an electronic image of all documents delivered to him. For documents filed electronically, the Registrar is not required to keep the original document but must ensure that the information given in that document is recorded in the register. The Registrar may direct that the records for a company that has been dissolved for two years are removed to the relevant Public Record Office (for England and Wales and Northern Ireland) or to the National Archives (for Scotland).

(c)   *Voluntary filing of translations (section 1106)*
A company may deliver to the Registrar a voluntary translation of documents that are subject to the 'Directive disclosure requirements', whether these documents have been previously filed or are being delivered to the Registrar for filing. The documents subject to these requirements are set out in CA 2006, s 1078 and comprise documents falling into the following categories:

(i)   for every company:
   (a)   constitutional documents;
   (b)   directors;
   (c)   accounts, reports and returns;
   (d)   registered office; and
   (e)   winding up;

(ii)   for public companies:
   (a)   share capital; and
   (b)   mergers and divisions.

The translation must be accompanied by form VT01 and can only be filed in paper format.

(d)   *Transliteration of names and addresses*
Names and addresses in documents delivered to the Registrar must only consist of the permitted characters and symbols as set out in the Registrar of Companies and Applications for Striking-Off Regulations 2009 (SI 2009/1803). However, there are exceptions to this and 'non-permitted' characters and symbols may be used in a number of instances, such as in relation to:

(i)   a memorandum of association;
(ii)   a company's articles;
(iii)   a court order;
(iv)   an agreement affecting a company's constitution (Chapter 3, Part 3 of CA 2006);
(v)   a valuation report (CA 2006, s 94(2)(d));
(vi)   a document delivered in respect of a company included in the accounts of a larger group required to deliver group accounts (CA 2006, ss 400(2)(e) and 401(2)(f)); and
(vii)   a charge instrument or copy charge instrument (CA 2006, Pt 25).

(e)   *Certification of documents*
Where a document delivered to the Registrar has to be certified as an accurate translation, or as a correct copy, the existing rules as to who is able to certify such documents will apply in relation to documents where the obligation to deliver arose before 1 October 2009. The new rules will apply where the obligation to deliver the document arises on or after 1 October 2009.

(f)   *Quality of documents*

As Companies House scans documents and forms delivered to the Registrar to produce an electronic image for online access, it is important not only that the original is legible, but that it can also produce a clear copy. Documents filed electronically must comply with the specifications set out by the Registrar in his rules on electronic filing.

Generally, every paper document sent to Companies House must state in a prominent position the registered name and number of the company. Paper documents should be on A4 size, plain white paper with a matt finish, while the text should be black, clear, legible and of uniform density. Letters and numbers must be clear and legible so that an acceptable copy of the document can be made.

Other powers of Companies House

[5.4] Companies House also has powers in other areas.

(a)   *Company names*
The Registrar of Companies has considerable powers to either reject an application made for the incorporation of a company under a particular name or to force a company to change its name in certain circumstances. In this regard, WebCHeck (see (c) below) has been enhanced to incorporate all the necessary search features for finding company names that would be considered the 'same as' under the Company and Business Names (Miscellaneous Provisions) Regulations 2009 (SI 2009/1085), as opposed to applying a strict alphabetical search which did not always identify a name that was the 'same as' an existing name. The Registrar's powers in this connection are discussed in **2.10** and **2.12** THE COMPANY CONSTITUTION.

(b)   *Fees*
The Act also grants the Registrar of Companies the power to levy statutory charges upon companies in certain circumstances. The fees currently applicable are those specified in the Companies (Fees) (Companies, Overseas Companies and Limited Liability Partnerships) Regulations 2009 (SI 2009/2101). While fees will continue to be set by regulations, the Registrar will in future be able to set fees for services not covered by the regulations. The circumstances and the fees payable are as follows.

UK companies	*Charge*	*Same day charge*
Electronic incorporation of a company	£14.00	£30.00
Paper incorporation of a company	£40.00	£100.00
Re-registration of a private company as a public company	£20.00	£50.00
Re-registration of a public company as a private company	£20.00	£50.00

Re-registration of a limited company as unlimited	£20.00	£50.00
Re-registration of an unlimited company as limited	£20.00	£50.00
Electronic registration of a company's change of name	£8.00	£30.00
Paper registration of a company's change of name	£10.00	£50.00
Registration of an annual return using electronic communications	£14.00	–
Registration of an annual return not using electronic communications	£40.00	–
Reduction in share capital by solvency statement	£10.00	£50.00
Voluntary striking off	£10.00	–
Administrative restoration	£100.00	–

Overseas companies	Charge	Same day charge
Registration of a UK establishment of an overseas company	£20.00	£100.00
Registration of a name under which an overseas company proposes to carry on business in Great Britain	£10.00	£50.00
Re-registration of a name under which an overseas company proposes to carry on business in Great Britain	£10.00	£50.00
Registration of the annual accounts of an overseas company	£20.00	–

The Limited Liability Partnerships Act 2000 introduced the concept of a limited liability partnership as an alternative to registration of a company as a means of obtaining limited liability. The Companies (Fees) (Companies, Overseas Companies and Limited Liability Partnerships) Regulations 2009 (SI 2009/2101) also set out the applicable fees on the incorporation of such a partnership and subsequent filing fees.

Limited liability partnerships (LLPs)	Charge	Same day charge
Electronic registration of an LLP on its formation	£20.00	£50.00
Paper registration of an LLP on its formation	£40.00	100.00
Registration of an annual return using electronic communications	£14.00	–

Registration of an annual return not using electronic communications	£40.00	–
Electronic registration of a change of name	£8.00	£30.00
Registration of a change of name	£10.00	£50.00

(c)   *Inspection of company records*
The public records of companies registered in the UK may be inspected by any person at Companies House. For companies registered in England and Wales, a company search can be undertaken at Companies House in Cardiff or London, and for companies registered in Scotland, a search can be undertaken at Companies House in Edinburgh.

Information about companies may also be accessed electronically using Companies House Direct, which can be viewed at Companies House, or provided by subscription to a user direct to the user's own computer system. In addition, WebCHeck (the link is available on the Companies House website) provides free access to general details about a company, such as the company's name, registered number, date of incorporation, its accounting reference date, and the last received annual return and accounts.

In addition to the information available on WebCHeck, Companies House Direct allows access to images of company accounts, the mortgage index and details of company directors. A register of directors and company secretaries includes lists of all directorships and secretaryships of individual officers as well as their home addresses, while a register of disqualified directors detailing all disqualification orders made under the Company Directors Disqualification Act 1986 is also available on the Companies House website. The Disqualified Directors Register provides details of the name, date of birth, and post town and the first part of the post code in respect of disqualified directors.

A fee is payable in respect of each company for which a company search is undertaken.

Electronic filing

[5.5] The Electronic Communications Act 2000 provided the legislative framework for the electronic incorporation of companies, and consequently the online incorporation of companies electronically has become the normal method of forming companies. The legislation is in line with developments in technology, and Companies House therefore provides a number of electronic services for the delivery of information electronically. These are:

(a)   *Software Filing*
The Software Filing service allows an increasing number of forms to be lodged electronically, together with audit exempt accounts and dormant accounts. The ability to file electronically using this service is supplemented by a validation process, involves a method of prepayment in the case of annual returns and is subject to companies having the minimum PC requirements for the system to operate. In addition,

companies which use the Companies House Direct service can download, view and print from their PC copies of document images such as accounts and annual returns.

(b)   *WebFiling*

The WebFiling service incorporates the electronic filing facility with internet technology and allows forms to be presented to Companies House via its website. A number of prescribed forms are available on the website for download, completion and filing manually. To use the service, all presenters are required to register and apply for a unique security code linked to their email address. A company authentication code is also necessary and is notified to the company secretary at the company's registered office address. As each transaction must be entered one at a time, WebFiling is not suitable for bulk use; in these circumstances the Software Filing service is more appropriate.

(c)   *PROOF*

Linked into the above services, Companies House offers the PROOF (PROtected Online Filing) service as a means of preventing the submission of forms to change the company's registered office and details of its directors for fraudulent purposes. Forms that can be submitted under this scheme include form AD01, and the various forms required for the appointment, termination and change of details of a director or secretary, along with the annual return shuttle document (form AP01). Companies wishing to take advantage of the PROOF service are required to register for either WebFiling or Software Filing, and to also complete form PR1 to opt into the service.

The annual return

General

[5.6] Section 854 of CA 2006 requires every company to make up and deliver to Companies House in each calendar year an annual return (form AP01) made up to a date no later than its 'return date' which is determined by reference to either:

(a)   the company's date of incorporation; or
(b)   the anniversary of the return date of the last filed annual return.

A company's return date may be changed by shortening the period between annual returns to less than a 12-month period; extensions beyond a 12-month period are not permitted.

The return must be filed at Companies House within 28 days of the return date accompanied by the prescribed fee (£30 for paper-based filing and £15 if filed electronically). Failure to do so renders the company and its officers liable to default proceedings (see **5.2** above).

The Companies Act 2006 (Annual Return and Service Addresses) Regulations 2008 (SI 2008/3000) specify the information to be provided in the annual return of a company and set out the conditions to be met by a service address.

They also serve to amend CA 2006, s 855(1) so that a company that keeps its records at a place specified in regulations under CA 2006, s 1136 is required to indicate the address of that place and the records kept there. In addition, whether or not the company's shares are admitted to trading on a regulated market (as defined in CA 2006, s 1173) will determine the information to be provided about its shareholders.

The 'shuttle document'

[5.7] This form was originally designed as a computer generated form, issued by Companies House to each company shortly before its 'return date'. However, Companies House has since ceased to issue shuttle documents and instead is providing companies with an authentication code to encourage electronic filing of the annual return using the WebFiling service. Previously, the shuttle document contained the following pre-printed details about the company:

(a)   company details including:
    (i)   company name and registered number;
    (ii)   registered office address;
    (iii)   the company's return date;
    (iv)   company type and principal activity; and
(b)   details of officers:
    (i)   particulars of the company secretary;
    (ii)   particulars of each director.

This information is available on the 'form' used for the WebFiling service, along with the issued share capital and details of shareholders (which ceased to be a feature of the pre-printed items appearing on the shuttle document).

Form and content of return

[5.8] Under CA 2006, s 855, each annual return must state the date to which it is made up (being a date no later than the 'return date') and, in addition, must contain the following information.

(a)   The address of the company's registered office and, if applicable, the address of the single alternative inspection location (SAIL) at which specified company records, including the register of members, registers of directors and secretaries, and register of debenture holders, are located.

(b)   The type of company and its principal business activities (given by reference to one or more categories of the Standard Industrial Classification (SIC) code).

(c)   The name and service address of every director of the company and, in the case of each individual director, his nationality, date of birth and business occupation.

(d)   The name and service address of the company secretary.

A new version of the Standard Industrial Classification, the numerical codes which are used to classify the principal business activities of companies in the UK, was adopted by the UK on 1 January 2008 but is being implemented by Companies House from 1 October 2011. The SIC 2007 codes replace the

2003 codings and brings the UK into line with the EUROSTAT System NACE and the UN System ISIC. From 1 October 2011, annual returns with a made up to date on or after that date will be required to use the new codes. Companies House will convert any SIC 2007 codes on annual returns filed before 1 October but it is recommended that the SIC 2003 classifications are used until that date. The 2007 SIC codes are available at www.companieshouse.gov.uk/infoAndGuide/sic/sic2007.shtml.

In addition to the above, the annual return of a company having a share capital must contain the following particulars with respect to its share capital and members.

(I)   The total number of issued shares of the company at the date to which the return is made up and the aggregate nominal value of those shares.

(II)   With respect to each class of shares denominated in sterling and any other currencies in the company:
   (i)   the nature of the class; and
   (ii)   the total number and aggregate nominal value of issued shares of that class at the date to which the return is made up; and
   (iii)   the prescribed particulars of rights (specifically the voting rights) attaching to each class of share.

(III)   For a private or non-traded public company, a list of the names of every person who:
   (i)   is a member of the company on the date to which the return is made up; or
   (ii)   has ceased to be a member of the company since the date to which the last return was made up (or, in the case of the first annual return, since the incorporation of the company);
   and, for a traded public company, the address of every person who is a member of the company on the date to which the return is made up.
   If the names are not arranged in alphabetical order, the return must have annexed to it an index sufficient to enable the name of any person in the list to be found easily.

(IV)   The number of shares of each class held by each member of the company at the date to which the return is made up, and the number of shares of each class transferred since the date to which the last annual return was made up (or, in the case of the first annual return, since the incorporation of the company), by each member or person who has ceased to be a member, and the dates of registration of the transfers (both acquisitions and disposals).
   The annual return may, if *either* of the *two* immediately preceding annual returns has given the full particulars of the members required above, give only such particulars as relate to persons ceasing to be or becoming members since the date of the last annual return *and* to shares transferred since that date. Thus, in such cases, the annual return would not need to include the foregoing particulars in relation to continuing members whose shareholdings have remained unchanged, except in the case of traded public companies where the details of shareholders that hold at least 5% of any class of share of the company must be disclosed

each year. This exception is not available for more than two consecutive years (that is, the full particulars must be given at least once in every three years).

From 1 October 2011, listed companies whose shares have been admitted to trading on a relevant market throughout the return period and that were subject to the Vote Holder and Issuer Notification Rules contained in Chapter 5 of the Disclosure and Transparency Rules (DTR5) issued by the FSA no longer have to disclose shareholder details in the annual return. This is a reflection of the fact that this information is already made available to the public under DTR by virtue of the disclosure of major shareholder notifications on the National Storage Mechanism (NSM), which is accessible at www.hemscott.com/nsm.do.

Listed companies that do not make such disclosures under DTR5 are still required to disclose shareholders which hold 5% or more of the company's issued share capital as at the made up to date of the annual return and must do so for every return filed. The Companies Act 2006 (Annual Return) Regulations 2011 (SI 2011/1487) remove the requirement for full disclosure of a shareholder list and associated transfers every three years. Companies which are not listed are still required to provide the names of shareholders who hold 5% or more of the company's issued share capital as at the made up to date of the annual return. The requirement to disclose a shareholder list and associated transfers every three years has also been removed for such companies by SI 2011/1487.

Information annexed to annual return – related undertakings

[5.9] Section 410 of CA 2006 requires disclosure of information about related undertakings in a company's accounts in accordance with the provisions of any regulations made under section 409 of the Act. By virtue of CA 2006, s 410(1), if the directors are of the opinion that due to the number of undertakings to be disclosed compliance would result in information being unduly excessive, the information need only be given in respect of:

(a) the undertakings whose result or financial position, in the directors' opinion, principally affected the figures shown in the company's accounts; and

(b) undertakings excluded from consolidation under CA 2006, s 405(2) or (3).

If advantage is taken of this exemption, the notes to the accounts should contain a statement that the information given relates to only these undertakings. In addition, the full information, comprising the information disclosed in the accounts as well as the information not so disclosed, must be annexed to the company's next annual return, being the return delivered to the Registrar after the accounts in question have been approved by the directors in accordance with CA 2006, s 414.

Failure to disclose the full information with the annual return will render the company and every director who is in default liable to a fine and, for continued contravention, to a daily default fine.

General filing administration

Prescribed forms

[5.10] The Companies Act 2006 specifies various circumstances in which a company must make a return to Companies House. There are over 200 circumstances specified under CA 2006 when a return is required to be made in a prescribed form. The forms required for these purposes are set out in APPENDIX 5C below.

Registration of resolutions

[5.11] In addition to the prescribed forms mentioned above and contained in APPENDIX 5C, CA 2006, s 30 requires that a copy of every resolution to which CA 2006, s 29 applies, must within *15 days* of it being passed, be filed with Companies House. The resolutions and agreements which must be registered pursuant to CA 2006, s 29 are:

(a) special resolutions;

(b) resolutions or agreements agreed to by all members of the company that, if not so agreed to, would not have been effective for its purpose unless passed as special resolutions;

(c) resolutions or agreements agreed to by all the members of a class of shareholders that, if not so agreed to, would not have been effective for its purpose unless passed by some particular majority or otherwise in some particular manner; and all resolutions or agreements that effectively bind all members of a class of shareholders though not agreed to by all those members;

(d) any other resolution or agreement to which this Chapter applies by virtue of any enactment.

(e) a resolution passed by the directors to change the name of a company to include the word 'limited', where directed to do so by the Secretary of State;

(f) a resolution to give, vary or revoke the authority of directors to allot shares pursuant to CA 2006, s 551;

(g) a resolution of the directors under CA 2006, s 664(1) to alter the memorandum of association of a public company, when it ceases to be a public company through the acquisition of its own shares;

(h) a resolution to give, vary, revoke or renew a company's authority under CA 2006, s 701 to purchase its own shares; and

(i) a resolution for the voluntary winding-up of the company passed pursuant to section 84(1)(a) of the Insolvency Act 1986.

For further information on general meetings and resolutions please refer to CHAPTER 7 MEMBERSHIP.

Summary

[5.12] Filing administration is a key element of a company secretary's role and is one which, if neglected, can result in considerable penalties being imposed upon both the company and its officers. To avoid any penalties, three key points must be borne in mind in relation to all forms and accounts presented to the Registrar of Companies:

(a)   such documents must be filed within the specified time limit;

(b)   in each case, they must bear the appropriate original signatures and be dated; and

(c)   in addition to being in a form approved by Companies House, the information contained on them must be clear and legible (see **5.3** above).

Disclosure and the Stock Exchange

General

UK Listing Authority

[5.13] Since 1 May 2000, the Financial Services Authority (FSA) has been the UK Listing Authority following the transfer of this function from the London Stock Exchange. This role was previously the responsibility of the Stock Exchange along with its role as a recognised investment exchange; these roles have been separated as a result of the transfer. The appointment of the FSA as the UK's competent authority was made under the Official Listing of Securities (Change of Competent Authority) Regulations 2000 (SI 2000/968). As the UK Listing Authority (UKLA), the FSA has responsibility for admitting to listing securities governed by Part VI of the Financial Services and Markets Act 2000.

A distinction is drawn between 'admission to listing' and 'admission to trading'. The UKLA is responsible for regulating those companies which seek admission to listing while the Stock Exchange regulates admission to trading. Initially, there was little impact on listed companies since the UKLA adopted the Listing Rules broadly in the form they were in prior to the transfer. However, the UKLA subsequently published a complete set of Listing Rules under the FSA banner and introduced a number of changes to the Listing Rules which principally sought to reflect the transfer of the UKLA to the FSA. In particular, these contained a new condition for listing that an issuer's listed securities must be admitted to trading, while a new continuing obligation required that such securities must be admitted to trading on a recognised investment exchange at all times.

More recently, the Listing Rules were amended to differentiate between companies that have a premium or a standard listing. The Rules define a standard listing as setting requirements that are based on the minimum EU directive standards, while a premium listing will include requirements that exceed these standards. Premium listings are applicable to equity shares of commercial companies, closed-ended investment funds and open-ended investment companies, with any other listing then being categorised as a standard listing.

In its introduction to the FSA Listing Rules, the UKLA indicated the objectives and principles which it will adopt in applying the Rules. In particular, the UKLA will:

(a) seek to strike a balance between the needs of issuers and investors so that issuers will have ready access to the market for their securities while also affording protection to investors;

(b) seek to promote through the Listing Rules and, in particular the continuing obligations, investor confidence in standards of disclosure, in the conduct of listed companies' affairs and in the market as a whole;

(c) require securities to be brought to the market in a way that is appropriate to their nature and number and which will facilitate an open and efficient market for trading in those securities;

(d) require an issuer to make full and timely disclosure about itself and its listed securities, both at the time of listing and subsequently;

(e) require issuers to provide holders of equity securities with an adequate opportunity to consider in advance and vote upon major changes in the company's business operations as well as matters of importance concerning the company's management and constitution; and

(f) apply the Listing Rules flexibly wherever possible so that there is an appropriate level of regulation (the UKLA will provide guidance on the application of the Rules in particular circumstances).

The FSA subsequently published a revised version of the Listing Rules. Chapters 9 to 16 in the original version, dealing with the continuing obligations of listed companies, became chapters LR7 to LR13. The changes to chapter 9 resulted in extensive re-ordering of the chapter and the inclusion of rules previously contained within other chapters rather than any real substantive changes to the content of this chapter. It no longer contains the rules on disclosure of price sensitive information since this now forms a separate sourcebook (the Disclosure Rules). However, chapter 9 now contains the rules from chapter 16 applying to directors (where these have not been deleted or included elsewhere in the revised Rules) and incorporates the Model Code as an annex to this chapter.

Companies are required to make announcements to a Regulatory Information Service in order to disseminate information to the market in the circumstances specified by the Listing Rules (see **5.14** below). The Listing Rules require hard copies of circulars and resolutions to be delivered to the UK Listing Authority. The UKLA will, where required by the Listing Rules, make available documents for public inspection at the Document Viewing Facility at the FSA's offices in Canary Wharf.

Stock exchange

[5.14] A company listed on the London Stock Exchange, in addition to its obligations under the Companies Act 2006, is required to comply with the requirements of the Listing Rules.

One of the main conditions of listing is the requirement to observe the continuing obligations set out in the Rules, which the Rules emphasise 'is essential to the maintenance of an orderly market in securities and to ensure that all users of the market have access to the same information at the same time'. The UKLA may take action against any company which fails to comply with any continuing obligation it is required to observe (see **5.17** below).

The FSA announced its intention during 2001 to allow listed companies to publish regulatory announcements through approved service providers – primary information providers (PIPs) – which would then disseminate the full text of the announcement to news vendors and secondary information providers (SIPs).

In response to the opening up of the market to other providers, the London Stock Exchange introduced at that time a number of enhancements to the Regulatory News Service (RNS) to enable the service to compete with these providers. The enhancements included further upgrades to the RNS internet submission mechanism (RNS Submit) to simplify the review and verification of text prior to publication and the launch of several new RNS services, including:

(a)   RNS Reach – for non-regulatory announcements;
(b)   RNS Mediastream – for video and audio content to be delivered alongside the full text announcements;
(c)   RNS Insight – a web-based service which allows monitoring, searching and analysis of RNS announcements; and
(d)   RNS Alert – an email-based service providing alerts on a real time basis of the publication of RNS announcements.

The FSA has previously approved a number of PIP services alongside the Regulatory News Services to act as Regulatory Information Services, and these currently include:

(i)   Announce;
(ii)   Business Wire Regulatory Disclosure;
(iii)   DGAP IR.COCKPIT;
(iv)   FirstSight;
(v)   marCo;
(vi)   News Release Express; and;
(vii)   PR Newswire Disclosure.

Notification of any matter required to be disclosed to the Exchange is made to a Regulatory Information Service (RIS). The Exchange's preferred method for making announcements is by electronic means, since this enables the RIS to process the information more quickly and efficiently for onward transmission to the market. Alternatively, announcements may be delivered by hand in hard copy form or by facsimile. The company should use the Announcement Validation Service (AVS) numbers issued to it when making announcements to validate the source of such information.

Continuing obligations

[5.15] The Listing Rules require a company to notify the RIS without delay of any information which will enable the company's shareholders and the public to make an assessment of its position, and of any major new developments which are not public knowledge and lead to substantial price movements in the company's listed securities and, for a company with listed debt securities, also have a significant effect on its ability to meet its commitments.

Listed companies are obliged by the Listing Rules to take all reasonable steps to ensure that any announcement made to the RIS or any information provided to the UKLA is not 'misleading, false or deceptive' and that any such announcement or information does not omit anything so as to make it misleading, false or deceptive.

In general, these obligations are in addition to any specific requirements of the Listing Rules to notify the Stock Exchange. The Exchange may, however, permit a company to dispense with the requirements to make information public where the directors can satisfy the Exchange that its disclosure may be prejudicial to the company's legitimate business interests. The circumstances in which a company must notify the RIS are numerous and include the following.

(a)   Any proposed change in the capital structure of the company, including the structure of its listed debt securities. Such changes must generally be notified as soon as possible.

(b)   Any appointment of a new director, or the resignation, removal or retirement of an existing director, or any changes to the role, functions and responsibilities of a director. This information must be notified to the RIS as soon as possible and in any case by the end of the business day following the decision or receipt of notice of the change by the company.

(c)   Any decisions of the directors relating to dividends must be notified as soon as possible after the board has approved the decision.

The Rules require all circulars, notices, reports, announcements or other documents issued by the company to be forwarded to the UKLA at the same time as they are issued. In addition, all resolutions passed by the company in general meeting, with the exception of resolutions which comprise the ordinary business of an annual general meeting, must be forwarded to the UKLA as soon as possible after the meeting in question. In each case, two copies of these documents are required.

The UKLA published in May 2000 an updated version of its continuing obligations guide (to replace the one issued by the Stock Exchange in September 1998). This guide is a useful summary of the key obligations which listed companies are required to comply with and is a helpful aid to company secretaries in ensuring that they meet the deadlines required by the Listing Rules.

The FSA Listing Rules are available in pdf format at http://fsahandbook.info/ FSA/html/handbook/LR. In addition, the UKLA Guidance Manual, originally issued in December 2001, provides guidance on a range of issues. It also seeks to formalise and publish certain procedures of the UKLA, and includes updated versions of the Price Sensitive Information Guide and the Continuing Obligat ions Guide.

Financial information

[5.16] For financial years beginning before 20 January 2007, a listed company is required to issue an annual report and accounts as well as a report covering the first six months of each financial year. The annual accounts must be published no later than six months after the end of the financial year, while the half-yearly report must be published within 90 days of the end of the relevant financial period. In exceptional circumstances, the UKLA may allow an extension to these time limits. However, following the Transparency Obligations Directive (Disclosure and Transparency Rules) Instrument 2006 (FSA 2006/70), a listed company is required to publish its annual report and accounts within four months of the financial year and its half-yearly report within two months of the relevant financial period, for financial years beginning on or after 20 January 2007.

Under the old rules, the company was required to notify the RIS as soon as possible following board approval of the preliminary statement of its annual results, the announcement of the half-yearly results and any decision relating to the payment of a dividend on the company's listed equity securities. These required the company to publish its preliminary statement within 120 days of the end of the relevant financial period. The preliminary announcement is now optional, although in the absence of such an announcement, a listed company is required to publish inside information as soon as possible to fulfil its obligations under the Market Abuse Directive.

The Accounting Standards Board (ASB) has previously published its recommendations for the information to be disclosed in the preliminary announcements, setting the minimum requirements for the information to be given in such announcements (although this provided more detail than was then required under the Listing Rules). In particular, the ASB recommendations required the inclusion of the following:

(1)   A narrative commentary highlighting the main factors which have influenced the company's performance during the financial period in question and the company's performance at the end of the period.
(2)   A summary profit and loss account which provides greater disclosure than currently recommended by the Listing Rules.
(3)   A statement of total recognised gains and losses which reports any material gains and losses that have been recognised during the financial period (other than those already indicated in the profit and loss account).
(4)   A summary balance sheet showing significant movements in key indicators and applying similar classifications to those used in the annual financial statements.

Where the half-yearly report is audited, the announcement to a RIS and any related press releases must include the auditors' report in full. However, where the auditors have merely reviewed the half-yearly report then a copy of the review report must be provided in full when the announcement is made to the RIS. For companies that do not publish quarterly reports, the Transparency Obligations Directive requires such companies to publish interim management statements between ten weeks after the beginning, and six weeks before the end, of the relevant six-month period. Such statements should disclose material events and transactions from the beginning of the period in question as well as the company's financial position and performance.

Monitoring and enforcement

[5.17] The UKLA monitors the information provided to it and will make contact with a company should the company fail to comply with the requirements of the Listing Rules. For instance, the Company Monitoring team will write to the company where notifications of major shareholdings are incomplete or the company secretary may be contacted by telephone where there appears to be a deficiency in the timing or content of announcements.

The UKLA is empowered to censure any company for its failure to observe any applicable obligation of the Listing Rules, to publish the fact that the company has been censured and to suspend or cancel the company's listing. The UKLA may also take action against the directors of the company concerned.

Appendix 5A

Publications available from Companies House

Ref. No.	Description	Date
Company Guidance		
GP1	Incorporation and Names	July 2011
GP2	Life of a Company – Part 1 Annual Requirements	April 2011
GP3	Life of a Company – Part 2 Event Driven Requirements	April 2011
GP4	Strike off, Dissolution and Restoration	June 2011
GP5	Late Filing Penalties	October 2010
GP6	Registrar's Rules and Powers	April 2011
GP7	Restricting the disclosure of your address	April 2011
Other Legislation		
GPO1	Overseas Companies registered in the UK	April 2011
GPO2	Limited Partnership Act	April 2011
GPO3	Newspaper Libel and Registration Act	May 2011
GPO4	European Economic Interest Groupings	May 2010
GPO5	Conducting Business in Welsh	May 2010
GPO6	The European Company: Societas Europaea (SE)	May 2010
GPO7	Cross Border Mergers	August 2011
GPO8	Liquidation and Insolvency	May 2010
GPO8s	Liquidation and Insolvency (Scotland)	May 2010
GPO8n	Liquidation and Insolvency (Northern Ireland)	June 2010

Ref. No.	Description	Date
Limited Liability Partnerships		
GPLLP1	Limited Liability Partnerships Incorporation and Names	July 2011
GPLLP2	Life of a Limited Liability Partnership	April 2011
GPLLP3	Life of a Limited Liability Partnership Strike off, Dissolution and Restoration	June 2011
GPLLP4	Limited Liability Partnership Late Filing Penalties	May 2010
GPLLP5	Limited Liability Partnership Liquidation and Insolvency	May 2010
GPLLP5s	Limited Liability Partnership Liquidation and Insolvency (Scotland)	May 2010
GPLLP5n	Limited Liability Partnership Liquidation and Insolvency (Northern Ireland)	August 2010

The above publications can be obtained by telephoning +44 (0)303 1234 500 or viewed on the Companies House website (http://www.companieshouse.gov. uk).

The Registrar of Companies also publishes a regular newsletter 'The Register' aimed at advising readers of current developments in company law and the activities of Companies House. Those interested can be requested to be put on the mailing list by emailing their full name and address to amendregister@companieshouse.gov.uk.

Appendix 5B

Companies House office locations

England & Wales

Crown Way Maindy Cardiff CF14 3UZ DX 33050 +44 (0)303 1234 500	Head Office for England & Wales providing all services.

London Information Centre 21 Bloomsbury Street London WC1B 3XD +44 (0)303 1234 500	Company search and document filing facilities.

Scotland

4th Floor Edinburgh Quay 2 139 Fountainbridge Edinburgh EH3 9FF LP – 4 Edinburgh 2 (Legal Post) *or* DX ED235 Edinburgh 1 +44 (0)303 1234 500	Head Office for Scotland providing all services.

Northern Ireland

Second Floor The Linenhall 32-38 Linenhall Street Belfast Northern Ireland BT2 8BG DX 481 N.R. Belfast 1 +44 (0)303 1234 500	Head Office for Northern Ireland

Stock Exchange

London Stock Exchange
10 Paternoster Square
London
EC4M 7L7
(020) 7797 1000

UK Listing Authority

UK Listing Authority
25 The North Colonnade
Canary Wharf
London
E14 5HS
(020) 7066 8333

Financial Services Authority   Document viewing facility
25 The North Colonnade
Canary Wharf
London
E14 5HS
(020) 7066 1000

Appendix 5C

Specified forms for use for returns to Companies House

The forms listed below comprise all forms to be used for filing purposes from 1 October 2009 onwards and fall into the following categories:

Company Forms

Limited Partnerships (LPs) Forms

Limited Liability Partnerships (LLPs) Forms

Non Companies Act Company Forms

Overseas Companies Forms

European Economic Interest Groupings (EEIGs) Forms

Societas Europaea (SE) Forms

Cross Border Merger Forms

Newspaper Libel and Registration Act Forms

The forms are also available in large print by contacting Companies House at +44 (0)303 1234 500.

Company forms

Functional Area	Form	Name of Form	CA 1985 Form ID
Accounts	**AA01**	Change of accounting reference date	225
Accounts	**AA03**	Notice of resolution removing auditors from office	391
Administration Restoration	**RT01**	Application for administrative restoration to the Register	
Annual Return	**AR01**	Annual Return	363
Annual Return	**AD02**	Notification of single alternative inspection location (SAIL)	
Annual Return	**AD03**	Change of location of the company records to the single alternative inspection location (SAIL)	
Annual Return	**AD04**	Change of location of the company records to the registered office	

Functional Area	Form	Name of Form	CA 1985 Form ID
Change of Constitution	CC01	Notice of restriction on the company's articles	
Change of Constitution	CC02	Notice of removal of restriction on the company's articles	
Change of Constitution	CC03	Statement of compliance where amendment of articles restricted	
Change of Constitution	CC04	Statement of company's objects	
Change of Constitution	CC05	Change of constitution by enactment	
Change of Constitution	CC06	Change of constitution by order of court or other authority	
Change of Name	NE01	Exemption from requirement as to use of "limited" or "cyfyngedig" on change of name	
Change of Name	NM01	Notice of change of name by resolution	
Change of Name	NM02	Notice of change of name by conditional resolution	
Change of Name	NM03	Notice confirming satisfaction of the conditional resolution for change of name	
Change of Name	NM04	Notice of change of name by means provided for in the articles	
Change of Name	NM05	Notice of change of name by resolution of directors	
Change of Name	NM06	Request to seek comments of government department or other specified body on change of name	
Change of Registered Office	AD01	Change of registered office address	287
Change of Registered Office	AD05	Notice to change the situation of an England and Wales company or a Welsh company	

Functional Area	Form	Name of Form	CA 1985 Form ID
Directors & Secretaries	AP01	Appointment of director	288a
Directors & Secretaries	AP02	Appointment of corporate director	288a
Directors & Secretaries	AP03	Appointment of secretary	288a
Directors & Secretaries	AP04	Appointment of corporate secretary	288a
Directors & Secretaries	TM01	Termination of appointment of director	288b
Directors & Secretaries	TM02	Termination of appointment of secretary	288b
Directors & Secretaries	CH01	Change of director's details	288c
Directors & Secretaries	CH02	Change of corporate director's details	288c
Directors & Secretaries	CH03	Change of secretary's details	288c
Directors & Secretaries	CH04	Change of corporate secretary's details	288c
Dissolution	DS01	Striking off application by a company	652a
Dissolution	DS02	Withdrawal of striking off application by a company	652c
Incorporation	IN01	Application to register a company	10,12
Investment Companies	IC01	Notice of intention to carry on business as an investment company	266(1)
Investment Companies	IC02	Notice that a company no longer wishes to be an investment company	266(3)
Liquidation	LQ01	Notice of appointment of an administrative receiver, receiver or manager	405(1)
Liquidation	LQ02	Notice of ceasing to act as an administrative receiver, receiver or manager	405(2)
Mortgage	MG01	Particulars of a mortgage or charge	395
Mortgage	MG02	Statement of satisfaction in full or in part of mortgage or charge	403a

Functional Area	Form	Name of Form	CA 1985 Form ID
Mortgage	MG04	Application for registration of a memorandum of satisfaction that part (or the whole) of the property charged (a) has been released from the charge; (b) no longer forms part of the company's property	403b
Mortgage	MG06	Particulars of a charge subject to which property has been acquired	400
Mortgage	MG07	Particulars for the registration of a charge to secure a series of debentures	397
Mortgage	MG08	Particulars of an issue of secured debentures in a series	379a
Mortgage	MG09	Certificate of registration of a charge comprising property situated in another UK jurisdiction	398
Opening of Overseas Branch Register	AD06	Notice of opening of overseas branch register	362
Opening of Overseas Branch Register	AD07	Notice of discontinuance of overseas branch register	362
Other Appointments	AP05	Appointment of a manager under Section 47 of the Companies (Audit, Investigations and Community Enterprise) Act 2004 or receiver and manager under Section 18 of the Charities Act 1993 or judicial factor (Scotland)	

Functional Area	Form	Name of Form	CA 1985 Form ID
Other Appointments	TM03	Termination of appointment of manager under Section 47 of the Companies (Audit, Investigations and Community Enterprise) Act 2004 or receiver and manager under Section 18 of the Charities Act 1993 or judicial factor (Scotland)	
Other Appointments	CH05	Change of service address for manager appointed under Section 47 of the Companies (Audit, Investigations and Community Enterprise) Act 2004 or receiver and manager under Section 18 of the Charities Act 1993 or judicial factor (Scotland)	
Registrar's Powers	RP01	Replacement of document not meeting requirements for proper delivery	
Registrar's Powers	RP02A	Application for rectification by the Registrar of Companies	
Registrar's Powers	RP02B	Application for rectification of a registered office or a UK establishment address by the Registrar of Companies	
Registrar's Powers	RP03	Notice of an objection to a request for the Registrar of Companies to rectify the Register	
Registrar's Powers	VT01	Certified voluntary translation of an original document that is or has been delivered to the Registrar of Companies	
Re-Registration	RR01	Application by a private company for re-registration as a public company	43(3)

Functional Area	Form	Name of Form	CA 1985 Form ID
Re-Registration	RR02	Application by a public company for re-registration as a private limited company	53
Re-Registration	RR03	Notice by the company of application to the court for cancellation of resolution for re-registration	54
Re-Registration	RR04	Notice by the applicants of application to the court for cancellation of resolution for re-registration	54
Re-Registration	RR05	Application by a private limited company for re-registration as an unlimited company	49(1)
Re-Registration	RR06	Application by an unlimited company for re-registration as a private limited company	51
Re-Registration	RR07	Application by a public company for re-registration as a private unlimited company	
Re-Registration	RR08	Application by a public company for re-registration as a private limited company following a court order reducing capital	139
Re-Registration	RR09	Application by a public company for re-registration as a private company following a cancellation of shares	147
Re-Registration	RR10	Application by a public company for re-registration as a private company following a reduction of capital due to redenomination	
Resolutions	Res CA2006	Special resolution on change of name	

Functional Area	Form	Name of Form	CA 1985 Form ID
Resolutions	**Written Res CA2006**	Written special resolution on change of name	
Share Capital	980(1)	Notice of non-assenting shareholders	
Share Capital	980(dec)	Statutory Declaration relating to a Notice to non-assenting shares	
Share Capital	984	Notice to non-assenting shares	
Share Capital	**SH01**	Return of allotment of shares	88(2)
Share Capital	**SH02**	Notice of consolidation, sub-division, redemption of shares or re-conversion of stock into shares	122
Share Capital	**SH03**	Return of purchase of own shares	169
Share Capital	**SH04**	Notice of sale or transfer of treasury shares by a public limited company (PLC)	169a
Share Capital	**SH05**	Notice of cancellation of treasury shares by a public limited company (PLC)	169a(2)
Share Capital	**SH06**	Notice of cancellation of shares	
Share Capital	**SH07**	Notice of cancellation of shares held by or for a public company	
Share Capital	**SH08**	Notice of name or other designation of class of shares	128(4)
Share Capital	**SH09**	Return of allotment by an unlimited company allotting new class of shares	128(1)
Share Capital	**SH10**	Notice of particulars of variation of rights attached to shares	128(3)
Share Capital	**SH11**	Notice of new class of members	129(1)
Share Capital	**SH12**	Notice of particulars of variation of class rights	129(2)

Functional Area	Form	Name of Form	CA 1985 Form ID
Share Capital	**SH13**	Notice of name or other designation of class of members	129(3)
Share Capital	**SH14**	Notice of redenomination	
Share Capital	**SH15**	Notice of reduction of capital following redenomination	
Share Capital	**SH16**	Notice by the applicants of application to court for cancellation of the special resolution approving a redemption or purchase of shares out of capital	176
Share Capital	**SH17**	Notice by the company of application to court for cancellation of the special resolution approving a redemption or purchase of shares out of capital	176
Share Capital	**SH19 (644 & 649)**	Statement of capital (Section 644 & 649)	
Share Capital	**SH19 (108)**	Statement of capital (Section 108)	
Share Capital	**SH50**	Application for trading certificate for a public company	117
Scottish Mortgage	466	Particulars of an instrument of alteration to a floating charge created by a company registered in Scotland	466
Scottish Mortgage	**MG01s**	Particulars of a charge created by a company registered in Scotland	410
Scottish Mortgage	**MG02s**	Statement of satisfaction in full or in part of a fixed charge for a company registered in Scotland	419a
Scottish Mortgage	**MG03s**	Statement of satisfaction in full or in part of a floating charge for a company registered in Scotland	419a

Functional Area	Form	Name of Form	CA 1985 Form ID
Scottish Mortgage	MG04s	Application for registration of a memorandum of satisfaction that part (or the whole) of the property charged (a) has been released from the fixed charge; (b) no longer forms part of the company's property for a company registered in Scotland.	419b
Scottish Mortgage	MG05s	Application for registration of a memorandum of satisfaction that part (or the whole) of the property charged (a) has been released from the floating charge; (b) no longer forms part of the company's property for a company registered in Scotland.	419b
Scottish Mortgage	MG06s	Particulars of a charge subject to which property has been acquired by a company registered in Scotland	416
Scottish Mortgage	MG07s	Particulars for the registration of a charge to secure a series of debentures by a company registered in Scotland	413
Scottish Mortgage	MG08s	Particulars of an issue of secured debentures in a series by a company registered in Scotland	413a

Limited Partnerships (LPs)

Functional Area	Form	Name of Form	Previous Form ID
Limited Partnerships	LP5	Application for Registration of a Limited Partnership	
Limited Partnerships	LP6	Limited Partnership Statement	

Limited Liability Partnerships (LLPs)

Functional Area	Form	Name of Form	Previous Form ID
Limited Liability Partnerships	LL IN01	Application for the incorporation of a Limited Liability Partnership (LLP)	LLP2
Limited Liability Partnerships	LL AP01	Appointment of member of a Limited Liability Partnership (LLP)	LLP288a
Limited Liability Partnerships	LL AP02	Appointment of corporate member of a Limited Liability Partnership (LLP)	LLP288a
Limited Liability Partnerships	LL CH01	Change of details of a member of a Limited Liability Partnership (LLP)	LLP288c
Limited Liability Partnerships Return	LLCH02	Change of details of a corporate member of a Limited Liability Partnership (LLP)	LLP288c
Limited Liability Partnerships Return	LL TM01	Termination of appointment of member of a Limited Liability Partnership (LLP)	LLP288b
Limited Liability Partnerships	LL AA01	Change of accounting reference date of a Limited Liability Partnership (LLP)	LLP225
Limited Liability Partnerships	LL AA02	Notice of removal of auditor from a Limited Liability Partnership (LLP)	LLP391
Limited Liability Partnerships	LL AD01	Change of accounting reference date of a Limited Liability Partnership (LLP)	LLP287
Limited Liability Partnerships	LL AD02	Notification of the single alternative inspection location (SAIL) of a Limited Liability Partnership (LLP)	
Limited Liability Partnerships	LL AD03	Change of location of the records to the single alternative inspection location (SAIL) of a Limited Liability Partnership (LLP)	

Functional Area	Form	Name of Form	Previous Form ID
Limited Liability Partnerships	LL AD04	Change of location of the records to the registered office of a Limited Liability Partnership (LLP)	
Limited Liability Partnerships	LL AD05	Notice to change the situation of an England and Wales Limited Liability Partnership or a Welsh Limited Liability Partnership (LLP)	LLP287a
Limited Liability Partnerships	LL AR01	Annual Return of a Limited Liability Partnership (LLP)	LLP363
Limited Liability Partnerships	LL DE01	Notice of change of status of a Limited Liability Partnership (LLP)	LLP8
Limited Liability Partnerships	LL NM01	Notice of change of name of a Limited Liability Partnership (LLP)	LLP3
Limited Liability Partnerships	LL DS01	Striking off of application by a Limited Liability Partnership (LLP)	LLP652a
Limited Liability Partnerships	LL DS02	Withdrawal of striking off application by a Limited Liability Partnership (LLP)	LLP652c
Limited Liability Partnerships	LL LQ01	Notice of appointment of an administrative receiver, receiver or manager by a Limited Liability Partnership (LLP)	LLP405(1)
Limited Liability Partnerships	LL LQ02	Notice of ceasing to act as an administrative receiver, receiver or manager by a Limited Liability Partnership (LLP)	LLP405(2)
Limited Liability Partnerships	LL RP01	Replacement of document not meeting requirements for proper delivery for a Limited Liability Partnership (LLP)	

Functional Area	Form	Name of Form	Previous Form ID
Limited Liability Partnerships	LL RP02A	Application for rectification by the Registrar of Companies for a Limited Liability Partnership (LLP)	
Limited Liability Partnerships	LL RP02B	Application for rectification of a registered office address by the Registrar of Companies for a Limited Liability Partnership (LLP)	
Limited Liability Partnerships	LL RP03	Notice of an objection to a request for the Registrar of Companies to rectify the Register for a Limited Liability Partnership (LLP)	
Limited Liability Partnerships	LL VT01	Certified voluntary translation of an original document that is or has been delivered to the Registrar of Companies for a Limited Liability Partnership (LLP)	
Limited Liability Partnerships	LL RT01	Application for administrative restoration of a Limited Liability Partnership (LLP) to the Register	
Limited Liability Partnerships Mortgage	LL MG01	Particulars of a mortgage or charge created by a Limited Liability Partnership (LLP)	LLP395
Limited Liability Partnerships Mortgage	LL MG02	Statement of satisfaction in full or part of mortgage or charge by a Limited Liability Partnership (LLP)	LLP403a

Functional Area	Form	Name of Form	Previous Form ID
Limited Liability Partnerships Mortgage	LL MG04	Application for registration of a memorandum of satisfaction that part (or the whole) of the property charged (a) has been released from the charge; (b) no longer forms part of the Limited Liability Partnership's (LLP's) property	LLP403b
Limited Liability Partnerships Mortgage	LL MG06	Particulars of charge subject to which property has been acquired by a Limited Liability Partnership (LLP)	LLP400
Limited Liability Partnerships Mortgage	LL MG07	Particulars for the registration of a charge to secure a series of debentures by a Limited Liability Partnership (LLP)	LLP397
Limited Liability Partnerships Mortgage	LL MG08	Particulars of an issue of secured debentures in a series by a Limited Liability Partnership (LLP)	LLP397a
Limited Liability Partnerships Mortgage	LL MG09	Certificate of registration of a charge comprising property situated in another UK jurisdiction by a Limited Liability Partnership (LLP)	LLP398
Limited Liability Partnerships Scottish Mortgage	LLP466	Particulars of an instrument of alteration to a floating charge created by a Limited Liability Partnership registered in Scotland	LLP466
Limited Liability Partnerships Scottish Mortgage	LL MG01s	Particulars of a charge created by a Limited Liability Partnership (LLP) registered in Scotland	LLP410

Functional Area	Form	Name of Form	Previous Form ID
Limited Liability Partnerships Scottish Mortgage	LL MG02s	Statement of satisfaction in full or part of a fixed charge by a Limited Liability Partnership (LLP) registered in Scotland	LLP419a
Limited Liability Partnerships Scottish Mortgage	LL MG03s	Statement of satisfaction in full or part of a floating charge by a Limited Liability Partnership (LLP) registered in Scotland	LLP419b
Limited Liability Partnerships Scottish Mortgage	LL MG04s	Application for registration of a memorandum of satisfaction that part (or the whole) of the property charged (a) has been released from the fixed charge; (b) no longer forms part of the Limited Liability Partnership's (LLP's) property by an LLP registered in Scotland	LLP419b
Limited Liability Partnerships Scottish Mortgage	LL MG01s	Particulars of a charge created by a Limited Liability Partnership (LLP) registered in Scotland	LLP410
Limited Liability Partnerships Scottish Mortgage	LL MG05s	Application for registration of a memorandum of satisfaction that part (or the whole) of the property charged (a) has been released from the floating charge; (b) no longer forms part of the Limited Liability Partnership's (LLP's) property by an LLP registered in Scotland	LLP419b

Functional Area	Form	Name of Form	Previous Form ID
Limited Liability Partnerships Scottish Mortgage	LL MG06s	Particulars of a charge subject to which property has been acquired by a Limited Liability Partnership (LLP) registered in Scotland	LLP416
Limited Liability Partnerships Scottish Mortgage	LL MG07s	Particulars for the registration of a charge to secure a series of debentures by a Limited Liability Partnership (LLP) registered in Scotland	LLP413
Limited Liability Partnerships Scottish Mortgage	LL MG08s	Particulars of an issue of secured debentures in a series by a Limited Liability Partnership (LLP) registered in Scotland	LLP413a

Non-Companies Act Companies

Functional Area	Form	Name of Form	Previous Form ID
Non Companies Act Companies	NC IN01	Application by a joint stock company for registration as a public company under the Companies Act 2006	680a/684
Non Companies Act Companies	NC IN02	Application by a joint stock company for registration as a private company under the Companies Act 2006	680a/684
Non Companies Act Companies	NC IN03	Application by a company (not being a joint stock company) for registration under the Companies Act 2006	680b

Overseas Companies

Functional Area	Form	Name of Form	CA 1985 Form ID
Overseas Companies	OS IN01	Registration of an overseas company opening a UK establishment	BR1
Overseas Companies	OS NM01	Registration of change of name of overseas company as registered in the UK	BR3
Overseas Companies	OS CC01	Return by an overseas company of an alteration to constitutional documents	BR2
Overseas Companies	OS AD01	Return by an overseas company of change of UK establishment relating to constitutional documents	BR7
Overseas Companies	OS AD02	Notice of location, or change in location, of instruments creating charges and register of charges for an overseas company	
Overseas Companies	OS AP01	Appointment of director of an overseas company	BR4
Overseas Companies	OS AP02	Appointment of corporate director of an overseas company	BR4
Overseas Companies	OS AP03	Appointment of secretary of an overseas company	BR4
Overseas Companies	OS AP04	Appointment of corporate secretary of an overseas company	BR4
Overseas Companies	OS AP05	Appointment by an overseas company of a person authorised to represent the company as a permanent representative in respect of a UK establishment	BR6
Overseas Companies	OS AP06	Appointment of a judicial factor (Scotland) for an overseas company	

Functional Area	Form	Name of Form	CA 1985 Form ID
Overseas Companies	OS AP07	Appointment by an overseas company of a person authorised to accept service of documents on behalf of the company in respect of a UK establishment	BR6
Overseas Companies	OS TM01	Termination of appointment of director of an overseas company	BR4
Overseas Companies	OS TM02	Termination of appointment of secretary of an overseas company	BR4
Overseas Companies	OS TM03	Termination of appointment by an overseas company of a person authorised to accept service of documents or person authorised to represent the company in respect of a UK establishment	BR6
Overseas Companies	OS TM04	Termination of appointment of judicial factor (Scotland) of an overseas company	
Overseas Companies	OS CH01	Return by a UK establishment of an overseas company for change of details	BR5
Overseas Companies	OS CH02	Return by an overseas company for a change of company details	BR3
Overseas Companies	OS CH03	Change of details of a director of an overseas company	BR4
Overseas Companies	OS CH04	Change of details of a corporate director of an overseas company	BR4
Overseas Companies	OS CH05	Change of details of a secretary of an overseas company	BR4
Overseas Companies	OS CH06	Change of details of a corporate secretary of an overseas company	BR4

Functional Area	Form	Name of Form	CA 1985 Form ID
Overseas Companies	OS CH07	Change of details by an overseas company for a person authorised to represent the company in respect of a UK establishment	BR6
Overseas Companies	OS CH08	Change of service address for a judicial factor (Scotland) of an overseas company	
Overseas Companies	OS CH09	Change of details by an overseas company for a person authorised to accept service of documents on behalf of the company in respect of a UK establishment	BR6
Overseas Companies	OS DS01	Notice of closure of a UK establishment of an overseas company	695(A)(3)
Overseas Companies	OS DS02	Notice of termination of winding up of an overseas company	703(P)(5)
Overseas Companies	OS LQ01	Notice of appointment of a liquidator of an overseas company	703(P)(3)
Overseas Companies	OS LQ02	Notice by an overseas company which becomes subject to proceedings relating to insolvency	703(Q)(1)
Overseas Companies	OS LQ03	Notice of winding up of an overseas company	703(P)(1)
Overseas Companies	OS LQ04	Notice by an overseas company on cessation of proceedings relating to insolvency	703(Q)(2)
Overseas Companies	OS MG01	Particulars of a mortgage or charge by an overseas company	
Overseas Companies	OS TN01	Transitional return by a UK establishment of an overseas company	

European Economic Interest Groupings (EEIGs)

Functional Area	Form	Name of Form	Previous Form ID
European Economic Interest Groupings	EE FM01	Statement of name, official address, members, objects and duration for EEIG whose official address is in the UK	EEIG2
European Economic Interest Groupings	EE FM02	Statement of name, establishment address in the UK and members of an EEIG whose official address is outside the UK	EEIG3
European Economic Interest Groupings	EE AP01	Appointment of manager of an EEIG where the official address of the EEIG is in the UK	EEIG3
European Economic Interest Groupings	EE AP02	Appointment of corporate manager of an EEIG where the official address is in the UK	EEIG3
European Economic Interest Groupings	EE CH01	Change of manager's details of an EEIG where the official address of the EEIG is in the UK	EEIG3
European Economic Interest Groupings	EE CH02	Change of corporate manager's details of an EEIG where the official address of the EEIG is in the UK	EEIG3
European Economic Interest Groupings	EE TM01	Termination of appointment of manager of an EEIG where the official address is in the UK	EEIG3
European Economic Interest Groupings	EF NM01	Statement of name, other than registered name, under which an EEIG, whose official address is outside the UK, proposes to carry on business in the UK	EEIG6

Functional Area	Form	Name of Form	Previous Form ID
European Economic Interest Groupings	EE NM02	Statement of name, other than registered name, under which an EEIG, whose official address is outside the UK, proposes to carry on business in the UK	EEIG7
European Economic Interest Groupings	EE MP01	Notice of documents and particulars required to be filed for an EEIG	EEIG4
European Economic Interest Groupings	EE MP02	Notice of setting up or closure of an establishment of an EEIG	

Societas Europaea (SE)

Functional Area	Form	Name of Form	Previous Form ID
Societas Europaea (SE)	SE AP01	Appointment of a member of a supervisory organ of a Societas Europaea (SE)	SE79a
Societas Europaea (SE)	SE AP02	Appointment of corporate member of a supervisory organ of Societas Europaea (SE)	SE79a
Societas Europaea (SE)	SE TM01	Terminating appointment of member of a supervisory organ of Societas Europaea (SE)	SE79B
Societas Europaea (SE)	SE CH01	Change of member's details of a supervisory organ of a Societas Europaea (SE)	SE79C
Societas Europaea (SE)	SE CH02	Change of corporate member's details of a supervisory organ of a Societas Europaea (SE)	SE79C
Societas Europaea (SE)	SE AS01	Amendment of Statutes of a Societas Europaea (SE)	SE82(1)(a)
Societas Europaea (SE)	SE CV01	Conversion of Societas Europaea (SE) to a Public Limited Company (PLC)	SE85

Functional Area	Form	Name of Form	Previous Form ID
Societas Europaea (SE)	**SE DT01**	Draft terms of formation of holding Societas Europaea (SE) involving a United Kingdom (UK) registered company or SE	SE68(2)(a)
Societas Europaea (SE)	**SE DT02**	Draft terms of conversion of a Public Limited Company (PLC) to Societas Europaea (SE)	SE68(3)(a)
Societas Europaea (SE)	**SE DT03**	Notification of draft terms of conversion of Societas Europaea (SE) to a Public Limited Company (PLC)	SE86
Societas Europaea (SE)	**SE FM01**	Formation of subsidiary Societas Europaea (SE) under Article 2(3) of Council Regulation (EC) No 2157/2001	SE5
Societas Europaea (SE)	**SE FM02**	Formation of holding Societas Europaea (SE)	SE6
Societas Europaea (SE)	**SE FM03**	Formation of subsidiary Societas Europaea (SE) under Article 2(3) of Council Regulation (EC) No 2157/2001	SE7
Societas Europaea (SE)	**SE FM04**	Transformation of a Public Limited Company (PLC) to Societas Europaea (SE)	SE8
Societas Europaea (SE)	**SE FM05**	Formation of subsidiary Societas Europaea (SE) under Article 3(2) of Council Regulation (EC) No 2157/2001	SE9(1)
Societas Europaea (SE)	**SE SC01**	Notice of satisfaction of conditions for the formation of holding Societas Europaea (SE) by a United Kingdom (UK) registered company or SE	SE70(1)

Functional Area	Form	Name of Form	Previous Form ID
Societas Europaea (SE)	**SE SS01**	Statement of solvency by members of Societas Europaea (SE) which is proposing to transfer from the United Kingdom (UK)	SE72(6)
Societas Europaea (SE)	**SE TR01**	Proposed transfer from the United Kingdom (UK) of Societas Europaea (SE)	SE68(1)(a)
Societas Europaea (SE)	**SE TR02**	Transfer to the United Kingdom (UK) of Societas Europaea (SE)	SE10
Societas Europaea (SE)	**SE TR03**	Transfer from the United Kingdom (UK) of Societas Europaea (SE)	SE11
Societas Europaea (SE)	**SE WU01**	Notice of initiation or termination of winding up, liquidation, insolvency, cessation of payment procedures and decision to continue operating of Societas Europaea (SE)	SE82(1)

Cross Border Mergers

Functional Area	Form	Name of Form	Previous Form ID
Cross Border Mergers	**CB01**	Notice of a cross border merger involving a UK registered company	
Cross Border Mergers	**LL CB01**	Notice of a cross border merger involving a UK registered Limited Liability Partnership (LLP)	

Newspaper Libel and Registration Act

Functional Area	Form	Name of Form	Previous Form ID
Newspaper Libel and Registration Act	NLR1	Initial Registration/Annual Return form for a Newspaper	
Newspaper Libel and Registration Act	NLR2	Newspaper Libel and Registration Act, 1981	

Chapter 6

The Directors

General

Definition of a director

[6.1] Section 250 of the Companies Act 2006 (CA 2006) defines a 'director' as any person occupying the position of director, by whatever name called. This would be determined by reference to facts, such as the nature of the duties performed by the person and the authority he exercises within the company. The scope of this definition is extended, by virtue of CA 2006, s 251, to include any person (known as a 'shadow director') in accordance with whose directions or instructions the directors of a company are accustomed to act.

Anyone deemed to be a director will be subject to the privileges and liabilities which attach to a director. For instance, CA 2006, s 1121 states that a director is an officer of the company and that, as such, he is liable to the relevant penalties if he or the company is in default of CA 2006 or other legislation.

Shadow directors

[6.2] A shadow director is also required to comply with the provisions of CA 2006 applicable to directors, including the following:

(a)   his details must be entered in the register of directors (CA 2006, s 162);
(b)   he must disclose any interests in contracts of the company by written notice to the directors (CA 2006, s 182); and
(c)   any service contract must be available for inspection by the members (CA 2006, s 228).

The term 'shadow director' may include outside persons or corporate bodies who, often for legitimate commercial reasons, influence the directors' actions or otherwise control the company. A controlling shareholder or a creditor may be regarded as a shadow director where the provisions of CA 2006, s 251 apply. For instance, *Re Tasbian Ltd (No 3)* [1992] BCC 358 has illustrated how a person's activities can be easily construed as those of a shadow director. In this case, the person appointed as a 'company doctor' to Tasbian Ltd by Castle Finance Ltd (which had provided finance to the company), had negotiated with trade creditors, the then Department of Trade and Industry and the then Inland Revenue on the company's behalf. He had also monitored the company's trading position on a regular basis, countersigned all company cheques, as well as proposing and implementing a new group structure. The judge ruled that the activities of the company doctor could fall within the definition of a shadow director, and this ruling was confirmed by the Court of Appeal.

For a person to be regarded as a shadow director, the directors must, as a body, be acting on his directions or instructions and must be accustomed to doing so.

A person is not deemed to be a shadow director in circumstances where the directors act on advice given by him in a professional capacity (CA 2006, s 251(2)), since there is no express or implied requirement for the directors to act. In addition, where the directors act in accordance with directions or instructions on an isolated occasion, a person will not be deemed a director.

Under CA 2006, s 251(3), a holding company will not be treated as a shadow director of its subsidiary companies by reason only of the directors of such subsidiaries being accustomed to act in accordance with its directions or instructions, for the purposes of the following:

(i)   general duties of directors (Chapter 2 of the Act);
(ii)   transactions requiring members' approval (Chapter 4);
(iii)   contract with sole member who is also a director (Chapter 6).

This section would appear to imply that other factors would need to be taken into account to determine whether or not the holding company should be regarded as a shadow director under the above sections.

Appointment

[6.3] The Companies Act 2006 requires that a private company must have at least one director, while a public company must have at least two directors. The Act further restricts a sole director from also occupying the position of secretary of the company. The Companies Act 2006 envisages a requirement for at least one director to be a natural person to avoid a corporate director holding office as a sole director of a company. This requirement was implemented on 1 October 2008. Companies with only corporate directors in place on 8 November 2006 had until 1 October 2010 to remedy this situation. Going forwards, the company will be required to have at least one individual who can, if necessary, be held accountable for the company's actions.

The first directors of the company, as named in the incorporation documents filed with the Registrar of Companies, are deemed to have been appointed upon the incorporation of the company. Their appointments are effective from the date of issue of the company's certificate of incorporation. Subsequent appointments are made by the directors (see PRECEDENT A, APPENDIX 6A), and/or the company in general meeting, in accordance with the provisions contained in the company's articles of association. Under CA 2006, s 160, the appointments of directors at a general meeting of a public company must be voted upon individually, unless all the members present at the meeting have first agreed to appoint the directors in a single resolution.

Within 14 days of the appointment of a director, the relevant notification (form AP01 or AP02) must be filed with the Registrar of Companies, providing details of the director's name, address, date of birth and occupation, together with a list of directorships currently held and any past directorships held within five years prior to that appointment (see **3.14 THE STATUTORY RECORDS**).

Directors' service addresses

[6.4] Sections 240–246 of the Companies Act 2006 sets out rules applicable to all company directors, such that a director will have the choice of either disclosing his residential address or a service address (such as the company's registered office address) on the public record, with his residential address being kept separately. However, specified public bodies and credit reference agencies will be able to obtain a director's residential address for designated purposes, although a director may apply to the Registrar under CA 2006, s 243(5) for higher protection so that his address may not to be disclosed to credit reference agencies on the grounds that the director:

(a)   is at serious risk of violence or intimidation as a result of the activities of a company of which he is a director;

(b)   has been employed by the police or security services; or

(c)   is providing, or has provided, goods or services to the police or security services.

Any director who on 30 September 2009 had a valid confidentiality order issued under the Companies Act 1985 has the same protection as a director who has made a successful application under CA 2006, s 243(5), while a director whose confidentiality order expired before 1 October 2009 was required to renew his order under CA 2006 (CA 2006, s 243(5)). Directors will be under an obligation to ensure that the service address is kept up to date to ensure that it is fully effective for the service of documents, while the Registrar has the power to ban for up to five years the use of a service address which proves ineffective and place the director's usual residential address on the public register.

Listed companies

[6.5] For companies listed on the London Stock Exchange, the appointment of a new director must be notified as soon as possible, and in any case, by the end of the business day following the decision, to a Regulatory Information Service. The announcement must disclose the date of appointment and whether the person appointed will be executive or non-executive as well as details of any specific functions or responsibilities held. In addition, companies must notify a Regulatory Information Service (see **5.14 DISCLOSURE AND REPORTING REQUIREMENTS**) of the following for a newly appointed director:

(a)   details of any other directorships of publicly quoted companies held in the last five years indicating which are current directorships (including directorships of companies quoted on other and overseas exchanges);

(b)   details of any receivership, liquidation (compulsory or creditors' voluntary), administration, company voluntary arrangement or any composition or arrangement with its creditors generally or any class of its creditors, where the director was an executive director at the time of or within the 12 months such events (similar disclosure is required where the director was a partner in a partnership);

(c)   details of any public criticism of the director by statutory or regulatory authorities (which includes designated professional bodies) and disclosure of whether the director has ever been disqualified by a court from acting as a director of a company or from acting in the management or conduct of the affairs of a company; and

(d)   any unspent convictions in relation to indictable offences.

A listed company must also notify a Regulatory Information Service of any changes in the above details ((a) to (d)) in respect of any current director. If no details are required to be disclosed about the new director, that fact must be notified. Where notification is required, it may either be made in the notification of appointment of a director or separately within five business days of the decision to appoint the new director.

Rotation of directors

[6.6] Many companies adopt articles of association which require a third of the directors of the company to retire by rotation at each annual general meeting and to be subject to re-appointment by the company in general meeting (see **PRECEDENT B, APPENDIX 6A**). The appointment (and re-appointment) of a director is defined as ordinary business of the company, for which an ordinary resolution is required. Article 21 of the PLC Model Articles/clauses 73 to 80 of Table A 1985 indicate the circumstances in which a director must retire at a company's annual general meeting. These are:

(a)   where a director is subject to retirement by rotation; and
(b)   where a director has been appointed by the board of directors since the last general meeting of the company.

At the first annual general meeting of a company to which the above clauses apply, all the directors of the company are required to retire from office and are subject to re-election by the members at the meeting. For subsequent annual general meetings, Table A 1985 requires that one third of directors, or the number nearest to one third, are subject to retirement by rotation. However, there may be circumstances in which some of the directors are not caught by these provisions.

For instance, clause 84 of Table A 1985 provides that a managing director or a director holding executive office is not subject to retirement by rotation. In addition, directors who were appointed by the board of directors between annual general meetings are not included in calculating the number of directors required to retire by rotation, although they are subject to retirement under clause 78 of Table A 1985. For example, for a company which has five directors, one of whom is the managing director, and two of whom were appointed since the last annual general meeting, the number of directors required to retire by rotation is one (being the number nearest to one third).

The directors subject to retirement by rotation are those who have been longest in office. For directors appointed on the same day, the director to retire would be decided by lot or by agreement among the directors. A director required to be re-elected at the annual general meeting will generally hold office until the end of the meeting in question should he not be re-elected. However, a retiring director, if willing to act, will be deemed re-appointed if the company does not fill the vacancy created by his retirement, unless it is resolved not to re-appoint the director or not to fill the vacancy.

It is essential that where directors are required to retire the company's articles are strictly adhered to, since failure to re-elect a director could have important consequences. For instance, in *Re New Cedos Engineering Co Ltd*

[1994] 1 BCLC 797, the directors of the company refused to register a transfer of shares. It was successfully argued that no valid board meeting had been held within the two-month period in which registration of a share transfer may be refused, since the directors had ceased to hold office by failing to be re-elected at a general meeting.

While CA 2006, s 161 and clause 92 of Table A 1985 provide that any acts of the directors are valid notwithstanding any defect in the appointment of any director which is subsequently discovered, the above case clearly demonstrates the need to follow any rotation clauses correctly. It would be prudent in such circumstances for any directors whose appointment is defective to be re-appointed by the board of directors or the members in general meeting, while also requesting the members to ratify any acts of those directors during the period in which they technically did not hold office (see **PRECEDENT C, APPENDIX 6A**).

The rotation clauses enable the company to remove a director at the expiry of his period of office if it wishes to do so. In some cases, it may be inappropriate or inconvenient to retain such clauses in the company's articles, although it may be useful to have alternative powers of removal in the articles in addition to the statutory provisions (see **6.11** below). If rotation clauses are not needed, it is advisable to amend the company's articles to remove these provisions. Where they are required, however, they should be followed strictly bearing in mind the possible consequences of failing to re-elect directors.

Executive, non-executive and alternate directors

[6.7] Regulation 84 of Table A 1985 permits the board of directors to appoint one or more of their number as managing director or to hold any other executive office, for instance, as finance director. Such directors are generally termed 'executive director'. Article 5 of the PLC Model Articles/regulation 72 of Table A 1985 further provides that the directors may delegate to executive directors such of their powers as they decide upon such terms and remuneration as they think fit. The terms of, and remuneration for, executive office are usually governed by a director's service agreement (see **14.18 EMPLOYMENT, HEALTH AND SAFETY**).

Such service contracts (or a memorandum of its terms) must be available for inspection at the company's registered office or at a place defined by regulations under CA 2006, s 1136 (such as the company's principal place of business (CA 2006, s 227)). Where any term of a director's service contract for a period exceeding two years states that the director's employment cannot be terminated by the company by notice or can only be terminated in specified circumstances, the agreement must first be approved by ordinary resolution of the company in general meeting (CA 2006, s 188). In addition, for any further contract entered into by the company with the director while the earlier contract has more than six months to run, the unexpired portion of the original contract is added to the period for which the subsequent contract will run. Any term which contravenes section 188 will be void to the extent that it contravenes the section, and any contract or further contract to which the relevant provisions apply are deemed to contain a term entitling the company to terminate it at any time by giving reasonable notice (CA 2006, s 189).

The Cadbury Committee in their Code of Best Practice proposed that where a director's term of office will exceed three years, shareholders' approval should be sought on the service contract. This was subsequently superseded in part by the requirements of the Greenbury Code, and as a consequence the Listing Rules define a director's service contract as 'a service contract with a director of the issuer with a notice period of one year or more with provisions for predetermining compensation or termination of an amount which equals or exceeds one year's salary and benefits in kind'. This position has not changed with the publication of the Combined Code or its more recent incarnation, the UK Corporate Governance Code.

The holding of executive office is dependent upon the holding of office as director and, as such, any director ceasing to hold office as a director, for whatever reason, will also cease to hold executive office at the same time. Executive directors are still subject to the provisions of the company's articles of association, although, where the articles require directors to retire by rotation, such rotation clauses will generally not apply to directors holding executive office (see **6.6** above).

Non-executive directors

[6.8] Non-executive directors do not hold executive office but are selected by the board of directors for appointment so that the company may benefit from a wealth of commercial experience and expertise gained outside the company. Such directors have the same responsibilities and liabilities as executive directors in terms of their statutory and fiduciary duties, even though they are not usually as involved in the company's affairs as are executive directors. However, they have the same rights of access to information afforded to executive directors of the company.

The Cadbury Committee's Code of Best Practice advised companies to select non-executive directors through a formal selection procedure. Although the decision should be made by the board as a whole, selection may be by recommendation of a nomination committee. The Code recommended that the majority of such directors are sufficiently independent of the management of the company so that they can exercise an independent judgement in any decision before the board. To enable a non-executive director to exercise this level of independence, PRONED (Promotion of Non-Executive Directors) recommended that, in particular, a non-executive director:

(a) should not have been employed by the company in an executive capacity within the five years prior to his appointment as a non-executive director;

(b) should not have commercial relationships with the company, of a regular or continuing nature, where he or his employing firm act as professional advisers to the company, or of a significant nature, where he is employed by a company which is a customer of or a supplier to the company on whose board he sits; and

(c) should not have a personal relationship with any other member of the board.

PRONED provides further guidance on the rights, terms and conditions of appointment of non-executive directors, and emphasises their role on various board committees, notably the audit committee, the remuneration committee and the nomination committee. While a number of organisations have endorsed the value of adequate non-executive director representation at board level, the importance of this role was again recognised by the Greenbury Committee in their Report on Directors' Remuneration.

The Greenbury Committee recommended that, to avoid potential conflicts of interest, a company's board of directors should set up remuneration committees exclusively comprised of non-executive directors to determine on behalf of the board, and on behalf of the shareholders, the company's policy on executive and specific remuneration packages for each of the executive directors. Such non-executive directors should have no personal financial interest, other than as shareholders, in the matters to be decided, no potential conflicts of interest arising from cross-directorships and no day-to-day involvement in running the business. The Hampel Committee supported the recommendations of the earlier committees and the position with regard to non-executive directors remains unchanged.

The role of the non-executive director was examined further in a review chaired by Derek Higgs on 'The role and effectiveness of non-executive directors' (the 'Higgs Review'), which recommended changes to the Combined Code. Some of the key features of the Combined Code which was agreed by the Financial Reporting Council and reflects the recommendations of the Higgs Review (and the Smith Report on Audit Committees: Combined Code guidance) are examined in **6.18** below.

Alternate directors

[6.9] A company's articles may provide for the appointment of an alternate director, who is a person appointed by a director to act in accordance with his instructions on the board of directors in the absence of that director (PLC Model Articles, article 25/Table A 1985, regulation 65). The appointment may be made by notice to the company at its registered office and is usually subject to the approval of the board. The appointing director may also revoke the alternate's appointment at any time by notice to the company. Where the appointing director ceases to hold office, for whatever reason, any alternate director so appointed will automatically cease to hold office.

An alternate director is generally entitled to receive notice of all board meetings, and of all committee meetings of which his appointor is a member. He may be deemed for all purposes a director and therefore his appointment would be required to be entered in the register of directors and notified to the Registrar of Companies. He would also be responsible for his own acts and defaults and, for this reason, is not deemed an agent of the director appointing him.

Remuneration of directors

[6.10] The Cadbury Committee's Code of Best Practice recommended that directors delegated the subject of remuneration to a remuneration committee (see **APPENDIX 6D**) made up wholly or mainly of non-executive directors, whose purpose is to recommend to the board appropriate remuneration for executive directors. For listed companies, the Greenbury Committee report went further than this by recommending that a remuneration committee should be established and consist exclusively of non-executive directors. The committee should make a report each year to the shareholders on behalf of the board, and the chairman of the remuneration committee should attend the company's annual general meeting to answer shareholders' questions about directors' remuneration. The report should form part of, or be annexed to, the company's annual report and accounts, and should give details of any service contracts with notice periods in excess of one year, giving reasons for the notice period. Although meetings of the committee may be open to executive directors, no such director may be involved in any decision on his own remuneration.

The remuneration to be paid to the directors of a company will usually fall into the following categories:

(a)　remuneration subject to the directors' determination:
- (i)　remuneration paid in respect of any executive office or services provided;
- (ii)　benefits to directors who have held executive office or employment;
- (iii)　expenses incurred within the discharge of directors' duties;

(b)　remuneration subject to approval in general meeting:
- (i)　any emoluments outside the scope of the above.

An alternate director is not entitled to receive any remuneration from the company for his services, unless there is provision for payment of alternate directors in the company's articles of association.

Article 23 of the PLC Model Articles/regulation 84 of Table A 1985 permits the directors to determine the terms and remuneration of any director holding the office of managing director or any other executive office and in respect of the provision by him of any services outside the scope of the ordinary duties of a director. Regulation 83 further provides that the directors may determine the expenses they are to be paid in connection with the discharge of their duties and regulation 87 authorises the directors to provide benefits, whether by payment of a gratuity, pension, insurance or otherwise on the retirement of any director who has held executive office or employment with the company.

The directors are generally entitled to such remuneration as the company in general meeting may by ordinary resolution determine (PLC Model Articles, article 23/Table A 1985, regulation 82). The level of remuneration may be determined in advance of the year in question, although, in practice, it is often confirmed at the general meeting at which the accounts disclosing such remuneration are laid. Approval of the accounts will not in itself authorise the payment of remuneration which has not been otherwise authorised, unless the shareholders are aware that in approving the accounts they are also being asked to approve the directors' remuneration.

Disclosure of the total emoluments paid to the directors in any year is required in the notes to the accounts of a company. For the purpose of approving the directors' remuneration at any general meeting at which the accounts are considered, it will be necessary to establish whether such emoluments are subject to the directors' determination or approval in general meeting.

As a consequence of the Greenbury Report on Directors' Remuneration, the Listing Rules were amended to incorporate its recommendations. The former Combined Code amended the information required to be disclosed in relation to the remuneration of directors. Under the Listing Rules a company's annual report to the shareholders must contain:

(i)   a statement of the listed company's policy on executive directors' remuneration;

(ii)   the amount of each element in the remuneration package for the period under review of each director by name, including, but not restricted to, basic salary and fees, the estimated money value of benefits in kind, annual bonuses, deferred bonuses, compensation for loss of office and payments for breach of contract or other termination payments, together with the total for each director for the period under review and for the corresponding prior period, and any significant payments made to former directors during the period under review; such details to be presented in tabular form, unless inappropriate, together with explanatory notes as necessary;

(iii)   information on share options, including SAYE options, for each director by name in accordance with the requirements of the Directors' Remuneration Report Regulations;

(iv)   details of any long-term incentive schemes, other than share options details of which have been disclosed under (iii) above, including the interests of each director by name in the long-term incentive schemes at the start of the period under review; entitlements or awards granted and commitments made to each director under such schemes during the period, showing which crystallise either in the same year or subsequent years; the monetary value and number of shares, cash payments or other benefits received by each director under such schemes during the period; and the interests of each director in the long-term incentive schemes at the end of the period;

(v)   an explanation and justification of any element of remuneration, other than basic salary, which is pensionable;

(vi)   details of any directors' service contract with a notice period in excess of one year or with provisions for pre-determined compensation on termination which exceeds one year's salary and benefits in kind, giving the reasons for such notice period;

(vii)   details of the unexpired term of any directors' service contract of a director proposed for election or re-election at the forthcoming annual general meeting and, if any director proposed for election or re-election does not have a directors' service contract, a statement to that effect;

(viii) a statement of the listed company's policy on the granting of options or awards under its employees' share schemes and other long-term incentive schemes, explaining and justifying any departure from that policy in the period under review and any change in the policy from the preceding year;

(ix)   for money purchase schemes, details of the contribution or allowance payable or made by the listed company in respect of each director during the period under review;

(x)   for defined benefit schemes:

(a) details of the amount of the increase during the period under review (excluding inflation) and of the accumulated total amount at the end of the period in respect of the accrued benefit to which each director would be entitled on leaving service or is entitled having left service during the period under review; and

(b) either:

    (i) the transfer value (less director's contributions) of the relevant increase in accrued benefit (to be calculated in accordance with Actuarial Guidance Note GN11 but making no deduction for any underfunding) as at the end of the period; or

    (ii) so much of the following information as is necessary to make a reasonable assessment of the transfer value in respect of each director:

        (1) age;

        (2) normal retirement age;

        (3) the amount of any contributions paid or payable by the director under the terms of the scheme during the period under review;

        (4) details of spouse's and dependants' benefits;

        (5) early retirement rights and options, expectations of pension increases after retirement (whether guaranteed or discretionary); and

        (6) discretionary benefits for which allowance is made in transfer values on leaving and any other relevant information which will significantly affect the value of the benefits.

(c) no disclosure of voluntary contributions and benefits.

Schedule 8 of the Large and Medium-sized Companies and Groups (Accounts and Reports) Regulations 2008 (SI 2008/410) sets out the requirements for the directors' remuneration report for financial years beginning on or after 6 April 2008. In particular, CA 2006, s 420 requires the directors of quoted companies to prepare a directors' remuneration report which includes disclosure of:

(a) information about the composition of the remuneration committee and performance-related remuneration and liabilities in respect of directors' contracts, such information being addressed in Part 2 of Schedule 8 and comprising:

    (i) circumstances surrounding the consideration by the directors of matters pertaining to directors' remuneration;

    (ii) a statement of the company's policy on directors' remuneration for the following financial year and for financial years subsequent to that;

    (iii) a performance graph which sets out the total shareholder return of the company on the class of equity share capital, if any, which caused the company to fall within the definition of a quoted company; and

    (iv) information concerning each director's contract of service or contract for services; and

(b)   detailed information about directors' remuneration set out in Part 3 of
         Schedule 8 and comprising:
         (i)   emoluments;
         (ii)   share options;
         (iii)   long term incentive plans;
         (iv)   pensions;
         (v)   excess retirement benefits of each director and, where appropri-
                 ate, of past directors;
         (vi)   compensation for loss of office paid to past directors; and
         (vii)   sums paid to third parties in respect of a director's services.

For the purposes of these regulations, a quoted company is defined as a
company whose equity share capital:

(i)   has been included on the official list in accordance with the provisions
        of Part VI of the Financial Services and Markets Act 2000;
(ii)   is officially listed in an EEA State; or
(iii)   is admitted to dealing on either the New York Stock Exchange or on the
        NASDAQ.

The directors' remuneration report must be approved by the board of directors
and signed on its behalf by a director or secretary of the company. Section 439
of CA 2006 provides that the directors' remuneration report is subject to the
approval of the members at the general meeting at which the annual accounts
for the financial year are to be laid. For this purpose, an ordinary resolution to
consider the directors' remuneration report must be tabled at the meeting. A
copy of the directors' remuneration report must also be delivered to the
Registrar of Companies.

The auditors are required to report on the auditable part of the remuneration
report (those items required by Part 3 of Schedule 8) and in their report give
their opinion on whether the directors have properly prepared the report in
accordance with CA 2006.

Failure to comply with the requirements of the new regulations with regard to
the signing of the report, its laying before the members and its delivery to the
Registrar of Companies may render liable to a fine the directors of a quoted
company who are in office immediately before the end of the period for laying
and delivering accounts for the financial period in question.

Removal

[6.11] The circumstances in which a director may vacate his office are
generally stated in the company's articles of association and usually comprise
the following statements which follow those specified by article 22 of the PLC
Model Articles (and its precursor, regulation 81 of Table A 1985):

(a)   that a person ceases to be a director by virtue of any provision of
        the Companies Act 2006 or he becomes prohibited by law from being
        a director;
(b)   a bankruptcy order is made against that person;
(c)   a composition is made with that person's creditors generally in satis-
        faction of that person's debts;

(d)　a registered medical practitioner who is treating that person gives a written opinion to the company stating that person has become physically or mentally incapable of acting as a director and may remain so for more than three months;

(e)　by reason of that person's mental health, a court makes an order which wholly or partly prevents that person from personally exercising any powers or rights which that person would otherwise have;

(f)　notification is received by the company form the director that the director is resigning from office as director, and such resignation has taken effect in accordance with its terms (see **PRECEDENT D, APPENDIX 6A**).

The company's articles may further provide that a director may be removed from office by resolution (of a specified majority) of the company, or that his office may terminate upon service of notice at the company's registered office by the company's holding company or majority shareholder. In the absence of any provisions in the articles of association, a director may nonetheless be removed from office by provisions contained in CA 2006.

Under CA 2006, s 168, the members may by ordinary resolution remove a director from office before his term of office has expired (see **PRECEDENT E, APPENDIX 6A**), provided that special notice (see **PRECEDENT F, APPENDIX 6A**) has been given to the company at its registered office of their intention to propose such a resolution at a general meeting convened for that purpose. It should be noted that the provisions of CA 2006, s 288 relating to written resolutions of members of private companies do not extend to resolutions passed under section 168.

The director in question is entitled under this section to receive a copy of the special notice and to prepare and have circulated to the members a written representation (unless upon application to the court, such representation is held to be defamatory). Furthermore, the director is entitled to attend and speak at the meeting at which his removal will be proposed.

The power of removal under CA 2006, s 168 co-exists with any such power contained elsewhere and cannot be set aside by anything in the articles or in any agreement between the company and the director. In addition, it is not the purpose of this section to deprive a director of any right to compensation or damages in respect of his appointment as a director or any appointment terminating with that as a director.

The resignation or removal of a director must be notified to Companies House (form TM01) within 14 days of the event and, in the case of a listed company, to a Regulatory Information Service as soon as possible and in any case by the end of the business day following the decision or receipt of notice of the change by the company.

Powers of directors

General

[6.12] The directors are responsible for the operation and management of a company both on a day-to-day basis and in the long term. Directors have extensive powers to manage the company and these are derived from the company's constitution. For instance, article 3 of the PLC Model Articles/regulation 70 of Table A 1985 empowers the directors to exercise all the powers of the company subject to the provisions of the articles.

Articles of association commonly contain specific provisions and restrictions relating to the exercise of their powers, for example, borrowing powers, although the limitation of legitimate actions is usually kept to a minimum so as to facilitate the efficient running of the company. There are also statutory provisions restricting the powers of directors to ensure that the company is managed for the benefit of shareholders and employees, including the Insolvency Act 1986, the Company Directors Disqualification Act 1986 and the Financial Services Act 1986.

The wide powers given to directors to act on behalf of the company mean that they are responsible for the arrangements relating to the fulfilment of the company's statutory duties. They can therefore be liable to penalties should the company fail to comply, and are sometimes personally liable for the consequences of their actions (eg for wrongful trading under the Insolvency Act 1986).

The directors act as agents of the company and cannot do anything which is not authorised by the company's constitution. Any act by them which is *ultra vires* the company will be void and ineffective, except where the transaction can be enforced by an outsider (see **11.2 COMMERCIAL CONSIDERATIONS**).

The directors' powers cannot be overruled by the members as they do not act as agent for some or even all the members. As such, their powers to appoint one of their number as managing director, to declare interim dividends and to sue in the company's name, have been treated as exclusive to them, and resolutions passed by members conflicting with these decisions are therefore ineffective. However, article 4 of the PLC Model Articles contains a reserve power for members which entitles them to direct the directors (by special resolution) to take, or refrain from taking, specified action, while not invalidating any of the directors' acts prior to the passing of the resolution. The members are also at liberty to alter the company's constitution by special resolution.

Directors should appreciate the obligations and responsibilities required of their office and understand the professional duty of care which a director as an officer of a company must bring to his position. The directors will commonly turn to the company secretary to enable them to carry out their duties in a professional manner.

Company secretary – role and relationship

[6.13] The company secretary is also an officer of the company as defined by CA 2006, ss 1121 and 1173 and, as such, he is liable to the various penalties incurred if he fails to comply with the requirements of the Companies Act 2006. It is his duty to draw the directors' attention to any action which is required to be taken, and he may be liable for damages resulting from his negligence, as well as any attempt, through the articles of association or any contract, to exempt any director, or other officer of the company, from liability in respect of negligence, default, breach of duty or of trust.

Section 1157 of CA 2006, does, however, provide that the courts may grant relief in any proceedings against an officer of the company, if it appears that the officer, although liable in respect of negligence, default, breach of duty or of trust, acted honestly and reasonably and under the circumstances of the case ought to be excused.

It is generally the duty of the company secretary to ensure that the board of directors acts in accordance with companies' legislation and the company's constitution (see **CHAPTER 1 THE COMPANY SECRETARY**). He should act on the instructions of the directors in filing all formal returns as required by the Companies Acts and maintaining the prescribed registers and records, as well as the minute book, the despatch of notices of general meetings and the company's report and financial statements.

The relationship of the company secretary to the board of directors and to individual directors will vary according to the size of the company and whether the directors hold executive or non-executive office (see **6.7** above). The directors will commonly rely on the company secretary for information and advice on all company issues, especially where they do not have first-hand experience, and the Cadbury Report (see **6.15** below) emphasised that all directors should have access to the company secretary on such matters. The report also recognised the importance of the company secretary's role in corporate governance matters, particularly in implementing the Code of Best Practice.

The Higgs Review further strengthened the role of the company secretary with regard to corporate governance. The Review made recommendations about the company secretary's role in relation to his accountability to the board on corporate governance issues, his responsibility for the induction and professional development of directors and for information flows within the board and its committees and between non-executive directors and senior management, and his involvement as secretary to all board committees. The Review also recommended that the appointment and removal of the company secretary should be a matter for the board as a whole.

The company secretary should therefore be able to advise, guide and warn the directors of the danger of disqualification and possible personal liability. The company secretary must be a competent and reliable person, and must be able to assist the directors in carrying out their duties. He must be able to carry out his duties in a satisfactory manner, without being biased towards any one director, as he is ultimately responsible for the performance of most of the duties imposed by the Companies Acts, which are generally delegated to him by the directors (see **1.1 THE COMPANY SECRETARY**).

Corporate governance

[6.14] Corporate governance remains a continually developing area which, since the Committee on the Financial Aspects of Corporate Governance under the chairmanship of Sir Adrian Cadbury first considered this issue, has seen the formation of further committees established to examine specific topics. The Study Group on Directors' Remuneration chaired by Sir Richard Greenbury and the Committee on Corporate Governance under Sir Ronald Hampel's chairmanship sought to develop the principles of corporate governance further. Turnbull, Higgs and Smith, amongst others, have considered other important aspects of corporate governance.

The Cadbury Report

[6.15] The Report of the Committee on the Financial Aspects of Corporate Governance (the 'Cadbury Report') was published on 1 December 1992. It defined corporate governance as the system by which companies are directed and controlled, and identified the three elements of governance as:

(a)   the board of directors;
(b)   the shareholders; and
(c)   the auditors.

The Cadbury Report, with its accompanying Code of Best Practice sought to clarify and redress the balance between the respective roles and responsibilities of the directors, the shareholders and the auditors. The report charged the directors with the responsibility for corporate governance, the shareholders with the responsibility to ensure that directors and auditors appointed by them fall within an appropriate governance structure with the auditors providing an external and objective check on the directors' statements.

The Code itself covered the role and structure of the board of directors, the appointment and independence of non-executive directors, the determination of the executive director' remuneration (subsequently superseded by the Greenbury recommendations) and the financial reporting and controls to be exercised by the board. The Code was primarily aimed at UK-registered companies listed on the London Stock Exchange, although the Code and the report's recommendations were regarded as relevant to many companies, whether public or private.

Since the Auditing Practices Board adopted the recommendations of the Cadbury Report in relation to directors' and auditors' responsibilities, a statement by the auditors on these matters has been required in their report on the accounts for financial periods ending on or after 30 September 1993.

The Greenbury Report

[6.16] The Greenbury Report on Directors' Remuneration was published on 17 June 1995. It sought to allay public concerns about the remuneration of directors by seeking to 'identify good practice in determining Directors' remuneration and prepare a Code of such practice for use by UK PLCs'. The Code was primarily aimed at listed companies, although its principles were also recommended for non-listed companies.

The Greenbury Code covered a number of areas comprising the composition and role of the remuneration committee, disclosure and approval provisions, remuneration policy and service contracts and compensation. The Code was intended to work alongside Cadbury although it extended and replaced the section in the Cadbury Code dealing with the remuneration of executive directors.

The Hampel Report

[6.17] The aim of the Hampel Committee was to review the implementation of the findings of the Cadbury and Greenbury Committees and the Report went on to endorse the overwhelming majority of the two earlier reports and their findings. According to the Hampel Report the 'objective of the new principles and code, like those of the Cadbury and Greenbury codes, is not to prescribe corporate behaviour in detail but to secure sufficient disclosure so that investors and others can assess companies' performance and governance practice and respond in an informed way'.

The Report itself set out seventeen principles (which follow) on which the final combined set of principles and code were based. The Code addressed the three elements of governance identified by Cadbury and covered the composition and role of the board of directors together with director' remuneration; the role of, and relationship with, the company's shareholders; and the board's accountability and its relationship with the company's auditors, as well as the function of the auditors.

(1) The board (Principle A.I)
Every listed company should be headed by an effective board which should lead and control the company. (Endorses Cadbury.)

(2) Chairman and CEO (Principle A.II)
There are two key tasks at the top of every public company — the running of the board and the executive responsibility for the running of the company's business. A decision to combine these roles in one individual should be publicly explained.

(3) Board balance (Principle A.III)
The board should include a balance of executive directors and non-executive directors (including independent non-executives) such that no individual or small group of individuals can dominate the board's decision taking. (Endorses Cadbury.)

(4) Supply of information (Principle A.IV)
The board should be supplied in a timely fashion with information in a form and of a quality appropriate to enable it to discharge its duties. (Endorses Cadbury.)

(5) Appointments to the board (Principle A.V)
There should be a formal and transparent procedure for the appointment of new directors to the board. The Committee recommended as good practice the adoption of a formal procedure for appointments to the board, with a nomination committee making recommendations to the full board. Individuals should also receive appropriate training following appointment and then as necessary to ensure that they are aware of their duties and responsibilities as director of a listed company.

(6) Re-election (Principle A.VI)

All directors should be required to submit themselves for re-election at regular intervals and at least every three years. Companies adopting Table A 1985 currently allow managing directors and executive directors to hold office without being required to retire by rotation.

(7)   The level and make-up of remuneration (Principle B.I)
Levels of remuneration should be sufficient to attract and retain the directors needed to run the company successfully. The component parts of the remuneration should be structured so as to link rewards to corporate and individual performance.

(8)   Procedure (Principle B.II)
Companies should establish a formal and transparent procedure for developing policy on executive remuneration and for fixing the remuneration packages of individual directors.

(9)   Disclosure (Principle B.III)
The company's annual report should contain a statement of remuneration policy and details of the remuneration of each director.

(10)   Shareholder voting (Principle C.I)
Institutional shareholders have a responsibility to make considered use of their votes.

(11)   Dialogue between companies and investors (Principle C.II)
Companies and institutional shareholders should each be ready, where practicable, to enter into dialogue based on the mutual understanding of objectives.

(12)   Evaluation of governance disclosures (Principle C.III)
When evaluating companies' governance arrangements, particularly those relating to board structure and composition, institutional investors and their advisers should give due weight to all relevant factors drawn to their attention. Investors should show some flexibility in interpreting the company's compliance with a code of best practice and ought to listen to the directors' explanations. Investors should then judge their explanations on their merits.

(13)   The AGM (Principle C.IV)
Companies should use the AGM to communicate with private investors and encourage their participation.

(14)   Financial reporting (Principle D.I)
The board should present a balanced and understandable assessment of the company's position and prospects. (Endorses Cadbury.)

(15)   Internal control (Principle D.II)
The board should maintain a sound system of internal control to safeguard shareholders' investment and the company's assets. The Report states that this covers financial, operational and compliance controls and risk management.

(16)   Relationship with auditors (Principle D.III)
The board should establish formal and transparent arrangements for maintaining an appropriate relationship with the company's auditors. (Endorses Cadbury.)

(17)   External auditors (Principle D.IV)

The external auditors should independently report to shareholders in accordance with statutory and professional requirements and independently assure the board on the discharge of their responsibilities in accordance with professional guidelines.

The Committee envisaged that the requirement for companies to confirm compliance with the Cadbury Code in the annual report and accounts would be superseded by a new requirement to make a statement to show how the principles of corporate governance are being applied and how the company is complying with the code. Any significant diversions from the code would need to be justified.

Combined Code

[6.18] Following the publication of its final report, the Hampel Committee produced a set of principles and code of good corporate practice which embraced the work of the Cadbury, Greenbury and Hampel Committees. The Committee submitted to the London Stock Exchange a Combined Code which sought to bring together Hampel and the earlier codes. The Stock Exchange followed this up with a consultation document inviting views on the cohesiveness of the draft Combined Code and when the code should apply to listed companies.

The final version of the Combined Code was published during June 1998 and a related amendment was made to the Listing Rules. Listed companies were required to comply with the new listing rule for accounting periods ending on or after 31 December 1998. As with the earlier Codes, the Combined Code was of relevance to non-listed companies.

The Combined Code differed from the code in the committee's final report in a number of respects. In particular, the Code made clear that in relation to the role of chairman and chief executive officer there should be a clear division of responsibilities at the head of the company which will ensure a balance of power and authority such that no one individual has unfettered powers of decision. Companies should also avoid paying more remuneration to directors than is necessary to attract and retain directors of the required calibre and no director should be involved in deciding his or her own remuneration.

Subsequently, the Turnbull committee published in September 1999 its final report on Internal Control: Guidance for Directors on the Combined Code. The Combined Code then required listed companies to report on their financial, operational and compliance controls as well as their risk management. The guidance applied in respect of accounting periods ending on or after 23 December 2000. One of the practical implications of the Code was that boards of directors need to assess the potential risks to which their business may be exposed. This may be addressed by producing a risk map to identify the key risk areas and establishing appropriate controls to address those risks. The Turnbull Review Group has since proposed some limited changes to the guidance, which are set out more fully in **4.31 ACCOUNTS AND AUDITORS**.

Following on from the Higgs Review and the Smith Report, the Financial Reporting Council agreed the final text of a new Combined Code during July 2003. The Code incorporated many of the Higgs and Smith recommendations and came into effect for reporting years beginning on or after 1 November 2003. The key features of the Code are:

(a)   new definitions of the role of the board, the chairman and the non-executive directors;

(b)   more open and rigorous procedures for the appointment of directors and from a wider pool of candidates;

(c)   formal evaluation of the performance of boards, committees and individual directors, enhanced induction and more professional development of non-executive directors;

(d)   at least half the board to be independent non-executive directors, with independence now defined (exemption for companies outside the FTSE 350);

(e)   the separation of the roles of the chairman and the chief executive is reinforced;

(f)   a chief executive should not generally go on to become chairman of the same company;

(g)   no individual to chair more than one FTSE 100 company;

(h)   closer relationships between the chairman, the senior independent director, non-executive directors and major shareholders; and

(i)   a strengthened role for the audit committee in monitoring the integrity of the company's financial reporting, reinforcing the independence of the external auditor and reviewing the management of financial and other risks.

In order to meet their obligations under the Listing Rules, listed companies have to describe how they apply the Code's main (and supporting) principles and either confirm that they comply with the Code's provisions or provide an explanation to shareholders where they do not.

The Financial Reporting Council subsequently consulted on further changes to the Combined Code and made a number of revisions (primarily those relating to Code provisions B.2.1, D.2.1, D.2.2 and Schedule C). The FRC introduced these revisions into the June 2006 version of the Combined Code ahead of the UK Listing Authority's consultation with listed companies. This further consultation was required before listed companies could be formally required under the Listing Rules to follow the new version of the Code. Further changes were made to the Code resulting in the June 2008 version which applies to accounting periods beginning on or after 29 June 2008.

Both the June 2006 and the June 2008 versions of the Combined Code are available online at www.frc.org.uk/corporate/combinedcode.cfm.

The UK Corporate Governance Code

[6.19] Following the FRC's latest review of the impact of the Combined Code, it published the UK Corporate Governance Code which seeks to address views on those parts of the Code which work well or require further reinforcement, any parts of the Code that have served to reduce the effectiveness of the board, the inclusion of other aspects of good governance practice, and the effectiveness of the 'comply or explain' mechanism. In producing the latest version of the Code, the FRC also considered the recommendations of the Walker Review of the governance of banks and other financial institutions, as well as their wider application to listed companies in other sectors.

The Code is now structured as follows:

(a)   Section A: Leadership;
(b)   Section B: Effectiveness;
(c)   Section C: Accountability;
(d)   Section D: Remuneration;
(e)   Section E: Relations with Shareholders.

The FRC also 'commissioned the Institute of Chartered Secretaries and Administrators (ICSA) to work with others on its behalf to update as necessary the good practice guidance from the 2003 Higgs Report . . . in the light of the proposed changes to the Code and economic and other developments'. As part of this remit, the FRC asked the ICSA to consider whether additional guidance should be provided on a number of related issues raised in Sections A (Leadership) and B (Effectiveness) of the Code. The result of this was draft guidance on 'Improving board effectiveness' which the ICSA published in March 2010 with a view to producing final guidance (following a second consultation in July 2010). The FRC subsequently published its Guidance on Board Effectiveness in March 2011 and this replaces the Higgs Guidance which has been withdrawn.

The UK Corporate Governance Code (formerly the Combined Code) applies to all companies with a primary listing (under the new listing regime), regardless of whether they are incorporated in the UK or overseas, for reporting years beginning on or after 29 June 2010 (see **APPENDIX 6G**).

The FRC published the Stewardship Code in July 2010 with the aim of enhancing 'the quality of engagement between institutional investors and companies to help improve long-term returns to shareholders and the efficient exercise of governance responsibilities'. The Stewardship Code defines this engagement as involving, amongst other matters, purposeful dialogue on strategy, performance and the management of risk, as well as issues being voted on by shareholders at general meetings. The FRC views the Stewardship Code as complementary to the UK Corporate Governance Code.

In addition, the ICAEW published the Audit Firm Governance Code in January 2010 to provide a code of good governance practice for audit firms involved in the audit of listed companies. The Code addresses six key areas of governance (leadership, values, independent non-executives, operations, reporting and dialogue) and is intended to apply for financial years beginning on or after 1 June 2010.

With the publication of the UK Corporate Governance Code, the Stewardship Code and the Audit Firm Governance Code, the three elements of governance defined by the Cadbury Report were reviewed and updated during the course of 2010.

Other codes of best practice

[6.20] In addition to the above Codes, a number of institutional investors have produced their own corporate governance guidelines against which they have indicated they will measure the effectiveness of boards of companies in which they invest. These guidelines are in some cases more exacting than the above Codes on particular issues of concern to institutional investors. Boards may find that they will need to address the concerns of their shareholders even though they are complying with or adhering to the codes and principles of Cadbury, Greenbury and Hampel.

Board meetings

[6.21] The Companies Act 2006 does not impose a requirement on the directors for the holding of board meetings. Indeed, regulation 88 of Table A 1985 merely provided that 'subject to the provisions of the articles, the directors may regulate their proceedings as they think fit', while article 19 of the PLC Model Articles enables the directors, subject to the articles, to 'make any rule which they think fit about how they take decisions, and about how such rules are to be recorded or communicated to the directors'. For many companies, it is usual for meetings to be conducted on an informal basis, particularly where the directors and shareholders are the same people, or there are few directors, or the directors can otherwise make decisions without notice or formality.

Unless the articles of association provide otherwise, directors can only exercise their powers collectively by passing resolutions at board meetings or by written resolution signed by all the directors. The company's articles will generally empower the directors to regulate their proceedings in respect of meetings. They should ensure that they comply with rules relating to:

(a)   the chairman's appointment (see **6.24** below);
(b)   notice (see **6.25** below);
(c)   quorum (see **6.26** below);
(d)   voting rights (see **6.27** below); and
(e)   recording of decisions (see **6.28** below).

The board of directors may comprise both executive and non-executive directors (see **6.7** above) and its composition should be such that power and authority is not reserved for too few members of the board. For this reason, the Cadbury Report advised that where possible the offices of chairman and the chief executive are not occupied by the same person and that the views of the non-executive directors, who should be sufficiently independent, carry significant weight in the board's decisions.

Matters specifically reserved for the approval of the board include the approval of the interim and final financial statements as well as the approval and recommendation respectively of the interim and final dividend. In addition, the board is responsible for the general management of the company, the appointment and removal of board and committee members as well as the company secretary. The Cadbury Committee also recommended that major capital projects, major contracts in the ordinary course of business and major investments, are subject to board approval (see **APPENDIX 6B**).

Committees

[6.22] The board of directors are generally authorised by the company's articles of association to delegate their powers to a committee comprising one or more directors (PLC Model Articles, article 5/Table A 1985, regulation 72). Such a committee will be formed for a particular purpose, for instance, the consideration of an item of business which cannot be properly discussed at a full board meeting without further examination.

Prior to setting up any committee, the directors should determine its relationship with the board, such as its terms of reference and its reporting requirements, as well as the regulations governing the proceedings of the committee, such as the number of directors that will constitute the quorum. Where the committee comprises two or more directors, Table A 1985 provides that, subject to any conditions imposed by the directors, the provisions of the articles governing the proceedings of directors will apply to the committee.

The board of directors may delegate responsibilities for the determination of executive directors' pay to a remuneration committee (see **APPENDIX 6D**) — for listed companies the Greenbury Committee's Code of Best Practice made this a requirement, and the selection and recommendation of suitable candidates for appointment as directors to a nomination committee (see **APPENDIX 6C**). The Cadbury Report principally dealt with the establishment of an audit committee (see **APPENDIX 6E**) to recommend to the board suitable auditors for appointment, to review the financial statements prior to submission to the board and to discuss any matters of concern with the auditors. All listed companies are advised to establish an audit committee composed of (at least three) non-executive directors, the majority of whom should be independent of the management of the company.

Company secretary's duties

[6.23] The company secretary's duties will vary according to the business to be conducted at the meeting but he must be ready to advise the chairman and the board, if requested to do so, on procedural points and to give his views on any matters referred to him. He should be in a position to alert the chairman to any proposed action which is unlawful or in conflict with the company's constitution, or any trust deed or any shareholders' pre-emption rights in the transfer or allotment of shares.

He must be aware of matters such as the inclusion of any other business which is not already on the agenda, particularly where a director is aiming to get a quick decision without the board having had time to carefully consider the matter. It follows that the company secretary should have available all necessary documents to enable him to perform his duties as required.

He must ensure that all confidential papers are removed and kept safely once the meeting is over.

Chairman

[6.24] The articles of association will generally provide for the appointment and removal of a chairman at meetings of the directors (PLC Model Articles, article 12/Table A 1985, regulation 91). The directors may appoint one of their number as chairman of the board and, in this role, he may preside at every meeting of the directors at which he is present. In his absence, Table A 1985 provides for the appointment of an alternative chairman for the purpose of conducting the board meeting.

The chairman must ensure that the meeting has been properly convened, in that notice of the meeting has been validly served on all directors in accordance with the company's articles. He should also establish that the meeting is properly constituted by ensuring that his appointment is valid and that the specified quorum is present at the meeting. He will be responsible for the regulation of the meeting and should therefore ensure that the meeting is conducted as required by the articles.

The chairman has a duty to ensure that the board meeting is a proper forum for debate. He should allow each director the opportunity to express his own views on any matter before the board, should he wish to, and to hear the views of other directors on that matter. He must not show partiality to any director, nor allow a director to monopolise the meeting so that debate is stifled.

The chairman may adjourn the meeting at any time should he feel that there is any cause to do so, subject to any conditions imposed by the company's articles.

Notice and agenda

[6.25] Unlike general meetings of the members, there is no statutory provision for the period of notice to be given to directors. Board meetings can therefore be at short notice or on specified dates as determined, so long as the directors are given reasonable notice or are notified in accordance with any provisions made in the articles of association. Indeed, written notice need not be given to the directors, unless required by the company's articles. However, all directors must be aware that in coming together the intention is to transact business of the company.

The articles usually provide that any one director may summon a meeting directly or request the company secretary to do so. If there is default in giving notice, the meeting will be irregular. The company secretary should ensure that all directors are given reasonable notice, so that they have sufficient time to enable them to attend, even if they have indicated that they will not wish to attend, otherwise the meeting may be invalid. Some articles may provide that where a director is absent from the UK, notice need not be given to that director (Table A 1985, regulation 88) although the Model Articles (in all its forms) remove this limitation. The notice of the meeting must contain:

(a)   the place of the meeting; and
(b)   the day, date and time of the meeting; and may also include:
(c)   the business to be transacted; and
(d)   the details of any special business to be transacted.

The agenda for the meeting may be circulated with the notice of the meeting, or it may alternatively form part of the notice (see (c) and (d) above). Any papers required to enable the directors to formulate their views on items to be discussed should be circulated with the agenda. The agenda will enable the chairman to conduct the business of the meeting in a logical manner and ensure that nothing is overlooked. It also helps the company secretary as he can make reference to the agenda to guide him in the drafting of the minutes after the meeting.

The company secretary should prepare a separate form of agenda for the chairman, giving more detail than those of the directors and containing the points to be taken into account in reaching a decision. There should be wide margins for use by the chairman should he wish to make any notes and the company secretary should refer to such notes, when preparing the minutes of the meeting.

Quorum

[6.26] The quorum (ie the number of directors required to be present to constitute a valid meeting) is generally fixed by the articles, although the articles may also provide the directors with the power to determine the quorum for board meetings (PLC Model Articles, article 10/Table A 1985, regulation 89). Table A 1985 provides that, unless the directors determine otherwise, two directors will comprise the quorum and permits, in the absence of their appointors, alternate directors to be counted in the quorum.

The quorum must be a 'disinterested' quorum entitled to vote on the matters to be discussed; thus the quorum must be comprised of directors who are entitled to vote on the particular matter before the meeting. If a director is interested in a contract and is not permitted by the articles to vote on it, he may not be counted for the purpose of the quorum with respect to that particular business. The meeting is irregular if the required quorum is not present and no business can be transacted.

A company's articles will generally specify the minimum number of directors required for the company, as in regulation 64 of Table A 1985, or will enable the members to determine the minimum by ordinary resolution. For many companies, the minimum number of directors will be equivalent to the number of directors comprising the quorum. In the case of a private company, the articles may provide that the minimum is one, and the quorum will be adjusted to one to enable the transaction of business by a sole director.

Where the number of directors falls below the number fixed as the quorum, the directors will be unable to transact valid business either in a meeting of the board, or by written resolution of the directors. Article 11 of the PLC Model Articles/regulation 90 of Table A 1985 provides that in this circumstance the continuing directors or the sole remaining director may act only for the purpose of appointing a director to fulfil the quorum requirement or to convene a general meeting.

Article 11/regulation 90 does not specify the business to be conducted at the general meeting but its purpose would presumably be to enable the directors to transact valid business. This may be achieved either by the members appointing a director to meet the quorum specified in the articles or to alter the provision in the articles so that the quorum is reduced to less than or equal to the number of directors then in office.

Where the number of directors falls below one, in the case of a sole director, it would then be necessary for the members to requisition a general meeting, by giving notice to the company at its registered office, to authorise the company secretary to convene a meeting at which a resolution could be passed to appoint new directors.

Voting

[6.27] Commonly, a company's articles of association will allow each director one vote on each resolution proposed at a board meeting, with the chairman being entitled to a second or casting vote in the case of deadlock (PLC Model Articles, article 14/Table A 1985, regulation 88). Where voting is exercised, this would usually be by a show of hands. However, decisions of the board are often made by consensus with the chairman determining the mood of the meeting and declaring the resolution carried or defeated on that basis.

The chairman may exercise his own vote in favour of a resolution and his casting vote either for or against the resolution. In exercising his casting vote, the chairman should consider whether or not the passing of a resolution by such a vote is in the best interest of the company, particularly where the directors propose to commit the company to a controversial or expensive course of action.

Similarly, each director owes a fiduciary duty to the company and should therefore exercise his vote in the interest of the company (see **6.32** below). For instance, the articles will usually provide that a director cannot vote on a resolution concerning a matter in which he has a material interest which conflicts or may conflict with the interest of the company (PLC Model Articles, article 14/Table A 1985, regulation 94). The provision may be relaxed in specific cases by the articles. Article 14/regulation 94 specifies the circumstances where it should not apply.

Having reached decisions on the items of business before the board, it is essential that the directors ensure all such decisions are implemented. This may involve delegation to the company secretary, such as in giving notice of a general meeting, or to a committee of directors where such business requires further consideration before a decision can be made (see **6.22** above). It is therefore common for the minutes of board meetings to indicate the person responsible for implementing a particular decision.

Minutes

[6.28] Section 248 of CA 2006 requires that a record of all meetings of the directors is kept. It is generally the company secretary's duty, as delegated by the directors, to keep a clear and concise record of the minutes of each meeting. Relevant dates and figures should be recorded, as well as the main considerations that led to a decision, and names should only be given if requested by the speaker, except where a formal resolution is proposed and seconded (see **1.15 THE COMPANY SECRETARY**).

Article 18 of PLC Model Articles/regulation 93 of Table A 1985 empowers a company to send out one or more copies of a proposed written resolution to each director for his consideration, with his consent to the passing of the resolution being indicated by signature on the document (see **3.46 THE STATUTORY RECORDS**). The resolution is deemed to have been passed, and thus valid and effective, on the date the document is signed by the last director. A leading case, *Hood Sailmakers Ltd v Axford* [1996] 4 All ER 830, examined the provisions of regulation 98 of Table A 1948 (the predecessor to regulation 93) and the impact upon it of regulation 106 (equivalent to regulation 88 of Table A 1985). Regulation 93 states that '[a] resolution in writing signed by all the directors entitled to receive notice of a meeting of the directors . . . shall be as valid and effectual as if it had been passed at a meeting of directors', while regulation 88 deems it unnecessary to give notice of such a meeting to a director who is absent from the United Kingdom. This would imply that if all directors save one were outside the UK written resolutions could be passed by the remaining director only. If this were the case, the effect would be to override the quorum requirement expressed in regulation 99 (equivalent to regulation 89 of Table A 1985). However, the *Hood Sailmakers* case has confirmed that all directors must sign this document for the resolutions to be valid.

A resolution in writing is equivalent to a resolution passed at a board meeting and should be entered in the minute book in the same manner as a board minute. Resolutions in writing are normally used where it is inconvenient to summon a board meeting, such as where there is not enough time to give notice for some urgent business or it is not possible for the directors to meet in the same place. Similarly, where the business to be conducted is routine in nature, this may be dealt with by written resolution. Decisions of a sole director are generally made by written resolution, since a meeting of the directors would only comprise one director in any case. A board meeting with a sole director would be appropriate where others have been invited to attend the meeting, such as the company secretary or the company's auditors.

The Act contains provisions requiring the minutes of all meetings of the company to be open to inspection by members of the company. However, no statutory right of inspection is given to the members to enable them to examine the minute book containing decisions of the directors. The directors' minute book is available for inspection by any director or alternate director of the company, and must be open for inspection by the company's auditors.

The minutes are defined in CA 2006 as 'evidence' of the decisions taken at a meeting. Their evidential value is considered more fully in **3.47 THE STATUTORY RECORDS**.

Modern technology

[6.29] The directors have been empowered by regulation 88 of Table A 1985 to regulate their proceedings in whatever manner they think fit, subject to any provisions in the company's articles, and this discretion has been extended by article 19 of the PLC Model Articles. As such, these provisions provide some scope for authority to use modern technology in the conduct of board meetings. For instance, meetings may be held over the telephone or the use of video-conferencing facilities would enable the directors to hold a meeting 'round the table' over long distances. However, this regulation is subject to other provisions in the articles and an explicit statement that directors may use such means to hold their meetings will avoid any ambiguity.

Meetings conducted by telephone or video-conferencing facilities may present a number of difficulties (both legal and practical), the most obvious one being the definition of a meeting established in *Sharp v Dawes* (1876) 2 QBD 26 (see **7.27 MEMBERSHIP**), that a meeting involves the coming together of two or more persons. Such meetings would not only appear to fail this test but also the quorum requirement.

Meetings conducted by telephone, even on a conference call, present difficulties due to the inability of each director to see the other and although impersonation is a potential problem, a more practical problem would be misunderstanding any decisions agreed or being unable to hear clearly what is being said. Such meetings would practically only take place between two or three directors where it is possible to bring 'together' all directors of the company without prior notice of a meeting. Any meetings conducted by telephone which excluded any director may be invalidated by the notice provisions.

With video-conferencing facilities, it is possible to conduct a meeting between several locations in a manner similar to a meeting where the directors are physically present in the same room, thereby overcoming some of the practical problems inherent with meetings over the telephone. Such facilities would be useful where the number of directors is large and they are dispersed between, say, two or three locations. Meetings conducted in this manner would require more formality, since it would be necessary to give sufficient notice to all directors.

For meetings held between several locations, issues around where the meeting actually took place, or where the meeting is held across different time zones, the date or time of the meeting, need to be addressed. To avoid ambiguity, it would be useful to establish rules relating to such meetings. For instance, the directors could determine that all meetings of a UK-incorporated company are deemed to be held in the UK and that the time of the meeting is to be expressed in Greenwich Meantime (GMT). Alternatively, the venue for the meeting may be determined by where the chairman of the meeting is located.

Where directors are separated by long distances, it is possible to pass decisions by written resolution of the directors. This would require sending copies of the resolution to each director by post and awaiting the return of each signed document before the resolution was passed. With the use of fax machines, it is possible to obtain a director's consent to a particular course of action within hours rather than days, by the transmission of a proposed resolution to each director and the receipt of a signed facsimile from each director. Any such signed resolutions should be supported by a copy of the resolution with the director's original signature.

Generally, it would be advisable, in the absence of any express provisions in the company's articles of association, for all meetings conducted by the above means to be confirmed in writing by the directors party to the decisions made, such as by written resolution of the directors. Alternatively, the directors should consider updating the articles to address such problems as the quorum requirement, so that they are able to take advantage of the flexibility offered by modern technology.

Duties of directors

General

[6.30] There are certain duties which a person running a business is obliged to carry out regardless of the legal form of the business. Essentially, these duties are to comply with specific business legislation such as employment, health and safety at work, consumer, income tax and VAT legislation. The duties of a company director are, however, considerably more onerous than those of a sole trader or partner.

While a director has a wide range of legal duties to fulfil, he also owes certain duties to the company. These have developed from a number of a common law duties (such as fiduciary duties and a duty of skill and care) and have been codified by a statement of general duties in CA 2006. Sections 171–177 of CA 2006 define the general duties owed by a director to the company. They are based on the common law rules and equitable principles but will operate in place of those rules. However, it is intended that the general duties will be interpreted and applied in the same way as common law rules or equitable principles. The general duties comprise:

(a)   duty to act within powers (CA 2006, s 171);
(b)   duty to promote the success of the company (CA 2006, s 172);
(c)   duty to exercise independent judgement (CA 2006, s 173);
(d)   duty to exercise reasonable care, skill and diligence (CA 2006, s 174);
(e)   duty to avoid conflicts of interest (CA 2006, s 175);
(f)   duty not to accept benefits from third parties (CA 2006, s 176); and
(g)   duty to declare interest in proposed transaction or arrangement (CA 2006, s 177).

The provisions of CA 2006 in relation to these general duties came into force on 1 October 2007, with the exception of those provisions which relate to conflicts of interest (that is, (e) to (g) above) which apply from 1 October 2008. As these duties are owed by the directors to the company, the company will be entitled to enforce them against directors. The general duties apply to all persons acting as director and to any person deemed to be a shadow director. However, in the case of shadow directors, there will be aspects of the statutory duties that must be applied differently. The courts will continue to be able to interpret and develop the provisions of the statutory statement in the light of changing business circumstances and needs.

The former common law position is now set out in **APPENDIX 6F**.

Duty to act within powers

[6.31] Under CA 2006, s 171, a director of a company must act in accordance with the company's constitution, and only exercise powers for the purposes for which they are conferred.

Duty to promote the success of the company

[6.32] Section 172 of CA 2006 requires a director to act in the way he considers, in good faith, would be most likely to promote the success of the company for the benefit of its members as a whole. In exercising this duty, a director must have regard (amongst other matters) to its strategic interests and stakeholders:

(a)   the likely long-term consequences of any decision, the impact of the company's operations on the community and the environment, and the desirability of the company maintaining a reputation for high standards of business conduct; and

(b)   the interests of the company's employees, the need to foster the company's business relationships with suppliers, customers and others, and the need to act fairly as between members of the company.

A director will be regarded as fulfilling this duty even if the purposes of the company consists of or includes purposes other than the benefit of its members, or if he is required by law to consider or act in the interests of creditors of the company.

Duty to exercise independent judgment

[6.33] Section 173 of CA 2006 states that a director of a company must exercise independent judgment. A director's ability to fulfil this duty is not impaired if he is required to observe contractual obligations under an agreement entered into by the company which restricts the future exercise of discretion by its directors, or he acts in a way authorised by the company's constitution.

Duty to exercise reasonable care, skill and diligence

[6.34] A director of a company must exercise reasonable care, skill and diligence. Section 174 of CA 2006 defines this as the care, skill and diligence that would be exercised by a reasonably diligent person with the general knowledge, skill and experience reasonably expected of a person carrying out the functions carried out by the director, and the general knowledge, skill and experience the director actually has.

Duty to avoid conflicts of interest

[6.35] A director must avoid any situation in which he currently has, or could have, an interest (either directly or indirectly) that does or may conflict with the company's interests (CA 2006, s 175). This section applies to the exploitation of any property, information or opportunity by the director (regardless of whether or not the company could take advantage of these) but not to a conflict of interest arising in relation to a transaction or arrangement with the company. Any situation which cannot reasonably be regarded as likely to give rise to a conflict, or relates to a matter which has been authorised by the directors, will not amount to a conflict of interest. A conflict of interest includes a conflict of interest and duty as well as a conflict of duties.

The directors of a private company may propose and authorise a matter provided the company's constitution does not contain a provision which invalidates the giving of such authorisation. However, for a public company, the directors must propose and authorise the matter in accordance with a specific term of the company's constitution. Any authorisation given is invalidated if, at the board meeting at which the matter is considered, it would only have been given if any interested directors were counted in the quorum or would not have been agreed to without including their votes.

Duty not to accept benefits from third parties

[6.36] Section 176 of CA 2006 places a duty on a director of a company not to accept a benefit from a third party conferred by reason of his being a director, or as a result of his doing (or not doing) anything as a director. A 'third party' is defined as a person other than the company, an associated body corporate or a person acting on behalf of the company or an associated body corporate. This does not include any benefits received by a director from a person by whom his services (whether as a director or not) are provided to the company, or any benefit which could not reasonably be regarded as likely to give rise to a conflict of interest.

Duty to declare interest in proposed transaction or arrangement

[6.37] Section 177 of CA 2006 requires a director of a company, who is in any way, directly or indirectly, interested in a proposed transaction or arrangement with the company, to declare the nature and extent of that interest to the other directors. This may be given at a meeting of the directors, or by notice to the directors in accordance with CA 2006, s 184 or s 185 (see **6.40** below)

Corporate manslaughter

[6.38] The Corporate Manslaughter and Corporate Homicide Act 2007 established that an organisation is guilty of an offence if the way in which its activities are managed or organised causes a person's death, and amounts to a gross breach of a relevant duty of care owed by the organisation to the deceased. The offence is called corporate manslaughter under the law of England and Wales or Northern Ireland, and corporate homicide under the law of Scotland.

The Act is intended to apply to a number of specified organisations including corporations which for the purposes of this Act are defined as any body corporate wherever incorporated (other than a corporation sole). A breach of duty of care by an organisation amounts to a 'gross' breach if the alleged conduct falls far below what can reasonably be expected of the organisation in the circumstances. An organisation is guilty of an offence under this section only if the way in which its activities are managed or organised by its senior management is a substantial element in the breach. Senior management encompasses those persons who play significant roles in:

(a)   the making of decisions about how the whole or a substantial part of its activities are to be managed or organised; or

(b)   the actual managing or organising of the whole or a substantial part of those activities.

It is the organisation that is guilty of the offence (and is consequently liable on conviction on indictment to a fine). While an individual cannot be guilty of aiding, abetting, counselling or procuring the commission of an offence of corporate manslaughter, this is clearly an issue for a responsible senior management to consider in the exercise of their duties.

Disclosure of directors' interests

General

[6.39] Directors are responsible to the members of the company for their actions. They must, in carrying out their duties, bear in mind the interest of the members and employees of the company, and must at all times act in good faith for the benefit of the company.

The Companies Act 2006 imposes certain duties on directors so that they cannot exploit their privileged position within a company and to avoid conflicts of interest. To achieve this aim directors are obliged to make full disclosure of certain interests, so that others connected with the company are kept fully aware of the true interests of the director. Directors therefore have a statutory duty in relation to:

(a)   disclosure of interests in transaction or arrangement (see **6.40** below);

(b)   loans to directors (see **6.41** below); and

(c)   obtaining approval of substantial property transactions (see **6.42** below).

A company listed on the London Stock Exchange is required by the Listing Rules to adopt a code of dealing in relation to the company's listed securities. The Model Code (which forms an annex to LR9 of the Listing Rules) sets a minimum standard, although a company may adopt a code with more exacting rules. The Code applies to dealings by the company's directors and by every person discharging managerial responsibilities, or any employee of the company, or any group company with access to inside information. The Model Code is a continuing obligation under the Listing Rules and companies are not required to adopt the Code each time it is amended.

Part V of the Criminal Justice Act 1993 introduced provisions relating to insider dealing and, by virtue of Schedule 6 to this Act, the Company Securities

(Insider Dealing) Act 1985 is repealed in its entirety. Section 52 of the 1993 Act provides that an individual who has information as an insider is guilty of insider dealing if he deals in securities that are price-affected securities in relation to this information in circumstances where the acquisition or disposal of shares occurs on a regulated market, or he relies on a professional intermediary or is himself acting as a professional intermediary. It is also an offence if a person in possession of such information encourages another person to deal in these securities in the above circumstances or improperly discloses the information to another person.

Section 53 contains defences to the above offences and Schedule 1 to the Act also provides special defences to a person whose business is as a market maker, or who can show that the information was market information or that he acted in conformity with the price stabilisation rules under section 48 of the Financial Services Act 1986. An individual guilty of insider dealing shall be liable on summary conviction to a fine not exceeding the statutory maximum (currently £5,000) or imprisonment for a term of not more than six months or both; or on conviction on indictment to a fine or imprisonment for a term of not more than seven years or both.

Disclosure of interests in existing transaction or arrangement

[6.40] Where a director has an interest (whether directly or indirectly) in any transaction or arrangement entered into by the company, he is obliged in accordance with CA 2006, s 182 to declare the nature and extent of his interest at a meeting of the directors, or by notice in writing (CA 2006, s 184) or by general notice (CA 2006, s 185) to the directors. A further declaration must be made if the earlier declaration of interest proves to be at the time or subsequently inaccurate or incomplete.

The requirement to disclose includes indirect interests such as the interests of connected persons as defined in CA 2006, s 252, except where such a person is also a director of the company. A 'connected person' under CA 2006, s 252 is defined as follows:

(a) members of the director's family (see CA 2006, s 253);
(b) a body corporate with which the director is connected (as defined in CA 2006, s 254);
(c) a person acting in his capacity as trustee of a trust–
  (i) the beneficiaries of which include the director or a person who by virtue of paragraph (a) or (b) is connected with him; or
  (ii) the terms of which confer a power on the trustees that may be exercised for the benefit of the director or any such person, other than a trust for the purposes of an employees' share scheme or a pension scheme;
(d) a person acting in his capacity as partner–
  (i) of the director; or
  (ii) of a person who, by virtue of paragraph (a), (b) or (c), is connected with that director;
(e) a firm that is a legal person under the law by which it is governed and in which–

(i)   the director is a partner;

(ii)   a partner is a person who, by virtue of paragraph (*a*), (*b*) or (*c*) is connected with the director; or

(iii)   a partner is a firm in which the director is a partner or in which there is a partner who, by virtue of paragraph (*a*), (*b*) or (*c*), is connected with the director.

Section 253 of CA 2006 defines those family relationships which comprise the members of a director's family. These generally include dependants such as children and stepchildren and adult members such as the director's spouse or civil partner and his parents. This section also includes any other person (whether of a different sex or the same sex) with whom the director lives as partner in an enduring family relationship. Under CA 2006, s 254, a director is regarded as connected with a body corporate if he and the persons connected with him are interested in at least 20% of the nominal value of the equity share capital of that body corporate or control the exercise of more than 20% of the voting power at any general meeting of that body.

Where the declaration is made in writing, this may either be by notice in writing or by a general notice. A notice in writing may be sent in hard copy form by hand or by post, or by an agreed means of electronic delivery provided the recipient has agreed to receiving notice in this manner. The making of the declaration is deemed to form part of the proceedings of the next board meeting after the notice has been given. A general notice may be given where a director has an interest in a specified body corporate or firm, or is connected with a specific person, and is to be regarded as interested in any arrangement or transaction the company may enter into with such parties.

A declaration is not required where the interest could not be regarded as reasonably giving rise to a conflict of interest, the directors are already aware of the interest, or the director's interest relates to the terms of his service contract.

A company's articles of association can provide that the interested director shall not vote or be counted in the quorum at a meeting at which a contract in which he is interested is discussed, unless his interest is as a shareholder or he represents an associate company. If the director does not disclose his interest, he is not covered by the protection in the articles of association which permit him to be interested in a contract and he may not be allowed to keep any private profit which he may make. If the breach of duty to disclose is subsequently discovered, the contract will be *prima facie* voidable and can be cancelled by the company, and the director will be liable to criminal proceedings and to a fine on conviction.

Directors' interests in a contract must be disclosed in the notes to audited accounts in accordance with CA 2006, s 412.

Loans to directors

[6.41] The general rule is that a company is prohibited from making a loan to a director of a company or of its holding company or giving a guarantee or providing security in connection with a loan made by any person to a director, without the members of the company first approving the transaction (CA 2006, s 197(1)). However, CA 2006 draws a distinction between loans which require the approval of the members of the company and loans which can be entered into without seeking such approval. For a public company, or a company associated with a public company, the approval of the members is required for a transaction which is:

(a)   a quasi-loan to a director of the company or its holding company, or the provision of a guarantee or security in connection with a quasi-loan made by any person to such a director (CA 2006, s 198);

(b)   a loan or quasi-loan to a person connected with a director of the company or its holding company, or the provision of a guarantee or security in connection with loan or quasi-loan (CA 2006, s 200); or

(c)   a credit transaction as creditor for the benefit of a director of the company or of its holding company, or a person connected with such a director, or the provision of a guarantee or security in connection with that credit transaction (CA 2006, s 201).

A resolution of the holding company is also required if the director is a director of the holding company. The resolution must be supported by a memorandum setting out the nature of the transaction, the amount of the loan and its purpose, as well as the extent of the company's liability. This memorandum must be made available for inspection by the members at the company's registered office for a period of 15 days prior to the meeting at which the resolution will be proposed and at the meeting itself.

Under CA 2006, the approval of the members of a company (whether public or private) is not required for transactions comprising:

(i)   a loan by a company for expenditure incurred, or to be incurred, by a director in the performance of his duties as an officer of the company or to avoid incurring such expenditure, provided the total value of the transaction and any other relevant transactions or arrangements does not exceed £50,000 (CA 2006, s 204);

(ii)   a loan by the company to a director for expenditure incurred, or to be incurred, by him, in defending any criminal or civil proceedings in connection with any alleged negligence, default, breach of duty or breach of trust by him in relation to the company or an associated company, or in connection with any application for relief under CA 2006, s 661(3) or (4) or s 1157 (see **6.51** below), or to avoid incurring such expenditure, where the terms provide for repayment if the director is convicted or judgment found against him (CA 2006, s 205);

(iii)   a loan by the company to a director for expenditure incurred, or to be incurred, by him, in defending himself in an investigation by a regulatory authority or against action proposed to be taken by that authority in connection with any alleged negligence, default, breach of duty or breach of trust by him in relation to the company or an associated company, or to avoid incurring such expenditure (CA 2006, s 206); or

(iv)   —

(a)   a loan or quasi-loan to a director, or the provision of a guarantee or security in connection with such a loan, by a company, the value of which, together with any other relevant transactions or arrangements, does not exceed £10,000;

(b)   a credit transaction, or the provision of a guarantee or security in connection with such a transaction, by a company, the value of which, together with any other relevant transactions or arrangements, does not exceed £15,000; or

(c)   a loan or quasi-loan to a director by a money-lending company, where the transaction is entered into by the company in the ordinary course of business, for no greater value and on terms no more favourable than for any unconnected person of the same financial standing (this also permits the making of home loans) (CA 2006, s 207).

A quasi-loan in these circumstances is a transaction under which the company agrees to pay, or pays otherwise than in pursuance of an agreement, a sum for a director or agrees to reimburse, or reimburses otherwise than in pursuance of an agreement, expenditure incurred by another party for the director:

(A)   on terms that the director (or a person on his behalf) will reimburse the company; or

(B)   in circumstances giving rise to a liability on the director to reimburse the company.

(CA 2006, s 199.)

The rules on loans to directors also apply to:

(I)   connected persons such as a spouse or minor children (defined in **6.40** above);

(II)   any company in which he is interested in at least one-fifth of the equity share capital; and

(III)   any company in which he can control the exercise of more than one-fifth of the votes.

Any transaction or arrangement which required members' approval but was entered into with a director without obtaining such approval is in breach of the Act and voidable at the instance of the company, unless restitution of the money or asset covered by the transaction or arrangement is no longer possible, the company has been indemnified for any loss or damage arising, or rights acquired in good faith by a person not party to these arrangements would be affected by the avoidance. The director concerned is also liable to make good any loss for which repayment is not obtained from a third party and to account for his own profit, unless he can prove that reasonable steps were taken to ensure that the Act was being complied with.

Where the approval of the members of the company, and where required, the members of the holding company, has not been obtained for a transaction subject to such approval, this can be remedied by the members passing a resolution to affirm the transaction or arrangement entered into by the company.

Substantial property transactions

[6.42] Should a director wish to purchase any substantial non-cash asset from a company or to dispose of such an asset to the company, then the approval of the members by an ordinary resolution at general meeting is required (CA 2006, s 190(1)). The term 'non-cash asset' applies to any property or interest in property other than cash, eg lease, shares, patents, copyrights, the benefits of book debts, etc (CA 2006, s 1163).

The following should be noted, when considering such a transaction:

(a)   shareholders' approval is only required if:
    (i)   the value of the assets is more than £5,000 and exceeds the lesser of £100,000 or 10% of the company's net assets;
    (ii)   the transaction is not between companies within a wholly-owned group.
(b)   a transaction which does not receive the approval of the members will generally be voidable; and
(c)   in relation to the transaction, if the board of directors exceeds any limitation of its powers under the company's articles, it will be voidable at the instance of the company in accordance with CA 2006, s 41 (see **6.44** below).

Where (c) applies, the directors will be liable to account to the company for any gain made directly or indirectly from the transaction and shall indemnify the company for any loss or damage which arises. The transaction can be ratified by the members in general meeting.

Intervention by the courts

[6.43] Generally, the courts are reluctant to intervene in the acts or decisions of the directors, except in the following circumstances where the directors:

(a)   have not acted honestly and in good faith (*bona fide*);
(b)   have exceeded their powers derived from the company's constitution (see **6.44** below);
(c)   have caused the company to act illegally; or
(d)   have in their actions breached the rules as established in the case of *Associated Provincial Picture Houses Ltd v Wednesbury Corporation* [1948] 1 KB 223, known as the '*Wednesbury Principles*', being that the directors have:
    (i)   taken into account matters which they ought not to take into account and acted in their own or a third party's interest;
    (ii)   acted for an improper purpose;
    (iii) refused to take into account or neglected to take into account matters which they ought to take into account;
    (iv)   done something which no reasonable board of directors could have considered to be in the company's interest, or which they actually thought would be injurious to its interests.

In order to safeguard their position directors should ensure that their reasons and the facts which they took into account, as well as the arguments against or for any proposed course of action, are fully recorded in the minutes of the board meeting.

Limitations on company's right to set aside a transaction

[6.44] Sections 39 and 40 of CA 2006 limit a company's right to have a transaction entered into by a third party acting in good faith with the company set aside by providing that:

(a) the validity of an act of a company shall not be called into question on the grounds of lack of capacity by reason of anything in the company's memorandum (CA 2006, s 39(1)); and

(b) in favour of a person dealing in good faith with a company, the power of the board of directors to bind the company, or authorise others to do so, shall be deemed to be free of any limitation under the company's constitution (CA 2006, s 40(1)).

A member may still bring proceedings to restrain acts which are beyond the company's capacity or beyond the directors' powers and the directors are therefore still under a duty to observe any limitations on their powers in the company's memorandum of association, as well as actions which, but for CA 2006, s 39(1), would be beyond the company's capacity. Such actions may only be ratified by special resolution of the company. Relief from liability relating to actions beyond the company's capacity may be agreed by a separate special resolution.

Section 40 of CA 2006 does not, however, affect any liability incurred by the directors, where they have exceeded their power, although these actions can be ratified by ordinary resolution of the company.

(i) For the purpose of CA 2006, s 40, a person is not to be regarded as acting in bad faith merely because he knows that an act is beyond the powers of the directors. He is presumed to be acting in good faith unless the contrary is proven.

(ii) Limitations on the directors' powers under the company's constitution include limitations derived from:

(A) a resolution of the company in general meeting or meeting of any class of shareholders; or

(B) any agreement between the members of the company or any class of shareholders.

Exception to limitation

[6.45] Section 41 of CA 2006 seeks to restrict the circumstances in which a director may contract with the company of which he is a director, a person connected with him or a company with whom the director is associated (see **6.40** above) where the company has acted *ultra vires* and under which the company may not have the transaction set aside.

This applies in circumstances where a company enters into a transaction with a director of the company or of its holding company or a person connected with him (see **6.40** above), and the board of directors, in connection with the transaction, exceeds any limitation on its powers under the company's constitution.

Section 41 states that such transactions are voidable at the instance of the company, notwithstanding the provisions of CA 2006, s 40 (see **6.43** above).

A private company limited by shares or by guarantee, having only one member, is permitted to enter into contracts with that member. However, where the sole member is a director of the company and the company enters into any contract with that member which is not:

(i)   reduced to writing; nor
(ii)   made in the ordinary course of the company's business,

the company is required, by virtue of CA 2006, s 231, to set out the terms of the contract in a written memorandum or record such terms in the minutes of the first board meeting following the making of the contract. For this purpose, a sole member who is a shadow director will be treated as a director under this section.

Liability of directors

General

[6.46] In carrying out his duties, certain standards are expected of a director. To avoid liability for acts done by him he must be able to show that he acted honestly and reasonably and that he ought fairly to be excused. He may be personally liable if he is negligent and makes a misrepresentation in that capacity.

Since the introduction of the Insolvency Act 1986 (IA 1986) and the coming into force of the Company Directors Disqualification Act 1986, there has been an increased possibility for directors to be disqualified and made personally liable for the company's debts. A liquidator or receiver has a statutory duty to report on the conduct of directors as well as shadow directors or failed companies. A report must be made to the Department for Business, Innovation and Skills if it is found that there have been activities which could lead to a director being declared unfit by the courts. (See **9.32** BORROWING AND SECURITY.)

Under the Company Directors Disqualification Act 1986, the director of a company may be disqualified from acting as a director of any company for a period of between 2 and 15 years, depending upon the nature of the offence committed under this Act. The circumstances in which an application may be made for the director's disqualification are as follows:

(a)   he has been guilty of three or more defaults in complying with companies' legislation in relation to the filing of documents with the Registrar of Companies during a period of five years prior to an application for his disqualification;

(b) he is, or was, a director of a company which has at any time become insolvent and that his conduct as a director of that company makes him unfit to be concerned in the management of a company;

(c) he has carried on business with the intention of defrauding the creditors of the company or any other person, or for a fraudulent purpose as defined under IA 1986, s 213 (see **6.48** below); or

(d) he was the director of a company which has gone into insolvent liquidation, and knew, or ought to have known that the company could not avoid insolvent liquidation; known as wrongful trading under IA 1986, s 214 (see **6.47** below).

A director who acts whilst disqualified or whilst an undischarged bankrupt is liable to imprisonment or a fine, or both, and is personally liable for debts incurred by the company whilst he was involved in the management of the company. Any person (including the company secretary) who knowingly acts on the instructions of a disqualified director is also personally liable. In both cases the liability is joint and several with the company and any other person who is liable.

In deciding whether to disqualify a director (or shadow director) the courts will take into account several factors such as:

(i) breach of faith or duty owed by the director to the company;

(ii) the use of the company's assets for the director's own benefit;

(iii) the company's failure to keep proper records or file statutory returns;

(iv) failure to produce annual accounts;

(v) causing a company's insolvency;

(vi) failure to supply customers with their goods even though they have been paid for; and

(vii) in an insolvency, failure to comply with duties relating to statement of affairs, attendance at meetings, surrender of company property.

Under CA 2006, the director of the company may be liable to default fines or other penalties (see above) for his failure to:

(A) file documents in due time with the Registrar of Companies, such as the annual return, audited accounts, various notifications and resolutions;

(B) convene and hold an annual general meeting;

(C) register a charge, which is registrable under CA 2006; or

(D) afford pre-emption rights to the existing members of a company, pursuant to CA 2006, s 561(1).

In addition, a director may incur personal liability under IA 1986 for:

(I) wrongful trading (see **6.47** below);

(II) fraudulent trading (see **6.48** below); or

(III) acting while disqualified (also under the Company Directors Disqualification Act 1986).

In the event that a company is struck off the register maintained at Companies House and is dissolved, either as a result of the Registrar of Companies taking action against the company (CA 2006, s 1000) or at the request of the directors (CA 2006, s 1003), the directors remain personally liable for any liabilities of the company for a period of six years from its dissolution (see **9.24**

BORROWING AND SECURITY.) This period of personal liability is reduced to two years if the company is removed from the register as a result of its liquidation under the procedures contained in IA 1986.

Most of the personal liability provisions of IA 1986 only apply where a company is in liquidation and involve the directors contributing to the company's assets for distribution by the liquidators.

With increasing interest in the civil liability of company directors, concerns have been expressed that suitably qualified individuals may be deterred from accepting positions as company directors. The key principles of director liability are not set out in legislation. The law does little to recognise that directors may face legal action for breach of duty (especially the duty of care and skill) even when they have acted in good faith and in the belief that their decisions were in the best interests of the company.

The Government has ruled out exemption or indemnification for fraudulent or other illegal conduct. Nor is it possible to insure against such liabilities. The Higgs Review, when considering the issue of directors' and officers' liability insurance, noted that 'the cost of [such] insurance is increasing and the coverage appears to be becoming less comprehensive'.

Wrongful trading

[6.47] Section 214 of IA 1986 implies that directors owe a duty to creditors where a company has gone into insolvent liquidation and the director knew, or ought to have known, that there was no reasonable prospect that the company should avoid this situation.

On application by the liquidator, the court may make a director personally liable to contribute to the company's assets (and disqualification for up to 15 years) where that director knew, or ought to have concluded prior to the liquidation, that there was no reasonable prospect that the company would avoid going into insolvent liquidation. A director will not be made personally liable where he can show that he has taken every step prior to liquidation to minimise the potential loss to the company's creditors.

In *Re Produce Marketing Consortium Ltd (No 2)* [1987] BCLC 520 the court, in deciding whether a director of an insolvent company knew that there was no reasonable prospect of the company avoiding liquidation, ruled that the director be judged by the standards of a person fulfilling that function with reasonable diligence, as well as the functions entrusted to that particular director. The two directors claimed they only became aware of the insolvent condition of the company when they received the draft accounts in January 1987. The court held that they must have had the knowledge at the time when the accounts should have been laid before the company in general meeting in July 1986, also that they were closely involved in the business and had delayed the preparation of the accounts.

It is a financial question as to whether a company is insolvent and any director with responsibility for accounting is therefore expected to display a greater degree of diligence in this area and is thus more likely to be found liable for wrongful trading. However, IA 1986 makes no reference to trading in the knowledge that the company cannot meet its liabilities. Directors may be able to continue trading whilst a company is technically insolvent if there is a *reasonable* prospect that they can trade out of the difficulties, or that an arrangement with creditors will solve the problems. This is to prevent the abuse of limited liability, and it is a test for negligence rather than for fraud; as such, the tests are objective.

In order to reduce the risk of being found liable for wrongful trading, a director should:

(a)   ensure that his job description is accurately defined;
(b)   ensure that the company has a system for producing accounts and information in a timely manner and within the limits set by companies' legislation; and
(c)   insist on his concern being recorded in board minutes where he can see that the company is insolvent but the other directors disagree.

The standard of skill and care to be shown by a director to avoid liability is the highest that he possesses and that a person carrying out his functions can reasonably be expected to possess.

Fraudulent trading

[6.48] Pursuant to IA 1986, s 213, a liquidator may apply to the court for an order making a director personally liable to contribute to a company's assets (and disqualify him for up to 15 years) where he is of the opinion that the director was knowingly party to the carrying on of the company's business with *intent* to defraud creditors. In the case of *Re William C Leitch Bros* [1932] 2 Ch 71 the 'intent' to defraud was held to be the continuance of business and the incurring of further debts when there was to the *knowledge* of the directors no reasonable prospect of creditors *ever* receiving payment of their debts.

In this way, fraudulent trading can be contrasted to wrongful trading in that with wrongful trading no 'fraudulent intent' need be proved, only negligence.

Section 993 of CA 2006 also makes a director liable to imprisonment (on conviction on indictment, a term not exceeding ten years) or a fine, or both, if the director was knowingly a party to carrying on business with the intention of defrauding creditors (whether the company's or not), or for any fraudulent purpose. This applies whether or not the company is in the course of being wound up.

Liability as a signatory

[6.49] The Companies (Trading Disclosures) Regulations 2008 (SI 2008/495) were introduced under the authority given in section 82 of the Companies Act 2006. These regulations require that any bill of exchange, promissory note, endorsement, cheque or order for money or goods purporting to be signed by, or on behalf of the company, must state the company's name in legible characters.

Any officer of the company who fails to comply with these regulations is liable to a fine and, in default of payment by the company, may become personally liable to the holder of any such cheque or bill of exchange. (See **11.11 COMMERCIAL CONSIDERATIONS**.)

Liability for contempt

[6.50] If a company is judicially restrained from carrying out certain acts, or gives an undertaking to that effect and the director whose duty it is to take reasonable steps to ensure that the order is obeyed, deliberately fails to do so and the order is breached, then that director may be personally liable and is in contempt of his duties.

In *Attorney General for Tuvalu v Philatelic Distribution Corp* [1990] BCLC 245 the Court of Appeal stated that although the director was not knowingly party to the breach, 'where a company was ordered not to do certain acts or gave an undertaking to like effect and a director was aware of the order or undertaking he was under a duty to take reasonable steps to ensure that the order was obeyed and if he wilfully failed to take those steps and the order or undertaking was breached he can be punished for contempt'. Accordingly the director in this case was committed to prison for contempt of court notwithstanding that he was not a party to the breach.

Indemnity for liability

[6.51] Sections 232–237 of CA 2006 serve to relax the prohibitions on provisions whereby a company seeks to protect its directors from liability for negligence, default, breach of duty or breach of trust.

Section 232 of CA 2006 makes void any provision which seeks to exempt a director from any such liability (s 232(1)) and treats as void any provision by which a company directly or indirectly provides an indemnity from such liability to any director of the company or of an associated company (s 232(2)). However, section 232(2) does not apply to a qualifying third party indemnity provision (as defined in CA 2006, s 234(2)) and does not prohibit the company from purchasing and maintaining insurance against such liability (see **13.54–13.59 INSURANCE ADMINISTRATION**).

Section 234 of CA 2006 defines a qualifying third party indemnity provision as any provision which does not provide any indemnity against any liability incurred by the director:

(a)   to the company or to the associated company;
(b)   to pay a fine imposed in criminal proceedings or a sum payable to a regulatory authority by way of a penalty in respect of non-compliance with any requirement of a regulatory nature; and
(c)   in defending any criminal proceedings in which he is convicted, in defending any civil proceedings brought by the company or an associated company in which judgment is given against him, or in connection with any application of CA 2006, s 661(3) or (4) (acquisition of shares

by innocent nominee) or CA 2006, s 1157 (general power to grant relief in case of honest and reasonable conduct), in which the court refuses to grant him relief.

Section 237 of CA 2006 requires the disclosure in the directors' report of any qualifying third party (and pension scheme) indemnity provision in force during the financial year in question. In addition, the qualifying indemnity provision must be available for inspection at the company's registered office or at a place defined by regulations in accordance with CA 2006, s 1136. Notice of the location of the provision must be given to the Registrar of Companies within 14 days of any change, failing which every officer of the company who is in default is liable on summary conviction to a fine not exceeding level 3 on the standard scale, and for continued contravention, a daily default fine not exceeding one-tenth of level 3 on the standard scale.

Articles of association will generally include an indemnity clause indemnifying officers of the company where proceedings are brought against them so that they will not have to bear the costs of any legal action brought against them, and article 85 of the PLC Model Articles/regulation 118 of Table A 1985 provides a model regulation on directors' and other officers' liability. An indemnity clause which follows regulation 118 may require amendment to allow a company to take advantage of the provisions of CA 2006, ss 232–237. Where, in any financial year, a company has purchased or maintained any such insurance, that fact must be stated in the directors' report.

Section 239 of CA 2006 authorises the members of the company to ratify by resolution the conduct of a director which amounts to negligence, default, breach of duty or breach of trust in relation to the company. A director in his capacity as a member is not permitted to participate in signing a written resolution to support any ratification or for his votes to be taken into account at a general meeting addressing this issue, although he may be counted in the quorum at such a meeting. Section 239 does not invalidate any decision taken by unanimous consent of the members, or any power of the directors to agree not to sue the director concerned, or to settle or release him from a claim made by them on the company's behalf.

In summary, companies are permitted to:

(i)   indemnify directors against most liabilities to third parties; and
(ii)   pay directors' legal costs upfront, provided that the director repays if he is convicted in any criminal proceedings or judgment is given against him in any civil proceedings brought by the company or an associated company.

These provisions allow the shareholders to agree a limit on directors' liability for negligence without permitting them to limit the liability of any directors who put personal interests before their duty to the company.

Appendix 6A

Precedents

A. Appointment of a Director

'It was resolved that pursuant to regulation [   ] of the Articles of Association of the company [   ] be and is hereby elected a Director of the company with immediate effect.'

B. Re-Election of Retiring Directors

(i) 'It was resolved that [   ] a Director who had been appointed since the last Annual General Meeting and in accordance with the company's Articles of Association, now retiring, be and is hereby re-elected a Director of the company.'

(ii) 'It was resolved that [   ] a Director retiring by rotation in accordance with the company's Articles of Association, be and is hereby re-elected a Director of the company.'

(iii) 'It was resolved that the Directors who had been appointed since the incorporation of the company and in accordance with the company's Articles of Association now retiring, be and they are hereby re-elected Directors of the company.'

C. Ratification of Directors' Acts

'(i) It was resolved that Messrs [   ] being the Directors who ceased to hold office by failing to be re-elected in accordance with the company's Articles of Association be and they are hereby appointed and re-elected as Directors of the company; and

(ii) All legal acts of the aforementioned persons acting as Directors of the company on behalf of the company in accordance with the authority given by the Articles of Association and exercised prior to the date of this resolution be and they are hereby ratified and confirmed notwithstanding any defects in any appointments that might otherwise cause their validity to be in doubt.'

D. Director's Resignation Letter

'The Directors

[   ] Limited

20[   ]

Dear Sirs

I hereby tender my resignation as a Director of the company with effect from the close of business at today's date and confirm that I have no outstanding claims whatsoever against the company.

Yours faithfully

. . . . ,

E. Removal of a Director

'It was resolved that [   ] be and he is hereby removed from his office as a Director of the company with immediate effect.'

F. Special Notice for the Removal of a Director

'The Directors

[   ] Limited

20[   ]

Dear Sirs

I/We hereby give notice pursuant to Section 168 and Section 312 of the Companies Act 2006 of my/our intention to propose the following ordinary resolution at the next Annual General Meeting of the company.

'That [   ] be and he is hereby removed from his office as a Director of the company with immediate effect'.

Yours faithfully

. . . . ,

Appendix 6B

Schedule of matters to be reserved for the approval of the Board of Directors

ICSA GUIDANCE ON MATTERS RESERVED FOR THE BOARD
Reference Number: 071011

1. STRATEGY AND MANAGEMENT

1.1 Responsibility for the overall management of the group. [CC A.1]

1.2 Approval of the group's long term objectives and commercial strategy. [CC A.1]

1.3 Approval of the annual operating and capital expenditure budgets and any material changes to them.

1.4 Oversight of the group's operations ensuring:

- competent and prudent management
- sound planning
- an adequate system of internal control
- adequate accounting and other records
- compliance with statutory and regulatory obligations.

1.5 Review of performance in the light of the group's strategy, objectives, business plans and budgets and ensuring that any necessary corrective action is taken. [CC A.1]

1.6 Extension of the group's activities into new business or geographic areas.

1.7 Any decision to cease to operate all or any material part of the group's business.

2. STRUCTURE AND CAPITAL

2.1 Changes relating to the group's capital structure including reduction of capital, share issues (except under employee share plans), share buy backs [including the use of treasury shares].

2.2 Major changes to the group's corporate structure.

2.3 Changes to the group's management and control structure.

2.4 Any changes to the company's listing or its status as a plc.

3. FINANCIAL REPORTING AND CONTROLS

3.1 *Approval of the half-yearly report, interim management statements and any preliminary announcement of the final results. [CC C.1; Audit; DTR 4]

3.2 *Approval of the annual report and accounts, [including the corporate governance statement and remuneration report]. (These items are often considered by the whole board but with the final formal decision being delegated to a committee (set up solely for that purpose). This allows time for any changes requested at the board meeting to be incorporated into the final document before publication.) [CA85 s 233, s 234C; DTR 4; LR 9.8; CC C.I; Audit]

3.3 *Approval of the dividend policy.

3.4 Declaration of the interim dividend and recommendation of the final dividend. [LR 9.7A.2; DTR 6.1.13]

3.5 *Approval of any significant changes in accounting policies or practices. [Audit]

3.6 Approval of treasury policies [including foreign currency exposure and the use of financial derivatives].

4. INTERNAL CONTROLS

4.1 Ensuring maintenance of a sound system of internal control and risk management including:

- receiving reports on, and reviewing the effectiveness of, the group's risk and control processes to support its strategy and objectives
- undertaking an annual assessment of these processes
- approving an appropriate statement for inclusion in the annual report. [CC C.2, C.2.1; Audit]

5. CONTRACTS

5.1 Major capital projects.

5.2 Contracts which are material strategically or by reason of size, entered into by the company [or any subsidiary] in the ordinary course of business, for example bank borrowings [above £xx million] and acquisitions or disposals of fixed assets [above £xx million].

5.3 Contracts of the company [or any subsidiary] not in the ordinary course of business, for example loans and repayments [above £xx million]; foreign currency transactions [above £xx million]; major acquisitions or disposals [above £xx million].

5.4 Major investments [including the acquisition or disposal of interests of more than (5) percent in the voting shares of any company or the making of any takeover offer].

6. COMMUNICATION

6.1 Approval of resolutions and corresponding documentation to be put forward to shareholders at a general meeting. [LR 13]

6.2 *Approval of all circulars, prospectuses and listing particulars [approval of routine documents such as periodic circulars about scrip dividend procedures or exercise of conversion rights could be delegated to a committee]. [LR 13; PR 5.5]

6.3 *Approval of press releases concerning matters decided by the board.

7. BOARD MEMBERSHIP AND OTHER APPOINTMENTS

7.1 *Changes to the structure, size and composition of the board, following recommendations from the nomination committee. [Nomination]

7.2 Ensuring adequate succession planning for the board and senior management. [CC A.4, A.7]

7.3 Appointments to the board, following recommendations by the nomination committee. [Nomination]

7.4 Selection of the chairman of the board and the chief executive. [Nomination]

7.5 Appointment of the senior independent director. [CC A.3.3; Nomination]

7.6 Membership and chairmanship of board committees. [Nomination]

7.7 Continuation in office of directors at the end of their term of office, when they are due to be re-elected by shareholders at the AGM and otherwise as appropriate. [Nomination]

7.8 *Continuation in office of any director at any time, including the suspension or termination of service of an executive director as an employee of the company, subject to the law and their service contract. [Nomination]

7.9 *Appointment or removal of the company secretary. [CA85 s 283, s 286; CC A.5.3]

7.10 *Appointment, reappointment or removal of the external auditor to be put to shareholders for approval, following the recommendation of the audit committee. [CA85 s 384; CC C.3.2; Audit]

7.11 Appointments to boards of subsidiaries.

8. REMUNERATION

8.1 *Determining the remuneration policy for the directors, company secretary and other senior executives. [Remuneration]

8.2 Determining the remuneration of the non-executive directors, subject to the articles of association and shareholder approval as appropriate. [CC B.2.3]

8.3 *The introduction of new share incentive plans or major changes to existing plans, to be put to shareholders for approval. [Remuneration]

9. DELEGATION OF AUTHORITY

9.1 *The division of responsibilities between the chairman, the chief executive [and other executive directors,] which should be in writing. [CC A.2.1]

9.2 *Approval of terms of reference of board committees. [CC A.4.1, B.2.1, C.3.1]

9.3 *Receiving reports from board committees on their activities. [Remuneration]

10. CORPORATE GOVERNANCE MATTERS

10.1 *Undertaking a formal and rigorous review [annually] of its own performance, that of its committees and individual directors. [CC A.6]

10.2 *Determining the independence of directors. [CC A.3.1]

10.3 *Considering the balance of interests between shareholders, employees, customers and the community. [CA06, s 172]

10.4 Review of the group's overall corporate governance arrangements.

10.5 *Receiving reports on the views of the company's shareholders. [CC D.1.1]

11. POLICIES

11.1 Approval of policies, including:

- Code of Conduct
- Share dealing code
- Health and safety policy
- Environmental policy
- Communications policy [including procedures for the release of price sensitive information]
- Corporate social responsibility policy
- Charitable donations policy. [CC A.1]

12. OTHER

12.1 The making of political donations.

12.2 Approval of the appointment of the group's principal professional advisers.

12.3 Prosecution, defence or settlement of litigation [involving above £xx million or being otherwise material to the interests of the group].

12.4 Approval of the overall levels of insurance for the group including directors' & officers' liability insurance [and indemnification of directors].

12.5 Major changes to the rules of the group's pension scheme, or changes of trustees or [when this is subject to the approval of the company] changes in the fund management arrangements.

12.6 This schedule of matters reserved for board decisions.

Matters which the board considers suitable for delegation are contained in the terms of reference of its committees.

In addition, the board will receive reports and recommendations from time to time on any matter which it considers significant to the group.

Items marked * are not considered suitable for delegation to a committee of the board, for example because of Companies Act requirements or because, under the recommendations of the Combined Code, they are the responsibility of an audit, nomination or remuneration committee, with the final decision required to be taken by the board as a whole.

CA06 refers to the Companies Act 2006

CA85 refers to the Companies Act 1985

CC refers to the Combined Code

DTR refers to the UKLA's Disclosure and Transparency Rules

LR refers to the UKLA's Listing Rules

References to Audit, Nomination or Remuneration refer to the board committee which will consider the item and make recommendations to the board for its final decision.

(Extracted from the 'ICSA Guidance on Matters Reserved for the Board' (Reference Number: 071011) and reproduced with the kind permission of the Institute of Chartered Secretaries and Administrators, www.icsaglobal.com.)

Appendix 6C

Nomination committee – terms of reference

ICSA GUIDANCE ON TERMS OF REFERENCE –
NOMINATION COMMITTEE
Reference Number: 101020

1. MEMBERSHIP

1.1 The committee shall comprise at least [three] directors. A majority of the members of the committee shall be independent non-executive directors.

1.2 Only members of the committee have the right to attend committee meetings. However, other individuals such as the chief executive, the head of human resources and external advisers may be invited to attend for all or part of any meeting, as and when appropriate.

1.3 Appointments to the committee are made by the board and shall be for a period of up to three years, which may be extended for further periods of up to three years, provided the director still meets the criteria for membership of the committee.

1.4 The board shall appoint the committee chairman who should be either the chairman of the board or an independent non-executive director. In the absence of the committee chairman and/or an appointed deputy, the remaining members present shall elect one of themselves to chair the meeting from those who would qualify under these terms of reference to be appointed to that position by the board. The chairman of the board shall not chair the committee when it is dealing with the matter of succession to the chairmanship.

2. SECRETARY

The company secretary or his or her nominee shall act as the secretary of the committee.

3. QUORUM

The quorum necessary for the transaction of business shall be [two] [both of whom must be independent non-executive directors]. A duly convened meeting of the committee at which a quorum is present shall be competent to exercise all or any of the authorities, powers and discretions vested in or exercisable by the committee.

4. FREQUENCY OF MEETINGS

The committee shall meet at least [twice] a year[1] and otherwise as required[2].

5. NOTICE OF MEETINGS

5.1 Meetings of the committee shall be called by the secretary of the committee at the request of the committee chairman.

5.2 Unless otherwise agreed, notice of each meeting confirming the venue, time and date, together with an agenda of items to be discussed, shall be forwarded to each member of the committee, any other person required to attend and all other non-executive directors, no later than [five] working days before the date of the meeting. Supporting papers shall be sent to committee members and to other attendees as appropriate, at the same time.

6. MINUTES OF MEETINGS

6.1 The secretary shall minute the proceedings and resolutions of all committee meetings, including the names of those present and in attendance.

6.2 Draft minutes of committee meetings shall be circulated promptly to all members of the committee. Once approved, minutes should be circulated to all other members of the board unless it would be inappropriate to do so.

7. ANNUAL GENERAL MEETING

The committee chairman should attend the annual general meeting to answer any shareholder questions on the committee's activities.

8. DUTIES

The committee should carry out the duties below for the parent company, major subsidiary undertakings and the group as a whole, as appropriate.

The committee shall:

8.1 regularly review the structure, size and composition (including the skills, knowledge, experience and diversity) of the board and make recommendations to the board with regard to any changes;

8.2 give full consideration to succession planning for directors and other senior executives in the course of its work, taking into account the challenges and opportunities facing the company, and the skills and expertise needed on the board in the future;

8.3 keep under review the leadership needs of the organisation, both executive and non-executive, with a view to ensuring the continued ability of the organisation to compete effectively in the marketplace;

8.4 keep up to date and fully informed about strategic issues and commercial changes affecting the company and the market in which it operates;

8.5 be responsible for identifying and nominating for the approval of the board, candidates to fill board vacancies as and when they arise;

8.6 before any appointment is made by the board, evaluate the balance of skills, knowledge, experience and diversity on the board, and, in the light of this evaluation prepare a description of the role and capabilities required for a particular appointment. In identifying suitable candidates the committee shall:

8.6.1 use open advertising or the services of external advisers to facilitate the search;

8.6.2 consider candidates from a wide range of backgrounds; and

8.6.3 consider candidates on merit and against objective criteria and with due regard for the benefits of diversity on the board, including gender, taking care that appointees have enough time available to devote to the position[3];

8.7 for the appointment of a chairman, the committee should prepare a job specification, including the time commitment expected. A proposed chairman's other significant commitments should be disclosed to the board before appointment and any changes to the chairman's commitments should be reported to the board as they arise[4].

8.8 prior to the appointment of a director, the proposed appointee should be required to disclose any other business interests that may result in a conflict of interest and be required to report any future business interests that could result in a conflict of interest[5]

8.9 ensure that on appointment to the board, non-executive directors receive a formal letter of appointment setting out clearly what is expected of them in terms of time commitment, committee service and involvement outside board meetings.

8.10 review the results of the board performance evaluation process that relate to the composition of the board;

8.11 review annually the time required from non-executive directors. Performance evaluation should be used to assess whether the non-executive directors are spending enough time to fulfil their duties.

The committee shall also make recommendations to the board concerning:

8.12 formulating plans for succession for both executive and non-executive directors and in particular for the key roles of chairman and chief executive;

8.13 suitable candidates for the role of senior independent director;

8.14 membership of the audit and remuneration committees, and any other board committees as appropriate, in consultation with the chairmen of those committees;

8.15 the re-appointment of any non-executive director at the conclusion of their specified term of office having given due regard to their performance and ability to continue to contribute to the board in the light of the knowledge, skills and experience required;

8.16 the re-election by shareholders of directors under the annual re-election provisions of the Code[6] or the retirement by rotation provisions in the company's articles of association, having due regard to their performance and ability to continue to contribute to the board in the light of the knowledge, skills and experience required and the need for progressive refreshing of the board (particularly in relation to directors being re-elected for a term beyond six years);

8.17 any matters relating to the continuation in office of any director at any time including the suspension or termination of service of an executive director as an employee of the company subject to the provisions of the law and their service contract;

8.18 the appointment of any director to executive or other office.

9. REPORTING RESPONSIBILITIES

9.1 The committee chairman shall report formally to the board on its proceedings after each meeting on all matters within its duties and responsibilities.

9.2 The committee shall make whatever recommendations to the board it deems appropriate on any area within its remit where action or improvement is needed.

9.3 The committee shall produce a report to be included in the company's annual report about its activities, the process used to make appointments and explain if external advice or open advertising has not been used.

10. OTHER

The committee shall:

10.1 have access to sufficient resources in order to carry out its duties, including access to the company secretariat for assistance as required;

10.2 be provided with appropriate and timely training, both in the form of an induction programme for new members and on an ongoing basis for all members;

10.3 give due consideration to laws and regulations, the provisions of the Code and the requirements of the UK Listing Authority's Listing, Prospectus and Disclosure and Transparency Rules and any other applicable Rules, as appropriate;

10.4   arrange for periodic reviews of its own performance and, at least annually, review its constitution and terms of reference to ensure it is operating at maximum effectiveness and recommend any changes it considers necessary to the board for approval.

11. AUTHORITY

The committee is authorised by the board to obtain, at the company's expense, outside legal or other professional advice on any matters within its terms of reference.

---

[1]   Some small companies and investment trusts may not need more than one scheduled meeting of the nomination committee each year.

[2]   The frequency and timing of meetings will differ according to the needs of the company. Meetings should be organised so that attendance is maximised (for example by timetabling them to coincide with board meetings).

[3]   When considering a new appointment the proposed new non-executive director's other commitments should be taken into account to ensure he or she has sufficient time to devote to the company. For an appointment to an FSA regulated company, FSA policy statement 10/15 page 26 states the FSA will consider the candidate's existing commitments when assessing their suitability for the role.

[4]   Code, B.3.1. This information should also be disclosed in the next annual report.

[5]   Companies Act 2006, s 175.

[6]   Provision B.7.1

(Extracted from the 'ICSA Guidance on Terms of Reference – Nomination Committee' (Reference Number: 101020) and reproduced with the kind permission of the Institute of Chartered Secretaries and Administrators, www.icsaglobal.com.)

Appendix 6D

Remuneration committee – terms of reference

ICSA GUIDANCE ON TERMS OF REFERENCE –
REMUNERATION COMMITTEE
Reference Number: 101019

1. MEMBERSHIP

1.1 The committee shall comprise at least [three] members, all of whom shall be independent non-executive directors. The chairman of the board may also serve on the committee as an additional member if he or she was considered independent on appointment as chairman. Members of the committee shall be appointed by the board, on the recommendation of the nomination committee and in consultation with the chairman of the remuneration committee.

1.2 Only members of the committee have the right to attend committee meetings. However, other individuals such as the chief executive, the head of human resources and external advisers may be invited to attend for all or part of any meeting, as and when appropriate and necessary.

1.3 Appointments to the committee are made by the board and shall be for a period of up to three years, which may be extended for further periods of up three-years, provided the director still meets the criteria for membership of the committee.

1.4 The board shall appoint the committee chairman who shall be an independent non-executive director. In the absence of the committee chairman and/or an appointed deputy, the remaining members present shall elect one of themselves to chair the meeting who would qualify under these terms of reference to be appointed to that position by the board. The chairman of the board shall not be chairman of the committee.

2. SECRETARY

The company secretary or his or her nominee shall act as the secretary of the committee.

3. QUORUM

The quorum necessary for the transaction of business shall be [two]. A duly convened meeting of the committee at which a quorum is present shall be competent to exercise all or any of the authorities, powers and discretions vested in or exercisable by the committee

4. MEETINGS

The committee shall meet at least [twice] a year and otherwise as required[1].

5. NOTICE OF MEETINGS

5.1 Meetings of the committee shall be called by the secretary of the committee at the request of the committee chairman.

5.2   Unless otherwise agreed, notice of each meeting confirming the venue, time and date together with an agenda of items to be discussed, shall be forwarded to each member of the committee, any other person required to attend and all other non-executive directors, no later than [five] working days before the date of the meeting. Supporting papers shall be sent to committee members and to other attendees, as appropriate, at the same time.

6. MINUTES OF MEETINGS

6.1   The secretary shall minute the proceedings and resolutions of all committee meetings, including the names of those present and in attendance.

6.2   Draft minutes of committee meetings shall be circulated promptly to all members of the committee. Once approved, minutes should be circulated to all other members of the board unless it would be inappropriate to do so.

7. ANNUAL GENERAL MEETING

The committee chairman should attend the annual general meeting to answer any shareholder questions on the committee's activities.

8. DUTIES

The committee should carry out the duties below for the parent company, major subsidiary undertakings and the group as a whole, as appropriate.

The committee shall:

8.1   determine and agree with the board the framework or broad policy for the remuneration of the company's chairman, chief executive, the executive directors, the company secretary and such other members of the executive management as it is designated to consider[2]. The remuneration of non-executive directors shall be a matter for the chairman and the executive members of the board[3]. No director or manager shall be involved in any decisions as to their own remuneration[4];

8.2   in determining such policy, take into account all factors which it deems necessary including relevant legal and regulatory requirements, the provisions and recommendations of the UK Corporate Governance Code and associated guidance. The objective of such policy shall be to ensure that members of the executive management of the company are provided with appropriate incentives to encourage enhanced performance and are, in a fair and responsible manner, rewarded for their individual contributions to the success of the company[5];

8.3   when setting remuneration policy for directors, review and have regard to the remuneration trends across the company or group[6];

8.4   review the ongoing appropriateness and relevance of the remuneration policy[7];

8.5   within the terms of the agreed policy and in consultation with the chairman and/or chief executive, as appropriate, determine the total individual remuneration package of the chairman, each executive director, company secretary and other designated senior executives including bonuses, incentive payments and share options or other share awards[8];

8.6   obtain reliable, up-to-date information about remuneration in other companies[9]. To help it fulfil its obligations the committee shall have full authority to appoint remuneration consultants[10] and to commission or purchase any reports, surveys or information which it deems necessary, within any budgetary restraints imposed by the board;

8.7   be exclusively responsible for establishing the selection criteria, selecting, appointing and setting the terms of reference for any remuneration consultants who advise the committee;

8.8 approve the design of, and determine targets for, any performance related pay schemes operated by the company and approve the total annual payments made under such schemes;

8.9 review the design of all share incentive plans for approval by the board and shareholders. For any such plans, determine each year whether awards will be made, and if so, the overall amount of such awards, the individual awards to executive directors, company secretary and other designated senior executives and the performance targets to be used[11];

8.10 determine the policy for, and scope of, pension arrangements for each executive director and other designated senior executives[12];

8.11 ensure that contractual terms on termination, and any payments made, are fair to the individual, and the company, that failure is not rewarded and that the duty to mitigate loss is fully recognised[13];

8.12 oversee any major changes in employee benefits structures throughout the company or group;

8.13 agree the policy for authorising claims for expenses from the directors;

9. REPORTING RESPONSIBILITIES

9.1 The committee chairman shall report formally to the board on its proceedings after each meeting on all matters within its duties and responsibilities.

9.2 The committee shall make whatever recommendations to the board it deems appropriate on any area within its remit where action or improvement is needed.

9.3 The committee shall produce a report of the company's remuneration policy and practices to be included in the company's annual report and ensure each year that it is put to shareholders for approval at the AGM.

10. OTHER

The committee shall:

10.1 have access to sufficient resources in order to carry out its duties, including access to the company secretariat for assistance as required

10.2 be provided with appropriate and timely training, both in the form of an induction programme for new members and on an ongoing basis for all members

10.3 give due consideration to laws and regulations, the provisions of the Code and the requirements of the UK Listing Authority's Listing, Prospectus and Disclosure and Transparency Rules and any other applicable Rules, as appropriate

10.4 arrange for periodic reviews of its own performance and, at least annually, review its constitution and terms of reference to ensure it is operating at maximum effectiveness and recommend any changes it considers necessary to the board for approval.

11. AUTHORITY

The committee is authorised by the board to obtain, at the company's expense, outside legal or other professional advice on any matters within its terms of reference.

---

[1] The frequency and timing of meetings will differ according to the needs of the company. Meetings should be organised so that attendance is maximised (for example by timetabling them to coincide with board meetings).

[2] The Code, D.2 and Schedule A, and D.2.2. Recommendations 29 – 34 of the final report of the Walker review of corporate governance in UK banks and other financial industry entities, published November 2009 states the remit of remuneration committees of Banks or other Financial Institutions should cover 'high end' employees. The Walker report is available separately from HM Treasury website at www.hm-treasury.gov.uk/walker_review_information.htm

[3] The Code, D.2.3.

[4] The Code, D.2.

[5] The Code D.1 Recommendation 35 of the Walker review, November 2009: remuneration committees of Banks or other Financial Institutions should seek advice from the board risk committee on specific risk adjustments to be applied to performance objectives.

[6] The Code, D.1.

[7] Taking account of the principles in Code, D.1. Recommendation 28 of the Walker review, November 2009: for Banks and Other Financial Institutions this should include responsibility for setting the over-arching principles and parameters of remuneration policy on a firm-wide basis.

[8] The Code, D.2.

[9] The Code, D.1.

[10] The Code, D.2.1.

[11] Recommendation 34 of the Walker review, November 2009: remuneration committees of Banks or other Financial Institutions should note the requirements for 'high end' employees to maintain a shareholding.

[12] The Code, D.2.2.

[13] The Code, D.1.4 and D.1.5 Recommendation 37 of the Walker review, November 2009 sets out disclosure requirements for remuneration committees of Banks and other Financial Institutions in relation to any additional enhanced benefits for executive directors or other 'high end' employees.

(Extracted from the 'ICSA Guidance on Terms of Reference – Remuneration Committee (Reference Number: 101019) and reproduced with the kind permission of the Institute of Chartered Secretaries and Administrators, www.icsaglobal.com.)

Appendix 6E

Audit committee – terms of reference

ICSA GUIDANCE ON TERMS OF REFERENCE – AUDIT COMMITTEE
Reference Number: 101017

1. MEMBERSHIP

1.1 The committee shall comprise at least [three] members. [Membership shall include at least one member of the risk committee.][1] Members of the committee shall be appointed by the board, on the recommendation of the nomination committee in consultation with the chairman of the audit committee

1.2 All members of the committee shall be independent non-executive directors[2] at least one of whom shall have recent and relevant financial experience. The chairman of the board shall not be a member of the committee[3].

1.3 Only members of the committee have the right to attend committee meetings. However, other individuals such as the chairman of the board, chief executive, finance director, other directors, the heads of risk, compliance and internal audit and representatives from the finance function may be invited to attend all or part of any meeting as and when appropriate and necessary.

1.4 The external auditors will be invited to attend meetings of the committee on a regular basis.

1.5 Appointments to the committee shall be for a period of up to three years, which may be extended for further periods of up to three years, provided the director still meets the criteria for membership of the committee.

1.6 The board shall appoint the committee chairman who shall be an independent non-executive director. In the absence of the committee chairman and/or an appointed deputy, the remaining members present shall elect one of themselves to chair the meeting.

2. SECRETARY

The company secretary or his or her nominee shall act as the secretary of the committee.

3. QUORUM

The quorum necessary for the transaction of business shall be [two] members[4]. A duly convened meeting of the committee at which a quorum is present shall be competent to exercise all or any of the authorities, powers and discretions vested in or exercisable by the committee.

4. FREQUENCY OF MEETINGS

The committee shall meet at least [four] times a year at appropriate times in the reporting and audit cycle and otherwise as required[5].

5. NOTICE OF MEETINGS

5.1 Meetings of the committee shall be called by the secretary of the committee at the request of any of its members or at the request of external or internal auditor if they consider it necessary.

5.2 2 Unless otherwise agreed, notice of each meeting confirming the venue, time and date together with an agenda of items to be discussed, shall be forwarded to each member of the committee, any other person required to attend and all other non-executive directors, no later than [five] working days before the date of the meeting. Supporting papers shall be sent to committee members and to other attendees as appropriate, at the same time.

6. MINUTES OF MEETINGS

6.1 The secretary shall minute the proceedings and decisions of all meetings of the committee, including recording the names of those present and in attendance

6.2 Draft minutes of committee meetings shall be circulated promptly to all members of the committee. Once approved, minutes should be circulated to all other members of the board unless it would be inappropriate to do so.

7. ANNUAL GENERAL MEETING

The committee chairman should attend the annual general meeting to answer shareholder questions on the committee's activities.

8. DUTIES

The committee should carry out the duties below for the parent company, major subsidiary undertakings and the group as a whole, as appropriate.

8.1 Financial reporting

8.1.1 The committee shall monitor the integrity of the financial statements of the company, including its annual and half-yearly reports, interim management statements, and any other formal announcement relating to its financial performance, reviewing significant financial reporting issues and judgements which they contain.

8.1.2 In particular, the committee shall review and challenge where necessary:

8.1.2.1 the consistency of, and any changes to, accounting policies both on a year on year basis and across the company/group;

8.1.2.2 the methods used to account for significant or unusual transactions where different approaches are possible;

8.1.2.3 whether the company has followed appropriate accounting standards and made appropriate estimates and judgements, taking into account the views of the external auditor;

8.1.2.4 the clarity of disclosure in the company's financial reports and the context in which statements are made; and

8.1.2.5 all material information presented with the financial statements, such as the business review/operating and financial review and the corporate governance statement (insofar as it relates to the audit and risk management).

8.2 Internal controls and risk management systems[6]:

The committee shall:

8.2.1 keep under review the adequacy and effectiveness of the company's internal financial controls and internal control and risk management systems[7]; and

8.2.2 review and approve the statements to be included in the annual report concerning internal controls and risk management[8].

8.3 Compliance, whistleblowing and fraud[9]:

The committee shall:

8.3.1 review the adequacy and security of the company's arrangements for its employees and contractors to raise concerns, in confidence, about possible wrongdoing in financial reporting or other matters. The committee shall ensure that these arrangements allow proportionate and independent investigation of such matters and appropriate follow up action;

8.3.2 review the company's procedures for detecting fraud;

8.3.3 review the company's systems and controls for the prevention of bribery and receive reports on non-compliance[10];

8.3.4 [review regular reports from the Money Laundering Reporting Officer and the adequacy and effectiveness of the company's anti-money laundering systems and controls];

8.3.5 [review regular reports from the Compliance Officer and keep under review the adequacy and effectiveness of the company's compliance function].

8.4 Internal audit

The committee shall:

8.4.1 monitor and review the effectiveness of the company's internal audit function[11] in the context of the company's overall risk management system[12];

8.4.2 approve the appointment and removal of the head of the internal audit function;

8.4.3 consider and approve the remit of the internal audit function and ensure it has adequate resources and appropriate access to information to enable it to perform its function effectively and in accordance with the relevant professional standards. The committee shall also ensure the function has adequate standing and is free from management or other restrictions;

8.4.4 review and assess the annual internal audit plan;

8.4.5 review reports addressed to the committee from the internal auditor;

8.4.6 review and monitor management's responsiveness to the findings and recommendations of the internal auditor; and

8.4.7 meet the head of internal audit at least once a year, without management being present, to discuss their remit and any issues arising from the internal audits carried out. In addition, the head of internal audit shall be given the right of direct access to the chairman of the board and to the committee.

8.5 External audit

The committee shall:

8.5.1 consider and make recommendations to the board, to be put to shareholders for approval at the AGM, in relation to the appointment, re-appointment and removal of the company's external auditor. The committee shall oversee the selection process for a new auditor and if an auditor resigns the committee shall investigate the issues leading to this and decide whether any action is required;

8.5.2 oversee the relationship with the external auditor including (but not limited to):

8.5.2.1 recommendations on their remuneration, whether fees for audit or non-audit services and that the level of fees is appropriate to enable an adequate audit to be conducted;

8.5.2.2 approval of their terms of engagement, including any engagement letter issued at the start of each audit and the scope of the audit;

8.5.2.3 assessing annually their independence and objectivity taking into account relevant [UK] professional and regulatory requirements and the relationship with the auditor as a whole, including the provision of any non-audit services;

8.5.2.4 satisfying itself that there are no relationships (such as family, employment, investment, financial or business) between the auditor and the company (other than in the ordinary course of business);

8.5.2.5 agreeing with the board a policy on the employment of former employees of the company's auditor, then monitoring the implementation of this policy;

8.5.2.6 monitoring the auditor's compliance with relevant ethical and professional guidance on the rotation of audit partners, the level of fees paid by the company compared to the overall fee income of the firm, office and partner and other related requirements;

8.5.2.7 assessing annually the qualifications, expertise and resources of the auditor and the effectiveness of the audit process, which shall include a report from the external auditor on their own internal quality procedures;

8.5.2.8 seeking to ensure co-ordination with the activities of the internal audit function;

8.5.3 meet regularly with the external auditor, including once at the planning stage before the audit and once after the audit at the reporting stage. The committee shall meet the external auditor at least once a year, without management being present, to discuss their remit and any issues arising from the audit;

8.5.4 review and approve the annual audit plan and ensure that it is consistent with the scope of the audit engagement;

8.5.5 review the findings of the audit with the external auditor. This shall include but not be limited to, the following:

8.5.5.1 a discussion of any major issues which arose during the audit;

8.5.5.2 any accounting and audit judgements;

8.5.5.3 levels of errors identified during the audit.

8.5.5.4 the effectiveness of the audit.

The committee shall also:

8.5.6 review any representation letter(s) requested by the external auditor before they are signed by management;

8.5.7 review the management letter and management's response to the auditor's findings and recommendations;

8.5.8 develop and implement a policy on the supply of non-audit services by the external auditor, taking into account any relevant ethical guidance on the matter.

9. REPORTING RESPONSIBILITIES

9.1 The committee chairman shall report formally to the board on its proceedings after each meeting on all matters within its duties and responsibilities.

9.2 The committee shall make whatever recommendations to the board it deems appropriate on any area within its remit where action or improvement is needed.

9.3 The committee shall produce a report on its activities to be included in the company's annual report.

10. OTHER MATTERS

The committee shall:

10.1 have access to sufficient resources in order to carry out its duties, including access to the company secretariat for assistance as required;

10.2 be provided with appropriate and timely training, both in the form of an induction programme for new members and on an ongoing basis for all members;

10.3 give due consideration to laws and regulations, the provisions of the Code and the requirements of the UK Listing Authority's Listing, Prospectus and Disclosure and Transparency Rules and any other applicable Rules, as appropriate;

10.4 be responsible for co-ordination of the internal and external auditors;

10.5 oversee any investigation of activities which are within its terms of reference;

10.6 arrange for periodic reviews of its own performance and, at least annually, review its constitution and terms of reference to ensure it is operating at maximum effectiveness and recommend any changes it considers necessary to the board for approval.

11. AUTHORITY

The committee is authorised:

11.1 to seek any information it requires from any employee of the company in order to perform its duties;

11.2 to obtain, at the company's expense, outside legal or other professional advice on any matter within its terms of reference;

11.3 to call any employee to be questioned at a meeting of the committee as and when required.

11.4 to have the right to publish in the Company's annual report details of any issues that cannot be resolved between the committee and the board[13].

---

[1] If the board has a separate risk committee.

[2] Guidance on circumstances likely to affect independence is given in Code provision B.1.1.

[3] Except on appointment, the Chairman of the company is not considered independent. Code provisions A.3.1, B.1.1 and note 5.

[4] As it is a Code provision that at least one member of the Committee has recent and relevant financial experience, it would be preferable for any quorum to include a member with recent and relevant financial experience, whenever possible.

[5] The frequency and timing of meetings will differ according to the needs of the company. Meetings should be organised so that attendance is maximised (for example by timetabling them to coincide with board meetings and/or risk committee meetings if the company has a separate risk committee)..

[6] If the company has a separate risk committee review of internal controls and risk management systems could be included in the duties of that committee.

[7] Code provision C.3.2.

[8] Unless this is done by the board as a whole.

[9] If the board has a separate risk committee whistleblowing and fraud (including the prevention of bribery) could be included in the duties of that committee.

[10] If the company has a separate risk committee prevention of bribery could be included in the duties of that committee.

[11] If the company does not have an internal audit function, the committee should consider annually whether there should be one and make a recommendation to the board accordingly. The absence of such a function should be explained in the annual report.

[12] If the board has a separate risk committee the duties of that committee could include review of the company's internal control and risk management systems.

[13] FRC Guidance on Audit Committees, October 2008, para. 3.5.

(Extracted from the 'ICSA Guidance on Terms of Reference – Audit Committee (Reference Number: 101017) and reproduced with the kind permission of the Institute of Chartered Secretaries and Administrators, www.icsaglobal.com.)

Appendix 6F

Duties of directors – common law position

Prior to the implementation of CA 2006 in relation to the general duties owed by a director to a company, the position of what duties a director owed was established by reference to common law principles and case law. The following reflects the common law position with regard to fiduciary duties, fair dealing and the duty of skill and care.

Fiduciary duty

In carrying out their duties, directors are in a fiduciary position, ie in a position of trust. Because of their fiduciary position, directors also owe certain duties to the company and must act *'bona fide'* in the interest of the company. The duty is owed primarily to the company and not to individual shareholders, or to creditors of the company. It is a subjective duty and the directors must act *'bona fide* in what they consider – not what the courts may consider – is in the interests of the company, and not for any collateral purpose' *per* Lord Greene MR in *Re Smith & Fawcett Ltd* [1942] Ch 304.

A director must not abuse his position as an agent of the company or trustee of the company's property. He must, therefore, not put himself in a position where there is a conflict of interest between his beneficiaries and his personal interests. Should any personal interests or conflicts arise, he is under an obligation to disclose the existence of the interest or conflict.

It appears that a fiduciary will not commit a breach of this rule merely by getting into a position of potential abuse, but that if he is in such a position, he is obliged to prefer the interest of the beneficiary. It therefore appears that a director will not be in breach of these rules if he were a director of a competing company. He may, however, find himself with conflicting duties to two separate beneficiaries.

The courts will only interfere if no reasonable director could possibly have concluded that a particular course of action was in the interest of the company.

In *Re W & M Roith Ltd* [1967] 1 WLR 432, a director entered into a service contract with his company in order to provide a pension for his wife in the event of his death. He did not give any consideration to the fact that the contract was not for the benefit of the company and accordingly the contract was held not to be binding on the company.

The interest of the company is not necessarily the same as its shareholders. Directors may, therefore, have to balance fairly the different interests of the company as a going concern, different classes of shareholders and those of present and future shareholders.

Fair dealing

Directors, by their fiduciary position, must comply with the fair dealing rule and not abuse their position or attempt to profit personally from it without complying with the requirements relating to full disclosure to, and the approval of, the rest of the board or shareholders. Thus, directors must not aim to enrich themselves without the knowledge and consent of the shareholders, otherwise personal liability will arise from the fact that a profit has been made.

In *Regal (Hastings) Limited v Gulliver* [1967] 1 AER 378, four of the directors and the company's solicitor had made a profit on the sale of a subsidiary company's shares to which they had subscribed in their own right. They were made to account for the profit. In summing up, Lord Russell said:

> The rule of equity which insists on those who by the use of a fiduciary position make a profit, being liable to account for that profit, in no way depends on fraud or absence of *bona fides*; or upon such questions or considerations as whether the profit would or should otherwise have gone to the plaintiff, or whether he took a risk or acted as he did for the benefit of the plaintiff, or whether the plaintiff has in fact been damaged or benefited by his action.

In this case it was pointed out that, if the directors had obtained the consent of Regal's shareholders in general meeting, they could have retained their profit. This case also highlighted the fact that the directors' profits need not be at the expense of the company before they have to account for it.

Thus, essentially, a director is expected to act honestly and in a reasonable belief that he is acting for the benefit of the company. He must not act outside the company's objects or make a personal profit from a transaction, even if it also benefits the company.

Duty of skill and care

Whilst a director may not be liable for making an error of judgement, he is expected to perform his duties to the best of his ability on the basis of his knowledge and experience. In general, an executive director would normally be expected to have the skills necessary to carry out his job but even non-executive directors must exercise reasonable skill and care in the exercise of their duties.

The case of *Re City Equitable Fire Insurance Co Ltd* [1925] Ch 407 defined the skill and care expected of a director as being the degree of skill and care that can reasonably be expected from the professional qualifications held by the director. This applies equally whether the director is a non-executive as well as an executive (*Dorchester Finance Co Ltd v Stebbing* [1989] BCLC 498). Furthermore, a greater degree of skill and care is expected from an executive director who is an experienced businessman than from an inexperienced non-executive director.

Thus, in general, although there are no clear guidelines to define the degree of skill and care expected of a director, the courts in determining possible liability will look at the qualifications and experience of the director and his status within the company (eg finance director or non-executive) to establish the degree of skill and care which he could reasonably have been expected to display.

Appendix 6G

The UK Corporate Governance Code (June 2010) – applicable to accounting periods beginning on or after 29 June 2010

THE UK CORPORATE GOVERNANCE CODE (JUNE 2010)

GOVERNANCE AND THE CODE

1. The purpose of corporate governance is to facilitate effective, entrepreneurial and prudent management that can deliver the long-term success of the company.

2. The first version of the UK Code on Corporate Governance (the Code) was produced in 1992 by the Cadbury Committee. Its paragraph 2.5 is still the classic definition of the context of the Code:

'Corporate governance is the system by which companies are directed and controlled. Boards of directors are responsible for the governance of their companies. The shareholders' role in governance is to appoint the directors and the auditors and to satisfy themselves that an appropriate governance structure is in place. The responsibilities of the board include setting the company's strategic aims, providing the leadership to put them into effect, supervising the management of the business and reporting to shareholders on their stewardship. The board's actions are subject to laws, regulations and the shareholders in general meeting.'

3. Corporate governance is therefore about what the board of a company does and how it sets the values of the company, and is to be distinguished from the day to day operational management of the company by full-time executives.

4. The Code is a guide to a number of key components of effective board practice. It is based on the underlying principles of all good governance: accountability, transparency, probity and focus on the sustainable success of an entity over the longer term.

5. The Code has been enduring, but it is not immutable. Its fitness for purpose in a permanently changing economic and social business environment requires its evaluation at appropriate intervals. The reviews preceding this one were in 2005 and 2007. The Preface, which should be regarded as an integral part of the Code, introduces the changes made in the current review.

6. The new Code applies to accounting periods beginning on or after 29 June 2010 and, as a result of the new Listing Regime introduced in April 2010, applies to all companies with a Premium Listing of equity shares regardless of whether they are incorporated in the UK or elsewhere.

PREFACE

1. The financial crisis which came to a head in 2008-09 triggered widespread reappraisal, locally and internationally, of the governance systems which might have alleviated it. In the UK, Sir David Walker was asked to review the governance of banks and other financial institutions, and the FRC decided to bring forward the Code review scheduled for 2010 so that corporate governance in other listed companies could be assessed at the same time.

2. Two principal conclusions were drawn by the FRC from its review. First, that much more attention needed to be paid to following the spirit of the Code as well as its letter. Secondly, that the impact of shareholders in monitoring the Code could and should be enhanced by better interaction between the boards of listed companies and their shareholders. To this end, the FRC has assumed responsibility for a stewardship code that will provide guidance on good practice for investors.

3. Nearly two decades of constructive usage have enhanced the prestige of the Code. Indeed, it seems that there is almost a belief that complying with the Code in itself constitutes good governance. The Code, however, is of necessity limited to being a guide only in general terms to principles, structure and processes. It cannot guarantee effective board behaviour because the range of situations in which it is applicable is much too great for it to attempt to mandate behaviour more specifically than it does. Boards therefore have a lot of room within the framework of the Code to decide for themselves how they should act.

4. To follow the spirit of the Code to good effect, boards must think deeply, thoroughly and on a continuing basis, about their overall tasks and the implications of these for the roles of their individual members. Absolutely key in this endeavour are the leadership of the chairman of a board, the support given to and by the CEO, and the frankness and openness of mind with which issues are discussed and tackled by all directors.

5. The challenge should not be underrated. To run a corporate board successfully is extremely demanding. Constraints on time and knowledge combine with the need to maintain mutual respect and openness between a cast of strong, able and busy directors dealing with each other across the different demands of executive and non-executive roles. To achieve good governance requires continuing and high quality effort.

6. The Code's function should be to help boards discharge their duties in the best interests of their companies. The FRC in this review has focussed on changing the 'tone' of the Code by making limited but significant changes to signal the importance of the general principles which should guide board behaviours. It is to be hoped that these changes will promote greater clarity and understanding with regard to the tasks of a board and that communication with shareholders will be more effective as a result.

7. Chairmen are encouraged to report personally in their annual statements how the principles relating to the role and effectiveness of the board (in Sections A and B of the new Code) have been applied. Not only will this give investors a clearer picture of the steps taken by boards to operate effectively but also, by providing fuller context, it may make investors more willing to accept explanations when a company chooses to explain rather than to comply with one or more provisions. Above all, the personal reporting on governance by chairmen as the leaders of boards might be a turning point in attacking the fungus of 'boiler-plate' which is so often the preferred and easy option in sensitive areas but which is dead communication.

8. The new Code recommends that, in the interests of greater accountability, all directors of FTSE 350 companies should be subject to annual re-election. As with all other provisions of the Code, companies are free to explain rather than comply if they believe that their existing arrangements ensure proper accountability and underpin board effectiveness, or that a transitional period is needed before they introduce annual re-election. The boards of smaller companies are also encouraged to consider their policy on director re-election.

Financial Reporting Council

June 2010

COMPLY OR EXPLAIN

1. The 'comply or explain' approach is the trademark of corporate governance in the UK. It has been in operation since the Code's beginnings and is the foundation of

the Code's flexibility. It is strongly supported by both companies and shareholders and has been widely admired and imitated internationally.

2. The Code is not a rigid set of rules. It consists of principles (main and supporting) and provisions. The Listing Rules require companies to apply the Main Principles and report to shareholders on how they have done so. The principles are the core of the Code and the way in which they are applied should be the central question for a board as it determines how it is to operate according to the Code.

3. It is recognised that an alternative to following a provision may be justified in particular circumstances if good governance can be achieved by other means. A condition of doing so is that the reasons for it should be explained clearly and carefully to shareholders[1], who may wish to discuss the position with the company and whose voting intentions may be influenced as a result. In providing an explanation, the company should aim to illustrate how its actual practices are both consistent with the principle to which the particular provision relates and contribute to good governance.

4. In their responses to explanations, shareholders should pay due regard to companies' individual circumstances and bear in mind, in particular, the size and complexity of the company and the nature of the risks and challenges it faces. Whilst shareholders have every right to challenge companies' explanations if they are unconvincing, they should not be evaluated in a mechanistic way and departures from the Code should not be automatically treated as breaches. Shareholders should be careful to respond to the statements from companies in a manner that supports the 'comply or explain' process and bearing in mind the purpose of good corporate governance. They should put their views to the company and both parties should be prepared to discuss the position.

5. Smaller listed companies, in particular those new to listing, may judge that some of the provisions are disproportionate or less relevant in their case. Some of the provisions do not apply to companies below the FTSE 350. Such companies may nonetheless consider that it would be appropriate to adopt the approach in the Code and they are encouraged to do so. Externally managed investment companies typically have a different board structure which may affect the relevance of particular provisions; the Association of Investment Companies' Corporate Governance Code and Guide can assist them in meeting their obligations under the Code.

6. Satisfactory engagement between company boards and investors is crucial to the health of the UK's corporate governance regime. Companies and shareholders both have responsibility for ensuring that 'comply or explain' remains an effective alternative to a rules-based system. There are practical and administrative obstacles to improved interaction between boards and shareholders. But certainly there is also scope for an increase in trust which could generate a virtuous upward spiral in attitudes to the Code and in its constructive use.

THE MAIN PRINCIPLES OF THE CODE

Section A: Leadership

Every company should be headed by an effective board which is collectively responsible for the long-term success of the company.

There should be a clear division of responsibilities at the head of the company between the running of the board and the executive responsibility for the running of the company's business. No one individual should have unfettered powers of decision.

The chairman is responsible for leadership of the board and ensuring its effectiveness on all aspects of its role.

As part of their role as members of a unitary board, non-executive directors should constructively challenge and help develop proposals on strategy.

Section B: Effectiveness

The board and its committees should have the appropriate balance of skills, experience, independence and knowledge of the company to enable them to discharge their respective duties and responsibilities effectively.

There should be a formal, rigorous and transparent procedure for the appointment of new directors to the board. All directors should be able to allocate sufficient time to the company to discharge their responsibilities effectively.

All directors should receive induction on joining the board and should regularly update and refresh their skills and knowledge.

The board should be supplied in a timely manner with information in a form and of a quality appropriate to enable it to discharge its duties.

The board should undertake a formal and rigorous annual evaluation of its own performance and that of its committees and individual directors.

All directors should be submitted for re-election at regular intervals, subject to continued satisfactory performance.

Section C: Accountability

The board should present a balanced and understandable assessment of the company's position and prospects.

The board is responsible for determining the nature and extent of the significant risks it is willing to take in achieving its strategic objectives. The board should maintain sound risk management and internal control systems.

The board should establish formal and transparent arrangements for considering how they should apply the corporate reporting and risk management and internal control principles and for maintaining an appropriate relationship with the company's auditor.

Section D: Remuneration

Levels of remuneration should be sufficient to attract, retain and motivate directors of the quality required to run the company successfully, but a company should avoid paying more than is necessary for this purpose. A significant proportion of executive directors' remuneration should be structured so as to link rewards to corporate and individual performance.

There should be a formal and transparent procedure for developing policy on executive remuneration and for fixing the remuneration packages of individual directors. No director should be involved in deciding his or her own remuneration.

Section E: Relations with Shareholders

There should be a dialogue with shareholders based on the mutual understanding of objectives. The board as a whole has responsibility for ensuring that a satisfactory dialogue with shareholders takes place.

The board should use the AGM to communicate with investors and to encourage their participation.

SECTION A: LEADERSHIP

A.1 The Role of the Board

Main Principle

Every company should be headed by an effective board, which is collectively responsible for the success of the company.

Supporting Principles

The board's role is to provide entrepreneurial leadership of the company within a framework of prudent and effective controls which enables risk to be assessed and managed. The board should set the company's strategic aims, ensure that the necessary financial and human resources are in place for the company to meet its objectives and review management performance. The board should set the company's values and standards and ensure that its obligations to its shareholders and others are understood and met.

All directors must act in what they consider to be the best interests of the company, consistent with their statutory duties[2].

Code Provisions

A.1.1   The board should meet sufficiently regularly to discharge its duties effectively. There should be a formal schedule of matters specifically reserved for its decision. The annual report should include a statement of how the board operates, including a high level statement of which types of decisions are to be taken by the board and which are to be delegated to management.

A.1.2   The annual report should identify the chairman, the deputy chairman (where there is one), the chief executive, the senior independent director and the chairmen and members of the board committees[3]. It should also set out the number of meetings of the board and its committees and individual attendance by directors.

A.1.3   The company should arrange appropriate insurance cover in respect of legal action against its directors.

A.2 Division of Responsibilities

Main Principle

There should be a clear division of responsibilities at the head of the company between the running of the board and the executive responsibility for the running of the company's business. No one individual should have unfettered powers of decision.

Code Provision

A.2.1   The roles of chairman and chief executive should not be exercised by the same individual. The division of responsibilities between the chairman and chief executive should be clearly established, set out in writing and agreed by the board.

A.3 The Chairman

Main Principle

The chairman is responsible for leadership of the board and ensuring its effectiveness on all aspects of its role.

Supporting Principles

The chairman is responsible for setting the board's agenda and ensuring that adequate time is available for discussion of all agenda items, in particular strategic issues. The chairman should also promote a culture of openness and debate by facilitating the effective contribution of non-executive directors in particular and ensuring constructive relations between executive and non-executive directors.

The chairman is responsible for ensuring that the directors receive accurate, timely and clear information. The chairman should ensure effective communication with shareholders.

Code Provision

A.3.1   The chairman should on appointment meet the independence criteria set out in B.1.1 below. A chief executive should not go on to be chairman of the same company. If, exceptionally, a board decides that a chief executive should become chairman, the board should consult major shareholders in advance and should set out its reasons to shareholders at the time of the appointment and in the next annual report[4].

A.4 Non-Executive Directors

Main Principle

As part of their role as members of a unitary board, non-executive directors should constructively challenge and help develop proposals on strategy.

Supporting Principle

Non-executive directors should scrutinise the performance of management in meeting agreed goals and objectives and monitor the reporting of performance. They should satisfy themselves on the integrity of financial information and that financial controls and systems of risk management are robust and defensible. They are responsible for determining appropriate levels of remuneration of executive directors and have a prime role in appointing and, where necessary, removing executive directors, and in succession planning.

Code Provisions

A.4.1   The board should appoint one of the independent non-executive directors to be the senior independent director to provide a sounding board for the chairman and to serve as an intermediary for the other directors when necessary. The senior independent director should be available to shareholders if they have concerns which contact through the normal channels of chairman, chief executive or other executive directors has failed to resolve or for which such contact is inappropriate.

A.4.2   The chairman should hold meetings with the non-executive directors without the executives present. Led by the senior independent director, the non-executive directors should meet without the chairman present at least annually to appraise the chairman's performance and on such other occasions as are deemed appropriate.

A.4.3   Where directors have concerns which cannot be resolved about the running of the company or a proposed action, they should ensure that their concerns are recorded in the board minutes. On resignation, a non-executive director should provide a written statement to the chairman, for circulation to the board, if they have any such concerns.

SECTION B: EFFECTIVENESS

B.1 The Composition of the Board

Main Principle

The board and its committees should have the appropriate balance of skills, experience, independence and knowledge of the company to enable them to discharge their respective duties and responsibilities effectively.

Supporting Principles

The board should be of sufficient size that the requirements of the business can be met and that changes to the board's composition and that of its committees can be managed without undue disruption, and should not be so large as to be unwieldy.

The board should include an appropriate combination of executive and non-executive directors (and, in particular, independent non-executive directors) such that no individual or small group of individuals can dominate the board's decision taking.

The value of ensuring that committee membership is refreshed and that undue reliance is not placed on particular individuals should be taken into account in deciding chairmanship and membership of committees.

No one other than the committee chairman and members is entitled to be present at a meeting of the nomination, audit or remuneration committee, but others may attend at the invitation of the committee.

Code Provisions

B.1.1   The board should identify in the annual report each non-executive director it considers to be independent[5]. The board should determine whether the director is independent in character and judgement and whether there are relationships or circumstances which are likely to affect, or could appear to affect, the director's judgement. The board should state its reasons if it determines that a director is independent notwithstanding the existence of relationships or circumstances which may appear relevant to its determination, including if the director:

- has been an employee of the company or group within the last five years;
- has, or has had within the last three years, a material business relationship with the company either directly, or as a partner, shareholder, director or senior employee of a body that has such a relationship with the company;
- has received or receives additional remuneration from the company apart from a director's fee, participates in the company's share option or a performance-related pay scheme, or is a member of the company's pension scheme;
- has close family ties with any of the company's advisers, directors or senior employees;
- holds cross-directorships or has significant links with other directors through involvement in other companies or bodies;
- represents a significant shareholder; or
- has served on the board for more than nine years from the date of their first election.

B.1.2   Except for smaller companies[6], at least half the board, excluding the chairman, should comprise non-executive directors determined by the board to be independent. A smaller company should have at least two independent non-executive directors.

B.2 Appointments to the Board

Main Principle

There should be a formal, rigorous and transparent procedure for the appointment of new directors to the board.

Supporting Principles

The search for board candidates should be conducted, and appointments made, on merit, against objective criteria and with due regard for the benefits of diversity on the board, including gender.

The board should satisfy itself that plans are in place for orderly succession for appointments to the board and to senior management, so as to maintain an appropriate balance of skills and experience within the company and on the board and to ensure progressive refreshing of the board.

Code Provisions

B.2.1   There should be a nomination committee which should lead the process for board appointments and make recommendations to the board. A majority of members of the nomination committee should be independent non-executive directors. The chairman or an independent non-executive director should chair the committee, but the chairman should not chair the nomination committee when it is dealing with the appointment of a successor to the chairmanship. The nomination committee should make available its terms of reference, explaining its role and the authority delegated to it by the board[7].

B.2.2   The nomination committee should evaluate the balance of skills, experience, independence and knowledge on the board and, in the light of this evaluation, prepare a description of the role and capabilities required for a particular appointment.

B.2.3   Non-executive directors should be appointed for specified terms subject to re-election and to statutory provisions relating to the removal of a director. Any term beyond six years for a non-executive director should be subject to particularly rigorous review, and should take into account the need for progressive refreshing of the board.

B.2.4   A separate section of the annual report should describe the work of the nomination committee[8], including the process it has used in relation to board appointments. An explanation should be given if neither an external search consultancy nor open advertising has been used in the appointment of a chairman or a non-executive director.

B.3 Commitment

Main Principle

All directors should be able to allocate sufficient time to the company to discharge their responsibilities effectively.

B.3.1   For the appointment of a chairman, the nomination committee should prepare a job specification, including an assessment of the time commitment expected, recognising the need for availability in the event of crises. A chairman's other significant commitments should be disclosed to the board before appointment and included in the annual report. Changes to such commitments should be reported to the board as they arise, and their impact explained in the next annual report.

B.3.2   The terms and conditions of appointment of non-executive directors should be made available for inspection[9]. The letter of appointment should set out the expected time commitment. Non-executive directors should undertake that they will have sufficient time to meet what is expected of them. Their other significant commitments should be disclosed to the board before appointment, with a broad indication of the time involved and the board should be informed of subsequent changes.

B.3.3   The board should not agree to a full time executive director taking on more than one non-executive directorship in a FTSE 100 company nor the chairmanship of such a company.

B.4 Development

Main Principle

All directors should receive induction on joining the board and should regularly update and refresh their skills and knowledge.

Supporting Principles

The chairman should ensure that the directors continually update their skills and the knowledge and familiarity with the company required to fulfil their role both on the board and on board committees. The company should provide the necessary resources for developing and updating its directors' knowledge and capabilities.

To function effectively, all directors need appropriate knowledge of the company and access to its operations and staff.

Code Provisions

B.4.1	The chairman should ensure that new directors receive a full, formal and tailored induction on joining the board. As part of this, directors should avail themselves of opportunities to meet major shareholders.
B.4.2	The chairman should regularly review and agree with each director their training and development needs.

B.5 Information and Support

Main Principle

The board should be supplied in a timely manner with information in a form and of a quality appropriate to enable it to discharge its duties.

Supporting Principles

The chairman is responsible for ensuring that the directors receive accurate, timely and clear information. Management has an obligation to provide such information but directors should seek clarification or amplification where necessary.

Under the direction of the chairman, the company secretary's responsibilities include ensuring good information flows within the board and its committees and between senior management and non-executive directors, as well as facilitating induction and assisting with professional development as required.

The company secretary should be responsible for advising the board through the chairman on all governance matters.

Code Provisions

B.5.1	The board should ensure that directors, especially non-executive directors, have access to independent professional advice at the company's expense where they judge it necessary to discharge their responsibilities as directors. Committees should be provided with sufficient resources to undertake their duties.

B.5.2   All directors should have access to the advice and services of the company secretary, who is responsible to the board for ensuring that board procedures are complied with. Both the appointment and removal of the company secretary should be a matter for the board as a whole.

B.6 Evaluation

Main Principle

The board should undertake a formal and rigorous annual evaluation of its own performance and that of its committees and individual directors.

Supporting Principles

The chairman should act on the results of the performance evaluation by recognising the strengths and addressing the weaknesses of the board and, where appropriate, proposing new members be appointed to the board or seeking the resignation of directors.

Individual evaluation should aim to show whether each director continues to contribute effectively and to demonstrate commitment to the role (including commitment of time for board and committee meetings and any other duties).

Code Provisions

B.6.1   The board should state in the annual report how performance evaluation of the board, its committees and its individual directors has been conducted.

B.6.2   Evaluation of the board of FTSE 350 companies should be externally facilitated at least every three years. A statement should be made available of whether an external facilitator has any other connection with the company[10].

B.6.3   The non-executive directors, led by the senior independent director, should be responsible for performance evaluation of the chairman, taking into account the views of executive directors.

B.7 Re-election

Main Principle

All directors should be submitted for re-election at regular intervals, subject to continued satisfactory performance.

Code Provisions

B.7.1   All directors of FTSE 350 companies should be subject to annual election by shareholders. All other directors should be subject to election by shareholders at the first annual general meeting after their appointment, and to re-election thereafter at intervals of no more than three years. Non-executive directors who have served longer than nine years should be subject to annual re-election. The names of directors submitted for election or re-election should be accompanied by sufficient biographical details and any other relevant information to enable shareholders to take an informed decision on their election.

B.7.2   The board should set out to shareholders in the papers accompanying a resolution to elect a non-executive director why they believe an individual should be elected. The chairman should confirm to shareholders when proposing re-election that, following formal performance evaluation, the individual's performance continues to be effective and to demonstrate commitment to the role.

SECTION C: ACCOUNTABILITY

C.1 Financial And Business Reporting

Main Principle

The board should present a balanced and understandable assessment of the company's position and prospects.

Supporting Principle

The board's responsibility to present a balanced and understandable assessment extends to interim and other price-sensitive public reports and reports to regulators as well as to information required to be presented by statutory requirements.

Code Provisions

C.1.1   The directors should explain in the annual report their responsibility for preparing the annual report and accounts, and there should be a statement by the auditor about their reporting responsibilities[11].

C.1.2   The directors should include in the annual report an explanation of the basis on which the company generates or preserves value over the longer term (the business model) and the strategy for delivering the objectives of the company[12].

C.1.3   The directors should report in annual and half-yearly financial statements that the business is a going concern, with supporting assumptions or qualifications as necessary[13].

C.2 Risk Management and Internal Control[14]

Main Principle

The board is responsible for determining the nature and extent of the significant risks it is willing to take in achieving its strategic objectives. The board should maintain sound risk management and internal control systems.

Code Provision

C.2.1   The board should, at least annually, conduct a review of the effectiveness of the company's risk management and internal control systems and should report to shareholders that they have done so[15]. The review should cover all material controls, including financial, operational and compliance controls.

C.3 Audit Committee and Auditors[16]

Main Principle

The board should establish formal and transparent arrangements for considering how they should apply the corporate reporting and risk management and internal control principles and for maintaining an appropriate relationship with the company's auditor.

Code Provisions

C.3.1   The board should establish an audit committee of at least three, or in the case of smaller companies[17] two, independent non-executive directors. In smaller companies the company chairman may be a member of, but not chair, the committee in addition to the independent non-executive directors, provided he or she was considered independent on appointment as chairman. The board should satisfy itself that at least one member of the audit committee has recent and relevant financial experience[18].

C.3.2   The main role and responsibilities of the audit committee should be set out in written terms of reference[19] and should include:

- to monitor the integrity of the financial statements of the company and any formal announcements relating to the company's financial performance, reviewing significant financial reporting judgements contained in them;
- to review the company's internal financial controls and, unless expressly addressed by a separate board risk committee composed of independent directors, or by the board itself, to review the company's internal control and risk management systems;
- to monitor and review the effectiveness of the company's internal audit function;
- to make recommendations to the board, for it to put to the shareholders for their approval in general meeting, in relation to the appointment, re-appointment and removal of the external auditor and to approve the remuneration and terms of engagement of the external auditor;

- to review and monitor the external auditor's independence and objectivity and the effectiveness of the audit process, taking into consideration relevant UK professional and regulatory requirements;
- to develop and implement policy on the engagement of the external auditor to supply non-audit services, taking into account relevant ethical guidance regarding the provision of non-audit services by the external audit firm, and to report to the board, identifying any matters in respect of which it considers that action or improvement is needed and making recommendations as to the steps to be taken.

C.3.3   The terms of reference of the audit committee, including its role and the authority delegated to it by the board, should be made available[20]. A separate section of the annual report should describe the work of the committee in discharging those responsibilities[21].

C.3.4   The audit committee should review arrangements by which staff of the company may, in confidence, raise concerns about possible improprieties in matters of financial reporting or other matters. The audit committee's objective should be to ensure that arrangements are in place for the proportionate and independent investigation of such matters and for appropriate follow-up action.

C.3.5   The audit committee should monitor and review the effectiveness of the internal audit activities. Where there is no internal audit function, the audit committee should consider annually whether there is a need for an internal audit function and make a recommendation to the board, and the reasons for the absence of such a function should be explained in the relevant section of the annual report.

C.3.6   The audit committee should have primary responsibility for making a recommendation on the appointment, reappointment and removal of the external auditor. If the board does not accept the audit committee's recommendation, it should include in the annual report, and in any papers recommending appointment or re-appointment, a statement from the audit committee explaining the recommendation and should set out reasons why the board has taken a different position.

C.3.7   The annual report should explain to shareholders how, if the auditor provides non-audit services, auditor objectivity and independence is safeguarded.

SECTION D: REMUNERATION

D.1 The Level and Components of Remuneration

Main Principle

Levels of remuneration should be sufficient to attract, retain and motivate directors of the quality required to run the company successfully, but a company should avoid paying more than is necessary for this purpose. A significant proportion of executive directors' remuneration should be structured so as to link rewards to corporate and individual performance.

Supporting Principles

The performance-related elements of executive directors' remuneration should be stretching and designed to promote the long-term success of the company.

The remuneration committee should judge where to position their company relative to other companies. But they should use such comparisons with caution in view of the risk of an upward ratchet of remuneration levels with no corresponding improvement in performance.

They should also be sensitive to pay and employment conditions elsewhere in the group, especially when determining annual salary increases.

Code Provisions

D.1.1   In designing schemes of performance-related remuneration for executive directors, the remuneration committee should follow the provisions in Schedule A to this Code.

D.1.2   Where a company releases an executive director to serve as a non-executive director elsewhere, the remuneration report[22] should include a statement as to whether or not the director will retain such earnings and, if so, what the remuneration is.

D.1.3   Levels of remuneration for non-executive directors should reflect the time commitment and responsibilities of the role. Remuneration for non-executive directors should not include share options or other performance-related elements. If, exceptionally, options are granted, shareholder approval should be sought in advance and any shares acquired by exercise of the options should be held until at least one year after the non-executive director leaves the board. Holding of share options could be relevant to the determination of a non-executive director's independence (as set out in provision B.1.1).

D.1.4   The remuneration committee should carefully consider what compensation commitments (including pension contributions and all other elements) their directors' terms of appointment would entail in the event of early termination. The aim should be to avoid rewarding poor performance. They should take a robust line on reducing compensation to reflect departing directors' obligations to mitigate loss.

D.1.5   Notice or contract periods should be set at one year or less. If it is necessary to offer longer notice or contract periods to new directors recruited from outside, such periods should reduce to one year or less after the initial period.

D.2 Procedure

Main Principle

There should be a formal and transparent procedure for developing policy on executive remuneration and for fixing the remuneration packages of individual directors. No director should be involved in deciding his or her own remuneration.

Supporting Principles

The remuneration committee should consult the chairman and/or chief executive about their proposals relating to the remuneration of other executive directors. The remuneration committee should also be responsible for appointing any consultants in respect of executive director remuneration. Where executive directors or senior management are involved in advising or supporting the remuneration committee, care should be taken to recognise and avoid conflicts of interest.

The chairman of the board should ensure that the company maintains contact as required with its principal shareholders about remuneration.

Code Provisions

D.2.1   The board should establish a remuneration committee of at least three, or in the case of smaller companies[23] two, independent non-executive directors. In addition the company chairman may also be a member of, but not chair, the committee if he or she was considered independent on appointment as chairman. The remuneration committee should make available its terms of reference, explaining its role and the authority delegated to it by the board[24]. Where remuneration consultants are appointed, a statement should be made available[25] of whether they have any other connection with the company.

D.2.2   The remuneration committee should have delegated responsibility for setting remuneration for all executive directors and the chairman, including pension rights and any compensation payments. The committee should also recommend and monitor the level and structure of remuneration for senior management. The definition of 'senior management' for this purpose should be determined by the board but should normally include the first layer of management below board level.

D.2.3   The board itself or, where required by the Articles of Association, the shareholders should determine the remuneration of the non-executive directors within the limits set in the Articles of Association. Where permitted by the Articles, the board may however delegate this responsibility to a committee, which might include the chief executive.

D.2.4   Shareholders should be invited specifically to approve all new long-term incentive schemes (as defined in the Listing Rules[26]) and significant changes to existing schemes, save in the circumstances permitted by the Listing Rules.

SECTION E: RELATIONS WITH SHAREHOLDERS

E.1 Dialogue with Shareholders

Main Principle

There should be a dialogue with shareholders based on the mutual understanding of objectives. The board as a whole has responsibility for ensuring that a satisfactory dialogue with shareholders takes place[27].

Supporting Principles

Whilst recognising that most shareholder contact is with the chief executive and finance director, the chairman should ensure that all directors are made aware of their major shareholders' issues and concerns.

The board should keep in touch with shareholder opinion in whatever ways are most practical and efficient.

Code Provisions

E.1.1   The chairman should ensure that the views of shareholders are communicated to the board as a whole. The chairman should discuss governance and strategy with major shareholders. Non-executive directors should be offered the opportunity to attend scheduled meetings with major shareholders and should expect to attend meetings if requested by major shareholders. The senior independent director should attend sufficient meetings with a range of major shareholders to listen to their views in order to help develop a balanced understanding of the issues and concerns of major shareholders.

E.1.2   The board should state in the annual report the steps they have taken to ensure that the members of the board, and, in particular, the non-executive directors, develop an understanding of the views of major shareholders about the company, for example through direct face-to-face contact, analysts' or brokers' briefings and surveys of shareholder opinion.

E.2 Constructive Use of the AGM

Main Principle

The board should use the AGM to communicate with investors and to encourage their participation.

Code Provisions

E.2.1   At any general meeting, the company should propose a separate resolution on each substantially separate issue, and should, in particular, propose a resolution at the AGM relating to the report and accounts. For each resolution, proxy appointment forms should provide shareholders with the option to direct their proxy to vote either for or against the resolution or to withhold their vote. The proxy form and any announcement of the results of a vote should make it clear that a 'vote withheld' is not a vote in law and will not be counted in the calculation of the proportion of the votes for and against the resolution.

E.2.2   The company should ensure that all valid proxy appointments received for general meetings are properly recorded and counted. For each resolution, where a vote has been taken on a show of hands, the company should ensure that the following information is given at the meeting and made available as soon as reasonably practicable on a website which is maintained by or on behalf of the company:

- the number of shares in respect of which proxy appointments have been validly made;
- the number of votes for the resolution;
- the number of votes against the resolution; and
- the number of shares in respect of which the vote was directed to be withheld.

E.2.3   The chairman should arrange for the chairmen of the audit, remuneration and nomination committees to be available to answer questions at the AGM and for all directors to attend.

E.2.4   The company should arrange for the Notice of the AGM and related papers to be sent to shareholders at least 20 working days before the meeting.

SCHEDULE A: THE DESIGN OF PERFORMANCE-RELATED REMUNERATION FOR EXECUTIVE DIRECTORS

The remuneration committee should consider whether the directors should be eligible for annual bonuses. If so, performance conditions should be relevant, stretching and designed to promote the long-term success of the company. Upper limits should be set and disclosed. There may be a case for part payment in shares to be held for a significant period.

The remuneration committee should consider whether the directors should be eligible for benefits under long-term incentive schemes. Traditional share option schemes should be weighed against other kinds of long-term incentive scheme. Executive share options should not be offered at a discount save as permitted by the relevant provisions of the Listing Rules.

In normal circumstances, shares granted or other forms of deferred remuneration should not vest, and options should not be exercisable, in less than three years. Directors should be encouraged to hold their shares for a further period after vesting or exercise, subject to the need to finance any costs of acquisition and associated tax liabilities.

Any new long-term incentive schemes which are proposed should be approved by shareholders and should preferably replace any existing schemes or, at least, form part of a well considered overall plan incorporating existing schemes. The total potentially available rewards should not be excessive.

Payouts or grants under all incentive schemes, including new grants under existing share option schemes, should be subject to challenging performance criteria reflecting the company's objectives, including non-financial performance metrics where appropriate. Remuneration incentives should be compatible with risk policies and systems.

Grants under executive share option and other long-term incentive schemes should normally be phased rather than awarded in one large block.

Consideration should be given to the use of provisions that permit the company to reclaim variable components in exceptional circumstances of misstatement or misconduct.

In general, only basic salary should be pensionable. The remuneration committee should consider the pension consequences and associated costs to the company of basic salary increases and any other changes in pensionable remuneration, especially for directors close to retirement.

SCHEDULE B: DISCLOSURE OF CORPORATE GOVERNANCE ARRANGEMENTS

Corporate governance disclosure requirements are set out in three places:

- FSA Disclosure and Transparency Rules sub-chapters 7.1 and 7.2 (which set out certain mandatory disclosures);
- FSA Listing Rules 9.8.6 R, 9.8.7 R, and 9.8.7A R (which includes the 'comply or explain' requirement); and
- The UK Corporate Governance Code (in addition to providing an explanation where they choose not to comply with a provision, companies must disclose specified information in order to comply with certain provisions).

These requirements are summarised below. The full text of Disclosure and Transparency Rules 7.1 and 7.2 and Listing Rules 9.8.6 R, 9.8.7 R and 9.8.7A R are contained in the relevant chapters of the FSA Handbook, which can be found at http://fsahandbook.info/FSA/html/handbook/.

The Disclosure and Transparency Rules sub-chapters 7.1 and 7.2 apply to issuers whose securities are admitted to trading on a regulated market (this includes all issuers with a Premium or Standard listing). The Listing Rules 9.8.6 R, 9.8.7 R and 9.8.7A R and UK Corporate Governance Code apply to issuers of Premium listed equity shares only.

There is some overlap between the mandatory disclosures required under the Disclosure and Transparency Rules and those expected under the UK Corporate Governance Code. Areas of overlap are summarised in the Appendix to this Schedule. In respect of disclosures relating to the audit committee and the composition and operation of the board and its committees, compliance with the relevant provisions of the Code will result in compliance with the relevant Rules.

DISCLOSURE AND TRANSPARENCY RULES

Sub-chapter 7.1 of the Disclosure and Transparency Rules concerns audit committees or bodies carrying out equivalent functions.

DTR 7.1.1 R to 7.1.3 R set out requirements relating to the composition and functions of the committee or equivalent body:

- DTR 7.1.1 R states than an issuer must have a body which is responsible for performing the functions set out in DTR 7.1.3 R, and that at least one member of that body must be independent and at least one member must have competence in accounting and/or auditing.
- DTR 7.1.2 G states that the requirements for independence and competence in accounting and/or auditing may be satisfied by the same member or by different members of the relevant body.
- DTR 7.1.3 R states that an issuer must ensure that, as a minimum, the relevant body must:
  (1)   monitor the financial reporting process;
  (2)   monitor the effectiveness of the issuer's internal control, internal audit where applicable, and risk management systems;
  (3)   monitor the statutory audit of the annual and consolidated accounts;
  (4)   review and monitor the independence of the statutory auditor, and in particular the provision of additional services to the issuer.

DTR 7.1.5 R to DTR 7.1.7 G set out what disclosure is required. Specifically:

- DTR 7.1.5 R states that the issuer must make a statement available to the public disclosing which body carries out the functions required by DTR 7.1.3 R and how it is composed.
- DTR 7.1.6 G states that this can be included in the corporate governance statement required under sub-chapter DTR 7.2 (see below).
- DTR 7.1.7 G states that compliance with the relevant provisions of the UK Corporate Governance Code (as set out in the Appendix to this Schedule) will result in compliance with DTR 7.1.1 R to 7.1.5 R.

Sub-chapter 7.2 concerns corporate governance statements. Issuers are required to produce a corporate governance statement that must be either included in the directors' report (DTR 7.2.1 R); or in a separate report published together with the annual report; or on the issuer's website, in which case there must be a cross-reference in the directors' report (DTR 7.2.9 R).

DTR 7.2.2 R requires that the corporate governance statements must contain a reference to the corporate governance code to which the company is subject (for companies with a Premium listing this is the UK Corporate Governance Code). DTR 7.2.3 R requires that, to the extent that it departs from that code, the company must explain which parts of the code it departs from and the reasons for doing so. DTR 7.2.4 G states that compliance with LR 9.8.6 R (6) (the 'comply or explain' rule in relation to the UK Corporate Governance Code) will also satisfy these requirements.

DTR 7.2.5 R to DTR 7.2.10 R set out certain information that must be disclosed in the corporate governance statement:

- DTR 7.2.5 R states that the corporate governance statement must contain a description of the main features of the company's internal control and risk management systems in relation to the financial reporting process. DTR 7.2.10 R states that an issuer which is required to prepare a group directors' report within the meaning of Section 415(2) of the Companies Act 2006 must include in that report a description of the main features of the group's internal control and risk management systems in relation to the process for preparing consolidated accounts.
- DTR 7.2.6 R states that the corporate governance statement must contain the information required by paragraph 13(2)(c), (d), (f), (h) and (i) of Schedule 7 to the Large and Medium-sized Companies and Groups (Accounts and Reports) Regulations 2008 where the issuer is subject to the requirements of that paragraph.
- DTR 7.2.7 R states that the corporate governance statement must contain a description of the composition and operation of the issuer's administrative, management and supervisory bodies and their committees. DTR 7.2.8 G states that compliance with the relevant provisions of the UK Corporate Governance Code (as set out in the Appendix to this Schedule) will satisfy these requirements.

LISTING RULES

Listing Rules 9.8.6 R (for UK incorporated companies) and 9.8.7 R (for overseas incorporated companies) state that in the case of a company that has a Premium listing of equity shares, the following items must be included in its annual report and accounts:

- a statement of how the listed company has applied the Main Principles set out in the UK Corporate Governance Code, in a manner that would enable shareholders to evaluate how the principles have been applied;
- a statement as to whether the listed company has:
  - complied throughout the accounting period with all relevant provisions set out in the UK Corporate Governance Code; or
  - not complied throughout the accounting period with all relevant provisions set out in the UK Corporate Governance Code, and if so, setting out:
    (i) those provisions, if any, it has not complied with;
    (ii) in the case of provisions whose requirements are of a continuing nature, the period within which, if any, it did not comply with some or all of those provisions; and
    (iii) the company's reasons for non-compliance.

THE UK CORPORATE GOVERNANCE CODE

In addition to the 'comply or explain' requirement in the Listing Rules, the Code includes specific requirements for disclosure which must be provided in order to comply. These are summarised below. The annual report should include:

- a statement of how the board operates, including a high level statement of which types of decisions are to be taken by the board and which are to be delegated to management (A.1.1);
- the names of the chairman, the deputy chairman (where there is one), the chief executive, the senior independent director and the chairmen and members of the board committees (A.1.2);
- the number of meetings of the board and those committees and individual attendance by directors (A.1.2);
- where a chief executive is appointed chairman, the reasons for their appointment (this only needs to be done in the annual report following the appointment) (A.3.1);
- the names of the non-executive directors whom the board determines to be independent, with reasons where necessary (B.1.1);
- a separate section describing the work of the nomination committee, including the process it has used in relation to board appointments and an explanation if neither external search consultancy nor open advertising has been used in the appointment of a chairman or a non-executive director (B.2.4);
- any changes to the other significant commitments of the chairman during the year (B.3.1);
- a statement of how performance evaluation of the board, its committees and its directors has been conducted (B.6.1);
- an explanation from the directors of their responsibility for preparing the accounts and a statement by the auditors about their reporting responsibilities (C.1.1);
- an explanation from the directors of the basis on which the company generates or preserves value over the longer term (the business model) and the strategy for delivering the objectives of the company (C.1.2);
- a statement from the directors that the business is a going concern, with supporting assumptions or qualifications as necessary (C.1.3);
- a report that the board has conducted a review of the effectiveness of the company's risk management and internal controls systems (C.2.1);
- a separate section describing the work of the audit committee in discharging its responsibilities (C.3.3);
- where there is no internal audit function, the reasons for the absence of such a function (C.3.5);
- where the board does not accept the audit committee's recommendation on the appointment, reappointment or removal of an external auditor, a statement from the audit committee explaining the recommendation and the reasons why the board has taken a different position (C.3.6);
- an explanation of how, if the auditor provides non-audit services, auditor objectivity and independence is safeguarded (C.3.7);
- a description of the work of the remuneration committee as required under the Large and Medium-Sized Companies and Groups (Accounts and Reports) Regulations 2008 including, where an executive director serves as a non-executive director elsewhere, whether or not the director will retain such earnings and, if so, what the remuneration is (D.1.2);
- the steps the board has taken to ensure that members of the board, in particular the non-executive directors, develop an understanding of the views of major shareholders about their company (E.1.2).

The following information should be made available (which may be met by placing the information on a website that is maintained by or on behalf of the company):

- the terms of reference of the nomination, audit and remuneration committees, explaining their role and the authority delegated to them by the board (B.2.1, C.3.3 and D.2.1);

- the terms and conditions of appointment of non-executive directors (B.3.2) (see footnote 9);
- where performance evaluation has been externally facilitated, a statement of whether the facilitator has any other connection with the company (B.6.2); and
- where remuneration consultants are appointed, a statement of whether they have any other connection with the company (D.2.1).

The board should set out to shareholders in the papers accompanying a resolution to elect or re-elect directors:

- sufficient biographical details to enable shareholders to take an informed decision on their election or re-election (B.7.1);
- why they believe an individual should be elected to a non-executive role (B.7.2); and
- on re-election of a non-executive director, confirmation from the chairman that, following formal performance evaluation, the individual's performance continues to be effective and to demonstrate commitment to the role (B.7.2).

The board should set out to shareholders in the papers recommending appointment or reappointment of an external auditor:

- if the board does not accept the audit committee's recommendation, a statement from the audit committee explaining the recommendation and from the board setting out reasons why they have taken a different position (C.3.6).

ADDITIONAL GUIDANCE

The Turnbull Guidance and FRC Guidance on Audit Committees contain further suggestions as to information that might usefully be disclosed in the internal control statement and the report of the audit committee respectively. Both sets of guidance are available on the FRC website at: http://www.frc.org.uk/corporate/ukcgcode.cfm

APPENDIX: OVERLAP BETWEEN THE DISCLOSURE AND TRANSPARENCY RULES AND THE UK CORPORATE GOVERNANCE CODE

Disclosure and Transparency Rules	UK Corporate Governance
D.T.R 7.1.1 R	**Provision C.3.1**
Sets out minimum requirements on composition of the audit committee or equivalent body.	Sets out recommended composition of the audit committee.
D.T.R 7.1.3 R	**Provision C.3.2**
Sets out minimum functions of the audit committee or equivalent body.	Sets out the recommended minimum terms of reference for the committee.
D.T.R 7.1.5 R	**Provision A.1.2**
The composition and function of the audit committee or equivalent body must be disclosed in the annual report	The annual report should identify members of the board committees.
	Provision C.3.3
DTR 7.1.7 R states that compliance with Code provisions A.1.2, C.3.1, C.3.2 and C.3.3 will result in compliance with DTR 7.1.1 R to DTR 7.1.5 R.	The annual report should describe the work of the audit committee.
	Further recommendations on the content of the audit committee report are set out in the FRC Guidance on Audit Committees
D.T.R 7.2.5 R	**Provision C.2.1**

The corporate governance statement must include a description of the main features of the company's internal control and risk management systems in relation to the financial reporting process.

While this requirement differs from the requirement in the UK Corporate Governance Code, it is envisaged that both could be met by a single internal control statement.

DTR 7.2.7 R

The corporate governance statement must include a description of the composition and operation of the administrative, management and supervisory bodies and their committees.

DTR 7.2.8 R states that compliance with Code provisions A.1.1, A.1.2, A.4.6, B.2.1 and C.3.3 with result in compliance with DTR 7.2.7 R.

The Board must report that a review of the effectiveness of the internal control system has been carried out. Further recommendations on the content of the internal control statement are set out in the Turnbull Guidance.

This requirement overlaps with a number of different provisions of the Code:

A.1.1: the annual report should include a statement of how the board operates.

A.1.2: the annual report should identify members of the board and board committees.

B.2.4: the annual report should describe the work of the nomination committee.

C.3.3: the annual report should describe the work of the audit committee.

D.2.1: a description of the work of the remuneration committee should be made available. *[Note: in order to comply with DTR 7.2.7 R this information will need to be included in the corporate governance statement].*

---

1   References to shareholders also apply to intermediaries and agents employed to assist shareholders in scrutinising governance arrangements.

2   For directors of UK incorporated companies, these duties are set out in the Sections 170 to 177 of the Companies Act 2006.

3   Provisions A.1.1 and A.1.2 overlap with FSA Rule DTR 7.2.7 R; Provision A.1.2 also overlaps with DTR 7.1.5 R (see Schedule B).

4   Compliance or otherwise with this provision need only be reported for the year in which the appointment is made.

5   A.3.1 states that the chairman should, on appointment, meet the independence criteria set out in this provision, but thereafter the test of independence is not appropriate in relation to the chairman.

6   A smaller company is one that is below the FTSE 350 throughout the year immediately prior to the reporting year.

7   The requirement to make the information available would be met by including the information on a website that is maintained by or on behalf of the company.

8   This provision overlaps with FSA Rule DTR 7.2.7 R (see Schedule B).

9   The terms and conditions of appointment of non-executive directors should be made available for inspection by any person at the company's registered office during normal business hours and at the AGM (for 15 minutes prior to the meeting and during the meeting).

10   See footnote 7.

[11] The requirement may be met by the disclosures about the audit scope and the responsibilities of the auditor included, or referred to, in the auditor's report pursuant to the requirements in paragraph 16 of ISA (UK and Ireland) 700, 'The Auditor's Report on Financial Statements'. Copies are available at: www.frc.org.uk/apb/publications/pub2102.html.

[12] It would be desirable if the explanation were located in the same part of the annual report as the Business Review required by Section 417 of the Companies Act 2006. Guidance as to the matters that should be considered in an explanation of a business model is provided in paragraphs 30 to 32 of the Accounting Standard Board's *Reporting Statement: Operating And Financial Review*. Copies are available at: www.frc.org.uk/asb/publications/documents.cfm?cat=7.

[13] 'Going Concern and Liquidity Risk: Guidance for Directors of UK Companies 2009' suggests means of applying this part of the Code. Copies are available at: www.frc.org.uk/corporate/goingconcern.cfm.

[14] The Turnbull guidance suggests means of applying this part of the Code. Copies are available at www.frc.org.uk/corporate/internalcontrol.cfm.

[15] In addition FSA Rule DTR 7.2.5 R requires companies to describe the main features of the internal control and risk management systems in relation to the financial reporting process.

[16] The FRC Guidance on Audit Committees suggests means of applying this part of t he Code. Copies are available at: http://www.frc.org.uk/corporate/auditcommittees.cfm.

[17] See footnote 6.

[18] This provision overlaps with FSA Rule DTR 7.1.1 R (see Schedule B).

[19] This provision overlaps with FSA Rules DTR 7.1.3 R (see Schedule C).

[20] See footnote 7.

[21] This provision overlaps with FSA Rules DTR 7.1.5 R and 7.2.7 R (see Schedule B).

[22] As required for UK incorporated companies under the Large and Medium-Sized Companies and Groups (Accounts and Reports) Regulations 2008.

[23] See footnote 6.

[24] This provision overlaps with FSA Rule DTR 7.2.7 R (see Schedule B).

[25] See footnote 7.

[26] Listing Rules LR 9.4; available at http://fsahandbook.info/FSA/html/handbook/LR/9/4.

[27] Nothing in these principles or provisions should be taken to override the general requirements of law to treat shareholders equally in access to information.

Chapter 7

Membership

Members and the company

Definition of a member

[7.1] Section 112 of the Companies Act 2006 (CA 2006) defines a member as being either a subscriber to the memorandum of association or some other person who has *agreed* to become a member of the company and has been *registered* as such in the register of members. With the exception of the members of a company limited by guarantee, the members of a company are thus its shareholders.

A shareholding in a company can be acquired in several ways, either by:

(a)   subscription to the memorandum of association;
(b)   acquisition by way of allotment or transfer; or
(c)   transmission.

However, until the person acquiring the shares by either of the methods above (except by subscription to the memorandum of association) is entered in the register of members of the company then, although he could be described as a shareholder, he could not be described as a member (CA 2006, s 112(2)). A person subscribing to the memorandum of association, however, automatically becomes a member without registration being required (CA 2006, s 112(1)).

An important point arising out of this definition is that CA 2006 commonly refers to 'members' not 'shareholders' in specifying their rights. Thus, even though a person may have acquired 99% of a company's issued shares he cannot exercise any of his rights as a member until registered in the register of members as holding the shares. However, the rights of members are commonly tied in with the shares that they hold, both by the Act and by a company's articles of association.

For companies limited by guarantee the situation is slightly different as the members do not hold shares. Instead of shareholdings, each person who wishes to become a member of a company limited by guarantee gives a guarantee that, in the event of the company being wound up, he will contribute the amount specified in the memorandum of association to the company's assets (usually £1). However, as with a company limited by shares, until the person giving the guarantee is registered in the register of members, he does not acquire the status of a member. Again, the subscribers to the memorandum of association automatically become members without registration being required.

Institutional shareholders

[7.2] Shareholders are the owners of a company and therefore institutional shareholders are obliged to act responsibly and in the best interests of their investors. Guidelines have been produced by the Institutional Shareholders' Committee on the responsibilities of institutional shareholders in the United Kingdom (UK). This code of best practice makes various recommendations such as having effective channels of communication with the board to enable a better understanding of each other's aims and requirements, supporting the board by positive voting unless they have good reason to do otherwise and to consider all offers of a takeover bid objectively.

Institutional investors have a fiduciary responsibility to those on whose behalf they are investing and. In June 1998 following a final report of the Hampel Committee, a Combined Code was produced and incorporated in the Listing Rules as Amendment 12. The Combined Code has since been revised following the Higgs Review but retains the key statements of the earlier Code as far as institutional shareholders are concerned. The following principles are applicable to institutional shareholders:

Main principles

Institutional shareholders have a responsibility to make considered use of their votes.

Institutional shareholders should enter into a dialogue with companies based on the mutual understanding of objectives.

When evaluating companies' governance arrangements, particularly those relating to board structure and composition, institutional investors should give due weight to all relevant factors drawn to their attention.

Supporting principles

Institutional shareholders should take steps to ensure that their voting intentions are being translated into practice.

Institutional shareholders should, on request, make available to their clients information on the proportion of resolutions on which votes were cast and non-discretionary proxies lodged.

Major shareholders should attend annual general meetings (AGMs) where appropriate and practicable. Companies and registrars should facilitate this.

Acquisition of shares

[7.3] As mentioned above there are several different methods by which a person may acquire shares in a company and accordingly become a member of it.

(a) *Subscription*
By subscribing to the memorandum of association of a company prior to its applying for registration, a subscriber automatically becomes a member on the date the company is incorporated (see **2.1 THE COMPANY**

CONSTITUTION and **7.1** above). In subscribing, the subscriber will state opposite his name how many shares he agrees to take and he will then sign the memorandum of association.

(b)   *Acquisition by allotment*

A person may become a member of a company by agreeing to purchase shares which the company has offered to issue. In effect, a contract is created between the company and the prospective member under which, in consideration for the payment by the member to the company of an agreed sum, the company will issue shares to the member. Usually the agreement to acquire shares in this manner will be indicated by the completion of an application form for shares in response to an offer for sale made by the company. On the allotment of the shares, the company will register the applicant in the register of members, and it is from that date that the person becomes a member, not from the date of allotment.

(c)   *Acquisition by transfer*

Subject to any restrictions which may exist in a company's articles of association, an existing member may transfer, either for consideration or otherwise, his shareholding in a company to another person. The transfer is effected by the completion of a stock transfer form (Stock Transfer Act 1963) by the transferor in favour of the transferee, the submission of the form (to HM Revenue and Customs (HMRC) Stamp Office) for stamp duty purposes and then the transferee's presentation of the form to the company together with the relevant share certificate for board approval and registration in the register of members (see **7.17** below).

(d)   *Transmission*

Although similar in many ways to a transfer of shares, a person may become entitled to the shares of another upon the death, bankruptcy or insanity of a member. In such circumstances, the person becoming entitled to the shares will submit to the company a notice of his entitlement (eg probate) together with a request that he now be registered in the register of members as the holder of the shares. Accordingly upon registration he becomes a member (see **7.23** below). It is important to note that a person who has not agreed to become a member cannot be registered in the register of members as one. In such circumstances, the person who has been erroneously registered may force the company to take his name off the Register. Such rectification of the register however will, in most circumstances, require the consent of the court (CA 2006, s 125).

Cessation of membership

[7.4] It would follow from the above and from CA 2006, s 112 that a person will cease to be a member of the company upon his ceasing to be registered in the register of members. This can be brought about in several ways:

(a)   voluntary transfer of shares (as **7.3**(*c*) above);
(b)   transmission on death (as **7.3**(*d*) above) or bankruptcy;
(c)   compulsory transfer of shares (eg enforcement of a lien); and
(d)   forfeiture (eg non-payment of calls due).

Restrictions upon membership

[7.5] Generally speaking, any person or legal entity may be a member of a company, subject to them having sufficient legal capacity. Thus, with the exception of minors and persons who are either bankrupt or insane (where agreement to become a member would be voidable), any person or corporation can be a member. However, CA 2006 has introduced several restrictions relating to the capacity of companies in certain instances to hold shares.

(a)　*Holding its own shares*
　　　CA 2006, s 658 expressly prohibits a company from holding its own shares. However, CA 2006, s 659 goes on to qualify this statement somewhat by specifically excluding certain transactions as not being acquisitions within the meaning of CA 2006, s 658, so long as the shares acquired are fully paid.
　　　CA 2006, s 690 further goes on to provide perhaps the most common exception to the general rule by setting out a procedure whereby a company with appropriate provisions/no restrictions in its articles may purchase its own shares (see **8.50–8.59 CAPITAL**).
　　　CA 2006, s 658(2)(b) states that any acquisition by a company of its own shares (unless being an exempt category) is void.

(b)　*Holding company*
　　　CA 2006, s 136 states that a company cannot be a member of its own holding company. An exception to this general rule exists in circumstances where the subsidiary is holding the shares of its holding company purely as a personal representative or trustee of a third party and that neither the subsidiary nor the holding company has a beneficial interest in the shares held. This situation arises where the company's employees hold shares in the company indirectly through a subsidiary company which acts as trustee for the employees.
　　　CA 2006, s 131(1)(b)/CA 1985, s 23(1) states that any transfer or allotment of shares (outside the limited exception) by a holding company to a subsidiary is void.

Shares

[7.6] Section 10 of CA 2006 has introduced a major change in that a limited company with a share capital no longer needs to have an authorised share capital. The information about shares subscribed for by the subscribers to the memorandum will be provided to the Registrar in the statement of capital and initial shareholdings. Previously, under CA 1985, s 2(5), every company is required to include a statement in its memorandum of association of the amount of share capital with which it proposes to be registered and that the share capital be capable of division into shares of a fixed amount. This constitutes a company's authorised (or nominal) share capital, for example:

'The share capital of the company is £1,000,000 divided into 1,000,000 ordinary shares of £1 each.'

The Act has many provisions relating to share capital (see below) but, apart from applying several general restrictions and obligations upon a company, does not specify the general rights which attach to shares. It is, in general, left to a company to determine what rights shall attach to its shares.

It is permissible for a company to denominate its capital in different fixed amounts of non-sterling currencies provided, in the case of a public company, the required statutory minimum (ie £50,000) is in sterling or the euro equivalent (see **2.23 THE COMPANY CONSTITUTION**).

Section 622 of CA 2006 introduces a new procedure for the redenomination of shares into a different currency by resolution of the members and there is nothing to prevent a public company's minimum share capital being redenominated in this way once a trading certificate has been obtained.

Under previous legislation in order to convert share capital from one currency to another, private companies would need to replace the existing share capital with new capital denominated in the desired currency by creating new shares and cancelling the old shares by capital reduction, requiring shareholder and court approval. Furthermore public companies were previously obliged to have a minimum share capital of £50,000 and only additional share capital to this can be denominated in another currency.

The rights and liabilities attaching to shares by the Act and by the articles of association are discussed in **7.7** below.

The Companies Act specifies further requirements with which a company must comply in respect of its share capital.

(a)   *Distinguishing numbers*
       CA 2006, s 543 requires that every issued share shall bear a distinguishing number. However, the section also provides that where all the issued shares are fully paid up and rank *pari passu* (equally between themselves) then the requirement for the shares to bear distinguishing numbers may be dispensed with by passing a resolution to this effect.

(b)   *Share transfers*
       Shares are the personal estate of a member and, subject to the Stock Transfer Act 1963, may be transferred by a member in the manner specified by a company's articles of association, for example, according to any pre-emption rights which may exist.
       The Stock Transfer Act 1963 specifies the form that a share transfer must take and under CA 2006, s 770 it is unlawful for a company to register any transfer not in the specified form or in any form approved of by the directors. Certain exceptions to this rule however exist under the Stock Transfer Act 1982 and where a person has become entitled to a share by operation of law (eg deceased member's executor) (CA 2006, s 770(1)(b)(i)).
       A company may specify the circumstances in its articles of association when it will and will not register transfers of shares. This power is subject however to CA 2006, s 774 which specifies the circumstances in which by operation of law a person must be recognised as having become entitled to shares (eg by grant of probate of a will) (see **7.23** below).

(c)   *Share certificates*

Within two months of the date of allotment or date of lodging of a transfer of any shares, a company is obliged to issue to the holder of the shares a certificate representing the shares which have been allotted or transferred (CA 2006, s 769) (see **7.24** below).

In respect of a transfer of shares the 'date of lodging' is deemed to be the date upon which a *duly stamped* transfer is lodged.

Membership and share rights

Rights of members

[7.7] The rights of the members of a company are usually linked with and expressed in terms of the rights attaching to the shares which they hold – although not exclusively so. For example, a member holding preference shares will have the same right to inspect the register of members of the company as a member holding ordinary shares, but the company's articles of association may give the two classes of shares different voting rights.

In companies limited by guarantee the rights of members attach solely to the member personally as no shares exist unless the company was formed before 22 December 1980. However, it is fairly common for such companies to create classes of membership which have lesser rights than full membership on such matters as voting; such membership is sometimes referred to as associate membership.

In essence, the rights and the liabilities attaching to shares and membership are defined by a combination of CA 2006 and a company's articles of association.

The Companies Act provides the members of a company with many rights specific to membership and also certain liabilities. The Act also provides for specific rights attaching to shares; these mainly relate to the variation of the rights of shareholders.

The principal rights of a member of a company are as follows.

(a) *Inspection of statutory books and records*
    The Act provides that a member may inspect various statutory registers of a company and request copies of the same (see **CHAPTER 3 THE STATUTORY RECORDS**) and to inspect directors' service contracts or written memoranda of the terms and conditions of a director's contract of service for both the company and any subsidiary of the company (CA 2006, s 229). A member may also request that a company provide him with a copy of its memorandum and articles of association (CA 2006, s 32).

(b) *To receive a copy of the annual accounts*
    CA 2006, s 423 provides that a member is entitled to receive a copy of the annual accounts of the company (see **CHAPTER 4 ACCOUNTS AND AUDITORS**) at least 21 days before the general meeting at which they are to be laid (usually the AGM).
    A member may also request that the company provide him with a copy of the latest accounts of the company (CA 2006, s 431).

By virtue of amendments to the Companies Act made by the Electronic Communications Act 2000 a company can send out accounts electronically to any person entitled to receive a copy of the accounts as long as that person has given prior consent and an address specific for that purpose.

Additionally, if the accounts from a listed public company have been received in the form of a summary financial statement, then a member may notify the company in the relevant manner prescribed by the Companies (Summary Financial Statements) Regulations 1995 (SI 1995/2092), of either or both of the following matters:

(i)   that he wishes to receive full accounts and reports for the financial year covered by the summary financial statements; and/or

(ii)   that he wishes to receive full accounts and reports for future financial years.

(c)   *To receive notice of general meetings*
Subject to any provisions to the contrary contained in the company's articles of association, a member is entitled, pursuant to CA 2006, s 310, to receive notice of all general meetings. Notices can be sent electronically (see **7.35** below for more details).

(d)   *To appoint a proxy*
CA 2006, s 324 further provides that a member may appoint a proxy or proxies to attend a general meeting on his behalf. A proxy need not be a member of the company and can speak and vote at the meeting. In addition, the appointment of a proxy can be contained in an electronic communication. A proxy may join in the demand for a poll (see **7.32** below).

(e)   *Elective regime*
Where a private company has elected to dispense with the requirements of the previous Companies Act 1985 relating to the holding of AGMs, the laying of the annual accounts before a general meeting and the annual appointment of auditors, a member may, by giving notice to the company, require that these elections be disapplied in respect of any year. Notice can be given electronically to an address specified for that purpose by or on behalf of the company. The Companies Act 2006 has since changed this to the extent that a private limited company is deemed to be in the elective regime unless it specifically opts in to holding AGMs and laying accounts, etc.

(f)   *Unfair prejudice*
Under CA 2006, s 994 a member has the right to petition the court to obtain relief where the member considers that any act (proposed or actual) will or has resulted in unfair prejudice to his interests or to the interests of the members generally.

(g)   *Petition court*
A member has the right under section 122 of the Insolvency Act 1986 to petition the court for the winding-up of a company if it is unable to pay its debts, if the members have fallen below two in the case of a public company or on just and equitable grounds.

Liabilities of members

[7.8] In addition to rights, a member also has certain liabilities imposed upon him by the Act as follows.

(a) *Contributions on winding-up*
     To contribute to the assets of the company in respect of any amounts outstanding on the shares which they hold in a winding-up (Insolvency Act 1986, s 74). Members of companies limited by guarantee would, in such circumstances, be liable to pay the amount of the guarantee which they have given. In certain circumstances persons who have been members within the twelve months preceding the winding-up can also be required to contribute to the assets of the company, but not beyond the amount which is unpaid on the shares which they held.
(b) *To pay calls on shares*
     To pay up when called upon to do so by the company, any amount outstanding on the shares which a member holds and which are unpaid (CA 2006, s 39(2)).

Share rights

[7.9] As well as the rights which attach to membership of a company, a member also has certain rights which attach to the shares which he holds. These rights are set out by a combination of CA 2006 and the articles of association.

Companies Act 2006

The rights set out in CA 2006 include the following.

Pre-emption rights

[7.10] Under CA 2006, s 561 a company proposing to issue shares is obliged to offer the existing members a proportion of the shares equal to the member's current shareholding (see **8.5 CAPITAL**). In certain circumstances a member's right may be disapplied pursuant to CA 2006, ss 567 and 570 (see **8.6–8.7 CAPITAL**) by resolution or through the company's articles of association.

Variation of class rights

[7.11] Special rights attached to a class of shares usually relate to dividends, voting, return of capital or distribution of surplus assets on a winding-up and will commonly be found in a company's articles of association. Where the rights are laid down as aforementioned, the provisions will determine how the shares can be varied. If it is unclear where the definition of rights is laid down, a scheme of arrangement, under CA 2006, s 895, may be necessary to clarify them.

(a) *Special rights in the articles*
     If the articles provide for a variation of rights procedure it usually takes the form of what is called a 'modification of rights article' whereby class rights can be changed by passing an extraordinary resolution at a

separate class meeting or by obtaining written consent of three-quarters of the holders of the issued shares of that class. The expressed procedure as set out in the articles must be complied with and any meeting required to be held must be done so in accordance with the provisions relating to the holding of general meetings in the articles. However, there must be a quorum of two who between them hold at least one-third in nominal value of the issued shares of that class.

In the situation where the articles do not provide for a variation procedure, CA 2006, s 630(4) details the statutory procedure to be followed. This is very similar to what is commonly found in the articles and requires:

(i)   three-quarters of the holders of the issued shares of the class in question to consent in writing to the variation; or

(ii)   the passing of an extraordinary resolution/special resolution (CA 2006, s 630(4)(b)) at a separate class meeting sanctioning the variation.

It should be noted that a written resolution of the members under CA 2006, s 288 could be used but that would mean obtaining the signature of *all* shareholders, not just of that particular class.

(b)   *Objection to variation*

If the articles state that a variation is subject to consent of a certain number of the holders of that class then CA 2006, s 633 may be applied. This gives minority members the right to challenge a decision to vary rights by making an application to the court within 21 days of the resolution being passed, to have the variation cancelled.

At least 15% of the dissentient holders of the issued shares concerned, who did not consent or vote for the resolution, must be party to the application. The court then has to decide whether the variation would unfairly prejudice the shareholders of the class represented. The variation will not have effect until it has been confirmed by the court.

Articles of association

[7.12] The articles of association is the document which sets out a company's internal rules (see **2.25–2.32, 2.38 THE COMPANY CONSTITUTION**) and accordingly the rights attaching to shares will usually be stated in them.

Voting

[7.13] The new Companies Act 2006 model articles set out much simplified and generic clauses relating to the internal administration of companies. Clauses 40 to 45 cover voting at general meetings.

Previously, regulations 54 to 63 of Table A 1985 set out the model voting rights attaching to shares. Regulation 54 states that 'subject to any rights or restrictions attaching to any shares' on a show of hands every member present at a general meeting has one vote (regardless of the number of shares held) and on a poll has one vote for each share of which he is the holder.

Where different classes of share exist the rights of members to vote on a show of hands is sometimes restricted (eg deferred shares) and different weightings can be attached to the number of votes shares of different classes carry on a poll (eg 'A' ordinary shares – one vote for every share held; 'B' ordinary shares – one vote for every ten shares held).

Regulation 57 further specifies that, unless all moneys due and payable in respect of shares held by a member have been paid, then that member's voting rights are suspended until such time as the amounts due have been paid. A company may specify in its articles other circumstances when voting rights may be suspended (eg public companies commonly reserve this right for circumstances when a member to whom a request under CA 2006, s 793 requiring the member to disclose the beneficial ownership of shares had not so disclosed beneficial ownership).

Dividends

[7.14] Part 23 of CA 2006 sets out the statutory provisions relating to the payment of dividends by a company. Additionally, regulations 28 to 33 of the new model articles (previously regulations 102 to 108 of Table A 1985) provide model regulations.

(a) *Statutory provisions*

CA 2006, s 830(1) provides that a company may not make a distribution except out of profits available for the purpose. A distribution is described in CA 2006, s 829(1) as being a distribution of a company's assets, whether in cash or otherwise. However, the following are specifically referred to in that section as not being distributions:

(i) an issue of shares as fully or partly paid bonus shares (see **8.13 CAPITAL**);

(ii) redemption or purchase of a company's own shares out of capital;

(iii) reduction of share capital; and

(iv) distribution of assets on a winding-up.

The profits available for distribution are defined as being a company's accumulated realised profits less its accumulated realised losses, so far as not previously distributed, capitalised or written off (CA 2006, s 830(2)). Sections 836–840 of CA 2006 further specify that, for the purposes of determining the profit available for distribution, reference must be made to the company's last annual, or interim, or initial accounts prepared in accordance with the Act. A public company is required to deliver these accounts to Companies House where they are used for the purposes of determining a dividend.

Problems have arisen where public companies have not filed interim accounts, which were required for justification of the payment of a dividend, prior to the distribution being made. Any dividend paid out in contravention of the provisions laid down in the Companies Act is illegal and therefore recoverable from the shareholders.

Further restrictions are imposed on distributions by a public company. CA 2006, s 831 states that a public company may only make a distribution at any time:

(i) if at the time of the distribution the amount of its net assets is not less than the aggregate of its called up share capital and undistributable reserves; and

(ii)   the distribution does not reduce the amount of the net assets to less than the aggregate of its called up share capital and undistributable reserves.

The undistributable reserves are defined by CA 2006, s 831(4) as being:

(A)   share premium account;

(B)   capital redemption reserve;

(C)   the amount by which the accumulated, unrealised profits exceed the accumulated unrealised losses (so far as not previously utilised, written off or reorganised as appropriate); or

(D)   any other reserve stated as not being capable of distribution either in the company's articles or any statute.

A company which has an exemption from the use of the word 'limited' in its name under CA 2006, s 60 (see **2.16 THE COMPANY CONSTITUTION**) is specifically required by the Act to have a clause in its articles of association prohibiting it from paying dividends (CA 2006, s 61(3), (4)).

(b)   *Articles of association*

A company's articles of association will usually make provision for the declaration of a dividend and its payment. These regulations may be modified as required by a company (see **2.25 THE COMPANY CONSTITUTION**). The new regulations of the model articles are more generic although it has generally retained the main thrust of the regulations as below mentioned.

(i)   *Declaration*

A company may by ordinary resolution declare dividends, but may not declare a dividend which exceeds the amount recommended by the directors. A final dividend is declared following the conclusion of the financial year in which the profits being distributed were earned. This is a matter commonly dealt with at the general meeting (AGM) (see **PRECEDENT H, APPENDIX 7B**).

(ii)   *Interim dividends*

Interim dividends are dividends which are paid between general meetings at which final dividends are declared. An interim dividend is declared during the course of the financial year in which the profits being distributed were earned. The power to pay interim dividends is one which is commonly delegated to the directors (see **PRECEDENT G, APPENDIX 7B**).

(iii)   *Right to receive dividends*

The articles of association will usually set out the rights of different classes of shareholder to receive dividends and, subject to any rights attached to shares, dividends are declared and paid according to the amounts paid up on the shares for which the dividend is paid.

(iv)   *Payment*

Payment of dividends is usually made by way of dividend warrant which details the gross amount of the dividend due to the shareholder, the tax credit (see **10.2 COMPANY TAXATION**) and the net amount payable, together with a warrant (or cheque) for the net amount.

(v)   *Unclaimed dividends*

Any dividend not claimed within twelve years of its declaration can be forfeited and cease to remain owing by the company if the directors so resolve. This is a longer period than the minimum required by statute. Under the Limitation Act 1980 the time limit for recovery is six years in England. In Scotland the time limit is five years under the Prescription and Limitation (Scotland) Act 1973.

(vi)   *Scrip dividends*

These are also known as stock dividends and are shares which are issued fully paid to shareholders instead of a cash dividend. They are different to bonus issues as the shareholder is usually given the choice of electing to take shares or cash. General authority for paying scrip dividends is required in a company's articles of association with specific authority being given by special resolution passed in general meeting.

(vii)   *Distribution in specie*

Dividends are generally satisfied by the payment of a cash amount. However, it is possible to satisfy the payment of a dividend by distributing assets of the company to its shareholders. This requires general authority to be given through the articles of association and for specific authority to be obtained from the shareholders by a special resolution passed in a general meeting.

(viii)   *Waiver of dividends*

Shareholders can waive their rights to receive a particular or future dividends in respect of all or part of their holdings. To be effective, the waiver should be in the form of a deed and should be executed and delivered to the company prior to the dividend being declared and paid (see **Precedent I, Appendix 7B**). The reason for this is to avoid any liability to tax due on declared dividends.

Alternatively the articles of association could be amended to include a provision giving shareholders the right to send notice to the company waiving their rights to a particular dividend, and consequently allowing the company to only declare and pay dividends to the shareholders who have not given such a notice.

(ix)   *Winding-up*

The rights of shareholders to participate in a distribution of the assets of a company on a winding-up will usually be determined by reference to any class rights existing in the articles of association. Regulation 117 of Table A 1985 provides that the liquidator may, with the sanction of an extraordinary resolution of the company, distribute the assets available for that purpose amongst the members. The usual presumption is that members holding shares with the same rights and paid up to the same extent rank equally on such a distribution with the amount paid relating to the proportion of shares held.

(c)   *Disclosure in accounts*

The changes made by the Companies Act 1985 (International Accounting Standards and Other Accounting Amendments) Regulations 2004 (SI 2004/2947) affect the accounting and auditing requirements of relevant companies for financial years beginning on or after 1 January 2005. For all companies that continue to prepare their accounts using UK GAAP the relevant changes are to the requirements as to how and where proposed dividends are disclosed in the accounts.

The changes described below apply only to accounts prepared in accordance with the Companies Act 2006, not to accounts prepared in accordance with International Accounting Standards. Many of these legal changes are being reflected in new UK Financial Reporting Standards. The requirement in paragraph 3(7) of Schedule 4 to CA 1985 for companies to show paid and proposed dividends as separate items in the profit and loss account has been removed.

Now, companies are required to show in the notes to the accounts:

(i)   any amount set aside to reserves or withdrawn from reserves, or proposed to be set aside or withdrawn;

(ii)   the aggregate amount of dividends paid in the financial year (other than those for which a liability existed at the immediately preceding balance sheet date);

(iii)   the aggregate amount of dividends liable to be paid at the balance sheet date; and

(iv)   the aggregate amount of dividends proposed before the date of approval of the accounts, and not otherwise disclosed under the previous two categories.

Class rights

[7.15] The share capital of a company may be divided into such class of shares as the company may determine. This is commonly done by the share rights being determined in the articles of association, although the articles may provide otherwise. In varying class rights account must be taken of CA 2006, s 630 (see **7.11** above).

The common classes of shares which a company's share capital may contain are as follows.

(a)   *Ordinary shares*

A company's ordinary share capital is commonly regarded as its 'risk' capital as the ordinary shares of a company will usually carry the main financial risk. They will normally confer on the holders full voting rights but will be subordinate to other classes of share in respect of dividends (eg preference shares). The ordinary shareholders usually stand to gain (or lose) the most on a winding-up, depending on the surplus assets available, as an ordinary share will usually participate past its capital value.

It is increasingly common for companies to divide their ordinary shares into different categories (eg 'A' ordinary shares and 'B' ordinary shares) and to attach different rights to each, for example, weighted voting rights between categories. Some companies have also issued non-voting ordinary shares, which bear all the characteristics of an ordinary share, but do not confer on the holder any right to vote at a general meeting. Companies are allowed to issue non-voting shares, ie shares that do not carry any voting rights, but this is rare in practice. Furthermore, the Listing Rules applicable to listed companies provide that non-voting shares must be clearly designated as such.

(b)   *Preference shares*

The common characteristic of preference shares is that they carry the right to a fixed dividend and will usually rank in priority to other classes of share for repayment on a winding-up.

(i)   *Dividend*

The dividend due on preference shares is, unless stated to be non-cumulative, deemed cumulative; thus, should a company fail to pay the dividend due, the dividend will accrue to the shareholder and become payable (together with the next dividend due) at the next payment date. A preference dividend must be satisfied before a dividend can be paid to the ordinary shareholders. Non-cumulative dividends are deemed lost if a company is unable to pay them in any particular year. The right to a dividend once declared is usually expressed as a percentage, eg 8% preference shares.

(ii)   *Voting*

Preference shares will not usually confer on the holders a right to vote at general meetings unless their dividend is in arrears, at which point they may be accorded such rights, or there is a proposed variation attaching to the shares.

(iii)   *Winding-up*

Preference shares usually only confer on the holders the right to the repayment of the capital sum of the share together with any dividends in arrears. However, it is possible for the shares to be deemed 'participating' in which case they will (after repayment of capital and outstanding dividends) rank equally with the ordinary shares on a distribution of surplus assets.

(iv)   *Conversion*

Preference shares may carry the right for the holders to convert them into ordinary shares at a particular time or upon the occurrence of a given event.

(c)   *Redeemable shares*

Where authorised by its articles of association, a company may issue redeemable shares (CA 2006, s 684). A model power for the issue of redeemable shares is given by regulation 21 of the new model articles/regulation 3 of Table A 1985. The terms and manner of the redemption must be determined in the articles of association, but in any event must be determined before the shares are issued (CA 2006, s 685). No redeemable shares may be issued where a company has no non-redeemable shares in issue.

The rights attaching to redeemable shares on such matters as voting, rights to dividend and to participate in a winding-up should be determined in the articles. It is common for redeemable shares to be issued as a hybrid version of preference shares (ie redeemable preference shares) (see **8.56 CAPITAL**).

(d)   *Founder shares*

These are shares usually issued to the founders or promoters of a company which confer on the holders enhanced rights over other classes of share. It is common for founder shares to give to the holders proportionately increased voting rights over the ordinary shares and an entitlement to participate in surplus profits over a specified level.

(e)   *Deferred shares*

Deferred shares are commonly shares which carry very few rights (ie their rights are deferred to the ordinary shares). A deferred share will usually carry no right to vote or participate in a distribution and only the right to repayment of their capital value on a winding-up.

(f)   *Other types of shares*

In addition to the above, many hybrid forms of share which combine the characteristics of these different classes exist. Examples are as follows:

(i)   preferred ordinary shares;
(ii)   cumulative redeemable preference shares;
(iii) cumulative redeemable participating preference shares;
(iv)   cumulative convertible non-participating preference shares;
(v)   non-cumulative convertible preference shares.

Such types of shares will commonly be used by venture capitalists when making an equity investment in a company.

Transfer and transmission of shares

Share transfers

[7.16] Under CA 2006, s 541 shares are deemed to be personal estate (moveable property in Scotland). They are transferable in the manner provided by the articles of association of a company. Section 770 of CA 2006 states that a proper instrument must be completed and presented to the company unless the shares have been transmitted by operation of law. However, CA 2006, s 784 gives the Secretary of State and the Treasury the power to make regulations allowing for the transfer of securities without a written instrument (see **7.20**).

The proper instrument of transfer required for fully paid shares of companies governed by the Companies Act is that set out in the Stock Transfer Act 1963. Under the 1963 Act the transferor's signature does not have to be witnessed nor be under seal (unless the transferor is a body corporate having a seal) and, where the shares concerned are fully paid, the transferee need not sign the form. Under CA 2006, s 770 it is unlawful for a company to register a transfer of shares not in this form (unless an exempt transfer under the Stock Transfer Act 1987).

Transfer procedure

[7.17] A transfer of shares takes place when a shareholder who wishes to sell his shares completes a stock transfer form and gives it with his share certificate to the purchaser in exchange for the agreed price. The purchaser then completes the bottom half of the form with his name and address, dates it and then presents it for payment of the appropriate stamp duty at HMRC Stamp Office. Once the stock transfer form has been stamped it can then be presented, together with the appropriate share certificate, for registration with the company (see PRECEDENT A2, APPENDIX 7B).

A new Stock Transfer form was introduced on 15 July 1996 for use where securities are transferred to a person who will hold them in uncertificated form. The address of the person to whom the securities are being transferred may be omitted.

If however the transferor only wishes to sell part of his shareholding then he must send the signed transfer to the company with his share certificate for endorsing with 'certificate lodged'. The stock transfer form is then returned, to be passed on to the transferee for the consideration, and can be presented to the company for registration.

Also, where the shares to be transferred are held jointly, then the stock transfer form must be signed by all the holders for the transfer to be valid.

If the shares being transferred are partly paid then the articles usually provide for both the transferor and transferee to sign the transfer form.

When a company receives a transfer for registration the following points should be borne in mind.

(a)   The details of the transferor and shares transferred should agree with the certificate(s) presented and the entry in the register of members.

(b)   The transfer form should be checked to ensure that it has been correctly completed and is stamped, denoting payment of the appropriate amount of stamp duty (see **7.19** below).

(c)   The company's records should be checked to ensure that there are no liens or other restrictions on the shares being transferred.

(d)   If the company has restrictions on transfers in its articles of association the transfer should be checked to ensure that it does not contravene any such provisions (see **7.18** below).

Once the company secretary (if there is one) or director is satisfied that the transfer is in order, it should be presented to the directors for their approval to its registration (see PRECEDENT A, APPENDIX 7B). Once this approval has been obtained, the register of members of the company should then be updated and amended, as appropriate, with the details of the new member being entered. The share certificate of the former member should be cancelled and filed with the stock transfer form. If the certificate of the former member has been lost or destroyed then the member should be asked to complete an indemnity (see PRECEDENT B, APPENDIX 7B). Only once the old share certificate (or an indemnity) has been lodged should a new certificate be prepared and issued. This must be done within two months of the transfer being lodged. The certificate will require signature by a director and the secretary of the company (or two directors) and be expressed as being executed by the company. The certificate can then be sent to the new member.

Pre-emption rights

[7.18] Many private companies and some public companies (except those that are listed where shares must be freely transferable) insert into their articles of association pre-emption rights which apply in circumstances where an existing shareholder wishes to sell all or part of his shareholding. In such situations the pre-emption rights will commonly require that the shareholder who wishes to sell must first offer his shares to the other shareholders in proportion to their existing holdings and in accordance with rules laid down in the articles with regard to notices, time limits etc.

Where pre-emption rights exist they must be observed, a company will be able to refuse to register a transfer of shares where the rights have been disregarded. This right of refusal is in addition to any other rights of refusal a company has contained in its articles of association. It should be noted that the directors' refusal to register a transfer must be in good faith, and for the benefit of the company. Where registration of a transfer in contravention of any existing pre-emption rights occurs, it is open to aggrieved members to contest its validity.

Stamp duty on transfer

[7.19] The person responsible for maintaining a company's register of members (usually the company secretary) is bound to ensure that all transfers accepted for registration are either stamped with the appropriate duty or certified as being exempt from stamp duty. He can request the adjudication of a transfer where he doubts that it has been properly stamped.

The current rates of stamp duty are set out in **APPENDIX 7A** to this chapter. Gifts *inter vivos* are exempt from stamp duty and are not subject to adjudication and the levy of a fixed stamp duty of £5.00. Such transfers may be submitted immediately for registration and need not be presented to the stamp office. The appropriate certificate on the reverse of the form must, however, be completed.

There are certain other transactions which are also exempt and are not liable to a fixed duty of £5.00; these are also listed in **APPENDIX 7A**.

CREST

[7.20] CREST is the electronic settlement system which allows shareholders to hold and transfer their securities in dematerialised form. CREST was introduced on the London Stock Exchange on 15 July 1996 to replace the previous settlement system, TALISMAN, which closed on 11 April 1997.

The legal procedures for the CREST system are contained in the Uncertificated Securities Regulations 2001 (SI 2001/3755) ('the Regulations') which provide for the system to be run by an approved operator. The operator is CRESTCo Ltd, a private company owned by various firms connected with all sectors of the equities market. CRESTCo has issued a manual which sets out the procedures in detail and the rules which apply.

Joining CREST

[7.21] In order for a company to be eligible to join CREST (to become a 'participating issuer') its articles of association need to permit securities to be transferred through CREST and thus the articles may need amending. Normally, this would be affected by the members passing a special resolution, however, the Regulations allow the board of directors to pass the relevant resolution and for notice of the directors' resolution to be given to all members either before or within 60 days of it being passed. The passing of the resolution effectively overrides any provisions in the company's articles which are inconsistent with shares being held in uncertificated form. CRESTCo has issued draft forms of notification.

The shareholders can resolve to revoke or reverse the directors' resolution by passing an ordinary resolution. A copy of the directors' resolution or of a resolution of the members preventing or reversing the directors' resolution must be filed with the Registrar within 15 days of it being passed.

In addition to joining CREST, the issuer must submit a separate application form to CRESTCo for each class of securities concerned.

A directors' resolution is not effective for loan stock or other securities whose rights are not set out in the articles. Instead, appropriate alterations will need to be made to the instrument creating the terms of the said securities. Similarly, a directors' resolution cannot be used if changes are required to the procedures for conversion and/or redemption of shares. Instead the articles would have to be altered by members' resolution.

In due course, the company should seek to remove any unnecessary or obsolete articles after entering into CREST.

Deposits of certificated shares into CREST are treated as if they were an exempt transfer and the stamp duty liability of £5.00 which normally applies to transfers for nil consideration does not apply. In addition, unless such deposits attract a liability to stamp duty reserve tax (SDRT) of 0.5% or 1.5% (as would be the case for transfers for consideration in money or money's worth), SDRT is not applicable (see **APPENDIX 7A**).

Statutory registers

[7.22] An entry on the register of members maintained by the participating issuer (eg the Registrar which has entered into the necessary agreement with CRESTCo Ltd) is *prima facie* evidence of title to the units of security which he is recorded as holding in uncertificated form.

The Registrar will update the register of members upon receiving an operator instruction. If relating to a transfer of title to uncertificated units of a security, this is the point at which legal title passes to the transferee.

Transmission of shares and the registration of documents

[7.23] Transmission of shares occurs when shares are 'transferred' by operation of law rather than by an act of a shareholder. For example, transmission encompasses the change in ownership in shares upon a shareholder's:

(a)   death;
(b)   bankruptcy; or
(c)   becoming of unsound mind and the subject of an order of the Court of Protection.

Where transmission occurs the entitled party must produce, to the company whose shares he is interested in, documentation to validate his claim. Where such documentation is received the following general points should be considered.

(i)   It should be ensured that the details of the shareholder concerned are the same in both the documentation submitted, the relevant share certificate(s) and the register of members.

(ii)   The share certificate(s) of the member concerned should be requested if not received at the same time as the documentation.

(iii)   The documents received should be recorded in a register of documents (date of receipt, type of document and date of return). Once the details of the documentation have been recorded in both the register of documents and register of members, a registration stamp or similar endorsement should be put onto the document.

(iv)   The share certificate should be endorsed in favour of the appropriate person and the company's registration stamp (as in (iii) above) impressed upon it. The endorsement on the share certificate should equate to the amended entry in the register of members (eg Messrs Y and Z, deceased).

(v)   The documentation and endorsed share certificate should be returned to the person entitled and an entry of the date they were returned made in the register of documents.

The common circumstances in which transmission will occur and the documentation required together with other circumstances when documentation may be presented to a company are discussed below.

(A)   *Probate*
       Grants of probate (or in Scotland, Confirmation) enable a person or persons named in the will of a deceased person to act as executor in respect of the estate of the deceased. A grant of probate includes a copy of the will and is issued under the impressed seal of the Family Division of the High Court. To help executors, 'office copies' of the grant will often be issued bearing an impression of the seal of the Court. Office copies do not include a copy of the will, but as the terms of the will are generally of no consequence to a company, office copies are sufficient for registration purposes as they indicate who is empowered to deal with the deceased's estate and should be accepted by the company as satisfactory evidence of the grant (CA 2006, s 774).
       On production of a probate for registration similar checks should be made as detailed in points (i) to (v) above. In addition the following is recommended:
       (I)   The date of death and registration of the probate should be entered in the appropriate folio of the register of members together with the name and address of the executor(s) to be

described as 'executor of . . . . deceased'. After the name of the member the word 'deceased' should be included. Legally they remain the registered shareholder.

(II)   The share certificate should be endorsed with the same details, ie date of death and registration of probate, name and address of executor(s).

(III)   Once the company has applied its registration stamp to the probate it should be returned to the person who lodged it together with the endorsed share certificate and if appropriate a new dividend mandate.

(IV)   Letters of request may be sent to the executor(s) if personal registration is required (see (E) below).

(B)   *Letters of administration*

Letters of administration (or in Scotland, Confirmation) are granted to a person to administer the estate of a person who has died without leaving a valid will (intestate) or without naming executors. Office copies of letters of administration are usually available in the same manner as for grants of probate.

(C)   *Confirmation*

This is the equivalent Scottish document to English probate and letters of administration.

(D)   *Bona vacantia*

Where a person domiciled in England and Wales has died without leaving a will and with no successor, then the High Court will appoint either the Treasury Solicitor, or the officers of the Duchy of Lancaster or the Duke of Cornwall to administer the estate of the deceased. The High Court will issue a document of *bona vacantia* to this effect. The equivalent Scottish document is *ultimus haeres*.

(E)   *Letters of request*

A letter of request is a document sent by an executor or administrator to a company authorising and requesting the company to enter their names as the holders of the shares standing in the name of the deceased in the register of members. The letter must be signed by all the executors/administrators of the deceased and should only be registered if a grant of representation (eg probate) has already been registered by the company.

The procedure for registration is similar to that which applies in the case of non-market transfers. Any subsequent change in the registered holder can then only be effected by a transfer in the normal way.

(F)   *Death of holding in joint account*

When a joint shareholder dies, the company does not have to concern itself with his executors or administrators. The remaining shareholder has full power to deal with the shares as the legal interest in shares passes to them by right of survivorship. A company will normally receive a certificate of death and upon receipt the name and address of the appropriate member should be deleted in the register of members.

(G)   *Change of name of shareholder*

A shareholder can change his name in a number of ways, for example, by marriage, the grant of an honour, succession to a title or by deed poll. When a company receives evidence of a name change the register of members and the member's share certificate should be amended as appropriate.

(H) *Change of address of shareholder*

Notifications of change of address should be signed personally by the shareholder. If there are circumstances that give rise to concern regarding the authenticity of the notification, then the shareholder should be sent the company's own form for completion.

(I) *Court of Protection orders*

The Court of Protection makes orders appointing receivers to deal with the income of persons described as 'the patient' when a person is proved to be incapable (through mental disorder) of managing his property and affairs. The equivalent Scottish document is known as an appointment of a judicial factor or *curator bonis*.

(J) *Lien*

A notice of lien is merely written advice that share certificates have been deposited with a person as security for a loan or other advance. Such a notice should not be acknowledged by a company as this would be contrary to the provisions of CA 2006, s 126.

It may be desirable, however, to keep an unofficial note of the notice in case the company wishes to exercise a lien over the shares or is asked to issue a duplicate certificate.

(K) *Bankruptcy order*

The effect of a bankruptcy order is to vest the property in the shares in a trustee for the benefit of the shareholder's creditors. Either the original order or an authenticated office copy of it or a copy of the *London* (or *Edinburgh*) *Gazette* should be presented to a company. The equivalent Scottish document is an act and warrant appointing a trustee in bankruptcy.

(L) *Stop notice*

A stop notice is an official notice given by the court preventing the transfer of, and sometimes the payment of, dividends on a shareholding because of the interest of a third party in the shares. There is no similar Scottish document.

(M) *Injunction*

An injunction or restraining order may be made by the court preventing the transfer of a shareholding. The order or an authenticated copy is sufficient for registration purposes. The equivalent Scottish document is an Interdict.

While the order is in force no transfer of the shareholding can be registered.

(N) *Rectification of register*

A court may order that the register of members of a company be rectified by the removal or addition of a person. The original order or an authenticated copy may be registered.

(O) *Restrictions on shares*

The Department for Business, Innovation or Skills, or the court, may order that the rights of transfer, renunciation, exchange and voting be removed from particular shares. In the event of the withdrawal of the order, this should be acknowledged to the sender and the entries made in respect of it deleted from the register.

(P)   *Powers of attorney*
        A power of attorney is the appointment by an individual or body corporate of a person or persons to act on his or its behalf on the terms and for the period specified in the power.

Share certificates

[7.24] A share certificate must contain at least the following information:

(a)   a certificate serial number;
(b)   the name of the company;
(c)   the name of the registered holder;
(d)   the number and description of the shares (this should be shown twice as a security measure);
(e)   a statement of the extent to which the shares are paid up; and
(f)   the date of the issue.

Companies that are listed on the Stock Exchange must also comply with the requirements of the Listing Rules.

The full name of the shareholder should be shown on the certificate together with any titles he may have (decorations or professional qualifications do not have to be shown). Where the shareholder is a body corporate, its full unabbreviated name should be shown. For joint holders it is only necessary to show the name of the first-named holder, although it is common practice to include the names of all the joint holders. Many certificates show the shareholder's registered address, being the full address that appears in the register of members. Increasingly, share certificates are omitting the address of shareholders as it has been recognised that addresses tend to become out of date very quickly.

(1)   *Execution of certificates*
        Under CA 2006, s 768, a share certificate issued under the common seal of a company is *prima facie* evidence of a member's title to the shares which the certificate represents. Accordingly, it is very important that precautions are taken for the accurate completion and security of share certificates. Companies are under no obligation to seal certificates but doing so gives the certificate greater evidential standing. Where a company has dispensed with the requirement to have a common seal (CA 2006, s 45), then a share certificate will be validly executed when signed by either two directors or one director and the company secretary (in the case of a public company or in the case of a private company, where the company has one) and expressed as being executed on behalf of the company (CA 2006, s 44(4)).
        If a certificate is signed without the director's authority, it will be void and not binding on the company (*South London Greyhound Racecourses Ltd v Wake* [1931] 1 Ch 496). However, where a certificate is

issued under the authority of the directors, even if fraudulently obtained, then the company is estopped from denying the holder's title. This can occur in circumstances where a transferee has lodged a forged transfer with the company or where the company secretary has fraudulently obtained the director's authority. Thus, it is now common practice for larger companies to have a forged transfer insurance policy to cover potential liabilities arising from the issue of share certificates.

(2) *Securities seal*

Although companies are no longer obliged to have company seals many public companies have adopted and continue to use 'securities seals'. Such seals are useful where the register of members is maintained by external Registrars, as the seal can then be kept in the custody of the Registrar who may seal the certificates without the need to send the certificates to the company for execution. The London Stock Exchange used to require listed companies to seal share certificates but this has since been abolished. Where seals are used, it is quite common for signatures to be omitted. Authority for this must be granted by the articles of association of the company.

(3) *Issue*

Under CA 2006, s 769, a company is required to have share certificates ready within two months after the date of allotment of shares or the date on which a valid transfer form is presented for registration. For listed companies the requirements are slightly more onerous as certificates must be available within one month after the expiry of any right of renunciation of renounceable documents, or within 14 days of the presentation of a valid transfer form.

Companies may issue more than one certificate in respect of each holding if authorised by their articles. Private companies are permitted to charge fees for these services. Listed companies are prohibited from charging a fee for replacing certificates.

(4) *Duplicate certificates*

The articles may provide that where a share is defaced, worn out, lost or destroyed then it may be renewed. When this occurs the shareholder should be asked to complete an indemnity in return for which a duplicate certificate (marked as such) can be prepared and issued to the member (see **PRECEDENT B, APPENDIX 7B**).

General meetings

General

[7.25] A general meeting is a meeting of the members of the company called either in circumstances specified by the Act or the articles of association, at which the members will consider, and if thought fit, pass the resolutions tabled at the meeting.

The Companies Act 2006 has introduced changes to the effect that private companies are no longer required to hold AGMs although they can still do so if they wish to. The concept of the EGM has been discontinued in the Companies Act 2006. With effect from October 2007 all company shareholder meetings will be called general meetings with the exception of public companies, when they hold AGMs, which they are still required to do under CA 2006, s 336. Such meetings will continue to be called AGMs.

Convening of general meetings

[7.26] A general power to convene general meetings vests in the directors of a company who must call a general meeting when required to do so by the Act or the company's articles of association, or when the directors wish.

In certain circumstances, general meetings may be convened by the members, the court and on the requisition of the auditors (see **7.46** below).

Section 307 of CA 2006 provides for the giving of notice of meetings to members (see **7.35** below).

Quorum

[7.27] A general meeting cannot be validly held unless a quorum of members is in attendance. A long-established principle of the common law is that a meeting is only validly constituted by the attendance of two or more persons (*Sharp v Dawes* (1876) 2 QBD 26). A company may determine its quorum requirements in the articles of association. Regulation 40 of Table A 1985 provides that a minimum of two members present either in person or by proxy is required to constitute a quorum.

Should a company's articles of association make no provision as to quorum, then under CA 2006, s 318, the quorum is deemed to be two members or qualifying persons personally present.

In the case of a private company, one person may be a quorum regardless of any provision in the articles if the company has only one member (CA 2006, s 318(1)).

The Act specifies one other instance in which one member may be a quorum and that is a general meeting called on the order of the court under CA 2006, s 306(4) (see **7.50** below).

Proxies

[7.28] Section 324 of CA 2006 provides that a member entitled to attend and vote at a general meeting is entitled to appoint another person or persons to attend and vote on his behalf. The proxy need not also be a member.

For a private company the right of a proxy extends to his also being able to speak at the meeting. This right now also extend to the proxy of a member of a public company under CA 2006, s 324.

The notice calling a general meeting of a company limited by shares must contain a statement that a member is entitled to appoint a proxy (CA 2006, s 325). To be valid, a form of proxy must be lodged with the company by a specific time prior to the holding of the meeting (usually 48 hours), thus allowing for the company to check the validity of appointments. Any provision in a company's articles which seeks to extend the period to longer than 48 hours is void (CA 2006, s 327). However, the period may be shortened (eg to 24 hours).

(For a sample form of appointment of a proxy see PRECEDENT C, APPENDIX 7B.)

In recent years questions have arisen as to the validity of faxed proxy appointments; more specifically when the original signed copy is not physically deposited at the designated office within the specified time laid down in the Articles. For the purposes of Part 8 of the Insolvency Rules 1986 it has been held that a faxed proxy form is acceptable if the signature placed thereon carries some distinctive or personal marking which has been placed there by, or with the authority of the creditor. Although this ruling did not apply to meetings held under CA 1985, some companies altered their articles to allow for faxed proxies.

Section 333 of CA 2006 allows for the appointment of proxies to be made using electronic communications to an address notified by the company for that purpose (subject to any conditions or limitations specified in the notice).

For companies employing registrars it will be the registrars who are initially responsible for checking proxy cards against the Register of Members and counting the postal proxy votes prior to the general meeting. If a company is to allow proxies to be submitted electronically, an alternative checking procedure will need to be adopted. If the proxy voting is close or the resolutions being proposed are controversial a poll may be demanded, in which case, scrutineers should be appointed by the company to check the proxy voting for any irregularities, and to carry out the poll count at the meeting itself (see **7.32** below).

When the shares of a company are traded on the Alternative Investment Market (AIM) or if the company is listed, it is obliged to send to all persons entitled to vote together with the notice, proxy forms providing for two-way voting on all resolutions to be proposed at the meeting. The form must also state that if it is returned with no indication as to how the proxy shall vote, the proxy will exercise his discretion as he thinks fit. If it is the intention of a member to abstain on a resolution he must mark his proxy card accordingly. Leaving the voting instructions blank does not generally constitute an abstention. The articles commonly provide for the instrument of proxy to be signed by the appointer, and sealed in the case of a corporation.

Section 326 of CA 2006 states that where proxies are sought at the company's expense and specify that a particular person is to act as a proxy, the invitation must be extended to all the members entitled to appoint a proxy for the meeting.

Where proxies have been revoked a vote given or a poll demanded by a proxy or an authorised representative of a corporation shall be valid where the authority of the person voted has been previously determined, unless a notice was duly deposited before the commencement of the meeting or any adjourned meeting at which the vote is given or the poll demanded.

If there are no provisions contained within the articles of association, after the meeting has begun, but before an adjourned meeting or a poll, notification of a revocation will only be effective if received before the meeting has started, since the adjournment and poll are regarded as continuations of the meeting.

If a member is present in person at the meeting he may vote despite having appointed a proxy. Where a member votes at the meeting, the proxy's authority will be impliedly revoked and if the proxy also votes this will invalidate his vote (*Cousins v International Brick Co Ltd* [1931] 2 Ch 90).

Authorised representative

[7.29] A corporation which is a member of a company may, under CA 2006, s 323, appoint a person or persons to be its representative at any meeting of a company which it is entitled to attend. Such representatives may be appointed by resolution of the directors of the appointing corporation (see **PRECEDENT D, APPENDIX 7B**).

It is advantageous from the appointing company's point of view to appoint a representative instead of a proxy. This stems from the fact that a corporate representative holds the same rights at a meeting as those of a registered shareholder. He may speak at the meeting and may vote on a show of hands and be counted in the quorum.

Additionally, the usual 48-hour notification rule for proxies to be appointed does not apply to a corporate representative, although it is common practice for the representative to submit prior to the meeting some proof of authority from his appointor.

Voting

[7.30] There are two forms of voting at a general meeting, being a show of hands and a poll. A company may determine the voting rights of members (usually related to the class of share held) in its articles of association. Regulations 40 to 42 of the new model articles provide for voting powers (previously provided for in regulations 54 to 63 of Table A 1985).

Show of hands

[7.31] The new model articles provides that, on a show of hands, every member present in person (or by an authorised representative) has one vote. Unless conferred by the articles, proxies have no right to vote on a show of hands. The chairman will usually count the hands raised and declare the result.

On a poll

[7.32] The new model articles provides on a poll that each member has one vote for every share which he holds. This procedure recognises the weighted rights of the larger shareholder who, on a show of hands, may be defeated by a larger number of smaller shareholders. On a poll, votes may be cast either personally, or by proxy.

The articles of association may make provision for the procedure on a poll but CA 2006, s 321 states that any provision in the articles is void in so far as it seeks to:

(a)   restrict the circumstances in which a poll may be demanded to other than on the question of the appointment of the chairman of the meeting or the adjournment of the meeting;

(b)   make ineffective a demand for a poll:

(i)   by not less than five members entitled to vote;

(ii)   by a member or members representing at least 10% of the total voting rights of members having the right to vote;

(iii) by members holding shares paid up to the extent of more than one-tenth of the total sum paid up on all the shares conferring a right to vote at the meeting.

Under CA 2006, s 329, a proxy may demand or join in the demand for a poll.

The voting process will generally be managed by the company's registrars and/or scrutineers appointed for this purpose. Firstly the validity of the demand should be checked by referring to the authority laid down in the articles and the identity of the person demanding the poll. The poll may be taken immediately, at the conclusion of the meeting, or at another time fixed by the chairman.

If the poll is to be held straight away, voting cards will be issued for completion and collected for checking, including those which the chairman holds in respect of shareholders who have appointed him as their proxy.

Any spoilt or incomplete cards will not be included together with any cards completed by members not shown on the register of members at the register's closing date.

Having counted the votes, the registrar, or appointed scrutineer, will produce a certificate recording the exercise of the votes. The chairman will then declare the result of the poll.

The Myners Report which undertook a 'Review of the impediments to voting UK shares' made recommendations to each party involved in the voting process. It was essentially aimed at listed companies where shares are held by nominees and the giving of instructions in the voting process is somewhat complicated by the number of parties involved and their interrelationships. The key recommendations for the company and consequently of concern for the company secretary are:

(a)   the introduction of electronic voting;

(b)   calling a poll on all resolutions at company meetings;

(c)   disclosing the results of the poll or the level of proxies lodged on each resolution;

(d)   that the results disclose the total votes or proxies received, and the manner in which those votes are exercised, whether for, against or consciously withheld in respect of the resolution being considered;

(e)   [amending the articles to] allow proxies to speak and vote on a show of hands.

Casting vote

[7.33] The new model articles allows, in the case of an equality of vote, the chairman to have a second or casting vote. In the event that the articles of association do not provide the chairman with a second or casting vote then he will not be entitled to one.

Majority requirements

[7.34] The Companies Act 2006 and a company's articles of association require resolutions to be passed by specified majorities. For the types of resolution, the majorities required and the circumstances in which they may be used see **7.55–7.63** below.

Notice of meetings

[7.35] Every general meeting which a company holds requires notice to be given to each person entitled to attend. The notice must be given within specified time limits and must contain certain particulars. The regulations surrounding the notice of meetings are found both in Chapter 3 of Part 13 of the CA 2006 and a company's articles of association.

The articles of association of a company may not reduce the length of notice required to be given to less than the minimum required by CA 2006, s 307. However, they may increase the length of notice required. The minimum periods of notice pursuant to CA 2006, s 307 are as follows:

(a)   in the case of an AGM, *21 days'* notice;
(b)   in the case of a general meeting, other than an AGM, *14 days'* notice.

Section 308 of CA 2006 allow companies to send out notice of meetings electronically to those entitled to receive them. The notice can either be sent directly to an electronic address supplied for the purpose by the recipient, or it can be published on a website and the recipient notified of their availability in a manner agreed with him. Any notice published on a website must be made available for the minimum periods of notice as in (*a*) and (*b*) above.

In addition, any notification concerning a meeting must:

(i)   provide the address of the website;
(ii)   provide the page on which the notice may be accessed and how it may be accessed;
(iii)   state that it concerns a notice of a meeting served in accordance with the Act;
(iv)   specify the place, date and time of the meeting; and
(v)   state whether the meeting is to be an AGM or general meeting.

If the articles of association of a company are silent on the dates upon which the service and receipt of the notice will be deemed to have occurred, then such dates may not be included in the period of notice. However, the articles of association will usually indicate whether the period of notice is to include or exclude the day of posting of the notice, the day of service and the day of the meeting itself. If the notice has been sent electronically, it shall be deemed to have been given 48 hours after the time it was sent. However the articles could provide otherwise so that notice is deemed to be delivered at the same time of sending. Proof that the electronic notice was sent in accordance with guidance issued by the Institute of Chartered Secretaries and Administrators shall be conclusive evidence that the notice was given.

It should be noted that one of the provisions contained within the UK Corporate Governance Code states that companies should arrange for the notice of the AGM and related papers to be sent to shareholders at least 20 working days before the meeting, thus giving shareholders more time to consider the contents of what they have been sent.

Agreement to short notice

[7.36] A meeting called by shorter notice than that specified by CA 2006, s 307 or the articles of association will only be valid if the following conditions are met.

(a)   In the case of an AGM, the short notice has been agreed to by all the members of the company entitled to attend and vote (CA 2006, s 337(2)) (see **PRECEDENT E.2, APPENDIX 7B**).

(b)   In the case of any other general meeting, the short notice has been agreed to by a majority of the members holding not less than 90% of the nominal value of the shares having a right to attend and vote at the meeting (CA 2006, s 307(6)(a)) (see **PRECEDENT E.1, APPENDIX 7B**).

The consent does not have to be given in writing although this is preferable. If the consent is given electronically it is advisable to retain the evidence securely.

Entitlement to receive notice

[7.37] Unless the articles of association determine otherwise, a notice of a general meeting must be given to every member of the company and to all persons entitled to a share in consequence upon the death or bankruptcy of a member and to the directors and auditors (CA 2006, s 310).

Regulation 112 of Table A 1985 additionally states that:

(a)   where joint holders of a share are concerned, the notice should be given to the first named in the register of members; and

(b)   if a member has a registered address outside of the UK he shall not be entitled to receive such notice unless he has given to the company an address within the UK where notices may be given to him.

Regulation 116 of Table A 1985 provides that a notice may be given by the company to a bankrupt or deceased person's trustee or personal representative to an address provided by them. However, in the absence of such an address, the notice may be given as if the bankruptcy or death had not occurred.

Even though a member may not be entitled to attend a meeting, unless the articles otherwise provide, he will still be entitled to receive notice. If a notice of a general meeting forms part of the statutory accounts, a footnote should be inserted to the effect that it is sent only for information to the holders of shares who are not entitled to attend and vote at the meeting.

If a person is entered into the register of members after notices have been despatched he is not entitled to receive the notice of the meeting. However, his usual rights of attendance and voting and to be counted in the quorum will still be applicable.

The company may also see fit to give notice of meetings to their solicitors and other advisers.

Section 313 of CA 2006 gives some form of relief in that if by accident any person so entitled to receive notice, failed to receive it, that fact shall not invalidate the proceedings at the meeting.

Contents of notice

[7.38] The name of the company together with details of the time, place and date of the meeting must be stated on the notice together with the general nature of the business to be transacted. If the meeting is to be an AGM this must also be described as such. Pursuant to CA 2006, s 325, a statement that a member entitled to attend and vote at the meeting has the right to appoint a proxy to attend and vote in his stead must appear on the notice. The notice should, by convention, be signed by or on behalf of the convening authority (CA 2006, s 44). This will usually be the secretary (in the case of a public company or in the case of a private company that has appointed a secretary) on behalf of the directors of the company (see **PRECEDENT F, APPENDIX 7B**).

In order for a notice to be valid it must state clearly the business to be transacted at the meeting, giving enough information to enable it to be fully understood. Where the proposed resolution contained in the notice is not self-explanatory it is customary to also attach an explanatory statement to the notice. This is necessary to enable members to make an informed decision about whether or not to attend the meeting.

It used to be necessary for listed companies to state in their notice convening an AGM the place and time at which copies of directors' service contracts would be available for inspection, or a negative statement if there are no such contracts available. The requirement to include such a note was removed following Amendment 8 to the Listing Rules and now the contracts must be available permanently.

Circulars

[7.39] If the company is listed, it is a requirement that for any business other than routine business at an AGM, the notice must be accompanied by an explanatory circular or if the business is to be considered on the same day as the AGM an explanation may be incorporated into the directors' report (Chapter 14, para 17 of the Listing Rules).

It is common practice, that where business is to be conducted at a meeting which is non-routine or complex, a circular is also despatched in conjunction with the notice, to provide shareholders with clear explanations as to why the business is being transacted. If any director has an interest in the resolution this is also likely to be disclosed in the circular.

Section 314 of CA 2006 also imposes a duty on a company to circulate at the requisition of the specified number of members, resolutions proposed to be moved or a statement with respect to business at any general meeting. This will be at the expense of the requisitionists (see **7.44** and **7.47** below). However, the former DTI investigated several proposals which have considered whether the costs of circulating the shareholders' resolution should be borne by the company.

Special notice

[7.40] The Companies Act 2006 requires that, in certain circumstances, special notice be given *to* the company of the intention to propose certain ordinary resolutions at a general meeting. The circumstances in which special notice must be given are:

(a)   the removal of a director (CA 2006, s 168(2));

(b)   removing an auditor before the expiration of his term of office (CA 2006, s 511(1));

(c)   the appointment of an auditor other than the retiring auditor (CA 2006, s 515(1));

(d)   filling a casual vacancy in the office of auditor; and

(e)   re-appointing as auditor a retiring auditor appointed by the directors to fill a casual vacancy.

Special notice was also previously required for appointing or approving the appointment of a director of a public company (or a subsidiary of a public company) who had attained the age of 70 (CA 1985, s 293). This has been repealed by CA 2006.

Section 312(1) of CA 2006 states that, where special notice is required to be given of any resolution, then the resolution is not valid unless notice of the intention to propose it has been given to the company at least 28 days before the meeting at which it is to be proposed. However, CA 2006, s 312(4) states that, where the meeting is called for a date 28 days or less after the special notice has been given, the notice is deemed properly given notwithstanding that CA 2006, s 312(1) has not been complied with.

On receipt of a special notice, the company must give its members notice of the resolution at the same time and in the same manner as it gives notice of the general meeting at which it is to be proposed. If this is not practicable, the company may give notice in a newspaper with an appropriate circulation, or by such other means as the company's articles of association specify at least 21 days/14 days before the meeting (CA 2006, s 312(3)). Notice of the relevant resolution must also be given to the persons to be affected by the said resolution, ie the director to be removed, the auditor to be removed, the retiring/resigning auditor and their replacement.

Annual general meetings

[7.41] The Companies Act 2006 no longer requires private companies to hold AGMs although they can still choose to do so if they wish. Public companies are still required to hold AGMs. Therefore the following will apply to public companies. Private companies that choose to hold AGMs will need to note the sections in Chapter 3 of Part 13 of CA 2006 covering general meetings.

Section 336 of CA 2006 requires a public company to hold an AGM within six months of its financial year end and CA 2006, s 337 further requires the company to describe it as the AGM in the notice convening the meeting.

Business of the meeting

[7.42] It is possible to call a general meeting of a company whenever necessary, but it is usual to defer non-urgent business until the AGM.

Accordingly, the AGM is the one occasion in a year when the directors must appear before shareholders and give them an account of their management of the company.

The Act does not specify what business is required to be transacted at an AGM, this is left to individual companies to include in their articles of association.

It is usual to include consideration of a company's annual accounts in the business of the AGM. The directors are required by CA 2006, s 437 to lay the accounts before a general meeting no later than the end of the period for filing the accounts in question, and a link between this and the AGM is obviously intended although not stated by the Act.

As well as the receipt of the annual accounts of a company, other business commonly transacted at the AGM includes:

(a)   the declaration of a final dividend;
(b)   the re-election of any retiring directors;
(c)   the approval of directors' remuneration; and
(d)   the re-appointment of auditors and the fixing of their remuneration (CA 2006, s 489(2)).

Other business which a company can conveniently deal with at the AGM are items such as:

(i)   authorising the directors to allot shares up to a specified level during the year (CA 2006, s 549) (see **8.4 CAPITAL**);
(ii)   disapplying pre-emption rights in respect of allotments of shares up to a specified level (CA 2006, s 561) (see **8.7 CAPITAL**).

Public companies commonly include items dealing with the directors' authority to allot shares and the disapplication of pre-emption rights in the business of every AGM so as to effectively roll over these authorities in each year.

(For a sample notice of the AGM of a company see **PRECEDENT F, APPENDIX 7B.**)

Conduct of the AGM

[7.43] The AGM is usually the one time of the year when the shareholders have the opportunity to speak on the business to be transacted and, where companies allow, for general questions to be asked on matters such as the past and future performance of the company and directors' remuneration.

It is extremely important therefore that careful preparation and planning are carried out well in advance of the meeting itself in order that the meeting can run as smoothly as possible.

In September 1996 the ICSA published a *Guide to Best Practice for Annual General Meetings* which contains 24 best practice points as well as other recommendations including how to communicate with shareholders, the timing and notice of the AGM, dealing with shareholders' questions and establishing procedures for dealing with disturbances.

Circulation of members' resolutions

[7.44] Under CA 2006, s 314, a company has a duty on the requisition in writing of a specified number of members and at the members' expense:

(a)   to circulate to members of the company entitled to receive notice of the next general meeting, notice of any resolution which may properly be moved and is intended to be moved at that meeting; and

(b)   to circulate to members entitled to have notice of any general meeting sent to them, any statement of not more than 1,000 words with respect to the matter referred to in any proposed resolution, or the business to be dealt with at that meeting.

The number of members required to requisition the company in this matter is as follows:

(i)   not less than 5% of the total voting rights of all the members having a right to vote at the meeting at which the requisition relates; or

(ii) not less than 100 members holding shares on which there has been paid up an average sum per member of not less than £100.

A copy of the requisition signed by the requisitionists must be deposited at the registered office of the company not less than six weeks before the meeting, where it requires notice of a resolution, and in other cases one week before the meeting. There should also be left with the requisition a sum reasonably sufficient to cover expenses unless the requests relate to the AGM of a public company and a sufficient number of requests are received before the company's year end, in which case there will be no charge.

A company may apply to the court for leave not to circulate such a resolution or statement if they (or some other person who is aggrieved) feel the resolution or statement is of a defamatory nature.

Default

[7.45] If a public company fails to hold an AGM in any year as required by the Act, the company and any officers of the company in default may, under CA 2006, s 336(3), be liable to a fine.

Extraordinary general meetings/general meetings

[7.46] The concept of extraordinary general meeting (EGM) has been discontinued by CA 2006. A general meeting which is not specified in the notice of the meeting as being an AGM is deemed to be a general meeting.

The directors have a discretion to call a general meeting at any time, and as often as they may wish (re-enacting Table A 1985, regulation 37). In practice, however, they will only call a general meeting if there is urgent business which cannot conveniently be left for consideration at the next AGM.

There are circumstances in which the directors are required to call a general meeting for a particular purpose, but, unlike an AGM, there are no provisions in the Act requiring general meetings to be held at specific intervals. A general meeting may transact whatever business is set out in the notice of the meeting.

In any of the following circumstances, the directors *are* required to convene a general meeting.

(a)   On the requisition of members of the company who hold at least *one-tenth* of the shares in the company carrying voting rights (CA 2006, s 303) (see **7.47** below).

(b)   On the resignation of an auditor who resigns in certain circumstances (CA 2006, s 518(2)) (see **7.48** below).

(c)   Within 28 days of the directors becoming aware that the net assets of a *public* company are half (or less) of its called-up share capital (CA 2006, s 656) (see **7.49** below).

(d)   In compliance with an order of the court (CA 2006, s 306) (see **7.50** below).

Requisition of a general meeting by the members

[7.47] Under CA 2006, s 303, members holding at least 10% of the paid-up share capital carrying voting rights at a general meeting may deposit at the registered office a requisition, signed by all of the requisitionists, requiring the directors to convene a general meeting.

The requisition must specify the objects of the meeting and thus it is usual to set out in the requisition the text of the resolution(s) which the requisitionists propose to move at the general meeting. The requisition must further be signed by all the members requisitioning the meeting and be deposited at the registered office of the company and may be in electronic form.

The directors must, upon receipt of a valid requisition, convene a general meeting for the objects specified in the requisition, although the directors may add further resolutions if they wish. The notice to convene the general meeting must be issued by the directors within 21 days of the deposit of the requisition. Furthermore, the directors are required to hold the meeting within 28 days of the dispatch of this notice (CA 2006, s 304(2)).

Should the directors fail to convene a general meeting following receipt of a valid requisition, the requisitionists, or a majority of them representing more than half their total voting rights, may convene the meeting, to be held within three months of the date of a deposit of the requisition. In such an instance, the requisitionists may recover from the directors any reasonable expenses which they have incurred in convening the meeting. However, the business of the general meeting must be confined to the purposes specified in the requisition.

The most common reason for a requisition is to remove directors from office (by an ordinary resolution, of which special notice is required under CA 2006, s 168). There is, however, no limit on the business for which a general meeting may be requisitioned.

General meeting on resignation of the auditor

[7.48] If an unquoted company's auditors resign, they are obliged by CA 2006, s 519 to state in their notice of resignation whether or not there are any circumstances which they consider should be brought to the notice of members or creditors of the company. If there are such circumstances, a statement of what they are must be included. For quoted companies the auditors will now always need to make a statement of the circumstances connected with their resignation.

If the auditor's notice of resignation states that there are circumstances which he thinks must be brought to the attention of the members or creditors, CA 2006, s 518(2) allows him, with his notice, to deposit a requisition calling on the directors to convene a general meeting to receive and consider the auditor's explanation of the circumstances surrounding his resignation.

The directors are then required to issue a notice within 21 days of the deposit of the requisition by the auditor, to convene a general meeting to be held within 28 days from the issue of that notice (CA 2006, s 518(5)).

General meeting on the financial situation of a public company

[7.49] Section 656 of CA 2006 imposes an obligation on the directors of a *public company* to convene a general meeting as a result of their becoming aware that the net assets of the company have fallen to, or below, the value of half its called-up share capital, for the purpose of considering whether any, and if so, what steps must be taken to deal with the situation.

In such a circumstance the directors must issue the notice to convene the meeting within 28 days of their becoming aware that the assets have fallen below the specified level and the meeting must be called for a date not more than 56 days from the date on which the directors became so aware.

General meeting by order of the court

[7.50] The court has an inherent power to order a general meeting of a company to be convened. However, it will not normally interfere in a dispute between directors and shareholders, as the shareholders have their own power to requisition a meeting as specified above.

The court has a general statutory power under CA 2006, s 306, either on its own motion or upon the application of a director or member of the company who would have power to vote at the meeting, to order that a general meeting be held and to give instructions for the conduct of the meeting.

This power is normally used to order that meetings be held when there is only one member available or willing to attend a general meeting and there is no other way of obtaining a quorum. Such a general meeting could not otherwise be held (*Re El Sombrero Ltd* [1958] Ch 900 and *Re Opera Photographic Ltd* [1989] 5 BCC 601).

Separate general meetings

[7.51] There are several circumstances under the Companies Act when a company must hold a separate general meeting of the holders of a class of share. The articles of association may further specify circumstances when class meetings must be held.

Variation of rights

[7.52] Section 334 of CA 2006 provides that in circumstances where a variation of the rights of a class of share is proposed, a class meeting must be held to pass a resolution approving the variation.

Reconstructions

[7.53] Sections 896 and 899 of CA 2006 provide that the court may, on the application of creditors or members or a class of creditors, convene class meetings (and creditors' meetings) in circumstances where a company is proposing a compromise between itself and its creditors (or a class of them) or its members (or a class of them) which requires a 75% majority of those attending and voting to make the compromise or arrangement binding.

The procedure for the convening, holding and passing of resolutions at class meetings are the same as for general meetings (unless the articles of association provide otherwise) except that the right to receive notice of and to vote at the meeting are usually restricted to the holders of the class of share in question.

Adjournment of meetings

[7.54] An adjournment of a meeting is, by common law, only a continuation of the original meeting, so unless otherwise provided for in the articles of association, there is generally no need to give notice of the adjourned meeting. Any irregularity in the convention of the original meeting will also affect the adjourned meeting. Proxies for the original meeting may be used for the adjournment. Regulation 39 of the new model articles and common law gives the chairman the power to adjourn a general meeting from time to time and from place to place. If, however, the chairman improperly attempts to adjourn a meeting, another chairman may be elected by the members and the meeting continued. In the case that the meeting has been adjourned properly, members would not be able to remain and carry on the proceedings. Additionally, if a poll is demanded on the question of adjournment, it should be taken immediately.

Where a meeting is adjourned for 14 days or more, at least seven days' clear notice must be given specifying the time and place of the adjourned meeting and the general nature of the business to be transacted (regulation 39 of the new model articles). Otherwise no new notice needs to be given, unless new business is proposed in place of or in addition to that proposed in the notice of the original meeting.

Furthermore, regulation 39 of the new model articles states that if there is not a quorum present after half an hour from the time appointed for the meeting, or if during a meeting the quorum ceases to be present, the meeting shall be adjourned to the same day and time the following week or a time and place as the directors may determine.

Resolutions

General

[7.55] Various decisions of a company are required by the Companies Acts, and the articles of association of a company, to be made by the members passing resolutions in general meeting. The articles of a company will normally determine the procedure and majorities required for particular resolutions. Under the Companies Act 2006, there are basically two types of resolution which are recognised, being ordinary and special resolutions.

Ordinary resolution

[7.56] An ordinary resolution is the normal means of securing the members' approval to business transacted at a general meeting. The ordinary resolution may be used for purely routine business (eg approval of the annual accounts), but may also suffice as approval of certain important or contentious business (eg the removal of a director).

No definition of an 'ordinary resolution' is contained in the Companies Act, but any resolution which is not defined as a 'special resolution' is deemed to be an ordinary resolution.

An ordinary resolution is carried by a simple majority of the votes cast at a general meeting, whether by a show of hands or on a poll.

As a general rule, it is not necessary to deliver a signed copy of an ordinary resolution to Companies House although there are a few exceptions, being:

(a)　the authorisation of directors to allot shares pursuant to CA 2006, s 551; and

(b)　the voluntary winding-up of a company pursuant to Insolvency Act 1986, s 84(1)(a) (Insolvency Act 1986, s 84(3)).

Unless the Act or a company's articles of association specify that a special resolution is required for a particular item of business, an ordinary resolution will usually suffice.

The articles of the company may provide that a special resolution shall be required in certain circumstances (eg in the instance of a subdivision of share capital). But in some situations the Act expressly overrides the articles in providing that an ordinary resolution is sufficient. For example, CA 2006, s 168 states that a director may be removed by an ordinary resolution of the company notwithstanding anything to the contrary in the articles of association.

Special resolution

[7.57] A resolution is deemed a special resolution pursuant to CA 2006, s 283 when it is described as such in the notice of the meeting. A special resolution to be passed must be carried by a three-quarters majority of votes cast at a general meeting. 14 days' notice is also required of a general meeting at which a special resolution is to be proposed.

A printed and signed copy of a special resolution must be delivered to Companies House within 15 days of its passing (CA 2006, s 30(1)).

The Companies Act specifically requires a special resolution to be passed to effect various actions of a company. Instances where a special resolution is required are:

(a)   an alteration to the objects clause where it has been entrenched in the articles of association;

(b)   an alteration to the articles of association (CA 2006, s 21(1));

(c)   a reduction of its capital subject to confirmation of the court (CA 2006, s 641);

(d)   various alterations of the company's status by re-registration (eg from a private to a public company) (see **2.43 THE COMPANY CONSTITUTION**);

(e)   a change of name (CA 2006, s 77);

(f)   a purchase of its own shares (CA 2006, s 694);

(g)   in disapplication of pre-emption rights (CA 2006, s 571);

(h)   when a company resolves that it be wound up voluntarily, it being unable to carry on its business because of its liabilities (Insolvency Act 1986, s 84(1)(c)); and

(i)   at a meeting of the holders of a particular class of shares, to sanction a variation of the rights attached to those shares under CA 2006, s 630 (or any corresponding provisions of the articles).

A company's articles of association may introduce further instances when a special resolution is required.

Written resolutions

[7.58] The Companies Act 2006 has brought about changes to written resolutions for private companies. With effect from October 2007, CA 2006, s 288 provides that anything which may be done by resolution of a *private* company in general meeting (or by resolution of a meeting of any class of members of the company) may, instead of a meeting being held, be done by a written resolution signed by or on behalf of *the requisite percentage of* members of the company (depending on whether the written resolutions are to be ordinary or special) who, at the date of the resolution, would be entitled to attend and vote at a general meeting. There are only two exceptions where the right to use the written resolution procedure is not allowed and they relate to the removal of a director or an auditor before the expiration of his term of office.

Previous notice is not required of such a resolution and physical signatures are not needed. Members are regarded as having signified their consent when the company receives from them an authenticated document, which may be in hard copy or electronic form, identifying the resolution and indicating their agreement. The date of the passing of the resolution is taken as being the date upon which the company has indicated in the resolution as being the last date for consent to be received before it lapses.

Section 300 of CA 2006 also ensures that any provisions in a private company's articles is void where it removes the ability of a private company to use the written resolutions procedure.

Written resolutions must be recorded in the company's minute book and as they are used to give effect to what otherwise would be either ordinary or special resolutions, the usual provisions of CA 2006, s 30 apply to the registration of the resolution at Companies House.

Amendment of resolutions

[7.59] An ordinary resolution may be amended even if the text of the resolution has been set out in the notice of the meeting.

The text of a special resolution must be set out in the notice of the meeting at which the resolution is to be considered. This has the result that there can be no substantial amendment of the resolution after the notice of the general meeting at which the resolution is to be proposed is posted, since the amended resolution would no longer be the same one of which notice had been given.

Resolutions passed at adjourned meetings

[7.60] Section 332 of CA 2006 provides that where a resolution is passed at an adjourned meeting of either the company, its directors or at a class meeting, then the resolution is deemed passed on the date on which it was passed (ie the date of the adjourned meeting being held and not at any earlier date).

Registration of resolutions

[7.61] Section 30 of CA 2006 requires that a copy of every resolution to which the section applies must, within 15 days of it being passed, be filed with Companies House (see **5.11 DISCLOSURE AND REPORTING REQUIREMENTS**).

Unanimous agreement of the members

[7.62] The procedures for convening, constituting and conducting a company meeting are intended to safeguard a minority of members, who may disagree with the resolutions passed at a general meeting or who may not be able to attend the meeting. Their safeguards are that the resolution must be passed by a simple or three-quarters majority; proper notice must be given for the meeting; a quorum of members must be present; and a vote on the resolutions proposed must be taken in the proper manner. If there are flaws in this procedure, the resolution may be invalid and accordingly will not be binding upon them.

Should, however, every member of a company who is entitled to attend and vote at a general meeting be in agreement with a resolution, it is pointless to invalidate the meeting because of some technical flaw in the procedure. This is illustrated by the case of *Re Express Engineering Works* [1920] 1 Ch 466, where a unanimous decision of a board meeting (all the members of the company being directors) was accepted in place of a resolution in general meeting.

In addition, the courts have recognised that the informal but unanimous agreement of the members, or an irregular general meeting which has produced the unanimous agreement of the members, will be accepted as a binding decision instead of a resolution duly passed at a general meeting.

Minutes of general meetings

[7.63] Section 355 of CA 2006 obliges a company to enter minutes of all general meetings into a book made for that purpose. It imposes a further requirement for a company to record written resolutions in the same way as those for general meetings.

Minutes are only *'prima facie'* evidence of the proceedings of a meeting and a member may still challenge the validity of these minutes (see **3.45 THE STATUTORY RECORDS**).

Appendix 7A

Stamp duties on share transfers

Rates of duty

Transfers on sale of shares (unless an exempt transfer or a fixed duty transfer) are liable to *ad valorem* stamp duty at the rate of 0.5% of the consideration, rounded up to the nearest multiple of £5.00.

Exempt transfers

The Stamp Duty (Exempt Instruments) Regulations 1987 (SI 1987/516) provide that certain documents (including a transfer operating as a voluntary disposition *inter vivos*) executed on or after 1 May 1987 are not liable to stamp duty. Exempt documents must bear an appropriate certificate and once certified, can be sent direct to the company secretary or Registrar for registration.

The categories of exempt transactions are as follows.

(a)   The vesting of property subject to a trust in the trustees of the trust on the appointment of a new trustee, or in the continuing trustees on the retirement of a trustee.

(b)   The conveyance or transfer of property the subject of a specific devise or legacy to the beneficiary named in the will (or his nominee).

(c)   The conveyance or transfer of property which forms part of an intestate's estate to the person entitled on intestacy (or his nominee).

(d)   The appropriation of property within section 84(4) of the Finance Act 1985 (death: appropriation in satisfaction of a general legacy of money) or section 84(5) or (7) of that Act (death: appropriation in satisfaction of any interest of surviving spouse and in Scotland also of any interest of issue).

(e)   The conveyance or transfer of property which forms part of the residuary estate of a testator to a beneficiary (or his nominee) entitled solely by virtue of his entitlement under the will.

(f)   The conveyance or transfer of property out of a settlement in or towards satisfaction of a beneficiary's interest, not being an interest acquired for money or money's worth, being a conveyance or transfer constituting a distribution of property in accordance with the provisions of the settlement.

(g)   The conveyance or transfer of property on and in consideration only of marriage to a party to the marriage (or his nominee) or to trustees to be held on the terms of a settlement made in consideration only of the marriage.

(h)   The conveyance or transfer of property within section 83(1) of the Finance Act 1985 (transfer in connection with divorce etc).

(i)   The conveyance or transfer by the liquidator of property which formed part of the assets of the company in liquidation to a shareholder of that company (or his nominee) in or towards satisfaction of the shareholder's rights on a winding-up.

(j)   The grant in fee simple of an easement in or over land for no consideration in money or money's worth.

(k)   The grant of a servitude for no consideration in money or money's worth.

(l)   The conveyance or transfer of property operating as a voluntary disposition *inter vivos* for no consideration in money or money's worth nor any consideration referred to in section 57 of the Stamp Act 1891 (conveyance in consideration of a debt etc).

(m)   The conveyance or transfer of property by an instrument within section 84(1) of the Finance Act 1985 (death: varying disposition).

If a transaction falls within one of the above categories a certificate in the following form should be contained within the transfer document:

I/We, hereby certify that this instrument falls within category [initial of category] in the Schedule to the Stamp Duty (Exempt Instruments) Regulations 1987.

Signature [transferor or transferor's Solicitor]

Description [eg transferor, solicitor for the transferor]

Dated

The certificate may be signed by the transferor or grantor, or by a solicitor on his behalf. (An authorised agent may also sign the certificate provided he states the capacity in which he signs.)

Fixed duty transfers

Transfers falling within any of the following categories attract a fixed duty of £5.00.

(a)   Transfer by way of security for a loan or re-transfer to the original transferor on repayment of a loan.

(b)   Transfer, not on sale and not arising under any contract of sale and where no beneficial interest in the property passes: (i) to a person who is a mere nominee of, and is nominated only by, the transferor; (ii) from a mere nominee, who has at all times held the property on behalf of the transferee; (iii) from one nominee to another nominee of the same beneficial owner where the first nominee has at all times held the property on behalf of that beneficial owner.

As with a transfer exempt from stamp duty, to establish that a transfer is only liable to a fixed duty of £5.00 a certificate should be completed which details the facts of the transaction.

Purchase of own shares

Stamp duty is payable on a purchase by a company of its own shares. The statutory return (form SH03) constitutes the document which is liable to stamp duty and is accordingly treated as the instrument transferring the shares on sale for stamp duty purposes (Finance Act 1986, s 66). The form, together with a cheque for the appropriate amount of stamp duty, should be sent to HMRC Stamp Office for stamping prior to lodging with the Registrar.

Stamp duty reserve tax

The Finance Act 1986 (section 86) introduced stamp duty reserve tax (SDRT) which is charged at the rate of £5.00 per £1,000 (or part thereof) on certain share transactions which do not attract stamp duty. SDRT is charged on certain agreements to transfer securities, where there is no transfer document and so no liability to stamp duty (eg shares held in electronic form under CREST). Renounceable letters of allotment and transactions closed within a stock exchange account are examples of items which attract reserve tax.

The Uncertificated Securities Regulations 1995 (SI 1995/3272) amended company law to allow for shares to be held in uncertificated form and to be transferred through an approved paperless transfer system. These regulations have since been replaced in their entirety by the Uncertificated Securities Regulations 2001 (SI 2001/3755).

The Stamp Duty Reserve Tax (Amendment) Regulations 1997 came into force on 20 October 1997 and made changes to the 1986 regulations to take account of paperless share dealing. Now the operator of CREST or a similar electronic system is liable to collect and pay SDRT incurred on chargeable transactions.

The two month period allowed for transfer documents to be produced and stamped before SDRT is charged does not apply unless there is still a stamped transfer document, in which case the stamp duty paid will cancel the SDRT charge.

To simplify calculations by the CREST operator, SDRT rates are charged at a flat percentage, eg 0.5%, but stamp duty rates remain the same.

Transfers arising from an agreement between persons who are not resident in the UK which are settled through CREST will be liable to SDRT.

Interest and penalties

Interest will be charged on duty that is not paid within 30 days of the execution of a document subject to stamp duty. The amount of interest will be rounded down where necessary to a multiple of £5.00, however no interest will be payable on calculated amounts of less than £25.00.

Penalties for late stamping will apply to all documents submitted late for stamping. There will be a maximum penalty of £300.00 (or the amount of duty owed if less) on documents submitted up to a year late, or £300.00 (or the amount of duty owed if more) where the documents are presented more than a year late.

Further information on the above can be found in the leaflet published by HMRC Stamp Office, entitled Stamp Duty Interest and Penalties, S010.

Appendix 7B

Precedents

A.1. Transfer of Shares

It was resolved that the undernoted duly stamped transfer of ordinary shares of £1 each in the company be and are hereby approved, and registered in the books of the company.

No. of Transfer	Transferor	Transferee	No. of Shares
1	Jerry Lai	Steve Martin	100
	Aquis Court	Aquis Court	
	31 Fishpool Street	31 Fishpool Street	
	St Albans	St Albans	
	Hertfordshire	Hertfordshire	
	AL3 4RF	AL3 4RF	

It was further resolved that a share certificate for the transferee be sealed and signed on behalf of the company in accordance with the Articles of Association of the company and issued in due course, and that the share certificate held by the transferor be cancelled accordingly:

A.2. Stock Transfer Form

STOCK TRANSFER FORM

(above this line for Registrars only)

Certificate lodged with the Registrar

Consideration Money £

(For completion by the Registrar/Stock Exchange)

Name of Undertaking.	
Description of Security.	

| Number or amount of Shares, Stock or other security and, in figures column only, number and denominations of units, if any | Words | Figures
(units of) |

Name(s) of registered holder(s) should be given in full; the address should be given where there is only one holder.
If the transfer is not made by the registered holder(s) insert also the name(s) and capacity (e.g., Executor(s)), of the person(s) making the transfer.

In the name(s) of

I/We hereby transfer the above security out of the name(s) aforesaid to the person(s) named below or to the several persons named in Parts 2 of Brokers Transfer forms relating to the above security:

Delete words in italics except for stock exchange transactions.

Signature(s) of transferor(s)

1. ....
2. ....
3. ....
4. ....

Bodies corporate should execute under their common seal.

Stamp of Selling Broker(s) or, for transactions which are not stock exchange transactions, of Agent(s), if any, acting for the Transferor(s).

Date

Full name(s) and full postal address (es) (including County or, if applicable, Postal District number) of the person(s) to whom the security is transferred.

Please state title, if any, or whether Mr., Mrs. or Miss.

Please complete in typewriting or in Block Capitals.

I/We request that such entries be made in the register as are necessary to give effect to this transfer.

Stamp of Buying Broker(s) if any	Stamp or name and address of person lodging this form if other than the Buying Broker(s)

Reference to the Registrar in this form means the registrar or registration agent of the undertaking NOT the Registrar of Companies at Companies House

FORM OF CERTIFICATE REQUIRED WHERE TRANSFER IS EXEMPT FROM *AD VALOREM* STAMP DUTY AS BELOW THRESHOLD.

[1] I/we certify that the transaction effected by this instrument does not form part of a larger transaction or series of transactions in respect of which the amount or value, or aggregate amount or value, of the consideration exceeds £1,000.

[1] I/we confirm that [1] I/we have been duly authorised by the transferor to sign this certificate and that the facts of the transaction are within [1] my/our knowledge [2].

[1] Delete as appropriate.

[2] Delete second sentence if certificate is given by transferor or his solicitor.

Signature(s)   *Description ("Transferor"," Solicitor", etc)*

....

....

....

Date

....

Notes

(1) If the above certificate has been completed, this transfer does not need to be submitted to the Stamp Office but should be sent directly to the Company or its Registrars.

(2) If the above certificate is not completed, this transfer must be submitted to the Stamp Office and duly stamped.

Page 2 of 2

B. Indemnity for Lost Certificate

'I, [Name of member] do hereby request that the company (or its Registrars) issue to me a duplicate certificate No. [certificate number] for [no. of shares] shares in the capital of the Company, the certificate having been mislaid, destroyed or lost, and in consideration of the Company so doing, I hereby indemnify the said Company against all claims and demands, monies, losses, damages, costs and expense which may be brought against or be paid, incurred, or sustained by the said Company by reason or in consequence of the said certificate having been mislaid, destroyed or lost, or by reason or in consequence of the issuing to me of the said duplicate certificate, or otherwise howsoever in relation thereto. I further undertake and agree, if the said certificate shall hereafter be found, forthwith to deliver up the same or cause the same to be delivered up to the company, its Registrars or their successors and assigns without cost, fee or reward.

Dated this [   ] day of [   ] 20[   ]

[Signature of member]'

C. Form of Proxy for use at General/Annual General Meeting

'I, [Name of member]

of [Member's address]

hereby appoint [name of proxy]

of [proxy's address]

or failing him the duly appointed Chairman of the meeting, as my proxy to attend and vote for me on my behalf at the General/Annual General Meeting of the company to be held at [place of meeting]

on [date of meeting] at [time am/pm of meeting]

and at every adjournment thereof.

Dated this [   ] day of [   ] 20[   ]

[Signature of member]'

D. Resolution of Board Appointing an Authorised Representative

'That [name of representative] be and is hereby appointed, pursuant to Section 323 of the Companies Act 2006, to act as the company's representative at any meeting of the members of [name of company].

This appointment shall remain in force until the company shall resolve otherwise or until [name of officer of the company] vacates the office of Director/Secretary/other officer of the company.'

E.1. Consent to Short Notice of a General Meeting

'We, the undersigned, being a majority in number of the members of the above-named company and entitled to attend and vote at the General Meeting of the said company convened by a Notice of Meeting [date of notice] and to be held on [date of meeting] and together holding 90% (in the case of a private company)/95% (in the case of a public company) and upward in nominal value of the shares giving that right, hereby agree to the holding of such meeting and to the proposing and passing of the Resolutions on the day and at the time and place set out in such Notice, notwithstanding that less than the statutory period of the notice thereof has been given to us.

Dated this [   ] day of [   ] 20[   ]

[Name of member]   [Name of member]
(Member)   (Member)'

E.2. Consent to Short Notice of an Annual General Meeting (for public company)

'We, the undersigned, being all the members for the time being of the company having the right to attend and vote at the Annual General Meeting of such company convened to be held at [place of meeting] on [date of meeting] at [time of meeting] (the attached notice being the notice convening the meeting), hereby agree:

(a)   in accordance with Section 307(4) of the Companies Act 2006 to the holding of such meeting notwithstanding that less than the statutory period of notice thereof has been given, and

(b)   to accept service of documents in accordance with Section 424(4) of the Companies Act 2006 notwithstanding that the said documents were sent less than 21 days before the meeting.

Dated this [   ] day of [   ] 20[   ]

[Name of member]   [Name of member]
(Member)   (Member)'

F. Notice of an Annual General Meeting (public company)

NOTICE IS HEREBY GIVEN THAT THE ANNUAL GENERAL MEETING OF [name of company]

WILL BE HELD AT [place of meeting]

ON [date of meeting] 200[   ] AT [time of meeting] AM/PM

BUSINESS

1   To receive and adopt the Directors' Report and the Audited Statement of Accounts for the year/period ended [   ].

2   To re-elect a Director.

3   To confirm the Directors' remuneration.

4   To declare a dividend.

5   To reappoint the retiring Auditors and authorise the Directors to fix their remuneration.

Dated this [   ] day of [   ] 20[   ]

REGISTERED OFFICE   BY ORDER OF THE BOARD
[registered office address of company]

SECRETARY [Signature of Secretary]

Note: A member entitled to attend and vote is entitled to appoint a proxy to attend and on a poll vote in his/her place. Such proxy need not be a member of the company.'

G. Board Resolution for an Interim Dividend

'It was resolved that an interim dividend for the year ended [date of accounting period] of [amount] on the ordinary shares of the company be [paid] [declared payable] on [date of payment] to all members whose name appears in the Register of Members on [record date].'

H. Declaration of a Final Dividend at General Meeting

'It was resolved that [the final dividend] [the dividend recommended by the directors on (date)] of [amount] for the year ended [date of accounting period] be [paid] [declared payable] on the ordinary shares of the company to all members whose names appear in the Register of Members on [record date] and that such dividend be paid on [date of payment].'

I. Deed of Waiver

The Directors

I, [   ] of [   ] being the registered holder of
[   ] shares of £[   ] each in the capital of
[   ] Limited whose Registered Office is situated at
[   ] ('the Company'), do hereby absolutely and irrevocably waive my
right and entitlement to the final dividend of [   ]p per share
recommended by the Directors and if considered fit to be approved by the shareholders
at the Annual General Meeting to be held on 20[   ].

Signed by me as a deed this [   ] day of [   ] 20[ ]

in the presence of:

Witness: [. . . . .]

Name: [. . . . .]

Address: [. . . . .]

Chapter 8

Capital

Maintenance of capital

[8.1] A general principle of company law is that capital, once raised, must be maintained. The issued share capital of a company is the fund to which creditors can look for payment of their debts. 'The whole of the subscribed capital of a company with limited liability, unless diminished by expenditure on the objects of the company shall remain available for the discharge of its liabilities' (*per* Kitto J in *Davis Investments Pty Limited v Commissioner of Stamp Duties (NSW 1957–58)*). Shares must not be issued at a discount (ie for less than their nominal amount) although payment in full is not required on allotment.

Serious loss of capital

[8.2] Under section 656 of CA 2006, should the net assets of a public company fall to a level of half or less of its called-up share capital, then the directors have a duty imposed upon them to convene a general meeting to consider what steps should be taken to deal with the situation. A problem that exists here for the directors of a public company is in determining the time at which the net assets have fallen to below one-half of the share capital. For the purposes of CA 2006, s 656 it would seem reasonable to assume that it is from the date that the audited accounts show this position as being the trigger date for the directors becoming aware of the situation. Upon discovery of the fact, the directors must within 28 days convene a general meeting, to be held on a date no later than 56 days from the date of discovery.

Issue of capital

[8.3] Capital is issued by the directors of the company and is represented by the shares which are taken up by the shareholders. In certain circumstances, the existing shareholders may have a right to have allotted to them a proportionate part of a new issue of shares (the application of pre-emption rights if incorporated into the articles of association). In addition, there are restrictions on offering shares to the public at large (see **8.9** below).

Section 555 of CA 2006 requires a company making an allotment of shares, to lodge with the Registrar of Companies *within one month*, a return of the allotment for registration. This is made in the prescribed form SH01. This return states the number and nominal amount of the shares allotted, the names and addresses of the allottees, and the amount (if any) paid or due and payable on each share whether on account of the nominal value of the shares or by way of premium. At the time of writing it is not clear as to the manner in which the registration is to be effected under the new Act. The implication is that a prescribed form of some description will probably be required.

If shares are allotted *otherwise than in cash*, a contract in writing constituting the title of the allottee to the allotment, together with the contract in respect of which the allotment was made, a return form SH01 must also be lodged with the Registrar of Companies. Form SH01 states the number and nominal amount of the shares so allotted, the extent to which they are to be treated as paid up, and the consideration for which they have been allotted. This shall be completed and lodged with the Registrar of Companies also within one month.

Authority to allot shares

[8.4] The Companies Act 2006 has made some changes to the allotment authority regime. With effect from October 2008, a private company with only one class of share capital will not need to go through this regime although it must still abide by whatever restrictions on allotments which may be imposed by its articles.

This new regime effectively differentiates between private companies with only one class of share capital and private companies with more than one class of share capital and public companies.

Section 550 of CA 2006 states that where a private company has only one class of shares, the directors may exercise any power of the company:

(a)   to allot shares of that class; or
(b)   to grant rights to subscribe for or to convert any security into such shares;

except to the extent that they are prohibited from doing so by the company's articles.

For private companies with more than one class of shares and for public companies, CA 2006, s 551 will apply. This basically states that the directors of those companies are permitted to allot shares in the company or grant rights to subscribe for shares or to convert other securities if the articles permit them to do so, or if there has been a resolution of the company granting them that authorisation.

Such authority may be general or specific to a particular issue and may also be conditional or unconditional. The authorisation must state either the maximum number or amount of shares that may be allotted and the expiry date of the authorisation. The expiry date may not be more than five years either from the date of incorporation of the company or from the date on which the resolution is passed by a general meeting of the company (see **PRECEDENT A, APPENDIX 8A**). An authority given in pursuance of CA 2006, s 551 may be revoked or varied at any time by the company in general meeting.

The authority may be renewed by the company in general meeting for further periods of no longer than five years, but such extensions of time must state the amount of securities that may be allotted within the period. It is common for many *public companies* to renew this authority each year at the annual general meeting (ie to effectively 'roll' the authority annually).

It should be noted that subscriber shares taken on formation, shares allotted in pursuance of an employee share scheme, and any right to subscribe for, or to convert any security into, shares in the company other than shares so allotted continue to be exempt under CA 2006, s 549(2).

A director who knowingly and wilfully contravenes CA 2006, s 549 is liable to a fine, but the validity of any allotment so made is not affected if the directors do not have sufficient authority to allot.

Pre-emption rights on issue

[8.5] Section 561 of CA 2006 provides that a company which is proposing to allot 'equity securities' must first make an offer of those securities, on the same or more favourable terms in proportion to the nominal value held, to each person holding relevant shares, and shares must not be allotted until the period allowed for acceptance of any such offer has expired, or all the offers made have either been accepted or refused.

The issue of any shares carrying the right to a fixed dividend and shares to be acquired under an employee share scheme do not fall within the definition of equity securities.

Exclusion

[8.6] Under CA 2006, s 567 the pre-emption rights may, as applying to a *private company*, be excluded by a provision contained in the articles. Moreover, any requirement or authority in the articles, if it is inconsistent with the statutory pre-emption provisions, will have effect as a provision excluding those provisions.

In practice, the articles of association of many private companies exclude the provisions of CA 2006, s 561(1) and may well provide non-statutory provisions.

Disapplication

[8.7] If the directors of a company, public or private, are generally authorised for the purposes of CA 2006, s 549 to allot shares, they may be given power by the articles or by a special resolution of the company to allot equity securities without application of the pre-emption provisions. Where the directors are authorised for the purposes of CA 2006, s 550 (private companies with one class of shares) or CA 2006, s 551 (private companies with more than one class of shares and public companies), whether generally or otherwise, the company may by special resolution resolve that the pre-emption provisions shall not apply to a specified allotment of equity securities (CA 2006, ss 569 and 570) (see **PRECEDENT B, APPENDIX 8A**). In this case the directors must circulate, with the notice of the meeting at which the special resolution is proposed, a written statement giving:

(a) their reasons for making the recommendation;

(b) the amount to be paid to the company in respect of the equity securities to be allotted; and

(c) the directors' justification of that amount.

In the case of public companies, it is common practice to link a resolution for the disapplication of pre-emption rights to a resolution authorising the directors to allot shares under CA 2006, s 549 and to propose such resolutions at the annual general meeting. However, for listed companies, the Stock Exchange will not regard a special resolution under CA 2006, s 570 as valid for a period longer than that ending 15 months from the date of the passing of the resolution or the next annual general meeting, whichever is earlier.

Certain cases will require specific shareholder approval, such as transactions with directors and substantial shareholders. Guidelines on pre-emption have been produced by the Stock Exchange and representatives of the institutional shareholders which, in general, approve of an annual disapplication provided it is restricted to an amount of shares not exceeding 5% of the issued ordinary share capital shown in the latest published accounts. A company is expected to observe cumulative limits in any rolling three-year period and not make use of more than 71/2% of issued ordinary share capital by way of non-pre-emptive issues for cash in any such period.

Payment

[8.8] Shares allotted by a company and any premium on them may be paid up in money or money's worth including goodwill and know-how. A public company is prohibited from accepting an undertaking by a person to do work or perform services for the company in payment for its shares, or any premium on them, and if it does so, the holder of shares is liable to pay to the company an amount equal to their nominal value and any premium treated as paid up by the company and interest at the appropriate rate. A company's shares may not be allotted at a discount (CA 2006, s 580). A public company may also not allot shares except as paid up at least as to one-quarter of its nominal value and the whole of any premium on it (CA 2006, s 586(1)).

The Registrar of Companies is aware of the payment up of share capital that had purportedly been satisfied by means of the allottee giving an undertaking to pay on demand the cash equivalent of one-quarter of the nominal value. The Registrar after having sought legal advice does not regard such undertaking as amounting to money or money's worth and has been advised that the use of this scheme is unlawful.

A public company is restricted from allotting shares as fully or partly paid-up otherwise than in cash if the consideration for the allotment is or includes an undertaking which is to be, or may be, performed more than five years after the date of allotment (CA 2006, s 587(1)). If the company allots shares in contravention of this provision the allottee remains liable to pay the company an amount equal to their nominal value plus any premium and interest at the appropriate rate (CA 2006, s 587(2)).

A non-cash consideration for shares in a public company must be valued in accordance with the provisions of CA 2006, s 596 before allotment. The valuation must be made by an independent person and a report must be made to the company during the six months immediately preceding the allotment of shares. A copy of the report must be sent to the proposed allottee. A copy of the report must also be delivered to the Registrar of Companies at the same time as the return of allotments.

An 'independent person' is defined as a person qualified at the time of the report to be appointed, or continue to be, an auditor of the company. If it appears to the independent person to be reasonable for the valuation to be made by someone who has requisite knowledge and experience to value the consideration and who is not an officer or servant of the company or its holding or subsidiary company, he may accept such valuation as the basis for his report.

The transfer from a person who is a subscriber to the memorandum in the case of a public company formed as such, or a person who is a member of the company on the date of re-registration in the case of a company re-registered as a public company, to a public company of non-cash assets where the consideration is equal to at least one-tenth of the nominal value of the company's issued share capital is prohibited, unless the conditions of CA 2006, s 598 have been complied with, during an initial period of two years from the date of incorporation or re-registration as a public company.

The conditions of CA 2006, s 598 are as follows:

(a)   the consideration must be independently valued under CA 2006, s 599;
(b)   the report with respect to the consideration must have been made during the six months immediately preceding the date of the agreement for the transfer of a non-cash asset;
(c)   the terms of the agreement must be approved by an ordinary resolution of the company; and
(d)   copies of the resolution and report must be circulated to the members not later than the giving of notice of the meeting at which the resolution is proposed.

Allotment of shares

Private company

[8.9] The ability of private companies to make allotments of shares is restricted by the provisions of CA 2006, s 755 and section 170 of the Financial Services Act 1986 which state that a private company commits an offence if it offers any shares for sale to the public. However, CA 2006, s 755(3) states that where a private company has offered its securities to the public, it would be required to re-register as a public company unless the court considers it undesirable or impractical to do so.

Public company

[8.10] Public companies may allot or offer to allot shares to the public. However, before they may do so, they must comply with the prospectus requirements of Part IV of the Financial Services Act 1986 or the Public Offers of Securities Regulations 1995 (SI 1995/1537) (see **8.14–8.22** below).

Issue of shares to existing shareholders

[8.11] There are basically two forms of share issue to existing shareholders whereby the shareholders may retain the same proportion of total equity as prior to the issue. These are rights and bonus issues.

Rights issue

[8.12] This is a form of raising additional capital from existing shareholders.

When offering shares in a rights issue, a company sends an explanatory letter to each member with a provisional allotment letter detailing the number of shares to which the member is entitled to subscribe and the price at which the shares are being offered. Attached to the letter will be forms of acceptance and renunciation. Should a member not exercise his right to the shares he may renounce them in favour of someone else. Ultimately, the member (or renouncee) will complete the form of acceptance and application and lodge it with the company, together with his payment for the shares.

The offer must conform to four requirements:

(a)   it must be in writing;
(b)   it must be delivered personally or by post;
(c)   it must specify a period being not less than 21 days within which the offer may be accepted; and
(d)   the offer must be on a 'rights basis' in proportion to the member's existing holding as a fraction of the holdings of all members eligible to receive the offer.

After the period of the offer has expired, the company may utilise any shares not accepted by the members to whom they were offered, either to issue them to outsiders or in different proportions between members.

Members have no automatic right to be offered shares which other members have not accepted. However, provisions in the articles of association may be included to such effect.

Bonus issue

[8.13] A bonus issue (sometimes called either a capitalisation or scrip issue) is also an allotment of shares to existing members in proportion to their present holdings. It differs from a rights issue in that no additional capital funds from outside the company are raised by the issue. Its purpose is to capitalise profits or reserves which would otherwise be available for distribution to the members. Thus no payment is required from the members for the bonus shares.

The shares being issued are paid up by the company applying either a credit balance from the profit and loss account or from reserves to the payment of the shares, which are then allotted to members. No statutory authority for this procedure exists, but it can only be done if the appropriate power to do so exists in the company's articles of association (regulation 34 of the new model articles/regulation 110 of Table A 1985). The power in the articles of association will also determine such matters as the requirement of the directors to obtain the authority of a general meeting before capitalising reserves and the proportions in which the bonus shares may be distributed. Bonus shares may not be issued at a discount (CA 2006, s 580) and a public company may not allot bonus shares as paid unless they are paid up to at least one-quarter of their nominal value (CA 2006, s 586).

The reserves which are capitalised may either be distributable profits, non-distributable reserves or a quasi-capital fund such as a share premium account or capital redemption reserve. The decision to capitalise, however, rests with the shareholders in general meeting.

Regulation of offers – the statutory framework

Introduction

[8.14] Generally, only a public limited company may make a public offer of shares (referred to hereafter as 'securities') because there are restrictions imposed on private companies offering securities to the public.

Securities may be either 'listed' or 'unlisted'. Listed securities are securities which are admitted to the Official List of the Stock Exchange; other securities are referred to as unlisted securities. Different statutory provisions apply depending on whether the securities to be offered are to be listed or unlisted. The relevant statutory provisions are briefly considered in turn below; where applicable, reference is made to where the provisions are dealt with in greater detail elsewhere in the chapter.

Listed securities

[8.15] The statutory provisions relating to listed securities are set out in Part IV (sections 142–157) of the Financial Services Act 1986. (These provisions replaced the provisions set out in Part III of the Companies Act 1985 and have since been amended by the Public Offers of Securities Regulations 1995 (SI 1995/1537).) The relevant securities to which Part IV applies are set out in Schedule 1 to the 1986 Act, and are as follows:

(a)   shares and stock in the share capital of a company (para 1);
(b)   debentures (para 2);

(c)   warrants or other instruments entitling the holder to subscribe for investments falling within (*a*) and (*b*) above (para 3); and

(d)   certificates which represent the above-mentioned securities (para 5) (but note that these securities are excluded from listing by the Stock Exchange listing rules referred to below).

Standard and Premium Listings

[8.16] The Financial Services Authority (FSA) has implemented changes (with effect from 6 April 2010) to the Listing Rules in order to bring greater transparency and clarity to the Official List and to the obligations that apply to the different categories of listed companies. The new regime categorises listed securities into two listing segments:

(i)   'Premium' – those securities that are generally subject to super equivalent standards; and

(ii)   'Standard' – those securities that are only covered by standards based on EU Directive minimum requirements.

Categories of 'Premium' listings: Equity shares: Commercial companies, Closed ended investment funds, Open ended investment companies

Categories of 'Standard' listings: Shares (eg equity shares/non equity shares), GDRS, Debt and debt-like securities, Securitised derivatives, Miscellaneous securities, eg Options and warrants.

Premium Listing Segment

[8.17] This segment will be restricted to companies that have listed equity shares. A listing in this segment will remain a pre-requisite for inclusion in the FTSE UK indices. Issuers seeking listing in this segment will still need to comply with the FSA's super-equivalent requirements by demonstrating a 3-year track record on admission to listing and complying with the continuing obligations on substantial and related party transactions.

Standard Listing Segment

[8.18] This exists for securities that do not meet the full requirements as mentioned above. The standard listing option for equity shares will be available for companies that meet the 25% free float requirement and publish an EU compliant prospectus.

Transfers

[8.19] Issuers will be able to transfer the listing of their shares between the two segments and categories subject to shareholders' approval generally, at a general meeting by a majority of at least 75%. Companies wishing to transfer a security into a new listing category will also be required to meet the eligibility requirements of that category in terms of working capital, financial reporting procedures.

No securities to which Part IV of the Financial Services Act 1986 applies are to be admitted to listing except in accordance with the provisions of Part IV (section 142(1)). Any application for listing is to be made to the Board of the Stock Exchange (which is the 'competent authority' (section 142(6)) in accordance with the provisions of Part IV and of rules made by the Stock Exchange for the purposes of those provisions ('Listing Rules'). The Listing Rules require that as a condition of admission to listing, a document known as 'listing particulars' must be submitted to the Stock Exchange; broadly, listing particulars are the equivalent to a prospectus where unlisted securities are being issued. Listing Rules and listing particulars, and the provisions of Part IV relating to them, are dealt with in greater detail in **8.24–8.31** below.

Unlisted securities

[8.20] The issue of unlisted securities is regulated by the Public Offers of Securities Regulations 1995 (SI 1995/1537) which came into force on 19 June 1995 and implement the Public Offers Directive (Council Directive 89/298/EEC). The regulations replace Part III of the Companies Act 1985, while also repealing Part V of Financial Services Act 1986 (which was never brought into force).

Part II of the new regulations apply to securities which have not been admitted to the Official List and are not the subject of an application for listing. The relevant unlisted securities subject to these regulations are set out in Schedule 1 of the Financial Services Act 1986 (see **8.15** above).

Registration and publication of prospectus

[8.21] A prospectus is required in relation to securities offered to the public in the United Kingdom (UK), although the regulations set out the circumstances where an offer is deemed not to be an offer to the public and therefore exempt from the requirement to register and publish a prospectus. The offeror who may or may not be the issuer is required to deliver for registration a copy of the prospectus to the Registrar of Companies prior to its publication.

Registration must occur before an offer of the securities is made. The prospectus must then be made available to the public free of charge from the time the securities are first offered to the public. The regulations also provide circumstances, for instance, where there is a significant inaccuracy in the original prospectus, where a supplementary prospectus is required to be delivered to the Registrar for registration.

Form and content of prospectus

[8.22] Prospectuses must be drawn up in accordance with Part II of the 1995 regulations which require more extensive disclosure than under the Companies Act but are less onerous than for listing particulars. The regulations impose on the persons responsible for the prospectus a general duty to disclose all relevant information similar to that imposed on those responsible for listing particulars under section 146 of the Financial Services Act 1986.

Schedule 1 of the regulations sets out the information to be included in the prospectus, while also providing circumstances in which there are exemptions to giving certain information. In general, the prospectus should contain general information about the name and registered office address of the issuing company together with details of the offeror if different from the issuer and the date of publication of the prospectus.

The prospectus should disclose the persons responsible for the prospectus and their advisers, the securities to which the prospectus relates and the offer as well as provide general information about the issuer and its capital. In addition, disclosure is required of details of the issuer's principal activities, its assets and liabilities, financial position and profits and losses together with details of its administration, management and supervision.

The capital markets

[8.23] An issue of securities can take a number of different forms:

(a)   public offer, by direct invitation by the company or an offer for sale by an issuing house;
(b)   placing or selective marketing, usually to institutional investors;
(c)   fixed price tender;
(d)   rights issue to the existing holders.

The primary market is the Stock Exchange Listed Market; minimum requirements as to the expected market value of securities apply and therefore a listing is only open to larger companies. Smaller companies may seek a quotation for their unlisted securities on the Alternative Investment Market (AIM) which replaces the Unlisted Securities Market (USM) and is designed to provide a regulated market with less onerous requirements for admission than for the Official List (see **8.32** below).

Official listing of securities

General

[8.24] As mentioned in **8.15** above, Part IV of the Financial Services Act 1986 contains the statutory requirements relating to the listing of securities on the Official List of the Stock Exchange. An application for listing must be made in accordance with section 143 of the FSA 1986 to the competent authority in such manner as the listing rules may require. The Board of the Stock Exchange has been designated the competent authority for the purposes of Part IV, and one of its functions is the making of listing rules. The listing rules are contained in the Financial Services Authority's 'Listing Rules'.

The Stock Exchange is primarily a market-place for trading the securities of companies. The requirements set out in the Listing Rules seek to secure the confidence of investors in the conduct of the market. They ensure that all applicants for listing are of a certain minimum size, have an adequate trading record and provide sufficient information about their history, prospects and financial condition to form a reliable basis for market evaluation. The second function, achieved by requiring all listed companies to accept the continuing obligations set out in Chapter 9 of the Listing Rules, is to ensure that all marketings of securities are conducted on a fair and open basis.

Reasons for seeking a public listing

[8.25] A company may wish to seek a public listing for the following reasons:

(a)   The character of the company may have changed. What started as a small business may have expanded to the extent that it is more suited to operate in the public domain.

(b)   The status is improved, which helps commercial and financial transactions.

(c)   The company has access to the market for additional capital which the existing shareholders may be unable or unwilling to provide.

(d)   The company may wish to make acquisitions and to be able to offer quoted shares as consideration.

(e)   A market in the company's shares may improve the effectiveness of executive or employee share schemes.

(f)   The shareholders may wish to realise a part of their investment; a flotation generally achieves a better price than a private sale.

(g)   The proprietors can retain effective control by holding a substantial stake whilst still realising their objectives.

(h)   A flotation may assist the proprietors in dealing with problems of succession.

Disadvantages of a public listing

[8.26] The disadvantages for a company seeking a public listing are as follows:

(a)   There is a considerable burden on the senior management in preparing for the flotation which may adversely affect the smooth running of the business.

(b)   The process of going to the market is expensive.

(c)   Public shareholders are more likely to expect a dividend so that the cash available for retention may be reduced.

(d)   Institutions and analysts need to be convinced of the company's worth and the proprietors and company will be subject to close scrutiny.

(e)   The FSA rules on the disclosure of information have to be complied with.

(f)   Dealings in the company's shares by directors are restricted by the Stock Exchange Model Code on directors' dealing.

Basic conditions to be fulfilled by an applicant

[8.27] A company seeking a public listing must fulfil the following requirements:

(a)   The expected market value of securities for which listing is sought must be at least £700,000 in the case of shares and £200,000 in the case of debt securities. However, securities of a lower value may be admitted to listing provided the Board of the Stock Exchange is satisfied that adequate marketability can be expected.

(b)   The securities must be freely transferable.

(c)   A company must have published or filed accounts covering a period of three years preceding application for listing. The Board of the Stock Exchange may accept a shorter period if it is desirable in the interests of the company or of investors and the Board is satisfied that investors will have the necessary information to enable them to arrive at an informed judgement on the company.

(d)   At least 25% of any class of shares must be in the hands of the public not later than the time of admission.

Listing particulars

[8.28] Listing particulars must not be published until they have received the formal approval of the Listing Department of the Stock Exchange in their final form. All new applicants were in the past required to publish listing particulars in accordance with Chapter 5 of the Listing Rules.

The Public Offers of Securities Regulations 1995 (SI 1995/1537) which implement the Public Offers Directive came into force on 19 June 1995, and made changes to the provisions of Part IV of the Financial Services Act 1986 in the context of public offers of securities which are the subject of an application for an official listing.

The principal change is the requirement that an issuer applying for listing of securities to be offered to the public in the UK for the first time is obliged to publish a prospectus rather than listing particulars before admission. The above regulations also introduced a regime for the pre-vetting of prospectuses by the Stock Exchange where no application for listing on the Exchange is involved. The purpose of this is to establish mutual recognition in other EU/EEA member states of UK prospectuses.

The contents requirements of listing particulars are set out in detail in Chapter 6 of the Listing Rules. A summary of the requirements is as follows:

Part A – Details of the persons responsible for the listing particulars, the auditors and other advisers.
The directors must make a declaration that they accept responsibility for the information contained in the document and that to the best of their knowledge and belief the information is in accordance with the facts and does not omit anything likely to affect the import of such information.
Part B – The securities for which application is being made.
Part C – General information about the issuer and its capital.
Part D – The group's activities.
Part E – Financial information concerning the issuer or group.
Part F – The management.
Part G – The recent development and prospects of the group.
Parts H–N – Additional information concerning debt securities.

Reference should be made to the Listing Rules for the detailed requirements of the contents.

In addition to the information specified by the listing rules as a condition of the admission of any securities to the Official List, Financial Services Act 1986, s 146 requires that any listing particulars shall contain all such information as investors and their professional advisers would reasonably require and reasonably expect to find for the purpose of making an informed assessment of the assets, liabilities, financial position, profits and losses and prospects of the issuer of the securities and the rights attaching to those securities.

Application procedure and publication

[8.29] Chapter 7 of the Listing Rules sets out the detailed procedure for application. Certain documents, including copies of the listing particulars, must be submitted for approval at least 14 days prior to the intended publication of listing particulars. An application for admission to listing signed by a duly authorised officer and an application by the sponsoring member firm signed by a partner or director of the member firm must be lodged with the Listing Department at least two business days prior to the hearing of the application by the Board of the Stock Exchange. In the case of securities of a class not already listed, the application must be supported by two firms of market-makers who are prepared to register as dealers in the security.

Once approved, the listing particulars must be published. The publication requirements vary according to the method by which the securities are to be brought to the market.

Persons responsible for particulars

[8.30] The persons responsible for listing particulars are:

(a)   the issuer of the securities to which the particulars relate;
(b)   each person who is a director of the company at the time when the particulars are submitted to the competent authority;
(c)   each person who has authorised himself to be named, and is named in the particulars as a director, or as having agreed to become a director of the company, either immediately or at a future date;
(d)   each person who accepts, and is stated in the particulars as accepting, responsibility for, or for any part of, the particulars;
(e)   each person, not falling within any of the foregoing categories who has authorised the contents of, or any part of, the particulars.

Persons responsible for listing particulars may be held liable to pay compensation to any person who has acquired any securities and suffered loss in respect of them as a result of any untrue or misleading statement in the particulars or omission from them.

Registration of particulars

[8.31] On or before the date on which listing particulars are published as required by the listing rules, a copy of the particulars must be delivered for registration to the Registrar of Companies, and a statement that a copy of the particulars has been delivered to the Registrar of Companies must be included in the particulars.

The Alternative Investment Market

General

[8.32] The Unlisted Securities Market (USM) closed entirely at the end of 1996. The USM was replaced on 19 June 1995 by the Alternative Investment Market (AIM) which is the market provided by the London Stock Exchange for transactions in AIM securities, being securities admitted to trading subject to the AIM Rules. AIM is a market designed primarily for emerging or smaller companies and the rules of this market are less demanding than those of the Official List or the former USM.

Admission to trading on AIM

[8.33] A company seeking admission of its securities to trading on AIM must satisfy on admission and continue to satisfy the Stock Exchange that it meets the following conditions.

(a)   It must be duly incorporated or otherwise validly established according to the relevant laws of its place of incorporation or establishment. An issuer which is a company incorporated in the UK must be a public company, while issuers incorporated or established outside the UK must be permitted to offer securities to the public.

(b)   The securities for which admission to AIM is sought must be freely transferable although any shares held by a shareholder which are subject to the restrictions imposed by CA 2006, s 793 may be discounted.

(c)   There must be no securities in issue of the class that are admitted to trading on AIM.

(d)   The issuer of AIM securities must have a nominated adviser and a nominated broker, although these roles may be performed by the same firm (see **8.34** below).

Companies seeking a listing on the Official List are required to demonstrate an acceptable trading record and meet other criteria, while the AIM Rules impose no minimum requirements on companies seeking admission to trading on AIM. However, a company which has as its main activity an independent business which has not been earning revenue for at least two years, must ensure that all persons who at the time of admission to trading on AIM are directors and employees agree not to dispose of their interest in AIM securities for a period of one year after admission to AIM subject to certain exemptions. Also, companies must now disclose any significant discrepancy between a company's actual performance and any public profit forecast.

At least ten days prior to admission, a new applicant must make a public announcement (via the Exchange's regulatory news service) giving details of its name and business; directors; major shareholders; promoters; and nominated adviser and broker.

Nominated adviser and nominated broker

[8.34] A nominated adviser must be independent of the issuer and must be a member firm of the Exchange or a person authorised under the Financial Services Act 1986. A nominated adviser must be entered on a list maintained by the Exchange and owes to the Stock Exchange the responsibilities set out in Chapter 16 of the AIM Rules. A nominated broker is a member firm of the Stock Exchange which assumes the responsibilities set out in Chapter 17 of the Rules.

If a company ceases to have either a nominated adviser or a nominated broker, trading in its securities will be suspended by the Exchange. Failure to replace either a nominated adviser or a nominated broker within one month of ceasing will result in the discontinuation of those securities to trading.

Application for entry to AIM

[8.35] An application for admission to AIM must be made in writing in a form prescribed by the Exchange and must be accompanied by an admission document if required. It must be received by the Exchange not less than 72 hours prior to the date the company wishes the securities to be admitted to trading.

When a company applies for admission it must publish a document in English containing information required by the Public Offers of Securities Regulations 1995 (SI 1995/1537) together with the additional information required by Chapter 16 of the AIM Rules. However, an admission document need not be published by an issuer applying for admission to trading on AIM of securities of a class already admitted, unless the issuer is required to publish a prospectus by virtue of the above regulations.

Continuing obligations

[8.36] The main obligations after entry to AIM are outlined in Chapter 16 of the AIM Rules. In particular, the directors must:

(a)   issue accounts within six months of the year end;
(b)   publish a half-yearly report within four months of the period end;
(c)   advise the Exchange without delay of the resignation, dismissal or change of any nominated adviser or nominated broker;
(d)   obtain shareholders' consent before issuing options or convertible loan stock; and
(e)   register all share transfers within 14 days of receipt.

The Rules also oblige the directors to disclose details of dividends, results, changes in capital structure, the cancellation of existing securities, material acquisitions or realisations of assets, directors' dealings in shares, changes in directors and any purchase by the company of its own shares.

Venture capital

General

[8.37] The term 'venture capital' is generally associated with investments made in unquoted companies with which a high level of risk is attached, but for which a high return is expected. No two investments made by venture capitalists will be the same, but such investments will generally have the following features:

(a)   equity participation or an option to convert debt into equity;
(b)   a medium to long-term (five or ten years) investment horizon; and possibly
(c)   active involvement in the management by the investor.

Companies qualifying for venture capital

[8.38] Any kind of business can successfully approach the venture capital market, provided it has an attractive investment proposal. Finance is available at most stages of development, such as:

(a)   start-up, requiring initial capital;
(b)   development and expansion, where additional capital is required to assist in the company's growth;
(c)   re-financing to release existing investors;
(d)   rescue of an unprofitable business with the prospect of a turn-around;
(e)   buy-out by the management or buy-in by another interested party.

Sources of venture capital

[8.39] Venture capital originated in the United States of America, and in the UK was only available from a few sources until the mid-1970s. However, the UK can now boast a wide range of providers of venture capital, including divisions or subsidiaries of clearing banks, merchant banks, major public companies, pension funds, insurance companies and investment trusts and Business Expansion Scheme funds.

Each fund has its own investment criteria, varying as to:

(a)   the size of investment, although as a broad guideline investments over £100,000 represent the lower threshold;
(b)   the preferred industry sector;
(c)   the state of development of the business;
(d)   the degree of involvement in the management of the business;
(e)   the overall return required, which itself will determine the percentage equity required.

In general, the higher the level of risk, the higher the return that will be expected. As an indication, a 20% compound rate of return would be expected of a low risk investment, rising to 60% or more for higher risks in, for example, a company starting up a new product/market. While some running yield on the investment may be sought, the overall return required will be estimated having regard to the expected length of the investment and profitable realisation by some form of 'exit route'.

Exit routes

[8.40] The venture capitalist will at some stage want to realise his investment in an acceptable manner. Typically, a fund will look for one of the following exit routes, depending on the suitability of the company:

(a)   Stock Exchange flotation (see **8.24** above);
(b)   Alternative Investment Market (see **8.32** above);
(c)   purchase of own shares (see **8.50** below);
(d)   acquisition by another company.

Alterations to capital

General

[8.41] Section 617 of CA 2006 allows a company limited by shares to alter its share capital in any of the following ways:

(a)   increasing its share capital by allotting new shares;
(b)   reduce its share capital in accordance with CA 2006, s 641;
(c)   consolidating and dividing its share capital into shares of a larger amount than its existing shares;
(d)   sub-dividing its shares, or any of them, into shares of a smaller amount;
(e)   converting all or any of its paid-up shares into stock and reconverting that stock into paid-up shares of any denomination;
(f)   cancelling shares not taken or agreed to be taken by any person and diminishing the amount of the share capital accordingly.

Any such alterations must be authorised by the company's articles of association and be approved by a resolution of the company in general meeting. The type of resolution required to approve the alteration (ie ordinary or special) will depend on the provisions of the articles of association, but will usually be an ordinary resolution.

Alterations must be notified to the Registrar of Companies within one month of their occurrence, accompanied by a statement of capital, which basically provides a 'snapshot' of the company's total share capital at a particular point in time.

Consolidation and division

[8.42] This is not a very common occurrence but would be used in circumstances where a company wished to combine shares with a low nominal value into fewer shares with a higher nominal value. Following consolidation, the register of members will require amendment and share certificates may also need to be recalled for amendment if any of the shares consolidated are in issue.

EXAMPLE

That the 100,000 ordinary shares of 10 pence each be and are hereby consolidated and divided into 10,000 shares of £1 each.

Sub-division

[8.43] Shares may be sub-divided by a company because shares of a smaller denomination are becoming more popular. The procedure is similar to that on conversion into stock and consolidation. The register of members will need to be amended and share certificates may also require amendment if any of the shares that are sub-divided are in issue.

EXAMPLE

That the 100 ordinary shares of £10 each be and are hereby sub-divided into 1,000 ordinary shares of £1 each.

Conversion and reconversion

[8.44] Stock can only be created from fully paid shares. The procedure followed is much the same as with a consolidation of shares except that it is not necessary to call in share certificates, nor will fractions occur.

Historically, the advantage gained by converting shares into stock lay in the fact that prior to the Companies Act 1948, stock did not require to be numbered, whereas shares did. However, the 1948 Act introduced a provision allowing companies to dispose of the requirement to number shares and thus the main advantage of stock was diminished.

Stock may also be reconverted into paid-up shares of any denomination, and the procedure is similar to that on conversion into stock.

Cancellation

[8.45] The procedure on a cancellation of, as it were, unwanted *unissued* share capital follows the preceding matters, but naturally does not involve any calling in of share certificates or any amendment to the register of members.

EXAMPLE

That the 10,000 ordinary shares of £1 each in the authorised capital of the company which have not been taken or agreed to be taken by any person be and are hereby cancelled and that the authorised share capital of the company be diminished by £10,000 accordingly.

A cancellation of capital should not be confused with a reduction of *issued* share capital under CA 2006, s 641 (see **8.46** below).

Reduction of capital

General

[8.46] A company's capital may be altered under CA 2006, s 641 by a reduction of its issued share capital. This type of alteration must be authorised by the company's articles of association and be approved by a special resolution of the company (see **PRECEDENT C, APPENDIX 8A**). The Companies Act 2006 has simplified the process for private companies limited by shares in that it may do so by passing a special resolution and supported by a solvency statement. In any other case, such reductions are, however, subject to confirmation by the court.

A company's issued share capital may be reduced in any of the following ways:

(a)   by extinguishing or reducing the liability on any of its shares in respect of share capital not paid-up;

(b)   by the cancellation of any paid-up share capital which is lost or unrepresented by available assets;

(c)   by paying up any paid-up share capital which is in excess of the company's needs.

Application for court order confirming the reduction

[8.47] In accordance with CA 2006, s 645, where a company has passed a special resolution reducing its capital by one of the methods described above (and the company is not a private company limited by shares), an application must be made to the court for an order confirming the reduction.

If the courts so direct or if the proposed reduction involves either:

(a)   diminution of liability in respect of unpaid share capital; or

(b)   the payment to a shareholder of any paid-up capital;

then the following applies:

(i)   at a date fixed by the court, every creditor who is entitled to any claim which would be admissible in proof against the company in a winding-up is entitled to object to the reduction of capital;

(ii)   the courts will settle a list of creditors entitled to object and may publish notices fixing days within which those creditors not entered on the list are to request that their names be entered and where they are to be excluded from the right to object to a reduction of capital.

The court has the power to dispense with the consent of a creditor on the company securing payment of his debt if:

(A)   the company admits the full amount of the debt or is willing to provide for it;

(B)   the company does not admit to the debt but the court fixes an amount after enquiry and adjudication as if the company were being wound up by the court.

Court order confirming reduction

[8.48] Under CA 2006, s 648, the court may issue an order confirming the reduction if it is satisfied with respect to every creditor who under CA 2006, s 645 is entitled to object to the reduction of capital, that either:

(a)   his consent to the reduction has been obtained; or

(b)   his debt or claim has been satisfied or determined.

The court may order the company to add the words 'and reduced' to its name for a period of time if it thinks appropriate, and may also request that the company publish the reasons for the reduction of capital.

Under CA 2006, s 649 the Registrar will register the court order confirming the reduction in capital upon the production of a copy of the order and minutes approved by the court showing:

(i)   the amount of the share capital;

(ii)   the number of shares into which the share capital is divided and the amount of each share;

(iii)   the amount (if any) paid on the shares.

The reduction becomes effective upon registration and in confirmation the Registrar issues to the company a certificate as conclusive evidence of the alteration.

Should a public company make application for its share capital to be reduced below the authorised minimum (ie £50,000 or euro equivalent), then the Registrar of Companies will not register such a reduction unless an application for the company to be re-registered as a private company is also submitted at the same time (see **2.44 THE COMPANY CONSTITUTION**).

Variation of class rights

[8.49] A company may, pursuant to CA 2006, s 334 vary the rights attaching to any class or classes of existing shares. This topic is covered in **7.11 MEMBERSHIP**.

Purchase of own shares

General

[8.50] A general rule against a limited company purchasing its own shares is contained in CA 2006, s 658, and is fundamental to the principle that capital must be maintained (see **7.5 MEMBERSHIP** and **8.1** above).

There are, however, a number of exceptions to this rule:

(a) acquisition of fully paid-up shares otherwise than for valuable consideration (CA 2006, s 659(1));
(b) redemption or purchase out of capital;
(c) acquisition of shares in a reduction of capital duly made (see **8.46** above);
(d) purchase of shares in pursuance of a court order under CA 2006, s 721(6) (powers of court on objection to redemption or purchase of shares out of capital), CA 2006, s 98 (litigated objection to resolution for company to be re-registered as private) or for protection of members unfairly prejudiced;
(e) forfeiture of shares, or acceptance of shares surrendered in lieu, in pursuance of the articles, for failure to pay any sum payable in respect of the shares.

There are a number of circumstances in which the purchase of own shares provisions might prove useful, in particular, for small and medium-sized private companies, where the unmarketability of unquoted shares is a burden. These include:

(i) the buying out of a dissident shareholder, who may be harming the company's business;
(ii) the buying out of the shares of a deceased shareholder where the personal representatives or beneficiaries under the will do not wish to keep them;
(iii) the buying out of the shares of a proprietor of a company who is retiring to make way for new management;
(iv) proprietors who might be unwilling to admit outsiders to a permanent share of the profits can obtain short-term equity finance with the possibility of the option of selling shares back to the company;
(v) outsiders who might be reluctant to become locked into an unquoted company will be more ready to invest if an additional market for their shares exists.

Although the considerations relating to the marketability of shares will not be applicable in the case of a public company, it may be advantageous to such a company to issue redeemable equity rather than permanent equity or loan capital to meet a need for medium-term finance.

Company law requirements

[8.51] Chapter 4 of Part 18 of CA 2006 specifies the procedures which must be followed. These provisions are designed to safeguard the interests of creditors and other shareholders.

Power to purchase shares

[8.52] Section 690 of CA 2006 gives power to a public or private company limited by shares or by guarantee and having a share capital, to purchase its own shares (including any redeemable shares) subject to any restriction or prohibition in the company's articles. Redeemable shares can therefore be purchased prior to their redemption date.

Following the purchase, there must be at least one member of the company holding non-redeemable shares.

Procedure

[8.53] The procedure is different, depending on whether the transaction is an off-market purchase or a market purchase.

The terms of a proposed contract for an off-market purchase (which, pursuant to CA 2006, s 693, means all purchases of shares made other than on a recognised investment exchange) must be authorised by a special resolution of the company (see PRECEDENT D, APPENDIX 8A) passed either at a general meeting of the company or, in the case of a private company, by written resolution, before the contract is entered into. In the case of a public company, the authority conferred by the resolution must specify a date on which the authority is to expire and that date must not be more than 18 months after the date on which the resolution is passed. The authority may be varied, revoked or renewed by special resolution

The shares to be purchased are disenfranchised for the vote on the special resolution. A vendor shareholder who holds shares other than those to be purchased can only vote on a poll in respect of those shares (CA 2006, s 695(4)(a)).

If the resolution is to be passed at a general meeting, a copy of the proposed contract or a written memorandum of the terms must be made available for inspection by members of the company at the company's registered office for not less than 15 days ending with the date of the meeting and at the meeting itself (CA 2006, s 696(2)) (see 3.47 THE STATUTORY RECORDS for inspection rights details). There is no provision for the shareholders to waive this requirement so, even if consent to short notice of the meeting is given, the 15-day period must still be adhered to. However, a private company may pass the resolution by written resolution (see 7.58 MEMBERSHIP), which would dispense with the 15-day inspection period, provided the documents are supplied to each member signing the resolution at or before the time at which the resolution is supplied to him for signature. The vendor shareholder is not regarded as a member who would be entitled to attend and vote on the resolution and he need not, therefore, sign the written resolution. If the procedural requirements are not observed the resolution is ineffective.

If the articles of association also contain pre-emption rights, the consent of all the members to waive those rights should be obtained. The following conditions must also be met.

(a) The shares to be purchased must be fully paid (CA 2006, s 686(1)).
(b) The terms of purchase must provide for payment on completion (CA 2006, s 691).

(c) The purchase price must be met out of distributable profits or from the proceeds of a fresh issue of shares made for the purpose (CA 2006, s 692). A private company may also make a purchase out of capital if the stricter procedural requirements of CA 2006, ss 709–723 are followed.

(d) Once purchased, the shares must be cancelled and the issued share capital of the company is diminished accordingly (CA 2006, s 706(b)). An issue of new shares for the purpose of making the purchase may be made up to the nominal amount of the shares to be purchased. If the shares were capable of being held as Treasury shares, then CA 2006, s 724 will apply and the shares may be held and dealt with in accordance with CA 2006, s 727 or s 729.

Treasury shares

[8.54] There are certain categories of companies, usually those that are listed or those which are traded on AIM and equivalent companies on the EEA, that may elect not to cancel shares which have been purchased back but instead hold them 'in treasury' for subsequent resale.

It is thought that the ability to hold repurchased shares in treasury for resale would provide additional flexibility, in that companies could carry a higher level of debt since they could subsequently resell the treasury shares fairly quickly if interest rates rose, necessitating a reduction in the company's gearing level.

Contingent purchase contract

[8.55] This is a contract entered into by a company relating to any of its shares which does not amount to a contract to purchase those shares, but under which the company may become entitled or obliged to purchase those shares. Purchase in pursuance of a contingent purchase contract may only be made if the contract is approved in advance by a special resolution before the contract is entered into (CA 2006, s 694(3).

Market purchases

[8.56] This requires only the authority of an ordinary resolution. The authority must:

(a) specify the maximum number of shares authorised to be acquired;

(b) determine both the maximum and minimum prices which may be paid for the shares; and

(c) specify a date on which it is to expire.

(CA 2006, s 701(3) and (6).)

The authority may be general or limited to the purchase of shares of a particular class or description and may be unconditional or subject to conditions (CA 2006, s 701).

The maximum and minimum price may be determined by:

, (i)   specifying a particular sum; or

(ii)   providing a basis or formula for calculating the amount of the price without reference to any person's discretion or opinion.

(CA 2006, s 701(7).)

Disclosure

[8.57] The special resolution authorising an off-market purchase or a contingent purchase contract must be filed with the Registrar of Companies within 15 days of its passing (CA 2006, s 30). The ordinary resolution for a market purchase must also be filed within 15 days.

Pursuant to CA 2006, s 707, within 28 days of the shares purchased being delivered to the company, the company must deliver to the Registrar of Companies a return currently on the prescribed form SH03 stating with respect to shares of each class purchased:

(a)   the number and nominal value of the shares;

(b)   whether the shares are potential treasury shares or not; and

(c)   the date on which they were delivered to the company.

In the case of a public company the return must also state:

(i)   the aggregate amount paid by the company for the shares; and

(ii)   the maximum and minimum prices paid in respect of shares of each class purchased.

Form SH03 should then be submitted to HMRC so that it can be stamped with the appropriate stamp duty before filing with Companies House.

However, following the changes announced in the 2008 Budget, the ad valorem stamp duty relating to the repurchase of shares now applies only where the consideration is £1,000 or more. For instruments executed on or after 13 March 2008 which fit this criteria, form SH03 does not need to be stamped by HMRC before being filed with Companies House, although the form must be certified that the transaction does not form part of a larger transaction, the consideration for which exceeds £1,000.

Also, form SH03 executed on or after 13 March 2008 does not need to be stamped by HMRC before filing with Companies House as the £5 fixed stamp duty applied to cancellation by a PLC of shares from treasury has been abolished.

Where a company enters into a contract for the off-market purchase of its own shares or a contingent purchase contract or a contract authorising the company to make a market purchase of its own shares, the company shall keep a copy of the contract or, if it is not in writing, a memorandum of its terms, at its registered office from the conclusion of the contract until the end of a period of ten years after the completion of all purchases under it. These copies must be open for inspection without charge to any member of the company and, if it is a public company, by any other person (CA 2006, s 702) (see **3.47 THE STATUTORY RECORDS** for inspection rights details).

Failure by company to purchase its own shares

[8.58] Should a company having made an agreement to purchase its own shares fail to do so, then the company is in breach of contract. Under CA 2006, s 735(2), a company may not be held liable in damages for its failure to purchase the shares. However, this subsection does not prevent an aggrieved shareholder from enforcing performance of the contract, excepting that the court may not grant an order for specific performance if the company can show that it is unable to meet the costs of the purchase out of its distributable profits (CA 2006, s 735(3)).

Where a company is wound up and shares are outstanding for purchase, then the shareholder may enforce the terms of the purchase against the company unless:

(a)   the purchase was to take place at a date later than that of the winding-up; or

(b)   the company was unable up to the date of commencement of the winding-up to lawfully make a distribution equal in value to the price at which the shares were to have been purchased.

(CA 2006, s 735(4) and (5).)

In such circumstances the debt due to the shareholder becomes a deferred debt in the liquidation.

Taxation

[8.59] The introduction of the purchase of own-share provisions was accompanied by some major changes in tax law which allow the purchase price for shares in unquoted trading companies to be treated as a capital payment and therefore subject to capital gains tax, rather than as a distribution which would give rise to a charge to advance corporation tax on the company and a liability to income tax to the vendor shareholder on any amount in excess of the nominal value plus premium on subscription.

Redemption of shares

General

[8.60] The provisions relating to the purchase of own shares are closely tied to the provisions under CA 2006, ss 684 and 685 permitting redemption of shares.

A limited company having a share capital may issue shares which are to be redeemed or are liable to be redeemed at the option of the company or the shareholder. It is subject to the following:

(a)   the articles of a private limited company may exclude or restrict the issue of redeemable shares;

(b)   a public limited company may only issue such shares if authorised to do so by its articles; and

(c)   no redeemable shares may be issued unless there are issued shares of the company which are not redeemable.

Redeemable shares may not be redeemed unless they are fully paid and the terms of redemption must provide for payment on redemption unless there is agreement between the company and the shareholder that payment may be postponed to a later date (CA 2006, s 686).

Terms and manner of redemption

[8.61] Section 685 of CA 2006 sets out conditions as regards the terms and manner of redemption which must be satisfied before redeemable shares may be issued. These are:

(a)   the date on or by which, or dates between which, the shares are to be or may be redeemed must be specified in the articles, or, if the articles so provide, may be fixed by the directors, in which case the date or dates must be fixed before the shares are issued;

(b)   any other circumstances in which the shares are to be or may be redeemed must be specified in the articles;

(c)   the amount payable on redemption must be specified in or determined in accordance with the articles. The articles must not provide for this amount to be determined by reference to any person's discretion or opinion;

(d)   any other terms and conditions of redemption must be specified in the articles.

Financing of redemption

[8.62] The general rule is that redeemable shares may only be redeemed out of distributable profits, or out of the proceeds of a fresh issue of shares made for the purposes of the redemption (CA 2006, s 687(2)). However, a private company may redeem or purchase its own shares out of capital under CA 2006, s 687(1). Pursuant to CA 2006, s 687(3), any premium payable on redemption must be paid out of distributable profits of the company, except that if the redeemable shares were issued at a premium, any premium payable on redemption may be paid out of the proceeds of a fresh issue of shares made for the purposes of the redemption (CA 2006, s 687(4)), provided this does not exceed the lesser of:

(a)   the aggregate of premiums received on the issue of the shares redeemed; and

(b)   the current amount of the company's share premium account (including any sum transferred to that account in respect of premiums on the new shares).

Failure to redeem

[8.63] Should a company fail to redeem any shares falling due for redemption, then the situation is the same as for a company failing to fulfil an agreement to purchase its own shares (see **8.58** above).

Capital redemption reserve

[8.64] When shares are redeemed or purchased wholly out of profits, the amount by which the issued share capital is reduced on cancellation of the shares shall be transferred to 'the capital redemption reserve' (CA 2006, s 733(1)). The capital redemption reserve is treated as share capital except that it may be applied in paying up fully paid bonus shares to be allotted to members of the company.

Where shares are redeemed or purchased wholly or partly out of the proceeds of a fresh issue of shares, the amount to be transferred to the capital redemption reserve is the difference between the nominal value of the shares redeemed or purchased and the proceeds of the fresh issue (CA 2006, s 733(3)).

If a private company redeems or purchases its own shares out of capital, different rules apply.

(a)   If the total of the permissible capital payment plus the proceeds of a fresh issue is less than the nominal value of the shares to be redeemed or purchased the difference must be transferred to the capital redemption reserve (CA 2006, s 734(2)).

(b)   If the total of the permissible capital payment plus the proceeds of a fresh issue is greater than the nominal value of the shares redeemed or purchased, the amount of any capital redemption, share premium account, or fully paid share capital and any amount representing unrealised profits of the company for the time being standing to the credit of any revaluation reserve maintained by the company, may be reduced by the amount by which the permissible capital payment exceeds the nominal value of the shares (CA 2006, s 734(3)).

Redemption or purchase of own shares out of capital

General

[8.65] A private company may, subject to any restriction or prohibition in its articles of association, make a payment in respect of the redemption or purchase of its own shares otherwise than out of its distributable profits or the proceeds of a fresh issue of shares (ie out of capital) (CA 2006, s 709(1)).

The payment which may be made out of capital is such an amount taken together with:

(a)   any available profits of the company; and
(b)   the proceeds of any fresh issue of shares made for the purpose of the redemption or purchase;

as is the price of redemption or purchase. This payment is known as the permissible capital payment.

(CA 2006, s 710 (1).)

There are special rules contained in CA 2006, s 712 for determining the availability of profits. The question must be determined by reference to profits, losses, assets and liabilities, depreciations, diminution in asset values, retentions to meet liabilities, share capital and reserves as disclosed in relevant accounts, ie such accounts as are necessary to enable a reasonable judgement to be made as to the amounts of those items. The directors are required to make a statement specifying the amount of the permissible capital payment within three months of the date of the accounts (CA 2006, s 714).

Procedure

[8.66] In order to make a payment out of capital for the redemption or purchase of its own shares, a company must carry out the following procedure:

(a)   The directors must make a statement specifying the amount of the permissible capital payment, stating that, having made full inquiries into the affairs and prospects of the company, they have formed the opinion:

(i)   that there will be no grounds on which the company could be found unable to pay its debts immediately following the payment out of capital;

(ii)   as regards its prospects for the year following the payment that, having regard to their intentions with respect to the management of the company's business during that year, the company will be able to carry on business as a going concern and be able to pay its debts as they fall due, throughout the year.

(CA 2006, s 714(3).)

The directors' statement must have annexed to it a report addressed to the directors by the company's auditors, stating that they have inquired into the company's state of affairs, that the amount specified in the declaration is the permissible capital payment and that it has been, in their view, properly determined and they are not aware of anything to indicate that the directors' opinion is unreasonable in the circumstances (CA 2006, s 714(6)).

Should a director make such a statement without having reasonable grounds for the opinion expressed in the declaration, then he is liable to imprisonment or a fine, or both (CA 2006, s 715).

(b)   The payment out of capital must be approved by a special resolution passed on or within a week of the date on which the directors make the statement (CA 2006, s 716). The member holding shares to which the resolution relates is disenfranchised from voting on the special resolution (CA 2006, s 717(3)). The statement and auditors' report must be available for inspection at the meeting at which the resolution is passed, or, if the written resolution procedure (see **7.58 MEMBERSHIP**) is used they must be supplied to the member at or before the time when the resolution is presented to him for signature.

(c)   Within one week of the date of passing of the special resolution above, the company must publish a notice in the *Gazette*:

(i)   stating that the company has approved a payment out of capital for the purpose of acquiring its own shares;

(ii)   specifying the amount of the permissible capital payment for the shares and the date of the resolution;

(iii)   stating that the statutory declaration of the directors and the auditors' report are available for inspection at the company's registered office;

(iv)   stating that any creditor of the company may, at any time within the five weeks immediately following the date of the resolution for payment out of capital, apply to the court for an order prohibiting the payment.

In addition, the company must also publish a similar notice in an appropriate national newspaper or give notice in writing to each of its creditors (CA 2006, s 719(1) and (2)).

(d)   A copy of the statement of the directors and the auditors' report must be delivered to the Registrar of Companies not later than the 'first notice date' which is the day on which the company first publishes the *Gazette* notice or the national advertisement, or notice to creditors, whichever is the earlier (CA 2006, s 719(4)). The statement and auditors' report must be kept at the registered office throughout the period beginning with the first notice date and ending five weeks after the date of the resolution and shall be open to inspection of any member or creditor (CA 2006, s 720) (see **3.47 THE STATUTORY RECORDS** for inspection rights details).

(e)   The payment out of capital for the purchase or redemption of the shares must be made no earlier than five nor more than seven weeks after the date of the resolution (CA 2006, s 723(1)).

There are changes introduced by CA 2006 in respect of simplifying the procedure for capital reduction for private companies which may impact on the procedure for purchase of own shares out of capital. See **8.50** above.

Objections by members or creditors

[8.67] Following the passing of a resolution approving a payment out of capital for the redemption or purchase of its shares, any member who did not consent to nor vote in favour of the resolution and any creditor may, pursuant to CA 2006, s 721, within five weeks apply to the court for cancellation of the resolution.

The court has various powers where an objection is lodged. It may approve arrangements for the purchase of dissentient members, or for the protection of dissentient creditors, it may make an order on such terms and conditions as it thinks fit, confirming or cancelling the resolution, and in confirming the resolution, it may alter or extend any date or period of time specified in the resolution.

Financial assistance by a company for the purchase of its own shares

General

[8.68] There has been a significant change brought about by CA 2006 in that the previous ban on giving of financial assistance by private companies for the purchase of its own shares no longer applies.

Where a person is acquiring or is proposing to acquire shares in a public company, it is unlawful for the company or any of its subsidiaries to give him any financial assistance directly or indirectly for the purpose of that acquisition, before or at the same time as the acquisition takes place (CA 2006, s 678(1)). Where a person has acquired shares in a company and any liability has been incurred by that person or any other person for the purpose of that acquisition, it is unlawful for the company or any of its subsidiaries to give financial assistance directly or indirectly for the purpose of reducing or discharging the liability so incurred (CA 2006, s 678(3)). The reference to 'person' is not limited to individuals but includes companies and other bodies corporate.

For the purpose of the foregoing:

(a)   a reference to a person incurring a liability includes his changing his financial position by making an agreement or arrangement (whether enforceable or unenforceable, and whether made on his own account or with any other person) or by any other means, and

(b)   a reference to a company giving financial assistance for the purpose of reducing or discharging a liability incurred by a person for the purpose of the acquisition of shares includes its giving such assistance for the purpose of wholly or partly restoring his financial position to what it was before the acquisition took place.

Thus, the recipient of the financial assistance need not necessarily be the acquirer of the shares in order for the provisions of the Act to apply.

If a company contravenes these provisions, it is liable to a fine and every officer of the company who is in default is liable to a fine or imprisonment or both (CA 2006, s 680).

Financial assistance

[8.69] Financial assistance is defined by CA 2006, s 677(1) as including:

(i)   financial assistance given by way of gift;

(ii)   financial assistance given by way of guarantee, security or indemnity, other than an indemnity in respect of the indemnifier's own neglect or default, or by way of release or waiver;

(iii)   financial assistance given by way of loan or any other agreement under which any of the obligations of the persons giving the assistance are to be fulfilled at a time when in accordance with the agreement any obligation of another party to the agreement remains unfulfilled, or by way of the novation of, or the assignment of rights arising under, a loan or such other agreement; or

(iv)   any other financial assistance given by a company the net assets of which are thereby reduced to a material extent or which has no net assets.

Under CA 2006, s 677(2), 'net assets' are defined as the aggregate of the company's assets less the aggregate of its liabilities, including provisions for liabilities and charges. This refers to the actual value of the company's net assets, as distinct from their book value.

Permitted transactions

[8.70] Under CA 2006, s 681, there are, however, some important exceptions and exemptions. The following types of transaction are specifically excepted from the prohibition (CA 2006, s 681(2))):

(a)   a distribution of a company's assets by way of dividend lawfully made, or a distribution made in the course of the company's winding-up;
(b)   the allotment of bonus shares;
(c)   a reduction of capital confirmed by order of the court;
(d)   a redemption or purchase of the company's own shares;
(e)   anything done in pursuance of an order of the court under CA 2006, s 895 (power of company to compromise with creditors and members);
(f)   anything done under an arrangement made in pursuance of Insolvency Act 1986, s 110 (liquidator accepting shares as consideration for sale of company property) or under an arrangement made between a company and its creditors which is binding on the creditors by virtue of Part I of the Insolvency Act 1986.

Also under CA 2006, s 678(2), a company is permitted to give financial assistance for the purpose of an acquisition of shares in itself or its holding company if:

(i)   the company's principal purpose in giving that assistance is not to give it for the purpose of any such acquisition, or the giving of the assistance for that purpose is only an incidental part of some larger purpose of the company; *and*
(ii)   the financial assistance is given in good faith in the interests of the company giving the assistance.

Where a person has already acquired shares in a company, the company or a subsidiary of the company, pursuant to CA 2006, s 678(4), is not prohibited from giving financial assistance if:

(A)   its principal purpose in giving that assistance is not to reduce or discharge any liability incurred by any person for the purpose of the acquisition, or the reduction or discharge of any such liability is only an incidental part of some larger purpose of the company giving the assistance; and
(B)   the assistance is given in good faith in the interests of the company giving the assistance.

These exceptions are intended to remove from the scope of the prohibition a transaction which has the incidental consequence, but not the main purpose, of providing financial assistance for an acquisition of the company's shares. An example might be where, for normal commercial reasons, a group of companies needs to increase its general level of borrowings after the acquisition of a new company and the new company assists in obtaining or securing the new borrowings.

Where the lending of money is part of the ordinary business of a company, the company is not prohibited from lending money in the ordinary course of its business (CA 2006, s 682(2)(a)). Restrictions exist on what may be done by a public company (see **8.73** below).

Employee share schemes

[8.71] Under CA 2006, s 682(2)(b) a company is not prohibited from providing financial assistance for the purposes of any employees' share scheme provided it does so in good faith in the interests of the company. Again, restrictions exist on what may be done by a public company (see **8.73** below).

A further exception in relation to the provision of financial assistance to employees was introduced into CA 1985 (now CA 2006, s 682(2)(c)). Under this exception, a company and any of its subsidiaries are permitted to provide financial assistance for the purposes of or in connection with anything done by the company (or a company in the same group) for the purpose of enabling or facilitating transactions in shares in the first-mentioned company between, and involving the acquisition of beneficial ownership of, those shares by:

(a)   the *bona fide* employees or former employees of that company or of another company in the same group; or

(b)   the wives, husbands, widows, widowers, children or stepchildren under the age of 18 of any such employees or former employees.

For the purposes of this exception, a company is in the same group as another company if it is a holding company, or subsidiary of that company, or a subsidiary of a holding company of that company (CA 2006, s 682(5)).

Loans to employees (other than directors)

[8.72] A company is not prohibited from making loans to persons (other than directors) employed in good faith by the company to enable them to acquire fully paid shares in the company or its holding company to be held by them by way of beneficial ownership (CA 2006, s 682(2)(d)).

Special restriction for public companies

[8.73] The exceptions described above are subject to a special restriction for public companies. A public company may take advantage of these exceptions only if the company has net assets which are not thereby reduced or, to the extent that its net assets are reduced, if the financial assistance is provided out of its distributable profits (CA 2006, s 682(1)(b)).

For the purpose of this restriction, the following definitions apply.

(a) 'Distributable profits' are those profits out of which the company could lawfully make a distribution equal in value to the financial assistance and includes, in a case where the financial assistance is or includes a non-cash asset, any profit which, if the company were to make a distribution of the asset, would be available for that purpose (CA 2006, s 683(1)).

(b) 'Distribution' has the meaning given by CA 2006, s 829 (CA 2006, s 683(1)).

(c) 'Net assets' means the amount by which the aggregate of the company's assets exceeds the aggregate of its liabilities (taking account of both assets and liabilities to be as stated in the company's accounting records immediately before the financial assistance is given) (CA 2006, s 682(3)).

(d) 'Liabilities' includes any amount retained as reasonably necessary for the purpose of providing for any liability or loss which is either likely to be incurred or certain to be incurred but uncertain as to amount or as to the date on which it will arise (CA 2006, s 682(4)(b)).

Appendix 8A

Precedents

A. Directors' Authority to Allot Shares

'That the Directors be and they are hereby unconditionally authorised for the purposes of Section 551, Companies Act 2006 to allot shares up to the amount of £[
] in the share capital of the company at any time or times during the period of five years from the date of this resolution.'

B. Disapplication of Pre-emption Rights

'That the rights of pre-emption contained in Section 569, Companies Act 2006 (private company with only one class of shares)/Section 570, Companies Act 2006 (private company with more than one class of shares and public companies) and Article [
] of the Articles of Association of the Company shall not apply to the allotment of [   ] ordinary shares of £1 each to be made by the Directors on [   ] 20[   ].'

C. Reduction of Capital

'That the capital of the company be reduced from [£] divided into [   ] ordinary shares of £1 each (which are all issued and paid up in full) to [£] divided into [   ] ordinary shares of 10 pence each and that such reduction be effected by returning to the holders of the said shares paid-up capital to the extent of 90p per share and by reducing the nominal amount of the said shares from £1 to 10 pence accordingly.'

D. Off-market Purchases of Own Shares

'That the off-market purchase(s) of shares in the capital of the company on the terms of the proposed contract(s) to be made between the company and [   ] as laid before the meeting and initialled by the chairman for the purpose of identification be and are hereby approved.'

Chapter 9

Borrowing and Security

Borrowing

General

[9.1] A company may require loan capital to achieve its objectives in addition to the share capital put into the company by its shareholders. Such loan capital may be secured or unsecured and where security is required by the lender this is usually achieved by way of a charge over the company's assets. A chargeholder will generally enforce his security on the occurrence of specified events and this may lead to the company's liquidation and subsequent dissolution. However, liquidation is not the only method whereby a company is dissolved since the company may be struck off and dissolved under Part 31 of the Companies Act 2006 (CA 2006). These matters are considered later in this Chapter.

Power to borrow

[9.2] A company may proceed to borrow and give security for borrowing in its own name, provided it has sufficient authority to do so in its articles of association. In general terms, a trading company has such authority as an implied power, as the borrowing of money can be regarded as incidental to its trading activities. This general assumption was extended into statute, by virtue of sections 108–110, and 112 of the Companies Act 1989; the implications of which were that as a company can no longer act *ultra vires*, then it must have an implied power to borrow (see **11.1 COMMERCIAL CONSIDERATIONS**).

However, the directors of a company may still be held personally liable by the members of the company, for committing the company to an act which is not expressly authorised in the articles of association. In terms of borrowing outside a company's powers, a director could incur substantial liability. It would therefore seem prudent practice to ensure that, for the protection of a director's position, an express power to borrow is given, and that any limit on the amount which may be borrowed is not exceeded.

It is common practice for the directors to be given an express power to borrow up to a specified limit, beyond which the authority of a general meeting is required. A company's constitution may contain a statement to the effect that 'the directors may borrow on behalf of the company and in the company's name such amounts as may be necessary for the business of the company'. Such an express power clearly gives the directors sufficient authority to exercise their borrowing powers on the company's behalf.

For a private limited company, no power to borrow need exist beyond that given in its articles of association. A company originally registered as a public limited company must, however, be in possession of a trading certificate under CA 2006, s 761 before it may exercise its borrowing powers (see **2.42 THE COMPANY CONSTITUTION**). Where a public company borrows without holding a trading certificate, the validity of the transaction cannot be questioned. However, the company and the officers responsible for the default become liable to prosecution (CA 2006, s 767).

Forms of borrowing

[9.3] Where the appropriate authority exists, a company may borrow in such manner as it thinks fit. Thus, borrowing can take the form of a mortgage on specific property, a floating charge on all a company's property or by way of a bond, debenture or debenture stock and either with or without security. If unsecured, it is usually called an 'unsecured note' or 'loan note'.

(a) *Bank loan or overdraft.* These methods would not normally be used to meet the company's long-term loan requirements, as banks are usually averse to the making of long-term loans for the purpose of capital developments. Moreover, the bank would almost certainly require some form of security, such as personal guarantees from the directors.

(b) *Issue of debentures.* This method would probably meet the company's requirements more adequately where a large loan is required for an extended period – where, for example, it is required for extensive capital development.

Debentures

[9.4] A debenture is defined by CA 2006, s 738 as including debenture stock, bonds and any other securities of a company, whether constituting a charge on the assets of the company, or not. In common usage, a debenture is usually regarded as a document which is described as a debenture and is used to evidence or acknowledge a debt. A debenture can either be secured or unsecured and either registered or unregistered. Some common terms used in relation to debentures are given below.

(a) *Debenture*
A debenture in its purest form is issued for a fixed amount and is not divisible or transferable into smaller amounts than its face value. It is usually issued in respect of a loan or series of loans and may be either secured or unsecured.

(b) *Debenture stock*
Debenture stock is a divisible form of a debenture (as described in (*a*) above). However, unlike a debenture, debenture stock will usually be created by a trust deed which sets out the conditions of issue, repayment and the payment of interest and its transferability (see **9.6** below). The form of transfer of debenture stock is specified in the Stock Transfer Act 1963 and transfers are generally exempt from stamp duty.

(c) *Registered debentures*
Most debentures and debenture stock are issued as registered in the name of the holder, rather than in bearer form. This has the advantage for both the issuing company and the holder that as registered

debentures are recorded in a company's statutory books, the title of the holder is documented and thus provides a measure of security to both parties should the document evidencing the existence of the debt be lost or damaged.

(d) *Convertible debentures/debenture stock*

These are a hybrid form of debentures/debenture stock that give an option to the holder to convert his debenture into shares in the company at a stated time or times and using a specified formula.

(e) *Secured debentures*

Debentures can be secured by either fixed or floating charges, or by a combination of both.

(i) *Fixed charge*

This will secure a particular item of property of the company (eg a building) and will restrict the company's ability to deal with that property without the consent of the debenture-holder.

(ii) *Floating charge*

This is a form of security that exists over the whole of the property and assets of a company as opposed to a particular item.

Fixed and floating charges are considered more fully in **9.7** to **9.10** below.

(f) *Unsecured debentures*

Unsecured debentures give no right of security to the holder. Because of this, unsecured debentures usually carry a higher rate of interest than secured debentures/debenture stock, due to the increased risk of loss of the capital sum. Unsecured debentures are commonly referred to as unsecured loan stock.

(g) *Redeemable debentures*

Although it is possible for a company to issue perpetual (ie irredeemable) debentures, it is rare in practice. Commonly, debentures/debenture stock when issued will be expressed to be redeemable on a specified date or dates or upon the occurrence of a specified event or events. Alternatively, debentures can carry a right to conversion (see (*d*) above) or to partial redemption and partial conversion.

The funding for redemption will commonly be made out of a sinking fund which is established in the terms of issue. A sinking fund is an account to which specified sums must be set aside by the company in order to finance the redemption.

Shares or debentures?

[9.5] When deciding between shares and debentures as a method of raising capital, the following factors ought to be considered.

(a) *Redemption*

If the company would prefer to have the opportunity to clear off the debt within a given period, debentures would obviously meet this requirement, as redeemability is an important feature of that type of security.

Against this, it might be argued that the advantage of redeemability can be gained by the issue of redeemable shares, but the rather stringent conditions laid down in CA 2006 for their issue and redemption frequently rule them out.

(b) *Interest*

Another way of making debentures more attractive than shares is to offer interest at a fixed rate which is payable (usually half-yearly) irrespective of the company's trading results.

Preference shares might be considered as an alternative, but the fixed dividend on such shares is dependent upon the company's trading results and may be passed over or carried forward.

(c) *Security*

If the company is in a position to offer adequate security to prospective debenture-holders, that would be yet another way of making debentures more attractive than shares.

On the other hand, the directors might regard the creation of a charge upon the company's assets as a disadvantage, in that it is likely to be restrictive as regards, for instance, the company's ability to dispose of the assets so charged. If, however, the security is in the form of a floating charge, this disadvantage can be put aside.

(d) *Economy*

Because the advantages of security and regular fixed rate interest can be included within the terms of issue of debenture stock, they can usually be issued at a lower rate of interest – that is, as compared with the rate of dividend that it would be necessary to offer to prospective preference shareholders.

(e) *Membership*

As debenture-holders are merely 'loan creditors' of the company, the raising of funds by way of debentures does not extend the membership and, therefore, by the same token there is no further spread of voting power.

Against this, it must be accepted that the preference shares of many companies carry no voting power. Furthermore, in recent years an increasing number of companies have appeared to favour the issue of non-voting ordinary shares.

(f) *Convertibility*

A debenture which provides for conversion into shares might prove attractive to the investor who is undecided between debentures and shares. This is the convertible debenture (see **9.4**(*d*) above).

(g) *Taxation*

Debenture interest is chargeable against profits, whereas dividend on shares is regarded as a distribution of profits – a very important consideration as regards taxation.

Issue of debentures

[9.6] Generally speaking, there are no provisions in CA 2006 relating to the issue of debentures. However, where an issue of debenture stock to the public is proposed, the regulations of the Financial Services Act 1986 relating to the issue of prospectuses apply. The regulations contained in the Listing Rules apply where the company making the issue is listed.

The trust deed creating the debenture stock will commonly detail the terms of issue. However, where a company is proposing to issue debentures which carry an option or right to convert the debenture stock into shares, then the provisions of CA 2006, s 549 regarding the directors' authority to allot shares apply (see **8.4 CAPITAL**). In addition, companies have been required since 6 April 2008 to register the allotment of debentures within two months of the date of allotment under CA 2006, s 741.

The purpose of the trust deed is to vest the charged property of the company in the names of trustees on behalf of the holders of the debenture stock and to set out the conditions regarding repayment, the payment of interest and the transferability of the debenture stock. A trust deed is not always required in the issue of debenture stock. However, the creation of one does offer a number of advantages:

(a)   the trust deed will usually contain a legal mortgage, which will generally rank in priority to other forms of security;
(b)   the appointment of trustees ensures that there is someone with a specific duty to act should the security be in jeopardy; and
(c)   the trustees can also act for the debenture-holders as a body to protect their interests.

Security

General

[9.7] Where a company borrows money, whether by way of the issue of debentures or by some other means (eg bank overdraft), it is common practice for the company to be required to give some form of security for the borrowing. It could be argued that there is an implied power for companies to grant security over its assets in a similar fashion to the power to borrow (see **9.2** above). However, because of the potential personal liability of directors where they act outside the power contained in a company's memorandum of association, it is generally advisable that this power is expressly stated.

Security may be given on any of the property of the company, be it real or personal, present or future, and can be secured either by way of a charge on specific property (fixed charge) or by way of a floating charge.

Fixed charges

[9.8] A fixed (or specific) charge is a charge which is granted over a particular property or asset of a company (eg a building) and is equivalent to a mortgage which a bank or building society would grant to an individual.

Once a charge has been created, a company cannot deal with the charged asset without the prior consent of the charge holder.

It is common practice, where a fixed charge has been created to secure the issue of a series of debentures, for the trust deed (see **9.6** above) to contain a clause appointing trustees for the debenture-holders in whom the fixed charge will vest. This has the advantage that should a debenture-holder transfer his debenture, then a transfer of the security is not also required, as would be the case if the trustees did not have this right.

A fixed charge holder ranks as the highest class of creditor in a winding-up. A fixed charge has priority over winding-up expenses and other creditors' claims, including preferential debts – which broadly comprise of taxation (although as a consequence of the Enterprise Act 2002 debts due to the tax authorities and social security contributions cease to rank preferentially), employee charges, and floating charges. However, where several fixed charges exist on the same property or asset, then the priority of ranking will depend upon the order of ranking established at the creation of the charges, as long as such charges have been registered at Companies House within the prescribed period (see **9.11** below).

Floating charges

[9.9] A floating charge is a charge which does not relate to any specific property or assets of the company but relates to the entire undertaking of the company. Thus, as a floating charge does not relate to specific assets, the company is not restricted in its freedom to deal with its assets in conducting its business. The terms of the deed creating a floating charge will usually specify the circumstances in which the charge will crystallise (ie attach to the property of the company subject to the charge). When crystallisation occurs, the floating charge effectively becomes a fixed charge and will give the holder the right to take possession of his security and to appoint a receiver to realise the security.

Subject to any fixed charges which may exist, a floating charge ranks in priority, in a winding-up, to ordinary and other secured creditors. Floating charges, whether crystallised or not, rank after winding-up expenses and (prior to the introduction of the Enterprise Act 2002) preferential debts.

Enforcing security

[9.10] An administrative receiver is appointed by or on behalf of debenture-holders as a receiver or manager of the whole or most of a company's property where such debentures are secured by a floating charge or by such a charge and one or more other securities (Insolvency Act 1986, s 29). An administrative receiver is normally appointed by the court on the application of a mortgagee or debenture-holder:

(a)   when repayment of the principal sum and/or payment of interest is in arrears;

(b)   when the security has crystallised into a specific charge by a winding-up order or resolution; or

(c)   where the security is at risk.

Another method of appointing a receiver is for the debenture-holder to execute a deed of appointment granting the receiver authority to act.

Under a fixed charge a receiver has no authority to manage the company but as long as the debenture confers this right, a receiver under a floating charge may be appointed as both receiver and manager. If a receiver is appointed in this way, under a floating charge, he can then manage the business provided that the charge is over the goodwill or business of the company. In practice, most bank debentures contain a fixed charge over certain identified assets and a floating charge over the general undertaking of the company.

The Enterprise Act 2002 introduced provisions into the Insolvency Act 1986 (IA 1986) which restricted the appointment of administrative receivers but expanded the use of administration. The procedures under administration aim to rescue the company as a going concern, achieve a better result for creditors as a whole, and realise property for the benefit of secured/preferential creditors. While the Act will restrict the use of administrative receivership, holders of floating charges prior to the enactment of the Act (in 2003) will retain the right to appoint an administrative receiver.

Registration of charges

General

[9.11] Every company is required by CA 2006, s 876 to maintain a register of charges and to enter in it particulars of charges specifically affecting the property of the company, and of all floating charges on the company's undertaking or any of its property (see **3.18–3.21 THE STATUTORY RECORDS**). Additionally, CA 2006, s 870 requires that if a company creates a fixed or floating charge over its assets, the charge must be registered with the Registrar of Companies *within 21 days* of its creation.

Pursuant to CA 2006, s 860(7), the following charges require registration:

(a)   a charge on land or any interest in land, other than a charge for any rent or other periodical sum issuing out of the land;
(b)   a charge created or evidenced by an instrument which, if executed by an individual, would require registration as a bill of sale;
(c)   a charge for the purposes of securing any issue of debentures;
(d)   a charge on the uncalled capital of a company;
(e)   a charge on calls made but not paid;
(f)   a charge on book debts of the company;
(g)   a floating charge on the company's undertaking or property;
(h)   a charge on a ship or aircraft, or any share in a ship; and
(i)   a charge on goodwill or on any intellectual property.

Section 861(5) of CA 2006 also deems that a charge includes a mortgage for the purposes of the Act.

Registration

[9.12] The Companies (Particulars of Company Charges) Regulations 2008 (SI 2008/2996) address the information to be provided to the Registrar of Companies when registering a company charge under CA 2006. The regulations specify the information required by the Registrar of Companies in respect of a charge created over an asset set out in CA 2006, s 860(7) as well as information to be provided following the acquisition by the company of property already subject to a charge.

A charge is registered by the delivery to the Registrar of Companies of the original charge document, together with a form MG01 which contains the following details:

(a) the date of the creation of the charge;
(b) a description of the instrument (if any) creating or evidencing the charge;
(c) the amount secured by the charge;
(d) the name and address of the person entitled to the charge; and
(e) short particulars of the property to which the charge relates; and
(f) the person(s) entitled to it.

Section 869 of CA 2006 further requires that the Registrar of Companies keep a register of charges in which these details for each charge registered with him must be entered. The issue by the Registrar of Companies of a certificate of registration of a charge is conclusive evidence that the charge has been duly registered, and that the particulars are complete.

If the Registrar of Companies detects any error or omission in the documents presented for the registration of a charge, the Registrar will return the documents to the presenter for correction and subsequent resubmission, unless the Registrar is able to exercise his power under CA 2006, 1075 to informally correct such documents. Unless the documents in corrected form are received at the registry within *21 days* of the creation of the charge, the Registrar will decline to register the charge.

Failure to register a charge

[9.13] If a charge required to be registered pursuant to CA 2006, ss 860 and 870 is not presented for registration *within 21 days* of creation, it becomes *void* against the liquidator or administrator and any creditor of the company. Furthermore, the loan secured by the void charge becomes *immediately repayable* by the company pursuant to CA 2006, s 874(3).

The position of the holder of an unregistered charge therefore depends on the course of events. He can demand immediate repayment or enforce his security against the company, unless the company should go into liquidation, in which case any other creditor who has obtained a right over the same asset will have priority. The position of the holder of an unregistered charge is therefore precarious.

Failure to register a charge pursuant to CA 2006, ss 860–868 renders the company and each of its officers liable to a fine under CA 2006, s 860(5).

It is possible to apply to the court for an order to extend the time limit for registration (ie to permit registration after the 21-day period has expired). An explanation of the reasons for the failure to register in time must be given. The court will usually permit late registration, unless there was a fraud, or the company has meanwhile gone into liquidation. In permitting late registration, the court will not deprive another creditor of his priority claim, if it is obtained after the 21-day period for the registration of an earlier charge has expired (CA 2006, s 873).

Although the direct consequences of the failure to register a charge affect the holder of the charge, there is also an impact on the company in that the loan secured by the charge becomes *immediately repayable*, even though it was lent for a fixed period, and the company and its officers may be fined.

Satisfaction of a charge

[9.14] A registered charge must be cleared from the register maintained by the Registrar of Companies on repayment of the full amount owing under the charge, or on the release of the property which is subject to the charge.

The requirement of CA 2006, s 872 for the registration of the satisfaction of a charge is that either a director or the secretary of the company must make a statutory declaration in the prescribed form (form MG02 or MG04 as appropriate). The declaration is then presented to the Registrar, who will enter a memorandum of satisfaction on the company's register of charges maintained on the public record.

Form MG02 is used when a debt has been paid off in full, and form MG04 when part of the property or undertaking subject to the charge has been released from it, or the property subject to the charge has been disposed of by the company.

Two practical points should be noted:

(a)   There is no time limit for delivering a statutory declaration. If it is overlooked at the time, it can be done even years later. Meanwhile, however, the file at Companies House will give misleading information.

(b)   It is not necessary to obtain the formal consent of the former holder of the charge to clear it from the file at Companies House. If the procedure for clearance is effected improperly, the charge holder may apply to the court for the reinstatement of the charge on the file and also claim damages from the company's officers if their action has caused him loss.

The satisfaction of a charge should also be recorded in the register of charges which is required to be maintained by the company.

Dissolution

General

[9.15] There are a number of circumstances in which a company may be struck off the register of companies and dissolved. In each case, the method by which dissolution is achieved involves following through procedures set out in

CA 2006 or IA 1986. The company may resolve to dissolve the company or the dissolution may be imposed on the company by its creditors or by the court. The circumstances giving rise to a company's dissolution generally fall into the following categories:

(a) the Registrar of Companies has cause to believe the company is no longer carrying on business and proceeds to strike the company off the register (see **9.16** below);

(b) the company is no longer trading, has no assets nor liabilities, and the directors resolve to apply to the Registrar for the company to be struck off (see **9.18** below); or

(c) the company is being wound-up under the provisions of IA 1986 (see **9.31** below).

A company may be dissolved and struck off under CA 2006 where it has no assets or liabilities, although a company with assets must be wound up under the provisions of IA 1986. It is important to note that the assets of a company which is inadvertently struck off either at the request of the company's directors or by the Registrar of Companies will become the property of the Crown (see **9.29** below). A company's dissolution may be effected by the Registrar in circumstances prescribed by CA 2006, or by application by the company's directors (see **9.17** below).

The process of restoration (see **9.27**) has been simplified with Companies House being able to undertake this by administrative means in the more straightforward cases, and with the current statutory court procedures being simplified in all other cases.

Striking off by Registrar

[9.16] Where the Registrar of Companies has reasonable cause to believe that a company is not carrying on business or is in operation, he may send to the company a letter inquiring whether or not this is the case (CA 2006, s 1000). This is generally indicated by the failure of the company to submit to Companies House an annual return or annual accounts within the required time limits. Failure by the company to respond to this letter within one month of its posting will result in the Registrar sending a second letter to the company within 14 days of the end of that month.

Should the Registrar receive from the company confirmation that the company is no longer in business or in operation, or receive no response within one month of sending the second letter, the Registrar may then publish in the *London Gazette* and send to the company by post notice that at the expiration of three months from the date of the notice the company will be struck off the Register of Companies and dissolved.

Where a company is being wound up and the Registrar has reasonable cause to believe that no liquidator is acting, or that the affairs of the company are fully wound up and the returns required to be made by the liquidator have not been made for a period of six consecutive months, the Registrar shall publish in the *Gazette* and send to the company or the liquidator (if any) notice of his intention to strike off and dissolve the company at the expiration of three months.

Following the expiration of the time mentioned in the notice, the Registrar may strike the company's name off the register and publish notice to that effect in the *London Gazette*. On publication of this notice, the company is dissolved.

Striking off procedure

[9.17] Sections 1003–1011 of CA 2006 set out the process whereby the directors of a private company may apply to the Registrar of Companies for the company to be struck off the register and impose certain responsibilities upon the directors of a company making such an application. The key elements of the procedure are examined below.

Application in prescribed form

[9.18] On application by a private company, the Registrar of Companies may strike the company's name off the register of companies (CA 2006, s 1003). An application by a company must be made on the company's behalf by its directors or by a majority of them in the prescribed form (form DS01), and submitted to the Registrar together with a filing fee of £10. During the three months prior to the application, the company must not have:

(a)   changed its name;
(b)   traded or otherwise carried on business;
(c)   made a disposal for value of property or rights which, immediately before ceasing to trade or otherwise carry on business, it held for the purpose of disposal for gain in the normal course of trading or otherwise carrying on business; or
(d)   engaged in any other activity, except one which is:
    (i)   necessary or expedient for the purpose of making an application under CA 2006, s 1003 or deciding whether to do so;
    (ii)   necessary or expedient for the purpose of concluding the affairs of the company;
    (iii)   necessary or expedient for the purpose of complying with any statutory requirement; or
    (iv)   specified by the Secretary of State by order for the purposes of CA 2006, 1003(1)).

A company shall not be treated as trading or otherwise carrying on business by virtue only of the fact that it makes a payment in respect of a liability incurred in the course of trading or otherwise carrying on business.

Other circumstances when application not permitted

[9.19] An application may not be made at a time when in relation to the company any of the following is the case:

(a)   an application has been made to the court under CA 2006, Pt 26 for the sanctioning of a compromise or arrangement and the matter has not been finally concluded;
(b)   a voluntary arrangement in relation to the company has been proposed under IA 1986, Pt I and the matter has not been finally concluded;

(c)   an administration order in relation to the company is in force under IA 1986, Pt II or a petition for such an order has been presented and has not been finally dealt with or withdrawn;

(d)   the company is being wound up under IA 1986, Pt IV, whether voluntarily or by the court, or a petition under that Part for the winding up of the company by the court has been presented and not finally dealt with or withdrawn;

(e)   there is a receiver or manager of the company's property; or

(f)   the company's estate is being administered by a judicial factor.

For (*a*) above, the matter is finally concluded if the application has been withdrawn, it has been finally dealt with without a compromise or arrangement sanctioned by the court, or a compromise or arrangement has been so sanctioned and has together with anything required to be done under any provision made in relation to the matter by order of the court, been fully carried out.

For (*b*) above, the matter is finally concluded if no meetings are to be summoned under IA 1986, s 3, meetings summoned under that section fail to approve the arrangement with no, or the same, modifications, an arrangement approved by meetings summoned under that section, or in consequence of a direction under IA 1986, s 6(4)(b) has been fully implemented, or the court makes an order under section 6(5) of that Act revoking approval given at previous meetings and, if the court gives any directions under section 6(6) the company has done whatever it is required to do under those directions.

Notice of application

[9.20] A person who makes an application under CA 2006, s 1003 is required to give notice of the application by providing, within seven days from the day on which the application is made, a copy of the application to every person who, at any time on that day, is:

(a)   a member of the company;

(b)   an employee of the company;

(c)   a creditor of the company;

(d)   a director of the company, other than any director who is party to the application;

(e)   a manager or trustee of any pension fund established for the benefit of the employees of the company; or

(f)   a person of a description specified by regulations made by the Secretary of State.

A document shall be treated as given to a person if it is delivered to him or left at his proper address or sent by post to him at that address.

Withdrawal of application

[9.21] A person who is a director of the company at the end of the day on which a person other than himself becomes a person within the categories listed in **9.20** (*a*)–(*f*) above, must provide to that person a copy of the application within seven days from that day. These duties cease to apply if the application is withdrawn before the end of the period for giving the copy application.

Should any of the events occur under which application for striking off cannot be made (see **9.18**, **9.19** above) a person who is a director of the company at the end of the day on which such an event occurs must ensure that the company's application is withdrawn immediately. An application under CA 2006, s 1003 is withdrawn if notice of withdrawal in the prescribed form (form DS02) is given to the Registrar of Companies.

Offences

[9.22] A person who breaches or fails to perform a duty imposed on him by CA 2006, ss 1003–1007 and 1009 is guilty of an offence and liable to a fine. It is a defence for the person accused of such an offence to prove that he did not know, and could not reasonably have known, of the existence of the facts which led to the breach, or in failing to perform a duty imposed on him that he took all reasonable steps to perform that duty. A person failing to give notice of an application to any party who, at the time of the application or subsequently, fell within the categories **9.20** (*a*)–(*f*) above with the intent to conceal the application will be liable to imprisonment or a fine, or both. Should a person make an application in circumstances where he is not permitted to do so, or fails to withdraw an application when such circumstances subsequently arise, would be guilty of an offence. Other offences include making a false application to the Registrar of Companies or giving false or misleading information in connection with such an application.

Notice by Registrar

[9.23] The Registrar shall not strike off a company until after the expiration of three months from the publication in the *London Gazette* of a notice stating that the Registrar may exercise his power under CA 2006, s 1003 in relation to the company and inviting any person to show cause why the Registrar should not do so. Where the Registrar strikes a company off the register notice of that fact shall be published in the *Gazette* and the company to which the notice relates is dissolved.

Liability of officers and members

[9.24] The liability (if any) of every director, managing officer and member of the company continues and may be enforced as if the company had not been dissolved for a period of six years from the dissolution of the company (see **9.27** below). If there is no officer of the company whose name and address are known to the Registrar of Companies, the letter or notice may be sent to each person who subscribed to the memorandum of association at the address shown in the subscription clause of the memorandum.

Objection to dissolution

[9.25] Where a company has been struck off the register of companies, an application may be made:

(a)   for the dissolution to be declared void; or
(b)   for the company to be restored to the register.

An application may be made by the liquidator of a company or by any other person appearing to the court to be interested for the court to make an order on such terms as the court thinks fit that the dissolution of the company be declared void. Once an order has been made, the liquidator or the interested person may take proceedings against the company as if it had not been dissolved. The person making the application to the court is under a duty to deliver to the Registrar of Companies an office copy of the order for registration within seven days after the making of the order or such further time as the court may allow. Failure to do so will render the person liable to a fine and, for continued default, to a daily default fine.

Application to declare dissolution void

[9.26] An application to declare a company's dissolution void may not be made after the end of a period of two years from the date of the dissolution of the company, unless it is for the purpose of bringing proceedings against the company:

(a)   for damages in respect of personal injuries including any disease and any impairment of a person's physical or mental condition; or

(b)   for damages under the Fatal Accidents Act 1976 or the Damages (Scotland) Act 1976.

Such applications may be made at any time, although no order shall be made on any such application if it appears to the court that the proceedings would fail by virtue of any enactment as to the time within which the proceedings must be brought.

Re-instatement of dissolved company

[9.27] The restoration of a company may be effected in two ways – by an administrative process involving application to the Registrar of Companies (CA 2006, s 1024) or by application to the court (CA 2006, s 1029). An application for an administrative restoration may be made by a former director or former member, while an application to the court for restoration may be made by any person specified in CA 2006, s 1029(2) or any other person appearing to the court to have an interest in the company's restoration.

(a)   *Administrative process*
        The Registrar shall restore the company to the register provided the following conditions are met:
        (i)   the company was carrying on business or in operation at the time of its striking off;
        (ii)   if any property or right previously vested in or held on trust for the company has vested as *bona vacantia*, the Crown representative (generally the Treasury Solicitor) has signified to the Registrar in writing consent to the company's restoration to the register; and
        (iii)   the applicant has delivered such documents relating to the company as are necessary to bring up to date the records kept by the Registrar and paid any penalties under CA 2006, s 453 that were outstanding at the date of dissolution or striking off.
        (CA 2006, 1025.)

An application for an administrative restoration is made to the Registrar of Companies using form RT01, accompanied by a statement of compliance (CA 2006, s 1026) confirming that the person making the application has standing to apply and that the requirements for administrative restoration have been met. An application to the Treasury Solicitor for a waiver letter and any asset that is bona vacantia is made on form BVC14 (available at www.bonavacantia.gov.uk/output/BVC14-Administrative-Restoration.aspx) upon payment of a fee (currently £69).

(b)   *Application to court*

An application for restoration of a company that has been struck off the register may be made to the court before the expiration of six years from publication in the *Gazette* of a notice under CA 2006, s 1000 or under CA 2006, s 1003(4). The application may be made by:

(i)   the Secretary of State;

(ii)   any former director of the company;

(iii)   any person having an interest in land or other property that was subject to rights vested in the company or that was benefited by obligations owed by the company;

(iv)   any person who but for the company's dissolution would have been in a contractual relationship with it;

(v)   any person with a potential legal claim against the company;

(vi)   any manager or trustee of a pension fund established for the benefit of employees of the company;

(vii)   any former member of the company (or their personal representatives);

(viii)   any person who was a creditor of the company at the time of its striking off or dissolution;

(ix)   any former liquidator of the company;

(x)   any person of a description specified in regulations under CA 2006, s 1006(1)(f) or s 1007(2)(f) where the company was struck off the register under section 1003 of the Act; or

(xi)   by any other person appearing to the court to have an interest in the matter.

(CA 2006, 1029.)

The court if satisfied that it is just that the company be restored to the register, may order that the company's name be so restored. Restoration may also be effected where in making an application under CA 2006, s 1003 a duty required to be performed was not so performed or there was a breach of duty.

Following the delivery of an office copy of the order to the Registrar of Companies for registration, the company is deemed to have continued in existence as if its name had not been struck off. The court may by the order make such directions and provisions as seem just for placing the company and all other persons in the same position as nearly as may be as if the company's name had not been struck off.

The directors of dissolved companies are generally required to bring their filing requirements up to date and therefore lodge with Companies House all outstanding documents (such as accounts and annual returns) in anticipation of the company's restoration. However, the requirement for filing such documents will depend on whether the directors intend to retain the company for future trading purposes. The alternatives appear to be:

(a)   If the intention is to restore the company merely to remove the asset it holds (ie the property), and for the company subsequently to be struck off when the property has been disposed of, then an undertaking will be required to this effect. In this case, the outstanding accounts and annual returns will not be required to be filed at Companies House.

(b)   If the intention is to retain the company on the public register following its restoration with a view to future trading or even in a dormant state (for example, for name protection purposes), then any outstanding documents will need to be filed at Companies House in advance of the application for restoration being made. Where the accounts are subject to audit, the company's auditors will be required to sign the audit report on those accounts, prior to the restoration of the company, as if the company were still in existence.

In both cases, the time limit for making an application is six years. However, two exceptions to this time limit arise in relation to a court-approved restoration:

(i)   where an application for an administrative restoration for a company (made within the six-year period) has been refused by the Registrar, and an application for its restoration has been made to the court within 28 days of the notice issued by the Registrar (even where this occurs after the six-year time limit); and

(ii)   in cases of personal injury, where an application for restoration may be made at any time for bringing proceedings against a company for damages for personal injury (see **9.26** above).

Discretionary payments by Treasury Solicitor

[9.28] There are guidelines on the Treasury Solicitor's website (www.bonava cantia.gov.uk) which indicate that the Treasury Solicitor is able to make discret ionary payments to former members of a dissolved company where the financial assets have vested in the Crown as *bona vacantia*. There are several circumsta nces where this may arise, although the two of relevance here are:

(a)   where the dissolved company can be restored; or
(b)   where it cannot be restored.

The criteria that the Treasury Solicitor uses to determine whether a company is capable of restoration or not are the usual company law principles. Where the Treasury Solicitor is able to make discretionary payments, these can only be made in respect of cash balances and only one payment will be made. The guidelines also specify that:

(i)   where the dissolved company can be restored the maximum payment is £3,000; and

(ii)   where the dissolved company cannot be restored the minimum payment is £750.

In situation (ii) above, the guidelines also specify that payments exceeding £50,000 require the specific consent of the Treasury. It is also possible that the Treasury may retain a portion of the fund, although in certain circumstances (which are not identified) the Treasury may agree to waive this amount.

Property of dissolved company

[9.29] When a company is dissolved, all property and rights whatsoever vested in or held on trust for the company immediately before its dissolution (including leasehold property, but not including property held by the company on trust for any other person) are deemed to be *bona vacantia* and:

(a)   belong to the Crown, or to the Duchy of Lancaster or to the Duke of Cornwall for the time being (as the case may be); and

(b)   vest and may be dealt with in the same manner as other *bona vacantia* accruing to the Crown, to the Duchy of Lancaster or the Duke of Cornwall.

The person in whom any property or right is vested by CA 2006, s 1012 may dispose of, or of an interest in, that property or right notwithstanding that an order may be made for the dissolution to be declared void or for the company to be restored to the Register of Companies. Where such an order is made it does not affect the disposition (but without prejudice to the order so far as it relates to any other property or right previously vested in or held on trust for the company), and the Crown or, as the case may be, the Duke of Cornwall shall pay to the company an amount equal to:

(i)   the amount of any consideration received for the property or right or interest therein; or

(ii)   the value of any such consideration at the time of the disposition, or, if no consideration was received, an amount equal to the value of the property, right or interest disposed of, as at the date of the disposition.

Disclaimer of property by Crown

[9.30] Where property becomes *bona vacantia* and vests in the Crown under CA 2006, s 1012, the Crown may disclaim its title to the property by notice signed by the Crown's representative, being the Treasury Solicitor or in relation to property in Scotland the Queen's and Lord Treasurer's Remembrancer. The right to execute a notice of disclaimer may be waived by or on behalf of the Crown either expressly or by taking possession or other act evincing that intention.

The Treasury Solicitor has previously exercised discretion, and not sought to collect *bona vacantia,* where the known net assets of a dissolved company were less than £500. In these circumstances, the Treasury Solicitor has not objected to a bank or building society making payment to the former shareholders of a dissolved company of a sole asset (whether in one or more accounts) of less than £500 without reference to the Treasury Solicitor should a request be received by the bank or building society for such a payment. However, the Treasury Solicitor's guidelines indicate that the current policy is to collect all cash balances, regardless of amount.

A notice of disclaimer is only effective if it is executed within 12 months of the date on which the vesting of the property under CA 2006, s 1012 came to the notice of the Crown representative, or where an application in writing is made to the Crown representative by a person interested in the property requiring him to decide whether or not he will disclaim, within three months after the receipt of the application. This period of three months may be extended by the court which would have had jurisdiction to wind up the company if it had not been dissolved.

A notice of disclaimer shall be delivered to the Registrar of Companies and retained and registered by him. Copies of the notice are required to be published in the *London Gazette* and to all persons who have notified the Crown's representative of their claim to be interested in the property. Where notice of disclaimer is executed under CA 2006, s 1013 relating to any property, that property is deemed not to have vested in the Crown.

Dissolution following winding-up

[9.31] The liquidation or winding-up of a company is effected under IA 1986, Pt IV, following which the company is struck off the register of companies and dissolved. Under the provisions of this Part, there are three methods of winding-up companies, which are as follows:

(a)   members' voluntary winding-up;
(b)   creditors' voluntary winding-up; and
(c)   winding-up by the court.

Voluntary winding-up may occur where the company's articles specify a fixed period for the company, that period has expired and the members have resolved to wind up the company; the company resolves by special resolution that it be wound up; or the company resolves that it cannot by reason of its liabilities continue in business (IA 1986, s 84).

The circumstances in which a company may be wound up by the court are specified in IA 1986, s 122 and include the following:

(i)   the company has by special resolution resolved that it be wound up by the court;
(ii)   the company has been a public company since its original incorporation and has not been issued with a certificate under CA 2006, s 761 (see **2.42 THE COMPANY CONSTITUTION**) and more than one year has expired since it was incorporated;
(iii) the company does not commence business within a year of incorporation, or suspends business for a whole year;
(iv)   except in the case of a private company limited by shares or by guarantee the number of members is reduced below two;
(v)   the company is unable to pay its debts; or
(vi)   the court is of the opinion that it is just and equitable that the company should be wound up.

The effect of a resolution being passed to wind up a company, or of the presentation to the court of a petition to wind up the company, is that the winding-up is deemed to commence from that moment (IA 1986, ss 86 and

129). Accordingly, the business of the company must cease, except as far as it may be required for the beneficial winding-up of the company (IA 1986, s 87).

Liability of directors in winding-up

[9.32] In conducting a winding-up, a liquidator is obliged to investigate the records of the company. He should consider whether any transactions were effected at an under-value or at preferential rates and whether any charges are void due to failure to register the charge or, in the case of floating charges, were created within one year of the beginning of the liquidation in favour of any person (within two years for a connected person). The liquidator should also consider whether there is any evidence of:

(a)   wrongful trading (see **6.47 THE DIRECTORS**);
(b)   fraudulent trading (see **6.48 THE DIRECTORS**); or
(c)   misfeasance (improper performance of a lawful act).

The liquidator has a duty to report any fraud or criminal act that he discovers in the course of a winding-up to the Department of Public Prosecutions (IA 1986, ss 218 and 219). Where the company is being wound up by the court the conduct must be reported to the Official Receiver. If the liquidator or the Official Receiver considers that the conduct of a director has been such as to make him unfit to be concerned in the management of a limited company, he must inform the Secretary of State.

Chapter 10

Company Taxation, Taxation of Company Cars, PAYE and National Insurance

Corporation tax

General

[10.1] Corporation tax is a tax which is levied on the worldwide profits of a United Kingdom (UK) resident company wherever the profits arise. The treatment of companies which are not resident in the UK is obviously different, but they too are chargeable to corporation tax on any profits which arise in the UK from a trade or business carried on by the non-resident company through a UK branch, agency or other form of permanent establishment.

For the purposes of corporation tax, 'profits' include both income and chargeable gains arising from the disposal of assets and 'company' means any body corporate or unincorporated association (although certain exceptions do exist, see *Conservative and Unionist Central Office v Burrell* [1982] 1 WLR 522). Partnerships, and Limited Liability Partnerships, although incorporated bodies, are not subject to corporation tax but to income tax, with each partner (or member of a Limited Liability Partnership) being jointly and severally liable for tax on the profits of the partnership. Local authorities and the charitable activities of registered charities are exempt from corporation tax. 'Profits' for this purpose does not include dividends received from UK companies.

A company which is incorporated in the UK is prima facie regarded as UK resident for corporation tax purposes. Where a company is incorporated outside the UK it will generally be regarded as UK resident if its central management and control is exercised in the UK.

An exception applies where a company which would be regarded as UK resident under these rules would also be treated as resident elsewhere under the tax legislation of another jurisdiction, and the UK and that other jurisdiction have concluded a double tax treaty with a residency tie-breaker clause. In such circumstances, if the company is treated as 'treaty resident' in the other country as a result of said double tax treaty, the company is treated, for UK tax purposes, as not resident in the UK.

Assessment

[10.2] Corporation tax is assessed on the profits of a company arising in each of its accounting periods and is then charged at the rate appropriate for the financial year in which the accounting period falls. A company's accounting period is deemed to commence on the date a company begins to trade, or otherwise becomes liable to corporation tax, or immediately after the previous accounting period finishes. An accounting period is deemed to finish on the earliest of the following dates:

(a) twelve months from the date of commencement of the accounting period;

(b) the company's accounting reference date, or if there is a period for which one company does not make up the accounts, the end of that period;

(c) the company ceasing to trade, or otherwise ceasing to be within the charge to corporation tax;

(d) the company beginning or ceasing to be resident in the UK; or

(e) the date that a winding-up petition has been passed.

Where a company makes up its accounts for a period that exceeds twelve months then the accounting period will be split into successive periods of twelve months and a second period of any shorter excess. The apportionment of profits or gains to the different periods is usually made on the basis of the number of days falling in each period unless otherwise stated.

For corporation tax purposes, a financial year commences on 1 April in each year and runs to 31 March in the following year (eg 1 April 2011 to 31 March 2012 is the 2011 financial year).

Where a company's accounting period straddles two financial years, the profits are calculated and then apportioned on a time basis between the financial years in which the accounting period falls, according to the number of days falling in each year.

Calculation of corporation tax

[10.3] In calculating the profits of a company which are liable to corporation tax, the following items, referred to here as taxable income, must be included:

(a) trading profits less capital allowances (Schedule D, Case I Profits), from which are deducted any losses arising from the same trade brought forward from previous years;

(b) income from property less allowable expenses (Schedule A);

(c) UK source investment income (other than dividends from UK companies) consisting mainly of interest and similar payments either gross or under deduction of tax (Schedule D, Case III); and

(d) income from overseas securities and possessions although with effect from 1 July 2009 most dividends from overseas companies will be exempt (Schedule D, Cases IV and V) and other miscellaneous items (Schedule D, Case VI).

As well as its taxable income, a company is also assessable on its chargeable gains (ie capital gains) less any allowable capital losses. These are subject to corporation tax but computed with reference to the capital gains tax legislation. From 1 April 2002 there is an exemption from 'chargeable gains' for trading companies/groups disposing of a 'substantial shareholding' (ie 10% or more) in trading companies/holding companies of trading groups (subject to certain conditions). A loss arising on such a disposal is disallowable for capital gains tax purposes (see **10.25** below). The taxable income and gains together constitute the profits chargeable to corporation tax.

From these chargeable profits may be deducted any allowable charges on income, being generally all amounts paid by the company where income tax has already been deducted (excluding interest) (eg gift aid payments, patent royalties paid before 1 April 2002 and annuities), trading losses of the current accounting period, certain trading losses from later accounting periods, losses (see **10.18** below) surrendered by other companies within the same tax group, management expenses/non-trading losses of the current period and non-trade deficits on loan relationships for the current period.

From 1 April 2002 the types of trade charges are more restricted as patent royalties no longer qualify as charges. Patent royalties paid before 1 April 2002 are treated as charges irrespective of the period to which they relate.

A company may set against its corporation tax liability:

(i)   any income tax already suffered on investment income received (see (*c*) above);

(ii)   surplus advance corporation tax brought forward at 6 April 1999, after taking account of the Shadow ACT regime (see **10.9** below); and

(iii)   double tax relief (credit for tax paid overseas on profits which would otherwise be taxed twice).

Corporation tax self-assessment (CTSA)

[10.4] Significant changes in corporation tax assessment and collection occurred on the introduction of CTSA for accounting periods ending on or after 1 July 1999.

Under the CTSA regime, a company is required to calculate, notify and pay its own tax liabilities without the need for HM Revenue and Customs (HMRC) to issue assessments. A company is also required to prepare and retain documentation to support the returns made. Under CTSA, companies are required to 'self-assess' their corporation tax liability for each accounting period, normally within twelve months of the end of the period of account in which the accounting period fell, and to file a corporation tax return form (Form CT600) within this period. HMRC permit a concession where a return is filed within seven calendar days of the filing deadline. In this instance, no late filing penalty should be levied and the return should not be considered to have been delivered late.

The presumption is that the submitted return reflects the company's correct corporation tax liability and that the tax paid is correct.

HMRC have a fixed period in which it may enquire into any return, known as the enquiry window. This is usually within twelve months of the filing due date. However, for accounting periods ending after 31 March 2008 of companies that are not members of a group or are members of a small group (as defined by section 383 of the Companies Act 2006), if the return is submitted in advance of the filing due date, the enquiry window will end on the first anniversary of the day on which the return was submitted

Where the return is delivered late, an enquiry may be opened any time up to and including the next quarter day following the first anniversary of the day on which the return was submitted, quarter days being 31 January, 30 April, 31 July and 31 October.

At the end of that period, or at the end of any enquiry, the taxpayer has some degree of finality. The position is made less certain by HMRC's discovery powers under which they may issue discovery determinations or assessments within six years after the end of the accounting period to which they relate or for up to 21 years after the end of an accounting period where negligent or fraudulent conduct is found.

Under CTSA, large companies (broadly those liable to the full rate of corporation tax (see **10.5** below) for their current and previous accounting periods or with chargeable profits in excess of £10 million) are required to pay their tax in quarterly instalments. Payments commence six months and fourteen days from the start of the accounting period, and are then payable at three-monthly intervals.

Companies within the quarterly instalment payment regime are required to pay 25% of their estimated/actual liability on each quarterly instalment date. Please note that companies that are not large pay their corporation tax on the 'ordinary' due date – nine months and one day after the end of the accounting period.

Rates of tax

[10.5] There are three rates of corporation tax which apply to companies, termed the full rate, the small companies rate (see **10.7** below) and the starting rate (see **10.6** below). The rates are as follows:

Financial Year(s)	Full Rate	Small Companies Rate	Starting Rate
2005	30%	19%	0%
2006	30%	19%	–
2007	30%	20%	–
2008	28%	21%	–
2009	28%	21%	–
2010	28%	21%	–
2011	26%	20%	–
2012	25%	20%	–

The full rate applies where company 'profits' exceed an upper limit, set at £1,500,000 for the financial year 2011. The small companies rate applies where profits do not exceed a lower limit, set at £300,000 for the financial year 2011. A different, marginal, rate of tax applies where profits fall between the thresholds. Profits for these purposes are profits chargeable to corporation tax, plus dividend income from non-group companies.

From 1 April 2004–1 April 2006, a minimum rate of 19% applied to distributed profits where the distribution was made to a non-corporate shareholder.

Budget 2011 announced the main rate for the financial year beginning April 2011 would instead drop by 2% to 26% to be followed by three further one per cent cuts to 23% by the financial year beginning April 2014.

(Source: www.hmrc.gov.uk/rates/corp.htm)

Starting rate

[10.6] For financial years to 2005, the starting rate of corporation tax of 0% applied to companies (other than Controlled Foreign Companies (CFCs) and Close Investment Holding Companies (CIHCs)) with profits (as defined) of up to £10,000 in the financial year.

Where a company's profits for the financial year 2005 were between £10,000 and £50,000, tax was charged on the excess over £10,000 so that the benefit of the 0% rate was gradually reduced until, at £50,000, it was eliminated. An effective marginal rate of 23.75% applied to profits within this band.

With effect from 1 April 2006, the 0% starting rate of corporation tax and the non-corporate distribution rate have been abolished.

Small companies rate

[10.7] Where a company's (other than a CFC or a CIHC) profits for the financial year 2011 exceed £50,000 but are no more than £300,000, the company will pay the small companies rate of corporation tax.

Where a company has profits for the financial year 2011 of between £300,000 and £1,500,000, tax is charged on the excess over £300,000 so that the benefit of the 20% rate is gradually reduced until it is eliminated once profits reach £1,500,000. The effective rate of tax paid in this 'upper' marginal band for the financial year 2011 is 27.5%.

The full rate of corporation tax of 26% for the financial year 2011 applies to companies with profits in excess of £1,500,000.

The thresholds of £10,000, £50,000, £300,000 and £1,500,000 relate to a stand alone company with a twelve-month accounting period and are all reduced proportionately for accounting periods of less than twelve months and where the company has associated companies (see **10.8**). For the purposes of the small companies rate only the Finance Act 2008 will remove the attribution of rights or powers held by business partners in determining control unless relevant tax planning arrangements are in place.

Associated companies

[10.8] Where the company has associated companies, the thresholds of £10,000, £50,000, £300,000 and £1,500,000 (and the £10m hurdle for quarterly instalment payments) are divided by the number of associated companies. In determining how many associated companies there are for the purposes of the small companies rate:

(a)   companies dormant throughout the relevant accounting period are ignored;

(b)   non-UK resident companies are included;

(c)   investment and holding companies are included;

(d)   companies are included if they were associated for any part of the accounting period.

Generally a company is regarded as an associated company of another if one of the two has control of the other or both are under the control of the same person or persons. Control for these purposes is as defined in **10.12** below.

Advance corporation tax

[10.9] Until 5 April 1999, advance corporation tax ('ACT') was generally payable at a rate of 25% of the net distribution whenever a company resident in the UK made a 'qualifying distribution'. This ACT could be offset against the company's corporation tax liability. For distributions after 5 April 1999 ACT has been abolished.

Many companies have surplus ACT brought forward at 6 April 1999. Broadly, companies are allowed to deduct surplus ACT from future corporation tax liabilities but only to the extent that they could have done so had the ACT regime continued in effect from 6 April 1999. The right to reduce the company's future corporation tax liability by reference to this surplus is restricted by the shadow ACT regime.

When a company makes a distribution after 6 April 1999, it is treated as having paid shadow ACT at a rate of 25% of the net distribution. The shadow ACT is set against the company's corporation tax liability for that accounting period. Although this does not actually reduce the company's corporation tax liability, the shadow ACT restricts the amount of 'real' surplus ACT brought forward which can be offset against the tax liability.

Income tax

[10.10] Where a company makes annual payments, for example, payments of interest to an individual, it is required to deduct income tax and account for this on its CT61(Z) return. Companies should generally deduct tax at the basic rate (20% for the 2011 financial year) on payments of interest and other annual payments. Where a company receives payments net of income tax, it can set the tax deducted against any income tax payable in that accounting period. Any tax deducted which is unutilised at the end of the accounting period can be set against the company's corporation tax liability.

From 1 April 2001, there is no requirement for companies to deduct income tax from relevant payments between UK resident companies.

Under the domestic law provisions implementing the EC Interest and Royalties Directive, with effect from 1 January 2004, outbound interest and royalty payments are exempt from withholding tax, provided that the beneficial owner is an associated company of another EU Member State or such a company's permanent establishment situated in another Member State. A company is an associated company of another company if it has a direct minimum holding of 25% of the capital or voting power in the other company or a third company (also resident in an EU Member State) has such a direct holding in both companies.

From 1 October 2002, where a company reasonably believes that the recipient of a cross-border royalty payment is entitled to relief from income tax under a double tax treaty, then the company may reduce the amount of withholding to the rate provided in the treaty.

Patent royalties paid before 1 April 2002 were treated as a charge on income. Patent royalties paid on or after 1 April 2002 are not charges but are dealt with under the rules for intangible fixed assets (see **10.16** below).

From 1 October 2002 payments by local authorities may also be made gross, as may payments to charities and other tax exempt bodies (whether by companies or local authorities).

Close companies

General

[10.11] The close company legislation was originally introduced to ensure that individuals could not avoid the higher rates of income tax by retaining income to be taxed in companies under their control.

Most close companies are private companies, but companies on the Alternative Investment Market may also be close. In some circumstances, a fully listed company may be a close company.

Definition of a close company

[10.12] Broadly, a close company is a company which is resident in the UK and either under the 'control' of five or fewer 'participators' or under the 'control' of participators who are its 'directors', whatever their number. A company is also close where those participators are entitled to the greater part of the assets on a winding-up of the company.

A 'participator' is generally defined as a person having a share or interest in the capital or income of a company, including an indirect interest (such as a loan creditor).

A person is taken to have 'control' of a company if he exercises, or is able to exercise or is entitled to acquire, direct or indirect control over the company's affairs. This includes possession of or the right to acquire the greater part of the share capital, voting power or rights to the assets on a winding-up.

A company cannot be close if it is:

(a)   a non-resident company for UK tax purposes;

(b)   a company controlled by one or more non-close companies (other than by reason of non-residence) and only close by taking a non-close company as one of the five or fewer controlling participators; or

(c)   a quoted company in which 35% or more of the voting rights attaching to the ordinary share capital are held by the public. The definition of public contains a number of restrictions to exclude holdings owned by persons who have an interest in or connection with the company.

Close investment-holding companies

[10.13] A close investment-holding company (CIHC) is a close company which exists wholly or mainly for the purposes of investment other than in land and buildings which are to be let to third parties. A company which deals in land or carries on any other type of trade is not treated as a CIHC. Nor is a company which holds shares in, or makes loans to, its subsidiaries which are themselves not CIHCs, as long as the holding company exists wholly or mainly for the purpose of holding shares in or making loans to such subsidiaries, or co-ordinating the administration of such subsidiaries.

Where a company is a CIHC at the end of its accounting period, then the company is charged to corporation tax at the full rate irrespective of the level of profits it makes.

Loans to participators

[10.14] If a close company makes a loan or advances money to a participator, or to an associate of a participator (other than a participator or associate which is a company non-resident in the UK) it has to pay corporation tax to HMRC at a rate of 25% of the amount advanced. This tax cannot be set against any other tax liability and represents a cash penalty for, broadly, as long as the loan is outstanding. If the loan is repaid, or written off, an equivalent proportion of the tax is repaid. The tax is payable on the same basis as the company's normal corporation tax payments under CTSA, unless the loan has been repaid in full before nine months after the end of the accounting period. Repayments of the tax are due nine months after the accounting period in which the loan was repaid.

The provisions do not apply if, broadly, a loan does not exceed £15,000 and it is made to a director or employee of the close company who works for it full time and who does not own more than 5% of the ordinary share capital in the company. Company law restrictions on loans to directors should, however, always be considered (see **6.38 THE DIRECTORS**).

Benefits to participators

[10.15] Expenses incurred by a close company in the provision of benefits, such as living expenses or accommodation, for any participator or his associate, will be disallowed for corporation tax purposes and will be treated as distributions, unless they are charged to income tax under Schedule E. For this purpose, the value of the deemed distribution is equivalent to the value of the relevant benefit for income tax purposes.

Taxation of intellectual property

[10.16] Prior to 1 April 2002, there was limited tax relief available for the cost of intellectual property, goodwill and other intangible assets acquired from a third party or created internally.

A new regime in respect of the taxation of intangible assets was introduced on 1 April 2002. Under the regime, a company can obtain tax relief for expenditure on intellectual property acquired after 1 April 2002 in most cases based on the amortisation reflected in the accounts. There is also provision for tax allowances at a fixed rate of 4% per annum on assets with an indefinite or longer life. On disposal of the assets, special roll-over relief will be available where proceeds are re-invested in certain relevant intangible assets. Profits or losses realised on disposal of assets under the new regime are taxable as trading profits or losses (Schedule D Case I). Assets that have been acquired or created before 1 April 2002 will continue to be subject to taxation under the old regime.

As well as applying to expenditure on the creation or acquisition of intangible assets (including abortive expenditure), the new regime also applies to any enhancement, preservation or maintenance expenditure. Relief under the new regime will therefore be available for the cost of internal development.

The rules for intangible assets apply to patent royalties recognised for accounting purposes on or after 1 April 2002, irrespective of when the patent right was created. Thus patent royalties paid are dealt with on an accruals basis as a deduction, under Schedule D Case I (trading), Schedule D Case VI (non trading) or Schedule A (property letting business).

Similarly, patent royalties received are dealt with on an accruals basis.

Taxation of research and development

[10.17] Expenditure on research and development (R&D) is written off in the accounting period in which it is incurred. Certain small and medium-sized enterprises (SMEs) are entitled to enhanced R&D tax relief at the rate of 175% (150% prior to 1 April 2008), and may claim R&D tax credits at broadly 24% of qualifying expenditure where a trading loss results. Subject to State Aid approval, from 1 April 2011 the rate of SME R&D Relief will increase to 200%. The rate of SME R&D Relief is planned to increase further to 225% from 1 April 2012 (source: www.hmrc.gov.uk/ct/forms-rates/claims/randd.htm).

Large companies may claim 130% (125% prior to 1 April 2008) relief for qualifying R&D expenditure incurred on or after 1 April 2002, as may SMEs where they carry out sub-contracted research and development for a large company. All of the above are subject to a de minimis £10,000 of qualifying expenditure per annum. The Chancellor announced in his Budget on 31 March 2011 that this limit will be removed for expenditure incurred on or after 1 April 2012.

With effect from 1 August 2008 the SME scheme has been extended to those companies with fewer than 500 employees (from companies with fewer than 250 employees). These companies will be able to claim relief at the rate of 175% for qualifying expenditure, instead of 130%. If the companies are loss making, they will also be able to claim the payable tax credit by surrendering their enhanced qualifying R&D expenditure for cash at the rate of 14%. In order to benefit from this change, there are also financial limits which the company must meet. The annual turnover must be less than 100 million euros or total balance sheet assets less than 86 million euros.

A cap of 7.5 million euros per R&D project in respect of the SME scheme was introduced with effect from 1 April 2008.

Tax losses

Corporation tax losses

[10.18] A trading loss is computed for corporation tax purposes in the same manner as a trading profit and may be utilised in the following ways.

(a)   A company may set a trading loss incurred in an accounting period against any profits (including capital gains) of the same accounting period. Relief is given in priority to charges on income and group relief.

(b)   A company incurring a trading loss for which it cannot claim full relief against profits of the same accounting period may set the unused losses against any profits of the preceding twelve months during which it was carrying on the same trade, setting the losses against the most recent profit first. The loss relieves income and gains after trading charges but in priority to non-trading charges. If the accounting period immediately prior to the loss-making period is for less than twelve months, two accounting periods will fall into the twelve-month carry-back period. If only part of an accounting period falls within the twelve months, profits are apportioned on a time basis. The profits apportioned are those before trade charges. For accounting periods ending between 24 November 2008 and 23 November 2010 an additional £50,000 of trading loss may be carried back beyond the preceding twelve months but no further than three years prior to the end of the accounting period.

(c)   Current year losses may also be group relieved to UK-resident companies headed by a common parent company (wherever that parent is tax resident) which owns, directly or indirectly, at least 75% of the ordinary share capital of each subsidiary company and which meets certain other requirements. Group relief is also available to UK branches of non UK-resident companies. Trading losses, charges on income in excess of profits, surplus management expenses of an investment company, non trade loan relationship deficits and Schedule A losses may be surrendered to fellow members of the group and used to reduce their profits of the same accounting period.

(d)   A company incurring a trading loss in an accounting period shall, to the extent it is not otherwise utilised as above, set the loss against the first available profit arising from the same trade in succeeding accounting periods. It is not permissible, for example, to defer claiming relief for a particular period so as to obtain relief for charges on income which do not relate to the company's trade. The loss may be carried forward indefinitely subject to the same trade continuing.

(e)   Where a loss is incurred during the last twelve months in which a company trades, to the extent it cannot be used against the profits of the accounting period in which it arises, the loss may be carried back and set against the profits of the accounting periods falling wholly or partly in the period of three years immediately before the loss arises. In determining the loss in the twelve months prior to cessation, charges paid wholly and exclusively for trade purposes can also be carried back. If the final trading period is of less than twelve months it will be necessary to time apportion any loss or excess trade charges of the previous accounting period falling in the final twelve months of trade.

(f)   Where a trading company pays charges on income which exceed the profits of the period against which they are deductible, the company may treat as a trading expense the smaller of the excess and the total trade charges, ie those incurred wholly and exclusively for the purposes of the trade. This amount is then eligible for loss relief as in (d) above. The excess of such charges over profits is not available for relief against the profits of preceding accounting periods as outlined in (b) above, otherwise than as part of a terminal loss on a cessation of trade (see (e) above).

Where a loss (ie an excess of debits over credits) arises on non-trading intangible fixed assets, a claim may be made to set all or part of the loss against other income and gains of the same accounting period. Any loss remaining unrelieved may be surrendered as group relief, or carried forward and treated as a loss on non-trading intangibles for the next accounting period.

Restrictions on setting trading losses against total profits

[10.19] Relief for trading losses is restricted in the following circumstances:

(a)   a loss incurred in a trade assessable under Schedule D, Case V (ie a trade controlled outside the UK) can only be relieved against future profits of the same trade;

(b)   a loss incurred in a trade not being run on a commercial basis with a view to profit can only be relieved against profits of the same trade.

Excess management expenses of investment companies

[10.20] An investment company is a company whose business consists wholly or mainly of the making of investments and which derives most of its income from them. In computing its taxable profits, an investment company is entitled to deduct its expenses of management (which are not defined by the legislation). Where the management expenses exceed the company's total profits for the period they are carried forward to the next accounting period and treated as if they were expenses actually incurred in the later period. Alternatively, excess management expenses can be surrendered as group relief, as noted in **10.18**(*d*) above.

From 1 April 2004 the requirement to be an investment company in order to claim a deduction for management expenses was removed. The relief for these costs has been extended to all companies with investment business.

Deficits on non-trading loan relationships

[10.21] Under the regime which deals with the taxation of corporate debt, net debits (ie losses) arising from non-trading loan relationships can be relieved in the following ways:

(a)   by set off against the company's total profits for the accounting period;
(b)   by surrender as group relief;
(c)   by carry back against profit arising in the preceding year from non-trading loan relationships; and
(d)   by carry forward for relief against non-trading profits (ie non-trading income and capital gains) of the next accounting period.

Relief for such losses must be claimed and can generally be taken in a combination of methods (*a*) to (*d*) above. Relief in (*a*) is given after relief for any trading loss brought forward but before any relief is given for a trading loss of the same or future period. Any deficits which are not relieved in the ways listed above are carried forward and treated as non-trading deficits arising in subsequent accounting periods.

Capital losses

[10.22] Allowable capital losses are deducted from chargeable gains of the same or any subsequent (but not earlier) accounting period. Companies are required to quantify the capital loss annually otherwise it will not be available to reduce capital gains. Special rules apply to determine the availability of capital losses for companies which join a tax group.

Certain restrictions are placed on losses being available for utilisation when the disposal giving rise to the loss is between connected parties.

With effect from 1 April 2000 companies within a capital gains group have been able to elect for one group company to be deemed to have disposed of a certain asset such that the gain or loss arising may be more efficiently utilised. Gains or losses arising on or after 21 July 2009 (the date of Royal Assent to the Finance Act 2009) will be permitted to be transferred within a group however arising (FA 2009, Sch 12).

Miscellaneous loss reliefs

[10.23] Where Schedule A losses arise, ie allowable expenditure exceeds the rent receivable under a lease of a UK property, the losses are pooled and relieved against any current year profits and future non-trade profits. They can also be surrendered as group relief.

Where in any accounting period a company incurs a loss in any transaction chargeable to corporation tax under Schedule D, Case VI, the company shall set the loss against any Case VI income in the same or any subsequent accounting period. Relief must be taken at the earliest opportunity.

By concession, deficiencies of income from sources overseas (taxed under Case IV/V) may be carried forward for set-off against future income from overseas sources.

Employee share schemes

[10.24] A statutory corporation tax deduction is available for the 'costs incurred' in the running of employee share schemes for accounting periods starting on or after 1 January 2003. The deduction is basically equal to the amount taxable (either as income or capital gains) on the employee, or for an approved scheme, the gain the employee makes.

There are various requirements relating to the company's business being within the charge to corporation tax. The eligible shares must be:

(a)   shares of a class listed on a recognised stock exchange;

(b)   shares in a company which is not under the control of another company;

(c)   shares in a company that is under the control of a company (other than a close company or a company that if resident in the UK would be a close company) whose shares are listed on a recognised stock exchange.

The shares must also be fully paid up, non-redeemable ordinary shares. The shares must be in:

(a)   the employing company;

(b)   a company that at the time of the award, is a parent company of the employing company;

(c)   a company that, at the time of the award, is a member of a consortium that owns the employing company or a company within (*b*) above; or

(d)   where at the time of the award the employing company or a company within paragraph (*b*) is a member of a consortium that owns another company, a company that at that time:

   (i)   is a member of the consortium or a parent in relation to a member of the consortium; and

   (ii)   is also a member of the same commercial association of companies as that company.

There are also conditions relating to the income tax position of the employee. It is irrelevant whether the share scheme is approved and when the incentives were actually awarded.

Substantial shareholdings

[10.25] Where a trading company (or the holding company of a trading group) disposes of a shareholding of at least 10% in a trading company (or a holding company of a trading group) then provided certain conditions are satisfied, any 'gain' arising on disposal is exempt from UK corporation tax on chargeable gains (and any loss is not an allowable loss). The main conditions which need to be satisfied are that the substantial shareholding must have been held for at least twelve months out of the two years immediately prior to the disposal and the activities of both the investing company and the company in which shares are disposed of must not consist to a 'substantial' extent of non-trade related activities, both before and immediately after disposal.

Time limits

[10.26] Many of the above claims must be made within two years of the end of the accounting period in which the loss was incurred, although some may be made within six years of the end of the accounting period. The Finance Bill 2009 includes provisions to reduce the time limits on most direct tax claims to four years with effect from 1 April 2010. Under CTSA, some claims, for example group relief, must be made on the corporation tax return (CT600) itself.

Disclosure of tax avoidance schemes

[10.27] The Finance Act 2004 contains provisions which impose obligations on tax advisers who promote tax schemes and taxpayers who implement them. Broadly, details of such schemes and arrangements must be notified to HMRC if they satisfy three tests:

(a) the scheme must be one of those specified in regulations as being 'connected with employment' or 'connected with financial products'; the scheme must confer a tax advantage in relation to income tax, capital gains tax or corporation tax (stamp duty and National Insurance contributions ('NICs') are currently excluded). The disclosure regime is extended, with effect from 6 April 2011, to require the disclosure of inheritance tax arrangements that seek to avoid IHT charges associated with transfers of property into trust (source: www. hmrc.gov.uk/aiu/disclosure-avoidance.htm);

(b) the definition of tax advantage is based on that set out in ICTA 1988, s 709, but is extended to include, for example, deferring tax payments or removing the obligation to withhold tax or account for tax under PAYE; and

(c) the tax advantage must be a main benefit or one of the main benefits that might be expected to arise from the scheme. As the test looks to benefit rather than purpose, commercially driven transactions can potentially be caught.

In many cases it will be the promoter (ie the adviser) who notifies HMRC, but where there is no UK promoter (and the overseas promoter is not making the notification), or a scheme is devised in-house, then the taxpayer is required to do so.

The time limit for notification by a promoter is five business days from the date that the scheme is made available for implementation. Where there is an overseas promoter then the taxpayer has five days from the start of implementation to notify, but if the scheme is devised in-house then the taxpayer needs only to notify at some point before the filing date for their tax return.

The information required must be sent to the new Avoidance Intelligence Unit and is set out in the regulations, but, broadly, HMRC must be supplied with enough information to enable them to establish how the scheme works. The promoter is, however, not required to disclose the name of the taxpayer concerned. HMRC will then (within 30 days) provide the necessary number for inclusion on tax returns.

The rules came into effect on 1 August 2004, but have a degree of retrospection as promoters need to notify anything promoted since 18 March 2004 and taxpayers need to notify anything implemented since 23 April 2004.

Value added tax

General

[10.28] Value added tax (VAT) is an indirect tax on transactions. It is charged on taxable supplies of goods or services made in the UK, by a taxable person, in the course of a business. In certain circumstances taxable persons must also account for VAT on goods and services received from overseas suppliers.

HMRC regulate the tax which operates within a framework of registration and self-assessment by the taxpayer and the submission of periodic returns. The submission of these returns is subject to a strict compliance code with penalties for non-compliance.

A taxable person must account for VAT chargeable on the supplies he makes (known as output tax), but is entitled to reclaim VAT incurred on goods or services which he purchases (known as input tax). Deduction of input tax is limited to the extent that such goods and services are used in the making of taxable supplies (see **10.32** below). VAT incurred on supplies used wholly for the making of exempt supplies (see **10.30** below) is not generally deductible.

Meaning of 'supply'

[10.29] VAT legislation considers two types of supply: supplies of goods and supplies of services. The passing of title to goods is a supply of goods. This is the case where the passing of title occurs immediately or at some future time, eg in a hire-purchase agreement. A supply of services is a wide concept incorporating anything which is not viewed to be a supply of goods.

To be liable to UK VAT a supply of goods or services must be deemed to have been made in the UK. There are special rules (known as the place of supply) for determining whether a supply is made in the UK. Presently the basic place of supply for services supplied to business customers has been where the supplier is based (subject to certain exceptions). However, from 1 January 2010 the basic place of supply of services supplied to business customers are deemed to be the country where the recipient is based, again subject to a number of exceptions.

Normally supplies are made for consideration, whether received in money or in some other non-monetary form. However, VAT legislation also treats certain other transactions, where no consideration is received, as if they were supplies for consideration. Examples include the provision of gifts of business assets; the assets of a business which remain in hand when it deregisters for VAT; and fuel provided to staff for their private use.

Certain transactions are specifically not treated as supplies, including the transfer of a business as a going-concern, where certain conditions, are satisfied and the receipt of dividends.

Liability of a supply

[10.30] VAT is calculated by applying the relevant VAT rate to the consideration received for a supply. For imported goods the value is the invoice price (plus other import duties, commission, freight etc) or the value according to the customs valuation rules.

There are a number of VAT liabilities for supplies of goods and services and these are summarised below:

(a)   *The standard-rate of VAT* – Supplies of goods and services are subject to the standard rate of VAT unless they fall within one of the exceptions outlined below. The standard rate of VAT increased from 17.5% to 20% on 4 January 2011. From 1 January 2010 to 3 January 2011 the standard rate was 17.5%. Prior to this the standard rate of VAT was 15%.

(b)   *The zero-rate of VAT* – These supplies are specified in VAT legislation and currently include, with some exceptions supplies of certain foods, books, certain supplies of buildings for domestic or charitable use, passenger transport, dispensed medicines and exported goods subject to proof of export. Zero-rated supplies are taxable supplies, but the rate of tax is nil. The value of these supplies counts towards the taxable turnover of the business.

(c)   *The reduced-rate of VAT* – There is also a reduced VAT rate which is currently 5%. The reduced rate applies to certain supplies of fuel and power, certain construction services, certain residential renovations and conversions, women's sanitary products, certain contraceptive products, and children's car seats.

(d)   *Exempt* – Supplies currently covered by the VAT exemption include some interests in land (subject to any options to tax that have been made), insurance, postage (only where supplied by the Royal Mail), some financial and insurance services, certain supplies of education and supplies of medical care. No VAT is chargeable on exempt supplies, and they do not form part of a businesses taxable turnover.

(e) *Outside the scope* – Certain supplies made by UK taxable persons are treated as being outside the scope of UK VAT. Supplies that are outside the scope of VAT include supplies of goods and services where the place of supply is not deemed to be in the UK and certain supplies that are mandatory within UK law. In these circumstances, such supplies fall outside the scope of UK VAT, although they may fall within the VAT regime of another country. VAT incurred by the supplier on purchases of goods and services used in making these supplies is typically recoverable if the supply would have been taxable if made in the UK, or if it falls within the special rules for financial or insurance services made to a person who belongs outside the EU.

Where several supplies are charged at a single inclusive price, the transaction will either be treated as a single supply with a single VAT treatment or in some instances a composite supply with several VAT treatments applied.

Taxable persons and registration

[10.31] VAT registered/registrable persons are those carrying on business (ie companies, partnerships, individuals or other legal bodies, eg charities, members' associations, etc) that are, or are required to be, VAT registered. Businesses must notify HMRC where their taxable turnover (ie the value of standard-rated, reduced rated and zero-rated sales) exceeds a certain VAT registration threshold on the basis of either *retrospective turnover test* or *forecasted future turnover test.*

Under the *retrospective test*, a business is liable to register for VAT if, at the end of any month, the value of its taxable supplies in the last twelve months has exceeded £73,000. Prior to April 2011, the threshold was £70,000.

Under the *forecast test*, a business is liable to register if at any time there are reasonable grounds for believing that the value of the business's taxable supplies will exceed £73,000 (formerly £70,000) in the next 30 days alone. The business must notify HMRC of its liability to register for VAT within 30 days of that date under both the retrospective and forecast registration tests.

Alternatively, a business may choose to register for VAT on a voluntary basis if it is making taxable supplies below the registration threshold or it intends to make taxable supplies in the future.

A business making only exempt supplies is not generally entitled to register for VAT, however there are some specific circumstances where a VAT registration is required. A business whose supplies are wholly or mainly zero-rated must notify HMRC if it exceeds the registration thresholds, but may be excused from registration. However, in this situation, registration is generally sought as the business can obtain repayment of VAT incurred on related costs/expenditure. A business that makes supplies of goods or services outside of the UK and, therefore, outside the scope of UK VAT should consider registration on a voluntary basis if those supplies would have been taxable if made in the UK or if they fall within the special rules for financial or insurance services made to a person who belongs outside the EU as it is also likely to be able to obtain repayments of VAT incurred on related costs and expenditure from HMRC.

Once a business is registered for VAT, it may apply for deregistration if the value of its supplies during the last twelve months has fallen below the deregistration threshold of £71,000 from 1 April 2011 (formerly £68,000).

(Source: www.hmrc.gov.uk/vat/forms-rates/rates/rates-thresholds.htm.)

Input tax and partial exemption

[10.32] Input tax is VAT suffered by a taxable person on goods or services supplied to him, or imported by him, which are used or to be used for the purpose of his business. The rules relating to the recovery of input tax are complex and restricted to the extent that it is attributable to the following activities: the making of taxable supplies, the making of supplies made outside the UK which would be taxable if made in the UK and the making of some supplies of financial services.

Before claiming credit for input tax the business should hold valid evidence to support deduction, eg a valid VAT invoice obtained from the supplier. There are rules regarding what must be shown on a VAT invoice which includes the supplier's VAT registration number, the date of supply, the name and address of the supplier and customer, details of the goods or services sold and the total amount of tax charged (this is not an exhaustive list).

UK VAT legislation does not permit the deduction of VAT on certain types of expenditure, for example VAT incurred on business entertainment.

A business that makes both taxable and exempt supplies may be 'partly exempt' and may suffer a restriction to the amount of input tax that it can deduct. If a restriction is necessary, deduction in each VAT accounting period is provisional subject an annual review.

Record keeping, returns and compliance

[10.33] A VAT registered person is normally required to keep business accounting records for six years (but can apply to HMRC to have this period reduced if there is a good commercial reason why this cannot be complied with).

HMRC undertake periodic visits to ensure that the correct amount of VAT is accounted for at the correct time.

When registering for VAT HMRC will allocate VAT accounting periods (although these may be changed on request). These accounting periods are usually quarterly (3-monthly) although a business in a net VAT repayment position (ie its input tax exceeds its output tax) may apply for monthly accounting periods. In addition, businesses that make supplies of less than £1,350,000 over a twelve-month period, may apply to submit one annual return, making prescribed regular interim payments to discharge its VAT liability throughout the year based on the business's estimated turnover.

Businesses must declare the amount of output tax due and the amount of input tax being claimed on their VAT return. Businesses must also show on the return the net value of goods and services supplied and acquired from other EU Member States.

If an error is made in calculating the value of VAT due, it must be adjusted either by making a voluntary disclosure of the error to HMRC, or by making an adjustment on a subsequent VAT return. The type of adjustment required is dependent on the size of the error made. VAT returns must be submitted to HMRC along with any payment in respect of the net VAT shown as being due by the last day of the month following the end of the VAT accounting period, eg the VAT return for the period ending 31 December must be in HMRC's possession along with any payment by no later than 31 January. Businesses who agree to pay HMRC by credit transfer get an extra seven days to submit their VAT return and payment to HMRC. Large businesses (whose total net VAT liability in the last year exceeded £2 million) are required to make monthly payments of VAT on account based on 1/24th of the business' previous year's net VAT liability. A balancing payment, making up the actual VAT liability for the period is then made with each return. Businesses have the option of paying their actual VAT liability on a monthly basis instead of making these payments on account.

Where input tax exceeds the output tax, HMRC will make a refund of the VAT to the business. If there is undue delay in making this payment a 5% repayment supplement may also be paid. HMRC are however, permitted to make 'reasonable enquiries' before making a repayment.

Retailers, certain businesses dealing in second-hand goods, and travel companies are required to use special schemes for calculating the amount of output tax due to HMRC.

Supplies of goods to other EU Member States can be subject to the zero-rate provided the UK business making the supply obtains its customer's valid EU VAT registration number and quotes this on its sales invoice, it must also retain suitable evidence that the goods have been dispatched from the UK within a prescribed timescale. If these conditions are not met, VAT must be charged at the standard rate. Exports of goods to customers in non-EU countries are zero-rated provided various requirements are satisfied, including obtaining adequate evidence of export.

Most UK businesses which sell goods to consumers based in other EU Member States are required to submit EC sales lists (ESLs) to HMRC on a VAT 101 form. ESLs are generally required to be made on a quarterly basis (although in certain circumstances monthly ESLs will be required) and must be submitted to HMRC within 42 days of the end of the relevant ESL period. From 1 January 2010 rules require businesses to complete ESLs for certain services supplied to customers in other EC Member States, as well as goods. In addition, the time limits for submission of ESLs are being reduced to 14 days from the end of the reporting period for paper ESLs and 21 days from the end of the reporting period for electronic submissions.

In addition, UK businesses that dispatch goods to customers based in other EU Member States with an aggregate value in excess of £270,000 and/or businesses that receive goods from suppliers based in other EU Member States with an aggregate value in excess of £270,000 per annum (effective from 1 January 2009), are required to make monthly Supplementary Statistical Declarations. These are known respectively as Intrastat 'Arrival' and Intrastat

'Dispatch' declarations. Intrastat declarations are made in respect of the movement of goods within the EU community and do not apply to supplies of services.

'Arrivals' and 'Dispatches' must be recorded on specific Intrastat forms and must be submitted to HMRC by no later than the end of the month following the end of the reference period. For example, for declarations in January the forms should be submitted by the end of February. HMRC have the powers to take criminal action in respect of non-compliance regarding the submission of Intrastat declarations and against the making of inaccurate Intrastat declarations.

Recovery of overpaid VAT

[10.34] HMRC are required to repay VAT which has been overpaid, however they may withhold payment where they believe that this would unjustly enrich the taxpayer. If an overpayment occurs the taxable person has three years to submit a claim from the end of the VAT accounting period in which the mistake was made. The three-year cap for correcting errors was extended to four years on 30 April 2010.

For further information on the correction of errors see **10.33** above.

Penalties and interest

[10.35] Offences and defaults in connection with VAT are dealt with by a system of financial penalties and surcharges which are imposed directly by HMRC and notified by means of assessment. Many of these penalties are based on the value of tax which has been under-declared and are cumulative. High level information on these is provided below.

(a)   *Failure to register at the appropriate time (Belated Notification Penalty)* – Default incurs a penalty of £50, or, if greater, a percentage of the net accrued tax due from the date VAT registration should have been effected to the date the business notified HMRC of its liability to be registered for VAT. The percentage varies depending on how late the registration liability is notified to HMRC. The penalty percentage ranges from 5% to 15%.

(b)   *Failure to submit a return or pay VAT by the due date (Default Surcharge)* – In these circumstances, HMRC issue a surcharge liability warning notice that prescribes a surcharge period extending over the next year. A further default during that period triggers an automatic surcharge of 2% of the VAT due. The surcharge period is then extended and the next default within that period attracts a surcharge of 5%. For each subsequent default within the surcharge period, the surcharge rises by 5% up to a maximum of 15%. A business will not normally be removed from the Default Surcharge regime until it has submitted a year's VAT returns on time and has discharged any liability arising from those returns on time.

(c) *Evasion involving dishonesty (civil evasion penalty)* – This incurs a penalty of up to 100% of the tax evaded, although HMRC can mitigate this penalty to such amount which they consider reasonable.

(d) *Regulatory breach* – Penalties are imposed for a breach of a regulatory requirement such as the requirement to produce documents on HMRC's demand. Such breaches are subject to a penalty of £5 per day, this is increased to £10 a day on the second breach and £15 a day for the third and any subsequent breaches within a two-year period. This is subject to a maximum penalty of 100 days and a minimum penalty of £50.

(e) *Failure to preserve records* – This is subject to a fixed penalty of £500.

(f) *Errors on VAT returns (for VAT periods prior to 1 April 2009):*

    (i) *Misdeclaration penalty.* For misdeclarations, a penalty will be incurred where a return is made understating liability to VAT or overstating repayment of VAT credit if the VAT which would have been lost (had the error not been discovered) equals or exceeds the lesser of £1 million and 30% of the 'Gross Amount of Tax' (GAT). GAT is the total amount of output tax plus input tax which should have been stated in the return for that period. If, however, the error arises as a result of HMRC issuing the taxpayer with an assessment which understates the VAT liability and this is not brought to HMRC attention within 30 days of the date of the assessment, the test is whether the tax which would have been lost equals or exceeds the lesser of £1 million and 30% of the 'True Amount of Tax' (TAT). TAT is the true output tax less input tax for the period in question.

    In both the above instances the penalty imposed is 15% of the tax which would have been lost if the inaccuracy had not been discovered.

    A person is not liable to a misdeclaration penalty if:

    (A) he is convicted of an offence or assessed to a penalty for tax evasion: conduct involving dishonesty; or

    (B) he has a reasonable excuse for the error; or

    (C) at the time when he had no reason to believe that HMRC were enquiring into his affairs, he furnished them with full information with respect to the inaccuracy concerned.

    Additionally, misdeclaration penalties are not normally imposed where:

    (1) the value of the error does not exceed £2,000 in a VAT period; or

    (2) the error is discovered in the period between the end of the VAT return quarter in question and the due date for the following return.

    (ii) *Repeated misdeclaration.* A misdeclaration which exceeds the lesser of 10% of the GAT and £500,000 is regarded as a 'material inaccuracy'. Where there is a material inaccuracy HMRC will issue a penalty liability notice to the taxpayer, if there are two or more further material inaccuracies in the eight periods following the issue of the notice, a penalty will arise. In such circumstances the penalty is charged in respect of the second and any subsequent material inaccuracies during the period of the notice.

The penalty for a repeated misdeclaration is 15% of the tax which would have been lost for the VAT accounting period in question if the inaccuracy had not been discovered.

(iii) *Default interest*. Simple interest at variable rates is charged on VAT which has been underdeclared or overclaimed. Interest is calculated from the date on which it should first have been paid to the date on which it is actually paid. It is chargeable even if penalties are also imposed. Where the tax underdeclared by one taxable person could be recoverable by another taxable person (known as commercial restitution) they may not seek to impose interest. This treatment is, however, discretionary.

(g) *Use of incorrect certificates* – A penalty equal to the tax undercharged is payable if a person to whom a supply is, or is to be, made gives a supplier an incorrect certificate showing that he qualifies for zero-rating or exemption.

(h) *Inaccuracies in ESLs* – If the information included on a minimum of three returns is materially misleading, and HMRC have issued timely warning notices to the taxpayer after the first and second offences, a penalty of £100 can arise if a third inaccurate ESL is submitted within two years of the issue of the second notice. After a penalty, the business must submit accurate returns for two years to set the 'penalty clock' back to the starting position.

(i) *Failure to submit ESLs* – Where an ESL is not received by HMRC by the due date and, following the issue by HMRC of a default notice, the business fails to submit the ESL within the next 14 days, a penalty becomes due. The first such default attracts a daily penalty of £5. Subsequent failures within the next year attract daily penalties of £5, £10 and £15 respectively for the first, second and third subsequent defaults. For each occasion of default, penalties are subject to a minimum of £50 and a maximum of 100 days.

Penalties may not be deducted in computing any profit or gain for direct tax purposes and are in addition to the amount of any assessment which HMRC may raise for any under-declaration of output tax or overclaim of input tax.

New penalty regime (which will replace the misdeclaration penalty and the civil evasion penalty) – All VAT returns submitted on or after 1 April 2009 will be subject to a new behaviour-based penalty regime. This new penalty system will fundamentally change the way misdeclaration penalties are determined. These penalties will apply to situations where VAT returns are submitted which understate the value of VAT due and will also apply in situations where HMRC have assessed the amount of VAT due and the taxpayer fails to inform HMRC that the amount is undervalued.

Under the old rules an error on a VAT return would be subject to a misdeclaration penalty of 15% of the potential loss to revenue if the error breached a prescribed arithmetic test. A penalty could be avoided however if a voluntary disclosure was made before the error was discovered by HMRC, and no penalty would be due if the error fell below certain de minimis limits.

The new penalty regime is now based on the behaviour of the taxpayer. If an error is discovered on a VAT return a penalty can be charged regardless of whether a voluntary disclosure is made or not. The amount of the penalty will be based on a percentage of the potential loss of revenue, the percentage being determined by the behaviour that led to the error occurring in the first place. Depending on the nature of the error and the level of disclosure from the taxpayer, the penalties can range from 0% to 100% of the potential loss of revenue.

There are four categories that a tax payer may fall within, which will determine the penalty factor that may be imposed.

(i)   An error is made despite the taxpayer taking reasonable care.

    (a)   In this case no penalty would be due.

(ii)   An error is made due to the taxpayer failing to take reasonable care.

    (a)   Here the taxpayer will face a penalty between 0 and 30% of the potential lost revenue.

    (b)   If an unprompted disclosure of the error is made to HMRC then the penalty will be between 0% and 30% of the potential lost revenue.

    (c)   If the error is only disclosed after the taxpayer is prompted to do so by HMRC then the penalty will be between 15% and 30% of the potential lost revenue.

(iii)   A deliberate error to understate VAT is made and the taxpayer makes no attempt to conceal this error.

    (a)   Here the taxpayer will face a penalty between 20% and 70% of the understated claimed VAT.

    (b)   If an unprompted disclosure of the error is made to HMRC then the penalty will be between 20% and 70% of the potential lost revenue.

    (c)   If the error is only disclosed after the taxpayer is prompted to do so by HMRC then the penalty will be between 35% and 70% of the potential lost revenue.

(iv)   A deliberate error to understate VAT is made and the taxpayer has made an attempt to conceal this error.

    (a)   Here the taxpayer will face a penalty between 30% and 100% of the potential lost revenue.

    (b)   If an unprompted disclosure of the error is made to HMRC then the penalty will be between 30% and 100% of the potential lost revenue.

    (c)   If the error is only disclosed after the taxpayer is prompted to do so by HMRC then the penalty will be between 50% and 100% of the potential lost revenue.

VAT and excise wrongdoing penalties

[10.36] From 1 April 2010 HMRC will apply wrongdoing penalties where a person:

(a)   issues an invoice that includes VAT which they are not entitled to charge;

(b)   handles goods on which Excise Duty has not been paid or deferred;

(c)   uses a product in a way that means more Excise Duty should have been paid;

(d)   supplies a product at a lower rate of Excise Duty knowing that it will be used in a way that means a higher rate of Excise Duty should be paid.

This penalty applies to anyone registered for VAT or excise, anyone who should be registered to pay VAT or excise duties and to other members of the general public.

Acquisitions from other EU Member States/importation

[10.37] Businesses purchasing goods from suppliers based in a different EU Member States are required to account for 'acquisition VAT'. This involves the customer accounting for output tax on the supply and where permitted input tax on the supply received. Where input tax on the supply is fully deductible accounting for acquisition VAT does not result in a VAT cost to the business.

Where a taxable person based in an EU Member State supplies delivered goods to non-VAT registered customers resident in another EU Member State, specific provisions known as 'distance selling' may apply. Under these rules if the value of the supplies made exceeds a prescribed threshold (which varies between countries) the following rules will apply:

(a)   the place of supply of the goods reverts to the customers country;

(b)   the supplier becomes liable to register for VAT in the country where the customer is based; and

(c)   the supplier is liable to account for VAT (at the appropriate rate) on any further sales made to non-VAT registered in that country.

For goods imported from outside the EU, VAT is due at the same rate as if the goods had been supplied in the UK. Any person, whether VAT registered or not, is liable to pay this VAT. VAT is also due on certain imported services.

There are special simplification rules in circumstances where businesses purchase goods in one EU Member State for direct delivery to customers in another EU Member State.

The European Union

[10.38] EU VAT legislation provides a framework for domestic VAT legislation in each EU Member State. The VAT legislation of each Member State must follow the principles laid down in EU legislation (most notably the Sixth VAT Directive). However, detailed interpretation can vary considerably across the EU Member States and in addition, individual EU Member States have the ability to derogate from certain parts of EU VAT legislation. As a result, although there is a degree of harmonisation across the EU, there is by no means a single unified VAT system.

A business which is VAT registered in an EU Member State may be able to recover UK VAT incurred in the course of its business in another EU

Member State by making an 8th Directive claim. These are made directly to the VAT authority in the country where the VAT was incurred. A number of conditions apply to 8th Directive claims, including the person making the claim must not have a liability to register for VAT in the country where the VAT was incurred.

Similarly, businesses established outside the EU may also claim recovery of UK VAT by making a 13th Directive claim. Once again these claims are subject to certain restrictions and cannot be made by a business which is liable to VAT registration in the relevant EU Member State.

All 8th Directive claims made on or after 1 January 2010 are required to be submitted to HMRC directly instead of the tax authorities in the country where the VAT was incurred. To facilitate this HMRC has introduced a new online system for all 8th Directive claims made on or after 1 January 2010.

Groups

[10.39] Two or more bodies corporate which are either established in the UK, or have a fixed establishment (ie a place of business) in the UK, and which are under common control may apply for a VAT group registration. The companies are then treated as a single entity for VAT purposes, trading through their representative member. This representative member submits a single VAT return accounting for all the VAT due on behalf of the VAT group although each member of the VAT group is jointly and severally liable for any VAT due. Any transactions between members of the group are disregarded for VAT purposes, although certain transactions between an overseas member of a group and a member in the UK are subject to a VAT charge.

Applications may be made for VAT grouping, de-grouping or changing the representative member and can be backdated by up to 30 days at HMRC's discretion. HMRC may refuse grouping or de-grouping where they consider it necessary for the protection of the revenue. In addition, where transfers of companies or assets into, or out of, a VAT group occur HMRC may direct the composition of the VAT group and/or the VAT liability of transactions between group members.

Where a VAT group acquires a business as a going-concern and the group is, or becomes partly exempt during the VAT (or longer) period in which the transfer takes place, the transfer may be treated as a self-supply and a restriction on input tax recovery could arise.

The advantages of VAT grouping may need to be balanced against the effect of including exempt or partly exempt companies within a group.

Small companies

[10.40] There are three measures available to ease the burden of accounting for VAT by small businesses. For these purposes a small business is defined by the level of its annual turnover (excluding VAT, exempt supplies and supplies of capital assets previously used in the business).

(a)   *Cash accounting* allows for VAT on both sales and purchases to be accounted for on a cash-paid basis and thus provides a measure of immediate relief for bad debts. A number of conditions must be met for a business to use cash accounting, in particular its use is not available to businesses with an annual turnover above £1,350,000 although if a business is on the scheme it can continue to operate cash accounting until its turnover reaches £1,600,000. Once this threshold is reached the business must revert to accounting for VAT on an invoice basis.

(b)   *Annual accounting* allows a business to account for VAT on an annual basis, instead of preparing quarterly returns. Under the scheme periodic payments totalling 90% of the liability for the current year, as estimated by HMRC, must be made by the business via direct debit. Any outstanding payment of VAT should then accompany an annual VAT return which must be submitted by the last day of the second month following the end of the accounting year. Any VAT reclaimable from HMRC as a result of an overpayment will be refunded at this time.

Annual accounting is not available to businesses with an annual turnover above £1,350,000. Once registered on the scheme businesses are required to leave the scheme if their turnover exceeds £1,600,000.

(c)   The *Flat Rate Scheme* allows businesses with an annual taxable turnover below £150,000 to calculate their VAT payments as a set percentage of their total taxable turnover. These percentages are provided by HMRC and are based on the type of business undertaken. Withdrawal from the scheme is compulsory when turnover in any twelve-month period exceeds £225,000, or turnover is expected to exceed £225,000 within the next 30 days alone.

Property

[10.41] The rules relating to property are detailed and complex. Briefly, the freehold sale of a commercial building or civil engineering work which is new or uncompleted is standard-rated. Most other grants of interests in, or rights over, commercial land and property are exempt. However, in certain circumstances the taxpayer has the right to opt to tax land or property and charge VAT at the standard rate on any future supplies of interest in that property. Subject to certain conditions these 'options' may be revoked within six months of being made. Once this initial period is over, however, options will remain irrevocable for 20 years.

The grant of a major interest (ie a freehold or a lease in excess of 21 years) in a new domestic dwelling, a new building intended for certain residential or charitable uses, or new dwellings arising from the conversion of previously commercial property may be zero-rated if made by the person constructing the building. All other grants of interests in non-commercial properties are exempt, without the taxpayer having the right to make an option as described above.

Appeals

[10.42] If any adverse ruling or assessment is received, it may be disputed by the taxpayer. A formal appeal must be made within 30 days of the ruling or assessment being issued. This period may be extended by agreement with HMRC.

Taxation of company cars

[10.43] Despite the upward trend in tax charges in recent years the company car may still be a benefit to employees when compared with the cost to them of obtaining a similar car themselves.

Higher paid employees, defined as those who receive remuneration, benefits and expenses at a rate exceeding £8,500 a year (pro-rated for part time workers), and all directors are taxable on the benefit of a car or van made available to them (or to members of their family or household) for private use. Private use for cars includes ordinary commuting travel from home to work; however, this does not apply to vans (see **10.47**). Individuals are taxed on the 'cash equivalent' of the benefit, determined in accordance with legislation.

Calculating the benefit

[10.44] Since 6 April 2002, the cash equivalent of a company car benefit is calculated by multiplying the list price of the vehicle by the 'appropriate percentage' determined with reference to the carbon dioxide (CO_2) emissions of that vehicle. With effect from April 2008, for cars which emit 120 grams (g) of CO_2 per kilometre of travel or less, the appropriate percentage will be 10%; therefore the taxable cash equivalent will be 10% of the list price of their vehicle.

For cars which emit above 120g of CO_2 per kilometre of travel, the appropriate percentage is based on published rates and rounded down to the nearest 5g of CO_2 per kilometre of travel. The cash equivalent will be between 15% (for cars which emit 135g/km of CO_2 or less) and 35% of the list price of the vehicle for the 2009/10 tax year. Each 5g increase in emissions will represent a 1% increase in the appropriate percentage. Some diesel cars will incur an additional 3% surcharge although the maximum applicable percentage will still be capped at 35%. These levels will remain the same for the 2009/10 tax year.

From 6 April 2010, the level of CO_2 emissions qualifying for the lower rate of 15% will be reduced by 5g to 130g and the levels for each 1% increment will similarly be reduced by 5g.

There are special rules for cars with certain fuels such as electric cars (9% flat rate), hybrid cars and bi-fuel cars.

From April 2011, the reductions currently given for electric/petrol hybrid cars and cars propelled by bi-fuels, road fuel gas and bio ethanol will be removed and the discount given for Euro IV standard diesel cars registered before

1 January 2006 will also be abolished. These amendments have the effect of changing the basis of how the appropriate percentage is determined from CO_2 emissions and fuel type, to CO_2 emissions alone.

The car benefit rules have been simplified for 2011/12 onwards.

From 6 April 2011:

(a)   there will be three letters to describe cars: E for electric only cars (as before), D for all diesels (previously types D and L) and A for all other types (previously types H, B, C, G and P);

(b)   there will no longer be any reductions for alternative fuels;

(c)   the diesel surcharge will apply to all diesels, whenever registered;

(d)   the £80,000 limit for the price of a car for car benefit purposes will no longer apply;

(e)   the lower threshold (the CO_2 emissions figure which sets the 15% rate) will be reduced from 130g/km to 125g/km;

(f)   the lowest appropriate percentage is 0% and applies to cars with CO_2 emissions of zero;

(g)   cars with CO_2 emissions of less than 75g/km have an appropriate percentage of 5%; and

(h)   cars with CO_2 emissions of 76g/km to 120g/km have an appropriate percentage of 10% and thereafter the rate is 15% increasing by 1% for every 5g/km to the current maximum of 35% (emissions of 225g/km and above).

The fuel benefit multiplier is increased from £18,000 to £18,800.

Green issues

[10.45] With effect from 6 April 1999, the Government removed the employee benefit tax charge on the following 'green' commuting benefits:

(a)   general subsidies paid directly to public transport bus services as long as employees are treated no more favourably than other members of the public and the service is available generally to employees of the employer (or each employer);

(b)   the provision of bicycles and cycling safety equipment as long as this is available to employees generally;

(c)   workplace parking for cars, bicycles and motorcycles; and

(d)   since April 2002, works buses (for one or more employers) with seating capacity of nine or more, as long as the bus is available generally to employees of the employer (or each employer).

Vouchers which may be provided in respect of any of these items will also be free of income tax and NIC.

Since April 2002 employees have not been able to claim capital allowances if they use their own bicycle for business travel, but they can obtain a tax-free mileage rate of 20p for business travel.

Rules permitting some employer-paid or employer-provided late-night office-to-home travel to not be treated as a taxable benefit have been extended to cover car-sharing arrangements, so that a tax charge will not arise if an employer pays for or provides the employee's home journey because the employee, due to unforeseen and exceptional circumstances, cannot get home in the shared car.

There is no requirement for employers to report a benefit in kind when a meal or refreshments are provided as an incentive to employees to participate in official cycle to work days.

Fuel

[10.46] Where a director or higher-paid employee (as defined in **10.43** above) has a car made available and fuel is provided for private use, the cash equivalent of this additional fuel benefit is chargeable to income tax.

For years prior to 2003/04, the cash equivalent was a 'scale charge' determined by the engine size and type of fuel of the relevant car. From 2003/04 the benefit is calculated with reference to the appropriate percentage of an annual fuel figure set by the Government. The appropriate percentage is the same as for the car benefit calculation. The annual figure is £18,000 for 2010/11. The fuel benefit multiplier is increased from £18,000 to £18,800 in 2011.

The fuel charge is an 'all or nothing' charge, ie there is no provision for increasing or decreasing the fuel benefit charge based on the degree of private mileage travelled; however it is possible to pro-rate the benefit if the provision of private fuel begins or ends during the tax year. The fuel benefit charge does not apply where a full reimbursement of private fuel costs is made and is required to be made, or where private fuel is not provided.

Vans

[10.47] A van for these purposes is a goods vehicle with a maximum design weight of up to 3,500kg. Goods vehicles in excess of this weight are designated by HMRC as Heavy Goods Vehicles and private use does not constitute a benefit in kind since these vehicles are not typically provided for private use.

From 6 April 2005 there have been significant changes to the company van benefit charge.

Prior to 6 April 2005 a van benefit charge was incurred if the van was made available for any private use including home-to-work commuting. After this date, if the private use of the van is restricted to home-to-work commuting no taxable benefit occurs; however, if there is additional private usage beyond home-to-work commuting a fixed scale rate charge of £3,000 will apply regardless of the age of the van. In addition, if fuel is provided for this unrestricted private use, an additional charge of £550 will apply. If all private fuel costs are reimbursed and required to be reimbursed by the employee this £550 fuel charge will no longer apply.

Vehicle design weight	Under 4 years old £	4 years old or more £

Up to 3.5 tonnes	3,000	3,000
Over 3.5 tonnes	–	–

National Insurance

[10.48] From 6 April 1991, employers have been liable to pay Class 1A National Insurance contributions on cars and fuel provided for the private use of directors or employees earning over £8,500 per annum. (See **10.64** below for further details).

Summary

[10.49] Cars remain a popular benefit for employees. Despite the increased tax charge, for many employees it is still more cost effective to have a company car than to provide a similar car personally out of taxed income. It is likely, however, to be advantageous for the employee with low private mileage to pay for his own private fuel. Many employers consider offering cash alternatives to the company car, not only for tax reasons, but also, for example, to reduce the burden of administering the company car fleet.

The current tax regime outlined above was intended by Government to remove any incentive for unnecessary business miles, to encourage employees to choose more fuel efficient cars and to encourage manufacturers to produce cars with lower CO_2 emissions.

PAYE administration

Duties

[10.50] Pay As You Earn (PAYE) is a tax collection system which requires an employer to calculate the income tax and NIC due from their employees in respect of their pay and certain benefits, to deduct this tax and NICs from gross payments made to the employees and to account for it and pay it over to HMRC. Failure by an employer to observe this duty to operate PAYE, even where specific instructions have not been received from HMRC, is likely to result in a liability for the tax and NICs that should have been withheld, with no automatic recourse to the employee, plus interest and possibly penalties. It is the employer's duty to determine whether an individual, whom they are paying, is an employee. If in any doubt they should contact their own PAYE district.

Records

[10.51] It is the duty of every employer to keep adequate records of his operation of the PAYE system for at least three years. These are liable to inspection by HMRC at any time.

Documents needed to operate a PAYE system

[10.52] Useful tables and guides published by HMRC in relation to PAYE are:

Table A   Pay adjustment
Tables LR and B–D   Taxable pay
Expenses and Benefits   A Tax Guide (480)
Day-to-day payroll (E
13)

Employer Further
Guide to PAYE and
NICs (CWG 2)

NI, SMP and SSP tables CA 35/36,
CA 38, CA 39,
CA 40, CA 43
What to do if your employee is sick (E 14)
National Insurance for Company Directors
(CA 44)

The basic forms required are:

P9D	Return of expenses and benefits paid to certain employees
P11	Deductions working sheet
P11D	Return of expense payments and benefits etc not covered by a dispensation for directors and employees earning at a rate of £8,500 a year or more. (For convenience, such employees are subsequently referred to as 'higher paid employees'.)
P11D(b)	Expenses and benefits statements: declaration and Class 1A NIC declaration
P14/60	Employee end of year return
P35	Employer's annual statement, declaration and certificate
P45	Details of employee leaving
P46	New employee certificate
P46(car)	Notification of a car provided for private use of an employee or director

New business

[10.53] A new employer must contact HMRC's 'New Employer' Helpline as soon as possible, in order to register with HMRC and receive all the necessary documentation.

Regular payroll

[10.54] It is the employer's duty to operate PAYE from the first instalment of pay. Whether a manual or computerised system is operated, the employer must follow the same basic steps and keep equivalent records. For each employee these steps are as follows:

(a)   Calculate the PAYE taxation by reference to PAYE Table A and Tables LR and B–D.

(b)   Calculate the National Insurance (NI) contributions due by reference to the NI Tables A–C for those who are not contracted-out and Tables C–G and S for those in contracted-out employment.

(c)   Calculate the amount of Statutory Sick Pay (SSP) and Statutory Maternity Pay (SMP) due by reference to CA 35/36.

(d)   Record these calculations on a deductions working sheet (P11) or equivalent.

(e)   Pay the employee's net pay and retain the total PAYE and NI less the permitted element of any SSP and SMP (see below).

(f)   By the 19th (22nd for electronic payments) of the following PAYE month pay to the Collector of Taxes the total PAYE and NI less SSP and SMP, using the paying-in booklet or by electronic means.

The Percentage Threshold Scheme (PTS) restricts the amount of SSP that employers can recover from the Government. Where the SSP payable in a month exceeds 13% of the total NI liability for that month the employer can recover the SSP, to the value of the excess over 13%, by reducing the monthly NI payment. If the SSP is 13% of the NI liability, or less, no SSP can be recovered.

The employer may recover either 104.5% of SMP paid if their annual Class 1 liability is £45,000 or less, or 92% of SMP paid if their annual Class 1 liability is more than £45,000.

New employees

[10.55] If a new employee produces or can obtain parts 2 and 3 of a new form P45 from his previous employer, this should be used to prepare a deductions working sheet for recording PAYE. Part 2 should be kept with the company's records; part 3 should be sent to the tax office immediately. The employee should keep part 1A for his own records. If the employer has 50 or more employees, part 3 of the form must be filed online. Online filing is mandatory for all employers from 6 April 2011.

If the employee cannot produce a form P45, a form P46 should be completed and the appropriate declaration signed. Dependent on whether statement A, B or C has been signed, tax should be deducted at basic rate or the appropriate emergency tax coding may be allocated on either a cumulative or non-cumulative basis and the form sent to the tax office. The P46 should be filed online for employers with 50 or more employees. Online filing is mandatory for all employers from 6 April 2011.

Employees leaving

[10.56] When an employee leaves his employment, a four part form P45 must be completed from the details recorded on his deductions working sheet. Part 1 must be sent immediately to the tax office and parts 1A, 2 and 3 should be given to the ex-employee. If a lump sum termination payment is being made, or if there is to be some other special arrangement, further advice should be sought. Part 1 should be filed online for employers with more than 50 employees. Online filing is mandatory for all employers from 6 April 2011.

Year-end procedures

[10.57] Following and as at 5 April each year the employer must:

(a)   complete a three-part form P14/60 for each employee, or magnetic tape equivalent;

(b)   complete a form P35 (P35MT), or substitute, for the employer;

(c)   pay by 19 April the balance of the PAYE and NI shown by the P35;

(d)   complete a form P11D for directors and 'higher-paid' employees recording all benefits and expenses provided to or paid on behalf of employees, and which are not covered by a dispensation from HMRC. From the tax year 1996/97, employers must attribute values to benefits on the P11Ds and provide employees with a copy of the information declared on their forms P11D;

(e)   complete a form P9D for all employees earning at a rate of less than £8,500 per year who receive certain types of benefits;

(f)   complete a form P11D(b) in respect of all the forms P11D;

(g)   give the P60 to each employee by 31 May following the tax year;

(h)   send the P14s and the P35 to their tax office by 19 May. Penalties will apply if these forms do not reach HMRC on or before this date;

(i)   send the P11Ds, the P9Ds and the P11D(b) to their tax office. The deadline for submission of these returns is 6 July following the end of the tax year by which date the employer must also have supplied the employee with a copy of the information on his form P11D or P9D, as appropriate; and

(j)   in preparation for the new tax year, change any employee who is on week 1/month 1 basis to a cumulative basis.

In addition to the above, the employer may choose to pay a lump sum of tax and NIC to HMRC in accordance with a PAYE settlement agreement (PSA). This payment replaces tax which the employees would otherwise have to pay themselves on benefits which HMRC regard as minor, irregular, or where it is impracticable to operate PAYE. The PSA should be agreed in advance with HMRC or in any case by 6 July following the end of the tax year concerned, and the tax ad NICs paid by 19 October following.

Employer Compliance Reviews

[10.58] Following a period of reorganisation and the publication of the 2006 Review of Links with Large Business, HMRC have now adopted a risk-based approach to Employer Compliance. This involves HMRC concentrating on those areas they perceive there to be particular risk. HMRC's Large Business Service (LBS) section have been using the risk-based approach for some years and it is intended that a customer relationship manager (CRM) will work closely with each business to ensure good ongoing compliance. LBS is sector-based and the risks LBS identify in one business will also be included in their review of other businesses in the same sector.

For those employers not dealt with by LBS, they will come under the remit of Local Compliance, which is split broadly into three areas according to the size of a business: Large & Complex, Small & Medium Enterprises (SMEi), and Individuals.

Employers falling into the latter two categories are unlikely to see any major changes in respect of employer compliance in the short term. Businesses considered to be Large & Complex (ie those with turnovers in excess of £30 million, complex structures and/or more than 250 employees) will be risk-assessed. The initial risk assessment may involve a desktop exercise and not involve the employer. However, the result will be shared with the employer. The larger employers in this category (ie turnover in excess of £200 million) will be appointed with a CRM. Businesses identified as 'low risk' will receive fewer HMRC interventions unless particular risks or issues arise. Businesses assessed as being 'not low risk' will receive increased attention from HMRC until they are able to demonstrate continued compliance and move towards a 'low risk' assessment.

Previously, Employer Compliance Reviews would have involved the inspection of pay, expense and benefit records. Under the risk-based approach HMRC will expect a business to be able to demonstrate systems, controls and procedures that are robust and fully compliant. On this basis large numbers of records should not be reviewed as part of an Employer Compliance Reviews

Personal Service Companies

[10.59] Where an individual provides personal services to a client through an intermediary (for example, a partnership, company or agency) and the worker is under a client's supervision, direction or control (such that he would actually be deemed to be an employee other than for the fact that the intermediary exists), the provisions of Part 2, Chapter 8 of ITEPA 2003 (also known as IR35) apply.

Under these provisions, the intermediary must account for PAYE/NIC on any income from 'relevant engagements' (ie those engagements where the individual is deemed to be an employee of the client) less any expenses incurred wholly, exclusively and necessarily by the individual in the performance of his services and a 5% flat rate deduction to cover administrative expenses of the intermediary. This PAYE/NIC must be accounted for regardless of whether the intermediary actually pays a salary to the individual.

Casual labour

[10.60] An employer paying £1 a week or more to any employee must deduct income tax at the basic rate from the full payment unless the employee has signed form P46 certifying that he or she has no other employment, in which case tax should be deducted using the current emergency code.

If the casual worker is employed for one week or less, form P46 does not need to be completed, although full details of the individual's name and address should be kept. Tax should be deducted by reference to the current emergency code unless the employee is known to have other employment. In that instance, tax at the basic rate must be deducted from the full payment. HMRC apply this procedure rigorously and may assess employers to tax and where appropriate National Insurance contributions, possibly on the grossed-up amount of such payments.

Settlement

[**10.61**] Most compliance and reviews reveal some discrepancies and HMRC will often calculate the tax and National Insurance contributions which have been 'lost' by extrapolating the results of a review covering a limited period. A new penalty regime was introduced for reporting periods from 2009/10 onwards. The period HMRC may look at is now dependent on whether there is a careless or deliberate error leading to a loss of tax. Penalties may also be sought, but may be partially mitigated according to whether an inaccuracy is careless, deliberate and/or concealed, whether unprompted disclosure is made and whether reasonable care was taken to prevent the error.

National Insurance

[**10.62**] Class 1 National Insurance expressed in its simplest form, is a deduction made from gross earnings in relation to a specific earnings period(s). Collection is normally made via the PAYE system.

A change in the way in which NICs for members of Contracted Out Money Purchase (COMP) schemes are worked out, recorded and reported took effect from 6 April 1997. New Contribution Table letters F, G and S were introduced to take account of these changes.

Rates

[**10.63**] The rates of National Insurance contributions are reviewed annually and are currently:

2011/12
Employer

Weekly Earnings	*Not Contracted Out (on all earnings)*	*Contracted Out Salary Related Schemes*	*Contracted Out Money Purchase Schemes*
Class 1 — Employers			
Up to £136	0%	0%	0%
£136–£817	13.8%	13.8% (Note 1)	13.8% (Note 2)

Employee (Note 3)	*Not Contracted Out*	*Contracted Out*
Up to £139	0%	0%
Balance up to £817	12%	10.4%
Over £817	2%	2%

Note 1: 3.7% rebate applies between £102 and £136 for salary related schemes.

Note 2: 1.4% rebate applies between £102 and £136 for money purchase schemes.

Note 3: Men aged 65 or over, and women aged 60 or over do not pay employees' contributions. Employer's contributions are however still payable. 1.6% rebate applies to contracted out schemes between £102 and £139.

Liability to National Insurance

[10.64] In calculating an employee's liability to National Insurance (NI), it is gross remuneration which is considered earnings. For this purpose, it is normally cash payments which are considered; in general, benefits in kind are excluded. However, anti-avoidance legislation has been introduced to bring certain non-cash payments into the charge for NI, for example, gold, diamonds, unit trusts and gilts and other readily convertible assets.

Where an employer meets an element of personal debt for the employee, the payment creates a liability for NI. In general, if the contract for supply of goods or services is between the employer and the provider then no Class 1 NI liability arises.

With effect from 6 April 2000 employers have been required to pay Class 1A NICs in relation tor taxable benefits provided to employees and most directors who are paid a rate of £8,500 a year, including taxable benefits and expenses, with some limited exceptions.

The main difference between 'earnings' for NI purposes and 'pay' and 'benefits in kind' for income tax purposes is that 'earnings' includes all cash payments from employment such as commission, fees, bonuses and cash payments in lieu of 'payments in kind' but certain payments are specifically excluded from 'earnings' for NI purposes.

These include:

(a)   reimbursed receipted business expenses;

(b)   any genuine redundancy or non-contractual compensatory payment; and

(c)   certain payments in kind (although note the extension of the Class 1A charge above). These may include the use of employer-owned or leased assets (such as houses or furniture), expenses contracted for and paid for by the employer, such as season tickets or medical insurance (BUPA) and paid for by the employer.

Employers are able to take account of all HMRC 'dispensations' in deciding whether NI should be paid on expense payments to employees.

Self assessment

[10.65] Self assessment gives people more responsibility and control over their tax affairs and imposes on employers a number of information requirements. The requirement for taxpayers to submit returns and self-assess their income tax liabilities affects mainly:

(a)   self-employed people;

(b)   business partners;

(c)   company directors; and

(d)   employees who pay tax at the higher rate.

The due date for paper returns is 31 October following the end of the tax year and 31 January following the end of the tax year for electronic returns.

To enable employees to comply with the tax return requirements, employers should, as noted at **10.57** above, provide the employees, by 31 May following the tax year, details of pay and tax deducted on form P60. In addition, the employer should evaluate benefits in kind provided to the employees, report these on forms P11D (or substitute) and provide a copy to the employees by 6 July following the end of the tax year. The employer is also responsible for providing similar information in respect of benefits the employer had arranged or facilitated from third parties.

The current penalty regime covers the late or incorrect submission of these documents.

Chapter 11

Commercial Considerations

Corporate capacity

Ultra vires

[11.1] Sections 39–47 of the Companies Act 2006 (CA 2006) contain a series of provisions dealing with the capacity of the company and the related issue of the authority of the board of directors to bind the company in relation to contracts made by the company with third parties.

The doctrine of *ultra vires*, as it was developed from the decision of the House of Lords in the case of *Ashbury Railway Carriage & Iron Company Ltd v Riche* (1875) LR 7 HL 653, dictated that a company may only do such acts as were specified in its memorandum of association and any act outside those objects was *ultra vires* and therefore void. This led to the practice of giving the company a comprehensive list of objects, stating that each was to be treated as a separate and independent object of the company by means of an independent objects clause, the effectiveness of which has been recognised by the House of Lords in the case of *Cotman v Brougham* [1918] AC 514. In order to further widen the capacity of the company the memorandum may include a subjective objects clause which would allow the company to carry on any other trade or business which, in the opinion of the directors, could be advantageously carried on in connection with, or ancillary to, the main business of the company. The doctrine was substantially modified by section 9 of the European Communities Act 1972, subsequently re-enacted as CA 1985, s 35, in relation to third parties dealing with the company in good faith.

Section 39 of CA 2006 distinguishes between the company's capacity and the powers of the directors to bind it. This provision abolishes the application of the doctrine of *ultra vires* to third parties, but retaining it in relation to the internal operation of the company, by allowing the members to bring proceedings to restrain an *ultra vires* act by the directors or to hold directors personally liable for the committing of the company to *ultra vires* acts.

The legislation covers the following points:

(a) the capacity of the company to enter into transactions;
(b) the drafting of the company's constitution so as to widen its capacity;
(c) the powers of the directors to bind the company;
(d) the ability of the members of the company to restrain an *ultra vires* act;
(e) the protection of third parties entering into contracts; and
(f) the ability of the members to ratify an *ultra vires* act.

The provisions of CA 2006 relating to corporate capacity were implemented on 1 October 2009, except section 44 of the Act which came into effect from 6 April 2008.

Capacity of the company in contracts

[11.2] Section 39 of CA 2006 provides that:

'(1)   The validity of an act done by a company shall not be called into question on the ground of lack of capacity by reason of anything in the company's memorandum.'

Thus, any transaction entered into by a company will be valid and enforceable by the company and by third parties involved in the transaction. However, where a company intends to enter into a transaction which is beyond its capacity, any member may bring proceedings to restrain the *ultra vires* act.

It remains the duty of the directors to observe any limitations on their powers flowing from the company's memorandum of association, and therefore the authority of the directors to bind the company continues to be restricted by the objects clause. However, any acts carried out by the directors which would have been *ultra vires* the company, but for CA 2006, s 39(1), may be ratified by a special resolution passed by the members of the company.

The form of company contracts

[11.3] Section 43 of CA 2006 provides that a contract may be made either:

(a)   by a company, by writing under its common seal; or
(b)   on behalf of a company, by any person acting under its authority, express or implied.

Any formalities required by law in the case of a contract made by an individual also apply to a contract made by or on behalf of a company.

Further provisions apply where a private company having only one member, who is also a director of the company, enters into contracts with that member (see **6.45 THE DIRECTORS**).

Sealing of documents

[11.4] Section 44 of CA 2006 provides that a document is executed by a company by the affixing of its common seal, but also goes on to state that a company need not have a common seal (see **1.14 THE COMPANY SECRETARY**).

The right to use the seal for the purposes of its business is usually vested in the directors. Article 81 of the PLC Model Articles/regulation 101 of Table A 1985 provides that the seal shall only be used by the authority of the directors or of a committee of the directors authorised by the directors. The article further provides that the directors may determine who shall sign any instrument to which the seal is affixed and unless they determine otherwise, it shall be signed by a director and the secretary or a second director.

Whether or not a company has a common seal, a document signed by a director and the secretary of a company, or by two directors, and expressed to be executed on behalf of the company has the same effect as if it were executed under the common seal. A document executed by a company which makes it clear on its face that it is intended to be a deed has effect upon delivery, as a deed, and unless a contrary intention is proved, it is presumed to be delivered upon its execution. In favour of a *bona fide* purchaser for valuable consideration, a document is deemed to have been duly executed by a company if it purports to be signed by either two directors or a director and the secretary. It will be valid as a deed, and will be delivered upon execution, that is to say, the signatories bind the company when they sign.

The Foreign Companies (Execution of Documents) Regulations 1994 (SI 1994/950) allow any foreign company to execute a document either by affixing its common seal or by any method valid under its own domestic law. The application of any English company law requirement relating to the execution of deeds by foreign companies need not be considered.

Power of directors to bind the company

[**11.5**] In relation to dealings by a third party with officers of the company, CA 2006, s 40(1) provides that:

> 'In favour of a person dealing with a company in good faith, the power of the board of directors to bind the company, or authorise others to do so, shall be deemed to be free of any limitation under the company's constitution.'

Under earlier companies' legislation a person was only protected in respect of 'transactions decided upon by the directors'. A person is now defined as dealing with a company if he is a party to any transaction or other act to which the company is a party. A person shall not be regarded as acting in bad faith by reason only of his knowing that an act is beyond the powers of the directors and shall be presumed to be acting in good faith unless the contrary is proved.

The protection from lack of authority derived from any limitation under the company's constitution is thus now wider than available previously and will include limitations deriving from a resolution of the company in general meeting or from any agreement between the members of the company.

The directors may not, however, use CA 2006, s 40 to enforce a contract against a third party unless the transaction has first been ratified by the company.

Transactions with directors

[**11.6**] Different rules apply when one of the parties to the transaction is a director of the company, its holding company or a person connected with them, and the board of directors exceeds any limitation on its powers under the company's constitution. In such cases the transaction is voidable by the company (CA 2006, s 41(2)). Whether or not it is avoided, the director who is a party to the transaction and any director of the company who authorised it, is liable to account for any gain to the company and to indemnify it against any loss suffered.

The transaction ceases to be voidable (CA 2006, s 41(3)) if:

(a) restitution of any money or other asset, being the subject matter of the transaction is no longer possible;

(b)   the company is indemnified for any loss or damage resulting from the transaction;

(c)   rights acquired bona fide for value and without actual notice of the directors exceeding their powers by a person who is not party to the transaction would be affected by the avoidance; or

(d)   the transaction is affirmed by the company.

A person who is not a director of the company but is connected with them is not liable if he can show that at the time the transaction was entered into he did not know that the directors were exceeding their powers.

Section 41 of CA 2006 is intended to prevent a director acting fraudulently by misusing his power to bind the company to a transaction from which he will benefit.

Constructive notice

[11.7] Section 40(2) of CA 2006 makes it clear that a party to a transaction with a company is not bound to enquire as to whether the company is permitted by its memorandum of association to enter into the transaction, or as to any limitation on the power of the board of directors to bind the company or authorise others to do so.

Under the doctrine of constructive notice a person is deemed to have notice of the details disclosed in any document kept at Companies House or made available for inspection by the company. However, CA 1985, s 711A(1) effectively abolished this doctrine in that a person shall not be taken to have notice of any matter merely because it has been disclosed in any document kept by Companies House, and is thus available for inspection, or has been made available by the company for inspection. The documents to which this section applied include annual returns, notifications of appointments and not just constitutional documents.

It was expressly stated in CA 1985, s 711A(2) that this does not impact upon the question of whether a person is affected by notice of any matter by reason of a failure to make such enquiries as reasonably ought to be made.

Notice of what is on the public file is, therefore, relevant to someone who has actually read it or in the circumstances ought to have done so. The question of when enquiries reasonably ought to have been made is one which the courts will have to settle. However, CA 2006, s 40(2) gives an exemption in relation to the question of the capacity of the company or the authority of the directors, as it states that there is no duty to enquire whether the transaction is permitted or as to any limitation on the power of the board to bind the company.

Powers of attorney

[11.8] Section 47 of CA 2006 gives a specific power to appoint attorneys to execute deeds on a company's behalf outside the United Kingdom. The appointment must be under seal (see **11.4** above) and the power of attorney may be either general or for a specific purpose.

Preliminary contracts

[11.9] A limited company only comes into existence on the issue of a certificate of incorporation by the Registrar of Companies. If a person purporting to act for a company, or as agent for it, enters into a contract or deed for, or on behalf of, a company at a time when that company has not been legally constituted, then, subject to any agreement to the contrary, the contract takes effect as one made by the person acting for the company or as agent for it and he is personally liable accordingly (CA 2006, s 51(1)).

Provisional contracts

[11.10] If a public company enters into a contract before the issue of a certificate to commence business (see **2.42 THE COMPANY CONSTITUTION**), and fails to comply with its obligation to obtain a certificate within 21 days of being called upon to do so, the directors of the company are jointly and severally liable to indemnify the other party to the transaction in respect of any loss or damage suffered by him by reason of the failure to comply (CA 2006, s 767(3)).

The contract remains valid and enforceable.

Personal liability of the officers of the company

[11.11] If any officer of the company or any person acting on its behalf signs, or authorises the signature, on behalf of the company any negotiable instrument or order for money or goods in which the name of the company is not mentioned in full, he is personally liable to the holder of the negotiable instrument or order for the amount of it if it is not paid by the company. In particular, the words 'limited' or 'public limited company' must not be omitted. 'The holder' is construed to mean, in the case of an order for money or goods, the person to whom the order is addressed.

Care must also be taken to ensure that the person who signs an agreement for the company clearly does so 'for and on behalf of the company' thereby establishing himself as an agent for the company, in order to avoid any personal liability. This is particularly important in the case of negotiable instruments because the agent will only be free from personal liability as far as persons who do not know of his representative capacity are concerned, if the intention to sign as an agent is stated on the instrument or is otherwise implied. Section 26 of the Bills of Exchange Act 1882 provides:

> 'Where a person signs a bill as drawer, indorser or acceptor and adds words to his signature indicating that he signs for or on behalf of a principal, or in representative character, he is not personally liable thereon; but the mere addition to his signature of words describing him as an agent, or as filling a representative character, does not exempt him from personal liability.'

Authority of directors to act on behalf of the company

[11.12] The articles of association generally define the powers of the directors. Express authority is given to the board of directors to exercise all the powers of the company subject to the provisions of CA 2006 and the articles (article 3 of the PLC Model Articles/regulation 70 of Table A 1985). The articles may also allow the delegation of the directors' powers to committees, managers, managing directors or other persons. Such delegation may be expressly given or by implication. The directors can be held liable for breach of duty if they exceed their powers (see **6.46 THE DIRECTORS**).

Criminal liability

[11.13] Where the entering into a transaction by the company gives rise to a criminal liability, questions arise as to whether the officer of the company is personally responsible or whether the company is vicariously liable for the act of its agent (see **14.34 EMPLOYMENT, HEALTH AND SAFETY**). It is a question of law whether, once the facts have been established, a person doing a particular thing is to be regarded as the company or merely as the company's servant or agent.

The Bribery Act 2010 received Royal Assent on 8 April 2010. It finally came into force on 1 July 2011 after an initial delay by the Ministry of Justice to allow further consultation on its principles and impact on UK business. It describes a number of circumstances in which a person will be found guilty of an offence under the Act and the conditions applicable to each of six cases set out on the Act. Section 3(2) defines the following functions and activities as falling within the remit of the Act:

(a)   any function of a public nature;
(b)   any activity connected with a business;
(c)   any activity performed in the course of a person's employment; and
(d)   any activity performed by or on behalf of a body of persons (whether corporate or unincorporate).

Section 5 of the Act also cites an 'expectation test' which states that ' . . . the test of what is expected is a test of what a reasonable person in the United Kingdom would expect in relation to the performance of the type of function or activity concerned.'

The Ministry of Justice has published guidance around the six principles established in the Bribery Act 2010 for bribery prevention to support a commercial organisation in implementing its provisions:

(i)   *Risk assessment* – knowing and keeping up to date with the bribery risks faced in the organisation's business sector and market.
(ii)   *Top level commitment* – establishing a culture across the organisation in which bribery is unacceptable, with clear, unambiguous and regular communication to all staff and business partners.
(iii)   *Due diligence* – knowing who the organisation does business with, knowing why, when and to whom the organisation is releasing funds and seeking reciprocal anti-bribery agreements, and being in a position to feel confident that business relationships are transparent and ethical.

(iv)   *Clear, practical and accessible policies and procedures* – applying to all staff and business partners under the organisation's effective control and covering all risks, such as political and charitable donations, gifts and hospitality, promotional expenses, and responding to demands for facilitation expenses or when an allegation of bribery comes to light.

(v)   *Effective implementation* – embedding anti-bribery in the organisation's internal controls, recruitment and remuneration policies, operations, communications and training on practical business issues.

(vi)   *Monitoring and review* – auditing and ensuring that financial controls that are sensitive to bribery are transparent, policies and procedures are regularly reviewed, and considering whether external verification would help.

The failure of a commercial organisation, such as a company, to prevent bribery may result in the organisation being guilty of an offence, although it is a defence if the company can prove it had adequate procedures in place designed to prevent the occurrence of such an event. An individual guilty of an offence is liable to imprisonment, a fine or both. On summary conviction, this can mean a prison term not exceeding 12 months and/or a fine not exceeding the statutory maximum, while on conviction on indictment, this is a term not exceeding 10 years and/or an unlimited fine.

While the Act sets out a number of defences for an individual, these are not generally available to an individual working for a commercial organisation.

Retention of company records

[11.14] A company's records need to be retained for various statutory reasons. Accordingly, it will frequently fall to the secretary of a company to draw up a policy for the retention of records and documents relating to the company's affairs.

In the majority of cases, legislation makes no specific reference to the length of time a particular record should be retained. In view of the increasing number of records required to be produced by a company in fulfilment of its statutory obligations and the availability of storage space, it is clear that any policy on retention of documents should ensure that records are retained for the shortest possible time.

In order to comply with CA 2006, s 388, the accounting records of a company (including all subsidiary records) must be preserved for a period of three years from the date when they were made in the case of a private company, and six years in the case of a public company. They must be kept at the registered office of the company or such other place as the directors think fit.

The length of retention is subject to any provision contained in rules made under section 411 of the Insolvency Act 1986. In addition, a company must ensure it also complies with other statutory requirements, such as those contained within the Taxes Management Act 1970, Limitation Act 1980, Value Added Tax Act 1994, and PAYE Regulations.

It is therefore desirable to comply with the other statutory requirements that accounting records should be retained for at least six years even by a private company (see **3.35** THE STATUTORY RECORDS).

All company records relating to the registration of the company, the company's constitution, meetings of the company and resolutions passed, should be retained for the life of the company. Minute books containing the minutes of proceedings of any general meetings of a company must be kept at the registered office of the company (CA 2006, s 358).

In a few cases, CA 2006 lays down a specific period of retention for certain documents as follows:

(a) A copy of any contract for purchase of own shares must be kept at the registered office of the company for a period of *ten years* from the date on which the purchase of all shares in pursuance of the contract is completed (CA 2006, s 702(3)).

(b) A report on interests in voting shares following investigation on requisition by the members, must be kept at the registered office for a period of *six years* from the day when it is first available, beginning with the day following that day (CA 2006, s 805(4)).

(c) A register of interests in shares of a public company must be kept for a period of *six years* after the company ceases to be a public company (CA 2006, s 819).

(d) An entry in the register of members relating to a former member of the company may be removed from the register after the expiration of *ten years* from the date on which he ceased to be a member (CA 2006, s 121)).

Some further suggested periods for retention of documents are contained in APPENDIX 11A to this chapter.

Patents, trade marks, copyright and designs

Patents

[11.15] An inventor wishing to protect his invention from being exploited by someone else without his consent can do so by acquiring a patent for the invention. In the UK the governing law for the application and enforcement of patents is the Patent Act 1977, as amended by the Patents Act 2004. The Patent Rules 2007 (SI 2007/3291) set out the detailed procedures and have recently been amended by the Patents, Trade Marks and Designs (Address for Service) Rules 2009 (SI 2009/546).

All UK patents last for 20 years from the date when the patent is filed. To keep a patent in force for the full 20 years, it is necessary that annual renewal fees are paid from the fourth anniversary of the date of filing. The patent gives the owner (the 'patentee') an exclusive right to the manufacture, use, or sale of the invention within the country or countries for which the patent has been granted.

To be patentable an invention must be concerned with the composition, construction or manufacture of something concerned with an industrial process or an article or apparatus of practical use. The invention must be new and not obvious to a person of ordinary skill experienced in the area in which the invention operates. If some other party exploits the invention without the patentee's consent, the patentee has the right to take legal action to prevent such exploitation. The patentee can licence another person or company to exploit the invention in return for royalties, or alternatively the patent can be sold outright by assignment. Note that the patentee himself may require a licence to work his own invention if a third party has a patent which covers his product.

It is not necessary to have a patent in order to put an invention into practice but, if an application is not made, somebody else subsequently making the same invention may be able to obtain a patent for it if the invention has been kept secret in the meantime. If the inventor decides to apply for a patent he must not publicly disclose the invention before filing an application, as this would prevent the grant of a patent or cause its subsequent withdrawal.

The method of application for a patent depends on where the inventor wishes to exploit his invention. If there is no intention of expanding into overseas markets, it is cheaper and simpler to file a national UK patent application. However, if the inventor is also seeking protection abroad, he can either apply for a patent under the European Patent Convention (EPC) or under the Patent Co-operation Treaty (PCT). In both cases the patent can be valid in the UK and, additionally, for certain other designated European or worldwide countries respectively. Further separate national filings may be required for protection in states which are not parties to these treaties. However, a UK application will usually be filed first, followed by any foreign applications being made up to twelve months later, based on the first UK application.

Obtaining a patent can be complex and the consequences of error serious. It is advisable to seek the advice of a registered patent agent who can perform the work involved in preparing, filing and processing an application. However, under the Copyright, Designs, and Patents Act 1988 (CDPA 1988), it is no longer the sole right of patent agents and solicitors to apply for or obtain patents on behalf of others.

Trade marks

[**11.16**] A trade mark is a means of identification. It is a symbol which a person can use to his benefit in the course of trade by distinguishing his own goods from similar goods of other traders. To achieve this, the trade mark must be distinctive in itself – in effect, the mark should be separately identifiable from the appearance or form of the goods to which it relates.

Registration of trade marks is not compulsory in the UK and it is not possible to register a trade mark in all cases (for example, where the mark is descriptive or too similar to known marks). Clearly, since registration confers a statutory monopoly, it would not be right to allow the registration of marks which are identical or are able to be confused with words or symbols (whether or not used as trade marks) which other traders in the goods or services are free to use in the ordinary course of business. The benefit of registration of a trade mark is that it confers a statutory monopoly in the use of that mark when related to the goods for which it is registered and the registered owner has the right to sue in the courts for infringement of the mark. The same considerations apply to service marks which may be used to distinguish the providers of certain services.

The Trade Marks Act 1994 (TMA 1994) regulates the application and registration of trade marks in the UK.

A trade mark is defined as 'any sign capable of being represented graphically which is capable of distinguishing goods or services of one undertaking from those of other undertakings' (TMA 1994, s 1).

Thus, trade marks can consist of the following:

(a) words (including personal names);
(b) designs;
(c) letters, numerals;
(d) shape of goods;
(e) musical sounds, colours, smells (but only where they can be represented graphically);
(f) computer generated images; and
(g) geographical names (where this has acquired a distinctive character, eg Champagne).

Under TMA 1994, s 63, the Comptroller-General of Patents, Designs and Trade Marks (referred to as the Trade Marks Registrar) is required to keep a Register of Trade Marks on which details of all trademarks and registrable transactions affecting them are kept. The 1994 Act contained transitional provisions dealing with the transfer of existing registrations under the previous system; it allows multi-class applications for goods and services; extends and improves the rights of trade mark owners with regard to trade mark infringement and introduced the current rules for registration. The Act carries a presumption that the trade mark is registrable, renewable every ten years on the payment of a fee (TMA 1994, ss 42–43).

Offences under the Act were created with regard to the fraudulent use of a mark, resulting in imprisonment for up to ten years and fines exceeding £5,000.

Companies seeking protection abroad can do so in three ways:

(i) by making an individual application in the chosen country;
(ii) by making an application which is effective throughout the EU, known as a Community Trade Mark; or
(iii) by making an application under the Madrid Protocol.

As with patents, it is advisable to instruct a trade mark agent to deal with the application, the processing of which can take between 12 and 18 months in the UK, assuming no objections to the mark are made.

Copyright

[11.17] To qualify for copyright under the Copyright, Designs and Patents Act 1988 (CDPA 1988), there must be a work which is original and literary, dramatic, musical or artistic in nature, or a sound recording, film, broadcast, or cable programme, or a typographical arrangement of a published edition. The definition expressly includes computer programs and extends to other work stored on a computer (CDPA 1988, s 3(1)(b)). Copyright will automatically apply and lasts at most for 70 years after the year in which the author dies or, in certain cases from the end of the calendar year in which the work was made (CDPA 1988, s 12 and Duration of Copyright and Rights in Performance Regulations 1995 (SI 1995/3297)). Computer generated programs enjoy protection for a period of 50 years from the date of creation.

The author of a work is the owner of the copyright in the first place unless:

(a) he is an employee working in the course of employment, when the employer will own the rights (CDPA 1988, s 11(2)); or

(b) the work is done under contract requiring transferral of the rights after production of the work.

The primary benefit of owning the copyright is that it gives certain rights to prevent:

(i) copying the whole or a substantial part of a work without permission;

(ii) trading in illicit copies, ie street trading of copied goods.

There are exceptions to copyright of which the exceptions for educational purposes are the most important and these are much tighter under the new law.

It is important to note that copyright only protects against actual copying and is not an absolute monopoly right.

'Moral rights' are one key aspect of copyright law that pertain to the author of copyright material and include:

(A) the right to be identified when a work is published commercially; and

(B) the right of objection to 'derogatory treatment' of the author's work.

(CDPA 1988, s 77.)

Moral rights do not cover computer programs and are not infringed unless the author asserts his right. Copyright contracts should take account of this new right separately from the ownership of the copyright itself, as there are various provisions in the Act relating to employees and contract work. Moral rights are not assignable, but pass under the estate of the author, either as he has directed or, if he has not done so, to the owner of the deceased's copyright.

Rights in performance

[11.18] The Copyright, Designs and Patents Act 1988 seeks to prevent amongst others unauthorised films, recordings, broadcasts and cable programmes of artists' performances. This means that consent should be sought before any live transmission or recording of their performances are made. The rights are personal and last 70 years from the year of any performance (CDPA 1988, ss 3–7). With films, the copyright lasts for 70 years from when the last of a number of people connected with the film die, eg principal director, author of screenplay, etc (Duration of Copyright and Rights of Performance Regulations 1995 (SI 1995/3297)).

Design right

[11.19] The Copyright, Designs and Patents Act 1988 treats industrial designs outside the scope of 'artistic' copyright, but at the same time provides some short-term protection to all original industrial designs. The right, known as unregistered design right, covers industrial articles of an original shape or configuration and applies automatically on either recording of the design or making an article to it and includes computer generated designs. The right lasts for 15 years from the end of the calendar year in which the design was made or was made into an article, whichever is the first, or if the articles made to the design are made available for sale or hire within 5 years of the end of the calendar year, 10 years from the date of availability for sale or hire, giving the owner the opportunity to prevent copying or import of copies. If marketing of a design is delayed beyond 5 years, then the term of protection is 15 years from the date the design was first created (CDPA 1988, ss 51 and 213–225).

There are some exceptions to unregistered design right and these include 'commonplace' designs (not defined), methods and principles of construction (though these may be patentable), surface decoration and, where the designed article is to fit into another article, the connecting parts. The purpose of the last exception is to exclude protection for spare parts and alternative designs which fit on to other articles. Also excluded are features which depend upon the appearance of another article with which the article is intended to be integral, apparently opening the door for producers of 'pattern' parts. There are also some complex restrictions on design right relating to nationality which excludes certain persons from design rights.

Registered design

[11.20] The registration of a design is possible by payment of a registration fee. This gives additional protection to unregistered design right in that it provides protection for five years renewable up to four more times, for five years each, on payment of a prescribed renewal fee. Articles which closely resemble the design, even if they have not been copied from the design, are included. To be registrable, the design must be new and a condition of 'aesthetic appeal' must apply; if an article's aesthetic aspects are not important to buyers, the registration will be refused. The same sort of exceptions apply as for unregistered design right (CDPA 1988, s 265).

Summary of provisions

[11.21] The Copyright, Designs and Patents Act 1988 extended the legislation enabling companies to protect their intellectual property, as follows:

(a)   The Act covers aspects of computer software and computer generated works which were not specifically covered in previous legislation.

(b)   The removal of copyright protection for drawings and blueprints for industrial articles and its replacement with unregistered design right makes the consideration of the benefits of registering designs important. The Act covers all designs and companies should consider the effect regarding competition against their products.

(c)   Contracts for works covered by the Act should cover all aspects of the legislation, including moral and employee rights, and not just copyright.

Useful addresses

[11.22] The UK Intellectual Property Office issues many advisory booklets on Copyright, Designs, Patents and Trade Marks and these are available at the following address:

Intellectual Property Office
Concept House
Cardiff Road
Newport
South Wales
NP10 8QQ

Telephone: 01633 814000
Website: www.ipo.gov.uk

There is a list of registered patent or trade mark agents available from the following addresses (respectively):

Chartered Institute of Patent Attorneys
95 Chancery Lane
London
WC2A 1DT

Telephone: (020) 7405 9450
Website: www.cipa.org.uk

Institute of Trade Mark Attorneys
ITMA Office
5th Floor
Outer Temple
222–225 Strand
London
WC2R 1BA

Telephone: (020) 7101 6090
Website: www.itma.org.uk

Appendix 11A

Document retention periods

The following table provides a summary of the key areas where a company is required to keep and maintain records, and the related recommended retention periods in each case:

Record	Recommended Retention Period	Remarks
Company records (including share registration)		
*Certificate of incorporation	Permanently	CA 2006, s 15
*Certificate to commence business (if any)	Permanently	CA 2006, s 761
*Certificate of change of company name	Permanently	CA 2006, s 80
Board minutes (signed copy)	Permanently (10 years under CA 2006)	CA 2006, s 248
Written resolutions of board	Permanently (10 years under CA 2006)	CA 2006, s 248
Minute books	Permanently (10 years under CA 2006)	CA 2006, s 248
Board committee minutes	Permanently (10 years under CA 2006)	CA 2006, s 248
Minutes of general & class meetings	Permanently (10 years under CA 2006)	CA 2006, s 355
Written resolutions of members/sole member	Permanently (10 years under CA 2006)	CA 2006, s 355
*Report & accounts (signed copy)	Permanently (6 years under VATA)	VATA 1994, Sch 11
Interim report & accounts	Permanently	
Circulars to shareholders (master copy)	Permanently	
Notices of general & class meetings (signed copy)	Permanently	
*Resolutions passed at above meetings (printed copies)	Permanently	CA 2006, s 32
*Memorandum & articles of association (signed original)	Permanently	
*Memorandum & articles of association (current)	Permanently	CA 2006, s 32

Record	Recommended Retention Period	Remarks
Register of sealed documents	Permanently (10 years under CA 2006)	CA 2006, s 248 Attention is drawn to the removal of requirements to have a seal but record of documents sealed is still needed
Proxy forms/polling cards	1 month after meeting if no poll demanded (1 year after meeting if poll demanded)	
Proxy forms used at meetings convened by court	At direction of court or 1 year after court supervision	
Results of a poll required to be made available on a website by a quoted company	2 years after publication on the website	CA 2006, s 341, 353
Report of an independent poll assessor	2 years after publication on the website	CA 2006, s 341, 353
*Register of directors & secretaries (original)	Permanently	CA 2006, s 275
Directors' service contracts	6 years after termination or expiry	TMA 1970
*Register of directors' interests in shares & debentures	Permanently	The requirement to keep this register was repealed on 6 April 2007
Register of interests in voting shares	Permanently	CA 2006, s 808
*Register of charges	Permanently	CA 2006, s 891
Register of members	Permanently	CA 2006, s 113 permits records of former members to be removed from register 10 years after cessation of membership
Register of debenture or loan stock holders	6 years after redemption	CA 2006, s 748 implies that this should be extended to 10 years, while a strict interpretation could imply that the register should be kept permanently

Record	Recommended Retention Period	Remarks
Forms of share and debenture application (originals)	3 years/6 years	CA 2006, s 388
Forms of acceptance & transfer	3 years/6 years	CA 2006, s 388
Renounced letters of acceptance & allotment	3 years/6 years	CA 2006, s 388
Renounced share certificates	3 years/6 years	CA 2006, s 388
Fully paid acceptance & allotment letters exchanged for a certificate	1 year after ceasing to be valid	
Share & stock transfer forms	10 years+	20 years where registered before 6 April 2008
Requests for designating or redesignating accounts	10 years+	20 years where registered before 6 April 2008
Letters of request	10 years+	20 years where registered before 6 April 2008
Redemption discharge forms or endorsed certificates	10 years+	20 years where registered before 6 April 2008
Forms of conversion	10 years+	20 years where registered before 6 April 2008
Signed forms of nomination	12 years + permanent microfilmed record	
Letters of indemnity for lost certificates	Permanently	
*Annual return	3 years	
Stop notices & other court orders	Until order no longer valid	10 years (20 years before 6 April 2008) where order provides evidence of the reason for any action taken
Powers of attorney (copy)	12 years after ceasing to be valid	
Dividend & interest payment lists (before disposal, an extract of outstanding warrants should be made)	Until annual audit, following payment, is complete	
Paid dividend & interest warrants	3 years/6 years, although 6 years after date of payment recommended	CA 2006, s 388

Record	Recommended Retention Period	Remarks
Dividend & interest mandates	Originals until 6 years after validity ceases	
Cancelled share/stock certificates	1 year from date of registration of transfer	
Notification of change of address (shareholders)	2 years	
Trust deed securing issue of debentures or loan stock	12 years after stock has been fully redeemed	
TALISMAN documents		
TALISMAN sold transfers	10 years+	20 years where registered before 6 April 2008
No subsale declaration forms	10 years+	20 years where registered before 6 April 2008
TALISMAN bought transfers	10 years+	20 years where registered before 6 April 2008
Property documents		
Deeds of title	Until sold or transferred	
Leases (signed copies)	15 years after expiry	
Agreements with architects, builders	15 years after completion	
Intellectual property records		
Documents evidencing assignment of trade/ service marks	6 years after cessation of registration	
Certificates of registration of trade/service marks	6 years after cessation of registration	
Intellectual property agreements & licences	6 or 12 years after expiry	
Materials for which copyright protection is claimed:		
Literary, dramatic and musical works	Life in being + 50 years	CDPA 1988
Artistic works, recordings, films, photos and broadcasts	50 years	
Accounting records		

Record	Recommended Retention Period	Remarks
To comply with CA 2006, s 386/CA 1985, s 221 (this obviously also includes all subsidiary records to support the annual accounts)	PLC – 6 years Ltd – 3 years	CA 2006, s 388
Budgets & periodic internal financial reports, eg to board	6 years	
Taxation returns and records	10 years	
VAT records	6 years	VATA 1994, Sch 11
Banking records, including Giro		
Cheques, bills of exchange & other negotiable instruments	6 years	
Paying-in counterfoils	6 years	
Bank statements & reconciliations	6 years	CA 2006, s 388
Instructions to banks	6 years after ceasing to be effective	
Charitable and political donations		
Deeds of covenant (donee)	6 years after last payment	TMA 1970
Documents evidencing entries in accounts re donations	6 years	CA 2006, s 388
Contractual and trust agreements		
Contracts under seal or executed as a deed	12 years after expiry	
Other contracts	6 years after expiry	
Trust deeds (original & copy)	Permanently	
Employee records		
Job applications & interview records	3 months after notifying unsuccessful candidates	Sex Discrimination and Race Relations Acts 1975 & 1976
Personnel and training records	6 years after employment ceases	
Senior executive records	6 years after employment ceases	
Payrolls & wage records (including details on overtime, bonuses & expenses)	6 years from the year end	FA 1998, Sch 18
Details of benefits in kind	6 years	TMA 1970
Labour agreements	10 years after ceasing to be effective	
Works council minutes	Permanently	
Income tax records (P45, P60, P58, P48 etc)	6 years	TMA 1970

Record	Recommended Retention Period	Remarks
Annual return of taxable pay and tax paid	6 years	TMA 1970
Health and safety		
Record and minutes of consultations with safety representatives and committees	6 years	HSSE, SRSC
Record of reportable accidents/accident book	3 years from date of entry	RIDDOR 1995, reg 7
Records of maintenance and examination	5 years	CLWR 2002, CAWR 2002, COSHH 2002
Air monitoring records	5 years (40 years under CAWR 2002 if health surveillance required)	CLWR 2002, CAWR 2002
Health surveillance of employees	40 years from date of last entry	CLWR 2002, CAWR 2002, COSHH 2002
General register and other records required to be kept under the Factories Act 1961 where no other provision is made	2 years from date of last entry	FA 1961, s 141
Radiation accident assessment	50 years	IRR 1985, reg 14
Radiation dosage summary	2 years from end of calendar year	IRR 1985, reg 13
Classification data	3 years	CHIPS 2002
Pension records		
All trust deeds & rules	Duration of scheme	
Trustees' minute books	Duration of scheme (6 years from the end of scheme year under OPS (SA) 1996	OPS (SA) 1996, regs 12-14
Accounts & supporting documents	6 years from the end of the scheme year	OPS (SA) 1996, regs 12-14
HMRC approvals	Duration of scheme	
Actuarial valuation reports	6 years from the end of the scheme year	OPS (SA) 1996, regs 12-14 6 years from date report signed
Documents relating to events notifiable under RBS(IP) 1995, regs 6, 8, 10, 11	6 years after the scheme year in which the event took place	RBS(IP) 1995, reg 15

Record	Recommended Retention Period	Remarks
Documents re. decision to allow retirement due to incapacity	6 years from end of scheme year in which the benefits began	RBS(IP) 1995, reg 15
Documents relating to events specified in RBS(IP) 1995, reg 15(4)	6 years from end of scheme year in which the event took place	RBS(IP) 1995, reg 15
Records of pensioners	12 years after benefit ceases	
Money purchase details	6 years after transfer or value taken	
Pension scheme investment policies	12 years after final cessation of any benefit payable under the policy	
Insurance		
Public liability policies	Permanently	
Product liability policies	Permanently	
Employers' liability policies	Permanently	
Other policies	Until claims under the policy are barred	
Claims correspondence	3 years after settlement	
Group health policies	12 years after the cessation of benefit	
Group personal accident policies	12 years after the cessation of the benefit	

The Registrar of Companies retains copies of some documents (marked * in the list). Some retention periods can be reduced by taking a power in the company's articles of association (marked + in the list).

Notes

CA 2006	Companies Act 2006
CAWR 2002	Control of Asbestos at Work Regulations 2002
CDPA 1988	Copyright, Designs & Patents Act 1988
CLWR 2002	Control of Lead at Work Regulations 2002
CHIPS 2002	Chemicals (Hazard Information and Packaging for Supply) Regulations 2002

Notes

COSHH 2002	Control of Substances Hazardous to Health Regulations 2002
FA 1961	Factories Act 1961
FA 1998	Finance Act 1998
HSSE 1996	Health and Safety (Consultation with Employees) Regulations 1996
IRR 1985	Ionising Radiations Regulations 1985
OPS (SA) 1996	Occupational Pension Schemes (Scheme Administration) Regulations 1996
RBS(IP) 1995	Retirement Benefit Schemes (Information Powers) Regulations 1995
RIDDOR 1995	Reporting of Injuries, Diseases and Dangerous Occurrences Regulations 1995
SRSC	Safety Representatives and Safety Committees Regulations 1977
TMA 1970	Taxes Management Act 1970
VATA 1994	Value Added Tax Act 1994

Chapter 12

Pensions

General

[12.1] Despite a rapid decline in the number of employers offering a final salary pension scheme, the UK still retains a strong occupational pensions movement. There are a number of reasons for this, among them being:

(a) to recruit and retain staff – a good pension scheme can be helpful in recruiting employees and keeping them subsequently. At the very least, the absence of a scheme may place an employer at a disadvantage to one that has a scheme in place;

(b) to support employment policies and spread cost – employers will wish staff to retire in a planned and orderly way without creating unexpected and substantial financial burdens. Failure to provide a scheme can lead to lower paid employees being reliant on means-tested State benefits; and

(c) to help industrial relations and public image – most employees and their representative organisations regard the existence of a pension scheme favourably and the employer's public image can be enhanced if it is seen that sick or elderly retired employees and their dependants are well treated.

What does the State provide?

[12.2] The Government does still have a role in the provision of retirement and death benefits. These benefits are summarised below.

State pensions

[12.3] The State pension scheme is in two parts. The first is a flat-rate pension. For 2011/12 this is £102.15 a week for a single person and £163.35 a week for a married couple. Most people in employment build an entitlement to the Basic State Pension, but the figures quoted above are subject to a sufficient National Insurance contributions (NICs) record. The Pensions Act 2007 reduced the number of qualifying years needed for a full Basic State Pension from 44 for men and 39 for women to 30 for both sexes with effect from 2010. Also, to qualify for any Basic State Pension at all, it was previously necessary to have earnings above the lower earnings limit for one qualifying year and to have at least 25% of the qualifying years needed for a full Basic State Pension. Both of these conditions were abolished from 2010.

The only employed people who are not entitled to State pensions are married women who elected to pay NICs at a reduced rate; this option is no longer available. As of April 2011, the Basic State Pension increases in line with the so-called 'triple guarantee', i.e. the highest of earnings, prices (CPI) and 2.5%. (Indexation was previously in line with RPI.)

Until April 2002, the second part of the State pension scheme was the State Earnings Related Pension Scheme (SERPS). This scheme started in April 1978 and its purpose was to allow employed people to build up earnings-related pensions. SERPS initially gave a maximum pension of 25% of revalued earnings between, the lower earnings limit (LEL) and upper earnings limit (UEL) for National Insurance purposes. However, under the terms of the Social Security Act 1988, this 25% maximum declined to 20% over a ten-year period from the year 2000.

From 6 April 2002, SERPS was replaced by a new State Second Pension (S2P). S2P provides extra benefits for moderate earners compared with SERPS. It was initially based on the same band of earnings as SERPS (LEL to UEL) but, from April 2009, the UEL has been replaced for S2P accrual purposes with a frozen 'upper accrual point' (UAP). For the tax year 2011/12 the LEL is £5,304 a year and the UAP is £40,040 a year.

The benefit structure of S2P, in 2011/12 terms, is shown below:

(a) all contributing employees earning more than £5,304 but less than £14,400 pa will be treated in S2P as if they had earnings of £14,400 pa;
(b) employees' rights to S2P will build up to a pension of:
  (i)   40% of earnings between the LEL and £14,400 pa;
  (ii) plus 10% on earnings from £14,400 to the UAP.

As of April 2011, S2P is uprated annually in line with CPI (rather than RPI, as previously).

Note that the Pensions Act 2007 reactivated the Labour Government's long-standing plan for S2P to become a flat-rate benefit. The mechanism by which this will be achieved is the introduction of the frozen UAP discussed above. Indexation of the existing flat-rate band of benefit will gradually eat away the remaining earnings-related component until the entire benefit is flat-rate. This is expected to be achieved by 2030.

After 40 years of work or credits, the revised scheme could be expected to deliver an entitlement of around £60 a week in today's terms – a significant reduction for high earners.

Besides these contributory State pension benefits, a growing number of pensioners have become eligible for means-tested State benefits in the form of the Pension Credit. This is a means-tested benefit made up of two elements. The guarantee credit ensures that nobody aged 60 or over need live on an income of less than £137.35 a week (£209.70 for couples). The second element of Pension Credit is the savings credit, available to those aged 65 and over, and payable to those who have made some additional retirement provision (eg private pension or capital assets). Its purpose is essentially to reduce the disincentive to saving generated by a means-tested system.

Some prospective changes to the state system are considered later in this chapter.

Equalisation of State pension ages

[12.4] State pension ages were long set at 60 for women and 65 for men. The Pensions Act 1995, however, provides for State pension ages to be equalised at the age of 65.

In the current legislated timetable, women's State pension age is due to be equalised with men's at 65 by April 2020. It is currently rising in steps of one month every two months, so that each single year increase takes two years to phase in. State pension age for both men and women is then due to increase from 65 to 66 between April 2024 and April 2026 in steps of one month every two months.

However, if measures in the 2011 Pensions Bill are passed women's State pension age will increase to 65 more quickly between April 2016 and November 2018. Between December 2018 and April 2020, men's and women's State pensions age will increase from 65 to 66.

The Government is also considering the timetable for future increases to the State pension age from 66 to 68.

Current legislation will increase State pension age in three phases:

(a)   from 65 to 66, phased in over two years starting from April 2024;
(b)   from 66 to 67, again phased in over two years, from April 2034; and
(c)   from 67 to 68, also phased in over two years, from April 2044.

The way this affects different age groups is as follows:

Age on 5 April 2006	Eligible for State pension from
46	between 65th and 66th birthday
38–45	66th birthday
37	between 66th and 67th birthday
29–36	67th birthday
28	between 67th and 68th birthday
27 or younger	68th birthday

However, this timetable is also under consideration by the Government, and the dates may yet be brought forward.

State death benefits

[12.5] As an example of State death benefit, let us take a look at the provision of lump sum death benefits. The Funeral Payment became available from 1988 but this payment is not only strictly means-tested, it is also repayable from the estate of the deceased. To obtain help from the Department for Work and Pensions (DWP) towards the cost of a 'simple funeral', the person organising the funeral has to be on income support or entitled to housing benefit or working families tax credit.

The other lump sum that the State pays when someone dies is the bereavement payment. This is a tax-free benefit of £2,000 and is based on the National

Insurance contribution record of the deceased. Entitlement to the benefit is restricted to those who are bereaved under State pension age and it is not paid at all if the spouse was entitled to a State retirement pension when he or she died.

The main income benefits are the widowed parent's allowance and the bereavement allowance, although it is not possible to receive both benefits at the same time. The bereavement allowance begins, for example, when the widowed parent's allowance ends.

Under SERPS as it originally stood, a widow or widower could inherit the whole of her or his deceased spouse's SERPS entitlement. Where a spouse dies after 5 April 2000, however, changes under the Social Security Act 1986 would have meant that the widow(er) could only inherit 50% of the entitlement. In all cases, the inherited pension, when added to any SERPS pension payable in the widow(er)'s own right, could not exceed the maximum SERPS pension payable to a single person. However, because of the failure of the DWP to tell people of the change, and some cases of incorrect advice, implementation was put back to October 2002 and has been phased in gradually over an eight-year period.

Apart from that earnings-related element, both the widowed parent's allowance and the bereavement allowance are flat rate benefits – £100.70 per week in each case, as from April 2011. The bereavement allowance may be reduced for younger widow(er)s and it is not payable at all to those who are bereaved under the age of 45.

Whilst paternalistic motivation is widely held to be in decline, the level of State retirement and death benefits has been a powerful reason why companies run pension schemes: very few companies wishing to be seen as good employers would be content to let their long-serving employees and their dependants live solely on State benefits.

Government incentives

[12.6] In common with all Governments in the developed world, the UK Government views with some concern adverse demographic trends, ie people are living longer and the birth rate is falling. Therefore, the contributory State pension scheme is expected to come under increasing strain and it is therefore to be expected that legislation should encourage companies and individuals to set up private pension provision. At present:

(a)   the Government gives rebates on employees' and employers' NICs for those pension arrangements which 'contract out' of S2P; and

(b)   valuable tax concessions are granted on employers' and employees' contributions to pension schemes, provided that these schemes are registered with HM Revenue and Customs (HMRC).

The attractions of benefit provision have increasingly been offset by new regulatory burdens.

Also, contracting out on a money purchase basis will be abolished from 6 April 2012. For the future of defined benefit contracting out, see **12.52**.

Types of pension scheme

[12.7] In the UK there are two main types of pension arrangement, the defined contribution scheme (also known as 'money purchase') and the defined benefit scheme (also known as 'final salary'). The main difference between them is the degree of risk sharing between the employees and the employer. In addition there are various hybrid arrangements. Risks in this context relate to such things as future salary inflation, future investment conditions (both up to and after retirement) and, to some extent, political risk.

Defined benefit schemes

[12.8] Under a defined benefit scheme the member is promised a pension, usually based upon length of service and salary at or close to retirement although it could be either a specific amount of pension (eg £50,000 per annum) or a specified ratio of final (or, increasingly, career average) salary (eg 2/3 of final pay). Whatever the promise, the member is, in the normal course of events, assured of that level of pension at retirement (assuming he or she remains with the employer to retirement).

Any variations in future inflation and investment returns will be reflected in the employer's costs of providing the scheme. In most schemes the employee also meets a part of the cost but this is usually at a fixed rate. In recent years final salary schemes have tended to bear a greater share of the impact of political changes than money purchase schemes. Changes to the taxation of dividends, increased longevity and new accounting measures have combined in recent years to discourage defined benefit provision. There has been a growing trend for many schemes to close to new entrants and, increasingly, to all future accrual, and there have been well-publicised cases of employers becoming insolvent, leaving behind schemes that are unable to meet their liabilities in full. (See **12.33** for the Pension Protection Fund compensation that now applies in such cases.)

Defined contribution schemes

[12.9] Under a defined contribution scheme the employer agrees to make contributions to the scheme on behalf of the employee. These benefits may be defined as a fixed amount, a fixed percentage of pay, or a graded amount (depending, say, on age) or may be arbitrary. The contributions paid in respect of an employee are paid into an individual account for each employee and accumulated, net of any expenses, up to retirement. The rate of accumulation will depend upon the investment vehicle which could be a 'with profits' or 'deposit administration' insurance contract which provides capital guarantees and which smoothes out variations in investment return, or a potentially higher yielding unit linked policy which is directly invested in stock exchange securities etc but is subject to the full and immediate impact of market variations.

In some arrangements the employee may have wide freedom as to how his pensions account is invested or this may be at the partial or total discretion of the pension scheme trustees. At retirement, the value of the employee's pension accumulation will then be available to buy a pension. Schemes vary in the extent to which they allow the member to choose a pension in the format that most suits his circumstances.

Clearly the employee is exposed to the full risk of variations in future investment performance up to retirement and investment conditions at retirement.

There are two types of defined contribution scheme. The first is an employer-sponsored, trust-based arrangement. The second is a group personal pension arrangement. This consists of individual personal pension or stakeholder plans (see below) to which the employer may contribute.

Hybrid arrangements

[12.10] The simplest type of hybrid arrangement is one under which the employee is provided a pension which is the better of a final salary pension promise or the pension which can be provided out of a money purchase accumulation.

Such hybrid schemes will either be referred to as a 'final salary scheme with a money purchase underpin (or guarantee)' or a 'money purchase scheme with a final salary underpin'. A money purchase underpin solves the problem of poor early leaver benefits under final salary schemes and thus makes them more attractive to younger mobile employees. A final salary guarantee under a money purchase scheme protects the employee against adverse investment conditions.

Another variation is to provide money purchase benefits up to, for example, 40 and then switch over to final salary benefits. This usually requires two schemes but a problem then has to be solved as to whether the money purchase credits should be translated into final salary benefits at age 40 or whether they should remain as separate additional benefits.

Also growing in popularity are defined lump sum (or 'cash balance') schemes whereby the member is allocated a defined fund at retirement (eg 25% of salary for each year's service) with which to buy an annuity. This tends to share risk between employer and employee.

The pros and cons of defined benefit schemes

[12.11] The main arguments *for* defined benefit (or final salary) schemes are:

(a)   they have traditionally been the form of pension most commonly provided in the UK;

(b)   the employee knows exactly what his retirement benefits will be in terms of his salary at retirement. The security this provides is normally particularly important to older and longer serving employees;

(c)   benefits on death in service and disability can be integrated easily into the benefit design, as can integration with State pension provision;

(d)   subject to certain regulatory constraints, the employer can control the pace of funding (ie it can choose a low initial rate of funding in the knowledge that the cost will gradually rise, or can deliberately incorporate generous margins for future contingencies etc);

(e)   the employer can benefit from any investment surpluses etc to reduce its future pension cost or to improve benefits; and

(f)   the scheme can sometimes be used as an element of a redundancy programme although the cost issues involved should be properly appreciated.

Some of the *difficulties* with final salary schemes are:

(i)   high salary inflation increases the cost of benefits already accrued thus resulting in additional costs to the employer. However, high inflation may be linked with increased equity returns from which the employer can benefit. Furthermore, the employer has some control over the level of salaries within his organisation;

(ii)   early leaver benefits are less valuable than benefits at retirement. This creates a divide between people who can receive a retirement pension (usually on leaving at age 50 or over) and those who cannot;

(iii)   final salary schemes provide effective security when a salary can be relied on to increase progressively through a career and the member can expect to stay with the same firm. In changing employment conditions, with changing earnings patterns and more frequent job changes this 'security' can be an illusion;

(iv)   final salary schemes have been more susceptible to political interference; this has tended to increase the costs of operating such schemes;

(v)   surplus and deficits may arise. This can lead to conflict over the use of any surplus and to sharply fluctuating costs; and

(vi)   the risk of the employer being unable to meet its liabilities.

The pros and cons of defined contribution schemes

[12.12] The main arguments *for* defined contribution (or money purchase) schemes are:

(a)   from the employer's perspective the future cost of the scheme is known; it is therefore limited and easier to budget for;

(b)   employees can exercise their judgement as to how to invest their own pension monies;

(c)   employees may be allowed to choose to take their retirement benefits in a manner which best suits their circumstances;

(d)   employees appear to be treated equally regardless of age or sex (depending on the scheme design); and

(e)   an option for the employees to take the promised employer's contribution as salary might be very attractive to younger employees with limited resources.

However, some of the *difficulties* with money purchase schemes are:

(i)   the employee bears all the risks of poor investment returns and of annuity rates at retirement being poor. This makes some employees feel insecure;

(ii)   the company may feel it has a residual moral responsibility to make up employees' benefits where these have been badly eroded by high inflation and/or poor investment performance;

(iii)   not all employees feel competent to make the choice of the investment medium and some employers/trustees are reluctant to make it for them;

(iv)   the final pension is not known until retirement. This makes it difficult for the individual to plan his retirement benefits;

(v)   money purchase does not recognise the increasing cost of pensions with age and the higher cost for women (who are expected to live longer). Thus, compared with final salary schemes, too much is provided for younger employees and too little for older employees. This can be corrected by using an age related contribution scale but then the overall cost would be susceptible to changes in the age distribution of the employees and might be seen as unfair by younger employees; and

(vi)   in general it is difficult to provide for the most suitable level of benefits for dependants on death in service under this type of scheme although it can be achieved by complex insurance arrangements.

Stakeholder pensions

[12.13] Stakeholder pension schemes were introduced in April 2001 under the Welfare Reform and Pensions Act 1999. Stakeholder pensions are the Government's attempt to encourage more people to save for their retirement by way of simple, flexible, defined contribution schemes offering good value for money. They may be set up as individual arrangements – in the same way as personal pension schemes – or as occupational schemes.

One of their key characteristics is stringent regulation. From 6 April 2005, charges are limited to 1.5% of the fund per annum for the first ten years of the policy's existence, and 1% thereafter. A default investment choice must be offered. From 6 April 2005, this must be a so-called lifestyling arrangement. So, where new members make no choice about investment, their funds will automatically be switched to lower risk/volatility investments as they approach retirement.

Members enjoy great flexibility as to the minimum contributions they pay, whether one-off or regular. Both contributions and benefits are subject to the same upper limits for tax relief as other private sector schemes.

Unless an exemption applies, employers are required to provide access to a stakeholder scheme for all their employees. This means consulting with employees to choose a stakeholder scheme and then to give them contact details and pass over employee contributions to the scheme provider in accordance with a payments schedule. This will give rise to indirect costs and an element of further regulatory burden – there are fines for non-compliance.

However, there are several exemptions from the requirement, the two most important being where employees can join an occupational or group personal pension scheme. The occupational scheme exemption is fairly straightforward: employees who can join a scheme within twelve months of starting work do not have to be given stakeholder access. The group personal pension (GPP) exemption is more complex. It is only if *all* employees have a right to join the GPP arrangement that any exemption applies; broadly, there must also be an employer contribution of at least 3% of basic pay and no penalties if contributions cease.

Employers with fewer than five employees are wholly exempt. Employees earning less than the LEL for National Insurance do not have to be given access but employers must beware of unlawfully discriminating against part-timers.

Employers need to assess the extent to which their arrangements exempt them from the access requirements. If they are not wholly exempt, there will be the task of weighing up the relative merits – not least the costs – of altering the entry conditions for their existing arrangements and going through the process of facilitating stakeholder access.

Legal and regulatory background

[12.14] Apart from European law, which is covered at **12.45** below, there are many areas of the law which impact upon the operation of pension schemes in the UK including the Pensions Acts 1995 and 2004; among the most important areas are those to do with:

(a)   trusts;
(b)   tax;
(c)   social security;
(d)   employment;
(e)   financial services; and
(f)   data protection.

Trust law and trustees' duties

[12.15] Most pension schemes in the UK are set up under trusts. There are two main reasons for this:

(a)   the pension scheme's assets are legally separated from those of the sponsoring employer; they are, therefore, protected from creditors should the company go into liquidation; and
(b)   it has been a requirement of HMRC that an occupational scheme is established under an irrevocable trust in order to benefit from valuable tax advantages.

A trust is where someone owns the assets but someone else is entitled to benefit from them. Trusts are administered by trustees. They are so called because they are trusted to look after the trust property. Over the centuries trust law has evolved so as to impose high standards of behaviour upon those who are placed in positions of trust. In a pension scheme the trustees own the assets and administer the scheme, but they do so solely for the benefit of the scheme members and other beneficiaries.

Leaving aside the legislative and regulatory points that have already been made, the role of trust law in pension provision has frequently been questioned. After all, the concept of a trust dates from medieval times, and derives from equitable, rather than common law rules. Is such a device appropriate for the present day and age? Should not pension rights be incorporated into the contract of employment, for example?

The Goode Committee, which was set up by the Government to enquire into, and to propose regulations for, the operation of pension schemes in the wake of the Robert Maxwell affair, considered this question and concluded that:

> 'trust law in itself is broadly satisfactory and should continue to provide the foundation for interests, rights and duties arising in relation to pension schemes.'

Why did the Committee come to this conclusion? There are several reasons for this, among them being:

(i)   while trust law is indeed of considerable antiquity, it has shown a remarkable ability to adapt to modern commercial requirements;

(ii)   a trust is not only a means of segregating assets for the protection of the beneficiaries, thus insulating them from the bankruptcy of the settlor, ie the employer, but it also provides a mechanism for the collective protection and representation of a group of people linked by a common interest;

(iii)   trust law provides for a high degree of fiduciary responsibility, ie the trustees have to act in good faith in the best interest of all the beneficiaries; it is surely right that this requirement be preserved; and

(iv)   contract law is in fact not sufficient to take over the obligations under a trust. Individual employment contracts do not, of themselves, provide the security resulting from a segregation of assets nor the collective mechanism that is important for the running of pension schemes. Additionally, contract law does not provide protection to all the beneficiaries of a pension scheme, eg the dependants of current members and early leavers who have deferred pensions under the terms of the scheme.

This viewpoint was reinforced by the Pensions Act 1995. Thus, it can be confidently predicted that trust law will, with some modification, continue as the basis of mainstream occupational pension provision in the UK for the foreseeable future.

Pension scheme trustees can be individuals, but it is possible to have corporate trustees and trust corporations. It is also common, especially with executive benefit schemes, for the sponsoring employer to act as trustee. This is not generally to be recommended because of possible conflicts of interest. (See also **12.29** for discussion of Pensions Acts 1995 and 2004 requirements for member-nominated trustees.)

All resignations and new trustee appointments have to be documented by means of deeds. This procedure, laborious though it may appear, is advantageous because it allows for the immediate vesting of the trust property in a new trustee.

Individual trustees are often directors or senior employees of the sponsoring organisation, but appointment of employee trustees who are selected, in some manner, by the scheme members is now required by legislation (see **12.29**, below). Also, some schemes have appointed independent trustees either to act alone or in addition to company and member appointed trustees.

Trustees' duties

[12.16] Besides being responsible for ensuring that contributions are collected and that employees are admitted to membership when they become eligible to join the scheme, trustees have a wide range of other equally important duties. The main duties can be summarised as follows:

(a) familiarisation with the provisions of the scheme and with trust and pensions law (see **12.39**: 'Trustees' knowledge and understanding');
(b) duty to carry out the provisions of the trust deed and rules of the scheme;
(c) duty not to discriminate;
(d) duty not to delegate unless authorised to do so;
(e) duty to act jointly;
(f) duty to invest;
(g) duty to keep accounts and other records, eg payment and transfer details and minutes of meetings;
(h) duty not to make a profit; and
(i) duty to be discreet.

Trustees' conduct in practice

[12.17] The trust deed governing the pension scheme will normally state how the trustees should carry out their duties. It usually specifies the following:

(a) where a unanimous decision is needed;
(b) how many trustees can constitute a quorum;
(c) whether written resolutions can be passed without a meeting;
(d) the procedure for appointment of a secretary; and
(e) the procedure for appointment of a chairman and whether the chairman is to have a casting vote.

At meetings the trustees will discuss how they should exercise their discretion. They will receive and discuss reports from professional advisers such as the actuary, auditor and investment manager. They will adopt accounts and minute the decisions taken in meetings.

Trustees' powers

[12.18] Trustees are given limited powers under general law and statute, for example certain restrictive powers of investment and limited powers to insure the trust property and to delegate administrative functions. Wider powers are generally given in a pension scheme trust deed. Examples are as follows:

(a) power of alteration;
(b) power to invest;
(c) power of delegation;
(d) power to augment benefits;
(e) power to accept incoming transfer values;
(f) power to wind up schemes; and
(g) discretionary powers.

There are certain discretionary powers which must be exercised by trustees. They can, and indeed must in some circumstances, call in advice, but must exercise the discretion themselves. Areas where trustees have to exercise discretion include:

(i)   payment of lump sum death benefits;
(ii) approval of ill health early retirements; and
(iii) consenting to amendments proposed by the employer.

Trustees' hazards

[12.19] Remedies for errors by trustees are enforceable by court action by a beneficiary for breach of trust. Breach of trust can be deliberate, negligent or accidental but there can be no successful action unless the beneficiary has suffered some loss. The Trustee Act 2000 offers a degree of statutory protection to trustees.

Companies should also give careful consideration to other ways of protecting trustees and scheme assets through indemnity insurance schemes.

Additionally, the Pensions Ombudsman has made numerous published decisions against trustees. Some of these findings have resulted from complaints about maladministration where trustees have been ordered to reconsider decisions; others have resulted in trustees being forced to make compensatory payments. The Ombudsman can rule on complaints made by individuals against employers, trustees and administrators, eg insurance companies. Appeals against his decisions are to the High Court and can only be made on points of law.

Tax law

[12.20] It was the Finance Act of 1921 which first set out the general principle that tax relief could be claimed in respect of occupational pension schemes for contributions made by companies and by employees.

Since then, the legislation has developed steadily and relentlessly. The general principle has, however, not changed a great deal since 1921, and may be summarised as follows:

> 'in return for generous tax reliefs given for employee and company contributions to pension schemes, benefits and contributions must be limited.'

Registered pension schemes (ie those which meet conditions set out in the Finance Act 2004 and register their status with HMRC) enjoy the following tax privileges:

(a)   the company may obtain corporation tax relief on its contributions;
(b)   the members are entitled to full tax relief (at their highest marginal tax rates) on their contributions;
(c)   the fund which backs the pension promises accrues free of all income and capital gains taxes, although tax credits on dividends from UK Equities received on and after 2 July 1997 cannot be reclaimed; and
(d)   a cash lump sum taken at retirement is tax-free, within certain benefit limits; pensions are taxable.

The Finance Act 2004 tax regime

[12.21] The Finance Act 1970 limits on the contributions to and benefits payable from approved pension schemes were replaced from 6 April 2006 by a single lifetime allowance on the amount of pension saving that can benefit from tax relief. The lifetime allowance is complemented by an annual allowance for tax relievable inflows of value to an individual's pension fund (whether funded by the member or the employer).

Key elements of the new regime are as follows:

(a)   The lifetime allowance for the 2011/12 tax year is £1.8 million. This will reduce to £1.5 million from April 2012 and is expected to be frozen at that level until at least 2015/16.

(b)   Individuals with large accrued benefits at 6 April 2006 were able to protect their benefits. A limited form of protection (termed 'fixed protection') is also available in respect of the reduction of the lifetime allowance to £1.5 million; in order to claim it and retain the £1.8 million limit, members must effectively give up active membership of all registered pension schemes.

(c)   A lifetime allowance charge operates to recoup tax relief on savings which exceed the lifetime allowance. This is 25%, with income from the excess taxed at marginal rates (giving an effective rate tax of at least 55% after income tax). The excess may be taken entirely in lump sum form (in which case a 55% charge is applied).

(d)   Pensions arising from defined benefit pension schemes are valued for the lifetime limit at 20:1 at all ages.

(e)   The annual allowance has been reduced from £255,000 (2010/11) to £50,000 (2011/12) and is expected to be frozen at that level until at least 2015/16. Individuals are able to obtain tax relief on contributions up to 100% of earnings within this limit (or £3,600 if higher), though there are further restrictions for those with earnings of £130,000 or more. Contributions above the allowance are permitted, but effectively without tax relief. An employer can claim relief in computing chargeable profits for the whole of its contribution, regardless of amount. To be deductible, however, employer contributions must be shown to be wholly and exclusively for the purposes of the employer's trade.

Some detailed changes are as follows:

•   Tax-free cash entitlement is set at 25% of the value of an individual's pension fund (up to the lifetime allowance). This is likely to allow greater tax-free cash for many people, and transitional protection is available for existing tax-free cash entitlements built up prior to 6 April 2006.

•   Minimum pension age increased from 50 to 55 from April 2010.

•   Members of occupational pension schemes are able to draw retirement benefits while still working for the employer, allowing them to phase themselves into retirement.

Many of the relaxations under the new regime are subject to individual schemes adopting them by making rule amendments.

Employment law

[12.22] Section 1 of the Employment Rights Act 1996 provides that pensions and pension schemes should be among the written details of the terms of employment given to employees within two months of starting employment. (See **14.13 EMPLOYMENT, HEALTH AND SAFETY.**)

However, more needs to be mentioned under this heading. There have been signs recently that employment tribunals are hearing more and more cases to do with pension rights. While decisions of employment tribunals carry no legal precedent (appeals against decisions are made to the Employment Appeals Tribunal) pensions are today being seen increasingly as part of the employment package. The major issue is the extent to which pension rights are transferred when employments are transferred, especially in compulsory competitive tendering situations. European Council Directive 77/187 provides that, when a business is sold, the purchaser must maintain the existing terms and conditions of employment of the employees of the business. In the UK, the Transfer of Undertakings (Protection of Employment) Regulations 1981 (SI 1981/1794) 'TUPE', brought the requirements of the Directive into UK law. Both TUPE and the Directive excluded occupational pensions schemes from the scope of their requirements but, through the Pensions Act 2004 the UK Government has now unilaterally withdrawn this exclusion – see **12.38**). (See also **14.30 EMPLOYMENT, HEALTH AND SAFETY.**) In addition, ECJ judgments in *Beckmann v Dynamco Wicheloe Macfarlane Ltd (C-146/00)* and *Martin v South Bank University (C-04/01)* have in effect determined that the exclusion in the Directive should not apply to early retirement benefits.

Transfer provisions in the public sector have long been, and remain, subject to more stringent provisions. Originally, the UK Government took the view that, where transfers of undertakings from the public to the private sector took place, pension rights did not have to be maintained. However, in April 1995, there was something of a volte-face on the part of the Government. It issued a circular to local authorities stating its view that a failure to maintain pension rights could render an authority liable to claims for constructive dismissal. The case of *Adams v Lancashire County Council and BET Catering Services Limited* [1996] IRLR 154, is the 'lead' case on this issue. The decision of the High Court on 17 January 1996 was that pensions were excluded both from the Directive and from the Regulations, although EU law did require Member States to adopt measures to protect employees' (and ex-employees') accrued pension rights. The Court of Appeal upheld this decision. By the passage of legislation relative to revaluation and preservation of deferred pensions, the UK Government had complied with this requirement.

Nonetheless, organisations tendering to provide public services under a Public Private Partnership or Private Finance Initiative must offer employees leaving the public service good quality pension arrangements meeting certain comparability and other requirements.

Under the Pension Schemes Act 1993, s 124(1) the Secretary of State may make payments out of the National Insurance Fund into an occupational pension scheme if he is satisfied that an employer has become insolvent and that at the time he became insolvent there remained unpaid contributions falling to be paid by him into the scheme.

Financial services law

[**12.23**] Under this heading reference is made to the Financial Services and Markets Act 2000 (replacing the Financial Services Act 1986). This Act states, among other things, that it is a criminal offence for anyone to give investment advice or to deal in investments unless he or she is registered to do so.

Therefore, pension scheme trustees run two risks, namely that:

(a)　they will handle the scheme investments themselves without being registered; and

(b)　they will, albeit unwittingly, find themselves in situations where they are giving investment advice to members.

The first of these can be overcome. Trustees can register under the Act but they normally delegate the investment of the assets to an investment manager who is registered. It is a fact that only the very largest pension schemes handle the investments 'in house', simply because they can afford to employ 'in house' investment experts.

It is the second risk that is perhaps more dangerous. If trustees give general advice to new employees as to whether they should join pension schemes they are not committing an offence because pension schemes themselves are not classed as investment under the Act. However, if a member comes along and asks 'what do you think of the personal pension contract offered by ABC Insurance PLC?' a trustee can only give general advice on the merits of the company pension scheme against a personal pension policy. If a trustee comments about, for example, the past performance of ABC Insurance PLC, whether this is likely to be repeated in the future and the charging structure of ABC's contract etc, then he or she is giving investment advice.

Similarly, if a scheme has a choice of AVC providers, eg P&R Building Society and ABC Insurance PLC, a trustee must not attempt to comment on the relative merits of the two alternatives by way of charges, investment performance, etc. A trustee can only give general advice as to the advantages of building society investments over insurance based investments or vice versa.

Social security law

[**12.24**] Along with tax law, social security law is one of the most important areas of law affecting occupational pension schemes, if only because of the plethora of both primary and secondary legislation emanating from the Department for Work and Pensions!

Changes in Legislation

[**12.25**] Key changes in DWP legislation are shown chronologically below. However, many of the more recent changes under the Pensions Acts 1995 and 2004 are discussed at greater length later in this chapter.

06/04/75　–　Leavers from this date aged 26 or over and with at least 5 years' pensionable service are entitled to preserved benefits

06/04/78	– Schemes must offer membership to men and women on equal terms (with some exceptions)
	– Start of SERPS and contracting out
01/01/85	– Contracted-out salary related schemes cannot offset revaluation of GMP against revaluation of other pension for leavers from this date ('anti-franking')
01/01/86	– Leavers from this date have a statutory right to a transfer value
	– Leavers from this date receive revaluation (in line with RPI or 5% if less) on their non-GMP pension accrued from 01/01/85
	– Entitlement to a preserved pension ceased to depend on the member being aged over 26
06/04/88	– Schemes are required to offer members an additional voluntary contribution facility
	– GMP and SERPS accrual rates are reduced
	– Scheme must increase GMP in payment by RPI or 3% if less
	– Widowers' GMPs are introduced
	– Contracted-out money purchase (COMP) schemes are introduced
17/08/90	– No payment of surplus to the employer can be made unless all scheme pensions increase in payment in line with RPI or 5% if less
12/11/90	– An independent trustee must be appointed to final salary schemes on the insolvency of the employer
01/01/91	– Leavers from this date receive revaluation on the whole of their pension in excess of GMP
02/04/91	– The Pensions Ombudsman begins to operate
09/03/92	– Schemes' ability to invest in employer-related investments is restricted
29/06/92	– Any deficiency in final salary scheme assets on winding up or the insolvency of the employer becomes a debt due from the employer
23/06/94	– During periods of paid maternity leave women must continue to accrue benefits on (notional) full salary
01/01/96	– Trustees are required to operate the scheme as if it contained a rule requiring full equal treatment of men and women as regards both membership conditions and benefits

Most of these measures have been consolidated into the Pension Schemes Act 1993.

The Pensions Acts 1995 and 2004

[12.26] The Pensions Act 1995 came into force on 6 April 1997, and made major changes to the regulation of UK occupational pensions. The Pensions

Act 2004 has built on the earlier framework, modifying some provisions and adding some major new ones.

Key provisions under the two Acts are described below.

The Pensions Regulator

[**12.27**] The Pensions Act 1995 established the Occupational Pensions Regulatory Authority (OPRA) as the principal authority for the regulation and supervision of occupational pension schemes in the UK. It had wide powers to deal with breaches of legislation by trustees but was criticised for being too reactive.

The Pensions Act 2004 therefore established a proactive Pensions Regulator to replace OPRA. The Regulator aims to focus on tackling fraud, bad governance and poor administration, and to encourage best practice through an increased education and guidance role.

The Regulator has extensive other powers, such as the power to issue an improvement notice, directing a scheme to take action to put right identified problems and prevent a recurrence, and the power to issue a freezing order to protect members' interests or scheme assets while an investigation is carried out.

All those involved with occupational pension schemes, including advisers, trustees and employers have a statutory duty to report material regulatory breaches to the Regulator. Further, regulations set out a list of 'notifiable events' that employers and trustees must report to the regulator as soon as reasonably practicable. These are events that might indicate a threat to the security of a defined benefit scheme.

As part of its educational role, the Regulator issues codes of practice containing practical guidance on meeting the requirements of legislation. Breach of a code does not, of itself, result in legal proceedings, but the code is admissible in evidence in any legal proceedings.

The role of pension scheme trustees

[**12.28**] The Pensions Act 1995 aimed to both clarify the powers and duties of the trustees of occupational pension schemes and to give to them new powers and duties. As examples of the former, trustees are required to:

(a)   have proper regard to the need for diversification of the scheme's investments as appropriate to the circumstances of the scheme;

(b)   maintain a separate scheme bank account; and

(c)   keep proper books and records (eg of their meetings, of any payment of pensions and benefits and of transfer details) (Occupational Pension Schemes (Scheme Administration) Regulations 1996 (SI 1996/1715)).

The Act gives to trustees certain powers that formerly could only be exercised by employers or employers with the consent of trustees, or trustees with the consent of employers.

Trustees are required to appoint the scheme actuary and auditor. While the latter appointment is usually made by trustees under the terms of their trust deed, it is quite common for employers to appoint scheme actuaries, who may, in practice, advise both the trustees and the employer in relation to the scheme. There is nothing in the legislation which forbids employers to appoint actuaries for the purpose of advising them on financial matters relating to pension schemes, but scheme valuations and certain statutory certification processes have to be conducted by actuaries who are appointed by the trustees. Crucially, trustees cannot rely on advice by an adviser who has not been appointed by them.

In the matter of pension scheme investments, trustees must (after consultation with the employer) prepare, and revise where necessary, in conjunction with their investment advisors, a written statement of the principles governing their decisions about investing the assets of the scheme.

Unless scheme rules require otherwise, trustees can take their decisions by majority.

Trustees are also required to set up and maintain procedures for settling disputes in occupational pension schemes.

No trustee, or anyone who is connected with him or her, can act as the auditor or actuary to the same scheme. Furthermore, no person can act, or continue to act, as a trustee if, among other things, he has been made bankrupt or has been convicted of an offence involving dishonesty. Trustees cannot be indemnified out of scheme assets for any fines that may be imposed on them, nor are they able to effect insurance to cover these instances from scheme resources.

Member-nominated trustees

[12.29] Trustees must ensure that arrangements are made for at least one third of the trustee body to be people nominated by the scheme members. Member-nominated trustees may only be removed with the consent of all the other trustees.

Until April 2006, employers had been able to seek members' approval to alternative arrangements, which need not include member representation (but which in practice often did). That provision was withdrawn by the Pensions Act 2004 (along with much of the overly prescriptive content of the initial legislation).

The Government has an existing statutory power to increase member representation further, to at least half the trustee body, but has not indicated that it intends to exercise that power. Many schemes have difficulty filling member-nominated trustee vacancies even on the one-third basis.

Statutory funding requirement

[12.30] The Pensions Act 1995 subjected every occupational pension scheme, other than money purchase arrangements and certain statutory schemes, to a complex minimum funding requirement (MFR). The MFR was highly prescriptive, allowed little allowance for each scheme's own circumstances and was administratively very burdensome.

The Pensions Act 2004 replaced the MFR from 22 September 2005 with a new statutory funding objective to ensure that schemes have sufficient and appropriate assets to cover their liabilities. The main elements of scheme-specific funding are:

(a)   a statement of funding principles setting out the trustees' policy for meeting the funding objective and remedying any failure to meet it;

(b)   an annual actuarial valuation (although these can take place every three years provided the trustees arrange for an actuarial report in the intervening years, outlining any changes since the last valuation);

(c)   a schedule of contributions, setting out how much the employer and employee will pay into the scheme.

If the funding objective is not met on the valuation date, the trustees must prepare, after taking actuarial advice, a 'recovery plan' setting out the steps to be taken to meet it and the period over which those steps will be taken.

Methods and assumptions used for calculating the liabilities, the statement of funding principles, recovery plan and schedule of contributions must be agreed with the employer (in most cases). In the absence of agreement, the trustees are able to modify future accrual, though again, only if the employer agrees. If the employer and trustees can't agree, trustees must inform the Regulator. Amongst other things, the Regulator is able to impose a schedule of contributions or itself modify future accrual.

Pension increases

[12.31] All defined benefit pensions accrued by reference to pensionable service from 6 April 1997 to 5 April 2005 have to be increased in payment in line with increases in retail price inflation, subject to a ceiling of 5% each year.

For service after 5 April 2005, however, defined benefit schemes are required to increase pensions in payment by the lesser of inflation and 2.5%. Schemes may, of course, offer benefits on a more generous basis than the statutory minimum.

The measure of inflation changed from RPI to the Consumer Prices Index (CPI) from April 2011. CPI tends to increase at a lower rate.

Money purchase schemes are not required to provide any pension increases.

Pensions and divorce

[12.32] The Pensions Act 1995 introduced new provisions for dealing with pension rights in all divorce, nullity and judicial separation proceedings. For divorce proceedings brought on or after 1 July 1996, courts in England and Wales have been required to take the value of pension rights into account when making financial provision orders. (The corresponding date in Scotland is 19 August 1996.) Courts are able to issue 'earmarking' orders instructing pension schemes to pay benefits to ex-spouses. Under English law the orders may apply to pension payments and lump sum benefits (eg benefits payable on retirement or death). Court orders apply to any pension payments made after 6 April 1997; attachment orders on lump sums can also be made. The value of pension benefits is based on cash equivalent transfer values; existing clean break settlements remain as courts seek to split other assets before issuing attachment orders to pensions; the ex-spouse does not become a scheme member; the courts have the power to override trustees' discretion or member's nomination regarding the payment of lump sum death benefits; and schemes will be able to charge for complying with requests from the courts for information on the pension rights of the parties.

Under the Welfare Reform and Pensions Act 1999, for divorce proceedings beginning after 30 November 2000, the courts have a further option. This is known as pension splitting or pension sharing. Under this option, part of the member's benefit rights are taken away and a completely separate benefit right is established in the name of the former spouse. This allows for a 'clean break' in a way that earmarking orders under the Pensions Act 1995 do not. Pension sharing leaves courts with three options when dealing with pension rights:

(i)   offsetting, where the value of pension rights is merely set against the value of other marital assets;

(ii)   earmarking, which diverts part of the member's benefit entitlement directly to the former spouse; and

(iii) sharing, which creates a separate legal benefit entitlement for the former spouse.

Pension Protection Fund

[12.33] The Pensions Act 2004 established a Pension Protection Fund (PPF) funded by levy and effective from 6 April 2005. The PPF is run by an independent board. Its purpose is to provide compensation to private sector defined benefit and hybrid schemes where the employer is insolvent and the scheme is in deficit. It has also taken over the functions of the former Pensions Compensation Board, paying compensation to defined benefit and defined contribution schemes in cases of fraud or misappropriation of assets.

The level of cover provided by the PPF is lower than originally anticipated. Broadly, it is as follows:

(a)   100% of the original pension promise for people who have reached normal pension age under the scheme;

(b)   90% for people below that age, subject to an overall benefit cap (at age 65 and after the 90% cap has been applied, this is £29,897.42 for 2011/12, indexed annually in line with earnings and actuarially ad-justed for other ages according to factors published by the PPF);

(c)   rights accrued after April 1997 will be indexed to prices, capped at 2.5% (pre-April 1997 rights will not be indexed); and

(d)   survivors' benefits for spouses will be calculated as 50% of the member's protected pension.

The levy is split into three parts. The main part is the pension protection levy made up of two elements: a flat rate scheme-based element and a risk-based element. The latter is based on the scheme's funding level and, if the PPF Board thinks it appropriate, one or more of the following:

(i)   the risk of employer insolvency;

(ii)   the nature of the scheme's investments when compared to its liabilities; and

(iii)   such other factors as may be set out in regulations.

The other two parts of the levy are the administration levy, covering the set up and ongoing costs of the PPF, and the fraud compensation levy, which replaces the existing compensation levy.

When an insolvency event occurs in relation to an employer there will be an 'assessment period' during which it will be established whether the scheme has enough assets to meet the PPF level of benefits. If not, the PPF will take over the scheme.

The Pensions Act 2004 contains measures to prevent employers from dumping their pensions liabilities on the PPF. These give the Pensions Regulator the power to:

(A)   require contributions from those involved in an act that has taken place with the purpose of avoiding a debt due to the scheme; and

(B)   require that 'financial support arrangements' are put in place where restructuring has left either service companies or subsidiaries with pension obligations that they cannot meet.

These so-called 'moral hazard' have become an important factor in corporate transactions and restructuring activity. It is possible to apply for a clearance notice to confirm in advance that a given set of circumstances will not lead to these powers being invoked.

Financial Assistance Scheme

[12.34] The Financial Assistance Scheme (FAS) was set up under the Pensions Act 2004 and its detailed operation is set out in regulations. It aims to compensate defined benefit scheme members who have lost out on their pension because their scheme was under-funded when it wound up prior to the introduction of the PPF. Initially, it only provided compensation where the employer is insolvent and has been unable to make up the deficit.

Regulations make FAS compensation broadly comparable to PPF compensation (see **12.33**).

Qualifying schemes

[12.35] Schemes are eligible if they started winding up between 1 January 1997 and 5 April 2005. The following schemes will qualify, ie those:

(a)   with an insolvent employer (for insolvencies up to 1 January 2009 the DWP will assume that the wind-up and employer insolvency are linked – after that date, evidence will be needed that such a link exists in order for the scheme to be eligible);

(b)   where a compromise agreement is in place and enforcing the debt on the employer would have forced it into insolvency; and

(c)   which started winding up between 1 January 1997 and 10 June 2003 (ie the date that the employer debt became full buy-out) with a solvent employer.

Additionally, in 2011 it was found that some schemes unexpectedly fell outside the PPF compensation provisions through not having an employer within the terms of the statutory definition. Regulations will therefore extend FAS eligibility where:

(i)   the scheme began to wind up between 23 December 2008 (the day after the last possible date to have done so in the existing FAS Regulations) and the day before the new regulations come into force (expected to be late 2011);

(ii)   the connection between the scheme and the last statutory employer was lost before 10 June 2011; and

(iii)   this last statutory employer had an insolvency event prior to 6 April 2005 and therefore would be unable to qualify for the PPF.

Compensation

[12.36] All members for whom benefits are unlikely to be met in full will be eligible for assistance of 90% of core pension rights accrued in their scheme, payable from the later of 14 May 2004 and scheme normal pension age (minimum age is 60, unless in ill health).

The cap on maximum assistance is £30,297.

Benefits accrued after April 1997 increased in payment by limited price indexation with 2.5% cap.

Changes to members' accrued rights

[12.37] Measures introduced from 6 April 2006 make it easier for trustees to change, without members' consent, benefit rights that have already been built up. The overall value of the rights must, however, be maintained. The process is subject to a variety of procedural constraints and actuarial certification.

Extending TUPE protection to pensions

[12.38] From 6 April 2005, the Pensions Act 2004 provides that where, on a TUPE transfer, the transferring employer provides an occupational pension scheme, the new employer must either offer membership of an occupational pension scheme or pay contributions to a stakeholder pension scheme. If the new employer's scheme is a defined benefit scheme it must satisfy the contracted-out reference scheme test (or an alternative standard set out in regulations). If it is a money-purchase occupational or stakeholder scheme, the employer must agree to match the employee's contributions to it, on a one-to-one basis, up to 6% of salary. There is no requirement to directly match the transferor's occupational scheme.

Trustees' knowledge and understanding

[12.39] From 6 April 2006, the Pensions Act 2004 requires trustees to be conversant with:

(a)   the scheme trust deed and rules;

(b) any statement of investment principles;
(c) where appropriate, the most recent statement of funding principles; and
(d) any other document recording policy on the administration of the scheme generally.

Also, where appropriate, trustees must have knowledge of:

(i)   the law in relation to pensions and trusts;
(ii)   the investment of assets;
(iii) scheme funding; and
(iv)   other matters set out in regulations.

The Regulator has published a code of practice on this subject, giving more details of the kinds of knowledge, training, experience or qualifications regarded as necessary to fulfil these requirements.

Employer consultation

[**12.40**] Employers are now required to consult before making changes to pension schemes, in order to ensure changes are developed in partnership. Only certain prescribed major changes fall within the scope of this requirement.

Vesting of pension rights

[**12.41**] A member's pension rights vest fully only after two years' pensionable service. The Pensions Act 2004 requires schemes to offer employees who have been scheme members for at least three months and leave during the two-year vesting period the choice of a refund of contributions or a cash equivalent transfer value.

Additional voluntary contributions facility

[**12.42**] Offering an additional voluntary contribution arrangement to members ceased to be compulsory from 6 April 2006.

Workplace access to information and advice

[**12.43**] Provisions within the Pensions Act 2004 make it possible for the Government to require employers to provide access to information and advice in the workplace. There have, as yet, been no signs of any intention to bring these measures into force.

Data protection law

[**12.44**] The Data Protection Act 1984 exempted from its requirements personal data held only for payroll and accounting purposes. The exemption was not, however, absolute. It was conditional upon the personal data not being used for any other purpose. A data user could not therefore claim exemption because the data was held for payroll reasons and then use the data for personal reasons.

Personal data held for one or more payroll purposes could be disclosed, *inter alia*:

(a)   to any person by whom the person is payable (for example a pension provider); and

(b)   for the purposes of obtaining actuarial advice.

Nevertheless, it is considered by many that the exemptions were too narrow and it was therefore usual for pension scheme trustees to register under the Act, especially if pension scheme data is held on a computerised system.

A major development has been the implementation of the Data Protection Act 1998, which came into force on 1 March 2000, replacing the Data Protection Act 1984. The objective is essentially the same – to protect people's right to privacy – but the measures are expanded to cover new types of data and to allow those on whom data is held to have better access to it.

Of the various detailed changes made, two in particular stand out as being of major concern to pension scheme trustees, and administrators and others who process information on behalf of the trustees. These are the inclusion of manual filing systems within the data protection requirements, whereas previously only electronic data were caught, and a requirement for members' consent to their data being processed.

The manual filing systems affected are those which store information structured by reference to individuals or by reference to criteria relating to individuals – in such a way that information about a particular member is readily accessible. This may exclude, for instance, pension scheme files such as actuarial reports mentioning particular members but which are not set up in such a way that information on a particular member can readily be retrieved.

The consent requirement is particularly onerous where 'sensitive personal data' are concerned. In terms of pension schemes, sensitive data will probably be limited to information concerning the member's health. However, under the Act, the term also encompasses information as to an individual's race, political opinions, religious beliefs, trade union membership, sex life or criminal offences. The member's specific consent is needed before any sensitive data can be processed. For non-sensitive data, consent is also needed (not necessarily *explicit* consent) unless, for instance, the data processing is necessary in order to comply with either a legal obligation to which the data controller (eg trustee) is subject, or a contract to which the member is subject.

Other measures concern changes to the registration process, the need for trustees to have a policy on data security and written contracts with third party data processors (eg administrators) governing security of personal data and improved data access rights for those on whom data are held. The range of penalties for non-compliance has also been strengthened.

The influence of European law

General

[12.45] As a member of the European Union (EU) the UK has a binding commitment (by virtue of the European Communities Act 1972) to uphold the principles contained in the Articles of the Treaty of Rome which the UK signed in 1973. The EU is conscious of the variety and differences in laws from one Member State to another and the ultimate intention of the Treaty of Rome was to harmonise the laws of the Member States.

By way of background, EU law takes three main forms, as follows:

(a)   Treaty Provisions – these are of direct application through the EU and may be enforced against Governments of Member States, private sector employers and individuals.

(b)   Directives – these are laws binding on the Member States and are designed to impose objectives which each Member State must introduce into its national legislation in whatever manner it chooses. If a directive is sufficiently precise in its terms it may be relied upon by an individual against the other individuals or private sector employers.

(c)   Decisions – these are issued by the Council, the Commission and the European Court of Justice (ECJ) and are binding only on those to whom they are addressed. Decisions can be addressed to Member States, national courts and individuals but are usually addressed to corporate bodies.

EU law has become very relevant to the pensions industry in recent years.

Sex equality

[12.46] Article 141 of the Treaty of Amsterdam states that:

> 'Each Member State shall during the first stage ensure and subsequently maintain the application of the principle that men and women should receive equal pay for equal work.'

The case of *Barber v Guardian Royal Exchange Assurance Group* [1990] IRLR 240 significantly extended the equal treatment requirements for pension schemes. In the *Barber* case the GRE pension scheme had a normal pension age of 62 for men and 57 for women. Mr Barber was made redundant at age 52. Under the scheme rules he was not entitled to an immediate early retirement pension although a female employee made redundant at age 52 would have been so entitled. The court held that benefits from a contracted out occupational pension scheme were 'pay' for the purposes of Article 119 provided they were derived from contract. There was a clear discrimination so Mr Barber's estate (Mr Barber having died meanwhile) was entitled to receive compensation.

Unfortunately, it was not immediately clear to what extent the ECJ's judgment was intended to be retrospective. In order to clarify the position, the Maastricht Protocol (1991) contained a provision to the effect that scheme benefits relating to employment before the date of the *Barber* judgment (17 May 1990) should not be considered as 'pay' and therefore are not required to be equalised (unless legal proceedings have already commenced).

While the issue of whether or not the *Barber* decision was intended to be retrospective is crucial, many other questions relating to pension provision were raised by this decision, some, but by no means all of which have been answered by subsequent test cases.

It would take too long to go through all the cases, but in summary:

(a)   the *Barber* judgment applies to all occupational pension schemes, whether or not they are contracted out;

(b)   equal treatment in occupational pension schemes is only required for service from 17 May 1990;

(c)   both employers and pension scheme trustees are responsible for ensuring conformity with the equal treatment requirements;

(d)   where men have a normal retirement age of (say) 65 and women 60, companies have to reduce the retirement age for men to 60 for service between 17 May 1990 and the date from which a common retirement age is adopted;

(e)   the use of sex based actuarial factors (for calculating transfer values for example) is permitted;

(f)   part-time employees (predominantly women) should be granted access to pension schemes along with their full-time colleagues. However, employers can exclude them if they can demonstrate objective grounds for doing so which are not related to gender; and

(g)   if a transfer is made from scheme A to scheme B, and the transfer value is not calculated in accordance with equal treatment principles, it is scheme B's responsibility to make sure that the transfer value is appropriately increased.

The European case law led to a provision being included in the Pensions Act 1995 requiring trustees to operate the scheme as if it contained a rule requiring full equal treatment of men and women as regards both membership conditions and benefits.

One subsequent major case law development was the European Court of Justice (ECJ) decision in *Preston v Wolverhampton Healthcare NHS Trust* [1998] IRLR 198, further clarified by a subsequent House of Lords ruling. This has given a clearer picture of the appropriate time limits and remedies for successful claims in cases of indirect sex discrimination against part-timers (see (f) above).

The decisions upheld existing UK law, in that part-timers who believe they have been unlawfully denied scheme membership must bring a claim no later than six months after leaving employment. However, if they are successful, backdated membership can be granted for the full period of their unlawful exclusion as far back as April 1976. (This overturned existing UK law allowing only two years retrospection from the date the claim was brought.) Employees have to make up the 'missed' contributions for backdating.

For employers, this raises the prospect of new sex equality claims and, potentially, substantial new liabilities.

In a more recent development (*Association belge des Consommateurs Test-Achats ASBL v Conseil des ministres*: C-236/09 [2011] 2 CMLR 994, [2011] Lloyd's Rep IR 296), the ECJ ruled on 1 March 2011 that applying differential male and female rates for insurance contracts invalidates the principle of equal treatment between men and women, and that such practice must cease by 21 December 2012. This will affect any purchaser of a pensions annuity, and could also, in due course, affect how defined benefit pension schemes set their actuarial factors. It is expected that the UK Government will need to amend the provisions of the Equality Act 2010 in order to comply with the ruling.

Other European equality legislation

[12.47] The EU Employment Framework Directive ('the Employment Directive') requires Member States to outlaw discrimination on grounds of sexual orientation, disability, age, religion and race. Implementation has been staggered, with age discrimination, the last aspect to be tackled, outlawed from 1 October 2006.

The age discrimination provisions are likely to prove the most burdensome of these measures for occupational schemes, in spite of exemptions to allow certain ostensibly discriminatory practices to continue. Key provisions in the UK regulations allow:

(a)   different ages for admission to the scheme and for entitlement to benefit, including different entry and benefit ages for different groups of employees; and

(b)   the use of age criteria in actuarial calculations.

The regulations go on to describe many specific scheme design features which will not be treated as discriminatory. Nonetheless, there are many common scheme design features that fall outside the exemptions and which must pass an 'objective justification' test if they are to continue.

Ongoing reform: automatic enrolment

[12.48] The Pensions Acts 2007 and 2008 contain major new measures intended to increase pension savings in the UK.

All eligible UK employees (those aged between 22 and State pension age, and who have earnings over £7,475 per annum in 2011 terms) must be automatically enrolled into a pension scheme – either the Government's new National Employment Savings Trust (NEST) scheme or a 'qualifying' scheme of their employer which offers at least a minimum level of contributions or benefits.

This measure will come into force from 2012, though complex phasing-in arrangements mean it will not be wholly operational until October 2017:

(a)   **October 2012 to October 2016:**
        –   Auto-enrolment will be staged by employer size, large through to small.

–   Employers using money purchase arrangements must contribute at least 1% of 'qualifying earnings', with a minimum total contribution of 2% qualifying earnings.

–   Employers with defined benefit schemes must allow opt-ins.

(b)   **October 2016 to October 2017:**

–   The minimum money purchase contribution rises to 2% employer; 5% total.

–   Auto-enrolment begins for employers with defined benefit schemes.

(c)   **October 2017 onwards:**

–   The minimum money purchase contribution rises to 3% employer; 8% total.

(Qualifying earnings is the band of earnings between £5,715 and £38,185 in 2010/11 terms.)

The legislation envisages that employers must automatically enrol relevant workers within one month of starting work (or the date they become eligible, eg on reaching age 22). Contributions must be calculated from day one and deducted on the first occasion the employee is paid. Under measures in the Pensions Bill 2011, however, all employers will be able to operate a 3-month waiting period. Once automatically enrolled, an employee will have one month to opt out by requesting an opt-out notice from the scheme (not the employer). The employer must then notify the scheme, and must refund all member contributions within one month. Employees who opt-out must be automatically re-enrolled at 3-year intervals.

Qualifying schemes

Qualifying defined benefit schemes

[12.49] Any contracted-out defined benefit scheme will meet the quality requirement. Where a scheme is not contracted-out it must meet a test scheme standard: broadly, 1/120th of qualifying earnings for each year of service, with a maximum of 40 years to count.

Qualifying defined contribution schemes (occupational and personal)

[12.50] An employer's defined contribution scheme must at least match the minimum contributions described above. So, once the reforms are fully implemented, the quality requirement is for a minimum overall contribution of 8% of qualifying earnings, of which at least 3% must come from the employer. The difficulty here is that qualifying earnings means all earnings, including commission, bonuses, overtime etc. Pensionable pay in most employers' schemes, on the other hand, will be based on basic pay only. The Government is, however, legislating for a simpler system for employers to certify that their defined contribution scheme meets the required contribution levels.

The NEST scheme

[12.51] NEST will be a trust-based occupational pension scheme run by a new trustee corporation and aimed at moderate to low earners. Minimum contributions are as described above. NEST will differ from other occupational pension schemes in many important ways:

(a) maximum contributions of £3,600 per annum (to be uprated between 2005 and 2012);

(b) no transfers in (except from members who have left occupational schemes after less than two years' service);

(c) no transfers out (unless the member has reached age 55 or is suffering from incapacity);

(d) no contribution refunds for early leavers.

Automatic enrolment will make far reaching changes to the UK pensions landscape. Besides the extra cost of contributions, its procedural complexity will be an unwelcome additional burden for most employers.

Pensions green paper

[**12.52**] In May 2011, the Government published its green paper on State pension reforms. The paper reflects its belief that the current system has become too complex for many people to understand and also gives rise to widespread means-testing. The paper sets out two options for reform.

(a) *Option 1* – Accelerate the transition of S2P to a flat-rate additional pension (which is due under current rules to be achieved by around 2030). This would be done by reducing the Upper Accrual Point (the upper limit on earnings which count towards benefit calculation) from its current level of £40,040 pa to about £14,000 over the next seven years. In the longer term, the flat-rate S2P would still be separate from the basic State pension, so there would still be some complexity in having two State pensions. Defined benefit contracting-out would continue, but with rebates reflecting the much lower S2P accrual rate.

(b) *Option 2* – Abolish S2P and provide a single-tier State pension at a level above the present minimum income guarantee. The Government proposes a level of around £140 pw in today's terms, assuming the member has a record of at least 30 years' NICs. No specific timetable is given for this option, but it would be shorter than the seven years in option 1. Defined benefit contracting out would be abolished. Transitional arrangements would be made for existing rights under S2P and under contracted-out schemes. The paper gives no details at this stage but basically anyone with an accrued S2P entitlement greater than the new flat-rate pension would receive that higher State pension. Those with accrued contracted-out rights would see an offset from the new flat-rate pension.

It appears that option 1 is based on accrual of £1.60 pw pension for each qualifying year of accrual. For someone paying NICs for 30 years, this would be expected to produce a broadly similar level of overall State pension to option 2. However, it does have the capacity to produce a higher amount for those paying NICs over a longer period. Option 2 is understood to be the Government's preferred approach though, at the time of writing, it has not confirmed how (or even whether) it intends to proceed with these measures.

Chapter 13

Insurance administration

Risk management and insurance

[13.1] The company secretary may be responsible for risk management or, more specifically, insurance which is one component of risk management.

Risk is a combination of events and likelihoods and is concerned with any situation in which unanticipated events result in the non achievement of the organisation's objectives.

Risk management may be defined as the identification, assessment, economic control and financing of those risks which threaten the assets or earning capacity of an organisation.

Assets not only include physical assets of the organisation but also intangible assets such as goodwill, intellectual property, trade marks, copyright etc and human resources. Threats to earning capacity include not only events causing a reduction in income, but also incidents resulting in an increase in costs, whether payable to maintain operations, or due to breach of legislation or contractual obligations arising from goods sold or services performed.

Risk management is an integral part of management in an organisation and can be a positive mechanism to operational managers in assisting them to achieve their objectives. It is a multi-stage process. The first stage is risk identification where one determines how the assets or the earning capacity of the organisation may be threatened. Only if such threats are recognised can one successfully deal with them.

The second stage is risk assessment where:

(a)   the impact of the risk is quantified to determine its potential severity; and

(b)   the likelihood of the risk occurring is established to measure its potential frequency.

The principal objective here is to measure the relative importance of the risk, which enables decisions to be made on priorities, and the most appropriate form of treatment adopted.

Following measurement of the exposure the next step is to ascertain how it may be eliminated or reduced. Loss reduction may take the form of:

(i)   pre-loss reduction – action taken following identification of a risk, but prior to the event occurring. Pre-loss risk control concentrates on reducing the frequency of an occurrence (eg ensuring guards on dangerous machinery); and

(ii)   post-loss reduction – focusing on reducing severity once the event has taken place (eg the installation of a sprinkler system).

Risks may also be controlled through non-insurance contractual transfer. Such transfers may be in the form of:

(A)   risk control transfers – requiring the transferee to perform and complete the action giving rise to the risk (eg subcontracting hazardous construction work); and

(B)   risk financing transfers – requiring the transferee to accept financial responsibility for losses arising from a particular exposure (eg indemnity agreements).

Once a risk has been identified and either avoided or reduced to the greatest extent practicable and economically viable, a decision has to be made as to whether the financial consequence of any residual risk can be:

(I)   retained by the organisation; or

(II)   transferred to the insurance market (assuming coverage exists).

The levels of risk which a company is able to retain depends upon:

(1)   the financial strength of the organisation;

(2)   the shareholders and the markets expectations;

(3)   the characteristics of the company; and

(4)   the post-loss goals of the operation.

The major benefits of risk retention are obtained by retaining the financial consequences of high frequency, low severity, and predictable losses, the costs of which are generally uneconomic to transfer.

For exposures which cannot be economically:

(a)   avoided or eliminated;

(b)   reduced through risk control and contractual risk transfer; or

(c)   retained by the organisation,

consideration may be given to insurance, providing coverage is available.

Insurance is a risk transfer mechanism which transfers the financial consequences of loss to a third party. If insurance protection is not available, consideration should be given to whether the activity giving rise to the risk should be continued.

The key features of an insurance contract are:

(i)   it is arranged in advance of an event and the agreement is documented in writing in the insurance policy; and

(ii)   the financial consequences of the loss are transferred to the insurer at the time of the incident.

There are a number of benefits of insurance which include:

(A)   compliance with legal or statutory requirements to insure;

(B)   indemnification against unexpected events and losses;

(C)   reduction in uncertainty through the substitution of the unknown costs of losses with the certainty of the known cost of the premium in that year;

(D)   release of funds held in reserve for unknown losses for more productive use; and

(E)   access to specialist risk management services provided by insurers.

However, the use of insurance as a risk financing tool is not without its criticisms. Most importantly, it may not provide full financial compensation in the event of a loss because of delays in restoration to full capacity and claim settlement; nor full compensation for permanent loss of market share and effect on public image etc.

Additionally, there may be practical problems such as financial failure of insurers, inadequate and inappropriate insurance arrangements, poor quality of service, volatility of premium costs and non-availability of the cover sought.

Risk transfer to insurers

[13.2] Risk transfer to insurers will normally take place in circumstances where:

(a)   there is a legal or statutory obligation to insure;

(b)   the size of the potential loss is such that it cannot be retained by the organisation; or

(c)   this is the most cost-effective method of handling the risk (subject to insurance coverage and capacity being available up to the limits required).

Insurance available

[13.3] There are three general areas of insurance covering:

(a)   loss or damage to the assets of the company;

(b)   loss of earnings; and

(c)   protection against statutory or common law liabilities.

Most insurance companies offer packages to cover these risks and in assessing the merits of them, consideration should be given as to whether they adequately provide protection for the organisation's assets, liabilities, risks and exposures which might include:

(i)   buildings, machinery and plant;

(ii)   stock;

(iii)   goods in transit;

(iv)   loss of income or increased costs;

(v)   crime;

(vi)   computer equipment;

(vii)   legal liability arising out of the operation of the business; and

(viii) terrorism.

Insurance policies should be carefully scrutinised to ensure that they cover the appropriate risks. It should also be considered whether insurance is, in fact, the optimum approach. Many risks can be managed without the use of insurance by identifying the risk and taking the appropriate preventative action.

The insurance broker

[13.4] Although all of the large insurance companies can offer expert guidance on many insurance issues and policies on a direct basis, they only offer their own policies for sale. There are advantages for the small company in the use of an insurance broker or consultant to reduce the overall cost of an insurance package and to advise on insurance needs. For larger companies or where complex risk issues are involved, it is usual for an insurance broker or consultant to be employed.

There are two main advantages in seeking this advice:

(a)   the broker or consultant has the experience of identifying risks and insuring against them that a company's own personnel may lack; and

(b)   the broker or consultant will be independent of the insurers and thus will be able to undertake a more objective assessment of a company's insurance requirements.

Insurance brokers are remunerated by a commission, included in the insurance premium, or by an agreed fee basis.

The loss adjuster and loss assessor

[13.5] In the event of a significant loss which is covered by the insurance arrangements it is normal practice for the insurers to appoint a loss adjuster to handle the negotiation of the claim.

The loss adjusters fees are paid by the insurer but he has a professional duty to:

(a)   be independent and impartial; and

(b)   assist the insured if he is unrepresented.

A loss assessor is appointed by and acts solely on behalf of the insured. It is the insured who is responsible for the payment of the loss assessor's fees, which may be based on time spent or on a success basis. To some extent, the appointment of a loss assessor by the insured removes some of the responsibilities that would otherwise fall on the loss adjuster. Insurance policies do not generally cover loss assessor's or claim preparation costs.

General principles and practice of insurance

[13.6] The following are key general principles and practices of insurance.

Utmost good faith

[13.7] The principle of utmost good faith forms the basis of the insurance contract. This places a responsibility on the insured to disclose any circumstances which are relevant or material. A material fact is one which would influence the judgment of a prudent insurer in setting the premium or determining whether to accept the risk.

Insurable interest

[13.8] Insurance may only be purchased in situations of risk where an 'insurable interest' exists. An insurable interest could be described as existing where:

(a)   there is a property or interest to insure (subject matter);
(b)   there is a relationship recognised at law between the insured and the subject matter; and
(c)   the happening of an insured event would cause the insured financial loss.

Indemnity

[13.9] Contracts of insurance are generally contracts of indemnity. Indemnity can be defined as returning an insured party to the same financial position it was in prior to the insured loss occurring. Neither profit nor betterment are allowed.

In property insurance the measure of indemnity is the lesser of the cost of repair of the damaged property or its value at the time of the loss. In practice, the insurers may pay for the cost of replacement on a new for old basis providing more than an indemnity settlement.

In respect of liability the measurement is the insured's legal liability to the employee or third party.

Average

[13.10] Average normally applies to material damage insurance and may sometimes be applicable to business interruption insurance. In circumstances where an average provision applies an insured will be considered their own insurer for any underinsurance and shall bear a rateable share of the loss. For example, if an insured only insures 90% of the total value at risk and an average provision operates any claim settlement will be reduced by 10%. Underinsurance must therefore be avoided to ensure an adequate indemnity.

Warranty

[13.11] A warranty imposes a duty upon an insured to maintain specific conditions which might otherwise give rise to an increase in risk. A breach of warranty, whether or not it is the cause of any loss, enables the insurer to void the policy at their option from the date of the breach. Warranties must therefore be strictly complied with.

An example is cash warranted to be kept in a safe overnight.

Excess

[13.12] This is the amount of loss to be borne by the insured, first, before the insurers pay. It may be stipulated as a monetary amount or, for business interruption insurance, a period of time. Only loss suffered beyond the excess will be met by the policy, eg loss £500,000 with an excess of £100,000 – policy pays £400,000.

Franchise

[13.13] A franchise operates as a threshold. It is necessary for the total loss to exceed the threshold before it can be claimed in full, eg loss £500,000 franchise £100,000 – policy pays £500,000. If the loss falls below the franchise no cover operates. A franchise may similarly be specified as a monetary amount or a period of time.

The insurance policy

Statutory policies – insurance policies required by law

[13.14] All businesses in the UK are legally obliged to have employer's liability insurance and motor third party insurance.

These compulsory insurances must be insured with an approved insurance company authorised to insure these risks. Approval is granted by the Department for Business, Innovation and Skills (commonly referred to as 'BIS') which supervises insurance companies who transact business in the UK. Companies may now, if they so choose, obtain insurance from an insurer who is authorised to insure these risks in another EU Member State and has notified BIS that it wishes to provide insurance in the UK.

Employers' liability

Legal requirement

[13.15] Under the Employers' Liability (Compulsory Insurance) Act 1969, every employer carrying on business in the UK must insure against legal liability for death, bodily injury or illness sustained by employees, while serving under a contract of service or apprenticeship, which arises out of and in the course of their employment.

Policy coverage

[13.16] The purpose of employers' liability insurance is to protect an employer against claims for damages brought by employees. The policy covers the employer's legal liability including:

(a)   negligence in failing to use reasonable care and skill in:
    (i)   providing suitable and safe plant;
    (ii)   providing a safe system of work;
    (iii)   providing a safe place of work; and
    (iv)   engaging suitable and competent employees;
(b)   breach of statutory regulations, eg Health and Safety at Work Act 1974; and

(c)   negligence of fellow employees (an employer will be vicariously liable if one employee negligently injures a fellow employee during the course of his/her employment).

The employers' liability policy responds to death, bodily injury or illness caused during the period of insurance. There may be a significant time period between the cause and the onset of the injury or illness, particularly in relation to exposure to toxic materials or the effects of noise. There may be a further period of time before the employee makes a claim. It is therefore important to retain records of historic policies to ensure that claims can be recovered under the appropriate policy.

The territorial limits operative on employers' liability insurance are Great Britain, Northern Ireland, the Channel Islands and the Isle of Man but cover also operates for employees who sustain death, bodily injury or illness whilst temporarily elsewhere in the world. Normally any action for damages must be brought within Great Britain, Northern Ireland, the Channel Islands and the Isle of Man.

The policy extends to indemnify any principals in like manner to the insured if it is necessary to do so to meet the requirements of any contract entered into by the insured with the principal.

A copy of the certificate confirming the insurance is in place is required to be displayed in a prominent place (eg a notice board) at each place of business.

Limit of indemnity

[13.17] The amount for which an employer is required to insure is £2 million for any one occurrence. It was common practice for insurers to provide cover, unlimited in amount, but with effect from 1 January 1995 insurers have generally imposed a limit of indemnity of £10 million for any one occurrence. Costs and legal expenses incurred in defending negligence claims made against the company by employees are inclusive of the limit of indemnity.

If the standard limit of indemnity is insufficient to cater for the maximum damages and costs which might arise from a single occurrence additional coverage will need to be sought.

Restrictions

[13.18] Legislation prohibits insurers avoiding liability due to an insured breaching a policy condition. In such circumstances the insurers will have to deal with the claim and compensate the injured employee. They will then have the right to recover from the insured the sum so paid any of which they have been obliged to pay under the provisions of the Employers' Liability (Compulsory Insurance) General Regulations 1971.

Excesses are not permitted under the Act, but it is permissible to include a policy term requiring the insured to reimburse insurers up to a stipulated sum in respect of any claim.

Motor

Legal requirement

[13.19] The Road Traffic Act 1988 requires that insurance exists for all vehicles used on the road against liability to any third party for death or bodily injury and damage to property. There is no requirement to cover damage to the insured vehicle.

Policy coverage

[13.20] There are three principal bases of motor insurance.

(a) Third Party only – unlimited liability to third parties in respect of death, bodily injury or damage to property arising out of the use of a vehicle. Property damage arising out of the use of commercial vehicles or vehicles bearing trade plates is normally limited.

(b) Third Party Fire and Theft – as above extended to include fire damage to and theft or attempted theft of the vehicle itself.

(c) Comprehensive – as above extended to include accidental damage of the vehicle itself and other specified extensions.

It is a requirement of the Road Traffic Act 1988 that a certificate of insurance or cover note has been issued by the insurer.

Third party coverage includes legal fees for representation and for defence. In addition, motor insurance policies normally pay costs of defence against a charge of manslaughter or causing death by reckless or dangerous driving in the UK if the charge arises out of an accident which is subject to indemnity under the policy.

Insured use

[13.21] There are two main classifications of insured use as far as a company is concerned:

(a) social, domestic and pleasure purposes and for the business of the policyholder excluding use for hiring, commercial travelling or for any purpose in connection with the motor trade; and

(b) as in (*a*) above but including carriage of passengers for hire or reward and use in connection with the motor trade.

It is normal practice to exclude use for racing, competitions, rallies or trials.

There may be restrictions on young or inexperienced drivers or persons convicted of serious motoring offences. Some policies severely restrict the cover provided if at the time of the accident the driver is under the influence of drink or drugs.

Foreign use

[13.22] Policy coverage applies in respect of an accident occurring in Great Britain, Northern Ireland, the Isle of Man and the Channel Islands and during sea transits between ports in these areas. In accordance with the EU Directive the policy includes cover in respect of the minimum requirements of those European Countries which have signed the Directive.

However, the insurer should be notified early of any proposed journey abroad to extend full policy coverage and for the issue of an international green card, for countries which are not party to the EU Directive. This green card is evidence that the insurance meets any local statutory requirements, so exempting the policyholder from having to effect insurance locally in most European countries. For countries which do not subscribe to the international green card system, insurance should be arranged locally.

For visits to Spain a bail bond is recommended. This is a guarantee provided by an insurer to secure the release of the policyholder or their vehicle from the custody of the authorities following an accident by the bearer. The bond is a guarantee and not insurance, and so is refundable by the bearer to the insurer if retained permanently by the authorities.

Minimum extensions

[**13.23**] It is usual to extend the policy to include:

(a)   Contractual Liability to Principal – liability assumed under an agreement with a principal for the execution of work or services;

(b)   Unauthorised Use – indemnity in the event of an accident occurring whilst a vehicle is being used without the knowledge of the insured for a purpose not permitted under the insurance policy; and

(c)   Unauthorised Movement – liability incurred in moving an obstructing vehicle without the authority of the owner.

Motor third party contingency cover

[**13.24**] Circumstances may arise where an employee uses his own vehicle on company business. Any claims from third parties arising out of this use may be covered by the employee's own insurance if business use is included. If not, then the employer may be vicariously liable. Contingent third party insurance covers this vicarious liability and indemnifies the employer. It does not cover the employee. Before giving permission to an employee to use his own vehicle on company business it is advisable to check that his insurance covers such business use by him.

Uninsured losses

[**13.25**] There are certain types of losses which may be incurred following a motor accident which are not covered under the insurance policy, eg hire charges of an alternative vehicle.

Legal expenses insurance can be arranged to meet the legal costs of seeking to recover uninsured losses suffered following a collision with a negligent third party.

Insurance policies to protect the business

[**13.26**] Common insurance policies include 'Material Damage', 'Business Interruption' and 'Third Party Liability' insurance.

Material damage

The risk

[13.27] The assets of a business will generally fall into three categories:

(a)   buildings;
(b)   plant, machinery and other contents; and
(c)   stock.

All are subject to possible loss, destruction or damage.

Policy coverage

[13.28] The material damage policy seeks to indemnify the insured in respect of loss, destruction or damage of physical assets. This indemnification may take the form of the insurer:

(a)   paying the value of the property at the time of the loss, destruction, or damage, in the event of a total loss;
(b)   paying the amount of the damage or the cost of repair in the event of partial damage; or
(c)   at its option reinstate or replace the property which has suffered damage.

Material damage insurance may be arranged to respond to loss, destruction or damage either from specified events or for all risks.

(i)   Fire and special perils
       The standard fire policy covers fire, lightning and to a limited extent explosion. At the insured's option the standard policy can be extended to include additional special perils such as:
       (A)   explosion;
       (B)   earthquake;
       (C)   riot and civil commotion;
       (D)   malicious damage;
       (E)   storm, tempest and flood;
       (F)   burst pipe; and
       (G)   impact.
       The insurer may also be prepared to grant cover for loss or damage arising out of:
       (I)   accidental damage;
       (II)   theft (normally restricted to that involving forcible and violent entry or exit);
       (III)   explosion, collapse and overheating of boilers, economisers and vessels;
       (IV)   sprinkler leakage; and
       (V)   subsidence.
(ii)   All risks
       The all risks policy covers loss, destruction or damage from any cause which is not specifically excluded. The standard all risks wording broadly covers fire, the special perils listed above (A–G) and accidental damage subject to some exclusions. Some of these exclusions may be avoided by the payment of an additional premium.

They include:

(1)   explosion of steam pressure vessels;
(2)   mechanical or electrical breakdown;
(3)   theft or attempted theft;
(4)   subsidence, ground heave and landslip; and
(5)   collapse and overheating of boilers, economisers etc.

Terrorism

[13.29] Cover for terrorist fire and explosion in the UK is limited in amount by insurers under their standard policy wordings. Full policy limits can be attained by purchasing terrorism cover from the material damage insurers, who then reinsure the risk with a facility set up by UK Insurers, Pool Re. This will attract an additional premium at standard rates established by Pool Re. The UK Government acts as a reinsurer of last resort to this facility. Depending on market conditions there may be alternative sources of terrorism insurance which can be explored.

Additional insurance

[13.30] The basic material damage policy may be extended to include:

(a)   goods in transit; and
(b)   money.

Goods in transit insurance can cover consignments by post, rail, road, sea or air carrier within preselected territories. Money insurance can cover cash and non-negotiable instruments in transit and at own premises in and out of business hours. Money insurance may additionally be extended to include personal accident assault to employees carrying cash.

Average

[13.31] Material damage policies are normally subject to average. In the event of underinsurance the insured will be penalised in any claim settlement.

In respect of buildings, machinery and plant, underinsurance caused by inflation can be avoided by utilising the 'day one basis'. The insured declares the cost of reinstating the property insured at the level of costs at the start of the period of insurance. An inflation provision is then applied to this figure. Providing the value declared at the commencement of the policy is adequate and the inflation provision sufficient the claim settlement will not be reduced by average.

Underinsurance on stock is most appropriately avoided by setting the sum insured at the absolute maximum which is envisaged will be held at any one time during the period of insurance and then agreeing with insurers that the premium they charge reflects this fact.

Reinstatement

[13.32] Being a contract of indemnity the measure of loss under the material damage policy is the value of the property at the time of loss or damage. This would include an appropriate reduction to allow for wear and tear. The indemnity contract can be amended so as to provide the full cost of reinstatement of buildings or machinery (but not stock) on a new for old basis (but not to include betterment). Consequently there would be no deduction to allow for the effects of wear and tear. Otherwise the insured should not be better off as a result of insurers meeting the full cost of reinstatement.

Minimum requirements

[13.33] It is recommended that the material damage policy includes the following.

(a)   Automatic reinstatement – automatic reinstatement of the sum insured in the event of loss.

(b)   Debris removal – the cost of removing building debris, damaged machinery and stock.

(c)   Professional fees – architects, surveyors and consulting engineers fees incurred in the reinstatement of property.

(d)   Public authorities – additional costs of reinstatement incurred in complying with building or other regulations.

(e)   Capital additions – automatic cover for alterations, additions and improvements to existing property.

The sum insured should be increased to include an estimated price for items (*b*) to (*e*) inclusive.

Areas to consider

[13.34] Some particular issues that should be considered are detailed below.

(a)   Buildings – in respect of leased premises, the insurance obligations of the landlord and the tenant should be examined carefully. It is also necessary to take into account any obligations to maintain the premises and/or the landlord's fixtures and fittings and ensure appropriate insurance is arranged. The landlord may be obliged to insure only against loss or damage to the basic structure of a building, caused by fire or related damage. Items such as flood or subsidence are not always required to be covered and a tenant should thus take particular care to ensure that his business is protected against these eventualities.

When insuring a building, it is advisable to insure on a re-instatement basis and to account for items such as architects' and surveyors' fees, demolition of the damaged structure and costs of meeting local authority requirements.

(b)   Plant, machinery and other contents – where plant and machinery are hired, clarification of the hirer's risks should be sought. It is common for the hirer to be responsible for all loss or damage to such equipment. Computer equipment is another area requiring particular attention. Risks to be assessed here are the costs of repairs falling outside any maintenance agreement and the cost of replacing any information corrupted or lost following a malfunction of the system.

(c)   Stock – an important consideration with stock is in relation to its transportation and storage. To avoid gaps in cover which could result in a loss to the company one should clarify the point at which stock becomes the company's liability on inwards transit.

(d)   Rent – ideally rent should be insured under the business interruption insurance arrangements which provides more appropriate and wider cover for rent than material damage insurance.

Business interruption

The risk

[**13.35**] Although a material damage policy is designed to cover such expenses as the cost of clearing debris, rebuilding premises and replacement of other physical assets, it is not intended to cover loss of income whilst replacements, repair or rebuilding are carried out. Neither does the material damage policy cater for the burden of extra expenses incurred in keeping the business in operation.

Overview of policy

[**13.36**] Business interruption insurance provides compensation to an insured who suffers loss of income following physical damage by an insured event.

The standard policy wording can be designed to cover both loss of income and costs incurred in avoiding such loss or can merely cover costs only. The trigger for the business interruption policy is an insured contingency causing damage to property used by the insured at their premises which causes interruption to their business.

Extension of the basic policy coverage may be required to cover certain scenarios and types of financial loss which are not covered under the standard wording. Business interruption insurers limit coverage under their standard policy wording in respect of terrorist fire or explosion. Full policy limits may be achieved by selecting the appropriate extension in a similar manner to material damage insurance.

Principles of business interruption insurance

[**13.37**] There are certain general principles to business interruption insurance which limit policy coverage and which need to be understood when arranging business interruption cover. These include the following.

(a)   Business definition – the business interruption policy only covers business activities which are defined. It is necessary for the business description to embrace all activities undertaken.
(b)   Premises definition – the standard business interruption policy only caters for consequential loss suffered as a result of insured damage occurring to premises which are defined. Therefore the standard business interruption policy does not cover loss suffered as a result of damage:
    (i)   to the insured's premises which are not defined and included in the 'premises' definition; or
    (ii)   to third party facilities.
However, the policy can be extended to cover such losses arising from damage to other premises upon which there is a dependency and property away from own premises.

(c) Material damage insurance provision – it is a condition of business interruption insurance that there must be a material damage insurance in force:
   (i) protecting the interest of the insured;
   (ii) covering the property which has suffered damage; and
   (iii) the material damage insurers must have accepted liability.

(d) Material damage provision waiver – the material damage insurance provision does not apply:
   (i) in circumstances where the material damage insurers avoid liability under their policy solely because the material damage loss falls below an excess or franchise and is therefore not recoverable under the policy; and
   (ii) to property in which the insured has no insurable interest, eg property owned by a third party.

Policy coverage

[13.38] There are three main types of business interruption policy.

(a) Increased Cost of Working Only Policy – this type of policy covers the additional expenditure reasonably incurred by the insured in order to minimise interruption to the business. It offers no protection for loss of income suffered. This basis of cover is only appropriate if it is possible to continue operating, at increased cost, following an incident without any effect on turnover.

(b) Gross Revenue Policy – this type of policy covers loss of revenue and any increased costs incurred to avoid or reduce a loss of revenue which would otherwise be incurred. It is necessary for such costs to be economic (ie costs incurred do not exceed revenue loss avoided). Insurers will normally exclude the element of variable costs which may reduce after an incident (eg savings in electricity consumption costs).

(c) Gross Profit (or Net Revenue) Policy – this type of policy covers loss of gross profit and any increased costs incurred in avoiding or reducing a loss in gross profit providing such costs are economic. Under a gross profit policy, it is necessary to specify these costs payable out of turnover that will be uninsured. To avoid underinsurance it is necessary to deduct only costs which are directly and proportionally variable with turnover under both a total and partial loss scenario (ie a 10% decrease in turnover should be accompanied by the same percentage reduction in the cost). Insurable gross profit is different to accounting gross profit, particularly in the treatment of wages, as all salaries and payroll are insured in full.

Average

[13.39] The insurance for increased cost of working only does not include either an average provision or an inflation provision. Business interruption insurance covering revenue or gross profit comes in two forms; one subject to average and one with no such provision.

The conventional form of cover in respect of gross profit and revenue includes an average provision. Therefore, if the sum insured is inadequate the insured will bear a share of the loss. There is no in-built provision for inflation during the period of insurance or the indemnity period.

Both gross profit and revenue cover may also be written on a non-average form known as the declaration linked approach. This method requires an estimate, calculated on a basis laid down in the policy, to be declared to insurers at the start of the period of insurance. The insured then benefits from an inflation provision up to 133 1/3% of declared value.

The non-average declaration linked form has significant advantages which include:

(a)   no penalty for underinsurance providing the declared value has been arrived at in accordance with the policy terms;
(b)   automatic provision for inflation during both the period of insurance and the indemnity period;
(c)   values based on current financial forecasts avoiding the need to accurately project income in future years; and
(d)   possibly, lower premiums because of a lower value declared to insurers.

Maximum indemnity period

[13.40] In addition to a monetary limit, the sum insured or limit of liability, there is a time limit, the maximum indemnity period. The indemnity period commences on the date of the damage and ceases when the results of the business are no longer being affected, providing this does not exceed a predetermined limit known as the maximum indemnity period. Hence it is not possible to claim for an indefinite interruption.

To establish an adequate maximum indemnity period consideration should be given to the period in which not only loss of income might be suffered but also additional costs incurred. The period needs to assume a catastrophic incident occurs (such as a major fire or explosion), and make allowance for:

(a)   debris removal, planning application and rebuild (where buildings are involved);
(b)   lead times for delivery (where machinery and equipment are involved);
(c)   additional allowance for any statutory or public authority requirements and any testing and commissioning; and
(d)   any additional period for recapture of lost market share.

The maximum indemnity period also needs to cater for ongoing expenses for which there are contractual obligations, eg lease and rent payments, to ensure such payments are protected for the maximum period contractually required.

The maximum indemnity period is normally defined in multiples of six months (eg 12, 18, 24 months etc) but there are generally no premium savings in selecting an indemnity period of less than 12 months.

Minimum requirements

[13.41] It is recommended that, as a minimum, the business interruption policy provides the following:

(a)   automatic reinstatement – automatic reinstatement of sum insured after a loss;

(b) payments on account – interim payments throughout the indemnity period; and

(c) professional accountancy fees – costs payable to professional accountants in providing and certifying particulars requested by insurers which form the basis of claim.

Extensions

[13.42] The standard business interruption policy covers consequential loss during the indemnity period as a result of:

(a) physical damage which is insured;
(b) to property used by the insured;
(c) which is at the premises of the insured.

There are a number of types of scenarios which are not covered by the standard policy wording but which can be covered by specific extensions at additional premium. These include interruption suffered as a result of:

(i)   a non damage incident such as bomb threat;
(ii) damage in the vicinity of the premises causing denial of access or a reduction in the number of customers in the area;
(iii) damage to customer premises resulting in a reduction in demand for the product;
(iv) damage to a suppliers' premises causing a shortfall in raw material or services provided; and
(v)   failure of utility supplies such as electricity, telecommunications, gas and water.

There are certain financial losses not catered for adequately by the standard business interruption policy but which also can be covered by specific extension at additional premium. These include:

(A) delay to income as a result of damage to property to be used at a future date;
(B) uneconomic additional expenditure incurred in maintaining the business;
(C) fines and penalties payable to third parties as a result of non performance of contract terms because of the insured damage;
(D) continuing research and development costs; and
(E) inability to recover outstanding debts because of destruction of debtor records.

Third party liability

The risk

[13.43] An organisation may incur liability in a number of ways, which include:

(a) negligence – omission to do something which a reasonable person would do or doing something which a prudent person would not do;
(b) nuisance – unlawfully disturbing a person's enjoyment of their property;

(c)   trespass – an unlawful act committed with force on the person or property of another;

(d)   strict liability – where the defendant will be liable even though reasonable care has been exercised;

(e)   contractual liability – amendments to common law liability assumed under the terms of a written contract;

(f)   statutory liability – liabilities created by Acts of Parliament; and

(g)   vicarious liability – where responsibility is assumed for the torts of others.

Policy coverage

[**13.44**] Public liability insurance protects an insured against legal liability for death of or bodily injury to third parties or loss of or damage to their property which happens in connection with the insured's activities. Product liability insurance indemnifies an insured against legal liability for death or bodily injury to third parties, or loss of or damage to their property caused by goods sold, supplied, repaired or serviced by the insured. The policies are commonly linked.

The policies will also indemnify the insured in respect of costs which the claimant has incurred as a result of the incident. This amount is usually in addition to the limit of indemnity (other than in North America).

Public and product liability insurance are both subject to territorial limits which stipulate where the death, injury or damage must occur for the policy to apply. It is important for the territorial limits to be sufficiently wide and ideally to be worldwide. Additionally, cover may be subject to a jurisdiction clause making reference to where actions by claimants against the insured may be covered by the policy. Similarly, the jurisdiction clause should be as wide as is possible to negotiate.

Most insurers exclude all claims arising out of pollution or contamination in North America. For other parts of the world, cover will normally not apply unless the claim arises out of a sudden, unintended, unexpected or unforeseen occurrence which takes place entirely at a specific time and place. Additionally any pollution and contamination cover will be subject to a limit of indemnity for the entire period of the insurance.

Basis of cover

[**13.45**] Public and product liability insurance can be available on a claims made or loss occurring basis. There are significant differences between the way these two types of coverage respond to claims:

(a)   the claims made basis provides cover for claims made in writing to the insured during the policy period irrespective of when the incident or cause giving rise to the claim occurred; and

(b)   the loss occurring basis responds to death, injury or damage caused to third parties during the period of insurance. The claim on the insured does not need to be made during this period.

The loss occurring basis is the form which is normally utilised in the UK.

Limit of indemnity

[13.46] Both public liability insurance and products liability insurance are subject to limits of indemnity, but the way in which these operate differs:

(a) under public liability insurance the limit of indemnity is the maximum that the insurer will pay out in respect of any one event which gives rise to a claim; and

(b) in respect of product liability insurance the limit of indemnity is the maximum that will be paid in respect of all events in any one period of insurance.

Minimum requirements

[13.47] As a minimum the public/product liability coverage should include:

(a) additional insureds – individual indemnity should be provided to directors, officers and employees, sport, social, first aid or medical staff, ambulance and fire services;

(b) cross liabilities – where the policy is in the name of more than one insured this makes it clear that liability of one insured to another is covered;

(c) indemnity to principals – where contractual obligations require this provides indemnity to a principal;

(d) tenant's legal liability – legal liability in respect of premises leased or rented to the insured;

(e) Defective Premises Act 1972 – liability for newly built, converted or adapted dwellings and landlord's liability for defects in premises;

(f) Consumer Protection Act 1987 – strict liability in respect of products supplied where an injured party need only prove that he has suffered injury caused by a defective product to be able to claim against the producer;

(g) Data Protection Act 1984 – liability arising out of the misuse of information retained about individuals on computer systems;

(h) overseas personal liability – personal liability for the insured's employees when outside the UK on business.

Extensions

[13.48] There are a number of types of liability which are excluded from the standard public/product liability policy but which can be included in certain circumstances. These include, *inter alia*:

(a) contractual liability – liability assumed under contract which would not otherwise have existed;

(b) property in insured's charge or control – inclusion of property belonging to others on which the insured is temporarily performing work;

(c) financial loss – liability for financial loss not dependent upon injury to persons or damage to property;

(d) contingent motor liability – legal liability arising out of a vehicle not owned or provided by the insured but used on the insured's behalf;

(e) design, plan or formula – liability arising out of defective design, plan, formula or specification of goods;

(f) labels and instructions – liability arising out of labels, pamphlets, instructions or other written material;

(g) product recall – expenses incurred in recalling or withdrawing a defective product from the market; and

(h) product guarantee – liability arising out of failure of a product to perform its intended purpose.

Professional indemnity

The risk

[13.49] Liability may arise from a breach of contract for services between a professional party and a client. It is implied in a contract for professional services that the professional will exercise a fair, reasonable and competent degree of care and skill. Any failure to do so which causes a loss to the client may result in the professional being sued for professional negligence. Case law has established that a professional may also owe a duty of care to another party who relies on the advice given. The standard of care expected of a professional person is the standard expected of an average member of his particular profession.

It is increasingly common for professionals to seek insurance to cover liability which may arise from a damages claim brought by a client. In the past such cover only tended to be sought by accountants, solicitors and architects. In the increasingly litigious climate, very few professionals now consider themselves safe. The number of actions for professional negligence has increased dramatically over recent years and damages and costs have spiralled, resulting in escalating costs of insurance and reduced availability in relation to certain professions.

Policy coverage

[13.50] The professional indemnity policy is designed to protect professional persons or others, who supply a skill or service, against their legal liability to compensate any third party who has sustained some form of injury, loss or damage due to their professional negligence. Cover is intended to apply to unintentional forms of conduct and does not include dishonest, fraudulent, criminal or malicious acts.

The professional indemnity cover provided is subject to claims arising within specific geographical limits. The geographical limits within a professional indemnity policy should be sufficiently wide to include all territories where a claim could arise.

Basis of cover

[13.51] Professional indemnity insurance is provided on a claims made basis. Provided the actual claim is made during the period of insurance it does not matter when the act of negligence giving rise to the claim took place. The policy may provide retrospective cover for acts of negligence committed prior to a specified date. Consequently an insured will be required to disclose all potential occurrences which may give rise to a claim in the future. Similar strict reporting requirements apply at each renewal. Failure to disclose a potential occurrence could prejudice cover.

The policy may also cover claims intimated during a discovery period after the expiry date of the policy. This is in respect of negligence occurring during the period of insurance for which claims are not made until after the policy ends.

Limit of indemnity

[13.52] The limit of indemnity will normally be a total limit for the entire period of insurance. In the event of a claim it is therefore necessary to reinstate the limit which has been eroded. Some insurers will offer a prepaid reinstatement at the time of setting up the policy. Costs and expenses incurred in the defence or settlement of any claim may be in addition to this limit, or included. It is common practice for policies to impose a degree of financial involvement by the professional should any damages claim be upheld.

Extensions

[13.53] There are a number of types of exposure which are not covered under the standard professional indemnity policy but which may be included in certain circumstances. These include:

(a)   dishonesty of employees – legal liability to others arising out of the dishonesty of employees (but not partners or directors);
(b)   libel and slander – legal liability in respect of libel or slander to title of goods and infringement of trademark, copyright or patent from matter contained in publications;
(c)   breach of warranty of authority – liability to a third party if the insured caused the third party to act on the strength of the insured's supposed authority;
(d)   loss or damage to documents – all risks cover on documents belonging to the insured or for which the insured is responsible; and
(e)   incoming/outgoing partners – liability for partners in respect of work performed in a previous practice/continuing liability for work performed once they have left.

Directors' and officers' liability

The risk

[13.54] Both executive and non-executive directors owe a duty of skill and care to both the company and to others.

Legal liability may arise from breaches of this duty such as:

(a)   negligent misstatements;
(b)   failure to carry out statutory responsibilities;
(c)   making unauthorised payments or allowing excessive company borrowing;
(d)   errors of judgement arising from a conflict of interest; and
(e)   through guarantees given in the course of business.

There are a variety of people or groups of people who can bring actions against directors and officers. These include:

(i)   shareholders;
(ii)   the company;
(iii) the Department for Business, Innovation and Skills;
(iv)   a receiver/liquidator;
(v)   company creditors; and
(vi)   regulatory bodies.

The Companies Act 2006 provides that a company may indemnify any director or officer of the company against any indemnity incurred by him in defending any proceedings (civil or criminal) in which judgment is given in his favour or he is granted relief by the court. See CHAPTER 6 (6.51).

Prior to the Companies Act 1989, there was doubt as to whether it was lawful for companies to purchase and maintain such indemnity policies on behalf of their directors or officers. However, companies may now purchase such policies, subject to the disclosure of their existence in the directors' report to the annual accounts.

Policy coverage

[**13.55**] A directors' and officers' policy provides cover under two sections:

(a)   one part protects the directors and officers in their personal capacity in circumstances where they cannot claim an indemnity from the company; and
(b)   the second part indemnifies the company in respect of costs and expenses it may have incurred in successfully defending a director or officer under the relevant sections of the Companies Act.

Basis of cover

[**13.56**] Directors' and officers' insurance operates on a claims made basis protecting directors and officers in respect of claims made against them during the period of insurance arising out of any wrongful act committed in their respective capacities.

Limit of indemnity

[**13.57**] The limit of indemnity is a total limit for all claims under the policy during the period of insurance and is inclusive of costs and expenses incurred in the defence or settlement of any claim.

Basic requirement

[13.58] The directors' and officers' insurance should ideally reflect the following:

(a) insured persons – the policy should provide blanket coverage for all past, present and future directors and officers of the company;

(b) company – the policy should include all subsidiary companies created or acquired on or before the inception date of the policy period;

(c) legal costs – the policy should include the provision for insurers to provide payment of defence costs as these are incurred; and

(d) directors' estates – the policy should automatically provide indemnity for claims made against the estates, heirs, legal representatives of the insured persons in the event of their death, incapacity or bankruptcy.

The standard directors' and officers' liability policy can be extended to include other areas of cover such as:

(i) protection for individual directors or officers of the company whilst acting in the capacity of a director or officer of another unrelated company; and

(ii) employment practices liability, such as claims arising from unlawful dismissal, sexual harassment, sexual/racial discrimination etc.

Exclusions

[13.59] Cover does not apply to losses arising out of dishonesty, fraud or illegal personal profit. Additionally, standard exclusions include:

(a) pollution and contamination;

(b) bodily injury/property damage;

(c) libel and slander;

(d) insured versus insured (ie the company suing a director or one director suing another);

(e) guarantees and warranties;

(f) professional liability; and

(g) fines and penalties.

Exclusions may vary between insurers, and it may be possible to modify these exclusions to some extent through negotiation and the payment of an additional premium.

Crime insurance

The risk

[13.60] A fraudulent or dishonest action of an employee or third party may result in loss of money or property. The risk may vary from low level pilferage by individuals to a major conspiracy between a group of employees, or a major funds transfer fraud carried out by a member of the public.

Policy coverage

[**13.61**] Crime insurance is designed to indemnify the insured against direct financial loss arising from the deliberate fraud or dishonesty of an employee or third party.

Basis of the cover

[**13.62**] The crime policy provides cover for direct financial loss arising from fraud or dishonesty committed during the period of indemnity, which is discovered either during the period of indemnity, or within a stipulated time period, normally 24 months after expiry of the period of indemnity or the cessation of the employment of the employee, whichever occurs first. The period of indemnity is the time during which the policy has been in force, not only the current year, but also any preceding years.

In addition to payment of the loss, insurers generally accept fees and expenses incurred in connection with a claim. The limit of indemnity under the policy will be inclusive of such costs.

When arranging crime insurance, it is usual for insurers to request the completion of a proposal form which sets out the systems of check that are in place to protect the business against the consequences of fraud or dishonesty.

In addition to electronic funds transfer fraud, a crime policy can be extended to cover other forms of loss such as:

(a)   loss or damage to money or other property including that arising from theft, mysterious unexplained disappearance; and

(b)   loss or damage to money or property whilst in transit.

Limit of indemnity

[**13.63**] The usual practice is to limit the indemnity to a specified amount.

Engineering

The risk

[**13.64**] Many organisations incur risks and responsibilities arising out of the use of boiler and pressure plant, lifting equipment, electrical equipment, mechanical machinery and computers.

The movement and installation of plant and machinery can additionally result in the loss of assets, the interruption of activities or liabilities being incurred.

Policy coverage

[**13.65**] Engineering policy coverage may be subdivided between:

(a)   the inspection of plant to comply with legislation; and

(b)   the insurance of plant and equipment against damage or breakdown.

Basis of cover

[13.66] The usual basis of cover will depend on the type of plant being insured.

(a)   Inspection – periodical inspection of plant may be required:
         (i)   to ensure the plant complies with the statutory requirements;
         (ii)   to meet the Health and Safety Commission's Guidance Notes, and Industry Codes of Practice;
         (iii)   to meet the operator's own needs to avoid faults, breakdowns and stoppages; and
         (iv)   to ensure the plant is in a suitable state of repair and adequately maintained for insurance purposes (if it is insured).

Legislation stipulates the maximum periods between inspection of particular types of plant. An insured may elect for more frequent inspection and the inspection of plant not subject to statutory inspection, particularly in circumstances where the plant is of a critical nature. Inspection services are available for most types of plant, whether or not the plant is actually insured.

(b)   Boiler/pressure plant – this covers all types of boiler and vessels which are subject to internal pressure. Cover may either operate:
         (i)   on a limited basis covering explosion or collapse only; or
         (ii)   on a wider basis covering sudden and unforeseen damage arising from any cause not specifically excluded.

In respect of steam plant, the policy should also cover damage to own surrounding property and third party liability arising from a steam explosion.

(c)   Lifts and lifting equipment – this covers lifts, cranes, hoists and all types of lifting and handling equipment. Cover is available for sudden and unforeseen damage arising from any cause not specifically excluded and/or breakdown.
         Cover can additionally be extended to include:
         (i)   damage to own surrounding property (either in consequence of damage to the equipment or arising out of the use of the equipment); and
         (ii)   goods being lifted or carried by the equipment (either in consequence of damage to the equipment or arising out of the use of the equipment).

(d)   Electrical and mechanical machinery – this covers all types of electrical and mechanical equipment including alternators, electric motors, engines, switchgear, compressors, electric pumps, turbines and fans. Cover is available for sudden and unforeseen damage arising from any cause not specifically excluded and/or breakdown. For high speed rotational items of plant the coverage can be extended to include own surrounding property.

(e) All plant and machinery – where an insured utilises boiler/pressure plant, lifts and lifting equipment and electrical and mechanical machinery, it is common practice to insure all plant at the premises on a sudden and unforeseen basis and breakdown.

(f) Computers – this covers all computer equipment, interconnecting cabling, telecommunication equipment, ancillary equipment and computer media. Cover is generally available in respect of:

(i) hardware and associated plant;

(ii) computer system records;

(iii) reinstatement of data; and

(iv) increased cost of working or business interruption.

Many computer policies specifically include additional benefits such as:

(A) accidental or malicious erasure, distortion or corruption of information on computer system records (eg by computer virus or disgruntled employees);

(B) incompatibility of computer systems records with replacement hardware;

(C) consulting engineers' repairs and investigations;

(D) avoidance measures impending loss;

(E) temporary repairs;

(F) property in transit/away for own premises;

(G) continuing rental costs;

(H) denial of access;

(I) failure or fluctuation in electricity supply;

(J) failure in distribution wiring; and

(K) failure of telecommunications and data transmission systems.

(g) Machinery movement – this cover can be tailored to cater for damage to machinery whilst being dismantled, erected or whilst in transit. Cover can either operate on a 'one off' basis for a specified period of time or as an annually renewable contract. Special consideration needs to be given where the transit is by sea or air.

(h) Erection, all risks – this provides cover against physical loss, destruction or damage to machinery and plant during transit/delivery to site, installation, erection and testing up until completion. Cover may specifically extend to include the maintenance period.

(i) Machinery, consequential loss – this covers loss of gross profit and/or increased cost of working following sudden and unforeseen damage and/or breakdown to plant or machinery. Cover can either be arranged on all plant and machinery or be restricted to specified items. In circumstances where loss, destruction or damage to new plant prior to use and production could result in delayed or lost income and increased costs, consideration should be given to advance profit cover.

Personal accident

The risk

[13.67] Everybody faces the risk of death and disablement arising out of an accident at work or home, whilst travelling or participating in hobbies or sports. Such an incident can cause the injured person and/or their dependants to suffer loss of income and/or incur extra costs. If the injured person is temporarily disabled their employer may have to maintain salary payments and employ a temporary replacement.

Policy coverage

[13.68] In the event of accidental bodily injury resulting in an insured person's death or permanent total disablement from any occupation within a specified time period (normally 12 or 24 months), the policy pays a fixed monetary sum or multiple of salary. A percentage of the lump sum is paid in the event of permanent partial disablement such as total loss of sight in one eye or total loss of one limb. Weekly benefits are payable, normally for a maximum of 104 weeks, in the event of temporary, total or partial disablement. The weekly benefits may be subject to a time excess or franchise before they become payable. Coverage may either be provided by way of a stand alone personal accident policy or an extension of other insurance policies such as motor or money policies.

Basis of cover

[13.69] Coverage is normally arranged on a group scheme basis to cover all employees of specified categories under a certain age and operates world-wide. Whilst benefits are normally based on multiples of salary, or percentages thereof, there will usually be a maximum limit in respect of any one person, and a separate limit in respect of an accumulation of employees killed or injured whilst travelling in an aircraft.

Coverage can be arranged on a 24-hour basis or be restricted to specified times and events, such as occupational accidents, non-occupational accidents, travel excluding commuting, sports, hobbies, criminal violence etc.

Coverage may extend to include legal expenses to pursue actions against negligent third parties causing bodily injury.

The lump sum payment for permanent total disablement will be dependent on the extent of coverage. The permanent total disablement may be:

(a) from gainful employment of any and every kind;
(b) from the insured's usual occupation and any other occupation for which the insured person is fitted by knowledge and training; or
(c) from the insured person's usual occupation.

Extension to basic policy coverage may be available in respect of:

(i) risks arising out of business travel outside the UK, such as medical expenses, baggage, personal effects and money, personal liability, cancellation and curtailment and replacement/rearrangement costs; and

(ii) sickness resulting in temporary total disablement of the insured person from their usual occupation.

Key man

The risk

[13.70] Many companies rely heavily on certain key directors and employees. Loss of such persons due to ill-health, disability or death can have a dramatic effect on a company due to:

(a) lost orders from personal contacts;
(b) loss of investor and bank confidence;
(c) costs incurred in finding and training a replacement;
(d) disablement costs such as salary and pension contributions; and
(e) general loss of confidence.

Overview of policy

[13.71] A policy can be taken out to cover these risks provided there is an insurable interest (ie the key man's function is vital) and that the level and period of cover is reasonable. The level of cover will normally be set at a multiple of salary.

The policy is not normally a personal benefit for the key person or the estate but a method of protecting the company. It can take the form of term assurance, life endowment assurance, health assurance or disability cover. The benefits can be taken in the form of a lump sum on death, instalments, or a regular income for disability.

Chapter 14

Employment, Health and Safety

Employment legislation

[14.1] Employment law is today recognised by company administrators as being of the greatest importance. Legislation in recent years has transformed the law in this area and has created new statutory rights for employees and obligations for employers. The European Union (EU) and the decisions of the European courts have had and will continue to play an increasingly important role in the development of the UK's domestic employment law. The employment section of this chapter seeks to outline the legislation governing individual employment, ie that directly applying between employees and employers and/or workers, along with the common law and EU law on relevant employment matters.

The legal rules governing employment law are derived from three principal sources:

(a)   the common law – including the law of contract by which the contract of employment is enforced, and the law of torts (wrongful acts which cause damage or loss) which governs, for example, an employer's liability for the acts of his employees, civil liability for industrial accidents and for forms of industrial action;

(b)   statute law – Acts of Parliament, regulations (statutory instruments) and statutory and non-statutory codes of practice; and

(c)   European legislation and judgments of the European Court of Justice (ECJ).

The main legislation applicable to employee rights and employer obligations is:

(i)   the Employment Rights Act 1996 (ERA 1996);
(ii)   the Employment Tribunals Act 1996 (ETA 1996);
(iii)   the Transfer of Undertakings (Protection of Employment) Regulations 2006 (SI 2006/246) (TUPE 2006); and
(iv)   the Equality Act 2010.

The Equality Act 2010 gathers up in one place the key discrimination laws, including equal pay, with effect from 1 October 2010.

The main legislation dealing with 'collective' employment rights, ie trade unions and trade disputes, is the Trade Union and Labour Relations (Consolidation) Act 1992 (TULR(C)A 1992), as amended by the Trade Union Reform and Employment Rights Act 1993 and the Employment Relations Act 1999 (see below). Other relevant employment legislation in force includes the Employment Tribunals Act 1996, the National Minimum Wage Act 1998 (see **14.90** below), the Public Interest Disclosure Act 1998 (see **14.96** below), the Working Time Regulations 1998 (see **14.22** below), the Data Protection Act 1998 (see **14.7** below) and the Human Rights Act 1998.

The Employment Relations Act 1999 (ERA 1999) covers 'blacklisting' of trade unions and the statutory right to be accompanied at disciplinary and grievance proceedings.

The EA 2002 introduced new ways of handling disputes in the workplace, by creating minimum statutory dismissal, disciplinary and grievance procedures. These troublesome provisions were repealed on 6 April 2009.

Administration of employment legislation

[14.2] Employment law is primarily administered by specialist employment tribunals and not the courts. There is a right of appeal on points of law only from employment tribunals to the Employment Appeal Tribunal (EAT) and from there to the Court of Appeal and the House of Lords. The employment tribunals were established to act relatively informally, consisting of a legally qualified chairperson and two lay members, appointed by the Secretary of State for Business, Enterprise and Regulatory Reform after consultation with organisations representing employees and employers. A considerable body of tribunal decisions has grown up around the interpretation of employment legislation.

The Employment Tribunals Act 1996 (ETA 1996) consolidated the previous law on employment tribunals. The Act covers amongst other matters the composition of tribunals (ETA 1996, s 4), procedure adopted in tribunals (ETA 1996, ss 6–15) and the membership, procedure and jurisdiction of the EAT (ETA 1996, ss 20–37).

The Employment Tribunals (Constitution and Rules of Procedure) Regulations 2004 (SI 2004/1861) ('the 2004 Regulations') came into force on 1 October 2004. They retained the 'overriding objective' introduced in July 2001. The overriding objective expressly requires tribunals to deal with cases justly. This means that, tribunals are required to ensure that the parties are on an equal footing, deal with the case in ways which are proportionate to the complexity and importance of the issues, ensure it is dealt with expeditiously and fairly and save expense. The parties have a duty to assist the tribunal to achieve the overriding objective, and the tribunal is required to give effect to the objective in exercising any powers under the 2004 Regulations.

Procedures for issuing and responding to claims, including prescribed forms have had to be used since 1 October 2005. A claim has to be submitted on a prescribed 'ET1' form and the response must be set out in a prescribed 'ET3' form. Tribunals can refuse to accept a claim that is not submitted on the correct form, and/or does not contain all the required information or is sent in late. Would-be claimants and employers need to be aware of the ACAS Code of Practice 2009 which sets out expected steps in grievance or disciplinary situations. The Code is not legally binding but may be taken into account by the employment tribunal. Under s 207A of TULR(C)A 1992, the employment tribunal has power to reduce or increase an employment tribunal award up to 25% for a failure to comply with the Code in claims set out in Schedule A2. This includes most routine employment tribunal claims including unfair dismissal.

The tribunal has a number of powers under the 2004 Regulations including:

(a) a general power to make case management orders;

(b) the ability to strike out all or part of a claim or response on the grounds it is scandalous, or vexatious or has no reasonable prospect of success;

(c) the ability to award legal costs against employees who have behaved unreasonably or vexatiously up to a maximum of £10,000 without separate assessment; and

(d) in a weak case, to require a deposit not exceeding £500 as a condition of continuing proceedings following a pre-hearing review.

The 2004 Regulations also enable the tribunal to make an order for costs against a party (or its representative) by reason of their conduct of proceedings. The tribunal also has power to make a preparation time order (up to a maximum of £10,000) at a fixed hourly rate (currently £31 from 6 April 2011, and increasing by £1 annually) where a party has incurred preparation costs but was not legally represented at the hearing.

The Advisory, Conciliation and Arbitration Service (ACAS) was established by the Employment Protection Act 1975, s 1 (now consolidated as TULR(C)A 1992, ss 247–253). Its role is primarily to bring about an improvement in industrial relations between workers and employers. It does this both by conciliating in trade disputes and in cases brought before an employment tribunal.

An employee or not?

[14.3] The employment status of individuals is one of the most regularly reviewed and most difficult issues in employment law. Every company secretary must know which persons within his organisation are 'employees' for the purposes of his company's rights and obligations under employment law. Whether an individual is an 'employee' has a crucial bearing on various matters such as the tax treatment of remuneration, the coverage of employers' liability insurance policies, the application of health and safety law, and many statutory employment protection rights including whether an individual can claim unfair dismissal (immediately on commencement of employment if it is an automatic unfair dismissal claim) or a statutory redundancy entitlement (see **14.93** and **14.95** below).

(See also **14.27** and **14.28** below, which consider the position of fixed-term employees and agency workers.)

There are traditionally two essential elements present in every employment contract:

(A) the obligation on the employee to personally provide his services; and

(B) mutuality of obligations between the employer and the employee.

In *Protectacoat Firthglow Ltd Szilagyi* [2009] IRLR 365 the Court of Appeal took a radically new approach to the question of whether a contract was a sham. Sedley LJ stated that the tribunal should simply ask itself what was the true relationship between the parties. Here, individuals given work were required to enter into a partnership with another individual and the company then purported to enter into a commercial arrangement with the firm. It was held that this did not reflect the true state of affairs. The men were told what to do and were subject to the control of the company. They were employees.

The second essential element, mutuality of obligations, was confirmed by the House of Lords in *Carmichael v National Power* [2000] IRLR 43. Mutuality is evidenced by an obligation on the part of the employer to provide work and an obligation on behalf of the employee to do the work provided.

The labels which the parties adopt for their relationships are not conclusive. In *Hall v Lorimer* [1994] ICR 218 the Court of Appeal decided that there is no single approach which is appropriate and all the details of the relationship were relevant in forming a view. The following 'tests' have been used by the courts in determining the relationship:

(I)   The control test – this looks at the extent that the employer controls the worker, ie his ability to tell the individual how and when to do his work (*Performing Rights Society v Mitchell and Booker* [1924] 1 KB 762).

(II)   The organisational test – this looks at whether the individual was part of, as opposed to accessory to, the employer's business (*Stevenson Jordan and Harrison Ltd v MacDonald and Evans* [1952] 1 TLR 101).

(III)   The mixed test – this looks at the entire relationship and its circumstances, in which control is only one element (*Ready Mixed Concrete (South East) Ltd v Minister of Pensions* [1968] 2 QB 497).

Relevant factors for reaching a decision on status include:

(A)   the parties' practice concerning tax;
(B)   the responsibility for expenses and equipment;
(C)   whether the employee performs exclusive service for the person for whom he works;
(D)   whether there is any obligation to provide or perform work and whether this obligation is to do the work personally;
(E)   the opportunity for the individual to profit from the performance of the organisation for which he works;
(F)   his degree of financial risk; and
(G)   his responsibility for investment and management.

The employment status of agency workers has until recently caused immense difficulty. On more than one occasion the Court of Appeal has suggested that an agency worker, particularly one in position for more than a year, might well be treated as having acquired an implied contract of employment with the end-user for whom they work. This notion has now been firmly crushed by a unanimous Court of Appeal decision in *James v Greenwich Council* [2008] ICR 545. The simple point at the heart of the decision is that one can only imply a contract if that is necessary to make an arrangement work. Where an individual already has a contract with an employment agency there is no need to imply alternative contractual provisions. Thus, an organisation looking to lay staff off without having to make redundancy payments would look to dispose of agency workers first of all.

In *Autoclenz Ltd v Belcher* [2011] IRLR 820, the Supreme Court revisited the issue of whether employment status was determined by looking at what the contract between the parties stated or by looking at the reality of the relationship, in circumstances where the would-be employees argued that the reality of the situation was different to the written contractual terms. In this case, although there was a clause in the contract stating that the employees were not under an obligation to accept work, the employees argued that that was not determinative because the reality was different – they were expected to attend for work and they had to supply their own services and not send a substitute. The Supreme Court held that the real situation trumped the terms of the written contract and it was not necessary for the employees to go as far as proving that the written arrangements were a sham.

Employing new staff

The advertisement

[14.4] An employer must not cause to be published an advertisement which indicates or might reasonably be understood to indicate that any application for the advertised employment would or might be determined by any extent with reference to the sex, race, disability, age, religion or belief or sexual orientation of the applicant. There are limited exceptions to this where, for example, being of a particular sex, race or religion is a genuine occupational qualification for the job. Generally, anything said in an advertisement does not form part of the employment contract. However, in some cases the courts have used advertisements as an aid to interpreting the contract, when the contract was silent on an important term, or where a term was ambiguous. For instance, in *Financial Techniques (Planning Services) Ltd v Hughes* [1981] IRLR 32, the contract of employment (see **14.13** below) failed to mention a profit-sharing scheme that had been described in detail in the advertisement, so the Court of Appeal implied a profit-sharing term into the contract (see **14.14** below for further details on implied terms).

Interviews — asking the right questions

[14.5] In employment law there is a difference in law between lying when asked direct and specific questions and failing to offer information which may otherwise be relevant. As a general rule there is no obligation on a job candidate to volunteer information. See the comprehensive analysis of the law made by Hamblen J in the recent case of *Cheltenham Borough Council v Laird* [2009] IRLR 621. The employer lost an action in which it claimed that the defendant had secured employment by concealing details of her mental health. The Judge strongly recommended that employers should ask of applicants whether they know of any factors or conditions which might affect the decision to offer employment. The employee will have a clear duty to answer honestly questions put. There is no duty to volunteer information. Company secretaries conducting interviews should diligently read submitted CVs or application forms for 'gaps' or unexplained occurrences, and ask the candidate directly about the circumstances.

The provisions of the Rehabilitation of Offenders Act 1974 must also be considered in this context. This Act sets limits on the extent to which an employer may take into account the criminal convictions of an applicant when making an appointment. Subject to certain exceptions, where a conviction is 'spent' within the terms of the Act, a question put to an applicant at an interview (or on an application form) about his past criminal convictions may be answered on the basis that it does not refer to a spent conviction. It is not lawful to exclude an applicant from employment if he has failed to disclose a spent conviction. The exceptions (specified by various statutory instruments) broadly relate to entry into certain professions, such as doctors, nurses, dentists, lawyers and accountants, and employment (i) in specific areas of the financial sector, (ii) in jobs connected with the administration of justice, and (iii) in the social and health services, and in teaching, where there is access to clients, patients and children. Where an applicant is being interviewed for a post which is covered by one of the specified exceptions, then provided that the questions being asked in the interview are in order to assess the suitability of the applicant for the post and he is informed that spent convictions must be disclosed, the applicant will be obliged to answer any questions about previous convictions, whether or not they are spent, and failure to disclose them would constitute a valid reason not to employ him.

Standard and enhanced disclosure of convictions is currently available to employers that recruit people to work with children, the elderly or vulnerable adults through the Criminal Records Bureau (CRB). The CRB is a nationwide database of criminal records which employers can access in relation to future and current employees. It should be noted that the CRB operates in England and Wales and the same type of checks are provided in Scotland by Disclosure Scotland except that Disclosure Scotland offers basic, standard and enhanced disclosure while the CRB in England and Wales only offers standard and enhanced disclosure. Basic disclosure contains details of convictions not spent under the Rehabilitation of Offenders Act 1974. At the time of publication the CRB in England and Wales has no plans to introduce a basic disclosure.

Employers wishing to use the CRB need to pay the appropriate fees, register with it to become a 'Registered Organisation' and appoint a 'Registered Person' to authorise disclosure applications. In order to keep this registration, employers must abide by the CRB's Code of Practice.

Section 60 of the Equality Act 2010 does, on the face of it, prohibit asking questions about the health of a job applicant before offering them work (conditionally or unconditionally) or before including an applicant in a pool from which it is intended to select a person to whom work will be offered. However, section 60(6) contains a vast range of exceptions to the prohibition and it is unlikely that many would be debarred from asking prudent questions which relate to the basic ability of an individual to do the work required of them.

Employees lying at interview

[14.6] Lying at an interview can be grounds for fair dismissal by an employer. In *Torr v British Railways Board* [1977] IRLR 175, Mr Torr was held to have been fairly dismissed from his job as a railway guard, when his employers discovered that he had been sent to prison for three years. The EAT held that:

> 'It is of the utmost importance that an employer seeking an employee to hold a post of responsibility and trust should be able to select for employment a candidate in whom he can have confidence. It is fundamental to that confidence that the employee should truthfully disclose his history so far as it is sought by the intending employer.'

Note that it is for the employer to seek the information and not for the employee to volunteer it.

Checking credentials

[14.7] An employer may use any selection process he likes provided it is not discriminatory (see 14.36 below) and where necessary it complies with the requirements of the Data Protection Act 1998. Indeed, some prospective employers may need to play detective about a candidate's background. Some employers require candidates to bring with them to their interview their certificates of school and higher education qualifications. It may also be regarded as a criminal offence for an employee to lie about a qualification in order to obtain or keep his employment, especially where professional qualifications are required to do the job (*R v Callender* [1992] 3 All ER 51). Professional qualifications can often be checked by searching the relevant professional register.

Until 1984 employers were only vicariously liable for the negligent acts their employees committed in the course of their employment (see 14.34 below). However, in 1984, the High Court ruled that the employer was liable for criminal acts. In *Nahhas v Pier House (Cheyne Walk) Management Co Ltd* [1984] 1 EGLR 160, a porter had been employed in a position of trust, yet his references had not been taken up. Had the employers done any form of check, they would have discovered large periods of unemployment created by imprisonment. The employers were held vicariously liable for the cost of jewellery, and the interest on that sum, stolen from Ms Nahhas.

In terms of data protection it is important when seeking personal data from individuals to ensure that the data is relevant to the post and not excessive in terms of making a recruitment decision. Any such information should only be used for the purposes for which it was obtained and cannot be used for any other purpose without consent. Care should also be taken to ensure that personal data gathered is securely held and either kept up to date or destroyed when no longer required. Further details of the Data Protection Act 1998 are outside the scope of this book, but a company secretary will need to ensure compliance with the Act with regard to both employee and client data and be familiar with the Employment Practices Data Protection Code (2005).

Making promises at interviews

[14.8] Assuming the recruiter has the authority to make offers or promises about the job at the interview, an oral promise may be binding. Company secretaries should pay particular attention to this point to avoid binding the company. For example, in the case of *Hawker Siddeley v Rump* [1979] IRLR 425, Mr Rump's oral promise at his interview that he would not have to be mobile was held to be a binding term. The written term of his contract which he later signed stated the opposite. The court held that since nobody had pointed out that the earlier term no longer applied, that this was an implied promise and took precedence over the conflicting written term (see 14.14 below for implied terms).

Making representations

[14.9] In normal cases where a person applies for a job advertised in the media, he is deemed to hold himself out to be competent for that job. However, where a job is barely described in the advertisement and is one for which an applicant could not be expected to know whether he is or is not competent, interviewing managers must take care not to make misrepresentations about the job. A recruiter who makes a misrepresentation which induces a person to enter into a contract may be sued for any losses sustained by him as a result of that misrepresentation, under the Misrepresentation Act 1967. The misrepresentation does not need to be fraudulent for the claimant to succeed, but there is a defence that, at the time the person made the representation, he had reasonable grounds to believe and did believe, up until the contract was made, the facts represented were true.

References

[14.10] Employers often make offers of employment subject to the receipt of 'satisfactory' references. On the face of it appears that there should be no dispute if the reference(s) do not satisfy the prospective employer. In fact, an employer has a duty to review the reference 'in good faith'. (See also **14.25** below.) In *Wishart v National Association of Citizens' Advice Bureaux (NACAB)* [1990] IRLR 393, Mr Wishart was turned down for a job of information officer because his references disclosed an alarming history of sickness absence. His explanation for this was that he had Hepatitis B. However, upon investigation, it was discovered that he had tested negative. In the light of the inconsistent explanations, his job offer was withdrawn on the basis of unsatisfactory references. He then sought an interlocutory injunction seeking to restrain the alleged breach of contract. The Court of Appeal held that the offer of employment subject to receipt of satisfactory references is permissible only if the references were subjectively satisfactory to the prospective employer. Notwithstanding this, it did recognise that although unlikely, it could be arguable that the test was objective in the sense that the prospective employer behaved in a manner inconsistent with a reasonable employer.

It should be noted that special rules (which are outside the scope of this chapter) apply to employers giving references for employees who are in areas regulated by the Financial Services and Markets Act 2000.

Employers reneging on job offers

[14.11] Once an offer of employment is made and accepted (whether orally or in writing), a collateral contract has been formed, ie a contract to employ, as the EAT decided in *Sarker v South Tees Acute Hospitals NHS Trust* [1997] IRLR 328. In this case, an employee whose contract of employment was terminated before she had even started work was entitled to bring a claim for breach of contract before the employment tribunal.

In other words, the prospective employer makes a warranty of employment to the other party that if he gives up his current employment, he will be given the new employment. In reliance on this warranty, the other party gives up his existing employment. Thus, if the prospective employer reneges on that contract, the other party may sue on it. Damages will be awarded on the basis of the financial loss suffered as a result of the breach by the prospective employer. The employee could claim loss of earnings until he obtains further employment (subject to his duty to mitigate his loss). This would usually be subject to the notice period in the new contract.

If employers wish to make offers of employment subject to the job applicant successfully passing an examination the results of which are not known at the time of the interview, it is essential that such conditions are expressly stated in the letter offering employment (*Stubbes v Trower Still & Keeling* [1987] IRLR 321).

Employers should ensure that all offers of employment are subject to the completion of satisfactory checks as to immigration status in order to avoid civil and/or criminal penalties for employing illegal workers (see **14.38** below).

Employee reneging on a job offer

[**14.12**] In a case where a prospective employee refuses to join the employer after originally having accepted the appointment, it is possible to sue that individual for the loss suffered by the employer as a direct result of the breach of contract. In most cases, this will be the cost of re-advertising and all recruitment costs if they would have been avoided had the employee given the required period of notice. The feasibility of this approach, will naturally depend upon the individual's ability to pay.

The contract of employment

General requirements

[**14.13**] A contract of employment made between an employer and an employee need not necessarily be in writing. An oral contract is as valid in law as one in writing. However, under the provisions of ERA 1996, s 1, there is a requirement for most categories of employee to be provided with a written statement of their main terms and conditions of employment, within two months of their commencing employment. The written statement is evidence of the contractual terms but is not the contract itself (unless the document is executed as a contract). Most employers will have a fuller written contract of employment which goes beyond the minimum information required in a written statement.

The requirement to provide a written statement of terms applies to all employees whether full or part-time (see **14.26** and **14.27** below). However, ERA 1996 does exclude certain classes of employees from the right to receive a written statement, for example, employees working wholly or mainly outside the UK and individuals employed for less than one month (ERA 1996, s 198). Employers are not required to provide a section 1 statement to the wider class of 'workers' (see **14.27** below). Under the Employment Act 2002 employees who are not provided with a written statement may claim an additional two to four weeks' pay as compensation in certain tribunal proceedings set out in Schedule 5 to the Employment Act 2002 (subject to the statutory weekly pay cap).

The terms and conditions of employment provided in the written statement must include details of the following:

(a) The names of the employer and employee.

(b) The date when the employment began.

(c) The date when the employee's continuous employment began (including any employment with a previous employer which counts towards the period).

(d) Details of wages or salary and the intervals at which remuneration is paid.

(e) Hours of work, and any terms relating to hours of work.

(f) Entitlement to holiday, including public holidays and holiday pay.

(g) Entitlement to sick leave and sick pay.

(h) Pension arrangements.

(i) Length of notice the employee is obliged to give and is entitled to receive from his employer to terminate employment.

(j) Where the employment is not intended to be permanent, the period for which it is expected to continue, or if it is for a fixed term, the date it is expected to end.

(k) The title of the job or a brief description of the work that he is employed to do.

(l) The place of work or, where the employee is required or permitted to work at various places, an indication of that and the name of the employer.

(m) Any collective agreements directly affecting terms and conditions.

(n) If the employee must work for more than one month outside the UK, the period for which he must work, the currency which he will be paid and any additional remuneration or benefits resulting from overseas work and any terms and conditions relevant to his return must be added.

(ERA 1996, s 1.)

A section 1 statement must also include a note of the disciplinary rules applicable to the employee, or must refer to a document, reasonably accessible to the employee, where such rules are contained. The statement must specify:

(i) a person to whom the employee can apply if dissatisfied with any disciplinary procedure relating to him;

(ii) a person to whom the employee can apply for the purpose of seeking redress of any grievance relating to his employment; and

(iii) the manner in which it should be made.

(ERA 1996, s 3(1).)

Written notification of changes to section 1 statements should be given to the employee at the earliest opportunity and, in any event, not more than one month after the change (ERA 1996, s 4).

The written statement may refer employees to other documents for details of pension entitlements and the sick leave policy, provided the employee has a reasonable opportunity to read the documents in the course of employment or they are reasonably accessible to the employee (ERA 1996, s 2). In addition an employer may, in the section 1 statement, refer the employee to a collective agreement.

Where an employer does not provide an employee with a section 1 statement, or provides a statement which is inaccurate or incomplete, the employee may apply to an employment tribunal (ERA 1996, s 11(1) and (2)). The employee must make a claim before the employment ceases or, if not then, within three months of the date on which employment ceased or, where it was not reasonably practicable for the application to be made within three months, within such period as the tribunal considers reasonable (ERA 1996, s 11(4)). A tribunal may state the particulars which should have been given and they are then deemed to have been included in a section 1 statement (ERA 1996, s 12).

Implied terms

[14.14] The employment relationship is governed not only by any express terms in the contract of employment, but also by terms which the law implies into the employment relationship. Implied terms which are commonly imposed upon employees include duties of fidelity and obedience, disclosure of information, performance of duties with due diligence and care, and not to make a secret profit. Both parties are also under a duty to give reasonable notice of termination if no notice period has been specified, and to maintain a relationship of mutual trust and confidence between each other.

There are various bases upon which courts may imply additional terms into contracts of employment. These include the following.

(a)   *Conduct* – which may evidence an agreement between the parties on a certain matter.

(b)   *The 'officious bystander' test* – a term may be implied if the court holds that it is so obvious that the parties are taken to have agreed to it.

(c)   *Custom* – terms which are regularly adopted in a particular context may be taken to have obviously been implied into every contract in that area.

(d)   *'Business efficacy'* – terms may be implied if it is necessary to give business efficacy to the contract, ie to make it work properly.

(e)   *Common characteristic* – a term may be implied if it is so characteristic of employment relationships that the employer and employee are taken to have necessarily agreed such a term.

The law, however, will not imply a term into a contract simply because it is reasonable. It will only imply a term which is reasonably seen as a necessary condition of the modern employment relationship (*Lister v Romford Ice* [1957] AC 555). Company secretaries should be aware of the possibility of relying on implied terms in relations with employees, or that employees may rely on them. In *Villella v MFI Furniture Centre Ltd* [1999] IRLR 468 the High Court implied a term into the employees' contracts concerning permanent health insurance. The implied term meant that the employer was unable to terminate the employee's contract of employment except for cause but excluding ill health, in circumstances which would prevent the employee benefiting under the scheme.

In a landmark decision *Malik and another v Bank of Credit and Commerce International (in compulsory liquidation)* [1997] ICR 606, the House of Lords held that dishonest business conduct by an employer potentially amounts to a breach of the implied term of mutual trust and confidence enabling an employee to recover 'stigma damages' for the damage to his reputation where the employer's conduct makes it more difficult for the employee to obtain work in the future.

However, a number of cases subsequent to *Malik* have made clear that there are limitations to the scope of the implied term of trust and confidence. In *Hill v General Accident Fire and Life Assurance Corporation Ltd* [1998] IRLR 641, the Court of Session in Scotland held that there is no overriding obligation for the contract of employment to be interpreted in a way which furthers the principle of mutual trust. The implied term of trust and confidence does not yet amount to an implied obligation that the employer must act reasonably. However, it is arguable that case law is leaning this way; indeed, cases such as *Johnson v Unisys* [2001] WLR 1076 refer to a duty to treat employees 'fairly' and in an 'even-handed manner'.

Two cases have been decided which show how the duty of trust and confidence can apply to very different factual situations. In *Horkulak v Cantor Fitzgerald International* [2003] EWHC 1918 (QB), [2003] IRLR 756, the conduct of an employers' chief executive was held to amount to a breach of the implied term of trust and confidence. The relevant conduct included using foul and abusive language, not allowing the employee a chance to respond to criticism and setting standards of performance which the chief executive did not reasonably believe could be attained by the employee. Rights during maternity leave were considered in *Visa International Services Association v Paul* [2004] IRLR 42 where it was held to be a breach of the duty of trust and confidence in failing to keep a woman, on maternity leave, informed of developments and job opportunities within her department.

Changing the contract terms

[14.15] Employment contracts can be changed at any time, but only with the agreement of both parties. Employers cannot unilaterally vary an employee's terms of employment. Employers who unilaterally impose changes in a contract can be sued for breach of contract, and may be brought to an employment tribunal to defend an unfair dismissal complaint if the employee is dismissed for refusing to agree to the changes or if the employee resigns and claims constructive dismissal. Changes imposed by the employer relating to one of the main terms of the contract are likely to constitute a fundamental breach, giving the employee the right to resign and claim damages for constructive dismissal (limited to the notice period if brought as a breach of contract claim) and unfair dismissal (where the employee has one year's service) Alternatively, the employee could work under the new terms but 'under protest' and bring a breach of contract claim. In practice, the terms of employment may not be contained in one single document (see **14.13** above), but may be contained in a variety of sources, including, typically, an offer letter, a 'contract' of employment, a staff handbook, various policies/memoranda, collective agreements and custom and practice. In *Bateman v Asda Stores Ltd* [2010] IRLR 370 the EAT decided that a clear power to vary terms which was contained in a staff handbook did empower the employer to harmonise terms of employment but the contractual right had to be exercised in compliance with the implied term of trust and confidence (in effect via consultation with staff, reaching agreement where possible). Not all of these types of other documents will necessarily be contractual, for instance, policies in staff handbooks are often specifically stated to be non-contractual. Whether a proposed change affects a contractual clause or a policy may be of importance, and, in some cases, radical changes in policy may lead to a breach of the implied term of trust and confidence even where the policy is non-contractual.

In the absence of carefully drafted provisions in a contract of employment which allow an employer the necessary flexibility to make changes, the employer requires the employee's consent to make changes, (and will always be fettered by the implied term of trust and confidence (see **14.14** above). Obviously, express consent is the ideal. Consent may, however, be implied, typically by the employee continuing to work after what is otherwise a unilateral imposition of changes, to the extent that the employee's conduct may be said to be evidence of acceptance. This approach is not recommended, especially where a change does not have an immediate effect. In this case the courts may be slow to conclude that continued working on the part of the employee without objection is evidence of consent. In *Aparau v Iceland Frozen Foods* [1996] IRLR 119, the EAT made a distinction between contractual terms which have immediate application, such as pay rates, and those such as mobility which do not, and upheld a cashier's claim of constructive dismissal when she was required to move to another store, even though a mobility clause had been introduced into her contract twelve months earlier.

Employers should be particularly careful with variations relating to remuneration. An employee facing a unilateral cut in wages can, as a matter of contract, refuse to accept the cut whilst continuing to work, and claim a contractual entitlement to be repaid the lost pay (*Burdett-Coutts v Hertford-shire County Council* [1984] IRLR 91). Under ERA 1996, s 13 (see **14.84** below), reductions in wages, overtime rates and the abandonment/modification of contractual bonus schemes would all result in a 'deduction' contrary to the ERA 1996 and would be actionable (*Bruce v Wiggins Teape (Stationery) Ltd* [1994] IRLR 536). Also, according to ERA 1996, s 104(1), any employee who is dismissed for asserting a statutory right is automatically unfairly dismissed. Arguably, an employee faced with a cut who resigns, claiming constructive dismissal (see **14.93** below), or who is given notice under the existing contract and an offer is made of a new contract, on reduced pay, could be regarded as having been dismissed in the context of a statutory right under ERA 1996 to continue to be paid at the agreed rate. In *Rigby v Ferodo* [1987] IRLR 61, the employer unilaterally imposed a reduction in wages. The court held that the employee, in continuing to work and receiving a reduced payment under protest, had not accepted the variation in terms and was therefore entitled to recover the difference between his contractual entitlement and the amount actually paid. The period of the damages was not restricted to the notice period because the employer had not sought to terminate the employment on notice (or at all).

More scope exists for changing contractual terms, where particular terms being altered are incorporated from a collective agreement. There will be no breach of contract where the employer has the right to vary the contract unilaterally, as in *Airlie and others v City of Edinburgh District Council* [1996] IRLR 516. Here, an employer reduced the bonuses payable under a collective agreement without the consent of the employees, but the agreement contained a code of practice allowing him to alter the bonus scheme. An employee's objection to changes negotiated with a union or already contained within the collective agreement will not prevail where the method of negotiating such terms are expressly incorporated into the contracts of employment, whether or not the employee was ever a member of the union, or has left (*National Coal Board v Galley* [1958] 1 AER 91). Also, the employer is not free to abandon the application of collectively derived but individually incorporated terms, even where the original collective agreement terminates (*Robertson and Jackson v British Gas Corporation* [1983] IRLR 302).

In *Henry v London General Transport Services Ltd* [2001] IRLR 132 the applicant's salaries were reduced as a result of a term contained in a collective agreement between the TGWU and the employer. The applicants claimed that they had not agreed to the new terms and their employer had made an unlawful deduction from wages. The EAT held that a collectively agreed term which allowed a reduction in salary could form part of employees individual contracts of employment by custom and practice if the custom of incorporating terms was certain and well known.

When proposing changes to contracts of employment to which consent cannot be obtained, it is preferable to give proper contractual notice to terminate (see **14.92** below), together with an offer of re-employment on the new terms and conditions, rather than run the risks inherent (including claims for unfair dismissal) with the imposition of unilateral changes. This should be done after:

(a)   following a fair procedure; and
(b)   consultation.

Whether the dismissals will then be fair or not (see **14.93** below) will be determined by applying principles established in *Hollister v National Farmers Union* [1979] IRLR 238, where it was held that an employer could fairly dismiss where there were 'sound, good business reasons' for introducing changes to terms and conditions. Employers must avoid statements such as 'Accept these terms or you will be dismissed'. Duress of this kind has been held to be an anticipatory breach of contract by the employer, entitling the employee to claim constructive dismissal. Employers must therefore ensure they carry out adequate consultation about the intended changes, without overtly threatening to give contractual notice of termination of the existing contract if this does not meet with success (*Greenaway Harrison Ltd v Wiles* [1994] IRLR 380).

Also under TULR(C)A 1992, s 188 there are collective consultation obligations where an employer is proposing to dismiss more than 20 employees in a 90–day period for a reason not related to the individual employee. This duty therefore applies where an employer is going to make large scale dismissals and make offers of re-employment on new terms to the dismissed employees, where it has been unable to get the employees' agreement to the change in terms.

Employers must remember, that a special regime applies to changes to employment contracts in the context of transfers of undertakings (see **14.30** below).

Unenforceable terms and illegal terms

[14.16] Any individual term which seeks to contract the employee out of the minimum statutory rights (eg those covering minimum statutory notice, discrimination, equal pay and unfair dismissal) is unenforceable. Illegal terms on the other hand, eg an agreement not to declare wages for tax, can make the contract itself unenforceable.

Promotions

[14.17] Employees who are promoted are effectively accepting a variation of their terms and conditions of employment. Continuity is not broken and the new contract immediately succeeds the previous one. Normally one or more of the fundamental terms of a contract are changed by the offer of promotion: position, duties, pay, overtime, benefits, mobility etc. The promotion gives the employer the opportunity to change the contract and for the employee to accept it. A promoted employee is entitled to rely on the terms of the original contract where these have not been revised or altered in the offer of promotion.

Directors' service contracts

[14.18] Company directors are not automatically employees of a company. However, it is common for many directors to hold an executive role within the company, thus becoming an employee. The Court of Appeal in *Secretary of State for Trade and Industry v Bottrill* [1999] IRLR 326 decided that a director was also an employee of the company even though he held a majority shareholding that meant he could veto his own dismissal.

In *Clark v Clark Construction Initiatives Ltd* [2008] IRLR 364 the EAT held that the fact that an individual had a controlling shareholding did not prevent a contract of employment arising. The issue was on what grounds it could refuse to give effect to the contract between Clark and the company. The circumstances in which it might be legitimate not to give effect to what was alleged to be a binding contract were firstly if the company was a sham; secondly, where the contract was entered into for an ulterior purpose; and thirdly, where the parties did not conduct their relationship in accordance to the contract. The EAT suggested a number of factors in determining whether the contract should be given effect or not. These were based on the parties' conduct and whether the contract had been identified or put in writing.

Where directors are regarded as employees the provisions relating to the contract of employment apply, together with the further requirements contained in the Companies Act 2006 (CA 2006). A director may be employed under the authority of the company's articles of association, by a resolution of the board containing the terms of appointment, by a letter written under the authority of the board or in a service agreement approved by the board.

Under CA 2006, ss 228–230, a company is required to keep at its registered office (or the place where the register of members is kept) a copy of each director's (including shadow directors) service contract where it is in writing for the duration of the contract and for at least one year from the date of termination or expiry of the contract. Where the contract is not in writing, a written memorandum of its terms (for example the written statement of the terms and conditions of employment) must be kept. These copies are open to inspection by the members at the place where they are kept and members may obtain copies for a small charge. Directors who are employed for less than twelve months or with less than twelve months before the termination of their agreement now fall within the ambit of these provisions. If the company is listed, then the Listing Rules require that directors' service contracts, or memoranda of their terms, be available for inspection by any person at the company's registered office at all times during business hours and at the annual general meeting for 15 minutes prior to the holding of the meeting.

Under CA 2006, s 188, a company is forbidden to enter into service contracts with its directors for periods which are or may be more than two years where the contract is not capable of being terminated by notice, or can only be terminated in specified circumstances, unless the term is first approved by a resolution of the company, or, where it is for the employment of a director of a holding company, by resolution of the holding company. Before any such resolution is passed, a written memorandum setting out the proposed agreement incorporating the terms must either be sent or submitted to every eligible member of the company at or before the time at which the proposed resolution is sent to him in the event of a written resolution, or, in the case of a resolution at a general meeting, available for inspection by members of the company both at the company's registered office for not less than 15 days ending with the date of the meeting, and at the meeting itself. Any such contracts or provisions not so approved are deemed void and the director's employment may be terminated on reasonable notice.

The Greenbury Code, Part D 'contracts and compensation' recommended that there is a strong case for setting notice or contract periods at, or reducing them to, one year or less. This statement was repeated in the Combined Code (a consolidation of the Cadbury and Greenbury Codes published in June 1998, and now annexed to the Listing Rules). The Listing Rules now require the disclosure to shareholders, in the company's annual report (as part of a report to the shareholders by the board of directors), of details of any directors' service contract with a notice period in excess of one year, giving the reasons for such notice period.

Section 1177 of CA 2006 repealed the general prohibition on companies paying directors remuneration free of income tax, which was conferred on companies by section 311 of CA 1985, following a recommendation of the Law Commission. A company is required to disclose in its annual accounts an estimate of the tax which it has undertaken to pay.

A further point worth noting is the position where a director's service contract conflicts with the company's articles of association. In such circumstances, the provisions of the articles will prevail, as the board may not override them. Articles of association will usually delegate the power to fix the terms and conditions of a director's employment to the board of directors. However, the power may be further delegated by the board to a committee of it, or to an individual director, for example, the managing director. In *Guinness plc v Saunders* [1990] 1 AER 652, a committee of the board purported to grant special remuneration to a director. The alleged oral contract between the director and the committee was held by the House of Lords to be void as the board had no power under the articles to delegate the power to a committee. A director cannot rely on ostensible authority or implied authority on the part of other members of the board; as any resolution of the board or a committee are deemed to be known by each director.

Section 182 of CA 2006 requires directors to disclose formally any interest they may have in existing contracts with the company to the board, including their contracts of employment and any subsequent variation to their terms and conditions, whilst section 177 of CA 2006 requires directors to disclose formally any interest they may have in proposed contracts.

An announcement must be made to the Company Announcements Office, of the appointment or resignation (or removal or retirement) of a director of a UK listed company and of any important changes being made in the functions or executive responsibilities of a director. There are additional formalities required by listed companies.

In addition, the Higgs Report on the role and effectiveness of non-executive directors, which was published in January 2003, increased the accountability of the boards of UK listed companies and gave non-executive directors a more demanding and influential role. The Report's recommendations were introduced as changes to the Combined Code and a revised Code was published on 23 July 2003. The revised Code included most of Higgs' proposals although some were watered down.

The Combined Code issued in 2003 was updated and replaced by the Combined Code on Corporate Governance issued in June 2006 and again in June 2008. In May 2010 the Financial Reporting Council published the UK Corporate Governance Code which applies to financial years beginning on or after 29 June 2010 (see **6.19** and **APPENDIX 6G**). Listed companies must report on how they have complied with the main and supporting principles of the UK Corporate Governance Code and also confirm if they have complied with the Code's provision. If a company has not complied with a provision they must explain why.

Sunday working

[14.19] The Sunday Trading Act 1994 reformed the law of England and Wales in regard to Sunday trading. These provisions have now been consolidated in Part IV and sections 101, 232 and 233 of ERA 1996. These Acts apply to two types of workers, shop workers and betting workers. Under these Acts, large shops (those with a floor area of more than 280 square meters) may open for up to six hours a day between 10am and 6pm on Sunday (except Easter Day and Christmas Day). There are also important provisions covering the employment rights of shop workers, which are:

(a)   the dismissal of 'protected shop workers' and (after a three-month period) 'opted-out shop workers' for refusing to work on Sundays is automatically unfair; and

(b)   that such workers have the right not to suffer any other detriment for refusing to work on a Sunday.

A 'protected shop worker' is a person who was employed as a shop worker when the Sunday Trading Act came into force, and continues to be so employed (until the date on which they were dismissed or suffered a detriment for refusing to work on Sunday); or a worker, irrespective of whether he was employed when the Act came into force, whose contract of employment is such that he is not required to work on Sunday.

The Act does not protect 'Sunday only' shop workers, nor does it prevent discrimination against those who are applying for shop work which may entail working on Sundays and who appear reluctant to do such work. A worker ceases to be 'protected' by giving his employer an 'opt-in' notice, stating that he wishes to work on Sundays and, after giving that notice, expressly agreeing to work on Sundays or a particular Sunday. A shop worker who, under his contract, may be required to work on a Sunday (but who is not employed to work only on Sundays), may give his employer an 'opting-out notice', ie a written statement that he objects to working on Sundays. After a three-month period starting with the date the notice was given, the employee has the same protection against unfair dismissal or suffering detriment as a protected shop worker. Employers must provide a statutory explanatory statement to employees who are or may be required to work on Sundays, within two months of the commencement of their employment. This statement describes the employment protection available and the ability to 'opt-out'. Thus, new employees and old employees who have opted in can be forced to work on Sundays. Old employees who have not opted in and new employees who have opted out cannot be forced to work on Sundays.

Time off

[14.20] There are various instances when employees have a statutory right to time off. These rights are contained in ERA 1996, Pt VI along with various other Acts detailed below:

(a) *Trade union officials and members* —— Officials of recognised trade unions have the right, under TULR(C)A 1992, ss 168–169, to time off with pay to carry out official union duties. Members of recognised trade unions have under TULR(C)A 1992, s 170, rights to reasonable time off without pay, to take part in trade union activities. There are no service requirements for these rights. An employee who is an official of, or member of, a recognised trade union may present a complaint to an employment tribunal that his employer has failed to permit him to take time off to carry out such duties, or (as the case may be) to take part in such activities (TULR(C)A 1992, ss 168(4), 170(4)). In addition, an employee who is an official of a recognised trade union may present a complaint to an employment tribunal that his employer has failed to pay him for time off to carry out such duties (TULR(C)A 1992, s 169(5)).

(b) *Public duties* – Employees who hold certain public offices, including being a justice of the peace or a member of a local authority, a statutory tribunal, a police authority, a board of prison visitors, a relevant health body, a relevant education body, the Environment Agency, the Scottish Environment Protection Agency or Scottish Water or a Water Customer Consultation Panel (ERA 1996, s 50), have the right to take time off without pay to perform duties. The amount of time off which the employer permits the employee will depend on the occasion and what is reasonable in the circumstances. Employers can pay regard to how much time off is required for the performance of the particular duty, how much time the employee has already been permitted under ERA 1996, s 50 or time off for trade union activities under TULR(C)A 1992 (see (a) above), and the circumstances of the employer's business and the effect the employee's absence will have on the running of that business. An employee may present a complaint to an employment tribunal if his employer fails to permit him to take time off under ERA 1996, s 50 (ERA 1996, s 51).

(c) *Health and safety representatives* – Under the Safety Representatives and Safety Committees Regulations 1977 (SI 1977/500) (as amended), safety representatives must be permitted time off with pay to undertake their duties or to undergo training. ERA 1996, s 44 provides protection for such employees not to suffer detriment in the exercise of these duties. The Health and Safety (Consultation with Employees) Regulations 1996 (SI 1996/1513) are applicable to employees not represented by safety representatives (ie non-unionised workplaces), and require employers to consult either with elected 'representatives of employee safety' or directly with employees. These representatives of employee safety have similar rights, as do safety representatives under the 1977 Regulations, to time off with pay for their duties, and the right (again set out in ERA 1996, s 44) not to suffer detriment as a result of the conduct of those duties. In addition, under ERA 1996, s 44 an employee has the right not to suffer a detriment where he took part (or proposed to take part) in consultation with the employer pursuant to the 1996 Regulations or in an election of representatives of employee safety under those Regulations, whether as a candidate or otherwise. A safety representative under the 1977 Regulations, or a representative of employee safety under the 1996 Regulations, may present a complaint to an employment tribunal that his employer has failed to permit him to take time off, or to pay him, for undertaking his duties or undergoing training (1977 Regulations, Reg 11; 1996 Regulations, Sch 2).

(d) *Occupational pension scheme trustees* – ERA 1996, ss 58–60, provide the right to time off for an occupational pension scheme trustee to perform his duties and to undergo training, with pay at his average hourly earnings. As with time off for public duties, the circumstances of the employer's business and the effect of the employee's absence on the running of the business will be taken into account. There is a similar remedy of complaint to an employment tribunal, normally within three months of an employer's failure to permit the time off. Occupational pension scheme trustees have the same rights as safety representatives not to suffer detriment in employment as a consequence of the conduct of their duties (ERA 1996, s 46). Dismissal as a result of carrying out such duties will be automatically unfair (ERA 1996, s 102).

(e) *Employees looking for work* – Employees who have been given notice of dismissal by reason of redundancy (see **14.95** below) are entitled to reasonable time off during normal working hours in order to look for new employment or make arrangements for training for future employment (ERA 1996, s 52). This only applies to employees who have had two years' continuous service at the time the notice of dismissal by reason of redundancy is due to expire. Employees taking time off in these circumstances are entitled to remuneration at their normal hourly rate (ERA 1996, s 53), and can also apply to an employment tribunal if an employer fails to permit the time off (ERA 1996, s 54).

(f) *Employee representatives* – An employee who is an employee representative for the purposes of Chapter II of Part IV of TULR(C)A 1992, or a representative for the purposes of TUPE 2006 (SI 2006/246), Regs 9, 13 and 15, or a candidate in an election in which any person being elected will be such an employee representative is entitled to take reasonable time off for him to be able to perform the functions of employee representative or candidate (ERA 1996, s 61). The representative has the right to remuneration at his normal hourly rate (ERA 1996, s 62) and the right to complain to an employment tribunal if this right is denied by his employer (ERA 1996, s 63). Like safety representatives and occupational pension scheme trustees, employee representatives have the right not to suffer detriment as a result of their position and exercise of their duties. Dismissal for such activities is also automatically unfair.

(g) *Ante-natal care* – An employee who is pregnant and has, on the advice of a medical worker (eg doctor or midwife) made an appointment to attend a clinic for the purpose of ante-natal care is entitled to be permitted by her employer to take time off during normal working hours to attend the appointment (ERA 1996, s 55(1)). To exercise this right the employee has to provide, if requested by her employer, a certificate from a doctor, midwife or registered nurse stating that the employee is pregnant, and an appointment card or some other document showing the appointment has been made (ERA 1996, s 55(2)). The employee is entitled to her normal hourly remuneration to attend such an appointment (ERA 1996, s 56) and has the right to complain to an employment tribunal if this is denied (ERA 1996, s 57). Ante-natal care is defined quite widely and can include, for example, parent-craft classes.

(h) *Young persons undergoing study or training* – Young persons in employment have the right to take paid time off work for study and training, by virtue of ERA 1996, ss 63A–63C. An employee who (*a*) is aged 16 or 17, (*b*) is not receiving full-time secondary or further education, and (*c*) has not attained the prescribed standard of achievement (as to which, see the Right to Time Off for Study or Training Regulations 2001 (SI 2001/2801)) is entitled to be permitted by his employer (or principal, where he has been sub-contracted) to take time off during the employee's working hours in order to undertake study or training leading to a relevant qualification (as defined). An 18-year-old employee who is undertaking study or training leading to a relevant qualification which he began before attaining that age has a similar right to time off.

The amount of time off that an employee is to be permitted to take is that which is reasonable in the circumstances having regard, in particular, to (i) the requirements of the employee's study or training, and (ii) the circumstances of the business of the employer (or the principal) and the effect of the employee's time off on the running of that business. An employee who is allowed time off is entitled to be paid for the time taken off at the 'appropriate hourly rate', and has the right to complain to an employment tribunal if the employer (or principal) has unreasonably refused the employee time off or has refused to pay him. An employee entitled to time off and to remuneration under these provisions also has the right (by virtue of ERA 1996, s 47A) not to suffer detriment in employment on the ground that the employee exercised (or proposed to exercise) that right or received (or sought to receive) such remuneration.

(i) *Time off for dependants* – Under ERA 1996, s 57A employees are entitled to take a reasonable amount of time off work during normal working hours where there is a domestic emergency involving family dependants. 'Dependants' are a parent, husband, wife, partner, child or other person living as part of the family or for whom the employee is the main carer. Time may be taken off, for example, where dependants are injured or unwell, where there has been a breakdown in care arrangements and for births, deaths and incidents involving a child at school. There is no legal requirement that time off for domestic emergencies be paid. An employee has a right to complain to an employment tribunal if the employer refuses to permit such time off (ERA 1996, s 57B). The employee has the right not to suffer a detriment as a result of time off and dismissal for such time off is automatically unfair (ERA 1996, s 99).

(j) *Time off for maternity and paternity leave* – see **14.46** to **14.53** and **14.54** and **14.55**.

Other terms and conditions

[**14.21**] In addition to statutory rights, like Statutory Maternity Pay (SMP) (see **14.52** below) and Statutory Sick Pay (SSP) see (**14.68** below), employees may have other legal entitlements provided for in the contract. As will be seen below, the Working Time Regulations 1998 have made provision for statutory entitlements in certain areas that previously were purely contractual.

Hours of work

[**14.22**] Before the Working Time Regulations 1998 (SI 1998/1833) (see below), working hours had been left to collective bargaining or individual contracts. However, some professions such as truck drivers, and the hours that children may work, are still separately regulated. The law protecting children was extended following the adoption of EU Directive 94/33/EC (the Young Workers Directive) in June 1994. Since 6 April 2003 young workers may not exceed an 8-hour day or a 40-hour week except in prescribed circumstances. Nor are young workers permitted to work during the hours of 10pm–6am, save in excepted industries, for example agriculture, retail trading, and hotels and catering. Young workers are workers between the ages of 15 and 18.

Broadly the Working Time Regulations (which are subject to numerous detailed exceptions outside the scope of this chapter) currently provide for: a maximum 48-hour working week (averaged over 17 weeks); a minimum daily rest period of 11 hours; a rest break of at least 20 minutes where the working day is longer than 6 hours; a minimum uninterrupted rest period of 24 hours (in addition to the daily rest periods of 11 hours) every week; paid annual leave of at least 4.8 weeks (increased to 5.6 weeks as of 1 April 2009); and an average limit of 8 hours in any 24-hour period on night work. Although under the Regulations, young workers are subject to the same broad limits on working time as adult workers, there are certain special entitlements applicable to them (again subject to exceptions).

Apart from their obligations under the Working Time Regulations 1998 (SI 1998/1833) , employers should in any case take care to avoid employees working excessive hours. The case of *Walker v Northumberland County Council* [1995] IRLR 35, illustrates the issue. The High Court held that the defendant council were in breach of their duty of care which they owed to the plaintiff employee as his employer in respect of a second mental breakdown he suffered as a result of stress and anxiety caused by his job as a social worker. The court held that an employer owes a duty of care to his employees not to cause them psychiatric damage by the volume or character of work that they are required to perform. The judge stated that there was no logical reason why the risk of injury to an employee's mental (as against physical) health should be excluded from the employer's general duty to provide an employee with a safe system of work and to take steps to protect him from reasonably foreseeable risks. This reinforced the earlier case of *Johnstone v Bloomsbury Health Authority* [1991] 2 AER 293, where the court held that whilst a contract of employment could impose a requirement on a hospital doctor to be available for 48 hours' overtime above the 40-hour week this had to be exercised in such a way as not to cause injury or damaged health. Employers should be aware of the liability that may arise from expecting workers to work excessively long hours.

The case of *Sutherland v Hatton* [2002] EWCA Civ 76, [2002] IRLR 263 concerned an employee teacher who had been forced to stop working because of psychiatric illness. The employee claimed that the psychiatric illness was caused by stress at work and that the employer was liable to them in damages. The Court of Appeal allowed her employer's appeal but in doing so they applied the following practical propositions to the facts:

(a) There are no special control mechanisms applying to claims for psychiatric illness or injury arising from the stress of doing the work the employee is required to do. The ordinary principles of employer's liability apply.

(b) The threshold question is whether this kind of harm to this particular employee was reasonably foreseeable. This has two components:
(i) an injury to health, which
(ii) is attributable to stress at work.

(c)   Foreseeability depends upon what the employer knows (or ought reasonably to know) about the individual employee. An employer is usually entitled to assume that the employee can withstand the normal pressures of the job unless he knows of some particular problem or vulnerability.

(d)   The test is the same whatever the employment; there are no occupations which should be regarded as intrinsically dangerous to mental health.

(e)   Factors likely to be relevant in answering the threshold question include:

    (i)   the nature and extent of the work done by the employee. Is the workload much more than is normal for the particular job? Is the work particularly intellectually or emotionally demanding for this employee? Are demands being made of this employee unreasonable when compared with the demands made of others in the same or comparable jobs? Or are there signs that others doing this job are suffering harmful levels of stress? Is there an abnormal level of sickness or absenteeism in the same job or the same department?

    (ii)   signs from the employee of impending harm to health. Has he a particular problem or vulnerability? Has he already suffered from illness attributable to stress at work? Have there recently been frequent or prolonged absences which are uncharacteristic of him? Is there reason to think that these are attributable to stress at work, for example because of complaints or warnings from him or others?

(f)   The employer is generally entitled to take what he is told by his employee at face value, unless he has good reason to think to the contrary. He does not generally have to make searching enquiries of the employee or seek permission to make further enquiries of his medical advisers.

(g)   To trigger a duty to take steps, the indications of impending harm to health arising from stress at work must be plain enough for any reasonable employer to realise that he should do something about it.

(h)   The employer is only in breach of duty if he has failed to take the steps which are reasonable in the circumstances, bearing in mind the magnitude of the risk of harm occurring, the gravity of the harm which may occur, the costs and practicability of preventing it, and the justifications for running the risk.

(i)   The size and scope of the employer's operation, its resources and the demands it faces are relevant in deciding what is reasonable; these include the interests of other employees and the need to treat them fairly, for example, in any redistribution of duties.

(j)   An employer can only reasonably be expected to take steps which are likely to do some good. The court is likely to need expert evidence on this.

(k)   An employer who offers a confidential advice service, with referral to appropriate counselling or treatment services, is unlikely to be found in breach of duty.

(l)   If the only reasonable and effective step would have been to dismiss or demote the employee, the employer will not be in breach of duty in allowing a willing employee to continue in the job.

(m)   In all cases, therefore, it is necessary to identify the steps which the employer both could and should have taken before finding him in breach of his duty of care.

(n)   The claimant must show that that breach of duty has caused or materially contributed to the harm suffered. It is not enough to show that occupational stress has caused the harm.

(o)   Where the harm suffered has more than one cause, the employer should only pay for that proportion of the harm suffered which is attributable to his wrongdoing, unless the harm is truly indivisible. It is for the defendant to raise the question of apportionment.

(p)   The assessment of damages will take account of any pre-existing disorder or vulnerability and of the chance that the claimant would have succumbed to a stress-related disorder in any event.

It was hoped that the House of Lords decision in *Barber v Somerset County Council* [2004] IRLR 475 would clarify the law in this area but it has neither approved nor disapproved the principles which the Court of Appeal laid down in *Sutherland v Hatton*. In this case the House of Lords put the responsibility back onto the employer to make inquiries and provide assistance and support in stress cases where the employer is put on notice of an employee suffering from a mental health problem.

In *Hartman v South Essex Mental Health & Community Care NHS Trust* [2005] EWCA Civ 6, [2005] IRLR 293 the Court of Appeal held that the general principles relating to stress at work cases were to be found in *Sutherland v Hatton*, however, care is required in their application to the particular facts of each case. The 16 factors set out above were referred to as 'useful signposts for judges faced with the, sometimes complex, facts of stress at work cases' but they were 'not intended to cover all the infinitely variable facts that are likely to arise in stress at work cases'. The principles are therefore good guidance for stress cases, but should not be looked at in isolation. The Court of Appeal added that they did not think that anything which was said by the House of Lords in *Barber v Somerset County Council* was intended to alter the practical guidance given in *Sutherland v Hatton*.

In *Intel Ltd v Daw* [2007] IRLR 346 the Court Of Appeal rejected the view in *Hatton* that an employer who provided treatment for stress was unlikely to be culpable. If the employer has damaged the employee, it is no answer to say that the employer has subsequently made the employee better. In *Dickins v O$_2$* [2008] EWCA Civ 1144, [2009] IRLR 58 the Court of Appeal doubted that stress injury was divisible and so a claimant who showed that the employer had materially contributed to injury was to pay full damages for the breakdown.

In *Hone v Six Continents Ltd* [2005] EWCA Civ 922, [2006] IRLR 49 the Court of Appeal applied the test in *Sutherland v Hatton* and in particular the 7th principle (see (g) above). Despite a lack of previous illnesses, a refusal to sign the Working Time Regulations opt-out and complaints about working hours influenced the Court of Appeal's decision that an impending injury to health, attributable to stress at work, was reasonably foreseeable. In this case it was noted that a reasonable employer should have appointed an assistant manager to help the employee as repeatedly requested by the employee.

Holidays

[**14.23**] Since 1 October 2007, under the Working Time Regulations 1998 (as amended), all workers have been entitled to 4.8 weeks' paid annual leave (this may include bank and any other statutory holidays). This increased to 5.6 weeks as of 1 April 2009. Following the ECJ's decision in *Broadcasting, Entertainment, Cinematographic and Theatre Union (BECTU) v Secretary of State for Trade and Industry* [2001] ECR 1-4881, [2001] IRLR 559, Regulation 13(1) which specified that workers must have 13 weeks' continuous service to qualify for paid annual leave has been ruled unlawful. A payment in lieu of the statutory entitlement cannot be made, except where the worker's employment is terminated. In such a case, compensation is payable; the amount is determined by a statutory formula. Untaken holiday cannot be carried over to the next holiday year save as set out below. There are detailed requirements in the regulations as to the dates on which leave can be taken, and as to notice. Public and Bank holidays may count towards the annual leave entitlement and often do for low paid workers. Therefore, the Government has legislated to increase the entitlement to paid annual leave to 5.6 weeks as detailed above. For full time workers this will mean 28 days' holiday. Part timers are entitled to a pro rata entitlement.

Following the ECJ decision in *Pereda v Madrid Movilidad* (ECJ C-277 08) [2009] All ER (D) 88 (Sep), the Government announced in May 2011 that it would be amending the Working Time Regulations 1998 to allow the carry-over of holiday to the next holiday year where an employee has been off on long term sick leave or on 'family' leave, and has been unable to take their holiday for that reason.

Miscellaneous

[**14.24**] Other rights to which employees may be contractually entitled are membership of the company pension scheme, subsidised sickness insurance, arrangements for time-off for medical appointments etc, stress counselling, provisions for London weighting, and relocation packages.

References

[**14.25**] Employers are generally under no legal obligation to provide a reference for a departing employee (save where the employee is working in an area governed by the Financial Services and Markets Act 2000 or where the refusal amounts to unlawful victimisation under the Equality Act 2010). However, where they do, then, according to the House of Lords in *Spring v Guardian Assurance* [1994] ICR 596, there is a general duty of care in negligence in relation to the contents of the reference. In this case, Mr Spring brought an action for negligence against Guardian Assurance plc following a reference written about him by two directors stating that: ' . . . this man has little or no integrity and cannot be trusted . . . '. The High Court accepted Mr Spring's description of the reference as 'the kiss of death'. The House of Lords ruled that a duty of care was owed both to the recipient and to the subject of the reference, saying that it was indeed a negligent reference as Mr Spring was undoubtedly 'a fool but not a rogue'. Mr Spring therefore won his claim that the reference was negligent and compensation for the fact that he suffered financial loss.

In relation to references and employers' liability for defamation, the *Spring* case also assists. Mr Spring lost his case for libel and malicious falsehood. A defamatory statement is one that is published, is false and derogatory without lawful justification. Such a statement must lower that person's reputation in the estimation of right-thinking people; expose him to ridicule or hatred or contempt and have a tendency to injure him in his office, profession or trade. The key to a successful claim for defamation is that the plaintiff must be able to show that the author of the statement was prompted by malice and deliberately false statements. Very few statements made about ex-employees or employees would fall into this category. In *Cox v Sun Alliance Life Limited* [2001] IRLR 448 the Court of Appeal upheld and followed the decision in *Spring*.

In *Kidd v Axa Equity & Law Life Assurance plc* [2000] IRLR 301 Mr Kidd's former employers gave a reference stating that they had received complaints about him from clients and that investigations into those complaints were continuing. As a result Mr Kidd was not taken on by his prospective employer. He sued his employers alleging they were in breach of a duty of care to provide a reference for him which was fair and not misleading. He believed the reference should have made clear that Mr Kidd had not yet been questioned in relation to the allegations.

The High Court held that an employer does not owe a duty of care to provide a reference which was fair, full and comprehensive, but an employer does owe a duty of care not to give misleading information. To succeed, an employee will need to prove that the employer did not take reasonable care to ensure misleading information was not given, that misleading information was given and that the misleading information was likely to have a material effect upon the mind of a reasonable recipient to the detriment of the employee. In Mr Kidd's case the information was not held to be misleading.

Part-time employees

[14.26] All part-time employees have the same statutory rights as full-time employees, including the following rights to:

(a) claim unfair dismissal after one years' continuous employment (see **14.93** below);

(b) claim statutory redundancy pay after two years' continuous employment (ERA 1996, s 155);

(c) claim 26 weeks' ordinary maternity leave (ERA 1996, s 71) and 26 weeks' additional maternity leave (ERA 1996, s 73);

(d) receive a written statement of terms and conditions of employment to be given within two months of joining (ERA 1996, s 1);

(e) receive itemised pay slips (ERA 1996, s 8);

(f) receive written reasons for dismissal, after one year's continuous employment (ERA 1996, s 92);

(g)   receive a minimum period of notice of dismissal (ERA 1996, s 86);
(h)   time off for trade union duties and activities (TULR(C)A 1992, ss 168 and 170);
(i)   time off for public duties (ERA 1996, s 50);
(j)   time off to look for alternative work or to arrange training when under notice of redundancy (ERA 1996, s 28);
(k)   a statutory guarantee payment (ERA 1996, s 28);
(l)   medical suspension pay (ERA 1996, s 64);
(m)   protection against dismissal on the grounds of pregnancy, childbirth or the taking of maternity leave (ERA 1996, s 99);
(n)   not be dismissed, to be selected for redundancy or to suffer detriment where health and safety matters are at issue (ERA 1996, s 100); and
(o)   protection against dismissal for asserting a statutory right (ERA 1996, s 104).

In addition to their rights under ERA 1996, part-time workers have also benefited under the Part-Time Workers (Prevention of Less Favourable Treatment) Regulations 2000 (SI 2000/1551), which came into force on 1 July 2000. The regulations ensure that part-time workers (ie both employees and workers) are treated no less favourably than their full-time counterparts, unless such treatment can be justified on objective grounds.

This means that part-time workers must receive (pro-rated where appropriate) no less favourable treatment regarding:

(a)   rates of pay;
(b)   access to pension schemes and other pension benefits;
(c)   access to training and career development;
(d)   holiday entitlement;
(e)   contractual sick pay, maternity pay, parental pay and career breaks; and
(f)   treatment in selection for promotion and transfer.

Part-time workers who believe they are being or have been treated less favourably and that the treatment is not justifiable have the right to make a written request for a written statement from the employer explaining the treatment. If a written statement is not received within 21 days or the statement is unsatisfactory, part-time workers may present a claim for compensation in the employment tribunal. In order to present a claim the part-time workers must identify a comparable full-time worker. Broadly, this is someone who works full-time for the employer, does the same or broadly similar work as the part-time worker and works under the same kind of contract as the part-time worker.

Fixed-term employees

[14.27] The Fixed-term Employees (Prevention of Less Favourable Treatment) Regulations 2002 (SI 2002/2034) came into force on 1 October 2002. The regulations implement the Fixed Term Work Directive in the UK and prevent fixed-term employees being treated less favourably than comparable permanent employees in terms of pay, pensions and other benefits unless the treatment can be objectively justified. Fixed-term employees are also entitled to be informed of vacancies in permanent posts. The regulations also repeal section 197(3) of ERA 1996 which enables fixed-term employees to waive the right to a statutory redundancy payment on the expiry of their fixed-term contract.

Fixed-term employees also have the right to claim unfair dismissal where they have been employed continuously for more than one year (see **14.86** below).

Under Regulation 8 of the 2002 Regulations, where an employer uses successive fixed-term contracts and the employee has been continuously employed in that way for four years or more, the employee will be deemed to be a permanent employee and any fixed term is of no effect, unless the employer can objectively justify the continuation of the use of a fixed-term contract.

Agency workers

[14.28] The law relating to agency workers and their employment status is extremely complicated. An agency 'temp' is usually on the books of an agency, works for an agency client, and may be employed by the agency (formally an 'employment business'). Day-to-day control rests with the client but the contractual relationship is usually said to be with the agency. Whether the worker is an employee of either the agency or the client or neither party will depend on the facts of the situation. See **14.3** above for the tests to apply when assessing employee status, ie is there mutuality of obligations between the parties, is there an obligation on the worker to personally provide their services, what level of control is exercised over the worker.

The Conduct of Employment Agencies and Employment Business Regulations 2003 (SI 2003/3319) came into force in 2004. The regulations aim to balance the rights of the work seekers with the commercial aims of the agency or business. There are different provisions applying to employment agencies and employment businesses and how they conduct their business. The regulations force employment agencies and businesses to state the basis on which they operate. This clarifies the obligations of all the parties and in particular where any employment liabilities in respect of work seekers will lie. The regulations impose strict requirements on the employment agency/business and the client hiring company with regard to provision of information between the parties including the work seekers. There are provisions limiting the circumstances in which employment businesses can charge transfer fees and also provisions allowing a hiring company to opt for an extended hire period, in certain circumstances, as an alternative to paying such a transfer fee. Companies should now be able to understand what rules they have to follow when engaging the services of an employment agency or employment business.

The European Commission put forward a draft directive giving temporary agency workers a right to be treated no less favourably than comparable workers in the business in which they are placed. In June 2003 it was put to one side when the European Council of Ministers failed to agree on the qualifying period for temporary workers. On 20 May 2008 the UK Government announced that it had agreed a deal with the unions and CBI on the rights of agency workers. The Agency Workers Regulations 2010 (SI 2010/93) came into force on 1 October 2011. The Regulations provide that after 12 weeks on assignment, agency workers are entitled to equal treatment including the same basic pay and annual leave (but not occupational sick pay) as comparable permanent employees. Equal treatment does not include the right to participate in occupational pension schemes, redundancy payment schemes or benefit schemes, eg company car or private health schemes.

Rights of workers

[**14.29**] It is important to note the difference in status between employees and workers. Workers are sometimes agency workers, and sometimes self-employed. Discrimination legislation applies to all situations where work is 'personally executed', and thus applies to most casual and freelance workers who are unable to send a substitute in their place. Workers are also protected under the Working Time Regulations, National Minimum Wage legislation and the Public Interest Disclosure Act 1998. They also have protection from unauthorised deductions from their pay (see **14.84** below).

Employment law establishes major duties regarding employees, but employers also owe duties to 'others', ie the self-employed, some freelancers and agency temps under the Management of Health and Safety at Work Regulations 1999 (SI 1999/3242) (see **14.72** below). These workers should therefore be included in any risk assessments.

Transfers of undertakings

[**14.30**] The Transfer of Undertakings (Protection of Employment) Regulations 2006 (SI 2006/246) (TUPE) give employees continuous employment rights when a trade or business is transferred by sale or other disposition. It includes contracting in/out situations and changes of contractor. A company secretary dealing with a TUPE situation should be aware of the potential need to negotiate indemnities and warranties where commercially possible, to limit the financial impact of TUPE related employment claims.

TUPE was intended to cover the requirements of the EU Directive 77/187/EEC, usually known as the 'Acquired Rights Directive (ARD)'. This Directive was revised in 1998 by Directive 98/50/EC and consolidated in 2001 by Directive 2001/23. The introductory paragraph to TUPE indicates that TUPE covers the 'rights and obligations relating to employers and employees on the transfer or merger of undertakings, businesses or part of businesses'. TUPE has three principal aims:

(a)   the protection of existing employment rights;
(b)   obliging employers to consult over transfers; and
(c)   the protection of employees against dismissal.

TUPE applies where there is a 'relevant transfer' (Reg 3). A relevant transfer is defined as:

(i)   a transfer of a business, undertaking or part of an undertaking or business situated immediately before the transfer in the UK where there is a transfer of an economic entity which retains its business identity (a 'business transfer') (Reg 3(1)(a)); or

(ii)   a client engaging a contractor to do work on its behalf, reassigning such a contract or bringing the work 'in-house' (a 'service provision change') (Reg 3(1)(b)).

The factors relevant to whether there has been a transfer of an 'economic entity' were considered in *Spijkers v Gebroeders Benedik Abbatoir CV* [1986] 2 CMLR 296 as follows:

(A)   the activities before and after the transfer;

(B)   the extent of the disruption of those activities; and

(C)   the use of the employees by the transferee.

This is not an exhaustive list of factors and the weight to be attached to each will vary considerably in each situation.

TUPE will apply whether or not property is transferred; as such, transfers of franchises also come within the definition. It is also worth noting that it is not necessary for assets to be transferred for TUPE to apply. It must however, be a stable economic entity that is transferred. All the circumstances of each particular case must be looked at (*Ayse Süzen v Zehnacke Gebäudereinigung GmbH Krankenhausservice* [1997] IRLR 255 and *Betts v Brintel Helicopters* [1997] IRLR 361; see also *ECM (Vehicle Delivery Service) Ltd v Cox* [1998] IRLR 416 (EAT)).

TUPE does not generally apply to the transfer of shares in a company which carries on an undertaking (*Initial Supplies Ltd v McCall* (1992) SLT 67), although company secretaries should note that TUPE can potentially apply in such a situation (*Millam v Print Factory (London) 1991 Limited* [2007] IRLR 526). Here, there was more than a mere transfer of shares. Activities were integrated and this meant that there was a transfer.

In order for there to be a service provision change, there must be an 'organised grouping of employees' before the change whose principal purpose is carrying on services for the client. It is expressly stated that the 'organised grouping of employees' may consist of only one employee (Reg 2(1)). There can therefore be a relevant transfer when a contract for services, such as a cleaning contract, is lost to a competitor. The employees of that cleaning company who are assigned to the particular contract will automatically transfer to the competitor.

There will not be a service provision change where:

(I)   the activities are carried out in connection with a single specific event or a task of short-term duration (Reg 3(3)(a)(ii)); or

(II)   the contract is wholly or mainly for the supply of goods for the client's use (Reg 3(3)(b)).

Effects of transfers on contracts of employment

[14.31] The effect of TUPE is to place those employed in the undertaking or grouping of employees to be transferred immediately before the transfer in the same relationship with their new employer as they had with their old employer. Rights and duties that automatically transfer to the employer following a relevant transfer include:

(a)   terms and conditions of employment (excluding occupational pension scheme rights which are subject to separate rules – see below);

(b)   claims regarding the payment of arrears;
(c)   outstanding legal claims (eg any discrimination claims before employ-
       ment tribunals);
(d)   outstanding personal injury claims;
(e)   disciplinary records; and
(f)   contractual requirements concerning confidentiality, the status of pat-
       ents etc.

The rights of employees who would have been employed immediately before
the transfer had they not been unfairly dismissed for a reason relating to the
transfer will also transfer. This means that the transferee can 'inherit' liability
for certain pre-transfer unfair dismissal claims.

The ECJ has defined 'immediately before' as not confined to events at the time
of the transfer but including cases where employees are dismissed some time
before a transfer, but solely or principally because of it (*P Bork International
v FAD* [1989] IRLR 41). This principle is now enshrined in the 2006
Regulations.

The new employer after a transfer is, in law, in exactly the same position as
was the previous employer. TUPE provides that any changes to the terms and
conditions of employment of transferring employees will be void if the sole or
principal reason for the changes is the transfer itself or a reason connected to
the transfer which is not an economic, technical, or organisational reason
entailing changes to the workforce (an 'ETO reason') (Reg 4(4)).

In *Wilson and others v St Helens Borough Council; Meade and another v
British Fuels Ltd* [1998] IRLR 706, one of the issues before the House of Lords
was whether transferees had any scope to vary the terms of employment after
a transfer, with the agreement of the employee. In view of the conclusion which
they had reached on the dismissal issue (see **14.33** below), the Lords stated that
it was not strictly necessary to deal with the variation issue. However, Lord
Slynn (with whom the other Law Lords agreed) stated that he did not accept
the argument that a variation was only invalid if agreed on as part of the
transfer itself. It might still be due to the transfer if it came later. However,
there must (or, at least, might) come a time when the link with the transfer was
broken or treated as no longer effective. Lord Slynn also stated that, where the
variation was not due to the transfer, it could validly be made, although he
accepted that it may be difficult to decide whether the variation is due to the
transfer or attributable to some separate cause.

Generally speaking, it will not be possible to justify a variation of terms and
conditions of transferring employees for the purposes of harmonising the terms
with those of existing employees. Even if employees agree to a change in their
terms and conditions, their agreement will be regarded by an employment
tribunal as ineffective in the circumstances. In this situation, the only effective
means of achieving a variation would be for the employer to terminate the
employment of the transferring employees and then immediately offer to
re-engage them on the new terms and conditions of employment. The dismissal
and re-engagement route will not break the employee's continuity of employment with the transferor but could expose the transferee to claims for unfair
dismissal. Therefore a compromise agreement may be advisable.

However, in *Power v Regent Security Services Ltd* [2008] IRLR 66 the Court of Appeal held that the effect of TUPE meant that although the transferring employees could not be deprived of any rights that transferred with them, it did not enable the transferee to avoid being bound by any new favourable terms it had agreed with the employees. TUPE also gives employers greater scope to vary the contracts of employees in an insolvency situation (Regs 8 and 9). The sole or principal reason for the change must be the transfer itself or a reason connected with the transfer which is not an ETO reason and it must be made with the aim of safeguarding employment opportunities by ensuring the survival of the undertaking or business. The changes will not be effective unless they are approved in advance by the appropriate representatives of the affected employees.

TUPE also applies to the transfer of part of an undertaking and in the case of *Fairhurst Ward Abbotts v Botes Building Limited* [2004] IRLR 304 the Court of Appeal confirmed that there is no requirement for the part of the undertaking transferred to be itself a separate economic entity before the relevant transfer takes place.

Occupational pension scheme benefits do not transfer under TUPE but benefits relating to old age, invalidity or survivor's benefits do (Reg 10). This provision codifies the ECJ decisions in *Beckmann v Dymanco Whicheloe Macfarlane Ltd C-164/00* [2002] IRLR 578 and *Martin v South Bank University* [2004] IRLR 74. In the *Beckmann* case the ECJ held that rights to early retirement benefits under an occupational pension scheme (for example enhanced redundancy pensions) will automatically transfer under TUPE to the transferee. The *Beckmann* decision has retrospective effect and transferees may be vulnerable to claims brought by employees (and former employees) whose pension benefits have been reduced as a result of a transfer.

Although occupational pension schemes do not transfer, Regulation 3(1) of the Transfer of Employment (Pension Protection) Regulations 2005 (SI 2005/649) provides that if the employee is, or is eligible to be, an active member of an occupational pension scheme run by the previous employer the new employer will be required, at a minimum, to allow the employee to participate in a contributory scheme where the new employer matches the employee's pension contributions up to a maximum of 6%.

An employer's obligation to make contributions to personal pension plans and stakeholder pension plans does transfer.

Duty to inform and consult

[14.32] Under Regulation 13 of TUPE 2006, trade unions or employee representatives elected for the purpose have a right to be informed and (in certain circumstances) consulted before a transfer takes place. The obligation to inform requires that the following information must be given to employees:

(a)   the fact that the relevant transfer is to take place, and the reasons for it;
(b)   the legal, economic and social implications of the transfer for affected employees; and
(c)   the measures which the employer envisages he will, in connection with the transfer, take in relation to those employees, or if he envisages no action, that fact (Reg 13).

There is no prescribed time limit on when the information should be given, but Regulation 13(2) says it should be long enough before the transfer to enable consultation to take place.

The obligation to consult is triggered if the transferee (new employer) envisages it will be taking measures (Reg 13(6)) which will affect the employees. Consultation must be undertaken with a view to seeking the employees' agreement to the measures. Merely providing an opportunity for employees to air their views will not be sufficient consultation.

Where an employer fails to inform and/or consult, a complaint may be presented to an employment tribunal within 3 months of the date of transfer. Compensation is set at up to a maximum of 13 weeks' pay for each employee. Unlike other statutory awards there is no limit on the amount of a week's pay. The transferor and the transferee will be jointly and severally liable for any award made by the employment tribunal for any failure to consult (Reg 15(9)).

There are conflicting EAT decisions as to whether compensation should be awarded for a mere technical breach of the duty to inform and consult. In *Baxter v Marks & Spencer plc* [2005] All ER (D) 26 (Oct), EAT it was held that no compensation should be awarded for a technical breach. However, in *Sweetin v Coral Racing* [2006] IRLR 252, the EAT held a maximum of 13 weeks' pay should be awarded as compensation unless there are circumstances which justify a lesser award. Until this conflict is resolved, it will be prudent for employers to adhere to the information and consultation provisions.

There are additional obligations to inform and consult in a collective redundancy situation under TULR(C)A 1992. If there is a failure to consult under TULR(C)A 1992 the tribunal may award such amount as it considers 'just and equitable' in all the circumstances having regard to the seriousness of the employer's default (s 189(4)(b)) and subject to a maximum of 90 days' pay for each affected employee (with no statutory cap). The Court of Appeal in *GMB v Susie Radin Limited* [2004] EWCA Civ 180, [2004] IRLR 400 set out principles for assessing an award for failure to consult and it was these principles which resulted in the EAT decision in *Sweetin* (see above).

TUPE also imposes an obligation on the transferor to provide certain basic information (called Employee Liability Information) to the transferee about the transferring employees before the transfer takes place, eg their identity, age and section 1 particulars (Reg 11). The information must be given not less than 14 days before the transfer, or as soon as is reasonably practicable. If the transferor fails to provide the necessary information, the transferee can present a claim to an employment tribunal and could be awarded compensation of up to £500 in respect of each transferring employee about whom the transferor has failed to provide the necessary information (Reg 12).

TUPE related dismissals

[**14.33**] A dismissal will be automatically unfair if its sole or principal reason is the transfer itself or a reason connected to the transfer that is not an ETO reason (Reg 7). If the dismissal is unconnected to the transfer or is for a reason connected to the transfer and there is an ETO reason then the employment tribunal will have to decide, using the criteria of reasonableness as with a non-TUPE-related unfair dismissal claim, whether in all the circumstances the decision to dismiss was fair. To bring a claim for unfair dismissal, employees must have at least one year's continuous employment.

In relation to pre-transfer unfair dismissals, the general rule is that liability is transferred to the transferee to the exclusion of the transferor. However, where the sole or principal reason for the pre-transfer dismissal is not the transfer itself or is an ETO reason connected to the transfer, then liability will remain with the transferor (Reg 4(3)).

Where prior to the transfer an employee objects to the transfer, his contract of employment will not automatically transfer and the employee will be treated as if he resigned (Reg 4(7)). The termination will not be treated as a dismissal by the employer. However, if the employee objects to a proposed post transfer detrimental change to his terms and conditions post-transfer, the employee is entitled to claim constructive dismissal and/or redundancy in addition to a common law claim for wrongful dismissal and the right of action is against the transferor (*University of Oxford v Humphreys and Associated Examining Board* [2000] IRLR 183).

It is important to note that the transfer itself does not amount to a dismissal, but operates as a novation of the contract. However, if the transferee fundamentally breaches the employee's contract of employment after the transfer, then the employee may be able to treat himself as constructively dismissed and his right of action in the employment tribunal would be against the transferee.

If the transfer involves or would involve a substantial change in working conditions to the material detriment of the employee, then the employee may resign (Reg 4(9)). In this situation, the employee will be treated as having been dismissed with notice by the employer (Reg 4(10)). The employee will therefore be precluded from bringing a claim in respect of damages for any notice period which he did not work.

The House of Lords in *Wilson v St Helens Borough Council* [1999] 2 AC 52 held that where dismissal has taken place before, on or following a transfer the dismissal remains effective even if the reason for the dismissal is connected to the transfer. The transfer did not render the actual dismissal void nor could the employees force the transferee to re-employ them on their old terms and conditions. Therefore the employee's remedy lies in claiming unfair dismissal in the employment tribunal.

To summarise, transferring employees who are dissatisfied with the transfer have the following options:

(a)   object without any good reason leaving them no claim;

(b)   treat the contract as having been terminated as a result of a substantial change to their working conditions to their material detriment, leaving them with a potential claim for unfair dismissal and notice pay;

(c)   claim that the change is a fundamental breach of contract entitling them to resign and giving them a claim for constructive unfair dismissal and wrongful dismissal; or

(d)   in certain situations, claim that their role is redundant and seek a redundancy payment accordingly if they have been dismissed (actually or constructively).

Vicarious liability

[14.34] At common law, an employer is liable for the tortious acts of his employees committed in the course of their employment. This has been interpreted very widely in the past and can often cover acts carried out by the employee outside normal working hours. For the purpose of ascertaining whether an employer is vicariously liable for torts of an individual engaged by him to perform certain duties, it is essential to determine whether that individual is an employee or an independent contractor. If the individual is an employee, then the employer will be vicariously liable for the torts committed by the employee *in the course of his employment*. If, however, the individual is an independent contractor, then the employer will only be liable for acts which come within his non-delegable duties. The employer does, however, have an option of obtaining an indemnity from the employee who committed the act which gave rise to the liability or, in certain circumstances, to dismiss him if the dismissal is for a potentially fair reason; an example would be serious misconduct (see 'Unfair dismissal' at **14.93** below).

In *Lister v Hesley Hall Ltd* [2001] IRLR 472 the House of Lords stated that an employer may also be responsible for acts which he has not authorised the employee to do provided they are connected to acts which he authorised the employee to do. Lister was a school worker who sexually abused boys who were in his care. The employer was held to be vicariously liable for the abuse as the tort was closely connected with his employment. Here, actions which could never be within the lawful course of work were yet held to be in the course of employment.

The approach of the House of Lords was followed by the Court of Appeal in *Mattis v Pollock (t/a Flamingo's Nightclub)* [2003] EWCA Civ 887, [2003] IRLR 603 where the employer was held to be vicariously liable for the injuries inflicted on Mr Mattis by an employee doorman. The employer was vicariously liable even though the employee had left his place of work, returned home and armed himself with a knife before the attack took place. In line with the House of Lords' reasoning in *Lister*, the Court of Appeal found that the attack was 'connected' to what the employer employed the doorman to do, because as part of his job he was encouraged to act in an aggressive and threatening manner towards customers.

In *Majrowski v Guy's & St Thomas' NHS Trust* [2006] UKHL 34, [2006] IRLR 695, the House of Lords held that employers are vicariously liable for their employees' breaches of statutory duties unless the particular statute specifically excludes liability. In this case it was held that the Protection from Harassment Act 1997 did not exclude such liability and therefore the employer was potentially liable for harassment conducted by an employee against Mr Majrowski.

The Court of Appeal in *Veakins v Kier Islington* [2010] IRLR 132 found that an employer was liable for the actions of an employee who had bullied the claimant in the workplace.

Employers' Liability (Compulsory Insurance) Act 1969

[14.35] The Employers' Liability (Compulsory Insurance) Act 1969 imposes upon every employer carrying on business in Great Britain an obligation to maintain insurance against claims by employees injured in the course of their employment. The insurance must be maintained under one or more approved policies with an authorised insurer against liability for bodily injury or disease sustained by employees arising out of and in the course of their employment in Great Britain. A copy of the current certificate of insurance must be displayed at each business premises in a position where it may be easily seen and read by employees.

Under the Employers Liability (Compulsory Insurance) Regulations 1998 (SI 1998/2573), the minimum aggregate amount of insurance an employer is required to maintain is not less than £5 million. Where the employer is a company with one or more subsidiaries this requirement is taken to apply to the company and its subsidiaries together, as if they are a single employer (Reg 3). An employer is not required to insure family members. Certain employers (specified in Schedule 2 of the Regulations) are exempted from the requirement to maintain insurance cover.

Discrimination

[14.36] The Equality Act 2010 (EqA 2010) has gathered together in one place the nine protected characteristics in employment law; namely, age, disability, gender reassignment, marriage and civil partnership, pregnancy and maternity, race, religion or belief, sex and sexual orientation. Generally speaking an employer will be liable for the discriminatory acts of its employees unless it has taken all reasonable steps to prevent discrimination (EqA 2010, s 109).

TULR(C)A 1992, s 137(1) makes it unlawful for an employer to refuse a person employment on the grounds that they are, or are not, a member of a trade union or that they refuse to become a member of, or refuse to resign from, a trade union. TULR(C)A 1992 removes the legal protection of a 'pre-entry' closed shop. Advertising for union, or non-union members, or instructing an employment agency to supply only one type of employee is also acting unlawfully.

After employment has begun, ERA 1996 contains provisions for the protection of employees from suffering detriment in employment (ERA 1996, ss 44–47). These protections include the right not to be discriminated against for:

(a)   carrying out health and safety duties (and certain other specified circumstances relating to health and safety);
(b)   refusing to work on Sundays (protected shop workers and betting shop workers);
(c)   acting as a trustee of an occupational pension scheme;

(d)   activities as an employee representative, or as a candidate for election as such;

(e)   making a protected disclosure (ERA 1996, s 47B) (see **14.96** below);

(f)   asserting certain rights under the Working Time Regulations 1998 (SI 1998/1833) (see **14.22** and **14.23** above) or the National Minimum Wage Act 1998 (see **14.90** below);

(g)   exercising the right to time off for study or training (see **14.20** above);

(h)   asserting rights under the Part Time Workers (Prevention of Less Favourable Treatment) Regulations 2000 (SI 2000/1551) (see **14.26** above);

(i)   asserting rights under the Fixed Term Employees (Prevention of Less Favourable Treatment) Regulations 2002 (SI 2002/2034); and

(j)   asserting rights to request a flexible working pattern under ERA 1996, ss 80F–80I.

Discrimination on the grounds of sex, race, disability, sexual orientation, age or religion or belief can be either direct or indirect.

Direct discrimination is the less favourable treatment of one person compared with another on any of the above grounds, such as refusing to employ people of a particular race.

Indirect discrimination is defined by EqA 2010, s 19(1) in these terms:

> 'A person (A) discriminates against another (B) if A applies to B a provision, criterion or practice which is discriminatory in relation to a relevant protected characteristic of B's.'

Certain exceptions to the basic principle of non-discrimination, however, are introduced by EqA 2010. Indirect discrimination can be justified where the employer demonstrates that the application of the provision, criterion or practice constituted a proportionate means of achieving a legitimate aim. Furthermore, what would normally amount to unlawful direct discrimination may be lawful if being of a particular sex, race, religion or belief, sexual orientation, age or having a disability is a requirement for the job. For example, a person working in a changing room might well be of the same sex as those using it. Someone working with the deaf might reasonably be preferred if they themselves used sign language.

There is no upper limit to the compensatory element which may be awarded in discrimination claims.

The employment tribunal can also make an additional award for injury to feelings. The Court of Appeal has set out guidelines as to the amount of the award in *Vento v Chief Constable of West Yorkshire* [2003] IRLR 102, as updated in *Da'Bell v NSPCC* [2010] IRLR 1. There are three bands depending on the severity of the discrimination as follows:

(a)   Lower band: £600–£6,000;

(b)   Middle band: £6,000–£18,000; and

(c)   Upper band: £18,000–£30,000.

Equal pay

[**14.37**] The Equality Act 2010 now enshrines the old equal pay legislation starting at section 64. The substantive law has not ben changed. The Act imposes a duty on employers to pay equal rates of pay to both sexes involved in 'like work', work rated as equivalent, or work of equal value, unless the employer can show that a variation in terms is due to a 'genuine material factor' which is not the difference of sex. A job evaluation scheme must have been implemented for work to be rated as equivalent. The methods for job evaluation are laid out in ACAS Guide No. 1. In the event of a dispute, it would fall to an employment tribunal to determine whether or not the work was 'like work', work rated as equivalent, or of equal value. In the case of work of equal value, the evidence of a member of an independent panel of experts will also be required. In *Levez v TH Jennings (Harlow Pools) Ltd (No 2)* [1999] IRLR 764 the limitation of an award to a maximum of two years' back pay under the Act has been held to be in breach of EC law requirements that there should be an effective remedy for discrimination. Arrears are now recoverable on the basis of comparable domestic law claims and backpay of up to six years prior to the date of the claim may now be awarded.

Applicants in equal pay cases can either rely on EqA 2010 or can directly rely upon EU law (Article 141, Treaty of Rome). Applications under Article 141 are also heard by employment tribunals. The ECJ has given a wide interpretation to the meaning of 'pay' which falls within Article 141. 'Pay' includes:

(a)   sick pay;
(b)   pension schemes supplemental to State provision;
(c)   occupational pension schemes linked to State retirement age; and
(d)   an award of compensation for unfair dismissal.

Equal Pay Questionnaires were introduced with effect from 6 April 2003 by the Equal Pay (Questions and Replies) Order 2003 (SI 2003/722). The questionnaire is intended to help individuals request key information from their employers to establish whether they are receiving equal pay, and if they are not, the reasons for this. The employer must respond to the questionnaire within eight weeks of receiving it. An employment tribunal may draw adverse inferences if the employer's replies are not received within the timescale without good reason. Employers are expected to answer the questions as fully as possible.

In May 2011 the Government announced that it was launching a consultation exercise on whether employment tribunals should have the power to order an employer to undertake an equal pay audit when the employer has lost a claim relating to unequal pay between male and female employees.

Immigration, Asylum and Nationality Act 2006 – employers' liability for illegal workers

[14.38] Since January 1997 employers have had a responsibility to check that all new employees are entitled to work in the United Kingdom. The rules governing employee checking, and the defence against conviction for employing illegal workers which such checks give employers, have been amended on several occasions since 1997. The latest rules came into force on 29 February 2008 when the relevant provisions of the Immigration, Asylum and Nationality Act 2006 (IANA 2006) came into force. The checks which are necessary will depend on when the employee in question was recruited. Further information can be found on the UK Border Agency (UKBA) website (see www. bia.homeoffice.gov.uk).

As a general rule, workers from any EEA member country are entitled to work in the UK. However, workers from the Czech Republic, Estonia, Hungary, Latvia, Lithuania, Poland, Slovakia and Slovenia (the so-called 'A8' countries) must comply with additional registration requirements if they wish to work in the UK for one month or more. Any such national must register with the Home Office and it is the responsibility of the employer to ensure that they do. After twelve months of legal working such nationals no longer need to be registered and can apply for a certificate confirming their right to work in the UK.

Additional rules also apply to workers from Bulgaria and Romania. Workers from Bulgaria and Romania require a work permit and an accession worker card showing their right to work in the UK, unless they are exempt from the requirement to obtain one or both of these documents.

Requests for documentary proof of the right to work in the UK should be made of each person to whom an offer of employment is made so as to reduce the risk of allegations of race discrimination. All job offers should be conditional upon the individual providing satisfactory evidence of his entitlement to live and work in the UK. This evidence should be provided before the individual starts work.

Staff responsible for hiring employees should know what to look for when asking for proof of a prospective employee's right to work. The Government has issued a code of practice for all employers giving guidance on 'the avoidance of race discrimination in recruitment practice while seeking to prevent illegal working'. Failure to adhere to the code is evidence admissible in a tribunal hearing.

Penalties for employing illegal workers

[14.39] The penalty for negligently employing an illegal worker is a fine of up to £10,000 per illegal worker. Knowingly employing an illegal worker is a criminal offence, punishable by a custodial sentence and/or an unlimited fine. Directors and HR professionals are those primarily at risk of a custodial sentence.

The Immigration, Asylum and Nationality Act 2006 provides a statutory excuse – effectively a defence to the offence of negligently employing an illegal worker – if the employer has checked the documentation of his workers before they start work. Employers must check certain documents and retain copies on file. If the job applicant has permanent leave to remain and has no restrictions on his employment or stay in the UK, then the check need only be made prior to the commencement of work. If the job applicant has restrictions on his right to remain, these checks must be repeated at least every twelve months following the date of the initial check (or more frequently if the leave to remain is due to expire earlier). Failure to complete the checks before employment starts, or at the time required, means the statutory excuse will not be available to the employer should it turn out that the worker does not have the right to work in the UK. The UK Border Agency has issued a Code of Practice on how to avoid race discrimination but at the same time comply with the duty to prevent illegal working.

Employing foreign workers

[14.40] The Immigration, Asylum and Nationality Act 2006 has introduced a new system for visa applications for the UK, which is being phased in on a staggered basis and will eventually replace the old system in its entirety.

A points-based system has been introduced for work permit applications, with points scored in a number of categories, including qualifications, prospective earnings, job offers and type of job, maintenance funds, and English language ability. In addition, the whole system has been structured into tiers, with different types of migrant (eg high value migrants, skilled workers, students and temporary workers) applying under different tiers. The points-based system and the new tiers are being phased in over the course of 2008 and 2009 as the present system is phased out. The old highly skilled migrant programme was fully replaced by Tier 1 from 1 July 2008. Tier 2 is expected to replace the old work permit arrangements from autumn 2008.

Sponsorship

[14.41] Under the new points-based system employers wishing to employ foreign workers need to apply for a 'sponsorship licence' from the UKBA. Sponsorship licence applications require a certain amount of suitability vetting by the UKBA to ensure that the employer is trustworthy and capable of carrying out its duties as an employer of migrants. Sanctions for those employers who fall foul of the legislation could include the downgrading or withdrawal of a licence resulting in an employer finding it more difficult, or no longer being able, to employ migrants – including those migrants already employed by that employer. The basic cost of a licence is £300 for small businesses (as defined in the Companies Act 2006) and £1,000 for all other sponsors. A UK head office can apply for a single sponsorship licence for all its UK subsidiaries. However, this needs to be weighed against the implications of one group company falling foul of the legislation which could result in the sponsorship licence being revoked for the entire group.

Holders of sponsorship licences must comply with a number of 'sponsorship duties'. A detailed analysis of these requirements is beyond the scope of this chapter, and more information in relation to this can be found on the UKBA website (see above).

Disability Discrimination

[14.42] A person has a disability where they have a physical or mental impairment which has a substantial and long-term adverse effect on their ability to carry out normal day-to-day activities. An impairment is long-term if it has lasted for twelve months, is likely to last twelve months or is likely to last for the rest of the life of that person. It is no longer the case that one must consider the list of eight factors when assessing the ability to perform normal activities. A past disability is also covered. There is statutory guidance on the matters to be taken into account in determining disability.

Perceived discrimination (ie where someone is assumed wrongly to have a disability) and associative discrimination (discrimination because of associating with a disabled person) are also covered, save in relation to the duty to make reasonable adjustments (see below).

Because of difficult case law over with whom a disabled person should compare themselves when assessing unfavourable treatment, the new Act refers to where such treatment occurs because of something arising in consequence of disability. An employer cannot be guilty of disability discrimination if he did not know and could not reasonably be expected to know that an individual was disabled (except in cases of indirect discrimination).

As well as having a duty not to discriminate on account of disability there is also a duty to make reasonable adjustments.

The new Equality Act 2010 preserves the duty under the previous legislation for an employer to make reasonable adjustments to any provision, criteria or practice applied by or on behalf of an employer, or any physical feature of the premises occupied by the employer that places a disabled person at a substantial disadvantage in comparison with persons without a disability. It also requires an employer to provide an auxiliary aid (eg an adapted chair or desk or special software) to remove the disadvantage.

The employer has a duty to take such steps as are reasonable in all the circumstances for him to take in order to prevent the arrangements having that effect. Examples of the steps which the employer may have to take include:

(A)　making adjustments to premises;
(B)　allocating some of the disabled person's duties to another person;
(C)　transferring him to fill an existing vacancy;
(D)　altering his working hours;
(E)　assigning him to a different place of work;
(F)　allowing him to be absent during working hours for rehabilitation or treatment;
(G)　giving him training;
(H)　acquiring or modifying equipment;
(I)　modifying instructions or reference manuals;
(J)　modifying procedures for testing or assessment;
(K)　providing a reader or interpreter; and
(L)　providing supervision.

In *British Gas Services Ltd v McCaull* [2001] IRLR 60, it was held by the EAT that the duty to make reasonable adjustments was not automatically breached merely on the basis that the employer was unaware of the duty. The test is an objective test and the employment tribunal must consider whether the employer took such steps as were reasonable in the circumstances.

Sexual orientation and religion or belief discrimination

[**14.43**] The Equality Act 2010 prohibits the following:

(a)　direct discrimination (treating people less favourably than others on grounds of sexual orientation or religion or belief);

(b)   indirect discrimination (applying a provision, criterion or practice which disadvantages people of a particular sexual orientation or religion or belief and which is not justified as a proportionate means of achieving a legitimate aim);

(c)   harassment (unwanted conduct that violates people's dignity or creates an intimidating, hostile, degrading, humiliating or offensive environment); and

(d)   victimisation (treating people less favourably because of something they have done under, or in connection with, the regulations, eg made a formal complaint of discrimination or given evidence in a tribunal case).

The law covers discrimination on grounds of perceived as well as actual sexual orientation (ie assuming – correctly or incorrectly – that someone is lesbian, gay, heterosexual or bisexual). The Act also now covers associative discrimination here and in all strands of discrimination, ie being discriminated against on grounds of the sexual orientation of those with whom you associate (for example, friends and/or family).

Discrimination on grounds of religion, religious belief or similar philosophical belief covers discrimination on grounds of perceived as well as actual religion or belief (ie assuming – correctly or incorrectly – that someone has or hasn't a particular religion or belief). The Act also covers association, ie being discriminated against on grounds of the religion or belief of those with whom you associate (for example, friends and/or family). It covers the lack of a belief as well as having a belief.

The law applies to all employers whatever their size and whether in the public or private sector (including the police). It applies to recruitment, terms and conditions, pay, promotion, transfers and dismissals.

Age discrimination

[14.44] The Equality Act 2010 makes discrimination (including associative discrimination) on account of age (actual or perceived) unlawful but it is possible to seek to justify that discrimination be it direct or indirect. Harassment and victimisation are also prohibited – both during and after employment. Both direct and indirect discrimination will be justified and lawful if they are a proportionate means of achieving a legitimate aim.

Employers may continue to use length of service criteria to reward staff as long as the qualifying period of service is not more than five years. Employers will also be able to use length of service criteria exceeding five years if they can demonstrate that they are fulfilling a business need in doing so.

Employees may complain of unfair dismissal at any age. The law removed the upper age limit on unfair dismissal claims, the tapering down provisions which reduce the award in the period leading up to the upper age limit and the upper and lower age limits on the basic award. The limit of 20 years' service counting towards the basic award has however been retained, as has the qualifying period of one year's service.

Selection for redundancy on the grounds of age is unlawful. The law removed some of the age-related criteria in statutory redundancy awards including lower age limits, the upper age limit of 65 (or the normal retirement age of the business in question) and the tapering down rule. The 20-year cap on the length of service that can be taken into account remains effective and the calculation of redundancy payments continues to be on the basis of length of service. The requirement that the employee has two years' continuous service before becoming entitled to a statutory redundancy payment is also maintained.

The default permitted retirement age of 65 was repealed in April 2011. Retirement is no longer one of the statutory 'fair' reasons for dismissal and the imposition by an employer of a compulsory retirement age will need to be justified, to avoid claims of age discrimination. Many retirements are consensual but an employer wishing to dismiss will need to find another 'fair' reason, eg redundancy, conduct, capability or some other substantial reason, to be able to resist an unfair dismissal claim.

Equal treatment and pension provision

[14.45] On 28 September 1994, the decision in six cases being heard together before the ECJ was announced. All involved the issue of sex equality and pension schemes. The cases arose from the ECJ's ruling of May 1990 in *Barber v Guardian Royal Exchange* [1990] IRLR 240. The case held that EU law outlawed pay discrimination between men and women, and that this also applied to benefits under private occupational pension schemes and retirement ages. In *Ten Oever v Stichting Bedrijfspensionenfonds voor het Glazenwassers en Schoonmaakbedrijf* [1993] IRLR 601 (the 'Ten Oever' case) the ECJ ruled that the *Barber* judgment did not apply retrospectively. In *Coloroll Pension Trustees Ltd v Russell* [1994] IRLR 586 the ECJ ruled that both employers and trustees are bound to apply the equal treatment rules, and employers could continue to rely on sex-based actuarial rates for the calculation of transfer values and commutation values for those leaving the scheme. It was not sexually discriminatory to take into account the actuarial assumption that women tend to outlive men, and consequently give rise to lower pension payments for men. The impact of *Barber* as clarified by *Coloroll* was that many pension schemes had to be amended in order to 'equalise' benefits between men and women. In a number of cases problems have arisen because of the way in which schemes attempted to equalise benefits. In *Vroege v NCIV* [1995] ICR 635 the ECJ ruled that employers will need to admit part-time workers to pension schemes, if barring them constituted discrimination. The ECJ reasoned that employers should have realised from its judgments in 1976 (in *Defrenne v Sabrena (No 2)* [1976] ECR 455) that barring part-time workers from pension schemes is frequently discriminatory and should have ended the practice long ago. This right is not limited by the *Barber* judgment and retrospective claims can be made back to April 1976.

In *Preston v Wolverhampton Healthcare NHS Trust* [2001] ICR 217 the House of Lords confirmed that the time limit of six months from the effective date of termination is not in breach of EU law notwithstanding that there is currently no provision for an extension of time. In situations where an employee is employed under a series of short-term contracts, time runs from the cessation of the last contract in the series.

In *National Power plc v Young* [2001] IRLR 32 the Court of Appeal held that if a claim is presented within six months of the effective date of termination, an equal pay claim relating to the employee's former employment may be pursued.

Statutory maternity rights

[14.46] The Employment Act 2002 made significant changes to statutory maternity rights and these rights were strengthened by the Work and Families Act 2006. The detail regarding maternity rights is to be found in the Statutory Maternity Pay (General) Regulations 1986 (SI 1986/1960) and the Maternity and Parental Leave etc Regulations 1999 (SI 1999/3312), as amended by the Maternity and Parental Leave (Amendment) Regulations 2002 (SI 2002/2789) and the Maternity and Parental Leave etc and the Paternity and Adoption Leave (Amendment) Regulations 2006 (SI 2006/2014).

Maternity rights fall into five main categories:

(a)   paid time off for antenatal care;
(b)   maternity leave;
(c)   maternity pay (Statutory Maternity Pay or Maternity Allowance);
(d)   protection against unfair treatment or dismissal; and
(e)   the right to return to work.

Requirements

[14.47] Pregnant employees are entitled to the following maternity rights:

(a)   Paid time off to attend appointments for antenatal care made on the advice of a registered medical practitioner, registered midwife or registered health visitor. Antenatal care is not restricted to medical examinations. This right applies regardless of the employee's length of service.

(b)   Ordinary Maternity Leave (OML) of 26 weeks from day one of their employment provided the pregnant employee complies with certain notification requirements.

(c)   A further 26 weeks of Additional Maternity Leave (AML) commencing at the end of the OML period (if they are already entitled to OML).

(d)   To complain of unfair dismissal on account of pregnancy (dismissal for a reason connected to pregnancy or for any pregnancy-related reason is automatically unfair, see **14.93** below).

(e)   Entitlement to the benefit of the terms and conditions of employment other than remuneration during the maternity leave which would have been applicable to her if she had not been absent and had not been pregnant or given birth to a child.

(f)   To work for up to ten 'keeping in touch' days during their maternity leave without bringing that leave to an end.

In addition to the above, since 6 April 2008, all women who are on compulsory maternity leave (the period of two weeks starting immediately after childbirth) are entitled to benefit from discretionary bonuses and, as previously, compulsory maternity leave periods should be taken into account in calculating discretionary bonuses.

In addition to these rights, pregnant employees may be eligible for payment of either Statutory Maternity Pay (SMP) (payable by their employer) or Maternity Allowance (MA) (payable by the social security office). Eligibility criteria for these payments are set out at **14.52** and **14.53** below.

All pregnant employees have a right to up to 52 weeks of maternity regardless of length of service, comprising of 26 weeks' OML and 26 weeks' AML. To qualify for this, the employee must notify her employer of:

(i)   her pregnancy;
(ii)   the EWC; and
(iii) the date on which she intends her OML period to start, which must be no earlier than the beginning of the 11th week before the EWC.

The employee must notify her employer no later than the end of the 15th week before her EWC or, if that is not reasonably practicable, as soon as is reasonably practicable. This notification need not be in writing unless the employer requests written notification.

An employee taking OML, and who has notified her employer of the date on which she intends to start her OML, may vary the date she has stated, provided that she notifies her employer of the variation at least:

(A)   28 days before the date varied; or
(B)   28 days before the new date,

whichever is the earlier, or, if that is not reasonably practicable, as soon as is reasonably practicable.

These notification requirements do not apply in the event that the employee's OML is triggered by pregnancy related illness in the last four weeks of pregnancy or her baby is born before her OML commences. In these two situations the employee must notify her employer of her pregnancy related illness or the birth of her baby as soon as reasonably practicable in order to be entitled to OML.

An employee's OML will commence on the earlier of:

(I)   the date which she has notified her employer as being the start of her OML; and
(II)   the day which follows the first day after the beginning of the fourth week before the EWC on which she is absent from work wholly or partly because of pregnancy.

Where an employee's baby is born before the commencement of OML then her OML will commence on the day following that on which childbirth occurs.

Protection from dismissal

[14.48] A woman who is pregnant or who is on OML or AML has the absolute statutory right not to be dismissed because of her pregnancy or for any other reason connected with her pregnancy or childbirth. It is unlawful for an employer to select an employee for redundancy because she is pregnant or for any other reason connected to her pregnancy or childbirth. It will be an automatic unfair dismissal (with no need for a year's qualifying service) to prevent an employee from returning from maternity leave. In addition to this it will be unlawful to dismiss an employee who does not return from her maternity leave at the correct time due to the fact that either her employer has not given proper notification of the date on which her leave is due to end and she reasonably believed that her leave had not ended; or her employer has given her less than 28 days' notice of the date her leave ends and it is not reasonably practicable for her to return to work on that date.

The Employment Rights Act 1996 also requires employers to provide written reasons for any dismissal of a woman who is pregnant or on maternity leave, regardless of the reason for the dismissal and even if totally unconnected with her condition. The employee does not have to request this statement of reasons, it must be provided automatically and applies regardless of the employee's length of service.

Although a woman dismissed on these grounds can pursue an unfair dismissal claim (see **14.93** below), she may also make her claim under sex discrimination law now enshrined in the Equality Act 2010. The advantage to her of seeking to establish a claim on this basis is that any compensation awarded under a heading of discrimination is not subject to a statutory maximum.

Although it may sometimes be fair to dismiss a pregnant employee, or an employee on OML or AML, for reasons of redundancy provided that her pregnancy or childbirth was not the reason for selection; there is a requirement under Regulation 10 of the Maternity and Parental Leave etc Regulations 1999 (SI 1999/3312) to offer a suitable alternative position where there is a vacancy (even though there may be other more suitable candidates).

The new contract must take effect immediately on the termination of her original contract, be suitable for the employee and appropriate in the circumstances. The terms and conditions of employment must not be substantially less favourable.

Suspension on grounds of pregnancy

[14.49] The Management of Health and Safety at Work Regulations 1999 (SI 1999/3242) contain rights for new or expectant mothers in relation to suspension from work on health and safety grounds. The rights protect women who are pregnant, who have recently given birth or are breastfeeding, if they have to be suspended from work because their job poses a risk to their health and safety. The rights include:

(a)   the right to have her working conditions or hours of work varied;

(b)   the right to be offered suitable alternative work where this is available;

(c)   where there is no suitable alternative work, the right to be suspended from work for as long as is necessary to protect her safety or health or that of her child and to be paid her normal remuneration during this period; and

(d)   it is automatically unfair for an employer to dismiss a woman rather than move or suspend her under these provisions.

Women who consider that their rights have been infringed can take their complaint to an employment tribunal, regardless of their length of service.

Return to work

[14.50] Employees can choose to do up to ten keeping in touch days during maternity leave (but not during the two-week compulsory maternity leave period). There is no specific requirement that these days be paid but the employee is normally paid her usual rate to avoid equal pay or national minimum wage issues. (In any event the employee is unlikely to agree to these days unless they are paid as normal)

Employers have a duty to notify employees who take OML or AML of the date on which their leave will end. Employers must give such notification within 28 days of receiving notification from the employee of the date she intends to start her OML or, where the employee subsequently varies that date, within 28 days of the date on which the OML commenced.

Employees who intend to return to work at the end of the OML or AML leave period do not have to notify their employers in advance of their return. However, an employee who intends to return to work earlier than the end of her leave period must give her employer not less than eight weeks' notice of the date on which she intends to return. If the employee attempts to return to work before the end of the leave period without giving such notice, the employer is entitled to postpone her return by up to eight weeks provided that date is not later than the end of the leave period. No remuneration is payable to the employee during such notice period given by the employer. These notification provisions do not, however, apply where the employer failed to notify the employee of the date when her leave period would end.

Regulation 18 of the Maternity and Parental Leave etc Regulations 1999 (SI 1999/3312) provides that an employee who returns to work after a period of OML is entitled to return to the job in which she was employed before her absence unless a redundancy situation has arisen. An employee who returns to work after a period of AML is also entitled to return to the same job unless there is some reason (other than redundancy) by which it is not reasonably practicable for her to return to the same job, ie a reorganisation, in which case the employer need only provide her with another job which is both suitable for her and appropriate for her to do in the circumstances.

Contractual rights during maternity leave

[14.51] During the period of both OML and AML an employee is entitled to benefit from all of her contractual terms save those covering remuneration, provided she satisfies the statutory notice requirements. This means that she will continue to accrue benefits like holidays, pension credits, service-related benefits, company cars and other perks. Under Regulation 26 of the Statutory Maternity Pay (General) Regulations 1986 (SI 1986/1960), employers must keep records for the three-year period following the end of the tax year in which a maternity pay period ends.

In relation to employer pension contributions these must be paid by the employer during the period of paid maternity leave at the normal rate as if the employee were at work. The employee need only contribute by reference to the actual maternity pay she is receiving.

Statutory Maternity Pay

[14.52] All employees are entitled to receive Statutory Maternity Pay (SMP) irrespective of whether or not they intend to return to work if:

(a)   they have worked for their employer for a continuous period of at least 26 weeks ending with the 15th week before the EWC (the qualifying week); and

(b)   their average weekly earnings in the eight weeks up to and including the qualifying week have been at least equal to the lower earnings limit (LEL) for National Insurance contributions.

SMP is payable for a maximum of 39 weeks and is set at the following rates:

(i)   six weeks at 90% of the employee's average weekly earnings; plus

(ii)   33 weeks at the SMP flat rate, which is set by the Government each year (£128.73 per week from 3 April 2011), or 90% of average weekly earnings, whichever is less.

SMP is based on the employee's average earning during an eight-week reference period ending with the qualifying week. However, following the ECJ ruling in *Alabaster v Woolwich plc* [2004] ECR 1-3101, [2004] IRLR 486 (ECJ) and the commencement of the Statutory Maternity Pay (General) (Amendment) Regulations 2005 (SI 2005/729), employees on maternity leave are entitled to have the earnings-related part of their statutory (and potentially any contractual) maternity pay recalculated to take account of any pay rise awarded between the start of the eight-week set period for calculating statutory maternity pay and the end of their statutory maternity leave (OML and any AML).

To gain her entitlement to SMP an employee must have complied with the notification rules, namely she must:

(A)   give her employer 28 days' notice of her intention to stop work and claim SMP;

(B)   have produced a copy of her maternity certificate (MATB1); and

(C)   have stopped work.

She can decide when to begin her leave and start receiving SMP but can do this no earlier than eleven weeks before the expected week of birth. She can, however, work up to the expected week of birth provided that she has not had to go on leave due to a pregnancy-related illness in the final four weeks of the pregnancy. Any sickness (even if pregnancy related) prior to the four-week period should be treated as normal sickness and SSP should be paid.

Employers may reclaim from HM Revenue and Customs (HMRC) 92% of the SMP they have paid out. 'Small Employers' (broadly those whose annual National Insurance Class 1 contributions are £45,000 or less) are able to recover 100% of any SMP paid out in any period plus an additional amount in compensation for the employer's portion of NICs paid on SMP.

Maternity Allowance

[14.53] Women who are not entitled to SMP but who have worked and paid NICs in any 26 weeks out of the 66-week period ending the week before the expected week of childbirth, and who earn, on average, a minimum of £30 per week are entitled to claim a maximum of 39 weeks' Maternity Allowance (MA).

The rate is £128.73 from 12 April 2011 or, if lower, 90% of normal weekly earnings.

Statutory paternity leave

[14.54] The Employment Act 2002 introduced statutory paternity leave and pay for the first time in the UK. The detail of ordinary paternity leave is to be found in the Paternity and Adoption Leave Regulations 2002 (SI 2002/2788). The regulations became operational on 6 April 2003. The Statutory Paternity Pay and Statutory Adoption Pay (General) Regulations 2002 (SI 2002/2822) deal with the issue of Statutory Paternity Pay (SPP). The rights to paternity leave and SPP allow an eligible employee to take paid leave to care for his baby or to support the mother of the baby following birth. Similar provisions apply on adoption of a child. Similar to the maternity leave scheme, there are two stages of paternity leave – ordinary paternity leave (OPL) and additional paternity leave (APL) – see below.

In order to be entitled to OPL the individual concerned must be employed under a contract of employment. In addition, the employee:

(a) must have been continuously employed by his employer for a period of 26 weeks by the 15th week before the expected week of the child's birth;

(b) must be either:
  (i) the father of the child; or
  (ii) married to (or the civil partner of) or the partner of the child's mother, but not the child's father; and

(c) have or expect to have:
  (i) if he is the child's father, responsibility for the upbringing of the child; or
  (ii) if he is the mother's husband (or civil partner) or partner but not the child's father, the main responsibility (apart from any responsibility of the mother) for the upbringing of the child.

If the child is born before the 14th week before the EWC and, but for the birth occurring early, the employee would have been employed continuously for the requisite 26 weeks, then he will be deemed to have the necessary length of service.

The former DTI's detailed guidance on paternity leave makes it clear that a 'partner' in this context can include a female partner in a same sex couple. An employee is still entitled to paternity leave if the child is stillborn after 24 weeks or the child is born alive at any stage of the pregnancy but later dies.

From April 2011 APL and additional statutory paternity pay were introduced under the Additional Paternity Leave Regulations 2010 (SI 2010/1055) and the Additional Statutory Pay Regulations 201 (SI 2010/1056). These allow fathers/partners to 'use up' any untaken maternity leave of the mother, if she returns to work early. It can be taken between 20 weeks and 12 months after the birth, up to a maximum of 26 weeks. These provisions also apply to adoptions.

Commencement of ordinary paternity leave

[14.55] An employee can choose to take his OPL:

(a)   in two blocks of one week each; or
(b)   as two consecutive weeks' leave.

Where there are multiple births the employee can still only take the above periods of leave. Employees do not receive separate paternity leave periods in respect of each child born at the same time.

Paternity leave can only be taken within the period of 56 days after childbirth. If the child is born early, paternity leave must be taken within the period from the actual date of birth up to 56 days after EWC.

An employee can choose to begin his period of OPL on:

(i)   the date on which the child is born;
(ii)   the date falling such number of days after the date on which the child is born as the employee may specify in a notice under Regulation 6; or
(iii)   a predetermined date, specified in a notice under Regulation 6, which is later than the first day of the EWC.

An employee must give his employer notice of his intention to take OPL, specifying:

(A)   the EWC;
(B)   the length of the period of leave that the employee has chosen to take; and
(C)   the date on which the employee has chosen that his period of leave should begin.

Such notice must be given to the employer no later than the 15th week before the EWC or, where that is not reasonably practicable, as soon as is reasonably practicable. An employer can ask the employee to sign a declaration to the effect that the purpose of his absence from work will be to care for a child or to support the child's mother and that he satisfies the conditions of entitlement set out above. HMRC has produced a model self certificate form SC3.

Once an employee has given the requisite notice, he may vary the date he has chosen as the beginning of his OPL providing:

(I)   he substitutes a different predetermined date; and
(II)   gives his employer at least 28 days' notice of the variation.

Where the employee has chosen to begin his period of leave on a particular predetermined date and the child is not born on or before that date, the employee must vary his choice of date and give his employer notice of the variation as soon as is reasonably practicable.

After the child is born the employee must give the employer notice of the date on which the child was born as soon as reasonably practicable after the birth.

The above notices need not be in writing unless the employer so requests.

Commencement of additional paternity leave

[14.56] To take APL the employee must give the employer at least eight weeks' written notice. The minimum leave which can be taken is two weeks and it must be taken in multiples of a week, up to the maximum of 26 weeks. The employee must also provide the employer with an employee declaration confirming details as to entitlement and a 'mother declaration' from the mother.

As with maternity leave the employee can do up to ten 'keeping in touch' days during APL.

Statutory Paternity Pay

[14.57] During OPL most employees will be entitled to receive Statutory Paternity Pay (SPP). Employees should give their employers 28 days' notice of their request to be paid SPP. Most employers will treat the notice that the employee wishes to take paternity leave as being notice that the employee is seeking payment of SPP during the leave period.

SPP will be paid to employees who have average weekly earnings above the LEL for National Insurance contributions (£102 a week for 2011/12). Average weekly earnings should be calculated by reference to the eight weeks immediately preceding the 15th week before the EWC.

If the employer determines that the employee is not entitled to receive SPP it must provide the employee with a written statement to this effect explaining why the employee is not entitled to SPP. The employer should do so by completing form SPP1 which is available from HMRC. SPP will be paid by employers for either one or two consecutive weeks as the employee has chosen.

SPP is paid at the prescribed statutory rate (£128.73 per week from 3 April 2011) or 90% of average weekly earnings, whichever is lower.

Employers will be able to recover the amount of SPP they pay out in the same way as they can currently claim back SMP (see **14.52** above). Employers will be able to claim back 92% of the payments they make, with those eligible for small employers' relief able to claim back 100% plus an additional amount in compensation for the employer's portion of National Insurance contributions paid on SPP.

Additional Statutory Paternity Pay

[14.58] During APL, eligible employees are entitled to ASPP at £128.72 (from 3 April 2011), or 90% of average weekly earnings, whichever is the lower (ie the same rate as SPP during OPL). To claim ASPP the employee must give eight weeks' notice. As with SPP the employer can recoup ASPP.

Statutory adoption leave

[14.59] The Employment Act 2002 set out the statutory scheme for adoption leave and inserted sections into the Employment Rights Act 1996. The rights to adoption leave and pay were subsequently extended by the Work and Families Act 2006. The detail of the leave entitlement is found in the Paternity and Adoption Leave Regulations 2002 (SI 2002/2788) (PALR Regulations), as updated by the Paternity and Adoption Leave (Amendment) Regulations 2004 (SI 2004/923) and the Maternity and Parental Leave etc and the Paternity and Adoption Leave (Amendment) Regulations 2006 (SI 2006/2014). The Paternity and Adoption Leave (Amendment) Regulations 2008 (SI 2008/1966) came into force on 23 July 2008 and amend entitlements to additional adoption leave, bringing it in line with the new additional maternity leave entitlements. They will apply to adopters where the adopted child is expected to start living with them from 5 October 2008 onwards.

As is the case with maternity leave, adoption leave is split into ordinary adoption leave (OAL) and additional adoption leave (AAL). Adoption leave and pay is not available in circumstances where a child is not newly matched for adoption, for example when a step-parent is adopting a partner's child.

Where a couple adopt jointly only one parent is entitled to adoption leave. The other parent, or indeed the partner of an individual who adopts, may be entitled to statutory paternity leave and pay.

The period of OAL is 26 weeks and the period of AAL is 26 weeks which are the same as the ordinary maternity leave and additional maternity leave periods. Employees can choose to begin a period of OAL on:

(a)   the date on which the child is placed with him for adoption; or

(b)   a predetermined date which is no more than 14 days before the date on which the child is expected to be placed with the employee and no later than that date.

Note that overseas adoptions have slightly different rules applied to them which are beyond the scope of this chapter.

Ordinary adoption leave requirements

[14.60] In order to be entitled to OAL an employee must:

(a)   satisfy the conditions set out in Regulation 15 of the PALR Regulations; and

(b)   comply with the notice and evidential requirements in Regulation 17 of the PALR Regulations.

Regulation 15 provides that an employee is entitled to OAL if that employee:

(i)   is the child's adopter;

(ii)   has been continuously employed for a period of not less than 26 weeks ending with the week in which he was notified of having been matched with the child; and

(iii)   has notified the adoption agency that he agrees that the child should be placed with him on the date of placement.

In this context a 'week' means the period of seven days beginning with Sunday.

The PALR Regulations provide that a person is notified of having been matched with a child on the date on which he receives notification of the adoption agency's decision.

In terms of Regulation 17 of the PALR Regulations an employee must give his employer notice of his intention to take OAL in respect of a child, specifying:

(A)   the date on which the child is expected to be placed with him for adoption; and

(B)   the date on which the employee has chosen that his period of leave should begin.

Such notice must be in writing if the employer so requests and must be given to the employer:

(I)   no more than seven days after the date on which the employee is notified of having been matched with the child for adoption; or

(II)   in a case where it was not reasonably practicable for the employee to give such notice, as soon as is reasonably practicable.

An employee who gives such notice may vary the date he has chosen as the date when the leave period will begin. Notice of such variation must be given at least 28 days before the date when the child is to be placed for adoption; or the predetermined date previously specified by the employee as the date when his leave will commence.

Evidential requirements

[14.61] Where the employer requests it, an employee must also provide the employer with evidence, in the form of one or more documents issued by the adoption agency that matched the employee with the child, of:

(a)   the name and address of the agency;

(b)   the date on which the employee was notified that he had been matched with the child; or

(c)   the date on which the agency expects to place the child with the employee.

The PALR Regulations impose a duty on employers to notify employees who have given notice of their intention to take OAL of the date on which the period of OAL to which the employee will be entitled (provided he meets the qualifying conditions) ends. Employers must give such notification within 28 days of the date on which the employee gave notice or, where the employee subsequently varies the date when he intends to commence his leave period, within 28 days of the date on which the OAL commenced.

The position with OAL is identical to the status of the contract of employment during ordinary maternity leave. An employee who takes OAL is entitled, during the period of leave, to the benefit of all terms and conditions of employment – except remuneration – which would have applied if he had not been absent. The employee is also bound by all obligations in his terms and conditions of employment during the leave period. Only sums payable by way of wages and salary are to be treated as remuneration. The right to receive pension contributions from the employer continues throughout the OAL period, as does the accrual of pensionable service.

Additional adoption leave requirements

[14.62] An employee is entitled to AAL in respect of a child if:

(a)   the child was newly placed with him for adoption;

(b)   he took OAL in respect of the child; and

(c)   his OAL period did not end prematurely as a result of either the placement of the child not proceeding, the death of the child, or the child being returned to the adoption agency under the relevant legislation; or the employee being dismissed during the OAL.

AAL entitles employees to take an additional 26 weeks' leave beginning on the day after the last day of the employee's OAL period. Therefore, employees who qualify for OAL and AAL can take a total of up to one year off.

There are no notification requirements placed on employees in respect of AAL. However, it should be noted that entitlement to AAL is dependent upon entitlement to OAL; the notification requirements in respect of OAL must therefore be met.

There are no notification requirements placed on employees who intend to return to work at the end of their AAL. Where an employee intends to return to work earlier than the end of his AAL he must give his employer at least eight weeks' notice of the date on which he intends to return. If an employee attempts to return earlier than the end of the AAL without giving such notice, the employer is entitled to postpone the employee's return to work by such a period that will ensure the employer has at least eight weeks' notice of the employee's return. However, in that situation the employer cannot postpone the employee's return to a date after the end of the AAL period.

The effect of AAL on the contract of employment is that adopters are entitled to receive all the same contractual benefits, apart from remuneration, that the adopter is entitled to during OAL.

Employees have the right to receive pension contributions throughout any period of paid adoption leave (ie up to 39 weeks). This period also counts towards pensionable service.

Return to work

[14.63] Prior to returning to work an employee is entitled to work for up to ten 'keeping in touch' days during his adoption leave without bringing that leave to an end. Payment for work carried out by the employee during the 'keeping in touch' days should be negotiated between the employer and employee.

An employee who returns to work after OAL is entitled to return to the job in which he was employed before his absence. An employee who returns to work after AAL is entitled to return from leave to the job in which he was employed before his absence, or, if it is not reasonably practicable for the employer to permit him to return to that job, to another job which is both suitable and appropriate for the employee in the circumstances.

An employee's right to return is to return:

(a)   on terms and conditions with respect to remuneration which are not less favourable than those which would have been applied if he had not been absent; and

(b)   with his seniority, pension rights and similar rights:

(i)   in the case of return from OAL, as they would have been if the employee had not been absent; and

(ii)   in the case of return from AAL, as they would have been if the period of his employment prior to AAL were continuous with the period of employment following it.

In other words, during OAL pension and other similar rights continue to accrue but there is no such accrual during AAL, just a right to the same benefits as the employee would have enjoyed if his period of employment before and after the leave was continuous.

The regulations provide that an employee is entitled not to be subjected to any detriment by any act, or any deliberate failure to act, by his employer because:

(A)   the employee took or sought to take OAL or AAL;

(B)   the employer believed that the employee was likely to take OAL or AAL; or

(C)   the employee failed to return after a period of AAL in a case where:

(I)   the employer did not notify the employee of the date on which his AAL ended and the employee reasonably believed that the period had not ended; or

(II)   the employer gave the employee less than 28 days' notice of the date on which the period would end, and it was not reasonably practicable for the employee to return on that date.

The above category has also been added to the list of situations where a dismissal for that reason is treated as being automatically unfair.

The PALR Regulations make specific provision for redundancy during adoption leave. Like maternity leave, an employee who is absent from work on adoption leave can lawfully be made redundant but there are specific measures which apply in such a situation. Where an employee on adoption leave has been selected for redundancy the employer must be careful in its assessment of whether there is alternative employment available. Where there is a suitable vacancy available, the employee on adoption leave is entitled to be offered that vacancy. If the employee is dismissed without such vacancy being offered to him, the dismissal will be automatically unfair.

In addition, an employee is treated as having been automatically unfairly dismissed if:

(a)   the reason for the dismissal is that the employee was redundant;

(b)   it is shown that the circumstances applied equally to other employees in the same undertaking who had similar positions to that held by the employee and who have not been dismissed by the employer; and

(c)   it is shown that the reason for which the employee was selected for dismissal was a reason of a kind specified above.

Statutory Adoption Pay

[14.64] Statutory Adoption Pay (SAP) will be paid to adopters eligible for OAL who have average weekly earnings above the LEL for National Insurance contributions (£102 per week for 2011/12). SAP will be paid by employers for up to 39 weeks and the rate will be the same as the standard rate of SMP. SAP is therefore paid at the prescribed statutory rate (£128.73 per week from 3 April 2011) or 90% of average weekly earnings, whichever is lower.

Parental leave

[14.65] Employees who have completed one year's continuous service are entitled to take 13 weeks' unpaid parental leave for each child born or adopted on or after 15 December 1999. During parental leave the employee remains employed and is guaranteed the right to return to the same job (or if not practicable a similar job of the same or better status and terms and conditions). Where the period of leave taken is less than four weeks the employee is entitled to return to the same job. Employers may put their own agreements regarding parental leave in place or rely on the fallback scheme provided in the Maternity and Parental Leave etc Regulations 1999 (SI 1999/3312). Employer schemes must be no less favourable than the fallback provisions. Special rules apply to parents of disabled children.

Flexible working

[14.66] The Employment Act 2002 (EA 2002) introduced a right for qualifying employees to request a variation to their terms and conditions of employment to allow flexible working patterns. The right to request flexible working is currently available to parents of children under the age of 17, parents of disabled children under 18, and carers of certain adults. In May 2011 the Government announced its intention to carry out a consultation looking at how to extend the right to request flexible working to all employees, including the design of a new system of flexible parental leave. The EA 2002 only gives employees the right to request a flexible working pattern and to have the request properly considered. Employers may refuse the request on various grounds specified in EA 2002, however a refusal without justification or a failure to follow the correct procedure could result in a compensatory award in the employment tribunal of up to eight weeks' pay (subject to the current (February 2011) statutory cap of £400 per week).

Discrimination issues may also arise if an employer turns down a flexible working request, eg if it normally agrees to a request by a female employee but does not for a male employee.

Future changes

[14.67] In January 2011 the Government announced proposals to introduce a new system of flexible parental leave. The main elements are a reduced 18-week period of maternity leave, the retention of ordinary paternity leave, the abolition of additional paternity leave and the introduction of a right to flexible parental leave, available to both parents, of up to 34 weeks (21 of which would be paid).

Statutory Sick Pay

[14.68] The Statutory Sick Pay (SSP) regime is set out in the Social Security Contributions and Benefits Act 1992 (as amended). SSP is payable to all eligible employees for periods of absence exceeding four or more days in a row (including weekends and holidays). SSP is not payable for the first three days but thereafter is payable for up to 28 weeks within any three-year period. Whether the employee will be paid at all during the first three days of absence will depend upon the employee's individual terms and conditions. The SSP scheme applies to all employers regardless of size.

Most large employers are obliged to bear the cost of SSP. The Statutory Sick Pay Percentage Threshold Order 1995 (SI 1995/512) (as amended) offers some relief for smaller employers. The Order allows any employer to recover the amount of SSP paid in a tax month which exceeds 13% of the employer's liability for National Insurance contribution (NIC) payments in the same tax month. A simple calculation is therefore required to ascertain whether or not there is an amount of SSP which can be recovered in a given tax month:

(a)   establish the gross Class 1 NICs liability for the tax month (exclude Class 1A NICs);
(b)   multiply the figure by 13%;
(c)   establish the total SSP payments in the same tax month;
(d)   if the amount at step (c) exceeds the amount at step (b), the difference can be recovered.

The rate of SSP from 6 April 2011 is £81.60 a week.

Certain categories of employee are not entitled to SSP, generally those who:

(i)   go off sick within eight weeks of having received, or being eligible for, one of a number of social security benefits;
(ii)   are earning less than the lower level of weekly earnings for National Insurance;
(iii)   are abroad in a country outside the EEA;
(iv)   have already received their full complement of SSP for that three-year period.

To be entitled to SSP, employees must also have complied with the agreed notification procedures. Notification of absence through illness can be required by the end of the first day of the illness, but if the employer does not specify a date, then the employee has seven days before he needs to notify his employer in writing. Notification arrangements are usually agreed between the employer and the employee or employees' representatives and normally include a self-certification form for the first seven days' absence and doctors' certificates thereafter.

Health and safety legislation

[14.69] The basis of UK health and safety law is the Health and Safety at Work etc Act 1974 (HSWA 1974). The Act sets out the general duties which employers have towards their employees and members of the public, and those duties that employees have to themselves and to each other. These duties exist 'so far as is reasonably practicable'. In other words, the degree of risk in a particular job or workplace needs to be balanced against the time, trouble, cost and physical difficulty of taking measures to avoid or reduce the risk. However, the case law in this area suggests that it is very difficult to establish that it would not have been reasonably practicable to ensure the safety of those concerned. The result is a very strict approach to liability in health and safety cases. The law requires that management look at what the risks are and take sensible measures to tackle them. The Management of Health and Safety at Work Regulations 1999 (SI 1999/3242) generally make more explicit what employers are required to do to manage health and safety under HSWA 1974. Like the Act itself they apply to every work activity.

The Government published in October 2010 the Young Report on health, claims and safety. Lord Young proposes that the law be radically revised so that employers are not swamped or intimidated by risk assessment and related duties. He suggests that much of the legislation imposing duties upon employers be simplified and contained in one set of codified rules. In an introduction to the report the Prime Minister gives it his unqualified backing.

Health and safety law has been subject to considerable change, mainly because of legislative developments emanating from the EU. Directives have resulted in a host of regulations in the UK. HSWA 1974 has been supplemented by the so-called 'six pack' of regulations (as amended). These are:

(a)   Management of Health and Safety at Work Regulations 1999 (SI 1999/3242);

(b)   Health and Safety (Display Screen Equipment) Regulations 1992 (SI 1992/2792);

(c)   Manual Handling Operations Regulations 1992 (SI 1992/2793);

(d)   Provision and Use of Work Equipment Regulations 1998 (SI 1998/2306);

(e)   Personal Protective Equipment at Work Regulations 1992 (SI 1992/2966); and

(f)   Workplace (Health, Safety and Welfare) Regulations 1992 (SI 1992/3004).

These and any other relevant regulations are detailed below.

The Health and Safety at Work etc Act 1974

[14.70] HSWA 1974 applies to virtually all workers and workplaces in the UK. It lays down the general principles for the health and safety of employees and others affected by work activity, and establishes the Health and Safety Executive (HSE), formed in 2008 following the merger of the Health and Safety Commission and the Health and Safety Executive. The Act lays down broad general duties and acts as a framework, with detailed health and safety regulations and Approved Codes of Practice (ACOPs) (including those that implement EU Directives) being made under the Act.

HSWA 1974:

(a)   imposes duties on employers, the self-employed and employees;

(b)   outlines the role of the HSE;
(c)   sets out enforcement provisions; and
(d)   details the penalties for non-compliance.

Employers' duties – Section 2 of HSWA 1974 requires every employer to ensure, so far as is reasonably practicable, the health, safety and welfare at work of his employees. Employers must provide and maintain plant and safe systems of work so that they are, so far as is reasonably practicable, safe and without risks to health. They must make arrangements to provide the necessary information, instruction, training and supervision to ensure the health and safety of employees. They must make arrangements to ensure so far as is reasonably practicable the safety and absence of risks to health in connection with the use, travelling, storage and transport of articles and substances. Employers must also maintain a safe working environment with adequate facilities and welfare arrangements (including safe access and egress). Section 2 does not detail what constitutes a 'safe system of work'.

In *R v Gateway Foodmarkets Ltd* [1997] IRLR 189, the Court of Appeal held that a company was in breach of its duty under section 2 for a failure at store management level to take all reasonable precautions to avoid the risk of injury to an employee, even though at senior management or head office level, all reasonable precautions had been taken. The HSE advocates that clear procedures should be adopted, and for serious hazards a written 'permit to work' system should be adopted. As mentioned above the duties under section 2 exist 'so far as is reasonably practicable'. This has been interpreted in the courts as meaning that the costs of carrying out the health and safety measures must not be disproportionate to the benefits to be obtained from doing it.

Section 2 of HSWA 1974 also requires every employer with five or more employees to prepare a written health and safety policy. It should detail the hazards present at the workplace, and the organisation and arrangements in force for implementing the policy. It should be revised 'as often as appropriate', be brought to the notice of employees, and state all persons within the organisation with health and safety responsibilities.

Section 2(6) of HSWA 1974 provides for employers to consult with safety representatives to enable co-operation to effectively promote health and safety, and to check the effectiveness of current arrangements. Where requested by two or more safety representatives, the employer must establish a safety committee. The Safety Representatives and Safety Committees Regulations 1977 (SI 1977/500), as amended by the Management of Health and Safety at Work Regulations 1992 (SI 1992/2051) set out in detail the function of such representatives and committees, and employers' duties to consult with them. With effect from 1 October 1996, the Health and Safety (Consultation with Employees) Regulations 1996 (SI 1996/1513) require an employer to consult all employees on health and safety issues, regardless of whether the employer recognises a trade union. Where there is no recognised union, these Regulations require an employer to consult either with elected 'representatives of employee safety' or directly with employees. (For the right of safety representatives and representatives of employee safety to time off work with pay, and the right not to suffer a detriment, see **14.20** above; and for protection against unfair dismissal, see **14.93** below.)

Section 3 of HSWA 1974 requires employers and self-employed persons to conduct their undertakings so as to ensure that persons other than employees are not exposed to risks to their health and safety. For cases regarding an employer's liability under this provision, see eg *R v British Steel plc* [1995] IRLR 310 (employer still liable even though senior management were not involved) and *R v Associated Octel Co Ltd* [1997] IRLR 123 (employer liable for negligence of independent contractor).

Section 9 of HSWA 1974 prohibits employers from charging employees for items of equipment protective clothing or anything else required by law.

Employees' duties – Section 7 of HSWA 1974 requires every employee to take reasonable care for the health and safety of himself and other people who may be affected by his acts or omissions at work. If there is a legal requirement on an employer to undertake safety measures, the employee must co-operate with his employer to fulfil his legal duty.

Directors' duties – Section 37 of HSWA 1974 provides that if a health and safety offence has been committed by the company with the consent or connivance of, or is attributable to negligence of, a director, manager or secretary of the company, that person will be guilty of an offence. The HSE and the Institute of Directors have published official guidance for directors on leading health and safety at work.

Corporate Manslaughter

[14.71] The Corporate Manslaughter and Corporate Homicide Act 2007 came into force on 6 April 2008, creating a new offence of corporate manslaughter in England, Wales and Northern Ireland and corporate homicide in Scotland. A company will be guilty of an offence if the way in which it manages or organises its activities causes a death and amounts to a gross breach of a relevant duty of care owed to the deceased. The management or organisation of the company's activities by the company's senior management must be a substantial element of the breach. Whether or not a duty of care exists is to be determined in accordance with the law of negligence, but specifically includes duties to employees and others, such as contractors. In determining whether or not there has been a gross breach of a duty of care, a jury is entitled to consider whether health and safety legislation has been complied with, the organisations safety culture and any relevant health and safety guidance.

In February 2011 the first company to be convicted of the new offence of corporate manslaughter was fined £385,000 (an amount higher than its annual turnover), payable in equal amounts over ten years. On 11 May 2011 the Court of Appeal dismissed an application by the company for leave to appeal against its conviction and fine. The fact that the fine would cause the company to be put into liquidation was found to be unfortunate, but unavoidable and inevitable (see *R v Cotswold Geotechnical Holdings Ltd* [2011] All ER (D) 100 (May)).

Management of Health and Safety at Work Regulations 1999

[14.72] The Management of Health and Safety at Work Regulations 1999 (SI 1999/3242) derive from the general duties outlined in HSWA 1974 and are set out in greater detail in the European 'Framework Directive' (89/391/EEC) 'on the introduction of measures to encourage improvements in the health and safety of workers at work', which mirrors HSWA 1974 but contains more specific requirements. The main requirements under the Regulations are for employers to:

(a)   carry out risk assessments;
(b)   implement preventative and protective measures;
(c)   make and record arrangements for implementing the health and safety measures identified as being necessary in the risk assessment;
(d)   appoint competent people to help implement the health and safety arrangements where possible appointing competent employees in preference to non-employees;
(e)   establish any emergency procedures;
(f)   arrange any necessary contacts with external services, especially as regards first aid, emergency medical care and rescue work;
(g)   provide understandable information and adequate training for employees; and
(h)   co-ordinate health and safety measures with other employers sharing the same workplace.

The central requirement is to carry out a 'suitable and sufficient' risk assessment (Reg 3), in order to decide what health and safety measures are needed. HSE guidance indicates that the level of detail in the risk assessment should be determined by the risks. Risk assessments must be recorded where five or more people are employed.

The Regulations require employers to assess the risks to the health and safety of 'new and expectant mothers' to ensure that they are not exposed to risks. The Regulations apply to employees who are pregnant, who have given birth or miscarried within the previous six months, or who are breastfeeding. Employers must assess risks, and ensure that workers are not exposed to risks identified by the risk assessment which would present a danger to their health and safety. The HSE has provided a list of known risks and agents. If there is still a significant risk, after taking reasonable preventative action, the employer must temporarily adjust the worker's hours or conditions of work to avoid the risk; offer her alternative work; or, if neither of the former is appropriate, give her paid leave from work for as long as it is necessary to protect her health and safety. ERA 1996, s 67(2) requires that any alternative work offered under the Regulations is not substantially less favourable than her normal terms and conditions and must be appropriate in the circumstances. (See also **14.49** above.)

The Regulations contain similar provisions requiring employers to carry out risk assessments prior to employing a 'young person' (defined as a person below the age of 18). The Regulations set down a list of factors to consider in reviewing the risk assessment, this includes paying particular attention to 'the inexperience, lack of awareness of risks and immaturity of young persons'.

Regulations on health, safety and welfare at workplace premises

[14.73] Under the framework established by HSWA 1974 and the Management of Health and Safety at Work Regulations 1999, specific regulations deal with health, safety and welfare at workplace premises. The main statutory requirements of which readers should be aware are as follows (all as amended):

(a)   Workplace (Health, Safety and Welfare) Regulations 1992 (SI 1992/3004);

(b)   Health and Safety (Safety Signs and Signals) Regulations 1996 (SI 1996/341);

(c)   Regulatory Reform (Fire Safety) Order 2005 (SI 2005/1541) and the Regulatory Reform (Fire Safety) Subordinate Provision Order 2006 (SI 2006/484) (in relation to England and Wales);

(d)   Fire (Scotland) Act 2005 as amended by the Fire (Scotland) Act 2005 (Consequential Modifications and Savings) Order 2006 (SSI 2006/475) (in relation to Scotland);

(e)   Electricity at Work Regulations 1989 (SI 1989/635) as amended by the Offshore Electricity and Noise Regulations 1997 (SI 1997/1993) and the Electrical Equipment for Explosive Atmospheres (Certification) (Amendment) Regulations 1999 (SI 1999/2550);

(f)   Gas Safety (Installation and Use) Regulations 1998 (SI 1998/2451); and

(g)   Health and Safety Information for Employees (Modifications and Repeals) Regulations 1995 (SI 1995/2923).

Regulations on equipment, plant and machinery

[14.74] Regulations made in this category cover employers' responsibilities for equipment, plant, machinery used at work (including display screen equipment) and personal protective equipment (PPE). The main statutory requirements of which readers should be aware are as follows (all as amended):

(a)   Provision and Use of Work Equipment Regulations 1998 (SI 1998/2306) as amended by the Police (Health and Safety) Regulations 1999 (SI 1999/860), the Pressure Equipment Regulations 1999 (SI 1999/2001) and the Noise Emission in the Environment by Equipment for use Outdoors Regulations 2001 (SI 2001/1701);

(b)   Supply of Machinery (Safety) Regulations 2008 (SI 2008/1597);

(c)   Personal Protective Equipment at Work Regulations 1992 (SI 1992/2966) as amended by the Personal Protective Equipment Regulations 2002 (SI 2002/1144), the Police (Health and Safety) Regulations 1999 (SI 1999/860) and the Ionising Radiations Regulations 1999 (SI 1999/3232); and

(d)   Health and Safety (Display Screen Equipment) Regulations 1992 (SI 1992/2792).

Regulations on physical hazards

[14.75] Regulations made in this category cover noise, radiation, manual handling, work related upper limb disorders (WRULDs)/repetitive strain injury (RSI), and vibration. The main statutory requirements are (all as amended):

(a)   Control of Noise at Work Regulations 2005 (SI 2005/1643);

(b)   Ionising Radiations Regulations 1985 (SI 1985/1333) as amended by Ionising Radiations Regulations 1999 (SI 1999/3232);

(c)   Manual Handling Operations Regulations 1992 (SI 1992/2793);

(d)   Control of Substances Hazardous to Health Regulations 2002 (SI 2002/2677); and

(e)   Control of Major Accident Hazards Regulations 1999 (SI 1999/743).

Regulations on first aid

[14.76] The Health and Safety (First-Aid) Regulations 1981 (SI 1981/917) as amended impose a general duty on employers to make adequate and appropriate first-aid provision for employees if they are injured or become ill at work. This includes providing first-aid equipment and arranging for first-aiders or an appointed person to administer first aid.

The accompanying Approved Code of Practice (ACOP) to the regulations is produced by the HSE and was last revised in 1997, giving employers greater flexibility in determining their own workplace first aid provision. The Regulations require the employer to make an assessment of first-aid requirements, and he should provide a suitable first-aid room or rooms should the assessment identify this as necessary. The ACOP states that at least one suitably stocked and properly identified first-aid container should be provided, be easily accessible and be placed near to hand washing facilities where possible. Employees should also be made aware of the first aid arrangements put in place by the employer.

Regulations on reporting of accidents and injuries at work

[14.77] The Reporting of Injuries, Diseases and Dangerous Occurrences Regulations 1995 (SI 1995/3163) (RIDDOR) require certain events relating to accidents and ill-health at work to be recorded, notified and reported by a 'responsible person' (normally employers) to the enforcing authority, which may be the HSE or the local authority environmental health department. Under RIDDOR, 'responsible persons' must notify enforcing authorities by the quickest possible means of the following:

(a)   the death of a person as a result of an accident arising out of or in connection with work;

(b)   a major injury suffered as a result of an accident arising out of or in connection with work;

(c)   an injury suffered by a person not at work (eg a visitor, customer, client, passenger or bystander) as a result of an accident arising out of or in connection with work;

(d)   a major injury suffered by a person not at work, as a result of an accident arising out of or in connection with work at a hospital; and

(e)   a dangerous occurrence.

'Accident' includes non-consensual physical acts of violence done to a person at work, and suicides on, or in the course of the operation of a railway, tramway, vehicle system or guided transport system.

Major injuries are listed in RIDDOR, Sch 1 as including:

(i)   any fracture, excluding fingers, thumbs and toes;

(ii)   dislocation of the shoulder, hip, knee or spine;

(iii)   any amputation;

(iv)   loss of sight (whether temporary or permanent);

(v)   a chemical or hot metal burn to the eye or any penetrating injury to the eye;

(vi)   any injury resulting from an electric shock or electrical burn (including one caused by arcing or arcing products) leading to unconsciousness or requiring resuscitation or admittance to hospital for more than 24 hours;

(vii)   any other injury leading to hypothermia, heat induced illness or unconsciousness; requiring resuscitation or admittance to hospital for more than 24 hours;

(viii) acute illness requiring immediate medical treatment, or loss of consciousness resulting from the absorption of any substance by inhalation, ingestion or through the skin; and

(ix)   acute illness requiring medical treatment where there is reason to believe that the illness resulted from exposure to biological agents or its toxins or infected material.

In addition to the notification requirement, the employer must submit a written report within ten days of the incident to the relevant enforcing authority. A report must also be submitted where by reason of an accident at work, a person has been incapacitated from his normal work for more than three consecutive days (excluding the day of the accident, but including any days which would not have been working days). Gas incidents must be reported within 14 days. Cases of disease must be reported forthwith if the employer has received a written statement by a doctor which diagnoses the disease as one listed as reportable in Schedule 3 to the Regulations. The employer is also required to report, in writing, the death of an employee if it occurs within one year of that employee suffering a reportable injury. RIDDOR, Reg 7 outlines the record-keeping requirements imposed on the employer.

In addition to the requirements under RIDDOR, employers must also ensure that all injuries, regardless of how minor, are recorded in an accident book. An accident book is required under the Social Security (Claims and Payments) Regulations 1979 (SI 1979/628) (as amended) for all premises covered by the Factories Act 1961 (s 175) or where ten or more people are employed at any one time for injuries in respect of which industrial injuries benefit may be payable. The book must contain the following information:

(A)   full name, address and occupation of the injured person;

(B)   date and time of the accident;

(C)   place where the accident happened;

(D)   cause and nature of the injury; and

(E)   name, address and occupation of the person giving notice, if other than the injured person.

Accident books are required to be kept for a period of three years from the date of the last entry.

Control of Asbestos Regulations 2006

[14.78] The Control of Asbestos Regulations 2006 (SI 2006/2739) (CAR Regulations) apply to employers, employees and the self-employed who work with asbestos whether the work requires a licence or not. The key issues covered in the Regulations are as follows:

(a)   Managing asbestos in buildings – reasonable steps must be taken to find out if there are materials containing asbestos in the premises. This can (but does not have to) include a survey. There may be no demolition, maintenance or any other work which exposes employees to asbestos unless there is a plan detailing how the work will be done and the details of the asbestos in the premises have been discovered.

(b)   Information, instruction and training – every employer must give adequate training (which includes information and instruction) to employees who are, or may be, exposed to asbestos, their supervisors and those who do work to help employers comply with the regulations.

(c)   Preventing or reducing exposure – employers have a duty to prevent exposure so far as is reasonably practicable. If exposure cannot be prevented, it must be reduced so far as is reasonably practicable without workers having to use masks.

(d)   Sampling, air tests and clearance certification – must be carried out by someone who is accredited by an appropriate body.

(e)   Health records and medical surveillance – for each employee who is exposed to asbestos, employers must keep a health record, ensure the employees are under adequate medical surveillance by a relevant doctor, provide regular medical examinations and keep the employee informed.

(f)   Washing and changing facilities – employers must provide adequate washing and changing facilities for employees who are, or may be, exposed to asbestos.

Enforcement of legislation

[14.79] Enforcement of HSWA 1974 is by the HSE, who appoint inspectors with powers to inspect workplaces, to institute prosecution proceedings for breaches of safe practices and to issue improvement notices for and prohibition notices against the carrying out of certain practices.

Improvement notices direct the employer to take certain actions or make improvements within a given time (not less than 21 days) when a health and safety law has been broken and is likely to be broken again. An employer can appeal to an employment tribunal, in which case the notice is suspended until the appeal is heard. An inspector must give the employer two weeks' notice of his intention to serve an improvement notice. The employer can then make informal representations, before the notice is served. Prohibition notices are served where a process carries a risk of serious personal injury. The notice forbids the process until the faults specified in the notice are rectified. If an appeal is made against a prohibition notice, it remains in force, unless the tribunal otherwise directs.

Other bodies which have powers of enforcement include the local authorities and fire authorities. It is quite possible that more than one body may have responsibility for the health, safety and welfare aspects of an employer's premises or operation. The local office of the HSE is able to determine who has responsibility for any particular part of an employer's premises or operations.

The police will investigate fatal accidents to ascertain whether the offence of corporate manslaughter or corporate homicide has been committed.

No smoking

[14.80] The Health Act 2006 introduced a ban on smoking at work, in enclosed public places and certain vehicles, and made it a criminal offence to smoke in a smoke-free place. Smoke-free premises must display no-smoking signs which comply with the Smoke Free (Signs) Regulations 2007 (SI 2007/923), eg they must be at least A5 in size and display the no-smoking symbol. Failure to display a sign can lead to a fine of up to £1,000. In addition, employers who fail to prevent smoking on their premises face fines under the Smoke Free (Penalties and Discounted Amounts) Regulations 2007 (SI 2007/764) of up to £2,500 if convicted in the Magistrate's Court. The only exemptions to the smoking ban are contained in the Smoke Free (Exemptions and Vehicles) Regulations 2007 (SI 2007/765) and include by way of example, designated smoking rooms in hotels or care homes and smoking by performers.

Wages and salary

[14.81] Pay is a basic element in the contract of employment, and the contract is therefore key to determining pay rights. The Employment Rights Act 1996 imposes certain obligations on the employer. As part of an employee's section 1 statement of particulars of employment, the employer is under an obligation to provide the following details (at a specified date no more than seven days before the section 1 statement):

(a)   the scale or rate of remuneration or the method of calculating remuneration; and

(b)   the intervals at which the remuneration is paid (ie weekly, monthly etc).

Pay

[14.82] The method of pay is a matter of agreement between the employer and employee. However, if employees have always been paid in cash and there is no provision within the employees' contracts allowing the employer to vary the method of payment, a unilateral change to cashless pay could amount to a breach of contract.

All employees are entitled to an itemised pay statement by virtue of ERA 1996, s 8. The statement must contain particulars of:

(a)   the gross amount of wages or salary;

(b)   the amounts of any variable and fixed deductions from that gross amount and the purposes for which they are made (unless a standing statement of fixed deductions has been given to the employee in writing, pursuant to ERA 1996, s 9);

(c)   the net amount of wages or salary payable; and

(d)   where different parts of the net amount are paid in different ways, the amount and method of payment of each part-payment.

If an employer fails to give a statement containing the above information, then the employee can apply to an employment tribunal to get one.

Pay period

[**14.83**] The period is not regulated. However, the period must be included in the written particulars of terms of employment (ERA 1996, s 1(4)(b)). Again, it cannot be unilaterally changed without the change constituting a breach of an employee's contract of employment. This could entitle the employee to present a claim for constructive (unfair) dismissal to an employment tribunal.

Restrictions on deductions made from wages by employers

[**14.84**] The ERA 1996, Pt II states that an employer shall not make any deduction from any wages of any worker (ie an employee or a worker) employed by him unless the deduction satisfies one of the following conditions:

(a)   it is required or authorised to be made by virtue of any statutory provision or any relevant provision of the worker's contract; or

(b)   the worker has previously signified in writing his agreement or consent to the making of it

(ERA 1996, s 13).

Deductions by statutory power include income tax and National Insurance contributions.

If the deduction is made pursuant to a relevant provision of the worker's contract, meaning any express or implied provision of the worker's contract, the worker must give written consent to the deduction before it is made.

Deductions cannot be backdated and made lawful by later agreement or consent (ERA 1996, ss 13(6) and 15(4)).

Thus, according to ERA 1996, s 13, a worker has the right to be paid wages properly due and any shortfall on such payment is effectively a deduction unless it is an error of computation. The case of *Yemm v British Steel* [1994] IRLR 117 makes clear that employers who make conscious decisions not to make a payment because they believe there is no contractual entitlement to it, are not making an 'error of computation'. 'Wages' includes fees, bonuses, commission, holiday pay, sick pay and maternity pay but does not include expenses. The House of Lords in *Delaney v Staples* [1992] IRLR 191 held that payments in lieu of notice do not amount to wages. Wages are payments in respect of services rendered during employment, therefore all payments in respect of termination are excluded unless mentioned in ERA 1996, s 27(1). ERA 1996, Pt II can be used to claim shortfalls, for example, non-payment of shift allowance or non-payment of a 'discretionary' bonus or commission (*Kent Management Services Ltd v Butterfield* [1992] ICR 272). An employment tribunal has also held that an employer's decision to erode a cashless pay supplement would be classified as an unlawful deduction (*McCree v London Borough of Tower Hamlets* [1992] IRLR 56).

The above also applies to situations where the employer might demand a payment from an employee, for example, the payment of a fine. Such demands must also conform with similar requirements.

Wages

[14.85] Wages means any sum payable to the employee by the employer in connection with his employment including:

(a)   any fee, bonus, commission, holiday pay or other emolument referable to his employment, whether payable under his contract or otherwise;

(b)   Statutory Sick Pay under Part XI of SSCBA 1992;

(c)   Statutory Maternity Pay under Part XII of SSCBA 1992;

(d)   Statutory Paternity Pay under Part 12ZA of SSCBA 1992;

(e)   Statutory Adoption Pay under Part 12ZB of SSCBA 1992;

(f)   a guarantee payment (under ERA 1996, s 28);

(g)   any payment for time off under Part VI of ERA 1996, or under TULR(C)A 1992, s 169 (ie payment for time off for carrying out trade union duties);

(h)   remuneration on suspension on medical grounds (under ERA 1996, s 64) and remuneration on suspension on maternity grounds (under ERA 1996, s 68);

(i)   any sum payable in pursuance of an order for reinstatement or re-engagement under ERA 1996, s 113;

(j)   any sum payable in pursuance of an order for the continuation of a contract of employment under ERA 1996, s 130 or under TULR(C)A 1992, s 164; and

(k)   remuneration under a protective award under TULR(C)A 1992, s 189.

(ERA 1996, s 27(1).)

Excluded from the definition are any payments:

(i)   by way of an advance under an agreement for a loan or by way of an advance of wages (but without prejudice to the application of section 13 to any deduction made from the worker's wages in respect of any such advance);

(ii)   in respect of expenses incurred by the worker in carrying out his employment;

(iii)   by way of a pension, allowance or gratuity in connection with the workers retirement or as compensation for loss of office;

(iv)   referable to the worker's redundancy; and

(v)   to the worker otherwise than in his capacity as a worker.

(ERA 1996, s 27(2).)

It should be noted that a non-contractual bonus paid to an employee by an employer shall be treated as wages payable on the day on which payment is made. Also vouchers, stamps or similar documents which are expressed as having a fixed monetary value and are capable of being exchanged for money, goods or services are also counted as wages (ERA 1996, s 27(3) and (5)).

Deductions and demands not covered by ERA 1996, s 13

[14.86] Deductions and demands not covered by ERA 1996 are those made in respect of the following ((d) to (f) apply to deductions only):

(a)   reimbursement of an overpayment of wages;

(b)   reimbursement of an overpayment of expenses;

(c)   disciplinary proceedings if those proceedings were held by virtue of statutory provisions;

(d)   payments made under a court order for an attachment of statutory provision requiring the employer to pay over earnings for sums due to a public authority;

(e)   where the deduction is to be made and paid over to a third party for sums due in accordance with a provision of his contract of employment and the employee has signified his agreement or consented in writing;

(f)   where there was no prior agreement, but the employee has agreed to the deduction by consent in writing (eg other attachment of earnings orders);

(g)   taking part in a strike or other industrial action, and the deduction is made (or the payment is required) by the employer on account of the worker's having taken part in that strike or other industrial action; and

(h)   where (in the case of a deduction) it is made with the prior consent of the employee, and the deduction or payment is for the satisfaction (whether wholly or in part) of an order of a court or tribunal requiring the repayment of an amount by the worker to the employer.

(ERA 1996, s 14.)

Note that union 'dues' and membership fees deducted after an employee has certified to the employer that he has resigned from a trade union are unlawful.

Unauthorised deductions

[14.87] If an unauthorised deduction is made from the pay of an employee (or the employer receives an unauthorised payment from the employee) under ERA 1996, the employee can complain to an employment tribunal. The claim must be presented to the tribunal within three months of the date the deduction was made. In the case of a series of deductions the claim must be presented within three months of the last deduction. The time limit can be extended by a tribunal where it was not reasonably practicable for the employee to present the claim in time. Where a tribunal finds a complaint well founded it shall order the employer to repay in full any unauthorised amounts deducted. Where only part of the deduction was unauthorised, or where the employer has already reimbursed the employee, the amount will be reduced accordingly.

(ERA 1996, ss 23–26.)

An employer who has been ordered to repay a deduction cannot recover the payment from an employee at a later date.

Retail employment — cash shortages etc

[14.88] In addition to the above, there are extra provisions covering employees in retail employment. These apply when an employer makes deductions from an employee's wages or salary on account of one or more cash shortages or stock deficiencies. Any deduction(s), in aggregate, from any wages payable to the employee on a pay day shall not exceed 10% of the employee's gross pay due to the employee on the day of payment (ERA 1996, ss 17, 18).

Employees who leave their employment are not subject to the 10% limitation. In this particular circumstance an employer can make deductions from the following:

(a)   final pay due under the contract for the last period of work prior to its termination for any reason (excluding payments relating to an earlier period); and

(b)   pay in lieu of notice paid to an employee after the payment of final pay,

whether the amount in question is paid before or after the termination of the employee's contract (ERA 1996, s 22).

The deductions and payment received include those arising out of the dishonesty or conduct of the employee resulting in the cash shortage or stock deficiency, or any other event for which the employee was contractually liable.

Before a retail employer can make deductions on account of cash shortages or stock deficiency the employer must have:

(i)   written to the employee stating the total liability; and

(ii)   required the employee to make the payment by means of a written demand issued to the employee on a pay day, or if this is not a working day, the first working day following that pay day.

The demand for payment must not be made earlier than the first pay day after the employee was notified of the total liability and no later than twelve months after the employer established the existence of the loss (ERA 1996, s 20).

Retail employment – definition

[14.89] Retail employment means carrying out retail transactions directly with, and collecting amounts payable in connection with retail transactions by members of the public or fellow employees or other individuals acting in their personal capacities. This does not have to be the employee's principal duty or carried out by the employee on a regular basis. 'Retail transaction' means the sale or supply of goods or the supply of services (including financial services) (ERA 1996, s 17(2)). 'Retail employment' therefore includes, for example, car park attendants, bus and rail conductors.

National minimum wage

[14.90] The National Minimum Wage Act 1998 (NMWA 1998) (as amended) sets out the powers of the Secretary of State to implement and set the level of the statutory national minimum wage (NMW), established a Low Pay Commission, and provides for the appointment of enforcement officers (drawn from HMRC) to enforce the Act's provisions.

The NMW applies to all workers over school leaving age working in the UK other than 'voluntary workers' at the following rates from 1 October 2011 (subject to variation), before deductions:

(a)   £6.08 per hour for those aged 21 and over;

(b)   £4.98 per hour for 18 to 20 year olds;

(c)   £3.68 per hour for 16 and 17 year olds; and

(d)   £2.60 for apprentices under 19, or 19 and over and in the first year of apprenticeship.

The Act excludes certain workers such as servicemen, share fishermen and prisoners; the genuinely self-employed are also excluded. The National Minimum Wage Regulations 1999 (SI 1999/584) (the NMW Regulations) (as amended by the National Minimum Wage Regulations 1999 (Amendment) Regulations 2007 (SI 2007/2318)), in force from 1 April 1999, exclude certain apprentices, certain trainees on Government training schemes, students on sandwich courses and teacher trainees while doing work experience, and homeless workers who do some work in exchange for being provided with shelter. The NMW Regulations also prescribe (in a detailed set of provisions) how to calculate a worker's hourly rate of remuneration to ensure it is at least the NMW.

Employers are required by the NMW Regulations to keep records to show that they are paying workers at a rate at least equal to the NMW. There is no prescribed format, and these records can be kept on a computer, but they must be capable of being produced in a single document. They must be kept for at least three years.

Enforcement officers may enforce payment of the NMW by serving an 'enforcement notice' on an employer (subject to a right of appeal to an employment tribunal), followed, if the enforcement notice is not complied with, by:

(i)   a 'penalty notice' (the penalty being double the amount of the applicable NMW in respect of each worker in respect of whom it applies); and

(ii)   proceedings on the worker's behalf (which can also be brought by the worker himself) to enforce payment of the NMW in the employment tribunal as an unauthorised deduction from wages, or by bringing a civil action for breach of contract.

There are also rights for the worker not to suffer detriment or to be unfairly dismissed in certain specified circumstances connected with the NMW.

NMWA 1998, s 31 sets out six criminal offences under the Act. It is an offence for an employer:

(A)   to refuse or wilfully neglect to remunerate the worker for any pay reference period at a rate which is at least equal to the NMW;

(B)   to fail to keep or preserve any record relating to the NMW;

(C)   to make, or knowingly cause or allow to be made, any false entry in an NMW record;

(D)   to produce or furnish, or knowingly cause or allow to be produced or furnished, any record or information which he knows to be false;

(E)   to intentionally delay or obstruct an enforcement officer; or

(F)   to refuse or neglect to answer any question, furnish any information or produce any document when required to do so by an enforcement officer.

Each offence under section 31 is punishable on summary conviction by a fine not exceeding level 5 on the standard scale which is currently £5,000.

Termination of employment

[14.91] The termination of a contract of employment can be brought about unilaterally by the employee, or by the employer, by mutual agreement, or by the completion (without renewal) of the term of a fixed-term contract. In each case, a considerable body of law, both statutory and common, has developed.

Notice of termination

[14.92] The period of notice required to terminate a contract of employment will usually be specified in the contract and is required to be specified in the written statement of employment particulars which employees are entitled to receive under ERA 1996, s 1.

Section 86 of ERA 1996 provides for statutory minimum periods of notice of termination to which employees with at least one month's service are entitled, notwithstanding anything to the contrary in their contract, or written terms and conditions of employment. An employee is also entitled to be paid during a period of notice whether there is work provided for him or not, or if he is off sick or on holiday under his contract of employment.

The statutory periods of notice start at a minimum of one week after one month's service up to a period of two years' service. Thereafter, an additional week's notice is required for each additional year's continuous service up to a maximum of twelve weeks' notice for continuous service of twelve years or more (ERA 1996, s 86(1)). The minimum notice from an employee is one week after one month's service. An employer may also give pay in lieu of notice. This can be given free of tax and national insurance deductions but only where there is no right to pay in lieu of notice provided for in the employee's contract and where the payment is essentially paid as damages for loss of notice (see *EMI Group Electronics Ltd v Coldicott* [1999] IRLR 630). The maximum amount that can be paid free of tax and National Insurance contributions is currently £30,000.

An employer who dismisses an employee without the requisite statutory notice period may be liable for an action of wrongful dismissal (see **14.94** below).

Unfair dismissal

[14.93] The right of an employee not to be unfairly dismissed is contained in Part X of ERA 1996.

An employee must have been continuously employed by the employer for a period of at least one year in order to qualify for protection from unfair dismissal. This applies whether the employee is full time or part time.

Once the fact of a dismissal has been established, ERA 1996 treats all dismissals as potentially unfair unless they fall within one of the 'potentially fair' reasons for dismissal, which are set out in section 98 of ERA 1996 (see below). Some dismissals are automatically unfair and also do not require the employee to have at least one year's continuous service to be protected. These are where the dismissal is:

(a)   related to pregnancy or childbirth, or maternity, paternity, adoption, parental or dependant care leave where there is a statutory right to that leave;

(b)   on the grounds that an employee has attempted to enforce a 'relevant statutory right' (eg the right not to have unlawful deductions from pay);

(c)   for a health and safety reason – either related to a serious imminent danger or an employee's activities as a representative related to raising health and safety issues at work;

(d)   of a shop or betting worker, for refusal to work on a Sunday;

(e)   related to the fact the employee is an occupational pension fund trustee;

(f)   on the grounds that the employee is acting as an employee representative or a candidate for election as an employee representative on a collective redundancy or TUPE transfer consultation;

(g)   on the grounds that the employee made a protected disclosure (see **14.96** below);

(h)   for asserting certain rights under the Working Time Regulations 1998 (SI 1998/1833) or NMWA 1998;

(i)   connected with trade union recognition, membership or non-membership, or participation in trade union activities (including protected industrial action);

(j)   for exercising or seeking to exercise the right to be accompanied to a disciplinary or grievance hearing, or for accompanying a fellow worker;

(k)   in connection with European Works Council activities;

(l)   for exercising or seeking to exercise any rights as a part-time worker or fixed-term employee;

(m)   in relation to a request for flexible working under EA 2002;

(n)   for the employee seeking to benefit from tax credits;

(o)   for the employee performing a function in relation to transnational information and consultation (Transnational Information and Consultation of Employees Regulations 1999 (SI 1999/3323)); and

(p)   connected with the employee carrying out jury service.

Some 'automatically unfair' dismissals require the employee to have at least one year's 'continuous service before a claim can be made. These include dismissals relating to:

(i)   a 'spent' conviction; or

(ii)   a TUPE transfer itself (see **14.30** above) or connected with such a transfer that is not an economic, technical or organisational reason involving changes to the workforce.

Where an employee is claiming unfair dismissal, he must present his claim to an employment tribunal within three months from the effective date of dismissal. This time limit may be extended at the employment tribunal's discretion where it determines that it was not reasonably practicable to present the claim within this timescale. This is generally not easy to establish.

From the employer's perspective, to avoid claims for unfair dismissal employees should not be dismissed without sufficient oral and written warnings being given and the employer must be able to show that he has acted fairly and reasonably in the circumstances surrounding the dismissal. Reference should be made to the ACAS Code of Practice on Disciplinary and Grievance Procedures (see below).

The 'potentially fair' reasons for dismissal are:

(i) reasons related to conduct;

(ii) redundancy (see **14.95** below);

(iii) contravention of an enactment whereby continued employment would constitute an offence;

(iv) reasons which relate to lack of capability or qualifications of the employee to carry out the work for which he is employed; or

(v) some other substantial reason of a kind such as to justify the dismissal of an employee holding the position the employee held.

(ERA 1996, s 98.)

In addition to showing a potentially fair reason for dismissal, the employer must use a fair procedure. Summary dismissal of an employee is seldom fair, except in extreme cases.

With effect from 6 April 2009 the new ACAS disciplinary code has replaced the statutory grievance and disciplinary procedures. The code is succinct and every company secretary should download it from the ACAS website and read it, slowly.

In determining whether a dismissal is fair, an employment tribunal will look at:

(A) whether in the circumstances, the employer acted reasonably or unreasonably in treating the event as sufficient reason for dismissing the employee (taking into account the size and administrative resources of the employer's undertaking); and

(B) the equity and substantial merits of the case.

(ERA 1996, s 98(4).)

If a claim for unfair dismissal is upheld, the remedy can be either an award of compensation (see below) to the employee or an order to re-engage or reinstate the employee. Compensation is also available for breach of an order to reinstate or re-engage an employee. Compensation is the most common remedy.

Where an employment tribunal makes an award of compensation there are two elements that it must consider:

(I) *Basic award*
    The calculation of this award depends upon the basic weekly pay (maximum of £400 from February 2011), length of service (maximum 20 years) and age of the employee and in summary is:
    (i) one and a half weeks' pay for each year of employment in which the employee was not below the age of 41;
    (ii) one week's pay for each year of employment not falling within (i) in which the employee was not below the age of 22;
    (iii) half a week's pay for each such year of employment not falling within either (i) or (ii).

The basic award maximum from February 2011 is £12,000.

(II)   *Compensatory award*

The maximum amount of any compensatory award which may be awarded is currently £68,400 (from February 2011).

Compensatory awards include losses such as loss of earnings, bonus, car allowance, pension, and can include elements of future loss. The employee is under a duty to mitigate their losses by taking reasonable steps to look for other work. A deduction can be made for contributory fault or where the employer can argue that the employee would have been fairly dismissed at a later date in any event (a so called 'Polkey' deduction). Employers should be aware of the potential uplifts to awards for failure to comply with the ACAS Code of Practice (see **14.2**).

(III)   *Injury to feelings*

This is awarded in discrimination cases only.

The maximum awards and other sums are reviewed every September against the movements in the Retail Prices Index, with changes taking effect on 1 February each year. Certain unfair dismissal situations relating to pregnancy, union membership, health and safety and breach of statutory duty have minimum compensation amounts and, as stated above, are also automatically unfair dismissals. The Employment Relations Act 1999 provides that where dismissal (or selection for redundancy) is automatically unfair for reasons of health and safety (ERA 1996, ss 100 and 105(3)) or for making a protected disclosure (ERA 1996, ss 103A and 105(6A)), there is no limit to the maximum compensatory award.

Wrongful dismissal

[14.94] Wrongful dismissal is a common law liability which arises when an employee is dismissed by an employer who acts in breach of his obligations to the employee under the contract of employment. Thus, the claim is one for breach of contract. A claim for wrongful dismissal will usually arise in the context of insufficient notice being given to the employee, with the usual remedy being damages.

From the employer's perspective, a defence to a claim of wrongful dismissal is that the behaviour of the employee constituted a breach of contract that in itself justified dismissal without notice.

A claim for wrongful dismissal does not impede an employee's statutory right to also claim unfair dismissal though they will not be awarded the same losses twice. Actions for wrongful dismissal and other claims for breach of contract related to the employment which arise or are outstanding on termination of employment may be heard in employment tribunals (Employment Tribunals Act 1996, s 3(2)), subject to a compensation limit of £25,000.

Redundancy

[14.95] Employers are required to consult employee representatives where there is a proposal to make 20 or more employees within a 90-day period, even where there is no recognised trade union. An employer is duty bound to consult with a trade union where the union is recognised. It is not possible for the employer to choose to consult employee representatives instead of a recognised union. However, employers often find that they consult with employee representatives for unrecognised groups of employees, and with the unions for recognised groups.

Broadly, an employee can be said to have been made redundant where the employer has closed its business in its entirety, has ceased to carry on a business at the employee's workplace or where the requirements of the business for the employee to carry out work of a particular kind have ceased or diminished or are expected to do so (ERA 1996, s 139).

To qualify for statutory redundancy pay, the employee must have been dismissed and have been employed continuously for a period of two years.

The amount of statutory redundancy pay to which an employee is entitled is based upon the employee's age, length of continuous employment (maximum 20 years), gross average weekly pay (maximum of £400 per week as at February 2011) at the date of his redundancy and is calculated as follows:

(a)   one and a half weeks' pay for each year of employment in which the employee was not below the age of 41;

(b)   one week's pay for each year of employment not falling within (a) in which the employee was not below the age of 22;

(c)   half a week's pay for each year of employment not falling within (a) or (c).

The time limit for claiming redundancy pay is six months, from the effective date of termination. Any suggestion that a redundancy dismissal was unfair brings the shorter, 3-month time limit to claim unfair dismissal into play

Statutory redundancy pay is allowable for corporation tax purposes and is not liable to income or capital gains tax in the hands of the recipient. Some employers offer their employees enhanced redundancy payments as part of their employment package. The House of Lords in *Mairs (Inspector of Taxes) v Haughey* [1993] 3 All ER 801, held that a payment made as compensation for loss of enhanced redundancy payments should be tax-free. Whether an employee is entitled to receive an enhanced redundancy payment will depend on the contractual terms and the factual circumstances at the time. In *Quinn v Calder Industrial Materials* [1996] IRLR 126 it was held that whilst, on previous occasions when redundancies were carried out, an enhanced redundancy pay scheme had been offered, this did not establish custom and practice entitling employees to the same enhancement in a future round of redundancies. However, in another case, enhanced payments had been made automatically on six previous occasions, had been viewed by the workforce as an expectation, and the employer had communicated with the employees in a way consistent with an entitlement; the Court of Appeal held that there was a legal entitlement to enhanced redundancy terms (*Albion Automotive v Walker* [2002] EWCA Civ 946.

Certain categories of employee are excluded from the right to receive a statutory redundancy payment, including employees:

(i)   who ordinarily are employed outside Great Britain; or

(ii)   who have been offered and unreasonably refused suitable alternative employment by the employer.

If an employee is offered alternative employment which is different in nature or has different terms and conditions of employment, the employee is entitled to a four-week trial period in the new job in which to decide if the employment is suitable. If, during or at the agreed end date of the trial period, either the employer or employee wishes to terminate the employment, the employee must be treated as having been dismissed for the reason that caused the original contract to end (ERA 1996, s 138(2)(4)), ie by reason of redundancy.

Public interest disclosure by employees

[14.96] The Public Interest Disclosure Act 1998 inserted sections 43A to 43L into ERA 1996. It aims to protect workers (defined so as to include contractors under the control of an employer, persons on training courses, and doctors, dentists, opticians and pharmacists providing services under statutory schemes) who report wrongdoing in one of six specified categories (a 'qualifying disclosure') set out below:

(a)   that a criminal offence has been committed, is being committed or is likely to be committed;

(b)   that a person has failed, is failing or is likely to fail to comply with any legal obligation to which he is subject;

(c)   that a miscarriage of justice has occurred, is occurring or is likely to occur;

(d)   that the health or safety of any individual has been, is being or is likely to be endangered;

(e)   that the environment has been, is being or is likely to be damaged; or

(f)   that information tending to show any matter falling within any one of the preceding paragraphs has been, or is likely to be deliberately concealed.

A worker is only protected if the qualifying disclosure is also a 'protected disclosure', ie it is made to a particular person. The first category of 'protected disclosure' is to the worker's employer. However, where the worker reasonably believes that the relevant failure relates solely or mainly to (i) the conduct of a person other than his employer, or (ii) any other matter for which a person other than his employer has legal responsibility, disclosure may be made to that other person. A worker who, in accordance with a procedure whose use by him is authorised by his employer, makes a disclosure to a person other than his employer, is to be treated for these purposes as making the disclosure to his employer.

A qualifying disclosure is also a 'protected disclosure' if it is made to an authorised regulator. The Public Interest Disclosure (Prescribed Persons) Order 1999 (SI 1999/1549), as amended by the Public Interest Disclosure (Prescribed Persons) (Amendment) Order 2005 (SI 2005/2464), authorises regulators for this purpose. The effect is that a worker will be protected if he makes a qualifying disclosure in good faith to a person specified in the Order, reasonably believing that (i) the failure disclosed falls within the matters in respect of which that regulator is prescribed, and (ii) that the information disclosed, and any allegations contained in it, are substantially true.

The other four ways in which 'qualifying disclosures' will be 'protected disclosures' are disclosures:

(1)   to a legal adviser, in the course of obtaining legal advice;

(2)   to a Minister of the Crown, where the worker's employer is either an individual appointed under any enactment by a Minister, or a body whose members are appointed by a Minister;

(3)   to another person other than those previously mentioned, but only if the worker makes the disclosure in good faith, reasonably believes the information to be substantially true, satisfies one of a number of stringent conditions (see ERA 1996, s 43G(2)–(4)) and in all the circumstances it is reasonable to make the disclosure;

(4)   in the case of 'exceptionally serious failures', another person where the worker makes the disclosure in good faith, he reasonably believes that the information disclosed (and any allegation contained in it) is substantially true, he does not make the disclosure for purposes of personal gain, the relevant failure is of an exceptionally serious nature, and in all the circumstances of the case, it is reasonable for him to make the disclosure (in determining this last point, particular regard will be had to the identity of the person to whom the disclosure is made).

Workers will have the right to complain to an employment tribunal if they have suffered any detriment as a result of making a protected disclosure, and dismissal for making a protected disclosure will be automatically unfair. There is no limit on compensation where dismissal (or selection for redundancy) is automatically unfair on the ground that a worker made a protected disclosure (ERA 1996, ss 103A and 105(6A)).)

In *Parkins v Sodexho Ltd* [2002] IRLR 109, the EAT upheld an employee's appeal against an earlier tribunal decision that claims under ERA 1996, s 100(1)(c) could not give rise to a claim for interim relief. The EAT held that s 43B of the Public Interest Disclosure Act 1998 required a breach of a legal obligation and a reasonable belief that such a breach had or was likely to occur and that it was this belief and subsequent disclosure which led to the employee's dismissal. Contrary to the tribunal's earlier decision, the EAT held there was no distinction between a legal obligation arising out of an employment contract and any other form of legal obligation.

Any provision in an agreement (including a contract of employment) which purports to prevent a worker from making a protected disclosure is void.

Trade Union recognition

[14.97] Section 1 of ERA 1999 amended TULR(C)A 1992 by inserting a new Schedule A1 which sets out legal procedures for obtaining union recognition and derecognition for collective bargaining purposes. The procedures, which are very detailed and enforced by the Central Arbitration Committee, are outside the scope of this chapter but it should be noted that a worker has the right not to be subjected to any detriment by any act or deliberate failure to act by his employer if the act or detriment is on the grounds that the worker:

(a) acted with a view to obtaining or preventing recognition of a union by the employer;
(b) indicated that he supported or did not support recognition of a union by the employer;
(c) acted with a view to securing or preventing the ending of bargaining arrangements;
(d) indicated that he supported or did not support the ending of bargaining arrangements;
(e) influenced or sought to influence the way in which votes were to be cast by other workers in a ballot;
(f) influenced or sought to influence other workers to vote or to abstain from voting in such a ballot;
(g) voted in such a ballot; or
(h) proposed to do, failed to do, or proposed to decline to do, any of the above.

If a worker suffers a detriment for any of the above reasons, he has a right to present a claim within three months to an employment tribunal. However, this does not apply if any ground above constitutes an unreasonable act or omission by the worker. If such a complaint is upheld, the tribunal may award such compensation as it considers just and equitable in all the circumstance, having regard to any loss. The usual rules of mitigation apply. Compensation is subject to a limit of the total of the basic award for unfair dismissal plus the maximum amount of possible compensation under ERA 1996, s 124(1) (currently £65,300).

If the worker is an employee and the detriment amounts to a dismissal within the meaning of ERA 1996, he may bring a claim to a tribunal on the grounds that he was unfairly dismissed and the reason or principal for his dismissal was one of the above grounds. There is no qualifying period of service to bring a claim under this section.

In addition, the dismissal of an employee is unfair if the reason or principal reason for the dismissal was that he was redundant but it is shown that:

(i) the circumstances constituting the redundancy applied equally to one or more other employees in the same undertaking who held similar positions to the employee and who have not been dismissed by the employer; and
(ii) the reason or principal reason that he was selected for redundancy was one of those reasons outlined at (a)–(h) above.

Further, protection has been provided against dismissal for those taking part in lawfully organised industrial action, by virtue of section 238A of TULR(C)A 1992.

Section 168A of TULR(C)A 1992 requires employers to allow time off for employees carrying out duties as union learning representatives. An employee who acts as a learning representative for an independent trade union is entitled to take time off during his working hours for a variety of different purposes in connection with his union functions. A learning representative is entitled to time off for:

(A)   analysing learning and training needs;
(B)   providing information and advice about learning or training matters;
(C)   arranging learning or training;
(D)   promoting the value of learning or training in relation to trade union members;
(E)   consulting his employer about carrying on such activities; and
(F)   preparing for the above activities.

In addition to this, learning representatives must also be granted time off in order to undergo training relevant to their functions as learning representatives. Other trade union members are also permitted time off in order to access the services provided by their learning representative. The above rights are only applicable where the trade union has given notice to the employer in writing that the employee is a learning representative of the union and that he has undergone sufficient training to enable him to carry on such activities. If an employee is refused time off he may complain to an employment tribunal.

Information and consultation

[14.98] The Information and Consultation of Employees Regulations 2004 (SI 2004/3426) came into force on 6 April 2005. From 1 April 2008, employers with 50 or more employees are required to inform and in certain circumstances consult with employees about business decisions and changes which may affect the employees. This can include changes to the workforce, introduction of new products, changes to the financial or management structure and redundancies. Under the Regulations employers can try to negotiate with employees for less onerous information and consultation obligations than provided for in the Regulations.

Chapter 15

Car Scheme and Property Administration

Car scheme administration

Introduction

[15.1] Recent years have seen a steady erosion of the tax benefits of company cars. Despite this the company car remains as one of the most popular benefits for employees as the cost to the employee of being provided with a company car is, in many instances, still less than providing themselves with a similar car. Accordingly, especially in the small to medium-sized company, the company secretary can commonly find himself responsible for car scheme administration.

Acquisition

[15.2] The best method of the acquisition of company cars is a question which raises many different points for the company secretary. Currently, outright purchase is the most common means of purchase of a company car. However, other means are available, being hire purchase, contract hire and finance leasing. The pros and cons of each are examined below.

Outright purchase

[15.3] Financing the purchase of a fleet of cars can provide a cash flow problem for companies, even where the fleet comprises only a few cars. Unless a business has unused cash resources and can use the benefit of capital allowances (given at the rate of 25% on a reducing balance basis up to a maximum of £3,000 per car per year), outright purchase has several disadvantages.

First, there is the question of a company's cash resources being invested in an asset which quickly depreciates; usually at an unpredictable rate. Also, a business is generally unable to reclaim the VAT paid on the purchase. From 1 August 1995, VAT is recoverable on cars purchased *exclusively* for business purposes but this is a very restrictive test which will not be satisfied if the cars are available for any private use. The main beneficiaries of the change are likely to be car leasing companies although genuine pool cars may qualify. Where VAT is recoverable on purchase, it must also be charged on the full selling price.

Then there is the question of the administration of the fleet. In most small companies, this is a responsibility which will commonly fall to the company secretary who then has to devote considerable staff time to matters such as buying and selling the cars, arranging insurance cover, organising servicing and repairs, as well as attending to the financial recording aspects.

A possible advantage of outright purchase is the possibility of being able to negotiate discounts with a seller. This is especially true when purchasing a large fleet.

A variation on outright purchase is hire purchase. Although the administrative problems are much the same as for outright purchase, a financing advantage is that interest payable on hire purchase is tax deductible. Also, capital allowances are available to the business from the outset of the hire purchase contract and the cost is spread over the period over which ownership is transferred.

Finance leasing

[15.4] Finance leases offer many advantages to a business. In general, leasing payments are deductible as trade expenses, subject to a restriction where the car costs more than £12,000, in which case a proportion of the rental is disallowed. Capital allowances are available to the lessor and the leasing rates reflect this. The lessor does not supply, maintain or sell the cars, but simply provides the finance to acquire the cars chosen by the lessee who bears the risk of their residual value (ie profit or loss). Accordingly, the administrative burdens of running a fleet to a large extent remain the problem of the lessee.

The two main forms of finance lease are:

(a)   the *open ended lease*, which is typically for a three-year period, but with an option to terminate at any time after a minimum period at a predetermined figure. The lessee pays or receives the difference between the sale proceeds and the predetermined settlement figure;

(b)   the *'balloon' lease*, which can be used if it is reasonably certain that the car will be retained until the end of the lease period. In addition to rental payments, a 'balloon' payment equivalent to the expected residual value of the car is payable at the end of the lease, whether or not the car is sold.

Contract hire

[15.5] Contract hire differs from finance leasing in that the lessor supplies and maintains the car, usually leaving the lessee with only insurance and fuel costs to pay, in addition to the hire charge which is tax deductible. The lessor also disposes of the car at the end of the contract. Bulk buying discounts and the expertise of the lessor in controlling maintenance costs and disposing of cars for the best prices, make contract hire competitive with the combined cost of finance rentals and maintenance incurred by the company itself.

The services which are offered by the lessor to the lessee under a contract hire agreement are usually a combination of the following:

(a)   buying the cars of the lessee's choice;
(b)   servicing and repair costs;
(c)   licensing the cars;
(d)   provision of replacement cars;
(e)   roadside assistance;
(f)   selling the car at the end of the hire period.

Accordingly, the majority of the car scheme administration is borne by the lessor rather than the lessee, which can be a considerable attraction to a company.

Property administration

Choosing and financing commercial premises

[15.6] It is essential that the location of a company be carefully researched to keep financial burdens to the minimum and to allow the business to develop successfully.

The main factors that should be considered when weighing up possible sites are:

(a)   availability of financial incentives (see **15.7** below);
(b)   costs and funding;
(c)   availability of labour;
(d)   availability of housing;
(e)   relocation of key staff;
(f)   preferred type of premises and availability;
(g)   time span for relocation; and
(h)   facilities, site access and communications.

It should be noted that the Building Regulations 1991 (SI 1991/2768) contain provisions applying to new buildings and conversions which include new stricter fire safety requirements. This is in addition to the Workplace (Health, Safety and Welfare) Regulations 1992 (SI 1992/3004) which came into force on 30 December 1993 (see **14.73** EMPLOYMENT, HEALTH AND SAFETY. Access and facilities for disabled people must be complied with (see **14.42** EMPLOYMENT, HEALTH AND SAFETY).

Financial incentives

[15.7] Government-backed financial incentives can be analysed into two main categories, namely tax relief and assistance with building costs.

Leasehold or freehold?

[15.8] The following options should be considered:

(a)   'short' property interests – eg a lease of less than 50 years;
(b)   'long' property interests – freehold or long leasehold.

In some instances there may be no choice since the 'long' interest may not be available or affordable, or the premises may have to be taken on whatever terms are available.

The main advantages of freehold ownership are:

(i)   elimination of uncertainty of future rent reviews;
(ii)   freedom from landlords' restrictions;
(iii) availability of an asset which can be used to generate liquid funds by borrowing on its value;
(iv) capital appreciation of the asset.

The main advantages of acquiring a lease are:

(A)   cash flow;

(B)   no necessity to obtain long-term mortgage funding.

Lease terms

[15.9] Leases are invariably long and complicated and somewhat difficult to understand. The following clauses will usually constitute the main terms of such documents.

(a)   *Rent payable and rent review* – this clause details the amount of rent payable to the landlord at the commencement of the lease together with the dates at which the rent may be increased during the lease.

(b)   *Break clause* – this clause will state whether the tenant can leave the premises and therefore maintain some degree of flexibility. Such a clause may also allow for the redevelopment of the premises.

(c)   *The obligation to repair* – this is an important clause as where the obligation is stated to be a 'full repairing and insuring one' the cost of carrying out repairs will fall entirely upon the tenant.

(d)   *Alterations/improvements* – a tenant may not be allowed to carry out alterations or improvements either at all, or at least without the landlord's consent. Under the Landlord and Tenant Act 1927, where a landlord's consent is required, the Act states that such consent may not be unreasonably withheld.

(e)   *Assignment and subletting* – the right to assign the lease is important as it will allow a tenant to market the remainder of the lease should the company no longer require the property.

(f)   *The obligation to insure* – if the landlord insures on a block policy, it is important that the tenant's interest is noted on it.

Licences

[15.10] A licence is a contractual document granting a company the right to occupy premises on the conditions set out in the contract. A potential disadvantage of a licence is that the normal rules on security of tenure as conferred by Part II of the Landlord and Tenant Act 1954 do not apply. However, in reality, few licences of business premises are not protected tenancies as, in general, the courts tend to dislike occupational insecurity for business tenants.

Commercial mortgages

[15.11] As with any request for mortgage finance, lenders consider both the type of property and the ability of the borrower to service the loan. There are many companies in the commercial mortgage market, comprising a mixture of banks, finance companies and insurance companies. Each has its own particular likes and dislikes, with regard to the type of property, and each has its own range of terms and conditions. The insurance companies tend not to lend against properties such as hotels, nursing homes, sports facilities and other restricted use sites, whilst banks and finance companies are often prepared to consider a wider range of buildings.

The borrower will usually be expected to produce accounts for the previous three to five years to prove a track record but, in addition, many lenders also seek personal guarantees from the directors. The interest rate charged may be fixed or variable; the banks will generally offer the choice to the borrower.

Lease renewal

[**15.12**] Under the Landlord and Tenant Act 1954 (Part II), business tenants are given the right to renew their tenancies at the expiry of the former lease where the provisions of the Act apply. Pursuant to section 23(1) of the Act, the Act applies so long as 'the property in the tenancy is or includes premises which are occupied for the purposes of a business carried on by him or for those or other purposes'. This will cover almost all types of business activity.

Termination of a business lease

[**15.13**] The Landlord and Tenant Act 1954 states that no lease may be brought to an end except in accordance with the Act. The effect of this statement, combined with the fact that most business leases are for a fixed term, means that a landlord must pursue the method of termination set down in the Act before he can regain possession.

To initiate the procedure, the landlord must service a notice of termination of the lease on the tenant under section 25 of the Act which will expire not earlier than the date of expiry of the tenancy under the lease. The notice can be served not less than six or more than twelve months before the date of the end of the lease and must be in the prescribed form and set out whether the landlord intends to oppose the grant of a new tenancy and, if so, on what grounds.

It is important to make sure that the section 25 notice is accurate. In *Morrow v Nadeem* [1978] 1 AER 237, the notice was served in the name of an individual, whereas the lease was held in the name of a company and in *Yamaha-Kemble Music (UK) v ARC Properties* [1990] 1 EGLR 261 the landlord was mistakenly named as ARC whereas the parent company PD was the lessor. Both notices were held to be invalid as the landlord's name is the most relevant piece of information.

A tenant must reply to the notice by issuing a counter-notice stating whether or not he is willing to give up possession of the property. This must be done within two months of the receipt of the notice. If such a counter-notice is not given, the tenant loses his right to apply to the court for a renewed tenancy (in default of a negotiated renewal).

Where negotiations for a renewal are proceeding but not yet finalised, the tenant must apply to the court for a renewed tenancy or he will lose the right to a new lease. This must be done not less than two months nor more than four months after service of the section 25 notice.

Should the parties fail to come to an agreement, the terms of the tenancy will be settled by the court under section 29 of the Act.

Should the landlord wish to modify the terms of the lease, he must have a 'fair and reasonable' case for doing so.

Once the landlord has given a section 25 notice to the tenant and the tenant has also replied that he would like to have a new tenancy, the landlord may apply to the court for an interim rent which will run from the date specified in the notice or the date of the tenant's request for a new tenancy, whichever is the later. The court must have regard to the existing rent, assuming an annual tenancy on values existing at the date when the interim rent starts to run (Landlord and Tenant Act 1954, section 24A).

New leases

[15.14] Should a landlord not wish to grant a renewed tenancy to a tenant, then he is restricted in his opposition by the terms of section 30(1) of the Landlord and Tenant Act 1954.

Section 30(1) of the Act defines the only reasons upon which a landlord may oppose a renewed tenancy as being:

(a)   the failure by the tenant to comply with repairing or other obligations;

(b)   the persistent delay in the payment of rent;

(c)   breaches by the tenant of other substantial lease obligations;

(d)   alternative accommodation has been offered by the landlord to the tenant;

(e)   a better return if the premises were let as a whole (in situations where the premises concerned are currently sub-let);

(f)   the landlord intends to demolish or reconstruct the premises[1];

(g)   the landlord wishes to occupy the premises.

Should the landlord obtain possession on any of the last three grounds specified above, the tenant may be able to claim compensation for the disturbance of his business and for any improvements which the tenant may have made to the premises.

---

[1]   Evidence of this intention will be required at the hearing. The landlord must have a fixed and *settled desire* to do what he claims and he must have a *reasonable prospect* of being able to do it and, in particular, that he has or will be able to obtain planning permission for what he intends to do. Planning permission will soon also be required for demolition.

Compensation

[15.15] As mentioned in **15.14** above, compensation may be paid by a landlord to a tenant in certain circumstances, and will be payable by the landlord to the tenant as soon as the tenant has quit the premises.

Calculation

[15.16] The amount of compensation payable was traditionally calculated by reference to the rateable value of the occupied premises at the date on which the landlord's notice is given, times the appropriate multiplier. This multiplier was announced from time to time by the Secretary of State for the Environment, Transport and the Regions by way of statutory instrument. If premises are occupied by the tenant or predecessors carrying on the same business for a period of at least 14 years, the tenant was paid twice the rateable value times the appropriate multiplier.

Prior to 1 April 1990, all premises, whether used for domestic or business purposes, were valued for rating purposes and the rateable value was easily obtainable. The appropriate multiplier was, until that date, three.

Following the introduction of the uniform business rate and the community charge, concern was expressed as to how compensation could be calculated under the new regime, particularly in relation to mixed premises, ie a combination of business and residential properties. Also, if the premises were used for business purposes only, the new uniform rate times the then existing multiplier of three led to concern amongst landlords.

It is clear that, as previously, the amount of compensation payable is calculated at the date the landlord serves his section 25 or section 26(6) notice. The rule relating to double compensation for businesses carried on at the premises for at least 14 years still exists in all cases. The compensation for business premises is calculated by reference to the new uniform business rate times the appropriate multiplier. This multiplier is discussed further below.

Mixed properties

[15.17] Subsections (5A) and (5B) of section 37 of the Landlord and Tenant Act 1954 (LTA 1954), introduced by the Local Government and Housing Act 1989 (LGHA 1989), state that if part of the holding is domestic property, one should disregard that part, take the uniform business rate valuation on the remainder of the property, add a sum equal to the tenant's reasonable expenses in moving out of the domestic property, and then apply the multiplier to the total sum. If the parties cannot agree upon the removal expenses, the courts will be asked to determine the sum.

Domestic properties

[15.18] Subsections (5C) and (5D) of section 37 of the LTA 1954, introduced by LGHA 1989, state that if the whole of the holding is domestic property, the rateable value shall be equal to the rent at which it is estimated it might reasonably be expected to let the premises from year to year when the tenant undertakes to pay all usual tenant's rates and taxes and bears the cost of repair and insurance. The calculation is again made as at the date the landlord served his section 25 or section 26(6) notice. If the parties cannot agree the calculation, the matter is to be referred to a valuation officer at the Commissioners for HM Revenue and Customs with the right of appeal to the Lands Tribunal.

The appropriate multiplier

[15.19] If the landlord served a notice under section 25 of the LTA 1954 (or section 26(6)) prior to 1 April 1990, the appropriate multiplier remains at three times the rateable value.

If the landlord serves his notice on or after 1 April 1990, the appropriate multiplier is one, unless the tenant has exercised an option introduced to him by LGHA 1989, Schedule 7 (see below). In the event that such an option has been exercised, the appropriate multiplier will be eight times the rateable value of the premises as on 31 March 1990.

The 1989 option

[15.20] Paragraph 4 of Schedule 7 to the LGHA 1989 uses the words 'in any case'. However, these words follow references to other parts of Schedule 7 which relate to mixed or domestic property. The debate which has arisen is whether the general words relate to any property protected by the LTA 1954. It is understood that the Department of the Environment, Transport and the Regions is of the view that it does relate to all protected properties, but a representative of the DETR has stated that it is not for the department to interpret statutes. The courts have not yet been given the opportunity to consider the matter. For the sake of safety it must be assumed, for the time being, that the section does relate to all business premises protected by the LTA 1954.

What is clear, is that the tenancy has to have been entered into before 1 April 1990, or entered into on, or after, that date pursuant to a contract made before 1 April 1990; the landlord's notice under section 25 or section 26(6) of the LTA 1954 must be given before 1 April 2000 and the tenant must give notice to the landlord that he wants to exercise his option. This notice must be given within the period the tenant has under the LTA 1954 for making an application to the court for a new tenancy. As stated above, if exercised, the tenant is entitled to eight times the rateable value registered on 31 March 1990.

Rent review

[15.21] In order to protect landlords from the effects of inflation, most new leases of business premises contain a clause allowing the rent to be reviewed periodically, thus enabling a landlord to increase the level of rent paid during the term of the lease.

In negotiating a lease a company should consider the following.

(a) The time period between reviews (eg every five years).
(b) The formula and method of determining the new rent.
(c) The provisions for arbitration in the event of failure to reach agreement about a rent (eg reference to an independent surveyor).
(d) Rent reviews will normally be initiated by the service of a notice. If the lease specifies that time is of the essence in a rent review, a landlord may lose his review right if he fails to deliver the appropriate notice at the appropriate time.

Repairs

[15.22] Leases will usually impose upon the tenant the obligation of repairing the property. In this connection there are several different terms that are commonly used. These are as follows.

(a) *To keep in repair* – the tenant has to repair the premises and maintain them during the period of the lease.

(b)   *To leave in repair/good tenantable repair* – the premises must be left in repair at the end of the lease to the standard that they were in at the time of grant of the lease.

(c)   *Full repairing and insuring* – the premises must be repaired and insured at all times by the tenant.

Where a landlord is obliged to do repairs, the lease will normally state that a notice of disrepair must be served on the landlord before his obligation will arise. Where the obligation to repair falls on the tenant, the landlord will normally have the right to enter and inspect the premises at least once each year.

Assignment

[15.23] A landlord may prevent a lease being assigned by inserting a bar against assignment in the lease. This will obviously affect the marketability, and accordingly the value, of the lease. Thus, it is more usual to find a clause in leases not barring assignment, but requiring the surrender of the lease to the landlord before assignment. Where the bar is qualified, the Landlord and Tenant Act 1927 provides that the landlord's consent shall not be unreasonably withheld.

Restrictive use

[15.24] There may be a provision that restricts the use to which the premises can be put. Where the clause is highly restrictive, it is likely to have a depressing effect on the rent payable.

Such restrictions are additional to any planning consent that may be required from the local planning authority to carry on a particular business.

The uniform business rate

General

[15.25] Businesses pay a uniform business rate (also called the non-domestic rate) on the rateable value of business premises. Business rates are calculated using the rateable value and the multiplier (see **15.26** below) set by the Government. Guidance is available on the Business Link website (see www.bus inesslink.gov.uk).

Rateable values are updated every five years. The latest revaluation was made as at 1 April 2010 (based on rateable values assessed at 1 April 2008) and is intended to reflect changes in the property market and redistribute the total tax liability for business rates. This means that some rates bills will rise but others will fall, and transitional relief will be available (see **15.27** below).

A special business rates relief is available to small businesses (see **15.28** below).

The Business Rates Supplement Act 2009 creates a new power for 'upper tier' local authorities in England and Wales to levy a local supplement on the business rate, and to retain the funds for investment in economic development in their area. Properties with a rateable value of £50,000 or less, are specified (in regulations) as exempt.

The multiplier

[15.26] The multiplier indicates the percentage, or pence in the pound, of the rateable value to be paid in business rates.

In England the standard multiplier for 2011/12 is 43.3 pence; therefore a business with a rateable value of £10,000 will pay business rates of £4,330 (excluding any discounts or reductions that may be available).

The small business rate multiplier was introduced in 2005/06 for businesses which qualify for small business rate relief. For 2011/12 the small business rate multiplier is 42.6 pence.

Transitional arrangements

[15.27] The revaluation at 1 April 2010 increased many rateable values, but decreased others. Transitional arrangements apply in England for the years up to and including 2014/15, as follows:

	Properties with rateable value of £18,000 or more (£25,500 or more in Greater London)		Properties with rateable value of less than £18,000 (£25,500 in Greater London)	
	Maximum decrease	*Maximum increase*	*Maximum decrease*	*Maximum increase*
2010/11	4.6%	12.5%	20.0%	5.0%
2011/12	6.7%	17.5%	30.0%	7.5%
2012/13	7.0%	20.0%	35.0%	10.0%
2013/14	13.0%	25.0%	55.0%	15.0%
2014/15	13.0%	25.0%	55.0%	15.0%

Small business rate relief

[15.28] The small business rate relief is available to all businesses whose rateable value is less than £18,000 (£25,500 in London). The small business rate relief depends on the rateable value of the property, as follows:

(a) if the rateable value is below £6,000 the rates are calculated using the small business multiplier (42.6 pence for 2011/12) and then reduced by 50%;

(b) if the rateable value is from £6,000 to £11,999, the reduction decreases on a sliding scale of 1% for every £120;

(c) if the rateable value is from £12,000 to £17,999 (£24,499 in London), the rates are calculated using the small business multiplier.

The small business relief is extended for periods between 1 October 2010 to 30 September 2012. For this period, eligible ratepayers will receive small business rate relief at 100% (instead of the current 50%) on properties with a rateable value up to £6,000 and a tapering from 100% to 0% for properties up to £12,000.

Table of Cases

V

W

Y

Table of Statutes

Table of Statutory Instruments

Index